Innovation and Transformation of Islamic Economics

Muhammad Ridhwan Ab. Aziz
Universiti Sains Islam Malaysia, Malaysia

Safeza Mohd Sapian
https://orcid.org/0000-0002-6905-5101
Universiti Sains Islam Malaysia, Malaysia

Suhaila Abdul Hamid
https://orcid.org/0000-0001-6945-6848
Universiti Sains Islam Malaysia, Malaysia

IGI Global
Scientific Publishing
Publishing Tomorrow's Research Today

Vice President of Editorial	Melissa Wagner
Director of Acquisitions	Mikaela Felty
Director of Book Development	Jocelynn Hessler
Production Manager	Mike Brehm
Cover Design	Jose Rosado

Published in the United States of America by
IGI Global Scientific Publishing
701 East Chocolate Avenue
Hershey, PA, 17033, USA
Tel: 717-533-8845 | Fax: 717-533-7115
Website: https://www.igi-global.com E-mail: cust@igi-global.com

Library of Congress Cataloging-in-Publication Data

Names: Muhammad Ridhwan Ab. Aziz editor | Safeza Mohd Sapian, 1973- editor | Suhaila Abdul Hamid editor
Title: Innovation and transformation of Islamic economics / [edited by] Muhammad Ridhwan Ab. Aziz, Safeza Mohd Sapian, and Suhaila Abdul Hamid.
Description: Hershey, PA : IGI Global Scientific Publishing, [2026] | Includes bibliographical references and index. | Summary: "This book offers insights and guidance on how to improve Islamic business operations, affairs and activities in achieving effectiveness and efficiency in Islamic financial institutions and Islamic organizations"-- Provided by publisher.
Identifiers: LCCN 2025014143 (print) | LCCN 2025014144 (ebook) | ISBN 9798337326559 hardcover | ISBN 9798337326566 paperback | ISBN 9798337326573 ebook
Subjects: LCSH: Economic development--Islamic countries | Finance--Islamic countries | Business enterprises--Islamic countries | Economics--Religious aspects--Islam
Classification: LCC HC499 .I56 2026 (print) | LCC HC499 (ebook) | DDC 330.917/67--dc23
LC record available at https://lccn.loc.gov/2025014143
LC ebook record available at https://lccn.loc.gov/2025014144

British Cataloguing in Publication Data
A Cataloguing in Publication record for this book is available from the British Library.

Table of Contents

Detailed Table of Contents

both policymakers and academic scholars about how emerging technologies impact financial integrity.

This article explores the integration of Enterprise Risk Management (ERM) with Artificial Intelligence (AI) in Islamic financial institutions, with a focus on risk identification, assessment, and management within the project environment. By leveraging a structured ERM framework, financial institutions can systematically identify, evaluate, and mitigate risks such as market fluctuations, credit risk, operational challenges, and sharia compliance violations. AI plays a critical role in improving risk detection, automating the identification of potential compliance issues (e.g., Riba, Gharar), and providing real-time predictive analytics to manage financial and non-financial risks. This article provides valuable insights into the potential of AI in transforming risk management practices, ensuring that Islamic financial institutions remain resilient and competitive in a rapidly changing financial ecosystem.

This chapter examines the role of Islamic finance in advancing financial inclusion in Algeria, where a significant share of the population remains unbanked or underbanked due to the incompatibility of conventional banking products with Islamic principles. By analyzing features such as profit- and loss-sharing, asset-backed financing, and social tools like zakat and Qard Hasan, the chapter highlights how these mechanisms can serve small businesses and marginalized groups. It also reviews recent policy reforms, including Islamic banking windows and dedicated regulatory frameworks, while identifying persistent challenges such as limited financial literacy and legal constraints. The analysis suggests that targeted policy measures and public education could unlock the potential of Islamic finance to foster inclusive economic growth and social justice, aligning financial services with the cultural and ethical values of

which encourages collective decision-making. Conversely, firm size, sales growth, and CRO presence exhibit negative or mixed effects, suggesting that governance structures must be effectively integrated for ERM to create value.

Strategic Human Resource Management (SHRM) is increasingly recognized as a critical lever for organizational success, particularly in complex environments like hospitals where work culture significantly impacts patient outcomes and staff well-being. This article explores the relationship between SHRM practices and the transformation of work culture within hospital settings. Through a literature review approach, drawing upon a curated collection of research articles, this paper synthesizes key themes and findings. The analysis indicates that targeted SHRM interventions, including leadership development, employee engagement strategies, robust knowledge management systems, and the cultivation of specific cultural attributes, are pivotal in driving and sustaining positive work culture transformations in hospitals. The findings underscore the necessity for hospital administrators and HR professionals to strategically align human resource practices with cultural change objectives to enhance organizational effectiveness, employee satisfaction, and the quality of care.

Drawing on daily returns from June 2018 to March 2024, this study evaluates how a multi-asset portfolio of Islamic finance equities (DJIM), sustainability indices (DJSW), WTI crude oil, and gold can jointly enhance risk mitigation and ESG alignment. Utilizing an R^2 connectedness framework that combines partial correlation networks, VAR modeling, and GFEVD, we quantify dynamic spillovers and shock transmissions as percentage contributions to forecast variance. Empirical results reveal that WTI and clean-energy benchmarks deliver the strongest hedging benefits across Minimum Variance, Minimum Correlation, and Minimum Connectedness portfolios. Islamic finance and sustainability indices, while offering moderate volatility reduction, assume a vital defensive role during market stress by upholding Shariah compliance and ethical mandates.

In the ASEAN region, greenwashing undermines ESG credibility, especially among high carbon-emitting firms, where discrepancies between sustainability claims and actual environmental impact lead to lower ESG scores. This study aims to examine the relationship between greenwashing on the ESG score moderated by carbon emission in the context of ASEAN region (Malaysia, Indonesia, Thailand and Singapore). Data from the 2,301 listed firms were downloaded from the Refinitiv Eikon database. The final data from 652 companies with 2,102 observations during the period 2020–2023 to test the study model effectively. By using random effects model, the findings indicate that greenwashing score negatively affects the ESG score for the companies. Furthermore, carbon emissions play a detrimental and significant moderating role in the association between greenwashing and ESG scores. Our findings addressing greenwashing requires coordinated action between firms, regulators, and rating agencies to ensure ESG disclosures reflect real progress not just public relations strategies.

Preface

INTRODUCTION

Over the past two decades, Islamic economics and Islamic finance have experienced remarkable growth and increasing global relevance. This expansion has unfolded alongside rapid technological change, particularly the rise of financial technology (fintech), which has reshaped how economic activities are organized, delivered, and governed. Within this evolving landscape, Islamic economics has demonstrated both resilience and adaptability—embracing digital innovation while remaining firmly rooted in its foundational ethical and Shariah-based principles.

Islamic economics represents a distinct and comprehensive economic framework derived primarily from the Qur'an and Sunnah, emphasizing justice, moral conduct, risk-sharing, and equitable distribution of wealth. Its intellectual foundations can be traced back to the Islamic Golden Age, when scholars articulated economic ideas that placed ethical considerations at the heart of trade, finance, and social relations. In contrast to conventional economic models that often prioritize efficiency and profit maximization, Islamic economics integrates moral responsibility, social welfare, and spiritual values into economic decision-making.

Core principles—such as the prohibition of riba (usury), the avoidance of excessive uncertainty (gharar), ethical investment, and obligatory redistributive instruments like zakat—aim to prevent wealth concentration, alleviate poverty, and promote social justice. These principles underscore an economic vision that seeks not only financial stability but also community resilience and sustainable development. In today's context, this ethical paradigm is increasingly relevant to global debates on financial inclusion, environmental stewardship, and socially responsible investment.

The Fourth Industrial Revolution and accelerating globalization have introduced profound technological transformations that affect lifestyles, production processes, and institutional structures. Digital technologies now enable greater efficiency in terms of cost, time, and energy, and Islamic economics is actively engaging with these developments. From Islamic banking, microfinance, insurance (takaful and retakaful), capital market instruments, and pension funds to Islamic businesses and social finance institutions, the application of Shariah principles continues to evolve in response to contemporary challenges.

This edited reference book, *Innovation and Transformation of Islamic Economics*, brings together scholarly insights and practical perspectives on how Islamic economic institutions and stakeholders can harness innovation while remaining faithful to the objectives of Shariah (Maqasid al-Shariah). The chapters explore strategies to enhance effectiveness and efficiency in Islamic financial institutions and organizations, highlighting the role of ethical governance, responsible investment, environmental, social, and governance (ESG) considerations, and digitalization in achieving sustainable and inclusive growth.

We envision this volume as a comprehensive resource for bankers, entrepreneurs, business leaders, policymakers, practitioners, academics, and students who seek to understand and contribute to the ongoing transformation of Islamic economics. By bridging theory and practice, tradition and innovation, this book aims to support the development of an Islamic economic system that serves the well-being of current and future generations.

We hope that this work will stimulate critical reflection, informed dialogue, and meaningful action toward advancing the innovation and transformation of Islamic economics in an increasingly complex global economy.

ORGANIZATION OF THE BOOK

Chapter 1 explores the strategic importance of intellectual capital efficiency in enhancing firm performance within digitally intensive economies, drawing empirical evidence from China. By unpacking the roles of within digitally intensive economies, drawing empirical evidence from China. By unpacking the roles of human, relational, and structural capital, the chapter underscores how skilled talent and ethical stakeholder engagement are critical drivers of resilience and competitiveness. The insights extend beyond the Chinese context, offering valuable reflections for Islamic economic transformation, particularly in aligning knowledge-based growth and digital innovation with Shariah principles.

Chapter 2 examines how strategic innovation, supported by government-led technological initiatives, influences the performance of Islamic SMEs in Ethiopia. The chapter demonstrates that enterprises actively engaging with public innovation programs achieve superior competitiveness and operational outcomes. It highlights the importance of collaborative networks, policy support, and a culture of innovation in strengthening Islamic SMEs, positioning them as key contributors to inclusive and technology-driven economic development.

Chapter 3 focuses on the role of Islamic crowdfunding in poverty alleviation across Indonesia's diverse regions. By analyzing the distribution and impact of zakat, infaq, and sadaqah (ZIS), the chapter reveals how Islamic social finance can address regional fiscal disparities and support community-based development. The findings illustrate the potential of Islamic crowdfunding as a complementary fiscal mechanism to promote social justice and reduce poverty, particularly in economically paradoxical regions such as Java.

Chapter 4 investigates regulatory and environmental factors shaping the adoption of blockchain technology in Anti-Money Laundering (AML) frameworks within Malaysia's financial sector. The chapter highlights the importance of regulatory clarity, ecosystem collaboration, and international alignment in accelerating blockchain adoption. It offers policy-relevant insights into how emerging technologies can strengthen financial integrity while aligning with Islamic finance's emphasis on transparency and accountability.

Chapter 5 addresses the transformative role of Artificial Intelligence in enhancing Enterprise Risk Management within Islamic financial institutions. By integrating AI driven analytics with Shariah-compliant ERM frameworks, the chapter illustrates how institutions can improve risk identification, compliance monitoring, and predictive decision-making. This contribution underscores AI's potential to reinforce resilience, governance, and ethical risk management in an increasingly complex financial environment.

Chapter 6 examines Islamic finance as a pathway to financial inclusion in Algeria, where conventional banking remains misaligned with societal and religious values. The chapter highlights how Shariah-compliant instruments—such as profit-and-loss sharing, asset-backed financing, zakat, and qard hasan—can serve marginalized populations and small enterprises. It also evaluates recent regulatory reforms while identifying structural challenges, positioning Islamic finance as a strategic driver of inclusive and socially just economic growth.

Chapter 7 explores the interrelationship between innovative strategy, human capital, and digital cost leadership in Islamic SMEs. The chapter demonstrates that human capital development plays a critical mediating role in translating innovation strategies into digital efficiency and competitive advantage. By emphasizing workforce training and people-centered innovation, this study reinforces the necessity of integrating technological advancement with human development in the digital era.

Chapter 8 examines how digital leadership styles influence organizational agility in the context of Construction 4.0. Drawing on empirical evidence from Malaysian construction firms, the chapter reveals that structured, people-centered leadership approaches—particularly transactional and servant leadership—are more effective in fostering agility than certain transformational traits. The findings provide important insights for managing digital transformation in technology-intensive industries.

Chapter 9 analyzes the strategic evolution of Islamic marketing and consumer behavior within the Takaful and Bancassurance sectors in Pakistan. The chapter highlights how Islamic values, ethical narratives, and digital technologies shape trust, engagement, and consumer decision-making. By integrating data-driven marketing, AI, and social media strategies with Shariah principles, the chapter offers a roadmap for building resilient and competitive Islamic financial business models.

Chapter 10 investigates the role of Enterprise Risk Management in enhancing firm value among Shariah-compliant companies listed on Bursa Malaysia. The findings emphasize the positive influence of board size and leverage, reflecting both agency theory and the Islamic principle of *shura*. At the same time, the chapter cautions that governance mechanisms must be effectively integrated for ERM to generate value, contributing nuanced insights into Shariah-compliant corporate governance.

Chapter 11 explores the interplay between Strategic Human Resource Management and work culture transformation in hospital settings. Through a comprehensive literature synthesis, the chapter demonstrates how leadership development, employee engagement, knowledge management, and cultural alignment are essential to improving organizational effectiveness and quality of care. The contribution underscores the strategic role of human capital in complex, service-oriented institutions.

Chapter 12 examines risk interconnections across Islamic finance equities, sustainability indices, and commodity markets. Using advanced connectedness and portfolio optimization techniques, the chapter shows how multi-asset diversification enhances risk mitigation while maintaining ESG and Shariah compliance. The findings highlight the defensive role of Islamic and sustainability indices during periods of market stress, reinforcing their relevance in ethical portfolio construction.

Chapter 13 presents a qualitative exploration of Takaful awareness and readiness among mosque committee members as key community influencers. The chapter identifies religiosity and ethical alignment as major drivers of acceptance, while trust, affordability, and information gaps remain significant barriers. It offers practical recommendations for Takaful operators to strengthen outreach strategies and deepen community-based financial inclusion.

Chapter 14 examines entrepreneurship as a catalyst for sustainable development, emphasizing innovation that transcends profit maximization. By integrating frameworks such as the triple bottom line and social entrepreneurship, the chapter illustrates how green technologies, inclusive business models, and digital tools can generate both ethical impact and strategic advantage. This contribution reinforces entrepreneurship's role in addressing global sustainability challenges.

Chapter 15 explores the empowerment of coastal communities in East Java through integrated Islamic microfinance to support sustainable ecotourism. By combining profit-sharing mechanisms with charitable funds, the chapter proposes a holistic model that addresses financial access, capacity building, and environmental sustainability. The study provides actionable insights for transforming coastal economies into resilient and inclusive development hubs.

Chapter 16 examines the acceleration gap between digital financial risks and regulatory responses in Indonesia's Islamic finance ecosystem. The chapter reveals a misalignment between the rapid evolution of fintech-related fraud and the delayed implementation of early warning systems. It underscores the urgency of embedding suptech and regtech solutions at the early stages of digital risk governance to ensure adaptive and proactive regulatory frameworks.

Chapter 17 investigates the impact of greenwashing on ESG performance in ASEAN countries, highlighting the moderating role of carbon emissions. The findings demonstrate that misleading sustainability claims significantly undermine ESG credibility, particularly among high-emission firms. The chapter calls for coordinated action among firms, regulators, and rating agencies to ensure that ESG disclosures reflect genuine environmental and ethical progress, aligning closely with the values underpinning Islamic economics.

CONCLUSION

As this edited reference book demonstrates, the innovation and transformation of Islamic economics is no longer a peripheral discourse but a central and evolving response to the complex realities of a rapidly changing global economy. Across its chapters, this volume brings together diverse empirical evidence, conceptual insights, and practical experiences that collectively reaffirm Islamic economics as a dynamic, ethical, and future-oriented economic paradigm. Rooted in the principles of justice, risk-sharing, and social responsibility, Islamic economics continues to show its capacity to adapt—embracing digital technologies, new governance frameworks, and sustainable business models without compromising its Shariah foundations.

The contributions in this book highlight that innovation in Islamic economics is inherently multidimensional. It spans intellectual capital development, digital leadership, fintech applications, risk governance, Islamic social finance, entrepreneurship, and ESG-aligned investment practices. Importantly, the chapters illustrate that technological advancement alone is insufficient; meaningful transformation requires human capital development, sound institutions, ethical leadership, and supportive regulatory ecosystems. Together, these elements enable Islamic economic institutions and enterprises to enhance resilience, competitiveness, and inclusivity in the digital era.

This volume also underscores the growing relevance of Islamic economics in addressing pressing global challenges, including financial exclusion, poverty, sustainability, climate risk, and governance integrity. By aligning economic activities with the objectives of Shariah (*Maqasid al-Shariah*), the studies presented here demonstrate how Islamic economics can contribute to balanced development that serves both material prosperity and social well-being. The integration of ESG principles, responsible innovation, and community-based finance further reinforces Islamic economics' role in advancing sustainable and equitable growth.

In bringing together perspectives from different regions, sectors, and methodological approaches, this book aims to bridge theory and practice while encouraging cross-disciplinary dialogue. We hope that policymakers, practitioners, academics, and students will find this volume not only a valuable reference but also a source of inspiration for future research, policy design, and institutional reform. Ultimately, the innovation and transformation of Islamic economics is an ongoing journey—one that calls for continuous learning, collaboration, and ethical commitment to ensure that economic progress remains firmly anchored in justice, sustainability, and shared prosperity.

Chapter 1
Intellectual Capital Efficiency and Firm Performance in the Digital Economy:
Evidence From China and Reflections for Islamic Economic Transformation

Syaima Adznan
https://orcid.org/0000-0002-0665-5994
Universiti Kebangsaan Malaysia, Malaysia

Soliha Sanusi
Universiti Kebangsaan Malaysia, Bangi, Malaysia

Aziatul Waznah Ghazali
https://orcid.org/0000-0002-1324-5248
Universiti Kebangsaan Malaysia, Bangi, Malaysia

ZhenQian Ji
Universiti Kebangsaan Malaysia, Bangi, Malaysia

ABSTRACT

This study examines the impact of intellectual capital efficiency (ICE) on firm performance in China's knowledge- and capital-intensive industries. Using panel data from 1,773 A-share firms (2016–2023) and a two-way fixed-effects model, ICE, measured as the average of human (HCE), relational (RCE), and structural

DOI: 10.4018/979-8-3373-2655-9.ch001

(SCE) capital efficiency, positively influences performance, with stronger effects in knowledge-intensive sectors. HCE and RCE are the most significant drivers, highlighting the value of skilled talent and strong stakeholder relationships, while SCE has a smaller positive effect. Findings highlight the need for targeted IC investment in digitally dynamic contexts to enhance resilience and competitiveness. Beyond China, the results have implications for Islamic economic transformation, where integrating ICE with digital technologies, guided by Shariah principles, can foster innovation, ethical stakeholder engagement, and the transition toward inclusive, knowledge-based economies.

INTRODUCTION

In the contemporary digital economy, the strategic importance of intellectual capital (IC) has been amplified. IC, encompassing human capital, relational capital and structural capital, has emerged as a critical driver of innovation, productivity, and long-term value creation. As organizations in both knowledge-intensive industries (KIIs) and capital-intensive industries (CIIs) navigate the complexities of technological transformation, globalization, and sustainability imperatives, the efficient use of intellectual capital becomes increasingly vital for firm performance and survival. Empirical studies consistently affirm the positive relationship between IC and firm success, highlighting its role in enhancing productivity, competitiveness, and sustained growth (Ahmed & Amir Hussin, 2024; Xu & Li, 2022; Adznan et al., 2022; Ramírez et al.,2021).

In KIIs such as software, banking, and information technology, where innovation and expertise are central, IC directly influences a firm's ability to compete and grow. For example, human capital drives innovation through skilled employees, relational capital builds customer trust, and structural capital supports efficient systems and sustainable practices (Aslam et al., 2024; Adznan et al., 2022; Buallay et al., 2019). These synergies translate into measurable improvements in firm performance, as shown by numerous studies. Similarly, in CIIs-such as manufacturing and utilities—where physical capital dominates, IC remains a crucial enabler of innovation and efficiency. Research by Xu & Li (2022) and Sharma et al. (2024) demonstrates that ICE, especially relational capital efficiency (RCE), significantly impacts company performance, such as return on assets (ROA). However, the relationship is not always linear; some studies argue that excessive investment in IC does not guarantee improved outcomes (Kim & Tran, 2024).

Despite growing evidence of IC's value, the literature remains heavily skewed toward knowledge-intensive sectors, with relatively limited empirical analysis in capital-intensive industries. Few studies have examined how ICE varies across different industry types within the same national context, particularly in a country undergoing both industrial modernization and digital transformation. The role of ICE has received limited attention in the context of the broader transformation of value-based economic systems, such as those envisioned in the Islamic economic paradigm. The Islamic economic system places strong emphasis on human development, stakeholders relationship and organizational process-dimensions that are intrinsically aligned with the components of intellectual capital. As Islamic economies embrace digital technologies, ICE emerges as a critical enabler of Shariah-compliant innovation and economic inclusiveness (Buallay et al.,2019; Aslam et al.,2024; Asutay & Ubaidillah 2024). Thus, understanding how ICE contributes to firm performance in digitally evolving markets, such as China, may also provide insight into how intellectual resources support innovation, institutional reform and structural transformation in Islamic economic systems.

This study seeks to bridge the gap by examining the impact of ICE on firm performance across both KIIs and CIIs in China. Although China and Islamic economies differ in their institutional and cultural foundations, both are committed to transitioning toward innovation-driven, knowledge-based economic models. China's strategic deployment of ICE, particularly in strengthening human and relational capital through digital technologies, offers valuable insights for Islamic economies seeking to achieve similar outcomes within a Shariah-compliant framework. China presents a compelling context for this investigation, given its dual role as a global manufacturing hub and an emerging leader in digital innovation. Government-led initiatives such as "Made in China 2025" and the broader national digitalization agenda have encouraged firms to move beyond traditional, resource-based strategies and embrace intangible assets as key drivers of competitiveness. These policy shifts highlight the urgent need for firms in both KIIs and CIIs to optimize their use of intellectual capital. However, the extent to which ICE influences firm performance across these diverse industry types remains underexplored, raising a critical research question: How does ICE impact firm performance across different industry types in China's dynamic and digitally transforming economy?

By utilizing a comparative lens and adopting the RBV as the theoretical foundation, the paper sheds light on how firms can enhance their performance by strategically leveraging these intangible resources. Furthermore, RBV's emphasis on industry-specific characteristics helps explain the divergent IC dependencies between KIIs and CIIs, offering a foundation for examining how industry differences moderate the relationship between ICE and FP. The inclusion of these insights can offer significant implications for Islamic economies seeking to leverage intellectual capital and digital innovation to achieve broader socio-economic goals grounded in Shariah principles (Asutay & Ubaidillah 2024). Therefore, supported by this theory, this paper reasonably predicts that ICE is closely related to FP, and this relationship varies depending on differences in industry characteristics. Our findings not only enriches the understanding of IC's role across varied industrial landscapes but also offers practical insights for managers and policymakers aiming to enhance organizational competitiveness in the digital age.

The remainder of this paper unfolds in the following manner. Section 2 offers a review of the existing literature on IC and ICE, culminating in the development of hypotheses. Section 3 details the methodological approach employed in this study, while Section 4 dives into a discussion of the results and key findings derived from the empirical analysis. To wrap things up, the concluding section provides a summary of the study's conclusions, acknowledges its limitations, and proposes directions for future research.

LITERATURE REVIEW AND HYPOTHESES DEVELOPMENT

Definition And Measurement of ICE

As financial markets evolve, IC has become a key intangible asset for enhancing firm performance and value creation (Kim and Tran., 2024; Jaunanda et al.,2024; Ramírez et al., 2021). IC encompasses the intangible, knowledge-based assets that fuel a company's competitive edge and overall success. It represents the collective expertise, innovative capacities, and relational networks embedded within an organization, making it indispensable in today's knowledge-centric economy. Unlike tangible or financial assets, IC's intangible nature poses unique challenges in terms of measurement and management. In addition, the steady growth of Islamic financial institutions (IFIs) reinforces their credibility and increasing significance within the global financial market. Therefore, it is essential for IFIs to place greater emphasis on understanding and developing their IC, as these knowledge-based resources play a significant role in driving both the structural and dynamic performance of Islamic economic system (Aslam et al., 2024; Asutay & Ubaidillah 2024).

ICE refers to the efficiency with which a company creates value using its IC (Pulic, 2000). It measures how effectively a company uses its IC to achieve financial performance. Since it is difficult to directly identify ICE in financial statements, most study adopts the Value-Added Intelligence Coefficient (VAIC) model proposed by Pulic (2000). The VAIC model provides information about the efficiency of value creation of a company's tangible and intangible assets, and has the advantages of simplicity and comparability. However, the limitation of this model is that it relies more on financial data and may not fully capture the actual value of intangible assets, especially in innovation-driven enterprises.

The VAIC model has also been widely criticized for its inability to account for relationship capital as a distinct and measurable component. This omission is particularly challenging given the growing recognition of external relationships—such as those with customers, suppliers, and strategic partners—as critical sources of competitive advantage and value creation. The failure to incorporate relationship capital not only limits the model's comprehensiveness but also leads to a potential underestimation of the key drivers of firm performance (Xu & Li, 2022; Ramírez et al.,2021). In response to these limitations, numerous studies (Ahmed & Amir Hussin, 2024; Asutay & Ubaidillah, 2024; Aslam et al. 2024) have adopted the Modified Value Added Intellectual Coefficient (MVAIC) model, which extends the original VAIC framework by explicitly integrating relational capital. This revised model provides a more holistic and accurate representation of the role of intellectual capital in enhancing organizational performance. In line with this approach, this study employs the adjusted MVAIC model to improve the precision in assessing the impact of ICE on FP.

ICE And Firm Performance (FP)

Consistent with RBV, ICE is a unique intangible resource that are valuable, rare, inimitable, and non-substitutable. It contributes to knowledge accumulation and innovation capabilities, thereby strengthening a firm's core competitiveness and ultimately enhancing FP. However, existing literature has not reached a consensus on the nature of the relationship between ICE and FP. While many studies report a positive link, findings vary across countries and contexts, suggesting that the influence of ICE may be moderated by external and internal factors. Most notably, several studies support a positive linear relationship, indicating that higher ICE leads to improved firm value and reduced financial distress. For instance, cross-national empirical analyses by Jaunanda et al. (2024) and Habib & Dalwai (2024) demonstrate that in countries such as China, Indonesia, Singapore, Malaysia, Thailand, the Philippines, and Egypt, enhanced ICE significantly improves market value and financial stability. These findings highlight the strategic importance of IC as an intangible asset within the economic environments of developing and emerging economies.

Additionally, Akgün and Türkoğlu (2024) found that firms in Europe experienced notable improvements in financial performance—particularly in profitability and market share—through investments in ICE. Their study, which examined listed companies during the financial crisis, emphasized that IC investments were instrumental in enabling firms to survive economic shocks and sustain long-term development. Similarly, Xu & Li (2022), focusing on manufacturing sector in China, reported that ICE positively contributed to enterprise development by enhancing competitive advantage, strengthening employee capabilities, and improving overall organizational performance.

Most studies reveal that ICE can promote FP but there are divergent findings across countries and contexts, suggesting that the role of ICE may be affected by a variety of factors. For example, the cross-national empirical analysis of Jaunanda et al. (2024) and Habib & Dalwai (2024) found that in countries such as China, Indonesia, Singapore, Malaysia, Thailand, the Philippines, and Egypt, improving ICE can significantly improve the market value and financial stability of enterprises. This shows that in the specific economic environment of these countries, IC as an intangible asset has strategic significance for the development of enterprises. In addition, Buallay et al. (2019) indicated that companies achieved significant improvements in financial performance by improving ICE, especially in terms of enhanced profitability and market share. They investigated the business success factors of European listed companies during the financial crisis and found that companies' investment in IC was a key factor in their ability to survive the crisis and achieve sustainable development. Aslam et al. (2024) investigated the mediating role of intellectual capital on the association between corporate governance mechanism and the ICE of Islamic banks. Their findings revealed that the inclusion of Shariah committee as a moderating variable has influenced positively the corporate governance and ICE of Islamic banks

Nevertheless, some studies have questioned the performance-enhancing role of ICE. For example, Kim & Tran (2024) pointed out that Vietnamese SMEs mainly rely on physical capital and financial capital for value creation, and have not yet been found to fully utilize human capital and structural capital. Therefore, in this context, the contribution of IC to FP is relatively limited. These findings highlight that the economic development stage and industrial structure of the country where the enterprise is located may affect the effectiveness of ICE. Several studies have suggested that there may be a nonlinear relationship between ICE and FP. Ryu et al. (2021) found relationship between IC and FP is a similar inverted U-shaped through analysis of Korean financial institutions. This finding suggests that ICE's positive effect on FP exits in the initial stage, but when the investment reaches a certain level, its marginal benefits begin to decrease and may even have a negative impact on FP. Similarly, Kim and Tran. (2024) used Vietnamese listed companies as samples to explore the impact of ICE on FP and found that the two showed an inverted U-shaped curve relationship. These research results show that although moderate investment in IC can effectively improve FP, overinvestment may lead to waste of resources and reduced benefits.

Judging from the existing literature, most studies focus on a specific industry in developed economies or emerging market countries, while research on enterprises of different sizes, industries or development stages is relatively limited. This research bias leads to certain extrapolation problems in the literature when summarizing the impact of ICE, that is, its conclusions may not be applicable to CIIs, thus limiting its applicability to different types of enterprises. In addition, although many studies have found that ICE has a positive impact on FP, the intensity and form of this impact may vary significantly across economies and industries. When managing and applying IC, firms in emerging markets may be constrained by institutional environments, cultural factors, and economic structures, such as greater financing constraints, more unstable legal and regulatory environment, and relatively weak intellectual property protection mechanism. These factors may affect the actual role of ICE in the market. In the Chinese context, the intensity of government regulation of enterprises is significantly higher than that of other emerging market economies, especially after the "Made in China 2025" strategy released in 2015, China promoted economic structural adjustment and emphasized technological innovation and industrial upgrading. However, strict policy supervision may constrain the independent operation and resource allocation of enterprises while promoting technological progress. Therefore, compared with other emerging markets, Chinese enterprises may show unique characteristics in the path and effect of ICE. However, previous literature has not focused on the situation of ICE in the Chinese market. Therefore, based on the discussion of the contributions and limitations of the existing literature, this paper proposes the following hypothesis:

H1. ICE has a positive impact on Chinese firm performance

ICE consists of three parts, HCE, SCE, RCE, and each component has different effects on FP. Among them, HCE is generally considered to be the core driving force for improving FP, especially in labor-intensive or knowledge-intensive industries (Asutay & Ubaidillah 2024; Majumder et al. 2023).

Human capital, primarily encompassing employees' skills, knowledge, and experience, has a direct bearing on a company's capacity for innovation, operational efficiency, and its competitive edge in the marketplace. Many studies have highlighted the positive impact of HCE on FP. For example, Jaunanda et al. (2024) discovered that boosting HCE levels can effectively mitigate the risk of a company facing financial difficulties, thereby bolstering its financial stability. Meanwhile, Adznan et al., (2022) conducted an analysis of Islamic banks and found that investment in human capital has a consistently positive impact on market performance, an effect that remained steady both before and after the financial crisis. Furthermore, Ahmed & Amir Hussin (2024), in their research on non-financial firms in Malaysia, found that improvements in HCE can significantly enhance a firm's financial performance.

Several studies have examined the positive impact of HCE on FP with much of the existing research concentrated in developing regions such as the Middle East, Southeast Asia, and others. Empirical studies focusing on Chinese firms remain relatively limited. In light of these contextual differences, the following hypotheses are proposed regarding the role of HCE:

H1a. HCE has a positive impact on Chinese firm performance

Relational capital plays a critical role in IC, encompassing the intricate web of connections, credibility, brand equity, and customer allegiance that businesses maintain with external stakeholders, including clients, suppliers, collaborators, governmental bodies, and community organizations. These relationship resources play an important role in improving the market competitiveness, technological innovation capabilities and financial performance of enterprises.

Existing studies have shown that RCE has a significant driving effect on a company's innovation capabilities and international market performance. Sharma et al. (2024) found that in India's textile industry, firms' RCE was positively correlated with FP. Customer, employee, supplier, and alliance networks in RC are critical factors influencing FP. Ryu et al. (2021) used Korean SMEs as a sample and found that RCE had a significant positive impact on technological innovation capabilities, and the improvement of technological innovation capabilities could significantly enhance the international performance of enterprises. This finding suggests that in a highly competitive market environment, cooperative relationships with external stakeholders are an important factor in promoting technological advancement and market expansion. In addition, the analysis of Buallay et al. (2019) on Islamic Banks in the Gulf Cooperation Council (GCC) pointed out that there is a significant positive correlation between ICE and FP, among which RCE has an impact FP significantly and positively.

However, current research on the role of relational capital in Chinese firms is still relatively limited. The business environment and government policies of Chinese enterprises are unique. Enterprises tend to rely more on government relations and business networks when building and utilizing relational capital, which may cause the impact of relational capital on FP to show characteristics different from those in other countries. Therefore, it is necessary to further explore the actual impact of RCE on FP in the Chinese context. Based on the above discussion, the following hypothesis is proposed:

H1b. RCE has a positive impact on Chinese firm performance

Structural capital is also an important component of IC, mainly including internal resources such as organizational processes, technology, systems, and intellectual property rights (Xu & Li, 2022). SC reflects the knowledge management system, innovation process, and operational efficiency within the enterprise, and is the supporting infrastructure for enterprises to transform human capital and relationship capital into actual performance. Although structural capital is theoretically considered to be an important factor in promoting firm innovation and performance improvement, there is no consensus in the existing literature on this issue.

Some literature believes that structural capital has limited impact on FP. For example, studies by Adznan et al. (2022) and Asutay & Ubaidillah (2024) show that in some industries, the correlation between structural capital investment and FP is weak, and companies with excessive Reliance on internal processes and technology may not lead to significant performance improvements. However, other studies point out that structural capital can effectively support the innovation activities of enterprises and thus improve performance. For example, studies by Majumder et al. (2023) and Xu & Li (2022) found that an enterprise's information management, technological systems, and innovation processes are important factors driving enterprise performance, which belong to structural capital.

Jaunanda et al. (2024) pointed out that improving SCE can help reduce the risk of a company falling into financial distress, thereby enhancing the company's financial stability. In addition, the research by Ryu et al.,(2021) emphasized that structural capital is a key factor in improving the competitiveness of SMEs. The study provides evidence that access to information and knowledge management, organizational culture, and process innovation capabilities have a positive and significant impact on SMEs' innovation capabilities, and that there is a positive relationship between this improvement in innovation capabilities and FP. Therefore, increasing investment in structural capital will help enhance the company's innovation capabilities and thus improve the company's overall performance.

Despite a wealth of research into structural capital, the landscape remains relatively uncharted when it comes to empirical studies on Chinese businesses. Investigating how efficiently structural capital is utilized, and its ultimate impact on performance, holds considerable theoretical weight and real-world implications for the Chinese market. Building on this, the hypothesis will be:

H1c. SCE has a positive impact on Chinese firm performance

ICE In Different Industries

Since different industries have differences in the degree of reliance on IC, information disclosure mechanisms, and government regulatory intensity, industries may significantly affect the impact of ICE on FP. Therefore, when further exploring the mechanism of ICE's impact on FP, it is necessary to deeply analyze the ICE mechanism in different types of industries and test whether the industry will change the impact intensity of ICE.

At present, the research on KIIs mainly focuses on the banking industry, pharmaceutical industry and other fields, which rely on the accumulation of intangible assets including IC. Several studies from the ASEAN-8 countries, Saudi Arabia, India, Bangladesh, and Nigeria have shown that ICE has a positive impact on FP, whether for commercial banks or Islamic banks (Asutay & Ubaidillah 2024; Aslam et al. 2024; Majumder et al. 2023; Buallay et al. 2019). These studies agree that firms in KIIs tend to rely more on efficient IC management to improve profitability and market competitiveness.

In contrast, research on CIIs has mainly focused on the manufacturing sector. Compared with KIIs that rely more on intangible assets such as human capital and innovation, CIIs (such as manufacturing) rely more on physical assets (fixed assets and technological equipment) (Xu & Li 2022). For example, Xu & Li (2022) found that among Chinese manufacturing listed companies, there was a significant positive correlation between IC investment and financial performance, and companies with more IC investment showed better financial performance. Similarly, Habib & Dalwai (2024) analyzed industrial firms in GCC countries and found that IC has a significant positive impact on FP. In addition, Sharma et al. (2024) focused on the Indian sugar mill industry and also concluded that IC and its components significantly affect financial performance.

Based on RBV, different industries have different core resources, so the role of ICE in FP in different industries may be different. In addition, the institutional environment of different industries, such as government supervision, market competition, and disclosure requirements, may affect the role of ICE in FP. This has also been reflected in previous literature. Jaunanda et al., (2024) highlighted that within manufacturing firms listed in China, Hong Kong, and Taiwan, the three components of IC play a pivotal role in enhancing FP. Notably, the impact of IC on FP is particularly pronounced in high-tech manufacturing sectors. Additionally, Xu and Li (2022) found that ICE exerts a greater influence on the profitability and operational efficiency of non-high-tech SMEs compared to their high-tech counterparts, though its effect on profitability remains somewhat limited. This suggests that differences in ICE across industries may stem from differences in industry attributes.

Existing literature also generally supports the key role of HCE and RCE in the performance of KIIs. For example, Jaunanda et al. (2024) shows that HCE is a core driver of firm profitability. Similarly, studies on Islamic banks (Asutay & Ubaidillah 2024) also confirm the crucial role of HCE in improving return on assets (ROA) and return on equity (ROE). Furthermore, Buallay (2019) demonstrated the significant effect of RCE on performance in Islamic banks. However, there is still no consensus on the role of SCE in different industries.

Therefore, the study makes the following hypothesizes:

H2. ICE has a greater impact on knowledge-intensive industries than on capital-intensive industries

H2a. HCE has a greater impact on knowledge-intensive industries than on capital-intensive industries

H2b. RCE has a greater impact on knowledge-intensive industries than on capital-intensive industries

H2c. SCE has a greater impact on knowledge-intensive industries than on capital-intensive industries

METHODOLOGY

This paper uses quantitative analysis methods for data analysis and uses Stata for empirical research. Stata has powerful panel data analysis functions, which can effectively process data characteristics and improve the accuracy of analysis.

Sample Selection

Aiming to explore how ICE influence the fiscal outcomes of KIIs and CIIs, this study will offer a China-based viewpoint to global IC research. Therefore, this paper uses the Organization for Economic Cooperation and Development (OECD) and the United Nations International Standard Industrial Classification (ISIC) to classify Chinese industries into two categories: knowledge-intensive and capital-intensive.

The China Association of Public Companies (CAPCO) released the latest industry classification standard on September 30, 2024, which divides China's industries into 19 categories, including: A (agriculture, forestry, animal husbandry and fishery); B (mining); C (manufacturing); D (electricity, heat, gas and water production and supply); E (construction); F (wholesale and retail); G (transportation, warehousing and postal services); H (accommodation and catering); I (information transmission, software and information technology services); J (finance); K (real estate); L (leasing and business services); M (scientific research and technical services); N (water conservancy, environment and public facilities management); O (residential services, repairs and other services); P (education); Q (health and social work); R (culture, sports and entertainment); S (public administration, social security and social organizations); T (international organizations). The OECD classification is based on the industry's R&D investment and human capital ratio, while ISIC divides industries into high-knowledge input industries and low-knowledge input industries based on the proportion of firm knowledge input. Therefore, according to the above standards, the classification results of 19 major industry categories are shown in Table 1. Among them, KIIs include 7 major industry categories and capital-intensive enterprises include 12 major industry categories.

This paper focuses on the IC efficiency and performance of listed companies in A-share market in China during 2016 - 2023 for the following reasons. In terms of the selection of sample companies, as China's most important capital market, the A-share market covers companies from all walks of life. Therefore, A-share listed companies are highly representative and can better reflect the overall situation of

Chinese companies. Secondly, A-share listed companies are strictly regulated by China's securities regulatory authorities and must disclose financial reports and non-financial information regularly. Therefore, choosing A-share listed companies as samples makes data acquisition more convenient and information more transparent and reliable. In terms of the choice of observation time, first, the State Council of China officially issued the document "Made in China 2025" on May 19, 2015, which clearly proposed that Chinese companies should "drive development with innovation", guide companies to increase IC investment, and promote the development of high-end manufacturing. Secondly, COVID-19 in 2020 has had a huge impact on the global economy and firm operations. The observation period of 2016-2023 can observe thc different effects of IC efficiency on FP before and after the pandemic. Furthermore, the study has excluded companies listed post-2016, those delisted at any point during our study, and any with incomplete data for the observation period. Ultimately, our sample consists of 229 from KIIs and 1,544 companies from CIIs, all sourced from the China CSMAR database.

Table 1. Results of industry classification

	Industry Code	**Number of Firms**
Knowledge-Intensive Industries	I, J, L, M, P, Q, R	229
Capital-Intensive Industries	A, B, C, D, E, F, G, H, K, N, O, S	1544

Variables

This section outlines the definitions of all variables used in the quantitative analysis, along with their respective measurement methods. As the main variable, existing literature generally uses VAIC to measure ICE. However, VAIC model fails to measure the impact of customer capital or RC separately, but includes them in SC. To study the impact of ICE components on performance separately, guided by Aslam et al. (2024), this paper uses three factors, HCE, RCE and SCE to study the impact mechanism of ICE on FP. Among them, HCE represents the ratio of firm value-added (VA) to all expenses related to employees, RCE represents the ratio of VA to all expenses related to marketing, SCE represents the ratio of VA to all R&D-related expenses, and VA is measured by gross income minus operating expenses.

The financial health of Chinese firms is often evaluated using two key metrics: Return on Assets (ROA) and Return on Equity (ROE). ROA serves as a gauge of a company's efficiency in generating profit from its assets, determined by dividing net income by the average total assets. On the other hand, ROE reflects the company's ability to generate returns for its shareholders, calculated by dividing net income by the average shareholders' equity. These metrics provide critical insights into a firm's operational and financial performance (Aslam et al. 2024; Sharma et al. 2024; Xu & Li 2022).

In this research, firm size (Size) and debt ratio (LEV) are incorporated as control variables within the regression model. Size is quantified by taking the natural logarithm of the company's total assets, while LEV is calculated as the ratio of total debt to total assets. These metrics align with methodologies established in prior studies (Xu & Li, 2022; Sharma et al., 2024).

Table 2. Variable symbols and measurements

Category	Variables	Symbol	Measurements
Dependent Variable			
Firm performance	Return on Asset	ROA	Ratio of operating income over assets
	Return on Equity	ROE	Ratio of operating income over equity
Independent Variables			
Intellectual Capital	Intellectual Capital Efficiency	ICE	(HCE+RCE+SCE)/3
	Human Capital Efficiency	HCE	VA/HC HC: all expenses related to employees
	Relational Capital Efficiency	RCE	VA/RC RC: all expenses related to marketing
	Structural Capital Efficiency	SCE	VA/SC SC: all expenses related to research and development
Control Variables			
	Firm Size	Size	Natural log of total firm assets
	Debt Ratio	LEV	Total debt / Total assets

Models

Given the diverse nature of firms in the Chinese A-share market, some firms may have missing data during 2016-2023. To ensure the stationarity of the variables, we conducted panel unit root tests using the Fisher ADF test, which is suitable for unbalanced panel data. The results indicate that all variables are stationary at level (I(0)), suggesting that cointegration tests are unnecessary. Consequently, we proceed with panel data regression analysis without differencing

To identify the most suitable panel regression approach, we employed a Hausman test to evaluate the merits of the Fixed Effects (FE) and Random Effects (RE) models. The test produced a p-value below the 0.05 threshold, signaling that the Fixed Effects model is the better fit, given that the assumptions underlying the Random

Effects model do not hold. As a result, we leaned into the Fixed Effects model for our analysis, making it the cornerstone of all further investigations.

This research employs four models to evaluate the study's hypotheses.

The study uses Model (1) to analyze the impact of ICE on FP.

$$ROA_{i,t} = \alpha_0 + \alpha_1 ICE_{i,t} + \alpha_2 Size_{i,t} + \alpha_3 LEV_{i,t} + \alpha_4 \varepsilon_{i,t}$$

$$ROE_{i,t} = \alpha_0 + \alpha_1 ICE_{i,t} + \alpha_2 Size_{i,t} + \alpha_3 LEV_{i,t} + \alpha_4 \varepsilon_{i,t}$$

Model (2) is used to test HCE, RCE, and SCE's influence. In addition, the results of coefficients can also be used to analyze the impact mechanism of ICE on FP.

$$ROA_{i,t} = \alpha_0 + \alpha_1 HCE_{i,t} + \alpha_2 RCE_{i,t} + \alpha_3 SCE_{i,t} + \alpha_4 Size_{i,t} + \alpha_5 LEV_{i,t} + \alpha_6 \varepsilon_{i,t}$$

$$ROE_{i,t} = \alpha_0 + \alpha_1 HCE_{i,t} + \alpha_2 RCE_{i,t} + \alpha_3 SCE_{i,t} + \alpha_4 Size_{i,t} + \alpha_5 LEV_{i,t} + \alpha_6 \varepsilon_{i,t}$$

Since industry characteristics may affect the impact of ICE on FP, it may not be enough to simply examine the main effect of ICE. We need to consider whether industry differences will amplify or weaken this effect. Based on this consideration, the industry interaction term (Industry × ICE) can quantitatively investigate the moderating impact of industry on the ICE-FP relationship, rather than simply performing a simple industry comparison analysis. The study will use Model (3) to examine the impact of industry differences on the relationship between ICE and FP.

$$ROA_{i,t} = \alpha_0 + \alpha_1 ICE_{i,t} + \alpha_2 (ICE_{i,t} * IndustryType) + \alpha_3 Size_{i,t} + \alpha_4 LEV_{i,t} + \alpha_5 \varepsilon_{i,t}$$

$$ROE_{i,t} = \alpha_0 + \alpha_1 ICE_{i,t} + \alpha_2 (ICE_{i,t} * IndustryType) + \alpha_3 Size_{i,t} + \alpha_4 LEV_{i,t} + \alpha_5 \varepsilon_{i,t}$$

To test the H2a-H2c, the study uses the model (4)-Z-test method to test whether the impact of HCE, RCE and SCE on KIIs is greater than that on CIIs. The coefficients used in the model are from Model 2. Z-test can determine if independent variables significantly impact dependent variables differently across two industries.

$$Z = \frac{\hat{\alpha}_1 - \hat{\alpha}_2}{\sqrt{SE\hat{\alpha}_1{}^2 + SE(\hat{\alpha}_2)^2}}$$

The above models are all two-way fixed effect models with fixed enterprise individuals and time. In the model, i=1, 2, 3...n denotes individual enterprises; t=1, 2, 3...n signifies time, and ε stands for the error term.

RESULTS AND FINDINGS

Descriptive Statistical Analysis

As illustrated in Table 3, the average ROA stands at 0.028, indicating that many companies struggle with inefficient asset utilization and challenges in generating profits. Additionally, the standard deviation of ROA is 0.064, with a minimum value of -0.223, highlighting that certain firms are operating at a loss and revealing substantial disparities in how effectively assets are managed across the board. A similar pattern emerges with ROE, where the average is 0.041, accompanied by a standard deviation of 0.129 and a minimum value of -0.6. This underscores the stark variations in profitability among companies, with some experiencing severe financial losses. These findings align with earlier studies on Chinese listed firms (Xu & Li, 2022), reinforcing the notion that profitability and asset efficiency remain pressing concerns in this context.

In terms of ICE, although the average value of ICE is low, at 36.799, the SD is large, at 98.858. This indicates that there are significant differences in ICE among firms. Among ICE's components—HCE, SCE, and RCE—SCE holds the highest average at 45.416, compared to HCE's 25.535 and RCE's 17.548. However, the study by Xu & Li (2022) showed that HCE is the most important component among HCE, SCE, and RCE. This is different from previous studies, and further analysis is needed to determine whether the impact of HCE on FP is different from previous studies. The SD for the three entities are 48.144, 154.331, and 49.826, respectively, which suggests a considerable degree of variance across the board. Moreover, the average LEV clocks in at 0.443, with a SD of 0.186. This signals that companies tend to lean on debt financing as a common practice, though the extent to which they do so swings wildly from one enterprise to the next.

Tables 4 shows the descriptive statistics of knowledge-intensive and CIIs. Comparing the data of the two industries, from the average value, the ICE (39.331), HCE (27.272) and RCE (19.377) of the capital-intensive industry are significantly higher than the ICE (17.035), HCE (16.807) and RCE (6.005) of the knowledge-intensive industry, and the ROA (0.030) and ROE (0.047) of the capital-intensive industry are also higher than those of the knowledge-intensive industry. This shows that there may be a positive correlation between ICE and FP, that is, the higher the ICE, the higher the ROA and ROE, which supports H1-H1b. The average SCE of the two industries is quite different. The SCE of the capital-intensive industry (48.548) is higher than the SCE of the knowledge-intensive industry (25.313), but the difference between the ROA and ROE of the two industries is not large, and further regression analysis is needed to discuss the impact of SCE.

Table 3. Descriptive statistics of full industries

VarName	Obs	Mean	SD	Min	Max
ICE	9871	36.799	98.858	0.274	765.768
HCE	9871	25.535	48.144	0.139	382.395
SCE	9871	45.416	154.331	0.140	1216.742
RCE	9871	17.548	49.826	0.265	414.780
ROA	9871	0.028	0.064	-0.223	0.190
ROE	9871	0.041	0.136	-0.600	0.307
Size	9871	22.902	1.329	20.369	26.673
LEV	9871	0.443	0.186	0.074	0.858

Table 4. Descriptive statistics of different industries

VarName	Obs	Mean	SD	Min	Max
knowledge-intensive industries					
ICE	1199	17.035	28.185	1.114	199.345
HCE	1199	16.807	25.528	0.558	173.350
SCE	1199	25.313	66.625	0.702	491.056
RCE	1199	6.005	7.443	0.436	54.154
ROA	1199	0.010	0.084	-0.223	0.190
ROE	1199	0.002	0.173	-0.600	0.300
Size	1199	22.470	1.090	20.254	26.673
LEV	1199	0.375	0.175	0.066	0.815
Capital-intensive industries					
ICE	8672	39.331	103.948	0.136	765.768
HCE	8672	27.272	54.801	0.088	448.701
SCE	8672	48.548	166.433	0.091	1289.430
RCE	8672	19.377	55.095	0.265	444.346
ROA	8672	0.030	0.061	-0.223	0.190
ROE	8672	0.047	0.129	-0.600	0.307
Size	8672	22.961	1.347	20.416	26.673
LEV	8672	0.452	0.185	0.077	0.860

Correlation Analysis

Table 5. Correlation results of variables in the full industry

	ROA	ROE	ICE	HCE	SCE	RCE	Size	LEV
ROA	1							
ROE	0.942***	1						
ICE	0.272***	0.318***	1					
HCE	0.214***	0.219***	0.644***	1				
SCE	0.259***	0.292***	0.699***	0.310***	1			
RCE	0.236***	0.282***	0.348***	0.059***	0.020**	1		
Size	0.131***	0.280***	0.285***	0.077***	0.201***	0.287***	1	
LEV	-0.333***	-0.076***	0.061***	-0.054***	0.036***	0.078***	0.474***	1

Table 6. Correlation results of variables in different industries

	ROA	ROE	ICE	HCE	SCE	RCE	Size	LEV
Knowledge-intensive industries								
ROA	1							
ROE	0.964***	1						
ICE	0.288***	0.314***	1					
HCE	0.163***	0.157***	0.591***	1				
SCE	0.291***	0.318***	0.724***	0.192***	1			
RCE	0.281***	0.289***	0.263***	0.110***	0.005	1		
Size	0.294***	0.356***	0.272***	0.018	0.313***	0.075***	1	
LEV	-0.218***	-0.042	0.078***	-0.070**	0.108***	-0.084***	0.237***	1
Capital-intensive industries								
ROA	1							
ROE	0.940***	1						
ICE	0.263***	0.307***	1					
HCE	0.214***	0.214***	0.642***	1				
SCE	0.251***	0.281***	0.688***	0.315***	1			
RCE	0.228***	0.274***	0.351***	0.036***	0.010***	1		
Size	0.105***	0.264***	0.271***	0.066***	0.175***	0.302***	1	
LEV	-0.361***	-0.095***	0.036***	-0.076***	0.011	0.076***	0.495***	1

To assess the linear relationship between key variables, this study performed a correlation analysis examining the interplay between ICE components (HCE, SCE, RCE) and FP metrics (ROA, ROE), alongside control variables such as Size and LEV. The results are detailed below.

Table 5 shows the results of the correlation analysis of the entire sample. As anticipated, a strong positive relationship exists between FP metrics—specifically ROA and ROE—and ICE along with its key components: HCE, SCE and RCE. The correlation analysis reveals that ICE significantly influences financial performance, with a coefficient of 0.272 ($p<0.01$) when paired with ROA. Furthermore, the correlation coefficients between ROA and HCE, SCE, and RCE are 0.214, 0.259, and 0.236, respectively, all reaching a significant level, which means that HCE, SCE, and RCE have a certain role in promoting performance. These findings underscore the pivotal role of intellectual capital in driving firm performance and lay a solid foundation for further empirical investigation across the industry.

As shown in Table 6, the correlation between ROA and ICE is 0.288, a figure significant at the 1% level. This correlation is stronger than what we see for the full industry and CIIs, suggesting that in KIIs, ICE really punches above its weight when it comes to influencing FP. We also see a correlation coefficient of 0.291 between ROA and SCE, highlighting how crucial SCE is within KIIs. While the ROA and RCE correlation coefficient in KIIs is lower than those for ROA and SCE, and ROA and HCE, it's still statistically significant. This indicates that both SCE and HCE play an outsized role in boosting a company's performance in this sector.

Moreover, when examining the relationship between ROA and SCE in KIIs, the correlation coefficient in CIIs is a mere 0.059, which pales in comparison. Interestingly, the correlation coefficient between ROA and HCE stands at 0.109, suggesting that HCE still plays a modest yet notable role in enhancing FP within CIIs. That said, it's clear that the influence of ICE on the FP of CIIs remains rather marginal when taken as a whole. There is also high positive correlation between ROA and ROE (correlation coefficient is 0.942, $p<0.01$), indicating that the two are consistent in measuring firm performance, providing a basis for the robustness analysis of using ROE as a replacement variable for ROA.

Variance Inflation Factor (VIF)

To mitigate the potential distortions caused by multicollinearity, we employed the Variance Inflation Factor (VIF) to assess each variable's influence on the regression analysis. The results are shown in Tables 9. According to Aslam et al. (2024), in a regression model, if the VIF of an independent variable is greater than or equal to 10, it serves as an indicator that multicollinearity exists within the model. Table 9's

VIF outcomes indicate all variables score below 2, confirming no multicollinearity issues in the models.

Table 7. Results of VIF

Variable	VIF	1/VIF		Variable	VIF	1/VIF
Size	1.520	0.656		Size	1.570	0.636
LEV	1.450	0.687		LEV	1.460	0.686
ROE	1.190	0.839		ROE	1.200	0.834
ICE	1.050	0.955		RCE	1.090	0.917
				SCE	1.050	0.950
				HCE	1.010	0.990
Mean	VIF	1.300		Mean	VIF	1.230

MULTIPLE REGRESSION ANALYSIS

As illustrated in Table 8, Model (1) demonstrates that ICE exerts a notably positive influence on both ROA and ROE across the entire sample, regardless of whether the analysis focuses on KIIs or CIIs. Specifically, the industry-wide data reveals that a one-unit rise in ICE corresponds to an increase of 0.0000750 units in ROA and 0.000171 units in ROE. Both coefficients are statistically significant at the 1% level, thereby robustly supporting H1.

Table 9 presents the outcomes of model (2), revealing that the three elements of ICE exert a positive and statistically significant influence on both KIIs and CIIs at the 1% level. H1a-H1c are thereby supported. Delving into the regression analysis for KIIs specifically, it becomes evident that a one-unit rise in HCE boosts ROA by 0.00106 units, while a similar increase in RCE leads to a 0.00367-unit gain in ROA. Additionally, a one-unit increase in SCE investment corresponds to a 0.000132-unit improvement in ROA. Notably, within the ICE framework, HCE and RCE wield a more substantial effect on FP compared to SCE. This pattern holds true for CIIs as well, where structural capital's influence on FP pales in comparison to that of human and relational capital. To quantify, a one-unit increase in HCE results in a 0.000133-unit rise in ROA, a one-unit increase in RCE yields a 0.000209-unit boost, and a one-unit escalation in SCE investment contributes a modest 0.0000267-unit enhancement to ROA.

The findings from Model (3) in Table 10 lend strong support to H2, highlighting that ICE significantly boosts FP in sectors where knowledge and innovation are paramount. The regression analysis reveals interaction coefficients of -0.000131 for ROA and -0.000269 for ROE, underscoring a notable trend: as industries shift from KIIs to CIIs, the incremental advantages of ICE begin to taper off. The results of Z-test, model (4), is shown in table 12. It further investigates the impact of HCE, RCE, and SCE on FP in different industries. The data in Table 11 show that the Z values of HCE, RCE, and SCE have reached a significant level, and H2a-H2c are confirmed.

Among the control variables, enterprise size has a significant positive relationship with enterprise performance. The theory of economies of scale can explain this conclusion, that is, large-scale enterprises can improve resource utilization efficiency, thereby enhancing the profitability and market competitiveness of enterprises, and thus promoting the improvement of enterprise performance. In addition, the leverage ratio of enterprises has a significant negative relationship with enterprise performance, that is, higher debt will increase corporate financial risks and bankruptcy costs, thereby affecting FP. When observing the regression coefficient of time, it can be found that when ROA is used as a measure of FP, KIIs are more affected by Covid-19 than CIIs. The data in Tables 8 and 9 show that after the outbreak of Covid-19 in 2020, the time regression coefficient of KIIs turned from positive to negative, but this phenomenon did not occur in CIIs.

However, when ROE is used as a measure of FP, both industries have seen a phenomenon of time regression coefficients turning from positive to negative after 2020, indicating that both industries have been impacted by Covid-19. The industry differences in ROA mainly reflect the impact of Covid-19 on the efficiency of asset utilization in different industries. Since KIIs are more dependent on human capital, they are more affected by Covid-19. The consistent results of ROE show that Covid-19 has a greater impact on the overall profitability of enterprises. Whether it is knowledge-intensive or CIIs, the net profit of enterprises has been negatively impacted by Covid-19, which in turn lowers the return on equity.

Results are consistent with existing literature in many aspects, while also revealing some new findings. The results of Model (1) confirm H1, that ICE has a positive impact on FP, which is consistent with the findings Akgün & Türkoğlu (2024) and Ramírez et al. (2021). The results of Model (2) support H1a-H1c, which follow the conclusion of Xu & Li (2022) on the impact of ICE components (HCE, SCE and RCE) on FP. In addition, in further industry analysis, this study found that among the components of ICE, HCE and RCE have a more significant impact, which is consistent with Ryu et al. 2021. Model (3) confirms H2 and further supports the explanation of FP by RBV. The results of Model (4) confirm H2a-H2c, which is partially consistent with Xu & Li (2022). Xu & Li (2022) studied the impact of ICE on FP of high-tech and non-high-tech small and medium-sized enterprises (SMEs) in China's manufacturing industry. They found that HCE had a greater impact on high-tech SMEs than non-high-tech SMEs, while SCE had a smaller impact on high-tech SMEs than non-high-tech SMEs. Unlike Xu & Li (2022), this study found that SCE had a greater impact in KIIs than in CIIs. The reasons for this difference may be sample differences and industry differences. First, Xu & Li (2022) only selected SMEs in China's manufacturing industry as the research sample, and they conducted relevant discussions at the firm level. This study selected China's A-share market and discussed the differences in ICE at the industry level. Second, Xu & Li's study only targeted firms in the manufacturing industry, while this study focused on the differences between KIIs and CIIs. In addition, in terms of control variables, the study found that the size of the enterprise was positively and significantly related to FP, while the leverage ratio was negatively and significantly related to FP, which is consistent with the research conclusions of Aslam et al. (2024). The study also found the impact of covid-19. Since KIIs are highly dependent on human capital, Covid-19 has had a greater impact on them. But at the same time, Covid-19 has also had an impact on the overall profitability of Chinese companies.

While this study focuses on the impact of ICE on firm performance in China's industrial sectors, the findings offer broader implications, particularly for the transformation of the Islamic economic system. The integration of digital technology enhances the effectiveness of ICE, and when framed within the ethical parameters of Islamic principles, this synergy can act as a powerful catalyst for institutional and systemic transformation (Aslam et al., 2024; Asutay & Ubaidillah, 2024). IFIs can therefore leverage ICE not only to improve performance but also to realign operations with their spiritual and developmental objectives, positioning themselves as leaders in promoting of value-based, digitally driven economic system.

Robustness Test

This study employs multiple robustness checks to ensure the validity and reliability of the empirical results. First, the study conducts a Hausman test to determine the appropriateness of the fixed effects model versus the random effects model. The test results reject the null hypothesis in all models, indicating that the fixed effects model is the preferred choice, thereby improving the reliability of the regression estimates. Second, the study substitutes ROE as an alternative dependent variable in place of ROA for regression analysis. The results obtained remain highly consistent with the original findings, suggesting that the observed relationships are not driven by a specific financial performance metric. Additionally, the study applies heteroscedasticity-robust standard errors in Stata to account for potential heteroscedasticity issues. As shown in Table 12, the results remain stable and consistent, further confirming the robustness of the findings. Consequently, this investigation's model outputs demonstrate strong reliabilit

Table 8. Regression results for model 1

	Full Industries		Knowledge-intensive Industries		Capital-intensive Industries	
	(1)	(2)	(1)	(2)	(1)	(2)
	ROA	ROE	ROA	ROE	ROA	ROE
ICE	0.0000750***	0.000171***	0.000702***	0.00150***	0.0000698***	0.000158***
	(8.69)	(8.85)	(5.45)	(5.56)	(8.54)	(8.47)
Size	0.0337***	0.0875***	0.0528***	0.113***	0.0309***	0.0851***
	(15.15)	(17.61)	(5.41)	(5.53)	(14.03)	(16.97)
LEV	-0.240***	-0.532***	-0.276***	-0.665***	-0.233***	-0.508***
	(-31.62)	(-31.38)	(-8.97)	(-10.29)	(-30.74)	(-29.47)
2016.year	0	0			0	0
	(.)	(.)			(.)	(.)
2017.year	0.0396	0.0562			0.0358	0.0453
	(0.77)	(0.49)			(0.76)	(0.42)
2018.year	0.0311	0.0241	0	0	0.0268	0.0138
	(0.65)	(0.23)	(.)	(.)	(0.61)	(0.14)
2019.year	0.0295	0.0206	0.00433	0.0157	0.0245	0.00812
	(0.62)	(0.19)	(0.67)	(1.17)	(0.56)	(0.08)
2020.year	0.0267	0.0142	-0.00138	0.00954	0.0225	0.00228
	(0.56)	(0.13)	(-0.21)	(0.70)	(0.51)	(0.02)
2021.year	0.0295	0.0174	-0.00223	0.0136	0.0260	0.00521
	(0.62)	(0.16)	(-0.34)	(0.99)	(0.59)	(0.05)
2022.year	0.0194	-0.00417	-0.0150**	-0.00425	0.0167	-0.0161
	(0.41)	(-0.04)	(-2.26)	(-0.31)	(0.38)	(-0.16)
2023.year	0.0152	-0.0150	-0.00853	-0.00326	0.0111	-0.0286
	(0.32)	(-0.14)	(-1.28)	(-0.23)	(0.25)	(-0.29)
_cons	-0.666***	-1.743***	-1.082***	-2.327***	-0.598***	-1.680***
	(-9.50)	(-11.14)	(-4.95)	(-5.08)	(-8.90)	(-10.98)
Control	Yes	Yes	Yes	Yes	Yes	Yes
Company	Yes	Yes	Yes	Yes	Yes	Yes
Year	Yes	Yes	Yes	Yes	Yes	Yes
F	127.8658***	131.3112***	20.4802***	22.6074***	119.1767***	117.3520***
p	0.0000	0.0000	0.0000	0.0000	0.0000	0.0000
r2	0.1359	0.1390	0.1455	0.1583	0.1434	0.1415

t statistics in parentheses
* $p < 0.1$, ** $p < 0.05$, *** $p < 0.01$

Table 9. Regression results for model 2

	Full Industries		**Knowledge-intensive Industries**		**Capital-intensive Industries**	
	(1)	(2)	(1)	(2)	(1)	(2)
	ROA	ROE	ROA	ROE	ROA	ROE
HCE	0.000190***	0.000400***	0.00106***	0.00226***	0.000133***	0.000268***
	(6.24)	(6.33)	(4.52)	(4.62)	(4.96)	(4.96)
RCE	0.000234***	0.000451***	0.00367***	0.00631**	0.000209***	0.000418***
	(7.00)	(7.17)	(2.82)	(2.17)	(6.75)	(7.02)
SCE	0.0000289***	0.0000737***	0.000132**	0.000266***	0.0000267***	0.0000679***
	(5.22)	(5.29)	(2.56)	(2.61)	(5.10)	(4.95)
Size	0.0292***	0.0787***	0.0441***	0.0950***	0.0269***	0.0771***
	(8.17)	(9.92)	(3.49)	(3.30)	(7.60)	(9.61)
LEV	-0.231***	-0.514***	-0.249***	-0.617***	-0.224***	-0.491***
	(-18.95)	(-16.66)	(-6.95)	(-7.38)	(-17.50)	(-14.96)
2016. year	0	0			0	0
	(.)	(.)			(.)	(.)
2017. year	0.0361***	0.0495**			0.0325***	0.0387**
	(4.34)	(2.53)			(4.06)	(1.96)
2018. year	0.0289***	0.0199	0	0	0.0241***	0.00848
	(4.61)	(1.25)	(.)	(.)	(3.66)	(0.50)
2019. year	0.0282***	0.0183	0.00610	0.0194	0.0227***	0.00455
	(4.55)	(1.17)	(0.88)	(1.22)	(3.47)	(0.27)
2020. year	0.0250***	0.0115	0.00243	0.0177	0.0201***	-0.00235
	(3.98)	(0.73)	(0.33)	(1.13)	(3.07)	(-0.14)
2021. year	0.0278***	0.0146	0.000898	0.0201	0.0234***	0.000390
	(4.58)	(0.95)	(0.12)	(1.27)	(3.70)	(0.02)
2022. year	0.0184***	-0.00547	-0.0111	0.00337	0.0147**	-0.0198
	(3.03)	(-0.36)	(-1.39)	(0.20)	(2.34)	(-1.23)
2023. year	0.0150**	-0.0147	-0.00354	0.00679	0.00994	-0.0307*
	(2.46)	(-0.96)	(-0.42)	(0.39)	(1.57)	(-1.91)
_cons	-0.572***	-1.562***	-0.929***	-1.995***	-0.513***	-1.514***
	(-6.96)	(-8.54)	(-3.33)	(-3.15)	(-6.29)	(-8.17)
Control	Yes	Yes	Yes	Yes	Yes	Yes

continued on following page

Table 9. Continued

	Full Industries		Knowledge-intensive Industries		Capital-intensive Industries	
Company	Yes	Yes	Yes	Yes	Yes	Yes
Year	Yes	Yes	Yes	Yes	Yes	Yes
F	1.1526e+10***	4.3650e+10***	18.5345***	17.4829***	2.0862e+10***	4.7673e+10***
p	0.0000	0.0000	0.0000	0.0000	0.0000	0.0000
r2	0.1553	0.1547	0.1932	0.1949	0.1616	0.1559

t statistics in parentheses
* $p < 0.1$, ** $p < 0.05$, *** $p < 0.01$

Table 10. Regression results for model 3 *Table 11. Z-test*

	(1)	(2)
	ROA	ROE
ICE	0.000332***	0.000698***
	(3.99)	(3.76)
ICE_IndustryType	-0.000131***	-0.000269***
	(-3.11)	(-2.86)
Size	0.0338***	0.0877***
	(15.18)	(17.64)
LEV	-0.240***	-0.532***
	(-31.63)	(-31.39)
2016.year	0	0
	(.)	(.)
2017.year	0.0396	0.0562
	(0.77)	(0.49)
2018.year	0.0311	0.0241
	(0.65)	(0.23)
2019.year	0.0294	0.0204
	(0.62)	(0.19)
2020.year	0.0266	0.0141
	(0.56)	(0.13)
2021.year	0.0294	0.0172
	(0.62)	(0.16)
2022.year	0.0193	-0.00431
	(0.40)	(-0.04)

	Z
HCE	3.9275***
RCE	2.6299***
SCE	2.0731**

$|Z| \geq 1.645, \alpha = 0.10$,
$|Z| \geq 1.960, \alpha = 0.05$,
$|Z| \geq 2.576, \alpha = 0.01$
*$\alpha < 0.1$, **$\alpha < 0.05$, ***$\alpha < 0.01$

continued on following page

Table 10. Continued

	(1)	(2)				Z
2023.year	0.0152	-0.0151				
	(0.32)	(-0.14)				
_cons	-0.667***	-1.746***				
	(-9.53)	(-11.16)				
Control	Yes	Yes				
Company	Yes	Yes				
Year	Yes	Yes				
F	117.2435***	120.2215***				
p	0.0000	0.0000				
r2	0.1369	0.1399				

t statistics in parentheses
* $p < 0.1$, ** $p < 0.05$, *** $p < 0.01$

Table 12. Robustness test

	(1)	(2)
	ROA	ROA
ICE	0.0000750***	
	(6.99)	
Size	0.0337***	0.0301***
	(9.73)	(8.47)
LEV	-0.240***	-0.233***
	(-19.52)	(-19.11)
HCE		0.0000967***
		(4.74)
RCE		0.000224***
		(7.01)
SCE		0.0000288***
		(5.47)
_cons	-0.665***	-0.590***
	(-8.33)	(-7.20)
Control	Yes	Yes
Company	Yes	Yes
Year	Yes	Yes

continued on following page

Table 12. Continued

	(1)	(2)
F	2.0988e+10***	1.9740e+10***
p	0.0000	0.0000
r2	0.1361	0.1504

t statistics in parentheses
* $p < 0.1$, ** $p < 0.05$, *** $p < 0.01$

CONCLUSION

This study investigates the impact of ICE on FP in the context of China, focusing on three core objectives: (1) to examine the influence of ICE and its components—human capital efficiency (HCE), relational capital efficiency (RCE), and structural capital efficiency (SCE)—on FP; (2) to assess the moderating effect of industry type on the ICE–FP relationship; and (3) to explore differences in ICE practices between knowledge-intensive industries (KIIs) and capital-intensive industries (CIIs). The empirical findings confirm that all three ICE components have a significant and positive effect on firm performance across Chinese industries. Notably, HCE and RCE exhibit a more substantial impact compared to SCE, indicating that firms rely more heavily on skilled human resources and external relational networks to enhance performance outcomes. Moreover, the influence of ICE is found to be stronger in KIIs than in CIIs, consistent with the greater dependence of KIIs on innovation and intellectual assets. These insights, while grounded in China's evolving industrial and digital context, offer valuable perspectives for countries and institutions seeking to align economic performance with ethical innovation, such as those pursuing transformation under the Islamic economic system. The study suggests that intellectual capital is more than a productivity tool—it is a strategic, ethical, and transformative asset. The synergy between ICE and digital technology offers new pathways for Islamic institutions to lead in areas such as financial inclusion, digital zakat and waqf, and Shariah-compliant innovation ecosystems.

A key contribution of this study lies in the reclassification of China's 2024 industry standards into KIIs and CIIs based on international benchmarks, enabling a robust industry-level comparative analysis. The inclusion of interaction terms further reveals the heterogeneous effects of ICE across sectors, contributing new insights to the literature on intellectual capital in emerging economies. The findings offer practical implications for managers and policymakers. For firms in KIIs, strategic investment in HCE and RCE can substantially boost performance, highlighting the importance of talent development and collaborative innovation. Meanwhile, firms in CIIs, although less reliant on ICE, should not overlook the benefits of integrating IC strategies—such as adopting digital technologies and fostering partnerships—to enhance competitiveness and resilience. Policymakers are encouraged to tailor support mechanisms, including R&D incentives and talent development programs, to promote effective IC utilization across sectors.

Despite its contributions, this study has certain limitations. The sample is restricted to A-share listed companies in China, excluding SMEs and unlisted firms, which may limit the generalizability of the findings. Future research should consider a broader range of firm types including Islamic banks, fintech companies, and Islamic social finance institutions and explore the dynamic effects of ICE across different economic cycles and regulatory environments. Such expansion would offer a more comprehensive understanding of ICE as a strategic asset for sustainable firm development in varying institutional contexts. Additionally, longitudinal research could explore how ICE development contributes to the realization of *Maqasid al-Shariah* over time, particularly within emerging digital Islamic economies.

REFERENCES

Adznan, S., Sori, Z. M., & Ramadili Mohd, S. M. (2022). Intellectual Capital Disclosure and Corporate Governance: Empirical Evidence from a Cross Country that Offering Islamic Bank Services. *Journal of Accounting and Governance, 18*, 147–164. DOI: 10.17576/AJAG-2022-18-11

Ahmed, Z. N., & Amir Hussin, M. R. (2024). The Effect of Intellectual Capital Efficiency on Malaysian Firm Performance: A Dynamic Panel Estimation. [MAR]. *Management Accounting Research, 23*(1), 57–84.

Akgün, A. İ., & Türkoğlu, S. P. (2024). Intellectual Capital and Performance of Listed Firms During The Global Financial Crisis: The Effects of Legal Origin. *The International Journal of Organizational Analysis, 32*(4), 759–785. DOI: 10.1108/IJOA-01-2023-3587

Aslam, E., Rehman, A. U., & Iqbal, A. (2024). The Mediating Role of Intellectual Capital in Corporate Governance and Financial Efficiency of Islamic Banks. *Corporate Governance (Bradford), 24*(1), 19–40. DOI: 10.1108/CG-06-2022-0276

Asutay, M., & Ubaidillah, . (2024). Examining the Impact of Intellectual Capital Performance on Financial Performance in Islamic Banks. *Journal of the Knowledge Economy, 15*(1), 1231–1263. DOI: 10.1007/s13132-023-01114-1

Buallay, A., Cummings, R., & Hamdan, A. (2019). Intellectual Capital Efficiency and Bank's Performance: A Comparative Study After the Global Financial Crisis. *Pacific Accounting Review, 31*(4), 672–694. DOI: 10.1108/PAR-04-2019-0039

Habib, A. M., & Dalwai, T. (2024). Does The Efficiency of a Firm's Intellectual Capital and Working Capital Management Affect Its Performance? *Journal of the Knowledge Economy, 15*(1), 3202–3238. DOI: 10.1007/s13132-023-01138-7 PMID: 40478946

Jaunanda, M., Sembel, R., Hulu, E., & Ugut, G. S. S. (2024). The Impact of Intellectual Capital Strategy on Firm Value and Financial Distress. *Corporate & Business Strategy Review, 5*(3), 148–158. DOI: 10.22495/cbsrv5i3art14

Kim, S. Y., & Tran, D. B. (2024). Intellectual Capital and Performance: Evidence from SMEs In Vietnam. *Asia-Pacific Journal of Business Administration, 16*(4), 860–875. DOI: 10.1108/APJBA-08-2022-0343

Majumder, M. T. H., Ruma, I. J., & Akter, A. (2023). Does Intellectual Capital Affect Bank Performance? Evidence from Bangladesh. *LBS Journal of Management & Research, 21*(2), 171–185. DOI: 10.1108/LBSJMR-05-2022-0016

Pulic, A. (2000). VAIC™–An accounting tool for IC management. *International Journal of Technology Management, 20*(5-8), 702–714. DOI: 10.1504/IJTM.2000.002891

Ramírez, Y., Dieguez-Soto, J., & Manzaneque, M. (2021). How Does Intellectual Capital Efficiency Affect Firm Performance? The Moderating Role of Family Management. *International Journal of Productivity and Performance Management, 70*(2), 297–324. DOI: 10.1108/IJPPM-03-2019-0119

Ryu, D., Baek, K. H., & Yoon, J. (2021). Open Innovation with Relational Capital, Technological Innovation Capital, And International Performance in SMEs. *Sustainability (Basel), 13*(6), 3418. DOI: 10.3390/su13063418

Sharma, D., Verma, R., Patil, C., & Nayak, J. K. (2024). Relationship Between Intellectual Capital and Firm Performance: Evidence from the Indian Sugar Mill Industry. *IIMT Journal of Management, 1*(1), 98–111. DOI: 10.1108/IIMTJM-11-2023-0054

Xu, J., & Li, J. (2022). The Interrelationship Between Intellectual Capital and Firm Performance: Evidence from China's Manufacturing Sector. *Journal of Intellectual Capital, 23*(2), 313–341. DOI: 10.1108/JIC-08-2019-0189

Chapter 2
Strategic Innovation's Effect on Islamic SME Performance Through Government-Supported Technological Development in Ethiopia

Fisseha Dejene Yadete
https://orcid.org/0009-0007-1002-4881
Bule Hora University, Ethiopia

Shashi Kant
https://orcid.org/0000-0003-4722-5736
DMI-St. Eugene University, Zambia

Chalchisa Amentie Karo
Ethiopian Civil Service University, Ethiopia

ABSTRACT

This article addresses the challenges faced by these enterprises in adopting innovative practices and the function of government initiatives in facilitating this process. The investigation employs a quantitative investigations approach, utilizing surveys and interviews to collect data from a sample of Islamic SMEs. This data is analyzed to explore the associations among strategic innovation, government support, and organizational performance, employing statistical techniques to identify substantial patterns and insights. Islamic SMEs that actively assimilated with government ini-

DOI: 10.4018/979-8-3373-2655-9.ch002

tiatives chaptered higher levels of innovation and improved operational influence, leading to augmented competitiveness in the market. The implications of these outcomes underscore the importance of fostering a culture of innovation within Islamic SMEs and leveraging government resources to support technological advancements. Additionally, the investigation emphasizes the need for collaborative networks and partnerships to further drive innovation and performance.

INTRODUCTION

Small and medium-sized enterprises (SMEs) are acknowledged as key contributors to economic development, innovation, and employment in a world economy that is becoming more and more competitive. SMEs' strategic innovation is essential to augmenting their competitiveness and resilience, especially in emerging nations like Ethiopia. This importance is heightened in the case of Islamic SMEs by their distinct operational frameworks, which are based on moral corporate conduct and community-focused objectives that are consistent with Islamic values (Andespa et al., 2024). In many international contexts, the significance of concentrating on Islamic SMEs is emphasized since these enterprises uphold moral principles that can outcome in sustained economic growth while offering communities vital services and goods.

The necessity for companies to change and adapt to changing consumer tastes, market dynamics, and technology breakthroughs gave rise to the idea of strategic innovation. It places a strong emphasis on creating and putting into practice innovative concepts that improve competitive advantage, streamline processes, and satisfy the needs of a constantly changing market. Empirical investigations over the years has manifests that companies that innovate continuously are better positioned to succeed better, especially when responding to rapid technical advancements or economic upheavals. According to investigations, government assistance greatly influences SMEs' ability to innovate by supplying the resources they need, easing the transfer of technology, and creating regulatory frameworks that are favorable(Lu et al., 2021).

The successful application of strategic innovation in Islamic SMEs is hampered by numerous practical issues, notwithstanding the expanding corpus of knowledge. These difficulties include a lack of qualified human resources, restricted access to funding, and a poor awareness of the latest technology developments (Afum et al., 2021). Additionally, Islamic SMEs' innovation processes are complicated by the unique obstacles they confront, such as adhering to religious precepts while implementing contemporary corporate techniques. As well as, a notable investigations gap is manifested by the paucity of empirical investigations examining the association among Ethiopian Islamic SMEs' success and government-supported technological growth.

This chapter aims to bridge these gaps by carefully analyzing the dynamics of strategic innovation and government support within the context of Islamic SMEs in Ethiopia. In doing so, it seeks to provide advice to future investigators and policy-makers as they create programs that foster technical advancement, augment operational efficiency, and ultimately augment the socioeconomic climate for SMEs(E. T. Kassa & Getnet Mirete, 2022). The comprehensive investigation presented here will address the investigations question, ***"How does strategic innovation, underpinned by government-supported technological progress, influence the success of Islamic SMEs in Ethiopia?"*** Because it seeks to determine the associations among innovation, government support, and SME performance, this question is essential. Additionally, it manifests the unique contribution Islamic SMEs provide to long-term economic expansion. As such, the outcomes of this investigation have the potential to inform policies that nurture an environment conducive to innovation, thereby enhancing the competitive edge of Islamic SMEs in Ethiopia and beyond (Alhyasat et al., 2025; Anwar et al.,2025). Consequently, the investigation's conclusions could influence laws that foster an innovative atmo-sphere, strengthening the competitiveness of Islamic SMEs in Ethiopia and elsewhere.

BACKGROUND OF THE INVESTIGATION

Ethiopia's small and medium-sized corporate (SME) environment is an essential part of the nation's economic structure(E. T. Kassa & Getnet Mirete, 2022). SMEs account for a sizable share of employment and make a big contribution to the GDP of the country. However, these companies frequently work in difficult conditions marked by a lack of cash, poor infrastructure, and shifting consumer preferences. In this regard, Ethiopian Islamic SMEs that follow Sharia law confront particular difficulties that may limit their ability to develop and innovate. A sophisticated grasp of the association among strategic innovation and government assistance is necessary due to the obligation to uphold Islamic principles while pursuing commercial success.

Al-Ameen's experience as a modest textile factory in Addis Ababa is a noteworthy case investigation that illustrates the difficulties experienced by Islamic SMEs in Ethiopia. The corporate, which has its roots in Islamic principles, specializes in creating apparel that conforms to both cultural and religious standards(Hassan, 2024). Despite its dedication to moral behavior, Al-Ameen finds it difficult to grow its corporate because of its restricted access to capital, which is made worse by Islamic financial institutions' possible reluctance to provide traditional loans. Because of this, the corporate has been unable to make investments in cutting-edge equipment or technology that would boost productivity and creativity. This circumstance is indicative of a larger pattern in which a large number of Islamic SMEs are hampered by both monetary constraints and the difficulties of upholding Sharia-compliant procedures (Andespa et al., 2024).

In order to augment product quality and market reach, Islamic SMEs, such as regional food processing companies, are attempting to implement innovative technology in the agro-processing industry (Cheah et al., 2022). This is another real-world example. These companies frequently use antiquated techniques that are time-consuming and reduce their ability to compete in a market that is changing quickly. In certain areas, government initiatives to promote technical advancement—like offering training courses and granting access to cutting-edge agricultural equipment—have proven potential. However, bureaucratic obstacles, SMEs' ignorance, and a lack of infrastructure to accommodate new technology frequently impede the implementation of these projects. These difficulties manifest how crucial it is to match government programs with the unique requirements and capabilities of Islamic SMEs in order to promote an innovative atmosphere.

As well as, empirical investigations suggests that community expectations and cultural considerations may complicate the strategic innovation process in Islamic SMEs (Andespa et al., 2024). These enterprises have to strike a careful balance among maintaining traditional values and fostering innovative growth, which occasionally outcomes in opposition to change. For example, many owners voiced concerns about sacrificing their cultural authenticity during a government-sponsored innovation session that aimed to integrate digital marketing tactics into Islamic SMEs. This situation emphasizes how innovation tactics must be customized to these companies' cultural frameworks in order to stay relevant while pursuing contemporary practices.

STATEMENT OF THE PROBLEM

A complex issue that has not received enough attention in the academic and real-world domains is the confluence of strategic innovation and government-sponsored technology development in Ethiopian Islamic SMEs (Lu et al., 2021). The ideal state imagines a dynamic environment where Islamic SMEs successfully use cutting-edge tactics to improve their performance, underpinned by strong governmental frameworks that encourage the use of new technologies(Enyioko & Onwusoro, 2018; Hasani et al., 2024). But this goal frequently stands in sharp contrast to the reality of today. Due to limited financial resources, poor technology infrastructure, and a lack of knowledge about the advantages of contemporary corporate methods, many Islamic SMEs find it difficult to innovate.

There is conflicting data regarding the real influences of government assistance on Islamic SMEs' capacity for innovation. Although some investigations manifests that government programs have improved the performance of SMEs, other investigations manifest that the advantages are not always available to diverse industries or kinds of enterprises(Rajeswari, 2025). These discrepancies point to a lack of knowledge on the ways in which different contextual elements—like the kind of government assistance, the unique traits of Islamic SMEs, and local economic circumstances—influence outcomes. For example, current investigations on the efficacy of specific government initiatives aimed at promoting innovation frequently yields conflicting outcomes; while some SMEs may gain a great deal from these initiatives, others may encounter bureaucratic obstacles that make them influential.

Additionally, there are still theoretical gaps in the literature on strategic innovation in Islamic contexts(Alhyasat et al., 2025; Cristofaro & Giardino, 2025). The majority of current frameworks is primarily geared toward traditional enterprises and has little relevance to the particular operational and ethical guidelines that regulate Islamic enterprises. As a outcome, there aren't many thorough models available to academics and professionals that discuss how innovative tactics and Islamic principles can be combined to improve corporate success. Additionally, there are gaps in our understanding of the unique requirements and difficulties experienced by Ethiopian Islamic SMEs. Without taking into consideration the unique socioeconomic and cultural circumstances of Ethiopian SMEs, many investigations have a tendency to extrapolate outcomes from other areas, which might outcome in suggestions that are not realistic.

These problems are exacerbated by practical and contextual difficulties. Islamic SMEs frequently face cultural opposition to implementing new corporate procedures or technology, which makes them reluctant to fully embrace innovation (Afum et al., 2021). These obstacles are further made worse by the absence of a supportive environment, such as training programs and mentorship programs designed specifically for Islamic corporate owners. These difficulties are exacerbated by the paucity of empirical investigations on the Ethiopian environment, which is underrepresented in the larger conversation about Islamic innovation and entrepreneurship. By focusing its investigation on the Ethiopian environment, this investigation seeks to close these imperative gaps and offer a more nuanced knowledge of how particular issues influence the innovation processes of Islamic SMEs(Aimal et al., 2025). This investigation will offer evidence-based suggestions for policymakers to create focused interventions that promote technological growth in Islamic SMEs by closely analyzing both the theoretical frameworks and the actual realities. Additionally, it aims to augment the theoretical underpinnings of SME growth in Islamic contexts by putting forth a model that combines strategic innovation with Islamic values.

RELATED THEORIES

Theory of the Resource-Based View (RBV): According to the Resource-Based View (RBV), a corporate's success and competitive advantage are largely determined by its distinct resources and capabilities(Naila, 2024). According to this notion, companies should use their internal resources—whether they are material (technology, cash) or immaterial (organizational culture, brand reputation)—to outperform their competitors in their respective marketplaces. This idea is especially relevant to Islamic SMEs because it emphasizes how crucial it is to acknowledge and capitalize on community connections and Sharia-compliant ethical values as imperative assets. Islamic SMEs can improve their competitiveness and overcome market obstacles while upholding their core values by concentrating on their unique skills and integrating them with strategic innovation.

Institutional theory: This theory looks at how formal and informal institutions influence the performance and behavior of organizations. According to this idea, organizations function in settings that are shaped by social norms, cultural standards, and regulatory frameworks (Rajeswari, 2025). Ethiopian Islamic SMEs' capacity for innovation is greatly influenced by government regulation and assistance. Islamic SMEs can more influence adjust to external mandates while pursuing innovations that align with their ethical framework by comprehending the interaction among institutional pressures and organizational practices. Thus, institutional theory sheds light on how Islamic SMEs negotiate social norms and state actions to promote innovation and expansion.

Diffusion of Innovations Theory: Everett Rogers created this theory to examine how novel concepts, methods, or technological advancements proliferate both inside and among societies and organizations (Naila, 2024). It emphasizes imperative elements that influence how innovations are adopted and spread, such as perceived benefits, compatibility, trial ability, complexity, and viability. This theory is especially pertinent to Islamic SMEs since it clarifies the difficulties these companies encounter when using cutting-edge procedures and contemporary technology. The rate and success of innovation adoption can be greatly influenced by variables like perceived dangers, cultural compatibility with Islamic beliefs, and the complexity of new technologies. Policymakers can create focused strategies that promote the spread of creative practices within the Islamic SME sector by comprehending these dynamics.

Dynamic capabilities theory: This theory focuses on how a corporate can integrate, develop, and reorganize its external and internal capabilities to deal with quickly changing circumstances. In order to sustain competitive advantage over time, this idea manifests the significance of ongoing learning, innovation, and adaptability. Given the rapid rate of technical breakthroughs and market shifts, Islamic SMEs must be able to create dynamic capacities. According to this notion, in order to prosper in the face of adversity, Islamic SMEs should develop the ability to innovate and modify their corporate models and procedures. In order to create resilience and promote sustainable growth, it emphasizes the need for constant investments in partnerships, human capital, and knowledge management.

Among these theories, the "*Dynamic Capabilities Theory*" serves as the primary theoretical foundation for this investigation. It provides a solid framework for understanding how Islamic SMEs in Ethiopia can acquire the abilities needed to innovate and adapt in a corporate climate that is continuously changing. By focusing on the dynamic capacities, this investigation may fully address how Islamic SMEs may make use of their unique resources and connect them with strategic innovation efforts supported by governmental frameworks. This lens makes it possible to conduct a comprehensive analysis of the internal and external support networks that have an influence on the performance of Islamic SMEs, giving practitioners and policymaker's useful data to encourage innovation and growth in this vital sector.

DEFINITION AND ORIGIN OF CONCEPTS

Strategic innovation: The application of novel concepts, procedures, or strategies that fundamentally change how a corporate operates in order to augment productivity, influence, or competitive advantage is known as strategic innovation(Anwar et al., 2025). It includes not just new goods or services but also revolutionary adjustments to organizational structures, corporate models, and procedures. Strategic innovation is the process of adding value in ways that rivals have not considered or that are specifically tailored to the demands of the market, especially in reaction to new trends or difficulties. The phrase "strategic innovation" came about as a outcome of the intersection of strategic management literature and innovation theory (Al-hyasat et al., 2025; Cristofaro & Giardino, 2025). Its theoretical foundations may be found in the writings of academics such as Michael Porter, who manifested the significance of value creation and competitive advantage in strategic management. But in the latter half of the 20th century, the idea of incorporating innovation as a strategic imperative gained traction, especially with the introduction of theories like Clayton Christensen's disruptive innovation, which emphasized how new technology may completely transform entire industries. Strategic innovation has expanded over time to include social, organizational, and corporate model advances in addition to technology breakthroughs.

Small and Medium Enterprises: SMEs, or small and medium-sized enterprises, are classified according to a number of factors, such as the number of workers, yearly income, and financial resources. SMEs are often defined as companies with less than 250 employees, though definitions might differ from one country to another. They are sometimes divided into three categories: micro (1–9), small (10–49), and medium (50–249) organizations. They are seen to be essential for promoting innovation, creating jobs, and advancing economic growth (E. T. Kassa & Getnet Mirete, 2022). As economies looked to recover and expand following World War II, the idea of SMEs was born. Government agencies and economic theorists started to divide corporates into various groups according to their size and economic contributions after realizing the importance of small enterprises in boosting the economy (Becha et al., 2025). Laws and policy frameworks that encourage the expansion and development of SMEs have established definitions of SMEs in several nations. Particularly as global economies have moved toward more diversified and entrepreneurial corporate environments, the focus on SMEs has continued to change.

Islamic SMEs: Enterprises that function in conformity with Islamic law (Sharia) and values are known as Islamic small and medium enterprises, or Islamic SMEs. While making sure that their operations adhere to Islamic rules, such as the proscription of interest (riba), excessive uncertainty (gharar), and unethical commercial methods, these companies place a high priority on moral behavior, social responsibility, and community welfare. Islamic SMEs are present in a wide range of industries, including manufacturing, services, retail, and agriculture. The idea of Islamic SMEs stems from the more general idea of Islamic economics, which became well-known in the middle of the 20th century as investigations started looking into how economic endeavors might be in line with Islamic values. A strong foundation for the expansion of Islamic SMEs has been made available by the recent decades' upsurge of interest in Islamic finance. The economic benefits that these enterprises make to both Muslim-majority and multicultural communities have also come to light as the number of Muslims worldwide has grown and diversified. The growth of Islamic SMEs has also been aided by the creation of numerous Islamic corporate groups and the expansion of financial products that adhere to Sharia law.

EMPIRICAL LITERATURE REVIEW

Strategic Innovation and SMEs Performance

Strategic innovation is essential to improving the performance of Islamic SMEs because it allows them to meet customer requests, adjust to changing market conditions, and maintain their competitiveness while abiding by Sharia law (Alhyasat et al., 2025; Cristofaro & Giardino, 2025). When innovation is incorporated into Islamic SMEs' strategic framework, it makes it easier to create new goods, services, and corporate models, which meaningfully boosts operational influence and responsiveness to the market. The enhancement of competitive advantage is one of the main ways that strategic innovation influences the performance of Islamic SMEs(R. Aslam et al., 2023). Islamic SMEs can set themselves apart from rivals by implementing creative strategies and providing distinctive goods that satisfy both ethical and consumer requirements. An Islamic-compliant textile corporate, for instance, might launch eco-friendly, ethically sourced textiles that appeal to both domestic and foreign consumers. In addition to drawing in a larger clientele, this kind of distinction fosters brand loyalty among customers who respect ethical consumption. According to numerous investigations, companies that strategically innovate frequently chapter augmented market share and customer happiness, which improves performance indicators overall.

Additionally, Islamic SMEs can streamline their internal operations through strategic innovation. These enterprises can save operating expenses and boost productivity by implementing creative management techniques and investing in new technologies. For example, Islamic SMEs can more influence allocate resources by streamlining operations through the use of digital solutions for inventory management and customer association management. According to investigations, SMEs who adopt process innovations see notable performance gains because they are able to react to consumer demands and market shifts faster. This flexibility is essential, particularly in industries where customer tastes and technology are changing quickly.

Facilitating market expansion is another aspect of how strategic innovation influences the performance of Islamic SMEs. Islamic SMEs might investigate new market potential beyond their conventional consumer bases by using creative marketing and customer engagement strategies(Alhyasat et al., 2025; Anwar et al., 2025). For instance, these enterprises can reach urban and foreign consumers who might not otherwise have access to their products by using social media platforms and e-commerce networks. According to empirical data, SMEs' reach and visibility can be greatly expanded by strategic innovations in marketing and sales channels, which will raise sales and revenue generation.

Additionally, Islamic SMEs can become more resilient to economic difficulties and external shocks by implementing strategic innovation. Many corporates were manifests to be vulnerable by the COVID-19 epidemic, but those that had already implemented new processes were frequently better equipped to withstand the crisis. For example, Islamic SMEs manifested greater levels of sustainability and adaptability when they switched to online sales or varied their product lines in response to shifting consumer behavior. These SMEs fortify their corporate models and guarantee long-term viability in the face of uncertainty by cultivating an innovative culture.

Strategic Innovation and Government-Supported Technological Development

By influencing the frameworks and procedures by which governments encourage and support innovation across a range of industries, including small and medium-sized enterprises (SMEs), strategic innovation has a substantial influence on government-supported technical advancement(Khalid & Jetin, 2025; Stutz & Matala, 2025). Since governments around the world understand that innovation is a vital component of economic growth, competitiveness, and technical advancement, this association is especially imperative. Giving policymakers a clear path forward is one of the main ways that strategic innovation influences government-sponsored technical progress. Government programs meant to promote technological advancement might benefit from the successful models, case investigations, and insights produced by enterprises—SMEs in particular—that embrace strategic innovation techniques(Alhyasat et al., 2025).

These creative methods demonstrate how new procedures or technology can boost competitiveness and productivity, which encourages governments to create focused initiatives that encourage comparable tactics in other sectors. As well as, according to strategic innovation in the private sector can encourage government-corporate collaborations, since innovative SMEs frequently aim to adopt advanced technologies and may need assistance that only government institutions can offer, like funding, investigations resources, or regulatory considerations(Anwar et al., 2025). These partnerships can outcome in public-private partnerships that not only propel technological development but also improve innovation ecosystems in particular regions or industries. By establishing bridges through strategic alliances, governments can augment their support to facilitate a wider range of technological advancements. As well as, the growing focus on R&D (Investigations and Development) programs is a clear indication of how strategic innovation influences government-supported technical development. Recognizing that cultivating an innovative culture necessitates dedication at the organizational and national levels, governments are more likely to invest in R&D grants or tax incentives when they witness successful strategic innovations within SMEs (Alhyasat et al., 2025).

Government Support for Technical Development and SMEs Performance

In order to improve the performance of Islamic small and medium-sized enterprises (SMEs), government support for technical development is essential. This assistance is essential for Islamic SMEs in order to bridge the technological and financial divide that these companies frequently encounter and to guarantee that the distinct moral principles that guide their operations are upheld and strengthened(Ha et al., 2025). Numerous factors, including as financial availability, capacity building, regulatory frameworks, and the development of innovation ecosystems, can be used to analyze this association. Financial aid and funding initiatives are among the main ways that government support influences Islamic SMEs(Yaseen et al., 2024). It is challenging for many Islamic SMEs to invest in the infrastructure and technology they need to become more competitive since they operate in resource-constrained situations. These financial costs can be reduced by government initiatives that offer grants, low-interest loans, or subsidies, enabling Islamic SMEs to make investments in cutting-edge technology and operational augmentments without sacrificing their commitment to Islamic finance principles. For instance, these companies can obtain the capital required for technological enhancements while adhering to their ethical obligations thanks to initiatives created especially to assist Sharia-compliant finance solutions.

Another crucial component of government assistance that has a big influence on how well Islamic SMEs function is capacity building and training programs(Yaseen et al., 2024). It's possible that many of these enterprises lack the abilities and know-how needed to successfully adopt cutting-edge technologies or creative techniques. Governments can close this gap by providing corporate management, digital literacy, and technical skills training programs designed especially for Islamic entrepreneurs. The performance of Islamic SMEs is meaningfully influenced by the regulatory environment that is made possible by government assistance. Islamic SMEs can better negotiate the challenges of adhering to both governmental and Islamic standards with the support of a regulatory framework. A climate that is favorable for the growth of Islamic SMEs is created by governments that streamline bureaucracy, cut down on red tape, and set clear rules for Sharia compliance. As well as, the performance of these enterprises can be directly improved by supportive policies that encourage the use and creation of new technologies. For instance, Islamic SMEs can align their operations with sustainable practices and the ideas of Islamic duty towards the environment and community if the government creates tax incentives for companies that invest in renewable energy technologies.

As well as, the operational capacities of Islamic SMEs can be meaningfully improved by government assistance in the form of infrastructure development, such as granting access to dependable internet connectivity, technology parks, and innovation hubs(Mohammadhossein & Atefeh, 2025). These companies may implement new technology thanks to improved infrastructure, which boosts output and influence. Investigations has indicated that areas with superior technology infrastructure see greater rates of innovation and SME expansion. By making such infrastructural investments, governments not only help Islamic SMEs operate better, but they also build a larger ecosystem that supports innovation and entrepreneurship.

Initiatives with government backing are also essential for promoting cooperation and alliances among the public and private sectors(Yaseen et al., 2024). Nevertheless, there are still obstacles to overcome before these programs can truly reach and help Islamic SMEs, even with the beneficial influences of government assistance. It's possible that many Islamic corporate owners are unaware of the government initiatives that are available to them or that bureaucratic obstacles will make it difficult for them to access them(Narendran et al., 2025). Additionally, government assistance's efficacy depends on how well these programs match the unique requirements and traits of Islamic SMEs. In order to better understand the particular needs of Islamic corporate groups and design assistance programs that meet those needs, officials must interact with them.

CONCEPTUAL FRAMEWORK

Figure 1. Conceptual framework

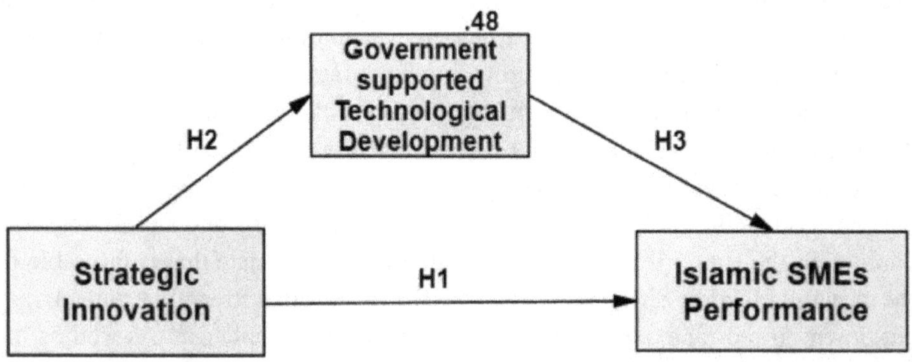

INVESTIGATIONS METHODOLOGY

The investigation used a quantitative investigations methodology to examine how government support and strategic innovation influence the performance of Islamic SMEs. To collect information about the experiences and perceptions of the variables of interest, 390 respondents—owners and managers of Islamic SMEs operating in different sectors of Ethiopia—were surveyed. This approach was chosen to enable statistically sound conclusions and to make it easier to identify associations among the variables(Zhang et al., 2025). The scale items were adapted from prior investigations to ensure reliability and validity, and a pilot investigation was conducted with a smaller sample to make necessary adjustments prior to the full-scale data collection(Teresi et al., 2022). The final questionnaire included a series of Likert scale items that allowed respondents to express their level of agreement or perception regarding each construct.

A structured questionnaire was developed, incorporating established scales to measure constructs such as strategic innovation, government-supported technical development, and overall corporate performance. The investigations employed exploratory factor analysis (EFA) as a prelude to factor analysis to evaluate the measurement model's validity(Cieri et al., 2025). Using the Kaiser-Meyer-Olkin (KMO) measure and Bartlett's test of sphericity, the data's appropriateness for factor analysis was assessed before to EFA. An acceptable sample size for factor analysis was indicated by a KMO value more than 0.70, which allowed for a meaningful interpretation of the underlying components. The variables' sufficient association to move further with the investigation was verified using Bartlett's test. The underlying factor structure was found by using EFA after the KMO and Bartlett's test. This allowed for the identification of imperative constructs and the removal of items that performed badly. The final measurement model was developed based on the EFA outcomes, and it was then examined using AMOS software's Structural Equation Modeling (SEM) feature.

SEM was used to examine the proposed connections among Islamic SMEs' performance, government assistance, and strategic innovation. This statistical method made it easier to evaluate both direct and indirect influences amongst the constructs, giving investigators a thorough grasp of how each variable influenced the others. The suitability of the model was assessed using the model fit indices, such as Chi-square, Root Mean Square Error of Approximation (RMSEA), and Comparative Fit Index (CFI)(Wang et al., 2025). The investigations were able to make inferences about the theoretical linkages suggested in the investigation since adequate fit indices manifested that the model adequately captured the data.

SCALE DEVELOPMENT

In order to guarantee the measurement of pertinent constructs with proven validity and reliability, the scale development for this investigation was painstakingly created based on an extensive evaluation of related literature. The success of Islamic small and medium-sized enterprises (SMEs), government support for technical advancement, and strategic innovation were among the constructs measured in the investigation(Bilal et al., 2024). A comprehensive evaluation of the corresponding dimensions was made possible by the operationalization of each construct using a number of questions drawn from earlier investigations. Items for the strategic innovation construct were modified from pre-existing scales that manifested enterprises' dynamic capacity for innovation and market adaptation. Imperative aspects of strategic innovation, such as corporate model, process, and product innovation, were emphasized in the literature. The inclusion of statements like "Our corporate regularly develops new products that meet customer needs" and "We implement new processes to augment our operational efficiency" was based on the writings of authors like, who offered a strong theoretical framework for comprehending innovation in SMEs. By combining the outcomes of investigations that looked at how government interventions might encourage innovation and technology adoption in SMEs, the government assistance for technological development construct was created (Audretsch & Belitski, 2021). Scholars like have manifested the significance of training initiatives, infrastructure support, and financial help. In order to ensure that each item accurately reflected the unique nuances of government support relevant to Islamic SMEs, the scale included items such as "Government funding has facilitated our technological advancements" and "We have benefited from government training programs that augment our technical skills."

DATA ANALYSIS

Table 1. KMO and Bartlett's test

Kaiser-Meyer-Olkin Measure of Sampling Adequacy.		**.850**
Bartlett's Test of Sphericity	Approx. Chi-Square	1419.738
	Df	91
	Sig.	.000

Source: Authors

Table 1 manifests the outcomes of sampling adequacy, which were used to determine if the data was suitable for factor analysis (Jusoh et al., 2023). The sample was big and representative enough to allow for factor analysis, as indicated by the KMO measure's value of 0.850, which also manifested a high degree of sampling adequacy. As well as, a Chi-Square value of 1419.738 with 91 degrees of freedom and a significance level (Sig.) of 0.000 was chaptered by Bartlett's Test of Sphericity. This outcome incorporates that there are associations among the variables that may be investigated using factor analysis, manifesting that the association matrix differs meaningfully from an identity matrix.

Table 2. Total variance explained

Component	Initial Eigenvalues			Extraction Sums of Squared Loadings			Rotation Sums of Squared Loadings		
	Total	% of Variance	Cumulative %	Total	% of Variance	Cumulative %	Total	% of Variance	Cumulative %
1	4.51	32.235	32.235	4.51	32.235	32.235	3.00	21.451	21.451
2	1.37	9.787	42.022	1.37	9.787	42.022	2.16	15.491	36.942
3	1.27	9.087	51.110	1.27	9.087	51.110	1.98	14.168	51.110
4	.949	6.782	57.892						
5	.871	6.223	64.115						
6	.773	5.519	69.634						

Extraction Method: Principal Component Analysis.
Source: Authors

Table 2 summarizes the Total Variance's outcomes. According to the investigations, the first component had a substantial contribution to the entire data structure, accounting for 32.235% of the total variance explained with a total eigenvalue of 4.51. This component likewise accounted for 32.235% of the total variation explained. With an eigenvalue of 1.37, the second component added 9.787% to the variance, augmenting the cumulative amount to 42.022%. With an eigenvalue of 1.27, the third component came in second, accounting for 9.087% of the variance and contributing to a total percentage of 51.110%. With eigenvalues of.949,.871, and.773 for the fourth, fifth, and sixth components, respectively, the subsequent components kept augmenting the variance, outcompeting in a total variance of 57.892%, 64.115%, and 69.634%. Interestingly, principal component analysis was the extraction technique used for this analysis, which successfully made it easier to identify imperative underlying elements in the dataset and improved comprehension of the constructs being assessed.

PRINCIPAL COMPONENT EXAMINATION

Confirmatory factor analysis (CFA), a statistical method, was used to analyze the principal component arrangement of a set of directed proxies. The perseverance of CFA is to incorporate the proposed connections among the latent components that underlie observable variables(Brimmell et al., 2025). To thoroughly assess the hypothesis about the associations among the directed proxies and their related latent conceptions, CFA was utilized in this investigation. The analysis sought to determine whether the conceptual framework appropriately represented the underlying structure based on predetermined theoretical expectations by comparing the model with the data. To determine the validity of the suggested model, which outlined the associations among the proxies, the CFA was carried out, as manifests in Table 3. The outcomes provided information about the model's suitability for capturing the relevant constructs by revealing the fit indices and statistical significance of the parameters. Chi-square, the Comparative Fit Index (CFI), and Root Mean Square Error of Approximation (RMSEA) (Sun et al., 2025) were among the fit indices that were employed in the analysis to assess how well the observed data fit the given theoretical framework.

Table 3. Covariances

Covariance			Approximation	S.E.	C.R.	P	Hy.
Government supported Technological Development	**<--->**	**Strategic Innovation influence**	**.242**	**.021**	**8.231**	***	**H2**
Government supported Technological Development	<--->	Islamic SMEs performance	.303	.032	7.692	***	H3
Strategic Innovation influence	<--->	Islamic SMEs performance	.254	.24	7.831	***	H1

Source: Authors

Table 3 manifests the imperative connections. With a C.R. of 8.231 and a S.E. of 0.021, the investigation manifests a positive covariance of 0.242 among the gender leadership gap and educational success, indicating a very substantial link ($p < 0.001$) that supports Hypothesis 2 (H2). A substantial association ($p < 0.001$) that supports Hypothesis 3 (H3) is also manifests by the covariance among educational attainment and workplace asymmetries, which is chaptered at 0.303 with a S.E. of 0.032 and a C.R. of 7.692. Additionally, the association among workplace asymmetries and the gender leadership gap is 0.254, with a statistically substantial ($p < 0.001$) C.R. of 7.831 and a S.E. of 0.24, supporting Hypothesis 1 (H1). The investigation's theoretical approach is substantiated by these strong covariances, which also manifest the interconnectedness of the dimensions and manifest how educational attainment influences workplace inequality and gender leadership dynamics.

Table 4. Validity concern

	CR	AVE	MSV	MaxR(H)	SIE	GSTD	IP
SIE	0.732	0.643	0.219	0.852	0.654		
GSTD	0.758	0.657	0.132	0.763	0.171	0.665	
IP	0.793	0.603	0.274	0.797	0.383	0.193	0.684

Note: SIE= Strategic Innovation influence; GSTD= Government supported Technological Development; IP= Islamic SMEs performance

Source: Authors

Table 4 addresses the validity concerns. With SIE at 0.732, GSTD at 0.758, and IP at 0.793 all over the permissible cutoff of 0.7, the CR values demonstrate good reliability. With SIE at 0.643, GSTD at 0.657, and IP at 0.603—all above the suggested value of 0.5—the AVE values, which manifest how much variance is captured by a construct in association to measurement error, are likewise satisfactory, manifesting convergent validity among the constructs. The scores of 0.219 for SIE, 0.132 for GSTD, and 0.274 for IP in terms of MSV indicate that although there are associations among the constructs, they are still sufficiently different from one another. As well as, with SIE at 0.852, GSTD at 0.763, and IP at 0.797, the MaxR(H) outcomes support the dependability of these structures.

Mediation Examination

Figure 2. Structure equation model

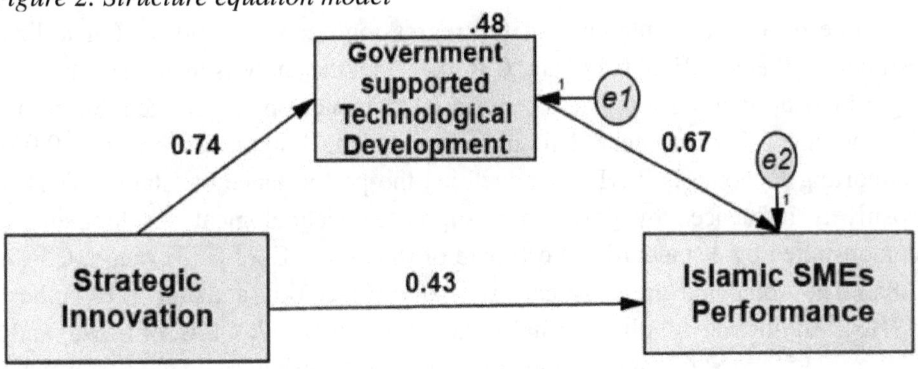

Table 5. Model fit indices

Sig.	Chi-Sq	RMR	Fitness Goodness	Fitness	TLI	RMSEA
0.004	1.954	.036	0.930	0.912	0.911	.028

Source: Authors

Table 5 gives information on model fit indices. A statistically substantial outcome is manifests by the chaptered significance level of 0.004. The discrepancy among the expected and observed covariance matrices is reflected in the Chi-square value, which is 1.954. With a chaptered Root Mean Square Residual (RMR) of 0.036, the residual variance appears to be within an acceptable range. Given that values above 0.90 are regarded as suggestive of a good match, the Index (CFI) is 0.912 and the Fitness Goodness Index is computed at 0.930, both of which manifest a strong model fit. The model's sufficiency is further supported by the stated Tucker-Lewis Index (TLI), which is 0.911. Last but not least, the Root Mean Square Error of Approximation (RMSEA) is 0.028, far below the generally recognized cutoff of 0.05, supporting the outcome that the model fits the data remarkably well.

Table 6. Regression examination

Relative			Approx.	S.E.	C.R.	P	Ass.
Government supported Technological Development	<---	**Strategic Innovation**	**.864**	**.143**	**7.583**	***	**H2**
Islamic SMEs performance	<---	Government supported Technological Development	.328	.131	2.853	***	H3
Islamic SMEs performance	<---	Strategic Innovation	.957	.192	7.958	***	H1

Source: Authors

Table 6 gives the outcomes of the regression analysis. With a standardized estimate of 0.864, S.E. of 0.143 and C.R. of 7.583, the analysis manifests that Strategic Innovation has a strong and substantial influence on Government Supported Technological Development. This indicates statistical significance at $p < 0.001$, supporting Hypothesis 2 (H2). As well as, the performance of Islamic SMEs is positively influenced by government-supported technological development, as demonstrated by a standardized estimate of 0.328, a S.E. of 0.131, and a C.R. of 2.853. These outcomes are statistically substantial ($p < 0.001$) and support Hypothesis 3 (H3). Additionally, with a normalized estimate of 0.957, a S.E. of 0.192, and a C.R. of 7.958, Strategic Innovation has a substantial influence on the performance of Islamic SMEs, supporting Hypothesis 1 (H1) and demonstrating the significance of this association ($p < 0.001$). When taken as a whole, these outcomes manifest how these dimensions are critically interconnected and how crucial government-supported technological development and strategic innovation are to improving the success of Islamic SMEs.

Table 7. Mediating function

	worth
Strategic Innovation → Islamic SMEs performance	.43
Strategic Innovation → Government supported Technological Development → Islamic SMEs performance	.74*.67=.48
	.91

Source: Authors

Table 7 manifests the mediating function. The outcomes manifest that strategic innovation has a direct influence on the performance of Islamic SMEs, as measured by a score of 0.43, which manifests how strategic initiatives have an instant influence on performance outcomes. As well as, the analysis manifests that Strategic Innovation has an indirect influence through Government Supported Technological Development. This indirect influence is 0.48, which is determined by multiplying the path estimates (0.74 for Strategic Innovation to Government Supported Technological Development and 0.67 for Government Supported Technological Development to Islamic SMEs Performance).

Together, these factors have a substantial overall influence on the performance of Islamic SMEs, as evidenced by the 0.91 overall influence of strategic innovation. Because both direct and indirect variables contribute to the link, the outcomes point to a partial mediation influence, manifesting the intricacy of the interactions among government-supported technological development and strategic innovation that influence the performance of Islamic SMEs.

DISCUSSION

The outcomes shed crucial light on the associations among government-backed technology development, strategic innovation, and the performance of Islamic SMEs. The performance of Islamic SMEs is strongly influenced by strategic innovation, as indicated by a standardized estimate of 0.43. This manifests how imperative creative activities are to enhancing corporate outcomes for Islamic small and medium-sized enterprises. Accordingly, enterprises that adopt strategic innovation are likely to realize enhancements in performance metrics since they can deploy new technologies efficiently and adapt to market shifts. Additionally emphasized is the indirect influence of strategic innovation through government-sponsored technology development, which points to a vital path for improving the performance of Islamic SMEs (Anwar et al., 2025).

The projected indirect influence of 0.48 manifests that, in addition to being directly realized, the benefits of strategic innovation are reinforced by enabling government support for technological advancement. This mediating function critically emphasizes the need for outside help to optimize the benefits of innovation, recommending stakeholders and policymakers to focus on creating technologically sophisticated environments that facilitate the growth of SMEs. The critical analysis manifests a modest mediation influence, and the overall cumulative influence of 0.91 indicates a substantial association across the constructs. Although strategic innovation has a direct and indirect positive influence on the performance of Islamic SMEs, this partial mediation suggests that other factors may also be at work and influence performance outcomes (Qasim et al., 2025). It draws attention to the intricate association among creative tactics and encouraging governmental frameworks, implying that a multifaceted strategy that incorporates both internal managerial tactics and external support networks may be necessary for Islamic SMEs to succeed.

MANAGERIAL IMPLICATIONS

The investigation's conclusions have a number of substantial management ramifications for Islamic SMEs looking to improve their performance with government assistance and strategic innovation. First and foremost, managers need to understand how imperative strategic innovation is to achieving corporate goals. Leaders may help employees be more creative and adaptable by cultivating an innovative culture inside their companies, which will eventually augment performance indicators. To better meet changing market expectations, this may entail rethinking product and service offerings, introducing training programs, or embracing new technology. Secondly, the investigation manifests the necessity for SMEs to aggressively pursue and utilize government assistance in technological advancement. For managers to have access to funds, grants, and projects that support technical growth, they need build trusting connections with legislators and government organizations.

These partnerships have the potential to give SMEs the infrastructure and resources they need to develop successfully, augmenting their marketability. Participating in government-led programs may also assist SMEs in keeping up with emerging trends and technology, which enables them to adjust to changes in the market more quickly. The chapter also emphasizes the value of a comprehensive strategy that incorporates both internal tactics and outside support networks. In order to ensure that strategic goals are supplemented by access to technology resources, managers should establish alignment among government funding and innovation activities.

In an augmenting competitive environment, this alignment can support a more thorough approach to performance enhancement, propelling long-term success for Islamic SMEs.

PRACTICAL IMPLICATIONS

The investigation's practical implications provide insightful information for Islamic SMEs and their stakeholders, manifesting doable tactics that can improve performance with government assistance and strategic innovation. First, integrating innovative techniques into their operations should be a top priority for Islamic SMEs. Small and medium-sized enterprises may boost productivity and stand out in the marketplace by cultivating an innovative culture, which will eventually boost their competitiveness and market share. As well as, it is imperative that Islamic SMEs actively participate in government initiatives and programs that promote technical advancement. This involves looking for grants, funding, and other resources that can aid in the adoption of new technology. To make sure their corporates can get the most out of these programs, managers should keep up with the latest government assistance options and work with the appropriate agencies. Better performance outcomes can outcome from such collaboration by giving SMEs the knowledge and infrastructure they need to improve their technical capabilities.

Islamic SMEs must also actively participate in government programs and initiatives that promote technical advancement. Outcome funding, grants, and other resources that can aid in the adoption of new technology is part of this. To guarantee that their companies can get the most out of these programs, managers should keep up with the latest government assistance options and work with the appropriate organizations. This kind of involvement may give SMEs the tools and information they need to improve their technology skills, which will improve performance outcomes.

THEORETICAL IMPLICATIONS

The investigation's theoretical implications provide a substantial contribution to the body of investigations already available on the association among organizational success, government-supported technical development, and strategic innovation, especially in the context of Islamic SMEs. First, by offering empirical proof of the direct and indirect influences of strategic innovation, the outcomes support and broaden accepted ideas about innovation and organizational success. This emphasizes how imperative it is to take into account, both internal and external strategies, which may be included into current frameworks that analyze the performance of small and medium-sized enterprises. As well as, by implying that government actions can improve the efficacy of innovation techniques, the identification of a mediating function for government-supported technological development augments the theoretical debate.

This realization motivates investigators to investigate the precise ways in which government assistance influences innovation and performance outcomes, Consequently cultivating a more profound comprehension of the contextual elements that influence the success of SMEs. It also suggests that theories of innovation ought to consider the influence of external support networks, as this may greatly influence an organization's ability to innovate. This investigation also adds to the body of knowledge on Islamic SMEs by analyzing the particular possibilities and difficulties they encounter while implementing strategic innovation.

The outcomes stimulate more investigations into the ways in which cultural and religious factors could influence innovative practices and associations among the government and this industry. The creation of more specialized theoretical models that take into account the unique traits of Islamic SMEs may outcome from this, improving strategic planning and policymaking. Essentially, this investigation manifests the significance of incorporating outside influences into preexisting scholarly frameworks and stimulates theoretical developments in the domains of innovation management and SME performance. This augments the general knowledge of how strategic initiatives may be successfully executed to drive performance in a variety of organizational settings by creating opportunities for future investigation to examine the intricate dynamics of innovation in many situations.

RECOMMENDATION

A number of suggestions may be made for Islamic SMEs looking to improve their performance through strategic innovation and government-backed technical development in light of the investigation's outcomes. First and foremost, it is prudent for these enterprises to make investments in developing a strong innovation culture. This may be accomplished via promoting risk-taking and innovation among staff members, putting training programs into place to improve skills, and creating an atmosphere that allows for the growth of fresh concepts. In order for innovation to be ingrained in the organization's vision and operational procedures, managers should make it a top priority as a fundamental corporate strategy. It's also critical to participate in government initiatives that offer technical assistance. Islamic SMEs have to aggressively look for collaborations with government organizations and take part in programs that support technological advancement and innovation.

This might include working together on investigations initiatives that can give access to funding and technical know-how, applying for grants, or joining technological incubators. These kinds of interactions can improve SMEs' competitive edge in the market in addition to bolstering their technological prowess. Building cooperative networks with other companies, academic institutions, and trade groups can also have a big influence. Islamic SMEs may access common resources, expertise, and best practices through partnerships, which can promote augmented creativity and productivity. By attending industry forums and seminars, SMEs may also remain up to date on new developments in technology and market trends, which will help them, adjust to changes more quickly.

FUTURE DIRECTIONS

Future investigations on the association among government-sponsored technical development, strategic innovation, and the success of Islamic SMEs should focus on a multifaceted approach that takes into account a range of contextual elements. Longitudinal investigations, which monitors the adoption of innovative practices over time and looks at how these changes influence performance and the function of government assistance in promoting sustained innovation, is one potential approach. As SMEs adjust to changing market needs and technology enhancements, this might offer insightful information on the long-term advantages and difficulties they encounter. The influence of digital transformation on Islamic SMEs' capacity for innovation may be a further investigations topic. Investigations should concentrate on comprehending how digital tools and platforms can improve innovation processes and, consequently, performance as corporates adopt them more and more.

Developing successful strategies and regulations that encourage technology integration will require examining the obstacles to digital adoption, particularly in the context of SMEs. As well as, comparative investigations that examine the experiences of Islamic SMEs in other nations or regions may manifest the many ways that legislative, cultural, and economic contexts influence innovative activities. By providing frameworks that may be tailored to local circumstances, such investigations may aid in identifying successful government assistance models and best practices. Examining how strategic innovation interacts with outside variables including consumer trends, market rivalry, and legislative changes might also be helpful. Comprehending these dynamics can provide SMEs with the information they need to overcome obstacles and seize opportunities in quickly evolving marketplaces.

CONCLUSION

To sum up, this investigation offers strong proof of the vital connections among Islamic SMEs' performance, government-supported technological development, and strategic innovation. According to the outcomes, governmental backing for technological breakthroughs further strengthens the influence of strategic innovation adoption as a driver of corporate performance. The analysis's substantial direct and indirect influences manifest how imperative it is for Islamic SMEs to use outside support networks in addition to investing in creative methods in order to maximize their performance outcomes. Additionally, the discovery of a partial mediation influence manifests how intricate these connections are, indicating that a number of factors play a function in Islamic SMEs' influence operation. Additionally, the discovery of a partial mediation influence manifests how intricate these connections are, indicating that a number of factors play a function in Islamic SMEs' influence operation. In order to assist these enterprises prosper in a competitive climate, policymakers are urged to create an atmosphere that supports technical advancement and innovation.

REFERENCES

Afum, E., Issau, K., Agyabeng-Mensah, Y., Baah, C., Dacosta, E., Essandoh, E., & Agyenim Boateng, E. (2021). The missing links of sustainable supply chain management and green radical product innovation among sustainable entrepreneurship orientation and sustainability performance. *Journal of Engineering, Design and Technology*. DOI: 10.1108/JEDT-05-2021-0267

Aimal, C., Dave, E., Ilyas, B., & Abid, S. (2025). Conceptualizing Corporate Social Responsibility Process Among Muslim SMEs in the UK : A Case Investigation Approach. In *Journal of the Knowledge Economy* (Issue 0123456789). Springer US. DOI: 10.1007/s13132-024-02567-8

Alhyasat, W., Alhyasat, E., & Khattab, S. A. (2025). *Technology trends in strategic management in the AI era : Systematic literature review. 0*(0), 1–18. DOI: 10.1177/01672533251322396

Anwar, U. A. A., Rahayu, A., Wibowo, L. A., Sultan, M. A., Aspiranti, T., Furqon, C., & Rani, A. M. (2025). Supply chain integration as the implementation of strategic management in improving corporate performance. *Discover Sustainability, 6*(1), 101. Advance online publication. DOI: 10.1007/s43621-025-00867-w

Aslam, R., Rehman, S., & Nasir, A. (2023). Investigating the association among government support and SMEs' sustainability through financial and green lenses. *Journal of Corporate and Industrial Marketing, 38*(11), 2379–2389. DOI: 10.1108/JBIM-05-2022-0191

Becha, H., Kalai, M., Houidi, S., & Helali, K. (2025). Digital financial inclusion, environmental sustainability and regional economic growth in China: Insights from a panel threshold model. *Journal of Economic Structures, 14*(1), 4. Advance online publication. DOI: 10.1186/s40008-025-00347-4

Bilal, M., Xicang, Z., Jiying, W., Sohu, J. M., Akhtar, S., & Hassan, M. I. U. (2024). Digital Transformation and SME Innovation: A Comprehensive Analysis of Mediating and Moderating Influences. *Journal of the Knowledge Economy, 0123456789*(1), 1153–1182. Advance online publication. DOI: 10.1007/s13132-024-02054-0

Brimmell, J., Edwards, E. J., Uiga, L., Wood, G., & Vaughan, R. S. (2025). The structure of executive functions in athletes: A latent variable approach. *Psychology of Sport and Exercise, 78*(January), 102808. Advance online publication. DOI: 10.1016/j.psychsport.2025.102808 PMID: 39855374

Cheah, J., Leong, S. Y., & Fernando, Y. (2022). Innovation strategies and organisational performance: The moderating function of corporate size among small- and medium-sized companies. *Benchmarking, 2018.* Advance online publication. DOI: 10.1108/BIJ-03-2021-0139

Cieri, F., Di Francesco, G., Cross, C. L., Bender, A., & Caldwell, J. Z. K. (2025). Dynamic neurocognitive adaptation in aging: Development and validation of a new scale. *Alzheimer's and Dementia. Alzheimer's & Dementia: Translational Research & Clinical Interventions, 11*(1), 1–9. DOI: 10.1002/trc2.70049 PMID: 39839075

Cristofaro, M., & Giardino, P. L. (2025). Sur fi ng the AI waves : the historical evolution of arti fi cial intelligence in management and organizational investigations and practices. DOI: 10.1108/JMH-01-2025-0002

Enyioko, N., & Onwusoro, C. (2018). Customer Association Management and Hospitality Industry in Nigeria. SSRN *Electronic Journal, 9*(1), 116–126. DOI: 10.2139/ssrn.2397245

Ha, A., Giran, A., Fadzline, P., Tamyez, M., & Fauzi, M. A. (2025). The paradoxes of sustainable HRM : Insights through the perspective of common good, green, social responsibility, and triple bottom line. 0(0), 1–19. DOI: 10.1177/01672533251320795

Hasani, T., Rezania, D., & Mohammadi, M. (2024). Towards a framework for successful metaverse adoption in Small and Medium-sized Enterprises: An exploratory investigation. *International Journal of Engineering Business Management, 16*, 1–34. DOI: 10.1177/18479790241257118

Khalid, A. M., & Jetin, B. (2025). *Introduction : Brunei Darussalam ' s Economy — Transition towards Development*. Springer Nature Singapore. DOI: 10.1007/978-981-97-6926-1

Lu, C., Yu, B., Zhang, J., & Xu, D. (2021). Influences of open innovation strategies on innovation performance of SMEs: Evidence from China. *Chinese Management Studies, 15*(1), 24–43. DOI: 10.1108/CMS-01-2020-0009

Mohammadhossein, S., & Atefeh, A. (2025). Modeling Factors Influenceing Digital Transformation : Suggestions for the Islamic Republic of Iran. In *Journal of the Knowledge Economy* (Issue 0123456789). Springer US. DOI: 10.1007/s13132-025-02654-4

Naila, D. L. (2024). Measuring the uptake of process innovation by SMEs in food industry : a resource-based view perspective. DOI: 10.1108/IJSBI-08-2024-0040

Narendran, R., Ng, E., & Almeida, S. (2025). Organizing Transgender People: Toward a Process-Based Theory of Representative Bureaucracy. *Nonprofit and Voluntary Sector Quarterly, 54*(6), 1473–1504. Advance online publication. DOI: 10.1177/08997640251317399

Qasim, D., Shuhaiber, A., & Rawshdeh, Z. (2025). Driving innovation performance: Exploring the mediating function of knowledge sharing in telecommunication companies. *Journal of International Entrepreneurship, 0123456789*(3), 677–703. Advance online publication. DOI: 10.1007/s10843-025-00383-y

Rajeswari, A. (2025). Intersecting Inequalities: Gender, Culture, Stereotypes, and Economic Justice. *Intersecting Inequalities : Gender, Culture, Stereotypes, and Economic Justice, 4*(1), 177–186. DOI: 10.56472/25835238/IRJEMS-V4I1P117

Stutz, C., & Matala, S. (2025). Manufacturing national consent for industrial policy : A microhistorical analysis of Finnish shipbuilding. *Journal of International Business Studies, 0123456789*. Advance online publication. DOI: 10.1057/s41267-025-00779-x

Sun, J., Li, L., Tian, X., & Fu, Y. (2025). Reliability and validity validation of the Chinese version of the family vitiligo influence scale. *BMC Public Health, 25*(1), 258. DOI: 10.1186/s12889-025-21439-7 PMID: 39838342

Teresi, J. A., Yu, X., Stewart, A. L., & Hays, R. D. (2022). Guidelines for Designing and Evaluating Feasibility Pilot Investigations. *Medical Care, 60*(1), 95–103. DOI: 10.1097/MLR.0000000000001664 PMID: 34812790

Wang, X., Zhou, Y., Li, L., Kueh, Y. C., Zeng, L., & Kuan, G. (2025). Psychometric properties of the Sport Mental Health Continuum – Short Form scale (Sport MHC-SF): Cross-cultural validation and measurement invariance of the Chinese adaptation. *BMC Psychology, 13*(1), 183. Advance online publication. DOI: 10.1186/s40359-025-02487-5 PMID: 40033429

Yaseen, M., Sajjad, W., Visetnoi, S., Amanah, S., & Saqib, S. E. (2024). Entrepreneurial Orientation and SMEs Efficiency With Government Financial and Non-Financial Incentives as Moderators. *SAGE Open, 14*(3), 1–23. DOI: 10.1177/21582440241281259

Zhang, X., Bilawal, M., Chenghuan, K., Afaq, M., & Jafri, H. (2025). A comparative investigation of economic activity and sustainable development in China and Three South Asian Countries. *Discover Sustainability, 58*(1), 170. Advance online publication. DOI: 10.1007/s43621-025-00885-8

Chapter 3
The Role of Islamic Crowdfunding for Poverty Reduction in Indonesia

Asnita Frida Sebayang
https://orcid.org/0000-0002-3481-5078
Universitas Islam Bandung, Indonesia

ABSTRACT

Indonesia has great strength from the Muslim population to promote regional economic growth. The study results indicate that the Muslim population is still concentrated in Java, as well as the number of poor people. On the other side, the economic power also relies on Java Island, with the highest contribution from Jakarta. The highest economic growth, however, is shifting to eastern Indonesia (especially Sulawesi and Papua). Java Island in Indonesia is experiencing a paradoxical economic development where economic strength is very high, but requires strong community-based support to overcome the complexity of poverty problems. The study results indicate the potential contribution of Islamic crowdfunding. There is a trend of increasing revenue from ZIS to more than 1 billion rupiah per year, and the role of filling the gap in regional fiscal capacity. The role of ZIS is increasing in Java and Sumatra, where it is being allocated effectively to reduce poverty.

INTRODUCTION

Development is defined as a continuous process to achieve prosperity. Various macro indicators describe efforts to achieve prosperity, such as gross domestic product, human development index, job availability, wage levels, and other indicators. The goals to achieve prosperity are always faced with various development problems/

DOI: 10.4018/979-8-3373-2655-9.ch003

issues such as unemployment and poverty. These development problems will disrupt the achievement of prosperity. In the Islamic approach, poverty is inevitable, where it is necessary to build access that connects the affluent with the poor with a pattern of mutual benefit and assistance. The Islamic thoughts are strongly encouraged to allocate their income to help the poor. On the contrary, the community is encouraged to be productive because the person who gives is in a more noble position than the one who receives.

The problem of poverty is also one of the major issues discussed in the Sustainable Development Agenda, placed as the first agenda item, support for poverty reduction efforts. These efforts relate to several elements of the SDGs, including efforts to prevent hunger, access to health, and education for all. These various dimensions seek to increase the economic capacity of the community to avoid extreme poverty. The importance of poverty reduction efforts is part of a systematic process by opening up various opportunities for income improvement, access to opportunities for a better life. However, poverty reduction efforts often face structural challenges, not only opening up opportunities but also obstacles from within individuals, as a series of complexities of education, health, and unemployment. The impact is that many poor people produce new poverty as a cycle that is difficult to break. The current development issues in Indonesia show in **Table 1** below.

Table 1. Selected economic indicators in Indonesia, 2022-2023

Indicators	Unit	Year	
		2022	**2023**
Population	person	275,773,800.00	278,696,200.00
Muslim Population	**Person**	**241,699,189.00**	**246,386,967.00**
Number of Poverty	Person	26,161,160.00	25,898,550.00
Human Development Index (HDI)	Index	73.52	74.11
Unemployment	Person	8,425,930.00	7,855,080.00
Zakat, Infaq, Sedekah (ZIS) Income-Original Islamic Crowdfund	**Rupiah**	**15,592,436,811,208.00**	**31,824,445,220,276.00**
GDP at Constant Price	Rupiah	11,710,223,200,000,000.00	12,301,475,100,000,000.00
GDP at Current Price	Rupiah	19,588,459,900,000,000.00	20,892,348,500,000,000.00
National Revenues	Rupiah	2,635,843,100,000,000.00	2,637,248,900,000,000.00
National Expenses	Rupiah	3,096,262,700,000,000.00	3,123,677,300,000,000.00

Source: Indonesia Statistics, 2024.

Islamic belief recognize that poverty is part of life. There are rich people, and on the other side, there are poor people. The principle of helping each other becomes a Muslim lifestyle. The Muslim society is taught to share their wealth with the surrounding community, both obligatory and/or recommended. For the wealth that has reached a certain value, there is an obligation to give in the form of zakat. Naturally, the Muslim community will maintain justice or maintain balance. This Islamic lesson is very important to ensure that all people around the Muslim community are not hungry and receive assistance from their surroundings. This potential can be a social capital strength for Muslim society to strengthen each other.

Poverty alleviation in the context of regional development is also complex because regions have different physical, economic, social, cultural, and environmental characteristics. In Indonesia, the complexity of poverty reduction is triggered by the geographical conditions of the vast archipelago so that it difficult to reach. In some outermost areas, mountains, coasts, and a number of other areas, accessibility is a major issue, so that transportation of basic material logistics is not easy. Differences in living standards in regions are not only due to differences in geographic (natural) potential but also due to differences in accessibility to new opportunities. This difference is evident in differences in regional fiscal capacity, which has implications for limited funding for poverty alleviation in the regions. Various financing alternatives, especially independent community financing, are still needed hugely.

Poverty remains a fundamental issue in global development, especially in low- and lower-middle-income countries. Todaro & Smith (2020) emphasize that despite improvements over the past half century, the World Bank estimated that in 2015, nearly 750 million people 2015 were still living on less than $1.90 per day based on 2011 US Purchasing Power Parity. Absolute poverty is defined as the inability of individuals to meet their basic needs, and this condition is still widespread in various parts of the world. In a conceptual context, Piwowarski et al. (2022) emphasize the importance of expanding the understanding of poverty in the future by including dimensions of absolute, relative, multidimensional poverty, and rights-based poverty. They argue that this approach is important to support the achievement of the first sustainable development goal (SDG), namely the eradication of poverty in all its forms.

The difference in fiscal capacity between regions does not allow the problem of poverty to be solved simultaneously by local governments. At that time, the Muslim community played a role in helping the surrounding community. The community can create an alarm of the condition of the community around it (at the local level) through the role of institutions, especially zakat collection bodies. The allocation of Islamic crowdfunding is not only in the form of direct assistance but can also be in the form of programs that open up new opportunities and productivity so that the community escapes the poverty trap in a sustainable manner. The conceptual framework the existence of Islamic Crowdfunding to support economic system shows in the figure below.

Figure 1. Conceptual framework of the role of Islamic crowdfunding in economic system

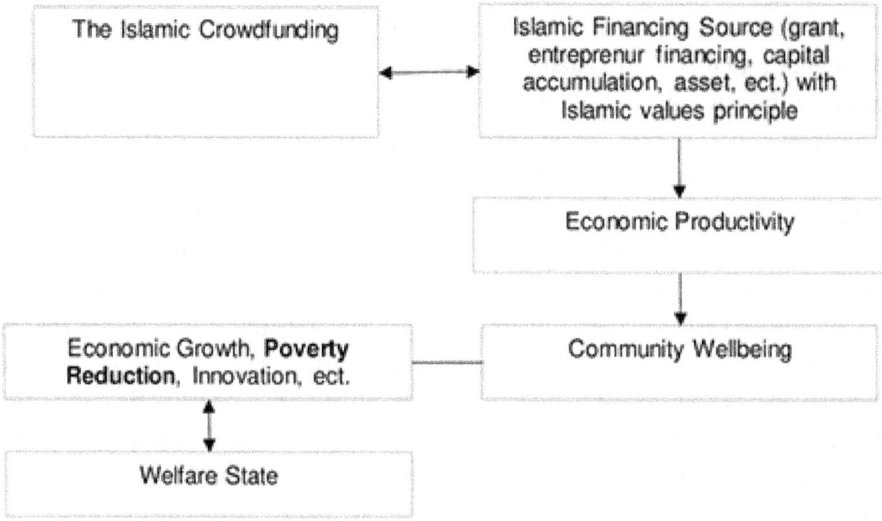

The long journey of development towards prosperity can be assisted by the participation of Muslim communities, especially in Muslim population areas. Increasing this role will produce a society that is "self-sustainable," so that it will help the government accelerate the improvement of the quality of development indicators. The intensive participation of the community in helping others is a social capital force. Meanwhile, all "capital" will influence the output according to the Cobb-Douglas production function theory. The transmission of Islamic crowdfunding into capital occurs from continuous accumulation.

In terms of structural resilience, zakat is considered a permanent solution to meet basic needs because it is carried out routinely every year and is designed to encourage balanced and comprehensive community development (Alhashmi, 2024). Zakat has advantages over other fiscal instruments because the tariff and usage have been regulated according to Sharia, as well as its function as an economic stabilizer and budget allocation tool (Al-Fatih, 2020). The integration of Islamic philanthropy, such as zakat, into Islamic socio-economic policies has been proven to be able to reduce poverty effectively in the short and long term (Iskandar et al., 2021). Even in a crisis such as the COVID-19 pandemic, zakat continues to contribute to the economic resilience of mustahik and encourages national economic growth by increasing community income and consumption (Herianingrum et al., 2024). In the context of fiscal policy, zakat has proven to be more effective than conventional subsidy mechanisms in addressing unemployment, especially among the highly educated (Raies, 2020), and has a direct impact on reducing hunger, inequality, and strengthening community economic empowerment (Gundogdu, 2019).

The presence of funding sourced from ZISWAF, either allocated in the form of cash transfers and/or programs, will elevate the position of aid recipients to aid providers. This philosophy will be a force for poverty alleviation because it is not only about providing aid but also changing mindsets. The strength of Islamic teachings will help people to rise from the brink of poverty. In terms of overcoming the inability to access basic public goods on a local scale, such as educational facilities, worship, health, access to clean water, sanitation, and others, can be provided from waqf allocations. Waqf is currently developing in the form of productive waqf, such as cattle/sheep farming, agriculture and agro-industry, and various other productive forms. This means that awareness of managerial capabilities and good governance must be the focus of the agenda of ZISWAF managers.

DEVELOPMENT ISSUES: MUSLIM POPULATION AND POVERTY IN THE REGION

Poverty is defined as the inability to meet basic needs. Although there is no standard definition related to poverty standards, conditions of deprivation can be reflected in the fulfillment of the needs for food, shelter, education, clean water, basic health, and various other needs. In line with the role of Java as a center of economic activity, the number of poor people is also the highest in Indonesia. The high number of poor people is influenced by tight competition to get jobs, which has implications for unemployment, the presence of migration to Java in the long term, which has an impact on density, and the existence of structural poverty, which produces new poverty. The new poverty that emerges becomes a social burden and a burden on the government because it will have an impact on slum areas, potential crime, unfair competition in the labor market, and various negative impacts that distort long-term economic growth.

The poverty conditions in the regions in 2023 are relatively varied between 2.7% (West Sulawesi) to 7.52 (Banten), but the highest number of poor people is in East Java Province, namely 4.19 million. The distribution of the poor population is on the island of Java. The development of the number of Muslim population, poor population, and poverty rates throughout Indonesia is presented in the following **Table 2**.

Table 2. Number of Muslim population, number of poor population, and poverty rate in regions in Indonesia, 2023

No	Province	Muslim Population (Person)	Poverty (Person)	Poverty Rate (%)
1	Aceh	5,356,635	807,000	6.03
2	North Sumatra	10,244,655	1,240,000	5.89
3	West Sumatra	5,528,423	340,000	5.94
4	Riau	5,870,015	486,000	4.23
5	Jambi	3,514,415	281,000	4.53
6	South Sumatra	8,508,999	1,046,000	4.11
7	Bengkulu	2,017,860	288,000	3.42
8	Lampung	8,598,009	971,000	4.23
9	Bangka Belitung Islands	1,344,903	69,000	4.56
10	Riau Islands	1,671,242	143,000	6.8
11	Jakarta	9,491,619	478,000	6.53
12	West Java	48,029,215	3,889,000	7.44
13	Central Java	36,773,442	3,792,000	5.13
14	DI Yogyakarta	3,433,129	448,000	3.69
15	East Java	40,179,566	4,189,000	4.88
16	Banten	11,686,756	826,000	7.52
17	Bali	434,941	194,000	2.69
18	West Nusa Tenggara	5,361,920	751,000	2.8
19	East Nusa Tenggara	523,523	1,141,000	3.14
20	West Kalimantan	3,320,719	353,000	5.05
21	Central Kalimantan	2,011,763	142,000	4.1
22	South Kalimantan	4,054,044	189,000	4.31
23	East Kalimantan	3,446,652	231,000	5.31
24	North Kalimantan	533,675	48,000	4.01
25	North Sulawesi	849,253	189,000	6.1
26	Central Sulawesi	2,450,867	396,000	2.95
27	South Sulawesi	8,359,166	789,000	4.33
28	Southeast Sulawesi	2,593,226	322,000	3.15
29	Gorontalo	1,191,484	184,000	3.06
30	West Sulawesi	1,217,339	164,000	2.27
31	Maluku	997,724	302,000	6.31
32	North Maluku	1,005,727	84,000	4.31
33	Papua	320,442	915,000	2.67

continued on following page

Table 2. Continued

No	Province	Muslim Population (Person)	Poverty (Person)	Poverty Rate (%)
34	West Papua	213,230	215,000	5.38
	Total	**241,134,578**	**25,902,000**	**4.61**

Source: Indonesia Statistics, 2024.

The above data indicates that poverty is a serious problem in Indonesia, namely, more than 25 million people are categorized as poor. This distribution also indicates that the Indonesian economy must spread to various regions as growth centers to mitigate the negative impacts of poverty. Various efforts can be made to overcome poverty.

As a large, archipelagic country, Indonesia is highly vulnerable to inequality and poverty. Poverty alleviation policies are difficult to access in remote areas. Development is currently shifting to new growth centers to achieve more equitable income distribution. In 2022 and 2023, the poor population was concentrated on the island of Java. The highest number of poor people in 2022 was on the island of Java, with 13,854,530 people, and the lowest was on the islands of Bali and Nusa Tenggara, with 937,620. Overall, East Java province had the highest number of poor people, reaching 4,181,290, and North Kalimantan province had the lowest poverty number, 47,460. Data identification results on the island of Sumatra showed that the highest number of poor people was in North Sumatra Province with 1,268,190, and the lowest was in Bangka Belitung with 66,780. On the island of Java, the highest number of poor people was in East Java with 4,181,290, and the lowest was in Yogyakarta Province with 454,030. On the islands of Bali and Nusa Tenggara, the highest number of poor people was in NTB Province with 731,940, and the lowest was in Bali Province with 205,680. In the provinces of Kalimantan, the highest number of poor people was in West Kalimantan Province with 350,250, and the lowest was in North Kalimantan Province with 47,460. On the island of Sulawesi, South Sulawesi has the highest number of poor people, at 777,440, and West Sulawesi has the lowest number, at 165,720. On the islands of Maluku and Papua, the highest number is in Papua Province, at 922,120, and the lowest is in North Maluku, at 78,870.

In 2023, the highest number of poor people was still in Java, with 13,621,340, and the lowest was in Bali and Nusa Tenggara, with 945,010. For each province as a whole, East Java province had the highest number of poor people, with 4,188,810 and North Kalimantan province with the lowest number of poor people, with 47,970. If we look at the distribution of poor people based on Sumatra Island, the highest number of poor people was in North Sumatra with 1,239,710 and the lowest was in Bangka Belitung with 68,690. The highest number of poor people in Java was in

East Java, with 4,188,810, and the lowest was in Yogyakarta, with 448,470 poor people. In Bali and Nusa Tenggara, the largest number of poor people was in West Nusa Tenggara (NTB) with 751,230, and the lowest was in Bali with 193,780 poor people. On the island of Kalimantan, the highest number of poor people is in West Kalimantan with 353,350 and the lowest number of poor people is in North Kalimantan with the number of poor people reaching 47,970. On the island of Sulawesi, the highest number of poor people is in South Sulawesi with the number of poor people reaching 788,850, and the lowest number of poor people is in West Sulawesi with 183,710. On the islands of Maluku and Papua, the highest number of poor people is in Papua Province, with 915,150, and the lowest number of poor people is in North Maluku, with 83,800. The above pattern indicates that centers of economic activity will be accompanied by pockets of poverty. Access to increasingly competitive resources in Indonesia's major cities means that not everyone has access to decent work.

The Table 2 above also indicates that the very large Muslim population in Indonesia can be mobilized as part of a community-based force. The more productive a Muslim is, the higher his income potential will be. This means that the potential for receiving zakat from his wealth is also higher. Likewise, with the potential for infaq, sedekah, and waqf. These efforts require a combination of economic capacity and spiritual capacity. For that reason, the awareness is still needed as a good Muslim.

The empirical findings from several studies confirm the effectiveness of various interventions in poverty reduction. Zhang et al. (2022) show that social entrepreneurship has the capacity to address rural poverty through the integration of farmers into the value chain of companies, which is considered a sustainable approach. Yerrabati (2023) confirms the significant role of entrepreneurship in reducing poverty severity, especially among groups below the $1.90 per day threshold, although it is found that women's entrepreneurship has a lower impact than men's. Liu et al. (2021) state that education, especially at a higher level, has a significant correlation with poverty reduction, and that improving skills through training helps strengthen households' capacity to escape the poverty gap. They state that basic literacy skills can reduce global poverty by 15 percent in one year.

Meanwhile, a study by Singh & Chudasama (2020) found that the effectiveness of poverty reduction was higher when implementing an integrated and multi-dimensional approach, such as providing microfinance through high-quality community organizations, building the capacity of the poor, and strengthening institutional governance. They concluded that this approach was superior to the market-based model. Research by Tri & Thanh (2023) in the context of Vietnam showed that strengthening production capacity in poor areas and increasing the distribution of benefits from growth were able to produce a more adaptive response to the dynamics of globalization. In terms of external roles, Mahembe & Odhiambo (2020) showed that foreign aid, especially in the form of grants and bilateral aid, has a significant contribution to reducing extreme poverty, especially in an environment that supports freedom of entrepreneurship.

Structural and productivity factors have also been shown to play an important role. Erumban & de Vries (2024) found that productivity growth in the manufacturing sector, as well as the shift of labor from low-productivity to high-productivity sectors, contributed significantly to poverty reduction in developing Asian countries. However, they noted that the agricultural sector did not show a significant impact. A study by Adeleye et al. (2020) also showed that although economic growth contributed to poverty reduction, income inequality weakened the effect. They emphasized that the interaction between inequality and growth is a crucial element that needs to be studied in depth in formulating more inclusive poverty alleviation policies.

The various proposals from previous studies related to poverty alleviation, such as; increasing the role of entrepreneurs, assistance in the form of cash transfers, empowering communities and their organizations, improving skills, and other programs. The proposals for various programs are based on increasing productivity to guarantee economic growth. Currently, many government policies have supported poverty alleviation, both multidimensional poverty and extreme poverty. Extreme poverty has various direct assistance programs for minimum living needs, such as cash transfers, family hope programs, and health insurance. Poverty that is structural and requires improvements in the quality of life and access to basic services, such as easy access to education through the Smart Indonesia Card/ Kartu Indonesia Pintar (KIP), provision of subsidies for decent housing, provision of sanitation and clean water, and various skills improvement programs. The reach of various programs based on government policies is still limited because the number of poor people is relatively high and spread across various regions with unique characteristics. Solving the problem of poverty based on ZISWAF is still highly needed because it needs to be approached not only in terms of material, but also with a holistic approach based on spirituality. There are fundamental changes that need to be touched on, namely changes in behavior and perspective. Poverty alleviation programs by zakat institutions and Muslim communities can help with these structural problems.

THE ROLE OF ISLAMIC CROWDFUNDING

The Conceptual of Islamic Crowdfunding and Its Recent Empirical Studies

The term "Islamic crowdfunding" refers to a financing concept based on Islamic ethical principles. This form of funding support manifests itself in various ways to support activities of Islamic value, including social welfare, entrepreneurship, and education. In the modern era, technology has played a significant role in the implementation of Islamic Crowdfunding, such as blockchain technology, the creation of platforms that ensure governance, particularly transparency and accountability in transactions, and various financing practices that guarantee the distribution of welfare without usury. The collection of funds is no longer carried out manually by waiting for donors at existing institutions but has expanded to a wide network that impacts society. Nelly et al. (2022) identified empirical studies on the development of Islamic crowdfunding in Indonesia. Their findings indicate that Islamic crowdfunding platforms began developing in 2009, driven by the needs of the business world for financing due to difficulties in accessing bank funds. The categories of financing through crowdfunding in Indonesia are: donations, rewards (gifts), assets, and equity. Islamic crowdfunding financing accesses capital, welfare, and economic growth. The challenges to the development of Islamic crowdfunding in Indonesia are public trust, innovation, and partnerships between crowdfunding operators and banks. The implementation of Islamic crowdfunding in Indonesia involves regulators, particularly Bank Indonesia, the Financial Services Authority (OJK), and the Indonesian Ulema Council, which ensure that Islamic principles are applied in its practice.

A study by Purwatiningingsih et al., (2024) applying a bibliometric analysis to Islamic crowdfunding research identified various aspects of the implementation of this form of financing, particularly in three main areas: social, support for start-up entrepreneurship, and education, which contribute to reducing poverty and promoting economic growth. One of the key issues in Indonesia involves fiqh studies and government regulations related to the digitalization of crowdfunding platforms. Arzam, F. et al. (2023) also analyzed the concepts and practices of Islamic crowdfunding through a literature review, applying content analysis to publications issued by Emerald Publishing. This study identified 30 relevant studies that applied Islamic crowdfunding with various implementation contracts dominated by mudharabah and salam contracts, which are practiced in entrepreneurship, and waqf applications. This study recommends that the implementation of Islamic crowdfunding should also be open to fundamental economic sectors such as agriculture and housing finance, with due regard to solutions that are in line with Islamic principles.

Fatimah, R. & Suryaman, H. (2024) conducted a case study of zakat institutions and found that the development of digitalization in Islamic crowdfunding has a positive impact on the amount of zakat funds collected because it can reach a wider range of fund donors. This study emphasizes that it is important for the management of zakat institutions to develop digital services. In the case study, several strategies developed by zakat institutions include; the development of an internal platform that can be accessed by the public, specifically a website used to provide information related to fund distributionas well as introduce various programs; strengthening collaborations with external institutions such as kitabisa.com and amalsholeh.com to expand the reach of services and the public; and utilizing social media platforms including WhatsApp, Instagram, and Facebook for their crowdfunding campaigns as well as to reach more donors.

As technology grows, Islamic crowdfunding is becoming more widespread, with more people able to donate. The quantity and quality of the Muslim community has the potential to grow even more, bringing prosperity to the surrounding community. Islamic guidance encouraging the Muslim community to be active in helping one another can be developed to have a greater impact with the power of various crowdfunding platforms.

Islamic crowdfunding funds, through previous studies, have been proven to provide many benefits to the community. For regions in Indonesia, the strength of Islamic teachings from the aspect of human relations can be social capital. The funds collected by the community can become initial funds for poverty alleviation issues. Legally, zakat institutions in Indonesia are protected by Law No. 23 of 2011 concerning Zakat Management, which states that zakat is managed by the National Zakat Agency (BAZNAS) and Zakat Institutions (LAZ). LAZ must be licensed. Regulations on zakat management already have legal protection regulated by Government Regulations and Ministerial Regulations. The rules of the game LAZ must meet various criteria that have been set by the government: legal entity, have a recommendation from BAZNAS, have a sharia supervisor, submit financial reports to BAZNAS and the public, and are prohibited from channeling the funds for political activities and from channeling them to things that violate sharia provisions.

Despite having a government-managed LAZ (Lembaga Zakat Al-Azlah), Indonesians are known for their generosity and habit of setting aside their wealth to share with the poor. Empathy for the surrounding environment is fostered from an early age through a culture of mutual assistance. It's easy to see local communities raising mutual aid funds, in the form of alms, for social needs. These funds are used by the community and for the community: to fulfill fardhu kifayah (obligatory obligations), assist poor households, assist orphans, and for other community needs. This practice positively influences various positive activities. Several forms of Islamic social fund allocation have an impact on poverty reduction.

Specifically for the allocation of zakat, religious guidance (QS At-Taubah verse 60) has categorized that 8 groups fall into eight categories of zakat recipients, two of which are the poor (people who have almost no assets or jobs so that they cannot fulfill their basic needs) and the poor (have income but are unable to fulfill their basic needs). Recipients of zakat are referred to as (mustahiq) in **QS. At-Taubah verse 60**, There is **8 group, including**:

1. *Fakir* are people who have almost no assets or jobs, so they cannot meet their basic living needs.
2. Poor are people who have an income, but it is not sufficient for their basic living needs.
3. *Amil Zakat* is the person assigned to manage zakat (collect, distribute, administer).
4. *Muallaf* are people who have just converted to Islam or whose faith is still weak, so that zakat can help strengthen their hearts towards Islam.
5. *Riqab* is a person who wants to free himself (in the present day, it is often interpreted more broadly as a person who is shackled in modern slavery or oppression).
6. *Gharim* (People in Debt) are people who have debts for lawful and urgent needs, but are unable to pay them off.
7. *Fii Sabilillah* are people who are fighting in the path of Allah. Previously, it was defined specifically as physical war on the battlefield; now it is understood more broadly as the struggle to uphold Allah's religion, Islamic education, preaching, health care, empowering the community, etc.
8. Ibn Sabil is a person on a long journey who runs out of provisions, even though he is rich in his place of origin.

The funds can be allocated by poor households to start businesses or encourage entrepreneurship. In many case studies in Indonesia, institutions such as mosques provide numerous opportunities to increase entrepreneurial capacity. This capacity, of course, needs to be supported by the availability of business capital. The availability of Islamic crowdfunding will help small business owners start their businesses. At the same time, the combination of capacity and capital will encourage opportunities for communities to transform their lives, from having no income to earning income. This increased capacity shifts the pattern from "zakat recipients" to "zakat payers."

Allocations for alms and charity are more flexible and can be realized by Muslims to help those around them more quickly. Communities with higher per capita incomes can allocate their wealth to address poverty issues in their communities, both directly and indirectly. The power of alms and charity can also manifest in the form of helping families (nuclear and extended families). Forms of mutual assistance within the extended family can also be a manifestation of Indonesia's unique local genius.

The allocation of Islamic crowdfunding in Indonesia also impacts access to education. Aid can finance schooling for poor communities. Indirectly, educational assistance will help break the cycle of poverty. A good education will indirectly transform productive and critical thinking, increasing a person's ability to think critically and find solutions to the problems they face. Better education also opens the door to job opportunities. Educated children from poor families have a greater opportunity to help themselves and/or their families escape poverty. This transformation will bring opportunities for increased income. This solution, while seemingly slow, offers long-term, sustainable benefits considering the challenges of poverty.

The Regional Economy Perspective

The role of Muslim communities in regional development is essential, considering that the economy must grow inclusively and sustainably. The fiscal capacity data above indicates the country's ability to resolve development issues to reach all regions in Indonesia. Alternative funding for the productivity of the poor is prominent because efforts on a local scale will accumulate nationally.

The role of ZISWAF in aggregate in Indonesia shows a positive trend with the strengthening of the institutional role of zakat collectors. In several regions, the trend of ZISWAF collection in the last three years by the National Zakat Agency has decreased, such as in Aceh, West Java, and Central Java. Meanwhile, in several other regions, there has been an increase, such as Riau, East Java, and West Nusa Tenggara. The amount ZISWAF in Indonesia region areas data show in Table 3 below.

Table 3. The ZISWAF collection among the regions in Indonesia

Province	Year		
	2022	2023	2024
Aceh Province	Already	241,643,748,097	232,082,230,866
North Sumatra	433,412,982,200	57,423,148,971	74,404,691,859
West Sumatra	233,024,494,105	169,968,729,165	211,754,424,639
Riau	154,985,378,702	217,633,539,334	229,771,895,025
Jambi	55,033,305,573	66,394,052,643	67,363,981,005
South Sumatra	90,613,920,625	50,249,184,842	53,289,561,392
Bengkulu	180,117,704,483	26,498,942,483	22,487,104,940
Lampung	80,820,349,600	31,703,110,979	32,691,522,026
Bangka Belitung Islands	70,308,437,595	22,802,225,290	21,286,854,769
Riau Islands	48,899,480,809	47,979,866,466	48,444,399,421
Jakarta	4,877,401,155,674	190,755,210,711	321,485,117,703
West Java	**3,369,828,095,134**	**584,026,331,461**	**620,947,572,815**
Central Java	**2,017,294,642,492**	**441,047,776,641**	**501,892,784,220**
DI Yogyakarta	2,498,109,588,195	67,587,379,973	79,719,226,573
East Java	174,165,517,105	405,460,297,005	432,672,681,523
Banten	451,738,448,413	136,071,457,050	142,362,407,765

continued on following page

Table 3. Continued

Province	Year		
	2022	2023	2024
Bali	7,375,877,000	16,459,789,100	39,134,195,614
West Nusa Tenggara	83,247,579,815	137,871,813,161	156,206,185,882
East Nusa Tenggara	147,402,000	1,422,135,211	2,140,889,000
West Kalimantan	145,336,389,337	16,223,901,712	16,924,209,748
Central Kalimantan	11,675,005,174	7,154,990,371	4,893,187,895
South Kalimantan	66,642,804,922	68,666,834,498	75,477,216,696
East Kalimantan	31,653,650,218	68,634,014,460	80,525,354,108
North Kalimantan	833,403,080	21,487,944,983	29,137,781,677
North Sulawesi	7,531,949,000	29,436,011,707	3,531,415,961
Central Sulawesi	86,311,446,444	10,294,622,278	11,992,087,563
South Sulawesi	264,687,772,209	130,117,522,147	140,703,692,267
Southeast Sulawesi	9,090,723,000	44,674,663,194	33,547,735,425
Gorontalo	20,000,000	26,903,391,071	30,315,338,134
West Sulawesi	58,676,749,304	16,182,193,417	14,849,071,820
Maluku	271,559,000	10,547,319,281	3,598,885,510
North Maluku	19,534,000,000	9,354,696,832	9,434,748,596
Papua	32,313,500,000	12,561,912,807	17,363,094,519
West Papua	31,333,500,000	599,346,945	1,645,827,499
Other institutions	**0**	**28,935,353,675,133**	**36,745,784,087,735**
Total	**15,592,436,811,208**	**32,321,191,779,419**	**40,509,861,462,190**

Source: National Amil Zakat Board, 2024.

Many studies have shown that Islamic philanthropy has been proven to play a significant role in overcoming economic problems. Several studies have shown that theoretically, zakat can drive the dynamics of the national economy (Herianingrum et al., 2024) and make a real contribution to reducing multidimensional poverty and supporting the achievement of the Sustainable Development Goals (SDGs) (Aziz et al., 2020). The zakat distribution program has proven effective in reducing poverty and income inequality, especially when considering gender differences in zakat receipts (Ayuniyyah et al., 2022). In addition, zakat also contributes to meeting basic needs through support for access to education, health services, decent housing facilities, and the provision of clean water and adequate sanitation (Ahmed et al., 2017; Razak, 2020). Thus, Islamic philanthropy is a potential solution to improving the quality of life of people in poor and vulnerable groups.

The zakat management models implemented in various countries show a diversity of institutional approaches that are adaptive to local contexts. Malaysia developed a centralized and technology-based system to ensure efficiency and transparency, while Turkey implemented a decentralized approach based on community participation, and Indonesia adopted a hybrid model that combines state supervision with private sector involvement (Mukhlishin et al., 2024). Specifically, Baitul Mal Aceh has succeeded in managing zakat as part of the Regional Original Income (PAD), and allocating it for both consumptive and productive assistance in supporting local economic development (Syahbandir et al., 2022).

The effectiveness of zakat in overcoming poverty is also reflected in its role in strengthening the micro and community business sector, especially through information technology-based distribution and modern management principles (Mongkito & Samdin, 2025). However, business assistance remains a crucial factor in ensuring the success of zakat-based empowerment programs, because without this synergy, improving the welfare of the mustahiq cannot be achieved optimally (Widiastuti et al., 2021). Similar findings show that although macroeconomic variables do not have a significant effect on mustahiq welfare, zakat empowerment programs accompanied by business assistance have a positive impact on business growth and improving welfare (Mawardi et al., 2023).

Optimizing zakat management requires improving the distribution system that takes into account the composite poverty index (IKB) and strengthening the government's role in collecting zakat (Choiriyah et al., 2020). Zakat is also identified as a supporting factor for economic growth in Muslim countries, the impact of which will be greater if accompanied by institutional transparency and increased effectiveness in collecting and distributing zakat (Ben Jedidia & Guerbouj, 2021). Strengthening cooperation between Zakat Collection Units and zakat collection institutions is also recommended to expand the scope of community empowerment programs, as shown by a study in Surakarta City (Yusran & Afiyah, 2024).

Beyond zakat, the global cash waqf model has also been proposed as a strategic alternative to alleviate poverty through cross-border mobilization and equitable redistribution of wealth among Muslim countries (Saiti et al., 2021). Cash waqf is considered more inclusive and accessible to the general public and can empower vulnerable groups such as single mothers and people with disabilities (Saiti et al., 2019). Effective cash waqf management is considered can improve the living standards of the poor and contribute to poverty reduction, especially when accompanied by global cooperation between waqf institutions and strengthening local institutions.

Management capacity is an important issue, so that the collection to distribution are based on good governance. Public trust must be maintained with the trustworthy attitude of the amil. The better the governance, the higher the level of public trust. In the next cycle, the managed funds will increase and can be reallocated for poverty reduction. At the same time, when the ZISWAF allocation is appropriately beneficial, the structural problem of poverty can be solved. It will be a dilemma when the amount of aid funds is very small, but the substance of the problem is very high. Economic growth really needs development partners who can ensure that the ZISWAF allocation is able to improve long-term welfare.

Muslim Population as a Social Capital Initiative

Indonesia's status as an archipelagic nation presents both positive and negative dimensions. If the population actively participates in solving social problems in their surroundings, it will significantly contribute to the country's prosperity. The government's efforts to address extreme poverty are relatively difficult to achieve across all Indonesian islands, especially the outermost ones. Public participation in helping others in extreme poverty alleviation efforts will be extremely beneficial. On the other hand, a population that is indifferent to others and far from Islamic teachings will become a society lacking empathy, thus hindering the achievement of poverty alleviation policies across Indonesia's various islands. The social strength derived from the Muslim population will become a significant social capital in poverty alleviation across the islands.

This potential for social capital will emerge from the strength of the population's collective strength, particularly the diverse Muslim population across islands. Access to public policies related to poverty alleviation across islands can be facilitated by strong Muslim solidarity. The following illustrates the distribution of the Muslim population across islands in Indonesia.

The island of Sumatra has a sizable Muslim population in most of its provinces. North Sumatra and West Sumatra have high Muslim populations, reflecting the majority of the population in these provinces. However, in the southern part of Sumatra, provinces such as Bengkulu and Lampung also have significant Muslim populations, although these are lower than those of the larger provinces in North Sumatra. Java has a high concentration of Muslims, with West Java and East Java being the provinces with the largest Muslim populations. This reflects the dominance of Islam on the island. The Special Region of Yogyakarta, although having a smaller Muslim population than West and East Java, still represents a significant number. The proportion of Muslims on Java is also related to issues of access to employment opportunities, education, healthcare, and various other amenities, which also impact migration to Java. The islands of Bali and Nusa Tenggara have distinct religious differences. Bali has a low Muslim population due to its predominantly Hindu population. Conversely, West Nusa Tenggara (NTB) has a high Muslim population, reflecting the dominance of Islam in the province. East Nusa Tenggara (NTT) also has a relatively low Muslim population, similar to Bali, though higher than Bali.

While not dominant, the Muslim community in Bali also exists and influences the development of the halal business.

The island of Kalimantan has a diverse Muslim population. West Kalimantan boasts a high Muslim population, reflecting the province's Muslim majority. On the other hand, East Kalimantan and North Kalimantan have smaller Muslim populations than West Kalimantan, with North Kalimantan having the lowest Muslim population on the island. Muslims in Kalimantan also live harmoniously with the local population despite religious and cultural differences in some areas.The island of Sulawesi has a varied Muslim population. South Sulawesi has a high Muslim population, reflecting the province's Muslim majority. However, provinces like Central Sulawesi and West Sulawesi have lower Muslim populations, with West Sulawesi having the lowest Muslim population on the island. In North Sulawesi, particularly in Manado and the surrounding areas, Muslims also coexist harmoniously with a predominantly Christian population.The Maluku Islands exhibit varying Muslim populations. North Maluku has a higher Muslim population than Maluku. North Maluku reflects a larger Muslim community, while Maluku has a smaller Muslim population. North Maluku also has a strong Muslim history, with the influx of Muslim preachers contributing to the development of the region. The island of Papua has a relatively small Muslim population. Papua has a higher Muslim population than West Papua, but it remains low compared to other islands in Indonesia. West Papua has the lowest Muslim population on the island.

The above conditions indicate that the Muslim population is spread throughout Indonesia, with varying proportions on each island. The presence of Muslims who practice good Islamic teachings and behavior will encourage a community that helps each other and cooperates in good deeds, especially in addressing poverty in their communities. This potential can be more easily realized if Muslim households also have the economic capacity (income) to meet their basic needs, allowing for allocations for aid to others. From an Indonesian cultural perspective, income is not the only instrument for helping fellow Muslims. Occasionally, opportunities to help the surrounding community arise through providing opportunities (jobs), sharing resource management, and other in-kind activities.

CONCLUSION

Regional economic development requires factual solutions by involving the Muslim community as an important resource. The condition of the country with limited fiscal capacity and a large population requires community participation as a source of sustainable economic growth. The Muslim population has strong funding sources through Islamic Crowdfunding, which has been proven to improve the community with various budget allocations that benefit the poor. Indonesia has more than 250 million people who can contribute to strengthening the perpetual social fund system with various beneficial programs. The community-based funding can fulfill the fiscal capacity gap in the regions. The role of the Muslim community in poverty reduction is a social responsibility. The form of strengthening the role of the Muslim community through increasing economic capacity so that they become payers of zakat, infak, sedekah, and waqf. The benefits of a productive community will encourage sustainable economic growth. Opportunities for increasing productivity must be on the agenda for allocating the use of ZISWAF so that the economic capacity of the community increases.

REFERENCES

Ahmed, B. O., Johari, F., & Abdul Wahab, K. (2017). Identifying the poor and the needy among the beneficiaries of zakat: Need for a zakat-based poverty threshold in Nigeria. *International Journal of Social Economics*, *44*(4), 446–458. DOI: 10.1108/IJSE-09-2015-0234

Al-Fatih, S. (2020). Strengthening Baznas As the Society's Trusted Zakat Agency To Increase the Welfare of Ummah. *Jurisdictie: Jurnal Hukum dan Syariah, 11*(1), 106-124. https://doi.org/DOI: 10.18860/j.v11i1.7841

Alhashmi, E. A. K. (2024). How to overcome poverty with zakat. *International Journal of Religion*, *5*(2), 1–13. DOI: 10.61707/tbxftv10

Arzam, Fauzi, M., Efendi, F., & Sulastri W. (2023). Islamic crowdfunding: A review literature. [RIEF]. *Review of Islamic Economics and Finance*, *6*(2), 171–186.

Ayuniyyah, Q., Pramanik, A. H., Md Saad, N., & Ariffin, M. I. (2022). The impact of zakat in poverty alleviation and income inequality reduction from the perspective of gender in West Java, Indonesia. *International Journal of Islamic and Middle Eastern Finance and Management*, *15*(5), 924–942. https://www.emerald.com/insight/content/doi/10.1108/imefm-08-2020-0403/full/html. DOI: 10.1108/IMEFM-08-2020-0403

Aziz, Y., Mansor, F., Waqar, S., & Haji Abdullah, L. (2020). The nexus between zakat and poverty reduction is the effective utilization of zakat necessary for achieving SDGs: A multidimensional poverty index approach. *Asian Social Work and Policy Review*, *14*(3), 235–247. https://onlinelibrary.wiley.com/doi/10.1111/aswp.12212. DOI: 10.1111/aswp.12212

Ben Jedidia, K., & Guerbouj, K. (2021). Effects of zakat on the economic growth in selected Islamic countries: Empirical evidence. *International Journal of Development Issues*, *20*(1), 126–142. DOI: 10.1108/IJDI-05-2020-0100

Choiriyah, E. A. N. M., Kafi, A., Hikmah, I. F., & Indrawan, I. W. (2020). Zakat and poverty alleviation in Indonesia: A panel analysis at the provincial level. *Journal of Islamic Monetary Economics and Finance*, *6*(4), 811–832. DOI: 10.21098/jimf.v6i4.1122

Fatimah, R., & Suryaman, M. (2024). Penggunaan Platform Crowdfunding dalam Upaya Peningkatan Penghimpunan Dana Zakat Infak dan Sedekah di LAZ Lidzikri Bandung. *As-Syirkah: Islamic Economic & Financial Journal, 3*(2), 847 -. DOI: 10.56672/syirkah.v3i2.209

Gundogdu, A. S. (2019). Poverty, hunger, and inequality in the context of zakat and waqf. *darulfunun ilahiyat, 30*(1), 49-64. https://doi.org/DOI: 10.26650/di.2019.30.1.0005

Herianingrum, S., Supriani, I., Sukmana, R., Effendie, E., Widiastuti, T., Fauzi, Q., & Shofawati, A. (2024). Zakat as an instrument of poverty reduction in Indonesia. *Journal of Islamic Accounting and Business Research, 15*(4), 643–660. DOI: 10.1108/JIABR-11-2021-0307

Iskandar, A., Possumah, B. T., Aqbar, K., & Yunta, A. H. D. (2021). Islamic philanthropy and poverty reduction in Indonesia: The role of integrated Islamic social and commercial finance institutions. *AL-IHKAM: Jurnal Hukum & Pranata Sosial, 16*(2), 274–301. DOI: 10.19105/al-lhkam.v16i2.5026

Mawardi, I., Widiastuti, T., Al Mustofa, M. U., & Hakimi, F. (2023). Analyzing the impact of productive zakat on the welfare of zakat recipients. *Journal of Islamic Accounting and Business Research, 14*(1), 118–140. DOI: 10.1108/JIABR-05-2021-0145

Mongkito, Abdul & Samdin, Samdin. (2025). The Role of Zakat in Poverty Alleviation and Farmer Welfare: The Theoretical Review. *Journal of Global Innovations in Agricultural Sciences*, 285-296. https://doi.org/DOI: 10.22194/JGIAS/25.1427

Mukhlishin, M., Wahab, A., Setiaji, B., & Tazhdinov, M. (2024). Zakat Maal Management and Regulation Practices: Evidence from Malaysia, Turkey, and Indonesia. *Journal of Human Rights. Culture and Legal System, 4*(2), 569–592. DOI: 10.53955/jhcls.v4i2.204

Nelly, Roos, & Harianto, Harianto & Abd. Majid, M. Shabri & Marliyah, Marliyah & Handayani, Rita. (. (2022). Studi Empiris Perkembangan Crowdfunding Syariah di Indonesia. Al-Kharaj: *Jurnal Ekonomi. Keuangan & Bisnis Syariah, 4*, 1383–1298. DOI: 10.47467/alkharaj.v4i5.926

Purwatiningsih, A., Purnamasari, S., Setyawati, H., Indriani, A., Prawitasari, D., & Fitria, S. (2024). Bibliometric analysis of Islamic Crowdfunding: A Literature Review of Its Journey. *F1000 Research, 13*, 531. DOI: 10.12688/f1000research.146797.1 PMID: 39822736

Raies, A. (2020). Islamic versus Conventional Fiscal policy: The effect of zakat on education and employment. *Academic Journal of Interdisciplinary Studies, 9*(1), 27–33. DOI: 10.36941/ajis-2020-0003

Razak, S. H. A. (2020). Zakat and waqf as instruments of Islamic wealth in poverty alleviation and redistribution: Case of Malaysia. *The International Journal of Sociology and Social Policy*, *40*(3/4), 249–266. DOI: 10.1108/IJSSP-11-2018-0208

Saiti, B., Dembele, A., & Bulut, M. (2021). The global cash waqf: A tool against poverty in Muslim countries. *Qualitative Research in Financial Markets*, *13*(3), 277–294. DOI: 10.1108/QRFM-05-2020-0085

Saiti, B., Salad, A. J., & Bulut, M. (2019). The Role of Cash Waqf in Poverty Reduction: A Multi-country Case Study. In Ghazali, E. M., Mutum, D. S., Rashid, M., & Ahmed, J. U. (Eds.), *Management of Shari'ah Compliant Businesses. Management for Professionals*. Springer., DOI: 10.1007/978-3-030-10907-3_3

Syahbandir, M., Alqarni, W., Hakim, A., & Muhiddin, B. (2022). State Authority for Management of Zakat, Infaq, and Sadaqah as Locally-Generated Revenue: A Case Study at Baitul Mal in Aceh. *AL-IHKAM: Journal of Law & Social Institutions*, *17*(2), 554–577. DOI: 10.19105/al-lhkam.v17i2.7229

Widiastuti, T., Auwalin, I., Rani, L. N., & Ubaidillah Al Mustofa, M. (2021). A mediating effect of business growth on the zakat empowerment program and the mustahiq's welfare. *Cogent Business & Management*, *8*(1), 1882039. Advance online publication. DOI: 10.1080/23311975.2021.1882039

Yusran, Q. Q., & Afiyah, I. (2024). Optimizing the Potential of Zakat to Alleviate Poverty Problems and Improve Community Economy in Surakarta City. *Journal of Ecohumanism*, *3*(3), 121–132. DOI: 10.62754/joe.v3i3.3394

Chapter 4
Regulatory and Environmental Enablers of Blockchain Adoption in Anti-Money Laundering:
Insights From Malaysia

Dahlia Fernandez
https://orcid.org/0000-0002-4238-1804
Universiti Kebangsaan Malaysia, Malaysia

Nurul Atasha Jamaludin
https://orcid.org/0000-0002-3545-3398
Universiti Kebangsaan Malaysia, Malaysia

ABSTRACT

Financial institutions now use blockchain technology as a transformative solution to enhance their Anti-Money Laundering (AML) compliance because of rising demands to combat complex money laundering schemes. This paper examines the policy and environmental elements which affect blockchain adoption within Malaysia's financial industry. The research uses secondary sources and international examples to determine essential factors for blockchain adoption which include regulatory clarity and strategic direction and international alignment and ecosystem collaboration. The adoption of blockchain technology faces challenges from fragmented legal frameworks and insufficient regulatory guidance yet Malaysia's digital economy agenda and cross-border cooperation create substantial opportunities. The research demonstrates that risk-based regulatory approaches combined with multi-stakeholder

DOI: 10.4018/979-8-3373-2655-9.ch004

participation will drive faster adoption of blockchain technology. The research provides knowledge to both policymakers and academic scholars about how emerging technologies impact financial integrity.

INTRODUCTION

The worldwide fight against money laundering has become an essential high-stakes priority for governments and financial institutions. The global financial system faces mounting pressure from regulatory agencies to improve Anti-Money Laundering (AML) compliance because criminals have developed sophisticated methods to launder illicit funds (FATF, 2023). The traditional AML frameworks depend on manual processes and legacy systems which produce inefficient operations and high compliance expenses and create vulnerabilities to fraud (Zetzsche et al., 2020).

Blockchain technology which supports Bitcoin cryptocurrency has proven to be a disruptive force for financial regulatory systems. The decentralized and transparent and immutable features of blockchain technology provide new ways to improve AML efforts through better transaction tracking and data verification and international cooperation (Dai & Vasarhelyi, 2017; Nik Man & Fernandez, 2023). The process of implementing blockchain technology into current AML practices extends beyond technical considerations. The implementation of blockchain technology depends on external factors which include national policy direction and regulatory frameworks and global standard alignment and industry partnerships and the broader digital ecosystem.

Malaysia provides an interesting case study due to its proactive stance on digital transformation, yet cautious adoption of blockchain in critical areas like AML. This chapter explores the policy and environmental determinants that influence blockchain integration in AML practices within the Malaysian financial sector. It aims to identify not only the challenges but also the opportunities for stakeholders to align innovation with compliance.

BLOCKCHAIN AND AML: AN EVOLVING RELATIONSHIP

Blockchain technology under the name Distributed Ledger Technology (DLT) functions as a revolutionary innovation which has the power to transform conventional financial compliance systems. Blockchain technology allows secure and transparent data recording and storage and sharing across a network of decentralized computers (nodes). The blockchain system stores transactions through blocks which include both timestamped transaction batches and cryptographic hashes linking each block to its predecessor thus creating an unalterable record chain. The blockchain structure makes it virtually impossible to modify recorded transactions because network consensus is required for any changes (Crosby et al., 2016).

The blockchain technology features of immutability and transparency along with decentralization and cryptographic security directly support Anti-Money Laundering (AML) practices. The financial crime prevention framework known as AML consists of policies and laws and technologies which identify and prevent and report money laundering and terrorism financing and illicit fund transfers. The evolution of sophisticated global financial crimes creates challenges for traditional AML systems because they depend on isolated data storage and disconnected reporting systems and human-based compliance processes (Arner et al., 2017).

Blockchain offers a paradigm shift in AML through the following mechanisms:

- Improved Transparency and Real-Time Monitoring:

Transactions on a blockchain can be instantly verified by all parties with access to the ledger. This feature allows compliance officers and regulators to trace the flow of funds across jurisdictions in real-time. Especially in permissioned blockchains used within financial consortia, the visibility into transaction history enables early detection of suspicious behavior (Zhang et al., 2019). For example, companies like Chainalysis and Elliptic already offer blockchain analytics platforms that assist banks and regulators in tracking illicit crypto transactions.

- Data Immutability and Tamper-Resistance:

Once recorded, blockchain data cannot be altered retroactively without detection, which preserves the integrity of transaction records. This immutability ensures that audit trails remain intact, providing a strong evidentiary basis for investigations. In contrast to traditional databases, where insiders might alter logs or delete suspicious entries, blockchain's consensus mechanism and distributed architecture protect the data against unauthorized modification (Dai & Vasarhelyi, 2017).

- Enhanced KYC and Customer Due Diligence (CDD):

Financial institutions spend considerable resources on duplicative KYC processes. Blockchain-based digital identity frameworks allow for reusable, verified identities that are cryptographically secured. When a customer's identity is verified by one institution, it can be shared across a network under strict permission protocols, reducing duplication, fraud risk, and onboarding time. Projects like Sovrin and uPort exemplify how self-sovereign identity (SSI) on blockchain can revolutionize KYC across borders (World Economic Forum, 2020).

- Smart Contracts and Automated Compliance Triggers:

Smart contracts are programmable codes stored on a blockchain that execute automatically when predefined conditions are met. They can be designed to enforce regulatory compliance rules such as blocking transactions from sanctioned entities, triggering alerts for high-risk transfers, or freezing funds for review. This automation can reduce manual errors, speed up response time, and ensure regulatory rules are consistently enforced (Tapscott & Tapscott, 2017).

- Cross-Border Collaboration and Standardization:

One of the biggest AML challenges is the fragmentation of regulations and lack of coordination across jurisdictions. Blockchain offers a shared infrastructure that can support harmonized compliance frameworks, particularly in multi-country financial ecosystems like ASEAN or the European Union. By enabling secure, standardized data sharing between regulators and institutions across borders, blockchain enhances the global fight against financial crime (FATF, 2023).

Despite its promise, the application of blockchain in AML is not without challenges.

Public blockchains, such as Bitcoin or Ethereum, are pseudonymous rather than anonymous, which means they require sophisticated analytics to link wallet addresses to real-world identities. Furthermore, integrating blockchain into traditional compliance infrastructure necessitates changes to legacy IT systems, legal frameworks, and internal workflows.

Nonetheless, the convergence of blockchain and AML presents a significant opportunity. As regulators become more familiar with the technology and industry standards emerge, blockchain is likely to evolve from an experimental innovation to a core element of next-generation compliance infrastructure. In doing so, it could drastically improve the effectiveness, efficiency, and accountability of AML efforts globally.

MALAYSIA'S POLICY LANDSCAPE AND DIGITAL AMBITION

The Southeast Asian nation of Malaysia has established its position as a digital innovation leader through its continuous efforts to modernize its economy by adopting advanced technologies (Zainol, Fernandez & Ahmad, 2017). The country's national initiatives demonstrate its ambition through the implementation of the Malaysia

Digital Economy Blueprint (MyDIGITAL) and the National Blockchain Roadmap 2021–2025 which outline digital transformation strategies for both public and private sectors (Ministry of Science, Technology and Innovation, 2021).

The MyDIGITAL Blueprint serves as a complete national plan which aims to make Malaysia a leading digital economy force in Southeast Asia. The blueprint contains six strategic thrusts which include the enhancement of digital trust through secure ethical technology adoption. The strategy places great emphasis on developing a solid digital infrastructure together with regulatory frameworks that enable blockchain along with artificial intelligence and big data analytics. The blueprint addresses the requirements to enhance cybersecurity alongside digital identity protection and data privacy safeguards which directly support Anti-Money Laundering (AML) objectives (Economic Planning Unit, 2021).

The Ministry of Science, Technology and Innovation (MOSTI) together with the Malaysian Industry-Government Group for High Technology (MIGHT) developed the National Blockchain Roadmap 2021–2025. This roadmap identifies five sectors including agriculture and Islamic finance and halal supply chain and renewable energy and public sector recordkeeping which should use blockchain for high-impact applications. The roadmap fails to explicitly mention AML as an area of focus but it supports regulatory blockchain applications and demands additional research about blockchain uses in governance especially for financial integrity and audit and compliance functions (Ministry of Science, Technology and Innovation, 2021).

The government established the Digital Investment Office (DIO) alongside the Malaysia Cyber Security Strategy 2020–2024 to promote secure technology adoption while drawing foreign direct investment into the digital economy. These initiatives work to build a thriving environment for financial technology (FinTech) which includes RegTech solutions that help with AML and compliance monitoring.

The strong policy base exists but blockchain technology integration into financial systems remains restricted especially when dealing with the sensitive field of AML. The implementation of blockchain technology faces three major barriers which industry observers and compliance professionals identify as the main hurdles:

- Regulatory Ambiguity: While financial regulators such as Bank Negara Malaysia (BNM) and the Securities Commission Malaysia (SC) have expressed openness to blockchain, there remains a lack of dedicated policy instruments addressing its role in AML specifically. Uncertainty about legal liabilities, data protection obligations, and cross-border data flow compliance continues to deter proactive adoption.
- Technological Gaps: Not all financial institutions possess the technical capability to implement blockchain-based solutions. Issues include integration

with legacy core banking systems, compatibility with existing risk management software, and interoperability across institutions.

- Human Capital and Industry Readiness: There is a shortage of blockchain-literate compliance professionals and internal capacity to assess the reliability of blockchain tools for AML. Additionally, many institutions remain hesitant due to the perceived novelty and risk associated with decentralization.

Multiple public-private initiatives exist to address these gaps. BNM operates the Financial Technology Enabler Group (FTEG) to facilitate FinTech regulatory discussions and Malaysia uses its Regulatory Sandbox Framework to enable both startups and established players to test innovative financial solutions including blockchain applications through controlled environments. The current sandbox projects have not dedicated many resources to AML-related use cases.

The DEPA (Digital Economy Partnership Agreement) between Malaysia and Singapore and Chile and New Zealand enables the country to establish platforms for standardizing blockchain-based compliance standards. Through these frameworks Malaysia gains international visibility and collaborative prospects to create blockchain governance systems which match worldwide AML developments.

The blockchain integration policy framework in Malaysia shows promise but the adoption process for AML remains slow and disorganized. The meaningful adoption of blockchain to protect Malaysia's financial system requires better coordination between national policy goals and specific sector regulations.

POLICY AND REGULATORY DETERMINANTS

Regulatory Clarity

The main challenge to blockchain adoption in AML practices stems from the absence of a unified regulatory framework which specifically addresses distributed ledger technologies (DLTs) in financial compliance. The Malaysian financial sector operates under Bank Negara Malaysia (BNM) and Securities Commission Malaysia (SC) issued legacy regulations. The bodies have recognized blockchain potential through policy statements and fintech consultations yet there exists no explicit legal framework to govern blockchain integration into AML protocols.

The absence of legal clarity leads industry players to adopt a "wait-and-see" stance especially in banking and securities sectors because regulatory compliance is non-negotiable (FATF, 2023). The lack of defined legal expectations creates concerns among institutions about unintentional regulatory breaches and potential enforcement risks. The regulatory uncertainty prevents organizations from testing and investing in blockchain-based AML solutions.

The regulatory bodies of Singapore and the European Union have established consultative frameworks and sandbox guidelines for DLT-based compliance tools which provide necessary clarity for innovation (MAS, 2021; European Commission, 2022).

Legal Fragmentation and Compliance Gaps

The blockchain regulatory framework in Malaysia exists as multiple separate systems which sometimes duplicate each other. The Capital Markets and Services Act 2007 (CMSA) controls digital tokens with security-like features but the SC Digital Asset Guidelines concentrate on ICOs and digital exchanges. The legal framework of blockchain technology for AML and financial oversight purposes remains unclear.

Different agencies use their institutional mandates to interpret blockchain functionality which results in poor inter-agency coordination and potential jurisdictional conflicts. Financial institutions face compliance ambiguity because of inconsistent regulations particularly when they participate in blockchain-based initiatives such as KYC consortiums and blockchain transaction monitoring platforms (Zetzsche et al., 2020).

The absence of defined data-sharing protocols between regulators and banks and fintech entities hinders the development of a unified AML infrastructure which undermines blockchain's goal to establish transparency and interoperability and build trust.

Alignment with Global Standards

The Financial Action Task Force (FATF) and Asia/Pacific Group on Money Laundering (APGML) serve as the main international standards for Malaysia to follow anti-money laundering regulations. The current FATF guidelines mainly address Virtual Asset Service Providers (VASPs) and digital currencies but do not provide sufficient guidance on blockchain infrastructure applications for AML beyond cryptocurrencies.

Financial institutions face a challenge because they need to innovate while following compliance rules in an environment where international regulatory guidance remains unclear. The lack of regulatory interoperability creates significant challenges for cross-border information exchange and blockchain-based KYC utilities and digital identity verification platforms (World Economic Forum, 2020; FATF, 2023).

The General Data Protection Regulation (GDPR) in the EU and Malaysia's Personal Data Protection Act (PDPA) create additional challenges regarding data immutability and the "right to be forgotten" which makes it difficult to align blockchain applications with privacy regulations across different jurisdictions (Zhang et al., 2019).

Government Direction and Strategic Investment

The Malaysian government has shown commendable strategic intent through the MyDIGITAL Blueprint (2021-2030) and the National Blockchain Roadmap 2021-2025, which lay the groundwork for positioning Malaysia as a regional digital leader. These blueprints articulate ambitions to leverage blockchain across various domains such as supply chains, education, and public services (Ministry of Science, Technology and Innovation, 2021).

However, when it comes to AML-specific applications, policy actions remain largely symbolic. There is a notable absence of:

- Targeted incentives for blockchain AML pilots
- Funding allocations for public-private compliance innovation
- Sandbox expansions to accommodate DLT AML use cases
- Guidance notes or circulars on how blockchain-based compliance tools should be regulated

Compared to countries like the United Kingdom, where the Financial Conduct Authority (FCA) has issued clear criteria for RegTech and blockchain trials, Malaysia still lacks the institutional mechanisms to de-risk innovation in AML contexts (FCA, 2021).

For blockchain to be effectively integrated into national AML efforts, the government must go beyond strategic rhetoric and deliver tangible policy instruments, such as tax incentives, regulatory relief, technical capacity-building grants, and a national sandbox for AML-focused blockchain projects.

ENVIRONMENTAL DETERMINANTS

The successful adoption of blockchain in Anti-Money Laundering (AML) practices extends beyond regulatory frameworks and technological innovation. The environmental context which includes ecosystem readiness, cross-border cooperation, and institutional capacity plays a vital role in determining blockchain's efficacy and scalability in the Malaysian financial system.

Ecosystem Collaboration

The successful implementation of blockchain technology requires all participants in the ecosystem to work together. The consensus-driven distributed system of blockchain requires multiple stakeholders including banks and fintech startups and regulators and legal entities and consumers to work together.

The financial and regulatory systems of Malaysia maintain separate institutional structures which prevent data architecture integration and limit the use of legacy systems. The majority of banks use their own KYC platforms while data sharing between institutions remains restricted because of privacy concerns and competitive advantage protection and unclear regulatory guidelines (Malaysia Digital Economy Corporation, 2021).

The absence of collaboration between entities prevents blockchain innovation from advancing while blocking the development of industry-wide solutions such as:

- Shared KYC utilities
- Consortium blockchains for transaction monitoring
- Common compliance standards across financial service providers

Countries such as the Netherlands (with the Dutch Blockchain Coalition) and Singapore (through MAS and the Singapore FinTech Association) have shown the value of consortium-based governance in developing blockchain applications for regulatory technology (RegTech). Malaysia must emulate such models through national forums, regulatory roundtables, and joint regulatory-fintech accelerators to foster innovation in blockchain AML.

Cross-Border Regulatory Cooperation

Money laundering is inherently a cross-border problem, funds are moved rapidly across jurisdictions, often through a complex web of shell companies and intermediaries. Therefore, the value proposition of blockchain lies in its ability to enable real-time, borderless surveillance of transactions, and support international AML investigations through transparent and verifiable trails.

However, Malaysia currently lacks comprehensive bilateral or regional data-sharing agreements specifically tailored for blockchain-based AML compliance. The absence of regional consensus on data standards, regulatory requirements, and surveillance protocols makes it difficult to implement a seamless blockchain AML framework (KPMG, 2022).

For example:

- There is no unified ASEAN strategy on blockchain-enabled compliance.
- Malaysia has not yet established memoranda of understanding (MoUs) with peer regulators in key markets such as Singapore, Thailand, or Indonesia to facilitate blockchain-based reporting.
- The interoperability of blockchain tools with international law enforcement agencies, such as INTERPOL or the Egmont Group, remains unexplored.

Malaysia could look to initiatives like Project Dunbar (a cross-border blockchain project between Singapore, Australia, Malaysia, and South Africa for multi-CBDC settlement) as a template for cross-border regulatory coordination in AML applications.

Infrastructure and Human Capital Readiness

The successful implementation of blockchain technology in AML depends on both technical infrastructure and human capital capacity. The digital infrastructure development in Malaysia through JENDELA and MyDIGITAL has been substantial but multiple technical barriers remain:

- The financial sector lacks sufficient blockchain-node hosting facilities throughout its institutions.
- The blockchain network faces issues with both speed and capacity to expand.
- The system faces major cybersecurity threats because of weak endpoint security measures and insufficient smart contract audit procedures.

Malaysia faces an essential shortage of AML and compliance professionals who possess blockchain technology expertise. Most compliance professionals lack training in:

- The fundamental operational principles of distributed ledger systems remain unfamiliar to most compliance professionals.
- The implementation of rule engines through smart contracts remains unfamiliar to most professionals.
- The analysis and tracing of blockchain data require specific skills that are not commonly found in the workforce.

The report by Arner et al. (2017) shows that compliance teams need to transform their role from document-based analysis to technology-based investigation which includes working with blockchain data structures and automated red-flag systems.

The following measures must be implemented to bridge these gaps in Malaysia:

- The country needs to establish blockchain certification programs at the national level for AML professionals.
- University programs should include blockchain and RegTech as part of their curriculum.
- The IT development sector should provide training to legal compliance teams through cross-training initiatives.
- The public sector needs to host bootcamps about blockchain technology through joint efforts between Bank Negara Malaysia (BNM), Securities Commission (SC), and MDEC.

A blockchain AML tool's effectiveness depends on both a strong technological base and employees who understand digital concepts.

STRATEGIC RECOMMENDATIONS

As blockchain technology continues to evolve, Malaysian policymakers and financial institutions must proactively shape a regulatory and operational environment that encourages responsible innovation while safeguarding against money laundering threats. Below are six strategic recommendations to support blockchain integration in AML practices:

Develop Blockchain-Specific AML Guidelines

Malaysia urgently needs clear and comprehensive regulatory guidance on how blockchain technologies can be integrated into AML protocols. These guidelines should address:

- Smart contract auditing standards, including code verification and assurance mechanisms.
- Use of blockchain for Know Your Customer (KYC) and Customer Due Diligence (CDD) procedures, with attention to identity validation, data sovereignty, and privacy concerns.
- Risk-based approaches to blockchain integration in line with FATF's updated Recommendations on Virtual Assets and Virtual Asset Service Providers (VASPs).
- Permissible technologies and approved vendors or consortia to avoid ambiguity in institutional procurement.

These guidelines should not only reflect international best practices but also be tailored to Malaysia's regulatory context. Input should be sought from BNM, the SC, legal experts, and technology stakeholders to ensure relevance and enforceability.

Expand and Institutionalize Regulatory Sandboxes

The existing regulatory sandboxes operated by BNM and SC in Malaysia need expansion and institutionalization for blockchain-based AML innovations. Specifically:

- Financial institutions and FinTech firms should be permitted to test DLT-enabled compliance tools such as automated suspicious activity reporting systems and blockchain-based KYC platforms.
- The regulators should enable cross-border pilot projects with neighboring regulators (e.g., MAS in Singapore, Bank of Thailand) to explore regional harmonization of AML rules.
- The financial sector should receive transparent information about sandbox results to speed up collective learning.

The successful outcomes of sandbox projects should receive expedited review for formal implementation through a risk-based regulatory approval process.

Foster Public–Private Partnerships and Incentives

The development of AML innovation requires more than government leadership alone. Strategic public–private partnerships (PPPs) can catalyze development and deployment by:

- The government should provide grants and matching funds to support blockchain AML pilot projects that involve startups and RegTech firms and university research centers.
- The government should initiate challenge-based programs which ask industry participants to develop blockchain solutions for particular AML challenges.
- The establishment of national AML innovation hubs will unite regulators with developers and compliance officers and researchers to create joint solutions.

The UK Financial Conduct Authority TechSprint model demonstrates how public-private partnerships succeed in creating functional RegTech solutions through international case studies.

Promote Interoperability and National Data Standards

The complete transformation of AML efforts through blockchain technology requires Malaysia to prevent solution development in isolated systems. The government should:

- The government needs to create a national digital identity framework that matches blockchain technology standards while following both the Personal Data Protection Act (PDPA) and AML requirements.
- Financial institutions should use open data standards to share transaction and identity data through permissioned privacy-compliant systems.
- The government should encourage financial institutions to use interoperable blockchain protocols (Hyperledger Fabric, Corda, Quorum) for banks and insurers and regulators to achieve integration and scalability.

SIRIM and MIMOS need to collaborate with regulatory bodies for developing local technical standards which match ISO/TC 307 (Blockchain and Distributed Ledger Technologies) standards.

Build National Capacity in Blockchain Compliance

The foundation of regulatory innovation depends on human capital. Malaysia needs to take the following steps to prepare for blockchain-based AML systems:

- The government should create certification programs and micro-credentials in blockchain compliance which should focus on auditors and risk managers and compliance professionals.
- The government should collaborate with universities and polytechnics to add blockchain governance and AML modules to their accounting and law and information systems curricula.
- The financial institutions should use knowledge-sharing platforms (e.g., forums, webinars, workshops) to exchange lessons learned from pilots and regulatory trials.

The regulatory bodies should participate in bilateral training programs with Estonia, the UAE and Singapore to acquire international expertise in blockchain governance and AML enforcement.

Engage in Regional and Global Collaboration

Malaysia should enhance its international positioning by:

- Participating in FATF working groups and IMF technical consultations to stay ahead of global trends in blockchain regulation.
- Advocating for regional blockchain standards under ASEAN frameworks, such as the ASEAN Digital Masterplan 2025.
- Collaborating with global RegTech alliances to tap into cutting-edge AML tools that are already being tested or deployed globally.

Such collaboration will help ensure that Malaysian institutions remain interoperable and competitive while upholding global AML commitments.

International Perspectives and Lessons Learned

Understanding how other nations have approached blockchain integration in Anti-Money Laundering (AML) practices can provide valuable lessons for Malaysia. Several countries have developed pioneering frameworks that balance innovation with compliance. Notably, Estonia, Singapore, and the United Arab Emirates (UAE) have positioned themselves at the forefront of blockchain-enabled financial regulation.

Estonia: A Blockchain Governance Pioneer

Estonia is often cited as a global leader in digital governance and blockchain application. Since the early 2000s, the country has embraced digital infrastructure, culminating in its blockchain-based data integrity systems known as KSI Blockchain.

- Estonia's e-Residency program provides global citizens access to Estonian digital services, including the ability to open bank accounts and establish companies remotely-subject to robust digital KYC checks (e-Estonia, 2022).
- Public registries, such as health, judicial, and business databases, are secured using blockchain for tamper-proof recordkeeping.
- AML compliance is enhanced by real-time transaction monitoring and secure data exchange across government agencies and financial institutions, ensuring fast and coordinated responses to suspicious activities.

The Estonian model emphasizes the central role of digital identity, cross-agency trust frameworks, and continuous government investment in cybersecurity, providing a potential model for Malaysia's e-government ambitions.

Singapore: Sandbox Innovation and Interoperability

Singapore's regulatory environment combines innovation-friendliness with strict financial oversight. The Monetary Authority of Singapore (MAS) has been instrumental in fostering blockchain adoption through initiatives like:

- Project Ubin, which explores the use of blockchain and distributed ledger technologies (DLT) for multi-currency payment settlements. The project's Phase 5 demonstrated the feasibility of using blockchain for AML-compliant cross-border payments (MAS, 2021).
- MAS's FinTech Regulatory Sandbox allows innovators to test blockchain-based AML solutions in a safe environment, guided by well-defined compliance protocols.
- The development of MyInfo, a digital identity and data-sharing platform integrated into financial institutions' KYC processes, showcases Singapore's success in achieving interoperability and regulatory trust.

Singapore's approach offers Malaysia insights into sandbox design, cross-border experimentation, and the value of aligning FinTech development with strong identity and data standards.

United Arab Emirates: Blockchain as RegTech

The UAE has integrated blockchain technology into its national economic transformation plans. The Emirates Blockchain Strategy 2021 and Dubai's Smart City initiative aim to digitize 50% of government transactions using blockchain.

Key AML-relevant initiatives include:

- The Central Bank of the UAE's (CBUAE) collaboration with private sector and international partners to launch KYC blockchain platforms for financial institutions (CBUAE, 2022).
- The use of blockchain to support eKYC processes by linking financial institutions with government databases, reducing duplication and enhancing fraud detection.
- The UAE's Risk-Based Supervision (RBS) model, which incorporates RegTech tools including blockchain-based analytics for compliance monitoring and enforcement.

Furthermore, the UAE has championed regional cross-border cooperation, working with the Gulf Cooperation Council (GCC) to harmonize digital finance regulations.

Key Lessons for Malaysia

From these case studies, several key lessons emerge that can guide Malaysia's policy and regulatory efforts:

- Leadership matters: Successful blockchain AML integration is often driven by strong, clear government mandates and dedicated taskforces.
- Sandbox-to-scaling pathways: Regulatory sandboxes should not be isolated experiments; they must be designed with clear roadmaps toward national implementation.
- Digital identity is foundational: All three countries prioritize robust digital identity systems, enabling more efficient and secure AML checks.
- Interoperability and regional cooperation: Aligning blockchain systems across borders enhances both compliance and competitiveness.

By adapting these global practices to its local context, Malaysia can leapfrog traditional hurdles and position itself as a regional RegTech leader.

LEGAL AND ETHICAL IMPLICATIONS

While blockchain presents powerful tools for enhancing Anti-Money Laundering (AML) efforts, its application raises complex legal and ethical questions. These challenges are particularly sensitive in heavily regulated environments like finance, where data protection, due pcess, and institutional accountability are paramount (Zhou et al., 2026; Fernandez & Aman 2022).

Data Privacy vs. Transparency

One of blockchain's most lauded features its radical transparency and immutability can be at odds with legal requirements for data minimization, access controls, and the right to be forgotten.

- Malaysia's Personal Data Protection Act (PDPA) prohibits the processing of personal data without consent and mandates data retention limits. Yet, blockchain's design especially public blockchains means once information is added, it is virtually impossible to erase or alter.
- The European Union's General Data Protection Regulation (GDPR) imposes even stricter obligations, including the right to rectification and erasure. This creates tension with blockchain's core principle of immutability.

- To address this tension, privacy-preserving blockchain architectures have been developed. These include:
  - o Zero-Knowledge Proofs (ZKPs) that validate information without revealing it
  - o Off-chain storage for personal data, with only hashes stored on-chain
  - o Permissioned blockchains that restrict access to sensitive data among vetted parties (Zhang et al., 2019)

These technologies offer pathways toward compliance, but their maturity and adoption levels remain uneven across jurisdictions.

Legal Liability and Automation

Blockchain AML systems often incorporate smart contracts, which are self-executing agreements with logic coded directly into the blockchain.

- Use Case: A smart contract might automatically freeze an account or flag transactions when thresholds are breached.
- Issue: If a false positive occurs (e.g., a legitimate transaction gets flagged), who bears the legal liability? The developer? The deploying institution? The regulator?
- Legal Uncertainty: The enforceability of smart contracts in Malaysia's legal system is still evolving. While Section 10 of the Contracts Act 1950 recognizes electronic agreements, courts have yet to address smart contract disputes directly.
- Legal scholars warn of the "black box problem," where institutions cannot fully explain or control how automated systems behave (Zetzsche et al., 2020). This creates a need for:
  - o Auditable codebases
  - o Human-in-the-loop governance
  - o Insurance and indemnity frameworks

Bias and Discrimination Risks

The increasing use of Artificial Intelligence (AI) and machine learning in blockchain AML tools creates an urgent ethical issue regarding bias detection.

- The training of algorithms with unbalanced datasets leads to discriminatory results that target specific demographic groups and geographic areas.

- The AML system could perform excessive monitoring on lower-income communities and foreign remittances that originate from particular nations.
- The solution to this problem requires regulators and institutions to take the following steps:
  - The law should enforce assessments to determine algorithmic fairness.
  - The documentation process for models should operate with complete transparency.
  - The use of AI tools in AML processes requires institutions to support third-party audits of these tools.

The ethical governance framework needs to expand its scope from code-based rules to include decision-making responsibility and system design inclusivity and digital compliance framework trust among the public.

Jurisdictional Conflicts and Cross-Border Enforcement

The worldwide nature of blockchain technology creates difficulties when AML violations occur across different jurisdictions:

- The process of a suspicious transaction beginning in Malaysia would use wallet addresses from Estonia while passing through a US-based exchange.
- The absence of treaties and cooperative frameworks creates regulatory fragmentation which enables actors to exploit jurisdictional gaps according to Arner et al. (2017).
- The following recommendations apply to Malaysia:
  - The country should join regional AML alliances that work to standardize blockchain technology.
  - The country should support the development of mutual legal assistance treaties (MLATs) which validate smart contract evidence.
  - The country should take part in blockchain governance initiatives at the global level through FATF and the Global Digital Finance (GDF) initiative.

FUTURE RESEARCH DIRECTIONS

Although the integration of blockchain into Anti-Money Laundering (AML) frameworks is gaining interest, the academic and practical understanding of its long-term implications remains fragmented. To inform robust policymaking and effective implementation, several research gaps need to be addressed in future studies.

Comparative Policy Studies Across ASEAN and Commonwealth Countries

The implementation of blockchain technology for AML purposes differs between countries because of their varying economic development levels and legal systems and technological readiness. The implementation of blockchain technology in Malaysia will benefit from comparative assessments of peer jurisdictions including Singapore and Australia and Estonia and the UK.

- Singapore (via Project Ubin and MAS regulatory sandboxes)
- Australia (through its National Blockchain Roadmap and AUSTRAC reforms)
- Estonia and the UK, which have adopted digital identity and blockchain compliance systems.

Key questions:

- How do legal frameworks influence adoption rates?
- What governance models have yielded the most resilient AML outcomes?
- How can regional alignment reduce regulatory arbitrage?

The research will reveal optimal practices together with acquired knowledge and regional regulatory standardization models.

Cost–Benefit Analyses for Institutions of Varying Sizes

The implementation of blockchain technology requires financial institutions to spend money on setup costs and training expenses and infrastructure improvements which tend to affect small and mid-sized institutions more heavily.

Research should:

- Analyze the total cost of ownership of blockchain AML platforms
- Quantify operational savings over time through efficiency gains
- Analyze the scalability and modularity of AML blockchain tools for institutions of different sizes

Policymakers should use this information to create compliance incentives that include financial support and tax benefits for smaller institutions.

Public Trust and Acceptance of Blockchain in Financial Oversight

Public confidence stands as the essential requirement for technology adoption beyond institutional factors. The literature lacks sufficient research about how typical citizens view blockchain systems when used for regulatory surveillance purposes.

Suggested focus areas:

- Perceived risks to personal data and privacy
- Trust in decentralized versus centralized oversight models
- Public attitudes toward automation in compliance and law enforcement

Quantitative surveys and qualitative interviews will establish trust frameworks which can direct ethical blockchain AML design.

Ethical Governance Models for Blockchain-Enabled Compliance

The implementation of blockchain technology for AML purposes creates moral dilemmas regarding surveillance practices and machine-based decision systems and accountability mechanisms. The field requires immediate interdisciplinary research between:

- Legal studies (smart contract enforceability, liability)
- Philosophy and ethics (bias, fairness, transparency)
- Technology policy (governance of decentralized platforms)

The research will help create responsible innovation guidelines through a multi-stakeholder framework that includes technologists, regulators, civil society and academia.

Longitudinal Impact Assessments

Most blockchain-AML studies are exploratory or conceptual. There is a lack of empirical data on how blockchain AML systems perform over time. Longitudinal studies can evaluate:

- Effectiveness in reducing money laundering cases
- Changes in reporting efficiency and false positive rates
- Shifts in institutional behavior and compliance culture

Such evidence is essential for determining whether blockchain is merely a techno-utopian promise or a truly transformative regulatory tool.

CONCLUSION

Blockchain technology represents an upcoming transformation for national Anti-Money Laundering (AML) compliance practices. Blockchain technology provides its ability to tackle AML system weaknesses through its core characteristics which include transparency and immutability along with real-time tracking and programmable automation.

The implementation of blockchain technology in Malaysia provides an opportunity to strengthen regulatory enforcement and enhance public trust in financial oversight while modernizing international compliance standards. Blockchain technology represents more than technical advancement because it requires policy changes and institutional and legal framework modifications for successful implementation in AML systems. The implementation of AML technology faces three main barriers because of the absence of standard regulations and weak digital infrastructure together with inadequate collaboration across industries.

Malaysia maintains explicit digital economy ambitions through both the MyDIGITAL Blueprint and National Blockchain Roadmap but practical blockchain-AML implementation has occurred at a slow and disorganized pace. Multiple actions must be taken to establish a connection between these existing gaps:

- The regulation needs to become clear to reduce institutional doubts and draw investment for AML technology.
- Policy coherence serves as an essential element which helps regulators and law enforcement organizations and financial institutions and emerging tech players maintain coordinated efforts.
- The development of blockchain AML solutions requires stronger partnerships between public and private organizations to support innovative applications of this technology.
- The protection of privacy and avoidance of algorithmic bias and citizens' rights defense in surveillance-intensive environments demands ethical foresight.
- The development of standards for compliance needs to be promoted at the regional level to establish unified expectations and enable cross-border data exchange between member states.

Malaysia stands ready to become a regulatory leadership entity that will define standards in this sector throughout ASEAN and the Global South region. The future requires Malaysian officials to develop capacity while conducting interdisciplinary research and experimenting through regulatory sandboxes that will enable responsible yet innovative policy implementation.

The successful integration of blockchain into AML frameworks requires both technological readiness and a complete governance structure which unites progressive innovation with responsible practices and compliance with national and international responsibilities.

ACKNOWLEDGMENT

We would like to acknowledge UKM Research Grant Scheme (EP-2024-033) for funding opportunities.

REFERENCES

Arner, D. W., Barberis, J., & Buckley, R. P. (2017). FinTech and RegTech in a Nutshell, and the Future in a Sandbox. *Research Handbook on Digital Transformations*, 89-102.

CBUAE. (2022). *Annual Report 2022*. Central Bank of the UAE.

Crosby, M., Pattanayak, P., Verma, S., & Kalyanaraman, V. (2016). Blockchain Technology: Beyond Bitcoin. *Applied Innovation*, *2*(6-10), 71.

Dai, J., & Vasarhelyi, M. A. (2017). Toward Blockchain-Based Accounting and Assurance. *Journal of Information Systems*, *31*(3), 5–21. DOI: 10.2308/isys-51804

e-Estonia. (2022). *Digital Transformation Case Study: Estonia*. https://e-estonia.com

FATF. (2023). *Anti-money laundering and counter-terrorist financing measures*. Financial Action Task Force.

Fernandez, D., & Aman, A. (2022). The Influence of RPA technology on Employee Skills in the Accounting Profession. *Jurnal Pengurusan*, *65*, 71–82.

KPMG. (2022). *The Pulse of Fintech H2 2022*. https://kpmg.com/my

Malaysia Digital Economy Corporation. (2021). *MyDIGITAL Blueprint*.

MAS. (2021). *Project Ubin: Central Bank Digital Currency (CBDC) and Blockchain Infrastructure*. Monetary Authority of Singapore.

Ministry of Science, Technology and Innovation. (2021). *National Blockchain Roadmap 2021–2025*.

Nik Man, N. H., & Fernandez, D. (2023). Potential Factors on Blockchain Adoption in Malaysian Public Sector Auditing. In *2023 16th International Conference on Developments in eSystems Engineering (DeSE)* (pp. 188–193). IEEE. https://doi.org/DOI: 10.1109/DeSE60171.2023.10162025

Tapscott, D., & Tapscott, A. (2017). *Blockchain Revolution: How the Technology Behind Bitcoin is Changing Money, Business, and the World*. Penguin.

World Economic Forum. (2020). *The Global Future Council on Blockchain: Building Value with Blockchain Technology*.

Zainol, Z., Fernandez, D., & Ahmad, H. (2017). Public Sector Accountants' Opinion on Impact of a New Enterprise System. *Procedia Computer Science*, *124*, 247–254. DOI: 10.1016/j.procs.2017.12.153

Zetzsche, D. A., Buckley, R. P., Arner, D. W., & Barberis, J. N. (2020). Decentralized Finance. *Journal of Financial Regulation*, *6*(2), 172–203. DOI: 10.1093/jfr/fjaa010

Zhang, Y., Xue, Y., & Liu, Y. (2019). Security and Privacy on Blockchain. *ACM Computing Surveys*, *52*(3), 1–34. DOI: 10.1145/3316481

Zhou, N., Fernandez, D., Aman, A., & Ghazali, A. W. (2026). Hyperautomation in Accounting: A Bibliometric Journey Through Artificial Intelligence and Robotic Process Automation Integration. *Journal of Advanced Research Design*, *138*(1), 42–64.

Chapter 5 Transforming Islamic Finance With AI: A Focus on Risk Management Strategies

Early Ridho Kismawadi
https://orcid.org/0000-0002-9420-5212
IAIN Langsa, Indonesia

Bayu Tri Cahya
https://orcid.org/0000-0001-9277-5740
IAIN Kudus, Indonesia

Erlindawati Erlindawati
Universitas Terbuka, Indonesia

ABSTRACT

This article explores the integration of Enterprise Risk Management (ERM) with Artificial Intelligence (AI) in Islamic financial institutions, with a focus on risk identification, assessment, and management within the project environment. By leveraging a structured ERM framework, financial institutions can systematically identify, evaluate, and mitigate risks such as market fluctuations, credit risk, operational challenges, and sharia compliance violations. AI plays a critical role in improving risk detection, automating the identification of potential compliance issues (e.g., Riba, Gharar), and providing real-time predictive analytics to manage financial and non-financial risks. This article provides valuable insights into the potential of AI in transforming risk management practices, ensuring that Islamic financial institutions remain resilient and competitive in a rapidly changing financial ecosystem.

DOI: 10.4018/979-8-3373-2655-9.ch005

INTRODUCTION

Islamic finance has emerged as an important pillar in the global financial system, with consistent annual growth exceeding 10% over the past decade, reaching global assets of over $4 trillion by 2024 (Islamic Finance Development Report, 2024). Based on sharia principles such as justice, transparency, and the prohibition of usury, gharar, and maisir, Islamic finance offers an ethical approach that is in line with modern society's need for sustainable and inclusive finance.

In a global context characterized by market volatility, geopolitical uncertainty, and rapid digital transformation, the integration of artificial intelligence (AI) in Islamic financial risk management is becoming increasingly relevant. AI, with its ability to analyse big data, predict trends, and automate decision-making, offers an opportunity to improve the resilience and efficiency of Islamic financial institutions

The rapid development of artificial intelligence (AI) technology is transforming various sectors, including finance, by introducing innovative solutions that improve efficiency (Gilvary et al. 2019; Javaid et al. 2023; Soori, Arezoo, and Dastres 2023; Yigitcanlar, Mehmood, and Corchado 2021), accuracy, and decision-making processes. In the realm of Islamic finance, where adherence to ethical principles and risk management is essential, the integration of AI offers significant transformation opportunities. Islamic finance operates under a unique framework that emphasizes risk sharing, social justice, and compliance with Sharia law, so it is important to adopt a robust risk management strategy that aligns with these principles.

Figure 1. Estimated share of worldwide spending on artificial intelligence (AI)-centric systems in 2023, by industry

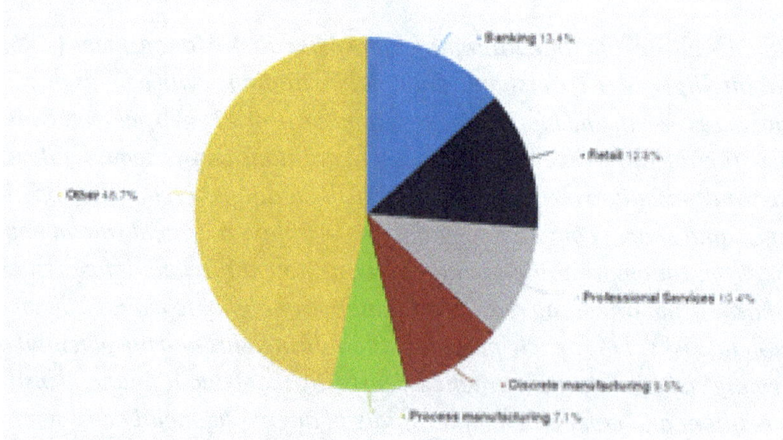

This transformation is reflected in global spending on AI, which is expected to reach $154 billion by 2023, with significant diversity across industries. The banking sector leads with 13.4 percent of total investment, followed by the retail sector with 12.8 percent, demonstrating their great commitment to AI adoption.

As financial markets become increasingly complex and connected, the ability to effectively identify, assess, and mitigate risk is crucial to the sustainability and growth of Islamic financial institutions. AI offers powerful tools to improve risk management strategies, allowing institutions to analyse large amounts of data, predict market trends, and make informed decisions that remain Shariah-compliant. However, the adoption of AI in Islamic finance also raises important questions regarding ethical considerations, data privacy, and potential algorithmic bias, which must be addressed to ensure that these technologies serve the interests of all stakeholders.

The ideal situation for Islamic financial institutions is to integrate artificial intelligence (AI) technology into the corporate risk management (ERM) framework seamlessly, so that it can identify, assess, and manage risks in real-time, accurately, and in accordance with sharia principles. AI is expected to predict market, credit, and operational risks, as well as optimize risk-based contracts such as mudarabah and musharakah, while maintaining transparency, fairness, and data privacy to support financial sustainability and stakeholder trust. Research shows conflicting results on the benefits of AI in Islamic finance. Some studies state AI improves efficiency and sharia compliance, but others mention risks such as algorithmic bias and data privacy violations that can violate sharia principles. This research addresses these non-conformities by systematically evaluating the benefits and risks of AI and proposing a governance framework to ensure sharia compliance.

Research on AI in Islamic finance has not been able to ascertain its long-term impact on financial stability and sharia compliance. Although AI models such as Bayesian networks are promising, data on their scalability in various contexts, such as the sukuk market, are still limited. The study fills this gap by analysing the effectiveness of AI and provides a basis for future long-term studies. Theories about the integration of AI in Islamic finance are still lacking, especially in aligning AI with sharia principles in ERM.

This research proposes a new theoretical framework that combines probability models and communication theories, such as the Shannon-Weaver model, to improve sharia-compliant risk management. The lack of understanding on how to apply AI practically in Islamic finance without violating sharia principles is an obstacle. This research provides practical guidance for applying AI to various Islamic financial instruments, such as murabaha, by ensuring sharia compliance. The application of AI varies across regions, such as the Middle East or Southeast Asia, due to regulatory and cultural differences. This research addresses this gap by analyzing AI applications in various global contexts to provide locally relevant strategies.

AI adoption faces challenges such as infrastructure costs, lack of AI literacy, and governance needs to address algorithmic bias and data privacy. This research proposes an AI governance framework integrated with ERM, interdisciplinary training, and sharia certification standards to address these challenges.

This research addresses these gaps through a systematic literature review, proposes a sharia-compliant AI-ERM model, and provides practical guidance for implementation. For researchers, the study offers a roadmap for interdisciplinary studies, while for policymakers, it recommends regulations that support innovation while maintaining privacy and sharia compliance, thereby strengthening an inclusive and sustainable Islamic finance ecosystem.

This chapter aims to explore the potential transformation of AI in Islamic finance, with a particular focus on risk management strategies. By examining current applications, challenges, and ethical implications, we seek to provide a comprehensive understanding of how AI can be leveraged to improve risk management practices while remaining aligned with the core values of Islamic finance. Through this exploration, we hope to contribute to the ongoing discourse on the intersection between technology and finance, highlighting the opportunities that AI offers to foster a more resilient and ethical financial ecosystem.

The implications of the application of artificial intelligence (AI) in risk management in the Islamic financial sector are broad and significant. The integration of AI can improve the ability of Islamic financial institutions to identify and manage risks more effectively, which in turn can improve the stability and sustainability of the financial system as a whole. However, the adoption of this technology also presents new challenges, such as the need to ensure compliance with Sharia principles and address ethical issues, including data privacy and potential algorithmic bias. Therefore, it is important for financial institutions to develop a framework that not only leverages AI technology, but also considers the social and ethical implications of its use. Thus, the application of AI in risk management can not only strengthen the position of Islamic financial institutions in the global market, but also contribute to the creation of a fairer and more inclusive financial system.

The contribution of this research lies in a deeper understanding of how artificial intelligence can be integrated into risk management strategies in the Islamic finance sector. By exploring existing applications of AI, the challenges faced, and emerging ethical implications, this paper provides valuable insights for stakeholders, including practitioners, academics, and policymakers. The research also highlights the importance of developing a balanced approach between technological innovation and adherence to Sharia principles, so that Islamic financial institutions can harness the potential of AI to improve the efficiency and effectiveness of risk management. Thus, this contribution not only enriches the existing literature, but also provides practical guidance for financial institutions in adopting new technologies responsibly and ethically.

METHOD

This literature review uses a systematic review approach to examine the integration of artificial intelligence (AI) in Islamic financial risk management. The literature is collected from academic databases such as Scopus and the Web of Science, the search process involves: (1) article identification, (2) filtering by title and abstract, and (3) full-text analysis. Thematic analysis is used to group findings into themes such as AI applications, sharia compliance, and ethical challenges. Validity is maintained through screening by two reviewers and transparent documentation

AI as a Driver of Innovation in Risk Management

Islamic finance is one of the fastest-growing sectors in the world, as demand for products and services that are in line with Islamic principles increases (Gani and Bahari 2020; Martín, Orden-Cruz, and Zergane 2020; Nagimova 2023). The basic principles in Islamic finance are fairness, transparency, and avoidance of activities that violate sharia such as riba, gharar (excessive uncertainty), and maisir (gambling) (Kismawadi 2024b; Ridho Kismawadi, Irfan, and Shah 2023). Artificial intelligence (AI) technologies offer significant opportunities to address complex challenges in the sector, while ensuring adherence to those principles. This article discusses three main aspects of the use of AI in the Islamic financial system, namely big data analysis and risk prediction, anomaly detection in transactions, and risk-based contract optimization.

Figure 2. Potential impact of generative artificial intelligence (AI) on productivity worldwide in 2023, by business functions (in billion U.S. dollars)

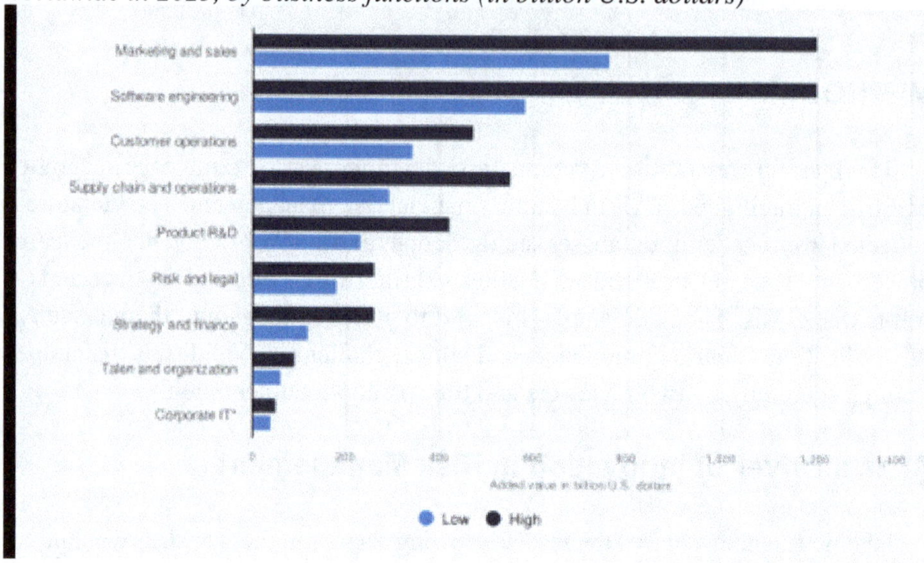

Generative artificial intelligence (AI) can have a significant impact on the productivity of various business functions, based on 63 use cases analyzed in 2023. Marketing and sales can benefit the most, with added value ranging from $760 to $1,200 billion, while software engineering can also see similarly high added value. In the context of risk management, generative AI's capacity to increase productivity extends to the development of sophisticated predictive models and real-time risk assessment tools, driving innovation by enabling businesses to proactively reduce uncertainty and optimize decision-making processes

In the world of finance, risk management is a crucial aspect to maintain the stability and sustainability of operations. Islamic finance, which is characterized by partnerships and risk sharing, requires a more in-depth risk management approach than conventional finance. AI enables deep analysis of big data to identify risk patterns that may not be visible with traditional approaches (Kismawadi 2024a). In the context of Islamic finance, AI helps identify investment risks, especially in contracts such as mudarabah (profit-based partnerships) and musharakah (capital-based partnerships). By utilizing more in-depth data, investment decisions can be made more carefully and in accordance with sharia principles. In addition, AI can be used for credit risk modeling by processing data from various sources such as payment history, economic trends, and social factors, so that predictions of customer payment ability can be carried out without involving the element of usury.

Sharia compliance is the main pillar in Islamic finance. However, the complexity of modern financial transactions makes the detection of activities that are not in accordance with sharia principles a big challenge. AI has the ability to detect suspicious transaction patterns automatically and in real-time, which was previously difficult to do manually. With transaction data analysis, AI can detect elements of riba or excessive profits in a financial contract, as well as recognize patterns that indicate the presence of gharar or maisir elements. For example, AI can be used to monitor customer transactions in real-time. If a flow of funds is detected to a non-halal company, the system will provide a warning and prevent the transaction. This not only ensures sharia compliance but also increases the credibility of Islamic financial institutions in the eyes of customers.

Risk-based contracts such as mudarabah and musharakah are the core of Islamic finance. This contract demands a fair sharing of risks and benefits between the parties involved. However, this process is often complicated because it requires accurate and transparent risk modelling. AI offers solutions with its ability to process big data and predict risk scenarios comprehensively. By utilizing AI technology, risk evaluations can be carried out faster, ensuring transparency and fairness, and providing dynamic adjustments in changing economic situations. For example, in musharakah projects for housing development, AI can be used to predict fluctuations in material prices, property market conditions, and potential demand. The results of this analysis help all parties draw up fair and realistic contracts, minimizing the potential for future conflicts.

The adoption of AI in the Islamic financial system has great potential to revolutionize the sector (Kismawadi 2024c). With AI's ability to analyse big data, detect anomalies, and optimize risk-based contracts, Islamic finance can achieve higher levels of efficiency, transparency, and fairness. However, the application of AI also requires attention to ethics, data privacy, and a deep understanding of sharia principles. Further research is needed to explore this potential, creating a more inclusive and sustainable Islamic finance ecosystem.

Risk Assessment and Mitigation with Artificial Intelligence (AI)

In this increasingly complex and connected world, artificial intelligence (AI) is increasingly playing a crucial role in risk management. AI not only helps in identifying and assessing risks, but also provides more efficient and sophisticated mitigation solutions. Therefore, AI can reinforce two main components in risk management: risk assessment and risk mitigation. The use of AI in risk management allows organizations to make faster, more precise, and more data-driven decisions, minimizing uncertainty and protecting organizations from existing threats.

Risk assessment is the first step in risk management that involves identifying, evaluating, and prioritizing risks (E R Kismawadi, Irfan, M., Al Muddatstsir, U. D., & Abdulkarim 2023). At this stage, AI can make a major contribution through big data analysis and machine learning. Prior to the advent of AI, risk assessment often relied on manual or semi-manual methods that required a lot of time and effort. However, AI can now automate this process by analysing much larger and faster volumes of data than humans, and can catch patterns that might have been missed with traditional approaches.

For example, in financial risk analysis, AI can process data from various sources such as the stock market, financial reports, economic news, and social media to detect trends and patterns that indicate potential risks. Machine learning algorithms can be trained to recognize signs of their vulnerability, such as unusual price fluctuations, alerts from news sentiment analysis, or macroeconomic indicators that indicate instability. AI can also detect hidden patterns that are difficult for human analysts to see. Thus, the process of identifying and evaluating risks becomes faster and more accurate.

AI also helps in evaluating the impact and likelihood of risks. In this case, AI-based predictive models, which use historical data and statistical algorithms, can provide better estimates regarding the level of impact of possible risks and the likelihood of such events occurring. For example, deep learning models can be used to analyse market trends and identify systemic risks that may not have been detected by using previous market data. In addition, AI can prioritize risks more precisely. By combining various factors, such as the likelihood of a risk occurring and its impact, AI can generate data-driven recommendations to prioritize which risks should be managed first.

Once the risk has been assessed, the next step is risk mitigation, i.e. the steps taken to mitigate or manage the impact of the risks that have been identified. AI provides a variety of innovative solutions for risk mitigation, increasing the efficiency and effectiveness of the mitigation strategies implemented.

One of the key mitigation strategies that AI can drive is risk reduction. AI can help reduce risk by automating and optimizing various processes to prevent or mitigate the impact of potential risks. In cyberspace, for example, AI can be used to detect cyber threats in real-time and take automated actions to mitigate the impact of potential attacks. AI technologies such as anomaly detection and pattern recognition allow the system to monitor network traffic and user activity, as well as detect suspicious behaviour. When there is an indication of a breach, AI-based systems can respond immediately, such as by blocking access or mitigating threats, before further damage occurs.

AI can also reduce risk through optimization and automation. In the manufacturing industry, for example, AI can be used to continuously monitor equipment and machinery, detect potential breakdowns before they occur, and provide early warnings to maintenance teams. This reduces the risk of machine failure that can disrupt production and cause large losses. By leveraging predictive algorithms and data analysis, AI can predict when machines need to be repaired or replaced, reducing downtime and the cost of sudden repairs.

AI can play a role in risk transfer. One obvious example is in insurance. In the insurance industry, AI helps in evaluating customer claims and risks more efficiently. AI algorithms can analyse historical data from various claims and use machine learning to assess individual or company risks. In this way, insurers can determine more accurate premium prices and reduce financial risk due to unexpected claims. Additionally, AI can also be used to determine whether or not a claim is legitimate by automatically analysing relevant data, which speeds up the claim process and reduces potential losses due to fraud.

Risk aversion can also be supported by AI. In this case, AI can be used to identify risks early, so that organizations can avoid actions that could worsen the situation or cause significant losses. For example, AI can monitor changes in market conditions or other external factors that could lead to economic crises or market instability. By analysing data in real-time, AI provides insights that allow organizations to take preventative measures early, such as suspending investments, withdrawing from risky markets, or changing operational strategies.

Risk acceptance can also be supported by AI, although in this context, AI plays a greater role in managing and minimizing the impact of the risks received. For example, in the aviation industry, the risk of engine failure or bad weather is difficult to avoid completely. However, AI can aid in contingency planning and provide data-driven recommendations that allow organizations to be better prepared for such risks. For example, using AI to predict the weather or analyse aircraft performance can assist airlines in minimizing losses caused by risks that have been accepted and planning a better response.

Artificial intelligence (AI) has changed the way we view and manage risk (Darwiesh et al. 2023; Iftikhar et al. 2020). With the ability to analyse big data and detect patterns that humans can't see, AI provides faster, more accurate, and more efficient tools for conducting risk assessments and risk mitigation. From identifying threats in the financial sector to improving cybersecurity and predicting machine failures in the manufacturing sector, AI enables organizations to take more precise and more informed actions in the face of risks. More so, AI also supports smarter decision-making in mitigation strategies, helping organizations to minimize the impact of risks and maintain their sustainability in a world of uncertainty. With the right application of AI, risk management can become more proactive, sophisticated, and responsive to evolving challenges.

Multi-Risk Assessment and Artificial Intelligence

In an increasingly complex and unpredictable world, organizations are often faced with a variety of risks that are interrelated and affect each other. To manage these risks effectively, a more comprehensive and integrative approach is needed. One method that is becoming increasingly popular is multi-risk assessment, which allows organizations to evaluate and manage different types of risks in one unified framework. This multi-risk assessment framework can involve different types of risks, such as financial, operational, environmental, and technological risks, which need to be analysed simultaneously to understand the relationships and impacts between them.

Figure 3. Share of professionals using generative artificial intelligence (AI) in organizations worldwide as of 2024, by function

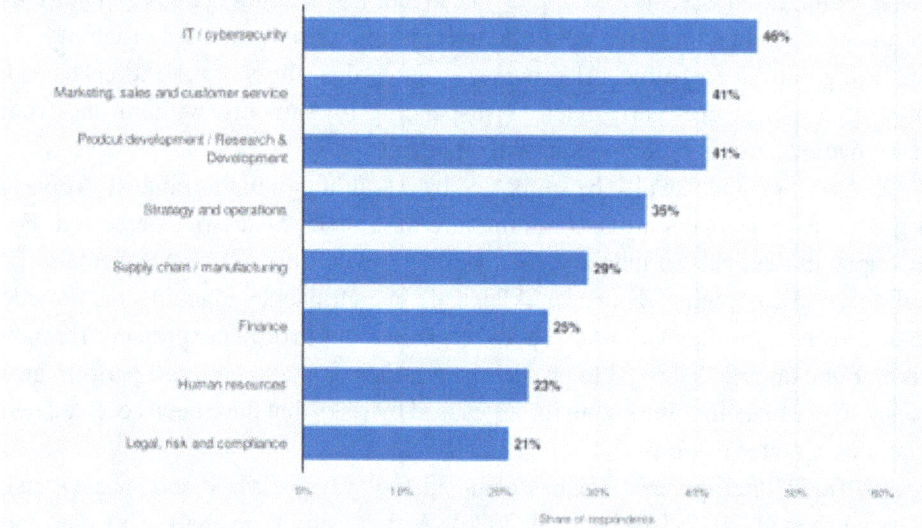

One of the most commonly used approaches is a three-level framework for multi-risk assessment, which includes three stages: initial assessment, semi-quantitative assessment, and quantitative multi-risk analysis using Bayesian networks. At each of these stages, artificial intelligence (AI) plays a crucial role in improving the accuracy, speed, and effectiveness of risk analysis. In particular, the adoption of generative AI (GenAI) is particularly prominent in IT and cybersecurity functions, where nearly half of the professionals surveyed in global organizations report their use in limited or large-scale implementations by 2024, improving the ability to address technological risks in a multi-risk framework

To implement multi-risk assessments more effectively, a clear and structured framework is needed. One of the most frequently used approaches is a three-level framework for multi-risk assessment, which includes three stages: initial assessment, semi-quantitative assessment, and quantitative multi-risk analysis using the Bayesian network. In each of these stages, artificial intelligence (AI) plays an important role in improving the accuracy, speed, and effectiveness of risk analysis (Hwang et al. 2025; Liu and Zhang 2025).

This three-tier multi-risk assessment framework begins with an exploratory first step and focuses on the identification and initial assessment of risks. This stage often uses a flowchart to help identify and group existing risks. The second step is a more in-depth risk assessment, using a semi-quantitative approach that combines qualitative and quantitative data to obtain a clearer picture of its level of vulnerability. The third step is a more detailed and accurate risk analysis, using a quantitative approach based on probabilistic models, such as the Bayesian network, to analyse risk interactions and impacts in a more complex way.

The first stage in the framework of multi-risk assessment is the initial assessment, which aims to identify the existing risks and classify them in certain categories. Typically, this stage is done using a flowchart or risk matrix, which provides an overview of the various risks that exist, as well as their potential impacts. At this stage, AI can play a role in automatically and quickly processing data to identify potential risks from various sources, such as historical data, financial statements, and relevant external factors (e.g., market trends, weather, or regulatory changes). AI can use natural language processing (NLP) techniques to extract information from unstructured documents (e.g., reports, emails, or news) and sentiment analysis to detect potential risks or threats that arise in the external environment. By automating the process of data collection and risk identification, AI accelerates initial assessments and provides a broader and deeper picture of the factors affecting the organization.

Once the risk is identified at an early stage, the next stage is a semi-quantitative assessment, which combines qualitative and quantitative data to provide a more in-depth assessment. In this stage, the risks that have been identified are measured using semi-quantitative criteria, such as the severity of the impact, the likelihood of the risk occurring, and the level of uncertainty that exists. AI can help in this stage with big data analysis to uncover the relationships between various risk factors and provide more objective assessments. For example, machine learning algorithms can be used to analyse historical data and estimate the likelihood of risk based on identified patterns. In addition, AI can also optimize assessments with multivariate analysis to evaluate the relationship between various risk variables simultaneously. With this approach, organizations can gain more accurate insights into the most relevant and significant risks, as well as how they interact with each other.

The final stage in the framework of multi-risk assessment is a more complex and in-depth quantitative multi-risk analysis. At this stage, the Bayesian network is used to analyse risks probabilistically and describe how various risks interact with each other and affect each other. The Bayesian network is a probabilistic model that makes it possible to analyse the cause-and-effect relationship between various risk factors and calculate the likelihood of the occurrence of various interrelated risk scenarios. AI plays a big role in this stage, especially with deep learning algorithms and probabilistic models that can analyse large amounts of data and identify highly complex patterns. In real-world applications, AI can be used to build Monte Carlo simulation models that allow organizations to evaluate various risk scenarios and calculate the overall impact of various possible events.

In Islamic finance, the application of AI and Bayesian networks in risk assessment is very helpful in identifying and managing various complex risks. For example, in murabaha financing involving commodities, AI can model the risk of fluctuations in commodity prices, such as oil, by analysing historical data and external factors, as well as calculating the possible impact on financing. In addition, in musharakah or mudharabah-based financing, AI can be used to predict the risk of infrastructure failure and the interaction between risk factors that affect project continuity. For credit risk in consumer financing, AI can analyse customer data and calculate the probability of default, while for sharia compliance, AI can check contracts to ensure transactions are free from riba or haram elements. Overall, AI and Bayesian networks help Islamic financial institutions to manage risk more effectively and improve sustainability and sharia compliance in their operations.

The application of artificial intelligence in multi-risk assessment provides a variety of significant benefits to organizations (Carpignano et al. 2009; Thiebes and Winkhardt-Enz 2023). First, AI allows for faster and more efficient risk assessment, reducing the time required to identify, evaluate, and analyse risks. With the ability to process large amounts of data and identify patterns that are invisible to humans, AI speeds up the decision-making process and allows organizations to respond to risks more proactively.

Second, AI improves the accuracy of risk assessments by reducing reliance on subjective assessments and increasing the use of objective and evidence-based data. By using ever-evolving algorithms, AI can provide more accurate risk predictions, as well as improve the accuracy of impact estimates and the likelihood of risks. Third, AI also makes it possible to analyse interactions between risks, which is difficult to do with traditional approaches. In multi-risk assessments, risks do not always stand alone; Often, one risk can trigger or exacerbate another. AI, primarily through the use of Bayesian networks, allows organizations to visualize these interactions and evaluate the cumulative impact of various interrelated risks. Fourth, AI can improve the ability to handle uncertainty in risk assessment. In many cases, risk comes with a high level of uncertainty, which can make predictions difficult. However, by using AI-driven probabilistic models, organizations can evaluate various possible scenarios and manage uncertainty more effectively.

Multi-risk assessment is a very useful approach to identify, evaluate, and manage various interrelated risks within an organization. By using a three-tier framework, which includes initial assessment, semi-quantitative assessment, and quantitative multi-risk analysis using the Bayesian network, organizations can gain a completer and more in-depth picture of the risks they face. Artificial intelligence (AI) plays a key role in improving the speed, accuracy, and depth of these assessments. From processing big data to analysing the complex relationships between various risks, AI enables organizations to make smarter decisions and be more responsive to existing threats. With the right application of AI, multi-risk assessments can become an even more powerful tool to help organizations manage uncertainty and ensure operational continuity in a world full of risks.

Enterprise Risk Management and artificial intelligence

The integration of Enterprise Risk Management (ERM) with artificial intelligence (AI) in Islamic finance offers great potential to manage risk more effectively and improve the performance of financial institutions (Özdemir and Selçuk 2021). Islamic finance, which emphasizes principles such as fairness, transparency, and compliance with sharia, requires a holistic approach in identifying, assessing, and managing the risks faced, ranging from market risk to sharia compliance risk. ERMs provide a systematic framework for managing these risks, while AI with its capabilities in big data analysis, machine learning, and risk prediction offers powerful tools to accelerate the process of risk identification and more informed decision-making. In the context of Islamic finance, AI can assist financial institutions in identifying potential risks related to market fluctuations, regulatory changes, and ensuring that the products and services offered are fully compliant with sharia principles, such as being free from riba, gharar, and maysir elements.

One of the main ways in which AI is powering ERM is with the ability to analyse data in greater depth and faster. For example, AI can model market risks that can affect mudarabah or musharakah-based financing by taking into account various external factors that can fluctuate, such as commodity prices or macroeconomic conditions. AI also allows for more accurate credit risk assessments, by analysing customer data in more depth, and helping to identify payment patterns that can predict the likelihood of default. Additionally, AI can monitor sharia compliance in financial transactions by automatically analysing investment contracts, transactions, or portfolios, ensuring that there are no violations of sharia principles that could damage the reputation and stability of Islamic financial institutions. With sentiment analysis using natural language processing (NLP) technology, AI can also help financial institutions monitor public perceptions of their sharia compliance and identify potential reputational risks early.

The integration of ERM and AI also has a significant impact on strategic decision-making. With AI's ability to analyse big data in real-time, Islamic financial institutions can make more informed decisions, be it in terms of investment, financing, or portfolio management. AI not only helps in assessing the potential gains and losses of various investment decisions, but also in anticipating risks that arise in the future, allowing Islamic financial institutions to take more proactive actions. For example, AI can provide risk simulations for projects funded through mudarabah or musharakah, allowing management to see the possible impacts of various scenarios and choose the most profitable path. In this case, AI is not only a tool for identifying and mitigating risks, but also for optimizing resource management and adjusting business strategies based on more in-depth risk analysis. To improving decision-making, the integration of ERM and AI also plays an important role in improving the financial performance of Islamic financial institutions.

By better managing risk, financial institutions can avoid losses that could disrupt their financial stability. For example, AI can be helpful in monitoring and managing market fluctuations, which is especially important in motherhood-based products that are vulnerable to external economic changes. Using predictive analytics, AI can predict how market changes will affect Islamic investment assets and portfolios, allowing financial institutions to adjust investment strategies more appropriately. This not only reduces potential losses but also opens up opportunities to achieve greater profits, maintaining the profitability and financial sustainability of the institution.

More than that, the integration of ERM with AI helps Islamic financial institutions to ensure sharia compliance in all their operations. In this increasingly complex world, with various regulations and market dynamics constantly changing, the supervision of sharia principles requires a more efficient and integrated approach. By using AI, Islamic financial institutions can easily monitor transactions and products offered, as well as ensure that everything is in accordance with applicable fatwas and sharia guidelines. AI is able to identify elements that violate sharia principles in contracts or transactions automatically, reducing the risk of violations that may not be detected by manual supervision.

The integration of ERM and AI in Islamic finance brings significant changes in the way financial institutions manage risk, optimize performance, and ensure sharia compliance. With AI capable of processing large amounts of data and providing accurate predictive analysis, Islamic financial institutions can make smarter, faster, and more informed decisions, whether in terms of investment, financing, or risk management. This integration not only helps financial institutions respond to existing risks, but also allows them to take advantage of new opportunities, increase customer confidence, and strengthen their position in the market. Ultimately, ERM and AI are working together to create a more transparent, more efficient, and more sustainable Islamic financial system, which can address future challenges while still adhering to the underlying sharia principles.

Project Risk Management Frameworks

A structured project risk management framework allows Islamic financial institutions to systematically identify, assess, and manage risks that can affect the institution's operations and sustainability. Islamic financial institutions, which operate with sharia principles, such as usury avoidance, fairness, and transparency, face unique challenges related to the risks that affect their financial projects. Therefore, the implementation of a good risk management framework is essential to ensure that the project runs in accordance with sharia principles and provides benefits to all parties involved.

The first step in a project risk management framework is planning, which includes the drafting of policies and procedures to manage risks throughout the project lifecycle. In Islamic financial institutions, this planning must involve understanding the risks associated with market uncertainty, changes in sharia policies, and potential violations of sharia principles, such as riba or gharar (ambiguity). After planning, risk identification is the next step that is no less important. Islamic financial institutions must identify risks that have the potential to arise from external factors, such as economic fluctuations and changing government regulations, as well as from internal factors, such as technological system failures or operational errors in financial transactions that are not in accordance with sharia. Here, artificial intelligence (AI) technology can play a crucial role in helping to identify risk patterns that are not directly visible to humans, especially when it comes to large or complex transactions.

Once the risks are identified, the next stage is a risk assessment, where Islamic financial institutions analyse the impact of those risks on the sustainability of their projects and operations. AI can be used to conduct big data analysis that includes historical data and market trends to assess the likelihood of certain risks. For example, AI can analyse financial data to identify trends in market fluctuations that can affect mudarabah or musharakah-based financing. In this case, AI can identify systemic risks that may not be detected through traditional analysis, giving Islamic financial institutions the ability to assess potential losses more accurately and in a timely manner. The use of risk matrices and AI-based probabilistic models can help classify risks based on their impact and prioritize risks that require immediate attention.

Once the risk is assessed, the next step is risk management. At this stage, Islamic financial institutions develop mitigation strategies to reduce or divert the risks that have been identified. In this sector, mitigation strategies can include risk transfer through sharia insurance, risk aversion through investment portfolio diversification, or risk acceptance with reserve preparation to overcome unexpected losses. In mudarabah and musharakah-based financing, Islamic financial institutions may choose to implement mitigation measures that include fair risk sharing between banks and business partners, as well as the use of more transparent instruments to avoid the presence of gharar (unclear elements). AI can play a role in helping to design and monitor mitigation strategies, by providing predictive analytics to determine the potential impact of investment decisions or policies taken.

Risk monitoring is the final step in project risk management, and at this stage, AI technology has a very vital role. AI can be used to monitor and analyse transactions in real-time, looking for anomalies that could signal a violation of sharia principles or other potential risks. For example, by utilizing machine learning algorithms, Islamic financial institutions can detect suspicious transaction activity, such as transactions that have the potential to involve riba or non-halal investments, before these problems develop into a bigger problem. AI can automatically identify specific patterns in transaction data that may indicate the presence of non-sharia risks, allowing financial institutions to take faster and more precise preventive measures. AI-driven risk monitoring can also speed up the process of detecting and mitigating smaller but repetitive operational risks, such as technical errors or lack of resources that may not be detected manually.

In Islamic financial institutions, the implementation of a structured project risk management framework is not only important to maintain the stability and sustainability of the institution, but also to ensure that every transaction and product offered is always in accordance with sharia principles. By using AI technology, Islamic financial institutions can strengthen their risk management in a more accurate and efficient way, allowing them to better identify, assess, and manage risks. For example, in the mudarabah and musharakah model, AI can help in monitoring the fair distribution of profits and losses between investors and business partners, as well as ensuring that there are no transactions involving elements of riba or gharar that can harm one party. In addition, AI can also assist Islamic financial institutions in adapting to evolving market dynamics and regulations, ensuring that the risk mitigation strategies implemented remain relevant to current market conditions.

In the Islamic finance sector, the risks faced are not only economic or technical, but also related to compliance with very strict sharia principles. Therefore, the implementation of risk management integrated with AI technology is very important to ensure that Islamic financial institutions can maintain the sustainability of their operations, meet customer expectations, and still comply with applicable Islamic regulations. AI can provide smarter and data-driven analysis, allowing institutions to make more informed and faster decisions in the face of existing challenges, as well as maintain the success of their Islamic finance projects.

The application of AI-driven project risk management in Islamic financial institutions allows for a more systematic and data-driven approach to managing risk. With the ability of AI to process big data, analyse patterns, and provide more accurate predictions, Islamic financial institutions can identify risks early, respond to them more quickly, and ensure that their projects are running in accordance with sharia principles. This not only reduces potential losses, but also strengthens the stability and sustainability of Islamic financial institutions in an increasingly dynamic and competitive market.

Figure 4. AI's role in risk management

AI strengthens risk management through data-driven decision support systems that enable proactive strategic transformation (Baryannis et al. 2019; Bussmann et al. 2021; Heaton, Polson, and Witte 2017). By analysing big datasets, AI algorithms can identify patterns, trends, and anomalies that are often undetected by human analysis. For example, in the context of supply chain management, AI can predict potential disruptions such as shipping delays or fluctuations in raw material prices based on historical and real-time data. This approach is in line with the principles of the Shannon-Weaver communication model, where AI acts as a "sender" of information that filters out "noise" in the data to produce clear signals in the form of risk mitigation recommendations.

AI's predictive capabilities allow organizations to anticipate risks before they occur, thereby improving operational reliability and supply chain continuity. For example, machine learning algorithms can leverage market, weather, or geopolitical data to predict external risks, while prescriptive analytics models recommend optimal mitigation strategies. This approach not only improves the accuracy of risk assessment, but also strengthens internal communication within the organization, ensuring that stakeholders receive relevant and actionable information for decision-making.

AI is revolutionizing risk management by automating routine tasks such as data collection, data cleansing, and initial analysis are time-consuming and prone to human error (Almaqtari 2024). By automating this process, AI improves efficiency and accuracy, allowing risk management professionals to focus on high-value strategic decision-making. In the communication framework, AI automation can be seen as the reduction of "noise" in communication channels, as described by the Shannon-Weaver model. By eliminating redundancy and errors in data processing, AI ensures that the information that reaches decision-makers is more accurate and timelier.

For example, AI-based tools can automatically categorize risk data from various sources, such as financial reports or news feeds, and generate structured risk reports. This not only saves time, but also improves consistency in the risk management process. Thus, AI allows organizations to allocate human resources to tasks that require creativity and critical judgment, such as the development of long-term strategies.

AI's ability to process and (Nene 2024), both structured and unstructured, provides a significant advantage in risk management. Machine learning algorithms can dig into insights from diverse data sources, such as social media, market reports, or operational logs, to uncover hidden patterns, correlations, and anomalies that human analysis might miss. In the context of communication theory, this ability mirrors the concept of "decoding" in the Shannon-Weaver model, where AI acts as a translator of raw data into meaningful information for decision-makers.

For example, in financial risk management, AI can analyse real-time transaction data to detect suspicious activity that indicates fraud (Bansal et al. 2024; Irfan et al. 2025). By integrating data from multiple sources, AI creates a holistic picture of the risk landscape, allowing organizations to make more informed decisions. This approach also supports the dynamics of interpersonal communication within organizations, as AI-driven insights facilitate more informed and collaborative cross-departmental discussions.

In a dynamic environment, the ability to monitor market operations and conditions in real-time is a critical aspect of risk management (Almaqtari 2024; Andronie et al. 2024). AI enables continuous monitoring by leveraging IoT sensors, market data feeds, and other sources of information to provide instant decision recommendations. In the framework of communication, this approach can be analogous to feedback in the Shannon-Weaver model, where AI provides immediate feedback to adapt risk management strategies to changing conditions. For example, in crisis management, AI can detect anomalies in operations, such as equipment failures or cybersecurity breaches, and recommend immediate response actions. This responsiveness is especially important in fast-paced environments, such as financial markets or global logistics. By providing real-time information, AI strengthens organizational communication by ensuring that all stakeholders have access to up-to-date data for quick and effective decision-making.

Figure 5. AI applications in risk management

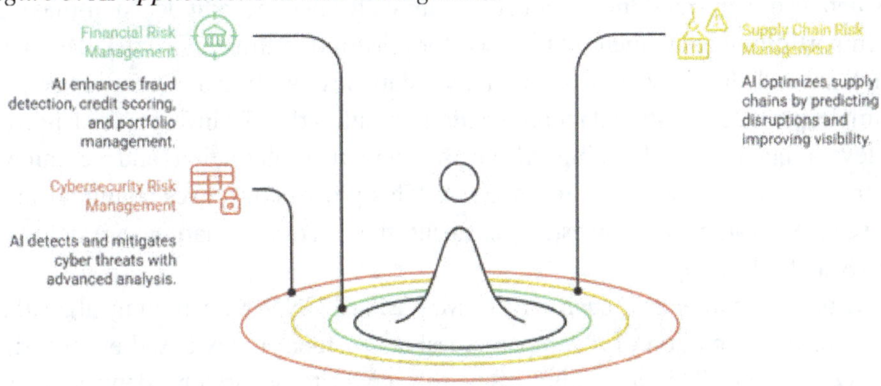

Artificial intelligence (AI) has been a key driver in transforming risk management across a wide range of domains, including financial risk management, supply chain, and cybersecurity (Kalkan 2024; Sruthy 2024; Szadeczky and Bederna 2025). By leveraging analytical, predictive, and adaptive capabilities, AI enables organizations to move from a reactive approach to a proactive approach in risk management. This article outlines the specific applications of AI in three key domains—financial risk management, supply chain risk management, and cybersecurity risk management—by integrating communication frameworks such as the Shannon-Weaver model to explain how AI improves information flow and decision-making. This approach ensures that the insights generated by AI can be effectively communicated to stakeholders, supporting collaboration

AI has revolutionized financial risk management by transforming operational workflows, driving product innovation, and improving precision in risk management (Moro Visconti 2024; Yüksel et al. 2025). AI algorithms and machine learning play a key role in detecting fraud by analysing patterns and anomalies in transaction data. By processing large volumes of data in real-time, AI can identify suspicious activity, such as money laundering, with a high degree of accuracy. Additionally, generative

AI can simulate fraudulent data to train detection models, improving the system's ability to recognize new threats. In the framework of the Shannon-Weaver model, AI functions as a "sender" that filters data to eliminate the "noise" of irrelevant transactions, thus generating clear signals for anti-fraud measures.

AI improves credit scoring accuracy by analysing customer data, such as transaction history, financial behaviour, and alternative data sources (e.g., social media)(Jannah et al. 2024; Nene 2024). AI algorithms enable personalized credit solutions, reducing loan default rates by predicting credit risk more accurately. This process mirrors the concepts of "encoding" and "decoding" in the Shannon-Weaver model, where raw data is transformed into actionable insights for better credit decision-making.

In portfolio management, AI is used for portfolio optimization, risk data management, and the provision of predictive statistics. AI-based robo-advisors, for example, provide investment recommendations tailored to the investor's risk profile. By leveraging machine learning, AI can predict market fluctuations and recommend diversification strategies to minimize risk. This process improves communication between AI systems and investors, ensuring that recommendations are delivered clearly and relevantly.

AI-based approaches, such as the MSVM+EFCNN data mining algorithm, allow for the formation of a company's risk assessment index based on historical data (Zhu 2024). This algorithm trains the model to accurately identify current risks, supporting strategic decision-making. In the context of communication, this approach facilitates feedback in the Shannon-Weaver model, where AI-generated risk data becomes the basis for cross-departmental discussions.

AI helps monitor and mitigate operational risks in banking transactions, such as system errors or process failures (Andronie et al. 2024; Kalkan 2024). By analysing operational data in real-time, AI improves banking outcomes and supports regulatory implementation. This approach reduces "disruption" in internal communication, ensuring that risk information reaches stakeholders quickly and accurately.

AI, combined with IoT technology, supports corporate social responsibility (CSR) strategies in financial risk management. AI can monitor and report compliance with environmental, social, and governance (ESG) standards, identifying profitable sustainable investment opportunities. Within the communication framework, AI facilitates external communication with stakeholders, such as transparent ESG reports, which increases public trust.

AI is transforming supply chain risk management by providing decision-making capabilities based on knowledge mining from big data. AI-based tools enable supply chains to become more agile and adaptive, reducing response times, increasing visibility, and mitigating the risk of disruptions. Key applications include: AI predicts potential disruptions, such as shipping delays or raw material shortages, by analysing weather, geopolitical, and logistics data. This allows organizations to take proactive actions, such as shipping rerouting. AI algorithms optimize inventory levels by predicting demand and identifying consumption patterns, reducing the risk of overstock or understock. AI improves communication with suppliers through performance data analysis, enabling better negotiation and mitigating the risk of supplier dependency. In the context of the Shannon-Weaver model, AI acts as an efficient communication channel, reducing "distractions" such as irrelevant data and ensuring that critical information about supply chain risks reaches decision-makers quickly.

AI makes a significant contribution to cybersecurity by offering advanced methods for the detection, analysis, and mitigation of cyber threats (Rahman et al. 2024). Key applications include: Machine learning and deep learning algorithms analyse large datasets to identify hidden patterns and adapt to new attack vectors. AI improves the speed and precision of threat detection, enabling real-time responses to potential breaches. AI, when combined with blockchain technology, creates a transparent and manipulation-resistant framework for storing and sharing security data.

This increases trust and reliability in security data communication. With continuous monitoring, the AI detects anomalies such as hacking attempts or malware, providing immediate response recommendations. In the Shannon-Weaver model, this reflects rapid feedback that allows organizations to dynamically adjust cybersecurity strategies. This approach also supports the dynamics of interpersonal communication within cybersecurity teams, where AI insights facilitate collaborative discussions to formulate effective mitigation strategies.

CONCLUSION

The integration of artificial intelligence (AI) in Islamic financial risk management offers transformative potential to improve efficiency, accuracy, and sharia compliance in the operations of financial institutions. By leveraging big data analytics, machine learning, and probabilistic models such as Bayesian networks, AI enables real-time identification, assessment, and mitigation of risks, including market, credit, operational, and sharia violations such as riba and gharar.

AI-powered Enterprise Risk Management (ERM) frameworks strengthen data-driven decision-making, ensuring transparency, fairness, and financial resilience while adhering to sharia principles. However, challenges such as data privacy, algorithm bias, and the need for technical expertise and infrastructure must be addressed through strong governance and interdisciplinary collaboration. The research not only fills gaps in the literature by providing an integrated framework for AI-based risk management, but also provides practical guidance for practitioners and policy recommendations to build a more inclusive, ethical, and sustainable Islamic finance ecosystem. With a balanced approach, AI can be a catalyst for advancing

Islamic finance amid complex global market dynamics, strengthening its position as a competitive and value-oriented financial system.

The integration of artificial intelligence (AI) in Islamic financial risk management has significant managerial implications for Islamic financial institutions. First, managers must invest in the development of technology infrastructure and human resource training to ensure effective adoption of AI, including expertise in machine learning and big data analytics. This requires a strategic allocation of resources to build a team that is competent in sharia technology and principles. Second, managers need to develop clear internal policies to ensure that AI algorithms are aligned with sharia principles, such as avoiding riba and gharar, through strict oversight by sharia boards and technology auditors.

Third, the application of AI allows managers to make faster, data-driven decisions, such as in credit risk assessments or portfolio management of mudarabah and musharakah, which can improve the operational efficiency and competitiveness of institutions. However, managers must also be proactive in managing ethical risks, such as algorithmic bias and data privacy violations, by implementing transparent AI governance guidelines. Thus, managers can leverage AI to strengthen financial stability while maintaining stakeholder trust.

In practical terms, the integration of AI in Islamic financial risk management offers a solution that can be directly applied to improve sharia efficiency and compliance. By using AI for big data analysis, financial institutions can identify market, credit, and operational risks in real-time, enabling faster responses to potential threats. For example, machine learning algorithms can detect anomalies in transactions that may indicate sharia violations, such as usury elements or non-halal investments, thereby improving the institution's compliance and reputation.

In addition, AI can optimize the risk assessment process in mudarabah and musharakah-based financing by predicting fluctuations in commodity prices or market trends, which aids in the formulation of fairer and more transparent contracts. However, practical implementation requires initial investment in technology and training, as well as collaboration with sharia experts to ensure that AI solutions are compliant with sharia fatwas and guidelines. With this approach, Islamic financial institutions can improve operational resilience and customer confidence.

From a theoretical perspective, this study enriches the risk management literature in Islamic finance by integrating the concept of AI into a sharia-based Enterprise Risk Management (ERM) framework. This research expands the understanding of how probabilistic models, such as Bayesian networks, can be applied to analyse multi-dimensional risks in the context of sharia, which were previously underexplored. In addition, the research contributes to Islamic financial theory by highlighting the importance of a balance between technological innovation and ethical compliance, reinforcing the principles of fairness and transparency. By integrating modern risk management theory with sharia values, this research opens up opportunities for the development of new theoretical models that accommodate the complexity of modern financial transactions while adhering to sharia principles. These implications encourage further research on the interaction between AI technology and ethical values in finance, broadening the academic discourse in this area.

To maximize the potential of AI in Islamic financial risk management, several recommendations can be considered. First, Islamic financial institutions should develop an AI governance framework that is integrated with ERM, which includes guidelines to ensure sharia compliance and algorithm bias mitigation. Second, investment in interdisciplinary training that combines technological expertise and sharia knowledge is needed to build internal capacity. Third, policymakers are advised to formulate regulations that support AI adoption while protecting data privacy and ensuring transparency, such as through sharia certification standards for AI algorithms. Fourth, financial institutions should leverage collaboration with academic institutions and technology providers to develop AI solutions tailored to Islamic financial needs. Finally, further research is recommended to explore the long-term impact of AI on financial stability and stakeholder trust, to ensure that technological innovation is aligned with the goals of inclusive and sustainable Islamic finance.

REFERENCES

Almaqtari, F. A. (2024). The role of IT governance in the integration of AI in accounting and auditing operations. *Economies*, *12*(8), 199. Advance online publication. DOI: 10.3390/economies12080199

Andronie, M., Blazek, R., Iatagan, M., Skypalova, R., U ă, C., Dijmărescu, A., Kovacova, M., Grecu, G., Pârvu, I., Strakova, J., Guni, C., Zabojnik, S., Chiru, C., Sedláčková, A. N., Novák, A., & Dijmărescu, I. (2024). *Generative artificial intelligence algorithms in Internet of Things blockchain-based fintech management* (Vol. 15).

Bansal, U., Bharatwal, S., Bagiyam, D. S., & Kismawadi, E. R. (2024). Fraud detection in the era of AI: Harnessing technology for a safer digital economy. In *AI-driven decentralized finance and the future of finance* (pp. 143–164).

Baryannis, G., Validi, S., Dani, S., & Antoniou, G. (2019). Supply chain risk management and artificial intelligence: State of the art and future research directions. *International Journal of Production Research*, *57*(7), 2179–2202. DOI: 10.1080/00207543.2018.1530476

Bussmann, N., Giudici, P., Marinelli, D., & Papenbrock, J. (2021). Explainable machine learning in credit risk management. *Computational Economics*, *57*(1), 203–216. DOI: 10.1007/s10614-020-10042-0

Carpignano, A., Golia, E., Di Mauro, C., Bouchon, S., & Nordvik, J. P. (2009). A methodological approach for the definition of multi-risk maps at regional level: First application. *Journal of Risk Research*, *12*(3–4), 513–534. DOI: 10.1080/13669870903050269

Darwiesh, A., El-Baz, A. H., Abualkishik, A. Z., & Elhoseny, M. (2023). Artificial intelligence model for risk management in healthcare institutions: Towards sustainable development. *Sustainability (Basel)*, *15*(1), 420. Advance online publication. DOI: 10.3390/su15010420

Gani, I. M., & Bahari, Z. (2020). Islamic banking's contribution to the Malaysian real economy. *ISRA International Journal of Islamic Finance*, *13*(1), 6–25. DOI: 10.1108/IJIF-01-2019-0004

Gilvary, C., Madhukar, N., Elkhader, J., & Elemento, O. (2019). The missing pieces of artificial intelligence in medicine. *Trends in Pharmacological Sciences*, *40*(8), 555–564. DOI: 10.1016/j.tips.2019.06.001

Heaton, J. B., Polson, N. G., & Witte, J. H. (2017). Deep learning for finance: Deep portfolios. *Applied Stochastic Models in Business and Industry*, *33*(1), 3–12. DOI: 10.1002/asmb.2209

Hwang, J., Youm, C., Park, H., Kim, B., Choi, H., & Cheon, S. M. (2025). Machine learning for early detection and severity classification in people with Parkinson's disease. *Scientific Reports*, *15*(1), 234. Advance online publication. DOI: 10.1038/s41598-024-83975-3

Iftikhar, A., Musa, S., Alam, M., & Su'ud, M. M. (2020). Artificial intelligence-based risk management in global software development: A proposed architecture to reduce risk using time, budget, and resource constraints. *Journal of Computational and Theoretical Nanoscience*, *17*(2–3), 878–885. DOI: 10.1166/jctn.2020.8735

Irfan, M., Parameswaran, S., Singh, K. A., & Kismawadi, E. R. (2025). Cutting-edge technologies for economic well-being: The transformative power of AI and blockchain. In *Driving socio-economic growth with AI and blockchain* (pp. 229–248).

Jannah, N., Bahri, M. I., Kismawadi, E. R., & Handriana, T. (2024). The effect of green brand image and green satisfaction on green brand equity mediated by green trust among outpatients. *Quality - Access to Success*, *25*(198), 381–390. DOI: 10.47750/QAS/25.198.40

Javaid, M., Haleem, A., Khan, I. H., & Suman, R. (2023). Understanding the potential applications of artificial intelligence in agriculture sector. *Advanced Agrochem*, *2*(1), 15–30. DOI: 10.1016/j.aac.2022.10.001

Kalkan, G. (2024). The impact of artificial intelligence on corporate governance. *Journal of Corporate Finance Research*, *18*(2), 17–25.

Kismawadi, E. R. (2024a). Blockchain technology and Islamic finance: Empowering small businesses for financial sustainability. In *Technopreneurship in small businesses for sustainability* (pp. 50–77).

Kismawadi, E. R. (2024b). Contribution of Islamic banks and macroeconomic variables to economic growth in developing countries: Vector error correction model approach (VECM). *Journal of Islamic Accounting and Business Research*, *15*(2), 306–326. DOI: 10.1108/JIABR-03-2022-0090

Kismawadi, E. R. (2024c). Sustainable Islamic financial inclusion: The ethical challenges of generative AI in product and service development. In *Exploring the ethical implications of generative AI* (pp. 237–258).

Kismawadi, E. R., Irfan, M., Al Muddatstsir, U. D., & Abdulkarim, F. M. (2023). Fintech innovations: Risk mitigation strategies in Islamic finance. In *Fintech applications in Islamic finance: AI, machine learning, and blockchain techniques* (pp. 35–58).

Kismawadi, E. R., Irfan, M., & Shah, S. M. A. R. (2023). Revolutionizing Islamic finance: Artificial intelligence's role in the future of industry. In *The impact of AI innovation on financial sectors in the era of Industry 5.0* (pp. 184–207).

Liu, Y., & Zhang, Z. (2025). Unlocking operational efficiency: How AI human capital investment enhances data processing efficiency. *Economics Letters*, *247*, 112147. Advance online publication. DOI: 10.1016/j.econlet.2024.112147

Martín, J. C., Orden-Cruz, C., & Zergane, S. (2020). Islamic finance and halal tourism: An unexplored bridge for smart specialization. *Sustainability (Basel)*, *12*(14), 5736. Advance online publication. DOI: 10.3390/su12145736

Moro Visconti, R. (2024). Artificial intelligence-driven FinTech valuation: A scalable multilayer network approach. *FinTech*, *3*(3), 479–495. DOI: 10.3390/fintech3030026

Nagimova, A. Z. (2023). Islamic capital markets: Prospects of the sukuk issuance in the post-Soviet countries. *World Economy and International Relations*, *67*(4), 81–91. DOI: 10.20542/0131-2227-2023-67-4-81-91

Nene, P. R. (2024). Can artificial intelligence replace assurance, governance and risk management professionals? *Risk Governance and Control: Financial Markets and Institutions*, *14*(2), 25–31. DOI: 10.22495/rgcv14i2p3

Özdemir, M., & Selçuk, M. (2021). A bibliometric analysis of the *International Journal of Islamic and Middle Eastern Finance and Management*. *International Journal of Islamic and Middle Eastern Finance and Management*, *14*(4), 767–791. DOI: 10.1108/IMEFM-06-2020-0277

Rahman, M. M., Pokharel, B. P., Sayeed, S. A., Bhowmik, S. K., Kshetri, N., & Eashrak, N. (2024). RiskAIchain: AI-driven IT infrastructure—Blockchain-backed approach for enhanced risk management. *Risks*, *12*(12), 206. Advance online publication. DOI: 10.3390/risks12120206

Soori, M., Arezoo, B., & Dastres, R. (2023). Artificial intelligence, machine learning and deep learning in advanced robotics: A review. *Cognitive Robotics*, *3*, 54–70. DOI: 10.1016/j.cogr.2023.04.001

Sruthy, S. K. (2024). Enhancing supply chain resilience through artificial intelligence: A strategic framework for executives. *Emerging Science Journal*, *8*(4), 1462–1473. DOI: 10.28991/ESJ-2024-08-04-013

Szadeczky, T., & Bederna, Z. (2025). *Risk, regulation, and governance: Evaluating artificial intelligence across diverse application scenarios* (Vol. 38). Palgrave Macmillan.

Thiebes, B., & Winkhardt-Enz, R. (2023). Challenges and opportunities using new modalities and technologies for multi-risk management. *Natural Hazards, 119*(2), 1137–1140. DOI: 10.1007/s11069-022-05516-3

Yigitcanlar, T., Mehmood, R., & Corchado, J. M. (2021). Green artificial intelligence: Towards an efficient, sustainable and equitable technology for smart cities and futures. *Sustainability (Basel), 13*(16), 8952. Advance online publication. DOI: 10.3390/su13168952

Yüksel, S., Eti, S., Dinçer, H., Gökalp, Y., Olaru, G. O., & Oflaz, N. K. (2025). Innovative financial solutions for sustainable investments using artificial intelligence-based hybrid fuzzy decision-making approach in carbon capture technologies. *Financial Innovation, 11*(1), 20. Advance online publication. DOI: 10.1186/s40854-024-00671-x

Zhu, J. (2024). Application of artificial intelligence data mining algorithm in enterprise management risk assessment. *International Journal of Information Systems and Supply Chain Management, 17*(1), 1–19. DOI: 10.4018/IJISSCM.342119

Chapter 6
The Role of Islamic Finance in Achieving Financial Inclusion in Algeria

Rached Lamraoui Boudoukha
https://orcid.org/0009-0001-6471-9044
International Islamic University Malaysia, Malaysia

Abdulmajid Obaid Hasan Saleh
International Islamic University Malaysia, Malaysia

Ashurov Sharofiddin
International Islamic University Malaysia, Malaysia

ABSTRACT

This chapter examines the role of Islamic finance in advancing financial inclusion in Algeria, where a significant share of the population remains unbanked or underbanked due to the incompatibility of conventional banking products with Islamic principles. By analyzing features such as profit- and loss-sharing, asset-backed financing, and social tools like zakat and Qard Hasan, the chapter highlights how these mechanisms can serve small businesses and marginalized groups. It also reviews recent policy reforms, including Islamic banking windows and dedicated regulatory frameworks, while identifying persistent challenges such as limited financial literacy and legal constraints. The analysis suggests that targeted policy measures and public education could unlock the potential of Islamic finance to foster inclusive economic growth

DOI: 10.4018/979-8-3373-2655-9.ch006

and social justice, aligning financial services with the cultural and ethical values of Algerian society. Ultimately, the chapter underscores Islamic finance as a strategic pathway toward sustainable financial development in Algeria.

INTRODUCTION

Financial inclusion refers to the process of ensuring that all individuals and businesses, regardless of their income level or geographic location, have access to useful and affordable financial products and services. This concept has gained global prominence owing to its direct impact on poverty reduction, entrepreneurship promotion, and economic development support (Khilafa & Boubelouta, 2023). Consequently, governments and financial institutions worldwide have implemented strategies to extend financial services to underserved populations, particularly to rural and low-income groups. These initiatives have been further supported by recent advancements in financing techniques and the ongoing technological revolution, which has introduced innovative service delivery models, especially in the aftermath of the COVID-19 pandemic. In this context, Islamic finance has emerged not only as a Shariah-compliant alternative to conventional finance but also as a system that fosters inclusive growth. Grounded in ethical principles, such as the prohibition of interest (Riba), avoidance of excessive uncertainty (Gharar), emphasis on risk-sharing, and real asset-backed transactions, Islamic finance offers a robust ethical and socially responsible approach to economic activity. Malaysia and Jordan have successfully integrated Islamic finance into their national financial inclusion strategies, supported by strong regulatory frameworks, digital platforms, and institutional coordination. By contrast, Algeria is still in the early stages of developing its Islamic finance sector, with limited infrastructure and fragmented implementation. However, with appropriate reforms and strategic investments, Algeria has the potential to emulate these models and significantly enhance its financial inclusion landscape through Shariah compliant solutions.

A qualitative descriptive approach was employed to explore the theoretical alignment between Islamic finance and financial inclusion objectives and to evaluate the operational outcomes of its implementation in Algeria. This approach facilitates a comprehensive assessment of the regulatory frameworks, institutional readiness, and sociocultural dynamics that influence the integration of Islamic finance. The remainder of this paper is organized as follows. The second section introduces the fundamental concepts of financial inclusion and Islamic finance, highlighting the compatibility of Islamic financial principles with inclusive economic objectives. The third section provides an overview of the current status of Islamic finance in Algeria and discusses key developments, existing institutions, and related policies.

The fourth section examines the potential role of Islamic finance in advancing financial inclusion in Algeria by addressing the needs of the unbanked and identifying the challenges that constrain its impact. The fifth section concludes the paper with findings and recommendations aimed at enhancing the contribution of Islamic finance to inclusive financial development in Algeria.

In the Algerian context, the problem statement can be described as the evolution of Islamic finance as a relatively recent phenomenon encountering both regulatory and institutional challenges. The initial legislation governing Islamic financial transactions in Algeria was enacted in 2018. However, it was subsequently repealed and replaced in 2020 by an amended and more comprehensive law aimed at regulating Islamic banking. Despite Algeria's predominantly Muslim demographic and increased government efforts to promote Islamic banking, financial inclusion remains a significant concern. A substantial portion of the population remains excluded from the formal financial system, often because of a lack of trust in conventional banks, the unavailability of suitable financial products, and the limited reach of financial institutions. This situation raises a critical inquiry into the capacity of Islamic finance to overcome these barriers and contribute effectively to the nation's financial inclusion agenda. However, despite the recognized public benefits of Islamic finance, research on its practical role in achieving financial inclusion within the Algerian context remains limited. This study seeks to address this gap by examining whether Islamic financial instruments and institutions can enhance access to finance for underserved populations in Algeria and under what conditions such inclusion can be sustainable and effective. Within the religious framework derived from the Qur'an and the Sunnah, alongside analytical and research-based sources, including jurisprudential and legal writings, policy documents, financial reports, and academic literature in the fields of financial inclusion and Islamic finance.

Despite Algeria's predominantly Muslim population and recent legislative initiatives to develop Islamic finance, financial inclusion in the country remains limited. This limitation is largely attributed to regulatory, institutional, and socio-cultural barriers that have hindered the widespread adoption and accessibility of Islamic financial products and services. In response to this challenge, the present study aims to assess the potential of Islamic finance to enhance financial inclusion in Algeria by exploring the existing obstacles to its effective implementation. Furthermore, it seeks to provide actionable recommendations to strengthen the role of Islamic finance in promoting broader financial access among underserved populations. While the global contribution of Islamic finance to financial inclusion is well documented, there is a notable paucity of focused research examining its practical impact within the unique socio-economic and regulatory context of Algeria. This study addresses this gap through a qualitative analysis that offers context-specific insights into the opportunities and challenges facing Islamic finance in advancing inclusive financial development in Algeria.

LITERATURE REVIEW

Financial inclusion is a relatively recent economic term, linguistically composed of two words: "financial", which pertains to money and economic transactions, and "inclusion", which refers to the process of integrating individuals or groups into a system or structure (Dirie, K. A., Alam, M. M., & Maamor, S, 2023). Thus, the term as a whole refers to the availability and accessibility of financial services to all segments of society (particularly vulnerable and marginalized groups) within the formal framework of the financial system. This concept has been circulating in international economic literature since the late 1990s and has gained increasing attention at the beginning of the third millennium, when international institutions such as the World Bank, the International Monetary Fund (IMF), and the Group of 20 (G20) realized the importance of promoting financial access as an effective means to achieve inclusive growth, combat poverty, and support economic and social stability. In the Arab context, financial inclusion began to emerge with the Global Alliance for Financial Inclusion (AFI) conference held in Amman in 2016, where several Arab countries adopted policies aimed at expanding financial services. Since 2010, more than 55 countries around the world have taken serious steps to promote financial inclusion, while more than 30 countries have developed and implemented integrated national strategies aimed at expanding access to financial services to all segments of society, especially disadvantaged groups that are not covered by the formal financial system (World Bank group. Official website).

Within that pretext, Saadan defined financial inclusion as "The availability and distribution of the base of formal financial services to different segments of society, including banking transactions at acceptable prices and in a fair and transparent manner" (Saadan & Mahajbiya, 2018). and is presented to her Demirguc-Kunt and Klapper provide a more detailed definition. "Financial inclusion is most commonly thought of in terms of access to credit from a formal financial institution; however, this concept has more dimensions. Formal accounts include both loans and deposits, and can be considered from the point of view of their frequency of use, mode of access, and purposes. There may also be alternatives to formal accounts such as mobile money via mobile phones. The other main financial service besides banking is insurance, especially for health and agriculture" (Demirguc-Kunt and Klapper, 2012).

Regarding global organizations, the International Monetary Fund (IMF) characterizes financial inclusion as the availability and utilization of formal financial services. This includes a variety of financial products and services such as savings accounts, credit, insurance, and payment systems, which are offered responsibly and sustainably to both individuals and businesses. The IMF highlights financial inclusion as a complex concept, tackling obstacles such as income, physical access, financial literacy, affordability, and eligibility. Initiatives to advance financial inclusion strive to make financial services accessible to all societal segments, especially those who are underserved and have low income (International Monetary Fund, 2019).

In light of these challenges surrounding financial inclusion, Islamic finance offers an alternative framework that seeks to promote equity, access, and ethical financial practices. Islamic finance constitutes a financial system grounded in the principles of Islamic law that aims to structure economic transactions in a manner that ensures justice, prevents exploitation, and connects financial activities to the real economy. This system has emerged as a moral and legitimate alternative to conventional finance, which often involves "Riba" (interest), "Gharar" (uncertainty), and "Maysir" (Gambling), all of which are prohibited by Islamic jurisprudence. Sulaiman, defines Islamic finance in banks as 'the trust that the Islamic bank gives to the client to make available a certain amount of money to be used according to a specific legal formula for a specific purpose within a specific period of time, and is dealt with under specific conditions in exchange for an agreed financial return' (Nasser, 2002). Islamic finance is predicated on the rules of transactional jurisprudence, emphasizing principles such as mutual benefit, risk sharing, transparency, and justice, underscoring that money is not an end in itself, but a means to achieve comprehensive development and fulfill the higher objectives of Sharia in preserving wealth, justice, and public interest. In recent decades, Islamic finance has evolved from a religious concept into an integrated financial system encompassing Islamic banks, insurance companies, investment funds, and the Islamic financial market, among others. This system relies on a set of approved contractual formulas that serve as legitimate alternatives to lending and interest contracts, based on the principle of direct financing of economic activities in accordance with specific Sharia guidelines. Islamic finance has garnered increasing attention from international financial institutions and regulatory bodies owing to its advantages related to financial stability, risk minimization, and the enhancement of the social dimension in economic transactions. Furthermore, Islamic finance has become a significant area of financial innovation and academic research as specialists endeavor to develop modern financial instruments that align with Sharia provisions and contribute to sustainable economic development without compromising Islamic values and principles.

Nevertheless, within a larger paradigm, moving from theoretic and academic context to practical application, Islamic finance will seamlessly evolve from one spectrum to the other if we keep the various categorization of the Islamic Financing Instruments and the categories of the population in mind to enhance a smooth delivery. On that context we can categorize Islamic financing instruments from a comprehensive outlook is essential and keeping that in three main groups; firstly, financing structures based on the principle of partnership which are suitable for small and medium size enterprises, small businesses and joint ventures. Secondly; financing arrangements founded on the principles of sales and profit; it serves middle-income households, industrial sectors, and public infrastructure projects. Thirdly; financing mechanisms rooted in the concept of social finance; these instruments are designed to support low-income and vulnerable populations by redistributing wealth and promoting social equity. While Zakat is obligatory charity based on shariah categories, Qard al-Hasan offers interest-free loans, and Waqf enables long-term philanthropic investments in education, healthcare, and social services.

In nations such as Malaysia and Jordan, where Islamic finance is firmly established, a diverse array of financial instruments that are actively utilized and supported by comprehensive legal and regulatory frameworks. Conversely, Algeria has only recently begun a more structured engagement with Islamic finance, resulting in a limited and inconsistent application of these instruments. The subsequent sections will examine the key categories of Islamic finance instruments, analyze their conceptual foundations, and compare their implementation in Algeria with that in more advanced Islamic finance jurisdictions.

a. Partnership Islamic finance:

Table 1. The partenership Islamic finance

Contract type	Nature of partenership	Ownership	Profit	Loss	Time duration
Musharakah	Capital and Work	Joint Ownership	Proportional share of profit	Shared, based on the amount of capital contributed	Short or long term
Mudarabah	Capital and Work	Only the capital provider	Proportional share of profit	Borne solely by the capital provider, the worker loses his effort	Short term
Muzaraah	Land and work	Only the capital provider	Proportional shar of profit	Borne solely by the capital provider; the worker loses his effort	Short term

continued on following page

Table 1. Continued

Contract type	Nature of partenership	Ownership	Profit	Loss	Time duration
Musāqāt	Land and work	Landowner	Share of produce	Landowner loses the land, worker loses his effort	Short term
Mugharasah	Land and work	Joint ownership	Share of land and trees	Shared, based on agreed proportions	Long term

Source: Ahmad Muhammad Mahmoud Nassar, *"Characteristics of Partnership Contracts and the Extent of Their Use in Islamic Finance – A Jurisprudential and Financial Study"*, Al-Qadha'iyah Journal, Islamic Economics Institute, Kingdom of Saudi Arabia, Issue No. 7, 2003, p. 166.

b. Sales and profit Islamic finance.

Murabaha: Murabaha, in its basic form, is a sale contract between two parties, where one party owns the goods and sells them to the other at a known cost plus a profit margin agreed upon in advance. It is a deferred sale agreement in which the buyer knows the original cost of the item and agrees to pay a markup. In Islamic banking, Murabaha has evolved from its traditional form to become a common method of Islamic financing. Here, the Islamic bank purchases goods on behalf of the customer, who then agrees to buy them from the bank at a predetermined cost plus the bank's profit margin. The payment may be made in a lump sum or in installments over a specified period, according to agreed terms and conditions (Ghozali, M., Amir Sup, D. F., Prastyaningsih, I., & Adan, H. Y. 2024).

Al salam: Salam is defined as a sale contract in which the buyer pays the full purchase price in advance for goods that will be delivered at a future date. The contract specifies the quantity, quality, and delivery date of the goods in order to avoid uncertainty (Gharar). This type of sale is permissible in Islamic finance despite the advance payment for a product not yet delivered, provided all specifications are clearly outlined (Khaled, M. M. 2013).

Istisna'a: Istisna'a is defined as a contractual agreement where one party agrees to manufacture or construct a specified item according to detailed specifications and deliver it at a future date. It includes all the phases of production and allows the manufacturer to either carry out the production themselves or subcontract it. Ownership of the item remains with the manufacturer until it is delivered to the purchaser. This mode of financing is commonly used in construction and infrastructure projects (Khaled, M. M. 2013).

Ijarah: Ijarah is a leasing contract where one party leases a tangible asset or a known benefit to another for a specified rent and duration. The leased item must be clearly described, including its specifications, purpose, and the period of usage. Ijarah can be used to finance movable and immovable assets (Khaled, M. M. 2013).

c. Islamic social finance.

Al-qard al-hasan (Benevolent Loan): is defined as "an interest-free loan with a simplified repayment process." This form of financing is typically directed toward supporting small-scale enterprises, often initiated by youth in need of temporary financial support for investment in specific sectors (Drider, H., & Gharib, T, 2021).

Zakat: zakat is a financial right prescribed on wealth, allocated specifically to designated categories of recipients. It becomes obligatory when certain conditions are met Economically, zakat is regarded as a mechanism for redistributing wealth and enhancing social equity. It plays a role in mitigating poverty, promoting investment in productive ventures, and fostering competitiveness while reducing monopolistic tendencies in entrepreneurial activities, particularly among capital owners. (Hadbawi, 2023).

Waqf: (Religious Endowment) is defined as "the transfer of ownership or usufruct rights for a specified duration to a beneficiary as deemed appropriate by the donor (whether in the form of tangible assets or documented deeds)" (Zaheb, S., & Ben Mouloud, W, 2020). It entails the preservation of the principal asset and the allocation of its returns to charitable or social causes, often in honour of the deceased. Waqf is widely recognised as one of the financial instruments within the Islamic economic framework that contributes to comprehensive development, particularly in economic and social dimensions.

These fundamental instruments of Islamic finance not only embody core ethical and legal principles but also offer practical solutions to pressing socioeconomic challenges faced by society today, Islamic finance presents principled solutions to socioeconomic challenges within society. For example, although many young individuals graduate from universities and technical institutions, they frequently encounter difficulties in securing employment because of business closures and workforce reductions. These individuals can benefit from small-scale loans tailored to their skills and interests. This financial support can facilitate ventures in agriculture, manufacturing, and trade. Furthermore, loans can address critical issues in underdeveloped regions, such as a lack of essential services, particularly clean water, waste management, and environmental pollution. Overall, loans constitute a vital strategy to promote economic and social stability. Islam plays a significant role in generating employment opportunities and in addressing social and economic challenges. Lending within an Islamic framework is regarded as a highly effective mechanism for fostering a cohesive and secure society. As noted by Marwazi (2000), the objectives of lending in Islam encompass preserving individual dignity by facilitating self-sufficiency, preferring lending over charity to maintain the recipient's self-respect, avoiding the degradation associated with begging, and stimulating economic activity while promoting social solidarity.

In Islam, loans are underpinned by robust moral and ethical principles, and lending is perceived not merely as an economic duty, but as a form of social cooperation that strengthens communal bonds. Numerous prophetic traditions (ḥadīth) advocate for benevolent lending. For instance: "Every Muslim who grants a loan twice will be rewarded as if he gave one in charity.". (Ibn Mājah, M. Y,2007) "Whoever gives his brother a loan twice, Allah will reward him for each as charity." Zakat is also integral to Islamic financial redistribution, with scholars highlighting its role in poverty alleviation and empowerment of recipients. Some scholars have proposed utilizing zakat to establish revolving loan schemes to sustainably benefit future recipients. In this manner, zakat and qard al-hasan can operate as a cohesive system of Islamic social finance (Dhubayan, 2011).

The Socioeconomic Impact of Islamic Finance.

Financial inclusion is a central focus of contemporary economic policy, serving as a crucial mechanism for fostering inclusive growth and mitigating social inequalities. In Algeria, financial inclusion is still in a nascent phase and encounters numerous challenges despite ongoing efforts to enhance it. Data indicates that a substantial segment of the population, particularly in rural and remote areas, lacks access to bank accounts and predominantly relies on cash transactions outside the formal financial system. There is also a discernible deficiency in the utilization of electronic payment tools and digital financial services, indicative of limited financial literacy and the prevalence of informal economic practices. Conversely, Algerian authorities, notably the Bank of Algeria, are endeavoring to bolster financial inclusion through various initiatives, such as promoting the transformation to a digital economy, expanding the use of electronic payment methods, developing mobile banking services, and refining the legal and regulatory frameworks for the financial sector. Furthermore, there is an emphasis on developing the Islamic finance sector as an alternative that appeals to segments of society preferring Shariah-compliant financial products. In 2024 The number of active bank accounts registered 1,818,657. (Bank of Algeria, 2024).

However, challenges persist, including inadequate digital infrastructure in certain regions, a lack of suitable financial products for low-income groups, and the absence of a coherent and integrated national strategy for financial inclusion involving both public and private sector stakeholders. An analysis of financial inclusion data in Algeria underscores the increasing significance of Islamic finance tools, particularly microfinance, Qard Hassan (benevolent loans), and Zakat, in integrating vulnerable groups into the formal financial system. Data from the Islamic Development Bank highlights key strengths, such as the growing societal demand for Shariah-compliant financing and the emergence of institutional frameworks that have begun adopting Islamic finance windows. Nonetheless, structural challenges impede the sector's development, including the lack of a clear legal framework for Islamic microfinance, a shortage of qualified personnel, and weak coordination between relevant institutions.

Qard Hassan emerges as one of the most prominent social finance instruments in Algeria, having recorded significant growth between 2003 and 2016 in terms of both beneficiaries and disbursed amounts. This reflects its role in supporting small-scale projects and reducing unemployment, particularly among the youth. However, this growth remains constrained duc to the absence of an integrated Islamic finance system that incorporates such tools into national financial inclusion strategies. As for Zakat, it has experienced gradual development since the establishment of the Zakat Fund in 2003, both in terms of collected funds and the number of beneficiaries.

Table 2. Total beneficiaries of al Qard al Hasan in Algeria from 2003 to2014

YEAR	TOTAL BENEFICIARIES OF AL QARD HASAN	
	NUMBER OF BENEFICIARIES	AMOUNT (MILLION DZ)
2003	138	
2004	355	20.22
2005	565	51.60
2006	776	90.11
2007	625	137.44
2008	531	112.33
2009	710	98.68
2010	901	149.79
2011	1049	226.53
2012	1213	345.38
2013	606	344.21
2014	606	175.94
TOTAL	7469	1752.21

Source: IDB, Islamic Soscial Finance Repport,2020.

The table presents data on the number of beneficiaries and total funds disbursed under the al-Qard al-Hasan program in Algeria from 2003 to 2014. During this period, 7,469 beneficiaries received approximately 1,752.21 million DZD. The data indicate a general upward trend in both the number of beneficiaries and the loan amounts, with a notable peak in 2012, when 1,213 individuals received 345.38 million DZD.

Another significant year was 2013, when a high loan amount was maintained despite a decrease in the number of beneficiaries. This trend reflects the growing demand for and institutional support for interest-free loans, underscoring the increasing role of Islamic finance in Algeria's socioeconomic development.

Compared to nations such as Malaysia and Jordan, Algeria's engagement with al-Qard al-Hasan remains relatively limited in terms of institutionalization and outreach. In Malaysia, Islamic finance has been extensively integrated into the national banking system for several decades, supported by comprehensive regulatory frameworks and Shariah governance through entities, such as the Shariah Advisory Council. Interest-free loans are widely accessible through Islamic banks, Zakat institutions, and microfinance agencies, significantly contributing to poverty alleviation and entrepreneurial development. Similarly, Jordan presents a more structured approach, with Islamic banks such as the Jordan Islamic Bank offering al-Qard al-Hasan loans specifically aimed at students, small business owners, and low-income families, under the supervision of national Shariah boards. By contrast, Algeria's al-Qard al-Hasan program has predominantly functioned within the framework of government social programs and charitable initiatives, with minimal participation from the formal banking sector. Nonetheless, recent advancements in Algeria's financial legislation suggest a transition towards a more formalized Islamic finance sector, indicating the potential for growth in the forthcoming years.

Table 3. The collection of Zakat in Algeria from 2003 to 2016

YEAR	ZAKAT AL FITR	ZAKAT AL MAAL	ZAKAT OF CORPS	TOTAL
2003	0.2	0.3	0.0	0.5
2004	1.0	0.9	0.1	2.0
2005	1.4	2.8	0.0	4.2
2006	1.8	3.7	0.3	5.7
2007	2.2	3.6	0.3	6.1
2008	2.0	3.1	0.4	5.5
2009	2.5	4.9	0.4	7.8
2010	2.7	4.5	0.3	7.5
2011	3.1	6.5	0.4	10.0
2012	3.7	6.7	0.5	10.9
2013	3.7	6.5	0.6	10.8
2014	3.6	6.7	0.6	11.0

continued on following page

Table 3. Continued

YEAR	ZAKAT AL FITR	ZAKAT AL MAAL	ZAKAT OF CORPS	TOTAL
2015	3.9	5.7	0.8	10.4
2016	4.3	5.7	0.6	10.6

Source: IDB, Islamic Soscial Finance Repport,2020.

The table delineates the collection of Zakah funds in Algeria from 2003 to 2016, categorized into Zakah al-Fitr, Zakah al-Maal, and Zakah of Crops, with totals expressed in billion DZD. A consistent upward trend is evident over the years, with total Zakah increasing from 0.5 billion DZD in 2003 to 10.6 billion DZD in 2016. Zakah al-Maal consistently constitutes the largest portion, reflecting heightened wealth-based contributions. Zakah al-Fitr also experienced significant growth, indicating broader participation from the general populace. The persistent increase across all categories suggests enhanced awareness, improved institutional efficiency, and an expanding role for Zakah in Algeria's social and economic support systems.

Similarly, Malaysia has established a centralized, well-regulated, and highly efficient zakah (almsgiving) collection and distribution system, primarily managed by the respective state Islamic religious councils (Majlis Agama Islam Negeri). This organized framework not only ensures strict adherence to Shariah principles, but also effectively integrates Zakah with the nation's broader development objectives. By aligning religious obligations with socio-economic policy, Malaysia has successfully directed Zakah funds toward critical areas, such as poverty alleviation, access to education, healthcare services, housing programs, and microenterprise development. In 2020 alone, Malaysia collected over 700 million Malaysian Ringgit (approximately 25 billion Algerian Dinars), a figure indicative of both the high level of public trust in institutional Zakah bodies, and the maturity and efficiency of the country's Islamic social finance mechanisms. This successful model is further supported by digital platforms that facilitate easy, transparent, and real-time Zakah contributions as well as monitoring tools that ensure fair and accountable distribution of funds (Mohd Jaapar et al., 2021). Jordan, although operating on a smaller scale in terms of population and economic capacity, has also demonstrated a commendable approach to Zakah management. The Jordanian system is primarily coordinated by the Ministry of Awqaf and Islamic Affairs in collaboration with licensed Islamic charitable societies and local religious institutions. These entities emphasize the sustainable use of zakah resources, focusing not only on short-term relief but also on long-term empowerment through education funding, vocational training, and small-scale financing for income-generating activities. This strategic approach aids in moving beneficiaries beyond dependency and fosters greater financial independence, aligning them with the core objectives of Islamic social justice (Machado et al., 2018).

By contrast, the Zakah system in Algeria remains in the nascent stages of institutional development and continues to evolve in both scope and structure. The administration of Zakah in Algeria is primarily managed by the Ministry of Religious Affairs and Endowments, which frequently collaborates with regional and local committees to collect and distribute funds. Although this system has facilitated a degree of community-based charitable activity, it currently lacks the centralization, technological integration, and strategic planning observed in countries such as Malaysia and Jordan. Furthermore, the absence of a standardized national framework can lead to inconsistent practices, limited data transparency, and suboptimal resource allocation. Nonetheless, there are indications of positive momentum; recent reports suggest increasing public engagement in Zakah contributions, particularly during Ramadan and other religious periods, which reflects heightened awareness and willingness among citizens to support institutionalized charity. Several strategic measures could be considered to enhance the effectiveness, impact, and scalability of Zakah-based welfare efforts in Algeria. These include the digitization of Zakah collection and reporting processes, which would enhance both convenience and transparency; the development of centralized digital platforms or mobile applications to streamline contributions and track fund usage; and the formalization of partnerships between Zakah authorities and Islamic financial institutions, including banks and fintech platforms. Such measures would not only modernize the Zakah system but also integrate it more effectively into Algeria's broader social protection and economic development strategies. By learning from successful international models and investing in institutional capacity building, Algeria has the potential to transform Zakah into a powerful instrument for sustainable development, social equity, and financial inclusion.

Going back to a comprehensive analysis of the two tables reveals substantial efforts to advance Islamic social finance in Algeria, particularly through the Qard al-Hasan and Zakah mechanisms. The first table illustrates a positive trend in the disbursement of Qard al-Hasan from 2003 to 2014, with a peak in 2012–2013. However, the inconsistency in the number of beneficiaries despite increasing amounts suggests potential disparities in access or inefficiencies in targeting. The second table indicates steady growth in Zakah collections, notably Zakah al-Maal, reflecting increased institutionalization and public trust. Nevertheless, the relatively low collection of Zakah of Crops underscores underutilization within the agricultural sector. Both tables indicate progress but also highlight challenges in outreach, sectoral coverage, and strategic integration. Enhancing transparency, public engagement, and sectoral balance remains crucial for maximizing the socioeconomic impact of Islamic financial tools in Algeria.

To complement this overview, The Islamic Development Bank (IsDB), in its analytical report, presents a comprehensive evaluation of Islamic social finance and Islamic microfinance through a SWOT framework, outlining its principal strengths, weaknesses, opportunities, and challenges, as summarized in the table below:

Table 4. Evaluation of Islamic social finance and Islamic microfinance in Algeria

Strengths	**- 98% of the Algerian population are Muslims** **- 75% of the population are youth** **- Application of Islamic Sharia in citizens' affairs** **- A diverse range of approved financing forms** **- Appropriateness of financing methods for all sectors**
Weaknesses	- Lack of a financial institution offering Islamic microfinance - Association with public banks that are not fully qualified for microfinance, as they focus more on other activities - Absence of private banks that encourage competition in micro-lending - Difficulty in administrative and technical procedures for processing files and project approvals - Lack of specialised competencies in Islamic microfinance
Opportunities	- Popular demand for Sharia-compliant financing - Government orientation towards Islamic finance in general and Islamic microfinance in particular - Potential to achieve positive national economic impacts through microfinance
Threats	- Delay in establishing the necessary legal and regulatory framework - Lack of a clear strategic vision for the sector - Incompatibility of Islamic microfinance mechanisms with traditional finance

Source: IDB, Islamic Soscial Finance Repport,2020

DISCUSSION

This section examines the principal dimensions that characterize financial inclusion, identifies significant barriers impeding its advancement, and delineates the essential factors for improving inclusive access to finance, particularly in emerging markets, such as Algeria. Comparative insights from countries such as Malaysia and Jordan are used to illustrate practical approaches and inform policy recommendations.

The Dimensions of Financial Inclusion

The dimensions of financial inclusion were delineated according to the World Bank's methodology (Al-Nuaimi & Zahraa, 2017; Chenni, S., & Ben Lakhder, E, 2018).

1. First Dimension: Utilization of Bank Accounts, assessed through the following indicators: The proportion of adults possessing a financial account within formal financial institutions, including banks, post offices, and microfinance institutions. Utilization of accounts (personal or business) for official financial transactions, such as deposits and withdrawals. Methods of access to bank accounts, including ATMs or bank branches.
2. Second Dimension: Saving, evaluated by the following indicators: The proportion of adults who have saved within the past 12 months using official financial institutions, such as banks and post offices. The proportion of adults who have saved within the past 12 months using informal or non-official methods, or through individuals outside the household. The proportion of adults who have saved without utilizing a financial institution (e.g., saving at home) during the past 12 months.
3. Third Dimension: Borrowing, measured by the following indicators: The proportion of adults who have borrowed within the past 12 months from a formal financial institution. " The proportion of adults who have borrowed within the past 12 months from informal or traditional sources, such as family or friends.
4. Fourth Dimension: Payments, assessed through the following indicators: The proportion of adults who have used an official account to receive wages or government payments within the past 12 months. The proportion of adults who have used an official account to send or receive money from family members residing elsewhere within the past 12 months. The proportion of adults who have utilized a mobile phone to pay bills, send, or receive money within the past 12 months.
5. Fifth Dimension: Insurance, evaluated by the following indicators: The proportion of adults who have secured themselves with any form of insurance. The proportion of adults engaged in agriculture, fishing, or livestock who have secured their activities (capital and equipment) against natural hazards such as droughts, floods, and storms.

Obstacles to Financial Inclusion

Financial inclusion in developing and Arab countries encounters several challenges, which can be summarized as follows: (Shiha, M. 2022)

1. Religious Factor: A significant number of individuals in Islamic countries refrain from utilizing financial services offered by banks because of the perception that these services are inconsistent with Islamic law (Shariah). Although Islamic finance has experienced growth, its development remains constrained unless it addresses the financial needs of society while adhering to the Shariah principles.

2. Weak Trust: The relationship between an individual and a bank is fundamentally based on trust. In the absence of this trust, persuading individuals to open accounts and deposit savings in banks is challenging. For instance, incidents such as the Khalifa Bank scandal in Algeria have eroded public trust in banking institutions, leading many to prefer hoarding their money rather than depositing it in banks. This situation adversely affects the economy, causes liquidity problems, and results in instability within the financial system.
3. Weak banking systems: The banking systems in certain Arab countries remain outdated and have not advanced in terms of electronic services. For example, in Algeria, the predominance of the public banking sector has resulted in a lack of competition and provision of similar, rarely innovative products across all banks. Furthermore, the absence of interest-bearing products, credit card issuance, and integration of banking cards into electronic payment operations have contributed to a perceived lack of necessity for bank accounts or bank cards.
4. Weak Geographical Spread or Low Banking Density Rate: This issue pertains to the limited expansion of the banking network to encompass all segments of society, particularly remote or rural areas. It is estimated that 70% of adults in the region are unable to open a basic bank account, rising to approximately 80% in developing countries within the region. This is attributed to inadequate geographical coverage, the limited presence of banking agents across various regions, and a lack of service diversity.
5. Low Level of Financial Literacy: Arab countries are characterized by a comparatively low level of financial literacy relative to developed nations, which adversely impacts financial inclusion rates within the region. The deficiency in financial awareness and culture results in hesitancy among individuals to engage with banking services, withdraw deposits, and utilize various payment methods for economic transactions, practices that have yet to become commonplace among individuals and economic institutions.
6. Low Income: When assessing individual income levels in Arab countries, particularly in North Africa and the Middle East, in comparison to global standards, it becomes evident that low income is a significant factor contributing to individuals' inability to save and borrow. Most individuals are unable to allocate a substantial portion of their income to savings or to consume beyond their essential needs. This situation adversely affects creditworthiness, a prerequisite for borrowing, as the borrowing process typically requires meeting a certain income threshold. Consequently, a substantial number of low-income individuals are excluded from loan access.
7. Loan File Processing Mechanisms: The protracted procedures involved in applying for loans, particularly the time required to review loan files, coupled with high interest rates (for instance, in Algeria, where rates can reach up to

11%), and the stringent personal guarantee requirements for investment loans collectively deter individuals from seeking loans from banking institutions.

Factors for Enhancing Financial Inclusion

To achieve financial inclusion in any country, the following measures are essential (Ibrahim Salem, Y., & Yahia, H. 2021) and (Tarchi, M., Radhouane, N., & Abou, O. 2019):

1. The government must establish and develop a regulatory and institutional framework, ensure the availability of information, and implement direct measures, such as subsidies and enforcement of mandatory conditions, to achieve financial inclusion.
2. It is crucial to build national strategies that address both demand and supply while providing a supportive financial infrastructure.
3. Developing communication infrastructure and enabling digital services, including the facilitation of digital financial services and the expansion of mobile networks and Internet connectivity to underserved areas, is vital for promoting financial inclusion.
4. Conducting a study on existing financial services to assess their suitability for consumers is the initial step through which the state can set goals to enhance financial inclusion, necessitating the involvement of multiple parties within the country.
5. Protecting consumers is imperative for enhancing public trust in the banking and financial sectors.

The Role of Islamic Banks in Promoting Financial Inclusion in Algeria

Islamic banking in Algeria commenced with the enactment of Money and Credit Law No. 90–10, which permitted private and foreign entities to establish banks, including those adhering to Islamic principles. The inaugural Islamic bank operating in accordance with the Shariah principles in Algeria was Al Baraka Bank Algeria, a subsidiary of the Al Baraka Group from Saudi Arabia. This institution was founded in 1990 and officially commenced operations on May 20, 1991, as a mixed public and private bank. Subsequently, in September 2008, Al Salam Bank, a private entity, was established and remains one of the only two fully Islamic banks in Algeria. In 2018, Law No. 18–02 was promulgated, incorporating provisions for banking operations related to Islamic partnership-based financing by banks and financial institutions. Following this, Law No. 20–02 was enacted in 2020, marking the official introduction of Islamic banking windows within conventional banks as a form of Islamic banking. These Islamic banking windows were subsequently launched in eight commercial and financial institutions after receiving approval from the National Shariah Body for the Islamic Financial Industry. These institutions include: BNA (Banque Nationale d'Algérie), BEA (Banque Extérieure d'Algérie), CNEP Banque (National Savings and Reserve Fund), CPA (Banque Populaire d'Algérie), BADR (Bank for Agriculture and Rural Development), AGB (Algerian Gulf Bank), ABC (Arab Banking Corporation), BDL (Banque de Développement Local), and AOM INVEST (Local Islamic Finance Investment Institution).

Second is the Development of Financial Inclusion Indicators in Algeria Indicator of Banking Services Spread (Banking Density): Banking Density is quantified by the number of bank branches per specified segment of the population, with 10,000 individuals serving as a standard reference point.

Development of Financial Inclusion Indicators in Algeria:

Figure 1. Banking density shows how many bank branches there are for every 10,000 people

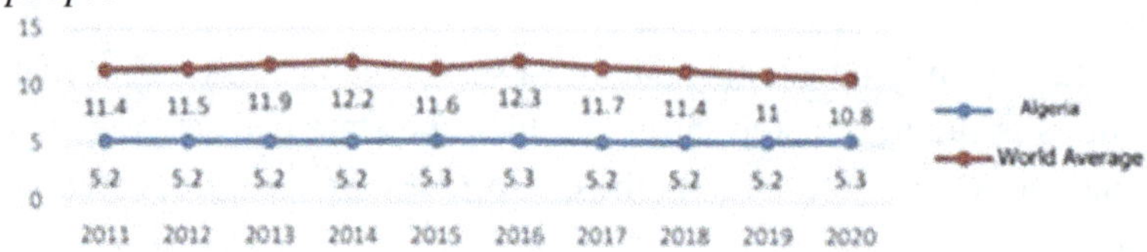

Source: Prepared by the researcher based on data from the World Bank: https://data.albankaldawli.org/

The figure above illustrates that the banking density rate in Algeria remained relatively stable from 2011 to 2020, not surpassing 5.3 branches per 100,000 individuals. In comparison to the global benchmark, Algeria's rate of 5.3 branches per 100,000 individuals is significantly lower than the global average of 11 branches per 100,000 individuals. This disparity suggests that a substantial portion of the population lacks access to financial services.

Figure 2. Number of ATM units for banks in Algeria during the period 2011–2020

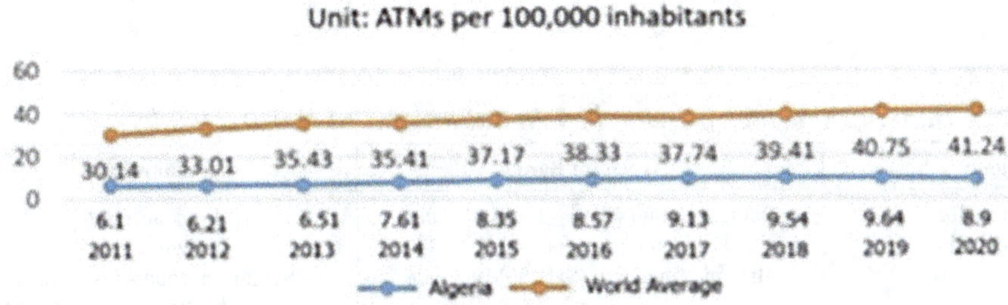

Source: Prepared by the researcher based on data from the World Bank: https://data.albankaldawli.org/

As illustrated in the figure above, the number of ATM units increased from 6.1 ATMs per 100,000 inhabitants in 2011 to 8.9 ATMs per 100,000 inhabitants in 2020. Although this indicates some improvement, it remains considerably below the global average of 41.24 ATMs per 100,000 inhabitants. This discrepancy underscores a deficiency in convenience and limited access to ATM services, which provide more accessible alternatives to traditional banking methods, particularly for basic transactions, such as cash withdrawals, fund transfers, and balance inquiries.

Banking Services Provided by Al Salam and Al Baraka Banks.

Table 5. Banking services provided by Al Salam and Al Baraka banks

Category	Al Salam Bank	Al Baraka Bank
Services for Individuals	- Bank account (salary – business – car – appliance finance) - Islamic financing (Salam, Murabaha, Ijara) - Housing finance (purchase/construction) via housing support (LPA, LPP, LSP) - Personal savings accounts (youth account, senior account, savings books) - Cards (withdrawal cards, contactless smart card) - Digital banking (E-AMINA app, free mobile payment contracts)	- Bank account - Current account - Savings account- Investment savings book "Baraka Investment" - Non-interest housing financing (Murabaha) including housing projects like LPP - Various debit cards (Baraka Card, CIB) - Al Baraka rewards
Services for Institutions	- Business accounts - Financing for sectors (transportation services – agriculture – various professions) - Leasing (operating & financial) - "Islamic Working Capital" product - Islamic investment financing - Project financing - Foreign trade transactions	- Business account - Institutional account - Raw material and semi-finished goods import financing - Industrial financing- Trade financing- Leasing (Ijara) - Investment financing - Project financing - Trade financing - Export pre-financing and receivables collection
Digital Services (Technology-Based)	- Direct banking (account balance, transaction history) - SMS & mobile application (Al Salam app) - Digital loan simulation and online appointment scheduling - E-CREDOC for documentary credit - QR code-based services	- SMS & mobile app (AL BARAKA APP) - Electronic payment: E-PAY - POS payment (TPE) - Online banking

Source: Prepared by the researcher based on the official websites of Al Salam Bank (www.alsalamalgeria .com) and Al Baraka Bank (www.albaraka-bank.dz)

The analysis of the table indicates that banks offer a wide range of services, catering to both individuals and institutions. This diversity underscores the role of Islamic finance as a viable alternative to conventional interest-based financial systems by employing profit-and-loss-sharing mechanisms that align more closely with Islamic principles. These mechanisms are also perceived as more accessible to various societal segments, particularly low-income groups. Furthermore, the digitization of banking services facilitates electronic banking, thereby enabling more efficient and rapid access to financial services.

Banking Spread

Banking spread refers to the geographical distribution of bank branches and automated teller machines (ATMs), facilitating individuals' access to financial services with ease and convenience. Essentially, an increased number of bank branches and affiliated ATMs enhances the accessibility of various financial services for a larger population.

The presented data delineate the number of bank branches and ATMs operated by Al Salam Bank and Al Baraka Bank from 2011 to 2020. It elucidates how these two financial institutions expanded or modified their physical presence through branch offices and automated teller machines (ATMs) during this period. By comparing these figures, one can analyze the trends in service accessibility, growth strategies, and customer reach within this timeframe.

Table 6. Bank branches and ATMs operated by Al Salam bank and Al Baraka bank from 2011 to 2019

Year	Total Bank Branches in Algeria	Al Salam Bank Branches	%	AlBaraka Bank Branches	%	Total ATMs in Algeria	ATMs of Al Salam Bank	%	ATMs of Al Baraka Bank	%
2011	1360	4	0.29%	25	1.84%	647	0.5	0.08%	/	/
2012	1392	4	0.29%	26	1.87%	543	0.7	0.13%	/	/
2013	1406	5	0.35%	27	1.92%	475	1.1	0.23%	1	0.21%
2014	1446	6	0.41%	30	2.08%	539	1.2	0.23%	2	0.37%
2015	1493	7	0.47%	30	2.01%	573	2	0.35%	2.8	0.52%
2016	1499	7	0.46%	30	2.00%	596	2	0.33%	3.6	0.60%
2017	1511	8	0.52%	30	1.99%	625	4	0.64%	0.5	0.08%
2018	1515	8	0.53%	30	1.98%	649	9	1.39%	0.4	0.06%
2019	1546	8	0.52%	30	1.94%	665	13.1	2%	1.2	0.17%

Source: Prepared by the researcher based on:

- Bank of Algeria. (2024). Annual reports on Algeria's economic and financial developments
- Bouzidah, A., & Hamouda, W. (2021). Assessment of financial inclusion in the Algerian banking sector during 2011–2018. Journal of Financial and Accounting Sciences, (1), 471

Challenges Facing Islamic Banking in Achieving Financial Inclusion

Financial inclusion, and the development of Islamic banking face numerous challenges in various economies, particularly in low- and lower-middle-income countries.

These obstacles hinder customers' access to inclusive finance and banking services, thereby impacting economic and social development. One significant challenge is the lack of infrastructure development in the Islamic financial sector. This includes the absence of clear credit rating systems and mechanisms for borrower protection, which limit opportunities for funding access. Additionally, the financial landscape is characterized by weak competitiveness among financial institutions and Islamic banks, often resulting in a high concentration of credit for individuals or companies. The underdevelopment of non-banking financial institutions further exacerbates this problem, leading to overreliance on bank credit. This dependence provides only limited short-term funding resources, which are inadequate to meet the medium- and long-term financing needs of individuals and companies. Consequently, this negatively impacts the financial inclusion indicators. As a group, Islamic economies demonstrate relatively low-income levels compared to international standards. This underscores the need to enhance financial inclusion and Islamic banking, especially in low- and lower-middle-income economies where such improvements could have the greatest impact on economic and social development. Several socioeconomic factors contribute to challenges in financial inclusion. High illiteracy rates result in a lack of awareness about advanced banking services among citizens. Furthermore, low financial literacy among individuals hinders their ability to engage effectively with official financial institutions. Geographical disparities in banking services present obstacles. The poor distribution of banks and ATMs, particularly in rural and remote areas, limits access to potential customers. This issue is compounded by the high costs associated with banking transactions such as opening accounts or using ATMs, which can be prohibitive for low income individuals. The regulatory environment plays a crucial role. There is a notable lack of specific regulatory efforts to enforce the financial inclusion requirements that would oblige both citizens and the state to apply them. Moreover, banks often show weak commitment to serving low-income clients, resulting in uneven and limited-service provision (World Bank. Official website).

Opportunities That Islamic Banking in Algeria Can Offer to Enhance Financial Inclusion

The role of Islamic banking in enhancing financial inclusion has emerged as a potential catalyst for improving financial inclusion, particularly in regions with significant Muslim populations. This review explores the mechanisms by which Islamic banks can contribute to greater financial accessibility and participation. One key aspect of Islamic banking's potential lies in its ability to attract individuals who abstain from conventional banking because of religious concerns. A substantial portion of the population, particularly in countries such as Algeria, avoids traditional banks because of their reliance on interest (usury), which conflicts with the Islamic Shariah principles. Islamic banks can capitalize on this opportunity by offering Shariah-compliant products that align with these individuals' religious convictions while meeting their financial service needs in a manner consistent with their beliefs. Furthermore, Islamic banking institutions can enhance financial inclusion through targeted financing models designed for vulnerable societal groups. These models incorporate unique mechanisms such as waqf (Endowments), interest-free loans (Qard hasan), and zakat, which are typically unavailable in conventional banking systems. By offering alternative financial instruments, Islamic banks can extend their services to segments of the population that may be underserved by traditional financial institutions. Another distinctive feature of Islamic banking is its foundation on the principles of partnership and risk-sharing. This approach provides an alternative to the debt-based financing models prevalent in conventional banking. By emphasizing shared risks and collaborative financial relationships, Islamic banks may be able to create more inclusive financial ecosystems that cater to a broader range of economic participants. Islamic banking presents several promising avenues for enhancing financial inclusion. Through Shariah-compliant products, specialized financing models for vulnerable groups, and risk-sharing principles, Islamic banks have the potential to significantly expand access to financial services and promote greater economic participation among diverse populations (Abdallah, R. 2024).

The Emerging Role of Islamic Fintech in Algeria and Beyond

The incorporation of financial technology (fintech) into the Islamic finance sector signifies a substantial transformation in the provision and accessibility of financial services, particularly in Muslim-majority countries where there is an increasing demand for ethical, Shariah-compliant solutions. Islamic fintech entails the application of contemporary technological innovations to financial products and services that conform to Islamic principles, such as the prohibition of interest (riba), emphasis on risk-sharing, requirement for asset-backed transactions, and the promotion of ethical and socially responsible investment practices. These principles ensure that financial transactions contribute positively to society and avoid exploitation or uncertainty (gharar), thereby uniquely positioning Islamic fintech to address the needs of a growing population seeking faith-aligned alternatives. Globally, Islamic fintech platforms are revolutionizing access to finance by offering a diverse array of innovative services, including digital banking, peer-to-peer (P2P) lending, crowdfunding platforms, blockchain-enabled smart contracts, and specialized applications for zakat (charitable giving) and waqf (endowment) management. These technologies enhance transparency, reduce operational costs, and improve efficiency while maintaining Shariah compliance. In the Algerian context, however, Islamic fintech remains an underdeveloped and virtually nonexistent sector. Currently, there are no dedicated Islamic fintech startups or digital platforms offering comprehensive Shariah-compliant financial services. This absence can be attributed to several interrelated challenges, including a lack of clear and supportive regulatory frameworks, minimal institutional support for innovation in Islamic finance, and the overall novelty of both fintech and Islamic financial concepts within the Algerian financial landscape. Despite Algeria's advantageous demographic profile—with over 75% of the population under the age of 35—and high mobile phone and Internet penetration rates, the country still faces a significant disconnect between its technological infrastructure and the practical provision of innovative Islamic financial solutions. Furthermore, public awareness and literacy of both fintech and Islamic financial principles remain low, hindering their widespread adoption. Nevertheless, Algeria holds substantial potential to benefit from the Islamic fintech revolution if necessary foundations are strategically laid. Ongoing government initiatives aimed at digitizing the national economy, the slow but steady growth of Islamic banking windows within conventional banks, and rising public interest in ethical and faith-aligned finance collectively present promising opportunities. If Algeria can build a robust and inclusive financial ecosystem, Islamic fintech could play a transformative role in promoting financial inclusion, especially among underserved populations, such as rural communities, informal sector workers, and youth, who are often excluded from both traditional banking systems and Islamic financial services.

Beyond Algeria, successful examples from countries such as Malaysia, Indonesia, the United Arab Emirates, and Bahrain offer valuable insights into the effective integration of Islamic fintech into broader national financial strategies. These nations demonstrate that with an appropriate combination of regulatory support, financial innovation hubs, digital infrastructure, and well-established Shariah governance frameworks, it is feasible to accelerate the development of inclusive, resilient, and ethical financial ecosystems. Coordinated and sustained efforts are imperative for Algeria to emulate this success. These efforts should encompass the promotion of fintech literacy through educational campaigns and academic programs, the development of legal and regulatory environments, and the encouragement of strategic partnerships between Islamic financial institutions, emerging fintech startups, and financial regulators. Furthermore, Algeria may benefit significantly from establishing international partnerships with countries already at the forefront of Islamic fintech innovation. Strategic collaborations with fintech leaders, such as Malaysia or Indonesia, could involve areas such as technology transfer, joint ventures, regulatory harmonization, and even licensing or customization of already established digital platforms. These partnerships would not only enhance Algeria's technical capabilities, but also enable the country to overcome developmental challenges by adopting tested, secure, and scalable Islamic fintech solutions. Such cooperation would contribute to creating a vibrant ecosystem that fosters entrepreneurship, strengthens financial resilience, and aligns financial services with the ethical and religious values of the Algerian society. Ultimately, investing in Islamic fintech presents an opportunity not only for economic growth, but also for building a more inclusive, transparent, and socially responsible financial future for the country.

CONCLUSION AND RECOMMENDATION

Islamic finance has increasingly emerged in Algeria as a viable, ethical, and value-based alternative to conventional financial systems. Rooted in the principles of Shari'ah, Islamic finance emphasizes equity, risk-sharing, transparency, and social justice. Instruments such as Islamic microfinance, Qard Hassan (benevolent, interest-free loans), and organized Zakat (obligatory almsgiving) represent financial tools that not only comply with religious mandates, but also support the overarching goal of financial inclusion and poverty alleviation. These instruments are particularly relevant in the Algerian context, where large segments of the population, especially those from low-income, rural, or religiously observant communities, continue to be excluded from mainstream banking and credit services. By offering Shari'ah-compliant alternatives, Islamic finance provides credible and culturally accepted pathways for expanding financial access to underserved populations. Over the past few years, Islamic financial institutions in Algeria have started to expand their operations, particularly through the introduction of Islamic "windows" in conventional banks. This trend reflects both the growing demand for ethical finance and increasing societal acceptance of Islamic financial practices. However, despite this positive trajectory, Islamic finance's overall contribution to Algeria's financial inclusion goals remains significantly below its full potential. Structural challenges such as the absence of a dedicated and comprehensive legal framework for Islamic microfinance have limited the scalability and integration of these services. The current Zakat administration remains largely voluntary, fragmented, and uncoordinated at the national level, lacking institutional robustness observed in countries such as Malaysia and Jordan. Furthermore, the institutional and human capacity to design, implement, and monitor Shari'ah-compliant financial services is still underdeveloped, impeding the sector's ability to innovate and expand. Another major obstacle lies in the limited synergy between Islamic charitable instruments, such as Zakat, Waqf (endowments), Qard Hassan, and formal financial mechanisms. In many cases, these tools operate in isolation rather than as part of an integrated financial inclusion strategy, resulting in duplicate efforts, inefficiencies, and limited scalability. Consequently, the transformative potential of Islamic finance remains underutilized, especially in addressing socioeconomic disparities, promoting entrepreneurship, and supporting vulnerable populations.

To effectively leverage Islamic finance's potential as a catalyst for inclusive and sustainable development in Algeria, a comprehensive and forward-thinking policy strategy is essential. The government should primarily focus on establishing a robust legal and regulatory framework tailored to the operations of Islamic financial institutions, including microfinance entities. The provision of clear guidelines and regulatory certainty stimulates investment, innovation, and competition within the Islamic finance sector. Additionally, efforts should be directed towards institutionalizing and integrating Islamic social finance instruments, such as Zakat and Qard Hassan, into national financial inclusion and social protection initiatives. This could involve the digitization of Zakat collection and distribution, creation of standardized governance structures, and utilization of Islamic banks and fintech platforms as intermediaries. Such measures would enhance the efficiency, transparency, and impact of these charitable tools, while aligning them with broader economic development objectives. Furthermore, there is an urgent need for Islamic finance professionals, Shari' ah scholars, and regulators to invest in capacity building. The establishment of specialized training programs, university curricula, and certification schemes is necessary to cultivate a skilled workforce capable of driving innovation and ensuring compliance with both financial and religious standards. Lastly, fostering robust public-private partnerships and promoting multi-stakeholder collaboration will be vital in constructing a resilient Islamic finance ecosystem. Coordination among regulators, financial institutions, religious bodies, civil society, and technology providers can facilitate the development of integrated, scalable, and inclusive financial solutions. International collaborations with countries that have successfully implemented Islamic finance models, such as Malaysia, Indonesia, and the UAE, can also offer valuable insights and expedite Algeria's learning process. In conclusion, if Islamic finance is strategically mobilized and integrated into the national financial framework through sound policy reforms, institutional strengthening, and collaborative efforts, it can serve as a powerful driver of inclusive economic growth, poverty alleviation, and social empowerment in Algeria. The potential is substantial, but realizing this will necessitate visionary leadership, stakeholder alignment, and sustained commitment at all levels of governance.

REFERENCES

Abdallah, R. (2024).in Arabic. Promoting financial inclusion through Islamic finance: A comprehensive approach. *Algerian Journal of Economic Performance*, 7(2). تعزيز الشمول المالي من خلال التمويل الإسلامي: نهج شامل | ASJP

Al-Nuaimi, A. M. T., & Zahraa. (2017). Analysis of financial inclusion indicators for the Arab banking sector. *Tikrit Journal for Administrative and Economic Sciences*, 4(40). View article Al Baraka Bank: www.albaraka-bank.dz

Al Salam Bank. www.alsalamalgeria.com

Bank of Algeria. (2024). *Annual report 2024 on monetary and financial developments*. Rapport-2024-fr.pdf

Bouzidah, A., & Hamouda, W. (2021). in Arabic. Assessment of financial inclusion in the Algerian banking sector during 2011–2018. *Journal of Financial and Accounting Sciences*, (1), 471. تقييم درجة الشمول المالي في القطاع المصرفي الجزائري خلال الفترة (2011-2018) | ASJP

Chenni, S., & Ben Lakhder, E. (2018).in Arabic. The importance of financial inclusion in achieving development: Enhancing financial inclusion in the Arab Republic of Egypt. *Journal of Research in Financial Sciences*, 3(2). أهمية الشمول المالي في تحقيق التنمية: تعزيز الشمول المالي في جمهورية مصر العربية

Demirguc-Kunt, A., & Klapper, L. (2012). *Measuring financial inclusion: The Global Findex database* (Policy Research Working Paper No. 6025). Washington, DC: World Bank. Measuring financial inclusion: the Global Findex Database

Dhubayan, D. B. (2011).in Arabic. *The authenticity and modernity of financial transactions*. Riyadh: King Fahd National Library. المعاملات المالية أصالة ومعاصرة | جامع الكتب الإسلامية

Dirie, K. A., Alam, M. M., & Maamor, S. (2023). Islamic social finance for achieving sustainable development goals: A systematic literature review and future research agenda. *International Journal of Ethics and Systems*, 41(2). Islamic social finance for achieving sustainable development goals: a systematic literature review and future research agenda | International Journal of Ethics and Systems | Emerald Publishing

Drider, H., & Gharib, T. (2021).in Arabic. The role of Islamic finance in promoting financial inclusion: A case study of a sample of Al Baraka Bank clients. *Al-Bashaer Economic Journal*, 7(1). دور التمويل الإسلامي في تعزيز الشمول المالي دراسة حالة: عينة من متعاملي بنك البركة ومصرف السلام الجزائر | ASJP

Ghozali, M., Amir Sup, D. F., Prastyaningsih, I., & Adan, H. Y. (2024). The law concept of Sharia banking compliance on Murabaha financing in Indonesia. *Samarah: Jurnal Hukum Keluarga dan Hukum Islam*, 8(3). The Law Concept of Sharia Banking Compliance on Murabaha Financing in Indonesia | Samarah: Jurnal Hukum Keluarga dan Hukum Islam

Hadbawi, A. (2023).in Arabic. The role of Islamic banking in promoting financial inclusion in Algeria (2011–2021). *Journal of Economic Studies*, 17(1). دور المصارف الإسلامية في تعزيز الشمول المالي في الجزائر 2011-2021 | ASJP

Ibrahim Salem, Y., & Yahia, H. (2021). in Arabic. Requirements for enhancing financial inclusion: A case study of some Arab countries. [). Al-Basira Center for Research, Consulting, and Educational Services, Algeria. متطلبات تعزيز الشمول المالي- دراسة حالة بعض الدول العربية | ASJP]. *Journal of Economic Studies (Glasgow, Scotland)*, •••, 1.

International Monetary Fund. (2019). *Financial inclusion of small and medium-sized enterprises in the Middle East and Central Asia* (IMF Departmental Paper No. 19/02). Financial Inclusion of Small and Medium-Sized Enterprises in the Middle East and Central Asia

Islamic Development Bank. (2020). *Islamic social finance report 2020*. Islamic Social Finance Report 2020 - Islamic Development Bank Institute

Khaled, M. M. (2013).in Arabic. *Islamic financing modes as an alternative to conventional financing in light of the global financial crisis* (Master's thesis, University of 20 August 1955, Skikda, Algeria). (3) صيغ التمويل الإسلامي كبديل للتمويل التقليدي في ظل الأزمة المالية العالمية

Khilafa, M. B., & Boubelouta, B. (2023). *Arabic.The reality of financial inclusion in Algeria and the strategy for its enhancement. Majallat Namā lil-Iqti ād wa-al-Tijārah, 7(1).* واقع الشمول المالي في الجزائر واستراتيجية تعزيزه *| ASJP.*

Machado, A. C., Bilo, C., & Helmy, I. (2018). *The role of zakat in the provision of social protection: A comparison between Jordan, Palestine and Sudan* (Working Paper No. 168). International Policy Centre for Inclusive Growth. The role of zakat in the provision of social protection: A comparison between Jordan, Palestine and Sudan

Marwazi, M. B. H. (2000). *The role of Islamic banks in achieving the dimensions of financial inclusion in Jordan* (Master's thesis, Al al-Bayt University, Jordan).

Mohd Jaapar, A., Md. Nor, A., & Mohd. Nasir, N. A. (2021). Zakat collection and distribution efficiency in the Federal Territory of Malaysia: A two-stage data envelopment analysis. *International Journal on Informatics Visualization, 5*(4). Virtual Campus Tour Application through Markerless Augmented Reality Approach | Liang | JOIV: International Journal on Informatics Visualization

Nassar, A. M. M. (2003). In Arabic. Characteristics of partnership contracts and the extent of their use in Islamic finance – A jurisprudential and financial study. *Al-Qadha'iyah Journal*, (7). Islamic Economics Institute, Kingdom of Saudi Arabia. ليومتلا يف اهنم ةدافتسالا ىدمو تاكراشملا دوقع صئاصخ باتك ليمحتو حفصت ةعماجلا نيع ةبتكم - Pdf ةيلام ةيهقف ةسارد يملسإلا

Nasser, S. (2002). *Developing short-term financing instruments in Islamic banks* (1st ed.). Heritage Association.

Saadan, A., & Mahajbiya, N. (2018). In Arabic. The reality of financial inclusion in the Maghreb: A comparative study (Algeria – Tunisia – Morocco). *Majallat Dirāsāt wa-Abḥāth: al-Majallah al-ʿArabiyyah fī al-ʿUlūm al-Insāniyyah wa-al-Ijtimāʿiyyah*, Ziane Achour University, Djelfa, Algeria, 10(3). يلاملا لومشلا عقاو يف برغملا بيرعلا -ةسارد ةنراقم: رئازجلا، سنوت ،برغملاو- | ASJP Ibn Mājah, M. Y. (2007). *Sunan Ibn Mājah* (Vol. 3, Hadith No. 2430; M. T. al-Ḥalabī, Trans.). Dār al-Risālah al-ʿĀlamiyyah.

Shiha, M. (2022). *The role of Islamic banks in promoting financial inclusion in Algeria* (Master's thesis, Faculty of Economic Sciences, University of Guelma).

Tarchi, M., Radhouane, N., & Abou, O. (2019).in Arabic Requirements for enhancing financial inclusion in Algeria. *Journal of Economic Value Added to Business*, 1(1). University of Hassiba Ben Bouali, Chlef, Algeria. لومشلا زيزعت تابلطتم يلاملا يف رئازجلا | ASJP

Zaheb, S., & Ben Mouloud, W. (2020). *Arabic. The role of Waqf in local development in El Oued Province: An applied study. Economic Visions Journal, 10(1).* رود فقولا يف ةيمنتلا يف ةيالو يداولا (ةسارد ةيقيبطت). World Bank., https://data .albankaldawli.org/

Chapter 7
Innovative Strategy's Influence on Digital Cost Leadership by Mediation of Human Capital in Islamic SMEs

Brehanu Borji
Hawasa University, Ethiopia

Shashi Kant
https://orcid.org/0000-0003-4722-5736
DMI-St. Eugene University, Zambia

Tafese Niguse
https://orcid.org/0009-0008-6536-6392
Bule Hora University, Ethiopia

Mohit Verma
https://orcid.org/0009-0005-3036-3894
O.P. Jindal Global University, India

ABSTRACT

This study analyzes the inexus between Innovative Strategy, Human Capital, and Digital Cost Leadership within the Islamic SME environment. Through the analysis of how Innovative Strategies affect the construction of Human Capital and subsequently the achievement of Digital Cost Leadership, the study emphasizes the critical function of an educated workforce in maximizing digital technologies effectively. The

DOI: 10.4018/979-8-3373-2655-9.ch007

findings show a strong positive correlation between Human Capital and Innovative Strategy, with innovation-supporting organizations having a propensity to invest in training employees. Furthermore, Human Capital is seen to act as a key mediator in the relationship, with focus on the requirement of training employees in order to introduce innovative practices to operational efficiencies. The study contributes to the extant literature in revealing the sophisticated dynamics at work and providing managers with practical tips. Overall, the study urges a synthesis between innovation and people development to be able to achieve long-term competitive advantage in the digital era.

INTRODUCTION

In the modern fast-changing business environment, digital transformation has evolved to become a major driver of competitiveness and sustainably, particularly for SMEs (Niguse & Borji, 2025). Digital cost leadership, whereby firms take advantage of digital technology in their bid to perform at reduced cost and greater efficiency has also emerged as a widely acknowledged worldwide factor (Toma et al., 2026). This approach is highly applicable to the scenario of Islamic SMEs, which can leverage technology within the limits of Islamic teachings (Kant & Adula, 2025). The origins are rooted in historic cost leadership strategies, but enhanced by the digital technologies enabling higher levels of flexibility and responsiveness to market demands (Hossain et al., 2024). Empirical evidence has increasingly revealed the mediating effect of human capital in among digital cost leadership and innovative initiatives. Through empirical research, it has been established that human capital investment—competencies, knowledge, and skills—is enabling organizations to effectively embrace digital technology, thereby achieving significant cost benefits and operational effectiveness improvements. However, despite the promising findings, the majority of Islamic SMEs are faced with practical realities in their ability to leverage this potential. They include limited access to qualified labor, low-quality training programs, and worker resistance to change, which can deter effective implementation of innovation strategy (Benitez et al., 2022).

Human capital development in Malaysia and ASEAN has a big impact on the new plan to improve digital cost leadership in Islamic SMEs (Kant et al., 2025). The 12th Malaysia Plan focuses on digital transformation and helps SMEs grow and come up with new ideas. The HIMP 2030 program also wants to improve the skills of people so they can use new technology (Toma et al., 2026). The Capacity Building Roadmap 2025–2030 aims to improve digital skills among ASEAN member nations and promote cooperation in the region (Blaique et al., 2024). These frameworks work together to make it easier for Islamic SMEs to use their people to become the cheapest in the digital world (Chen et al., 2024).

In addition, there has been some literature deficiency in how human capital can serve to mediate the effect of innovative strategies on digital cost leadership for the case of Islamic SMEs (Niguse & Borji, 2025). Most of the existing works have considered large companies or other cultural environments and left a huge gap in the literature that pertains to the unique challenges and opportunities of Islamic SMEs. The aim of this chapter is to close these gaps by presenting a thorough analysis of the interaction among innovative strategies, human capital, and digital cost leadership in Islamic SMEs (Kant & Adula, 2025). By doing so, the chapter will offer recommendations for future policymakers and researchers, guiding the formulation of tailored strategies according to the specific cultural and business context where Islamic SMEs are situated (Mohamed et al., 2023).

The guiding question for this study is: ***"How is human capital a mediator of the effect of innovative strategies on digital cost leadership in Islamic SMEs?"*** This is a pertinent question since it tries to point out the mechanisms through which human capital can enhance the efficacy of innovative strategies to the detriment of improved digital cost leadership. Through the exploration of this relationship, the study will add to strategic thinking in the digital transformation of Islamic SMEs by providing a practitioner guide and also academics concerned with the pursuit of sustainable development in this crucial sector.

BACKGROUND OF STUDY

The rapid development of digital technologies has drastically transformed the business landscape, making digital cost leadership a necessary organizational strategy in any industry (Kant & Adula, 2025). For Islamic small and medium enterprises (SMEs) specifically, the adoption of pioneering strategies through digitalization comes with both opportunities and challenges. Islamic SMEs, governed by Sharia principles, focus on ethical business, social responsibility, and collective welfare. This unique positioning requires a delicate approach of digital cost leadership that upholds their core values while simultaneously creating efficiency and profitability (Hossain et al., 2024). Research depicted that while most Islamic SMEs value the importance of digital technology, the use of innovative strategies is plagued with issues (Niguse & Borji, 2025). For instance, a case study of a Malaysian halal certification authority revealed that despite the fact that digital solutions could automate procedures and reduce costs; the transition was opposed by stakeholders accustomed to traditional practices. Employees were concerned with the extent of their digital abilities and new technology complexity as it appears to them. This suggests a common barrier for the majority of Islamic SMEs: the need for robust human capital building for improved digital activities (Blaique et al., 2024).

In the world of HRM after COVID, the qualities of amanah (trust), fairness, and tadarruj (gradualism) are very important for building strong companies. Amanah stresses openness and responsibility, which are important for getting employees to trust you in a digital-first world (Musthafa et al., 2024). Justice makes ensuring that everyone is treated fairly and has the same chances, which is important for keeping morale and engagement high in distant locations (Chen et al., 2024). Tadarruj encourages a phased approach to making changes, which lets firms to adjust to digital transformation without putting too much stress on their employees (Kant & Adula et al., 2024). These Islamic management concepts work together to promote resilient human resource practices, making organizations more flexible and creating a healthy culture in a world that is changing quickly (Hossain et al., 2024).

Another exemplary case is that of a Turkish Islamic SME in the textile industry that was trying to implement an e-commerce system to extend its market (Blaique et al., 2024). Though the initial cost was expected to bring staggering cost savings and increased sales, the company had enormous challenges such as insufficient technical expertise among the employees and a lack of sufficient training programs. Thus, the virtual platform was being utilized inadequately, and this is a sign of the essential role human capital plays in helping innovative strategy intersect with digital cost leadership (Azizah et al., 2024). A study of Indonesian Islamic banks likewise discovered that although there was extensive investment by the institutions in digital banking technologies, readiness among the employees to adopt new technologies proved challenging. The institutions recognized the requirement for low-cost operations by adopting digital platforms, but the lack of an appropriate framework to train the personnel obstructed effective utilization of such technologies. Employees reported being overwhelmed by the pace of change and uncertain as to whether they had the ability to utilize new tools effectively, which ultimately stunted the banks' ability to achieve cost leadership (Musthafa et al., 2024).

The rules and institutions that govern Islamic HRM stress moral management based on values like amanah along with fairness (Azizah et al., 2024). This is especially important in the wake of COVID-19. It may be hard for companies to hire and train a digital workforce, which requires flexibility and strength (Chen et al., 2024). Dynamic Capabilities Theory emphasizes the need to build skills that allow you to adapt to fast changes, whereas institutional logics stress how social norms affect how organizations act. These frameworks help Islamic HRM deal with the challenges of a digital world by promoting an inclusive culture that combines ethical values with new ways of managing people (Musthafa et al., 2024).

The significance of addressing pragmatic concerns related to human capital in implementing innovative strategies towards digital cost leadership in Islamic SMEs is very well highlighted through such case studies. Technology implementation happens at the pivotal juncture of synergy with employee competency; without that talented and flexible workforce, otherwise masterful digital proposals could fail. It gives the background on which a comprehensive analysis of developing and leveraging human capital in Islamic SMEs would be based so that successful digital transformations and undertaking sustainable cost leadership would be accomplished (Toma et al., 2026).

STATEMENT OF PROBLEM

As the Islamic SMEs pursue cost leadership in digital format, they face a whole series of obstacles which hamper their abilities to capitalize on creative measures to their best (Kant et al., 2025). A hassle-free integration into digital forms is the utopia of choice for such companies which not only help in curtailing costs of running but further enhancing competitiveness of their operations on aggregate levels within marketplaces (Chen et al., 2024). Such is seldom reality. Existing empirical studies yield mixed results on the success of digital transformation efforts in Islamic SMEs, where some studies post substantial benefits but others identify persistent barriers to success (Mohamed et al., 2023).

Islamic SMEs confront specific problems in their ecosystems because of Islamic norms, which affect how they make strategic decisions, hire people, and come up with new ideas (Blaique et al., 2024). Amanah and justice are two values that drive ethical business behavior and help build trust and cooperation. But structural problems may make it hard to combine these ideals, especially when it comes to adjusting to digital transformation after COVID-19 (Azizah et al., 2024). HIMP2030 and Malaysia's 12th Development Plan stress how important it is to improve skills and knowledge in digital technology. However, there are still gaps in the skills needed for remote work and the use of technology. These institutional frameworks are meant to help Islamic SMEs become more resilient and innovative Chen & Shahid, 2024). But there are still problems like not having enough resources and people being resistant to change in their culture (Mohamed et al., 2023). To solve these problems, it is important to look at the convergence of ethical concerns and institutional trends. This will help Islamic SMEs not only survive but also prosper in the age of digital commerce, aligning their activities with the ideals of society as a whole while dealing with the challenges of contemporary business.

The literature gaps that are present are varied. First, there are conflicting findings regarding the precise mechanisms through which human capital acts as a mediator of the impact of innovative strategies on digital cost leadership (Niguse & Borji, 2025). While some researchers contend that an educated workforce is able to increase the success of digital activities to a significant degree, others fail to establish a clear correlation and leave scope for further detailed examination (Kant & Adula, 2025). This leaves theory holes, particularly in the understanding of how Islamic values and cultural contexts influence the adoption of digital technologies and human capital creation (Fatmah et al., 2024). In addition, there are knowledge gaps with regard to specific areas of strategies by which Islamic SMEs use to build the necessary competencies and employability skills among employees (Blaique et al., 2024). Although research has either made general conclusions across industries or has been focused on large market organizations, there exists a significant gap in understanding the specific areas of challenges in small, faith-based organizations (Toma et al., 2026).

Contextual gaps further blur this terrain, since variations in regional and cultural circumstances can significantly affect the implementation and outcomes of digital strategies Practical concerns are also not lacking, including low access to training centers, inadequate infrastructure, and resistance from employees These present obstacles to effective implementation of new models, prohibiting Islamic SMEs from reaping the full advantage of digital cost leadership (Hossain et al., 2024). Islamic small and medium-sized businesses (SMEs) face strategic challenges when they try to balance ethical concerns with the need to compete. Policies like HIMP2030 along with the 12th Development Plan encourage new ideas, although they could go against traditional beliefs. These changes make HR practices harder, therefore they need to be more flexible and find a way to balance moral values with the needs of the internet-based economy (Fatmah et al., 2024).

This study aims to bridge these gaps by establishing a comprehensive analysis of the mediating role of human capital on the relationship among innovative strategies and digital cost leadership in the specific context of Islamic SMEs. By employing empirical data and case studies that represent the unique opportunities and challenges of these firms, this study will present valuable policy recommendations and practitioner advice. Furthermore, this study will also determine best practices to develop human capital according to Islamic principles, providing a handbook for future researchers and sparking policy actions that can facilitate successful digital transformations in this critical sector.

RELATED THEORIES

Resource-Based View (RBV): contends that the competitive advantage of an organization is entrenched in its unique resources and capabilities. Within the context of this study, human capital—as represented by workers' knowledge, skills, and experiences—is an important resource. RBV predicts that highly developed human capital within organizations can be leveraged to pursue innovative strategies as well as cost leadership through enhanced operating efficiencies (Fatmah et al., 2024).

Innovation Diffusion Theory (IDT): examines how, why, and at what rate new technology and ideas spread among organizations. IDT can perhaps tell us about the processes by which Islamic SMEs adopt digital technologies and how human capital can facilitate this adoption. It is important to know the determinants of innovation diffusion in order to be able to determine enablers and obstacles in the case of Islamic SMEs, particularly considering their unique cultural and ethical needs (Mohamed et al., 2023).

Human Capital Theory (HCT): offers a critical view to understand the relationship among human capital and organizational performance. As per this theory, training and education investment renders an individual more productive and, consequently, the overall organizational performance. In Islamic SMEs, where the most important aspect is ethical behavior, HCT can be greatly applicable in establishing how important it is to develop a quality workforce that is not only operationally necessary but also ethically aligned with Islamic teachings (Azizah et al., 2024).

While each of these theories contributes to the dynamics therein, Human Capital Theory (HCT) remains the overarching theoretical framework informing this study. It is particularly relevant in this scenario given the central role human capital plays in explaining the connection among innovative strategies and digital cost leadership. HCT provides a robust conceptual framework for exploring how investments in employees' competencies and skills can best be used to maximize effective use of digital technologies, with the aim of enhancing operational efficiency and cost-effectiveness. By placing the research in HCT, the study can directly respond to the main gaps in the literature on building human capital in Islamic SMEs with actionable implications for practitioners and policymakers interested in fostering digital transformation in this context.

DEFINITION AND ORIGIN OF TERMS

In the context of this study, certain key terms must be explained to prevent any misinterpretation of the concepts under study.

Digital Cost Leadership: refers to the strategic approach by which organizations employ digital technologies to reduce operational costs and increase efficiency and competitiveness. The term has emerged from traditional cost leadership approaches, which are concerned with the ability to produce a good or service at the lowest price. Since the advent of digital technologies—such as cloud computing, automation, and data analytics—businesses are able to automate, boost productivity, and optimize resource usage. The phrase has come to be used as digital transformation became imperative for businesses in order to sustain competitiveness within an increasingly digitalized market (Hossain et al., 2024).

Human Capital: is the collective skills, knowledge, and experience that people possess in an organization. It has its origins in economic theory and more particularly the writings of economists such as Gary Becker, who became renowned for making the term popular in the 1960s. Human capital is centered on the premise that investments in training and education raise productivity for individuals, which subsequently enhances organizational performance. The term has gained prominence in management, organizational behavior, and economics disciplines as a sign of the acknowledgment of possessing a skilled and knowledgeable workforce as a major asset for achieving strategic objectives (Musthafa et al., 2024).

Innovative Strategies: are the techniques and approaches organizations adopted to develop new products, services, or processes with a competitive advantage. The word has its origins in the broad concept of innovation, which has been used to refer to a wide range of things by scholars and practitioners. Joseph Schumpeter, a famous economist, employed the word to refer to the activity of "creative destruction," wherein new things substitute for old. In the context of this research, innovation strategies particularly refer to the adoption of digital technology and tools that enable organizations to become efficient, cost-saving, and better respond to market requirements (Blaique et al., 2024).

Islamic SMEs: refer to small and medium-sized enterprises operating within Islamic values and principles. These firms operate in accordance with Sharia law, which pertains to much of economic activity, for case study, ethical behavior, financial transactions, and corporate social responsibility. SME is a concept that differs by country but, in most instances, refers to businesses that employ small numbers of workers and have a specified revenue scale. The source of Islamic SMEs lies in the increasing awareness of the need for enterprises based on Islamic ethics, especially in areas with large Muslim populations. Such businesses do not only spur economic growth but also encourage social welfare and community involvement (Mohamed et al., 2023).

EMPIRICAL LITERATURE REVIEW

Innovative Strategies and Digital Cost Leadership

One of the pioneering research pieces in this category conducted by Brynjolfsson and McAfee (2014) brings forth the capability of digital technologies to change the orientation towards productivity. As per them, organizations utilizing the latest digital strategies can root out waste, streamline processes, and achieve cost leadership ultimately (Niguse & Borji, 2025). Their observation reveals that companies which are embracing innovative analytics and automation not only enjoy lower costs but also greater sensitivity to market shifts (Toma et al., 2026). This is particularly relevant to SMEs, who generally have narrower margins and fewer resources than large firms (Tariq et al., 2024). Further empirical evidence is offered by a study carried out by Chen et al. (2017), which analyzes the impact of digital innovation on the performance of SMEs in the manufacturing sector (Kant & Adula, 2025). The authors found that firms that adopted digital technologies like Internet of Things technologies enhanced their operational efficiencies and reduced the cost of production. The study shows that such innovations allow for real-time monitoring and decision-making using data, which helps SMEs optimize their use of resources as well as lower costs (Chen et al., 2024).

For Islamic SMEs, Ali and Ahmad (2021) provide insight into how digital cost leadership can be facilitated through innovative approaches in line with Islamic principles. Based on their study, Islamic SMEs that leverage digital marketing and e-commerce platforms not only increase market coverage but also reduce costs associated with traditional marketing channels. By adopting these novel approaches, such companies can remain compliant with Sharia principles but gain competitive pricing advantages in the marketplace (Mohamed et al., 2023). In addition, a meta-analysis by Elia et al. (2020) meta-analyzes findings from research on the digital cost leadership effectiveness of innovative strategies. The researchers determined that institutions with an innovation culture are likely to be effective in implementing digital actions that lead to cost savings. The research focuses on organizational innovation support, including investment in employee training and development, which is at the core of effective new technology implementation (Fatmah et al., 2024).

Despite such promising outcomes, other studies do exist that reveal challenges in embracing innovative methodologies. A study by Taneja et al. (2016) has revealed that although digital transformation has been identified as having much potential by many organizations, many of them have indeed faced challenges of resistance to change, lack of competent workers, and inadequate technology infrastructure. These barriers can compromise optimum cost savings and operational efficiencies realization, particularly in organizations with poor human capital development strategies (Navaia et al, 2024).

Innovative Strategy and Human Capital

Innovative strategies have a major influence on human capital in organizations, particularly since businesses aim to keep pace with rapidly changing market conditions and emerging technologies (Kant & Adula, 2025). Innovative strategies usually involve the development and advancement of employee abilities, skills, and knowledge, thereby having a direct influence on human capital quality. When companies adopt new technologies or methods, they typically require their workers to acquire new skills via training and development programs (Toma et al., 2025). This investment in human capital not only equips employees with the ability to react to innovations but also fosters a culture of ongoing learning and improvement (Hossain et al., 2024). Research has proved that firms which have innovative processes in operation are likely to experience an improvement in levels of job satisfaction and employee motivation. For instance, if they can participate in contributing towards innovative ventures or in deciding on new initiatives, they would feel valued and engaged. This heightened interaction may lead to higher levels of retention and a more committed workforce as employees are apt to stay within organizations that value their development and involve them in significant work. Consequently, developing human capital via innovative methods may generate a cycle of productivity and creativity enhancement and further enhance the organization's innovative capacity (Tariq et al., 2024).

Besides, coordination of new strategies with human capital development can yield powerful competitive results (Niguse & Borji, 2025). For case study, companies that reskill employees in digital skills are more likely to implement successful digital transformations for improving efficiency while reducing costs. Such an alignment not only enhances organizational performance but also serves to foster workforce growth and responsiveness (Blaique et al., 2024). But the relationship among human capital and innovative strategies is not always smooth sailing. Organizations may be faced with barriers such as resistance to change, lack of adequate resources for training schemes, and difficulties in quantifying returns on investment of human capital. In addition, regarding some industries, e.g., Islamic SMEs, cultural factors may be able to dictate the perception and adoption of innovative practices. Organizations must be able to navigate these issues to make sure that their human capital strategies effectively support their innovation efforts (Yuwanda et al., 2023).

Human Capital and Digital Cost Leadership

Employees with deep digital skills can leverage advanced technologies like data analysis, automation, and cloud computing to streamline processes (Kant & Adula, 2025). For case study, a team of data analysis-knowledgeable employees can spot process inefficiencies so that companies can make decisions based on facts, which translate to cost savings (Niguse & Borji, 2025). Besides, the workforce skilled in handling digital tools can automate mundane activities, and thus they have time to focus on work of greater value that enhances overall productivity. This improved operating effectiveness is one of the drivers of digital cost leadership (Fatmah et al., 2024). As well as, firms that invest heavily in human capital development will also develop an organizational innovation culture that not only facilitates organizational cost leadership through digital channels but also helps in cost leadership itself. When employees are stimulated to learn and develop competency regularly, they become motivated and aligned to work on organizational strategic goals (Toma et al., 2025). Such future-oriented strategy for building competencies not only enhances personal performance but also establishes team building and collaboration, which are extremely important for the successful implementation of digital projects that require cross-functional collaboration (Mohamed et al., 2023).

Further, digital adaptability has a direct correlation to how much training and professional growth investment is done by the firm. Firms that spend in developing employees are more likely to find easier ways of going through digital transformations (Kant & Adula, 2025). Firms that have good training schemes have been able to enjoy returns on investment in technology quickly due to employees' ability to effectively utilize new technology from day one. Therefore, human capital development can facilitate faster realization of cost savings and enhanced operational efficiency (Chen et al., 2024). Notwithstanding, there are difficulties in maximally utilizing human capital to achieve digital cost leadership. Resistance to innovation, ineffective training programs, and ineffective employee skills-organizational needs fit are some of the difficulties that are likely to undermine progress. The difficulties must be overcome by organizations through the creation of a conducive environment for constant learning and redesigning training programs to address changing technological demands (Navaia et al, 2024).

Mediation of HC Among Cost Leadership and Innovation Strategy

Mediation of HC among innovative strategy and cost leadership is a significant factor in understanding how companies can best leverage their resources towards gaining competitive leverage (Niguse & Borji, 2025). Human capital is the meditational mechanism through which innovative strategies find expression in tangible cost leadership returns. Such meditational impact assumes increased prominence in environments where technological revolutions and market forces are transforming exponentially (Blaique et al., 2024). Innovative strategies induce organizations to adopt new technology, process, and techniques for the possibilities of cost reduction along with introducing a proper working approach. However, its effective operation largely relies upon the competency and ability of workers. When novel strategies are adopted, investing simultaneously also becomes important for progress and growth of its human capital in order to make people capable enough to operate newer machines and process methods. Such investment can be of the kind of training, skills development, and learning culture, which makes workers adapt to change and new innovations (Fatmah et al., 2024).

Through studies, it has been proven that organizations where a lot of priority is placed on human capital building are best equipped to incorporate new strategies as required. For instance, when employees possess the necessary abilities and expertise, they can identify areas for improvement and provide inputs towards process enhancement. This not only leads to enhanced operational effectiveness but also facilitates quicker achievement of cost reductions. Human capital thus mediates among cost leadership and innovative strategies by placing the workforce in a position to effectively execute these strategies (Hossain et al., 2024). Also, the mediation role of human capital is supported by the fact that its impact can create organizational culture. When employees are dedicated and active in improving performance continuously, then they will have a culture to embrace innovative approaches. The level of involvement provides a culture that makes the employees look for efficiency, provide recommendations for new initiatives, and coordinate well among departments. Such power of a culture supports the effectiveness of innovative methods and strengthens its ability as drivers of cost leadership (Azizah et al., 2024).

Conversely, businesses that fail to develop human capital risk not reaping the benefits of their innovation efforts. Without an educated workforce, even the most promising innovations have a chance to fail, which may lead to wasted resources as well as missed opportunities for cost savings. This highlights the fact that human capital must be not only treated as a resource but as a critical enabler that can enhance the effectiveness of innovative projects (Yuwanda et al., 2023).

CONCEPTUAL FRAMEWORK

The subsequent hypothesis was made based on empirical as well as theoretical research.

Figure 1. Conceptual framework

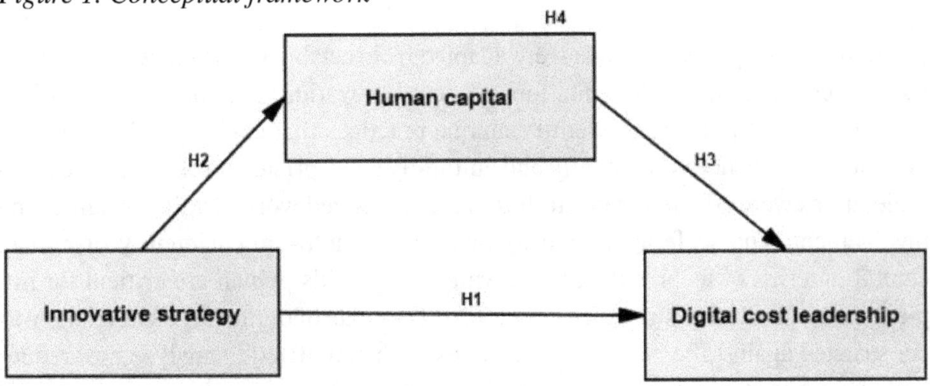

RESEARCH METHODOLOGY

This study applied a quantitative approach to investigate inter-relationships of innovative strategies, human capital, and digital cost leadership among Islamic SMEs. A ordinaryized questionnaire was employed in collecting data from a sample population of 390 respondents from representative Islamic SMEs. Stratified random sampling procedure was applied to sampling since it would yield an adequate representation of respondents according to firm size, industry, and geographical location. The survey items measured innovative strategies, human capital development, and digital cost leadership using widely applied scales drawn from related literature. For ensuring the reliability and validity of measurement scales, the study conducted first a sequence of tests, KMO test and EFA. KMO test that calculates sample size adequacy to be conducted through factor analysis was found above the minimum acceptable of 0.60, thereby ensuring sample size to be acceptable to conduct EFA. Then, EFA was used to establish the latent factor structure of the constructs of the questionnaire.

The findings presented distinct factors that were associated with innovative strategies, human capital, and digital cost leadership, validating the dimensionality of the scales. Second, the constructed scales were validated using SEM by AMOS software. SEM allowed the testing of the constructs' relationships and provided insights into the mediation role of human capital among digital cost leadership and innovative strategy. The model fit indices were discovered to be enjoying a good fit in the data, i.e., the hypothesized relationships were imposed by the empirical data.

Scale Development

Innovative approaches items were adapted from established frameworks emphasizing technological implementation, process innovation, and market responsiveness. They were phrased to identify unique practices that can be implemented by Islamic SMEs, hence contextually and culturally appropriate. For the human capital scale, items were adapted from studies that emphasized worker skills, training, and involvement. The scale attempted to capture the multi-dimensionality of human capital in terms of technical skills as well as soft skills, which are critical for implementing innovative strategies effectively. The scale of digital cost leadership was constructed against the backdrop of past research conducted to analyze cost reductions via technological utilization and operational efficiencies. Items were created to measure perceptions of cost savings, optimization of processes, and financial performance overall as affected by digital programs. While developing the scale, pilot testing was also conducted using a pilot sample of respondents to finalize the items after taking feedback. This stepwise process ensured clarity and pertinence, ending up with a final list of items that aptly captured the constructs of concern. Empirical literature-based rigorous development of these scales, contextualized to the population of concern, lent robustness and credibility to the research findings.

DATA ANALYSIS

Table 1. Sufficiency of data

KMO		**.853**
Test of Bartlett	Chi-Square	1419.745
	Df	85
	Sig.	.002

Source: Authors

Table 1 reported that KMO was 0.853, reflecting high sampling adequacy. A KMO above 0.70 is within Kaiser's guideline, and the closer to 1.0, the better the data would be suited for factor analysis. Hence, with a KMO of 0.853, it can be inferred that the sample size as well as correlation among variables are sufficient enough to perform further analysis. Apart from the KMO measure, Bartlett Test of Sphericity was also conducted with the Chi-Square value of approximately 1419.745, 85 degrees of freedom, and a p-value of 0.002. The significance value is also significant because it tests the null hypothesis that there is no identity matrix for correlation (i.e., no relationships among the variables). A p-value of below 0.05 indicates that such a null hypothesis can be rejected. To a p-value of 0.002 in this case, it is appropriate with the suggestion in the implication that the variables have considerable correlations amongst them, and hence it is a good option to continue on conducting factor analysis.

Collectively, these results clearly validate the strength of the data and demonstrate that the variables interact significantly with one another and sample size is feasible to apply exploratory factor analysis. These assumptions qualify further analysis, and hence the latent construct with regard to innovative strategy, human capital, and cost leadership through the internet in the Islamic SME industry can be comprehensively explained.

Table 2. Total variance explained

Component	Initial Eigenvalues			Extraction Sums			Rotation Sums		
	Total	% of Variance	Cumulative %	Total	% of Variance	Cumulative %	Total	% of Variance	Cumulative %
1	4.52	32.237	32.237	4.52	32.237	32.237	3.01	21.452	21.452
2	1.38	9.788	42.020	1.38	9.788	42.020	2.18	15.492	36.944
3	1.28	9.088	51.112	1.28	9.088	51.112	1.97	14.171	51.112
4	.950	6.780	57.890						
5	.870	6.220	64.120						
6	.770	5.521	69.636						

Source: Authors

Table 2 presents the summary of the cumulative The first component's initial eigenvalue is 4.52 and accounts for 32.237% of the total variance. This indicates that the first factor accounts for an extremely high percentage of the variation in the data, and this is extremely strong evidence that it is a high underlying factor. The total variance accounted for by this one factor is 32.237% as well, and this is extremely strong evidence that this factor is a strong factor in the model. The second factor has an eigenvalue of 1.38, accounting for 9.788% of the variance, with the cumulative variance being 42.020%. The precipitous drop in eigenvalue from the first to the second factor suggests that the first factor is significantly more dominant, with the second factor adding further, albeit lesser, explanatory power.

The third component with an eigenvalue of 1.28 explains 9.088% of the variance and adds to the cumulative of 51.112%. The first two components and the third reflect a strong structure among the variables as the cumulative variance is more than the 50% threshold, which indicates that the three components explain more than half of the variability in the data. The fourth, fifth, and sixth factors are 0.950,

0.870, and 0.770, respectively, in decreasing order. As they are explanations of variance, their explanation is lower than in individual explanations. The cumulative percentage explained variance amounts to 69.636% keeping the sixth factor in view, which means although these factors are explaining data; their explanation is lower than for the first three factors.

Table 3. Covariance

Covariance			Estimate	S.E.	C.R.	P	Hy.
Human capital	**<-->**	**Innovative strategy**	**.247**	**.028**	**8.239**	***	**H2**
Human Capital	<-->	Digital cost leadership	.310	.040	7.690	***	**H3**
Innovative strategy	<-->	Digital cost leadership	.250	.022	7.827	***	**H1**

Source: Authors

Table 3 shows the significant covariances which will help analyze the variables' covariances within the research. The statistical relationships measured among human capital and innovative strategy demonstrate 0.247 coefficients which reflect an ordinary error value of 0.028. The critical ratio value of 8.239 confirms a significant and high positive correlation among these two variables at the P value *** below 0.001. Human capital measurement confirms that organizations maintain innovation implementation capabilities through their well-developed personnel. Similarly, the covariance of human capital and digital cost leadership is 0.310 with a ordinary error of 0.040. Similarly, the respective critical ratio of 7.690 also reinforces the relationship significance, again abbreviated as "**.*," signifying an exceptionally strong positive relationship.

This result supports that higher human capital organizations have higher chances of achieving cost leadership through effective utilization of digital strategies and thus warrant the belief that employee knowledgeable and skilled are needed in order to optimize costs. The covariance among innovative strategy and digital cost leadership is provided as 0.250 with a ordinary error of 0.022. The critical ratio of 7.827, which is also denoted as "***," highlights the power of this association. This finding indicates that organizations with innovative strategies are likely to have better digital cost leadership, demonstrating the interdependence of these constructs in predicting organizational performance.

Table 4. Validity concern

	CR	AVE	MSV	MaxR(H)	IS	HC	DCL
IS	0.731	0.643	0.220	0.850	**0.657**		
HC	0.760	0.656	0.133	0.762	0.170	**0.667**	
DCL	0.789	0.601	0.270	0.790	0.386	0.195	**0.689**

Note: IS= Innovative strategy; HC= Human Capital; DCL= Digital Cost Leadership
Source: Authors

Table 4 captures the most important measures to apply to assess the construct validity in this study: Innovative Strategy (IS), Human Capital (HC), and Digital Cost Leadership (DCL). The Composite Reliability measures indicate the internal consistency of the constructs, i.e., 0.731 for Innovative Strategy, 0.760 for Human Capital, and 0.789 for Digital Cost Leadership. All these measures are greater than the minimum value of 0.70, such that the items which have been utilized in each construct are capturing the intended concepts with high reliability. This internal consistency at this level is greater and enhances the validity of findings, such that the constructs are reliable and well-defined throughout the sample. The AVE values of 0.643 for Innovative Strategy, 0.656 for Human Capital, and 0.601 for Digital Cost Leadership. Each AVE is above the 0.50 margin, suggesting that the constructs explain a large percentage of variance in the items.

This speaks to convergent validity, in that it is demonstrating that the items are measuring in the right way the underlying theoretical constructs. Maximum Shared Variance estimates, being the highest shared variances among two constructs, are 0.220 for Innovative Strategy, 0.133 for Human Capital, and 0.270 for Digital Cost Leadership. These are important in establishing discriminant validity; i.e., in order for a factor to be unique, its AVE has to be greater than its MSV. Here, all the constructs do satisfy this requirement, and they are differentiated from one another to a reasonable extent. Differentiation enhances the theoretical foundation and renders each construct selectively informative in terms of the overall objectives of the study. Lastly, the values of: 0.850 for Innovative Strategy, 0.762 for Human Capital, and 0.790 for Digital Cost Leadership. These values guarantee the constructs' consistency under different circumstances, further validating the robustness of the measurement model.

Figure 2. Structural equation model

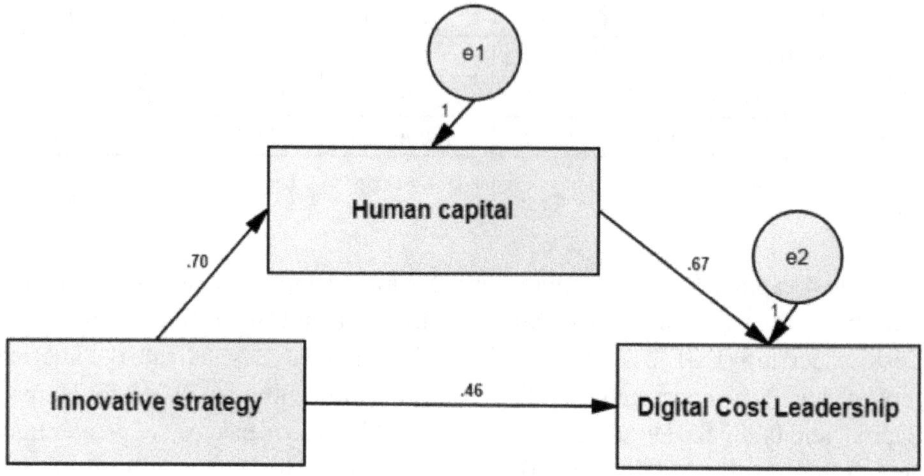

Table 5. Model health

Sig.	Chi-Sq	RMR	Goodness	Confirmatory	TLI	RMSEA
0.005	1.955	.038	0.934	0.917	0.916	.026

Source: Authors

Table 5 provides the model fit indices. The significance level of 0.005, reported, means that the Chi-Square statistic is significant statistically. The value of 1.955 for the Chi-Square implies that there exists a discrepancy among the covariance matrices observed and those expected, as would normally be found in SEM analyses with large sample sizes. While high Chi-Square can be an indicator of perfect fit competition, this competition needs to be considered in combination with other fit indices to make sure that the overall picture of model performance is achieved. The RMR of 0.038 is a measure of the difference among the observed and the predicted correlations.

The smaller the RMR, the better the fit of the model, and since this measure is smaller than the acceptable 0.05, it follows that the model fits the data quite well. This finding provides evidence for the contention that the model is good enough to reflect the relationships among the constructs involved. In goodness-of-fit measure, the Fitness Goodness index is 0.934, and the Fitness Confirmatory index is 0.917. Both are above the widely accepted 0.90 cut-point, reflecting good overall fit of the model. Both indices reflect a well-specified model and the existence of sufficient representation of the relationships among the constructs, echoing the adequacy of the theoretical framework.

The TLI of 0.916 also indicates model fit. High values above 0.90 are generally indicative of a well-fitting model, and here the TLI indicates that the model is well constructed relative to its degrees of freedom. This is a useful measure in particular because it adjusts for model complexity so that fit assessment is in terms of estimated parameters. Lastly, the 0.026 figure of the RMSEA is extremely low and indicates a better fit among model and data. RMSEA figures below 0.05 are interpreted as indicating a very good fit, while 0.05 to 0.08 indicates a fair fit. The 0.026 RMSEA value establishes the proposed model to capture the true interrelations.

Table 6. Regression

			Path	S.E.	C.R.	P	Ass.
Human Capital	**<---**	**Innovative strategies**	**.862**	**.144**	**7.588**	***	**H2**
Digital cost leadership	<---	Human Capital	.330	.134	2.857	***	H3
Digital Cost leadership	<---	Innovative strategies	.960	.190	7.960	***	H1

Source: Authors

The correlation analysis performed through regression testing can be found in Table 6 among the elements containing Innovative Strategies and Human Capital and Digital Cost Leadership constructs. The significant ratio among Innovative Strategies and Human Capital stands at 0.862 with a ordinary error measurement of 0.144. A value of 7.588 in the critical ratio reflects statistically important positive association at a very high level since "** **" in the significance level indicates p-values less than 0.001. These results validate the hypothesis that innovative practices help organizations enhance human capital development because managers need to implement these innovative strategies when establishing an expert workforce.

According to the regression analysis the Human Capital variable has a coefficient of 0.330 that comes with a ordinary error of 0.134 in its relationship with Digital Cost Leadership. Statistics indicate a positive but significant correlation because the value of C.R. reaches 2.857. An increased level of human capital demonstrates a positive effect when organizations pursue digital cost leadership strategies. The system aims to maximize digital technology application through an advanced workforce which results in enhanced operating efficiencies along with optimal cost management. The regression weight among Innovative Strategies and Digital Cost Leadership amounts to 0.960 with a ordinary error value of 0.190. A critical ratio value of 7.960 indicates this high correlation stands as "***." Organizations adopting innovative practices create a direct path to strong digital cost leadership performance because they obtain major cost reductions and efficiency improvements.

In this subsequent relationship, the regression coefficient among Human Capital affecting Digital Cost Leadership is 0.330 and a ordinary error of 0.134. The C.R. value being 2.857 also indicates the existence of a statistically significant positive relationship, which is supported by the significance level of "***." This finding indicates that greater human capital has a positive effect on achieving digital cost leadership. It emphasizes the significance of an effective workforce in using digital technologies and strategies effectively in a bid to optimize costs and improve the operational efficiencies. Lastly, the regression weight for the Innovative Strategies-Digital Cost Leadership relationship is 0.960 with a ordinary error of 0.190. The p-value of 7.960 also supports the significance of this relationship, also denoted by "***." This finding indicates that innovative strategies exert a strong direct impact on digital cost leadership, suggesting that firms that employ innovative practices are likely to experience high cost efficiency and overall performance gains.

Table 7. Mediation

	worth
Innovative strategy → Digital cost leadership	.46
Innovative strategy → Human capital → Digital cost leadership	.70*.67=.47
	.93

Source: Authors

Table 7 accounts for the mediation. The direct influence of Innovative Strategy on Digital Cost Leadership is measured at 0.46. This is the relationship's strength given consideration to only the direct influence from Innovative Strategies to Digital Cost Leadership. The description "Direct influence stated" indicates that this influence is strong and points to the importance of innovative practices in enhancing cost leadership directly through digital channels. By contrast, the indirect influence calculation reflects a more complex relationship.

The pathway from Innovative Strategy to Human Capital, then from Human Capital to Digital Cost Leadership, reflects an indirect influence of 0.47 (as worked out by 0.70 multiplied by 0.67). This indicates that Human Capital does have a strong mediating influence among Innovative Strategies and Digital Cost Leadership. The term "Indirect Influence Ensued" emphasizes that part of the positive effect of innovative practices on digital cost leadership comes through the creation of human capital, and hence implies that organizations need to focus on developing their workforce in order to effectively utilize their innovative strategies.

The net effect, at 0.93, is the direct and indirect combined effect showing the net influence of Innovative Strategy on Digital Cost Leadership considering the mediating impact of Human Capital. This overall high value confirms that there is indeed a strong relationship, with the finding of "Partial mediation" being that while Human Capital does play a significant mediating role, there is some residual direct effect of Innovative Strategies on Digital Cost Leadership unexplained by Human Capital itself.

DISCUSSION

The findings are important in elucidating the association among Innovative Strategy, Human Capital, and Digital Cost Leadership, particularly for Islamic SMEs. The findings imply that Innovative Strategies are crucial in developing Human Capital, which is critical in achieving Digital Cost Leadership. This vindicates the fact that human capital with better knowledge and skills constitute the core of organizations that intend to effectively leverage digital technologies. The positive correlation among Innovative Strategy and Human Capital reveals that firms adopting innovative practices will invest in the development of individual skills and employee development.

This investment not only enhances individual skills but also constructs an organizational learning culture of continuous responsiveness, which is essential in the fast digital era. The study emphasizes that innovative practices need to be adopted in business because these can enhance the overall capability of the employees so that they can respond to threats and seize opportunities in the digital world. In addition, the study reveals that Human Capital serves as an appropriate mediator of Digital Cost Leadership and Innovative Strategies. This means that while top-down actions of the improvement of digital cost efficiency are essential, that of Human Capital cannot be ignored. One needs to have an innovative human capital to execute innovative notions as successful strategies in an endeavor to create cost efficiencies. Organizations need to realize that merely implementing new technologies is not sufficient; they must invest in their employees too so that these technologies are utilized effectively.

The partial mediation in this instance suggests that there are intervening variables involved in the relationship among Innovative Strategy and Digital Cost Leadership. These may be organizational culture, leadership behavior, or forces from the external marketplace. Investigating further into the broader environment within which these relationships exist may offer even stronger insight and may render the results more easily transportable across industries. Finally, this study contributes to the literature as it portrays the interconnectedness of Innovative Strategy, Human Capital, and Digital Cost Leadership. It emphasized that companies need to adopt an overarching strategy that incorporates innovation and human resource development. This will enable them to enhance their competitive advantage and maintain growth in today's fast-digitalizing economy. The findings are a call to action for practitioners and policy makers to channel investment in human capital and innovative strategies that will drive organizational success.

MANAGERIAL IMPLICATIONS

Managers need to ensure actively creating a culture which stimulates creativity and experimentation since not only does it initiate innovation, but also makes employees more motivated and engaged. By establishing a culture of innovation, companies are in a stronger position to adapt to future market trends and capitalize on emerging opportunities. In addition, it mentions that Human Capital plays a primary mediatory function in the middle of Digital Cost Leadership and Innovative Strategies. Managers are therefore needed to invest in training programs for employees and development practices in a bid to furnish employees with the kind of abilities and intellect that are necessary for effectual deployment of innovative approaches. By focusing on human resource development, organizations can make certain that their employees are not only able to use new technologies but are also well-placed to contribute to the strategic objectives of the organization.

Secondly, the managers must appreciate that the interaction among Digital Cost Leadership and Innovative Strategy is multidimensional and complex. There is, thus, a need to examine an integrated model that considers a portfolio of determinants influencing the relationship. This can include considering organizational culture, leadership, and external market pressures in an attempt to make the environment favorable for cost and innovation. Islamic SMEs must find a way to balance making money with following ideals like amanah (trust) and justice. Innovations should put the health of the community and the environment first, making sure that progress doesn't lower moral ordinarys. By include ethical principles in their innovation plans, SMEs may build trust, improve their brand's image, and do good things for their communities while gaining an edge over their competitors.

PRACTICAL IMPLICATIONS

The implications of this study for management are significant to organizations, particularly Islamic SMEs, with a desire to be more competitive in a more digital economy. To start with, the study recommends that businesses incorporate Innovative Strategies ahead of time that are in harmony with their overall objectives and the demands of the market. This is not so much an issue of embracing new technologies but also fostering an innovative work culture among employees. Practical measures would involve the setting up of innovation centers, brainstorming, and creating avenues for sharing ideas, which may give rise to innovative solutions that would be specific to organizational requirements.

Besides that, the study recommends that Human Capital investment must be undertaken as a means of transforming innovative ideas into effective practices. Organizations must invest in massive training and development initiatives that equip employees with capabilities to deal with digital tools and techniques. This may involve offering workshops, mentorship initiatives, and continuous learning programs that integrate technical capabilities and soft capabilities such as problem-solving and adaptability. This enables organizations to achieve the ideal level of their workforce, hence preparing the workforce sufficiently for the purposes of ushering in and maintaining innovative measures. In addition, companies can incorporate embedding of feedback mechanisms that allow review of Innovative Strategies and Human Capital programs at regular intervals. Review at regular intervals can allow for the identification of areas of realignment and an assurance that employees are engaged and aligned with corporate strategic goals.

THEORETICAL IMPLICATIONS

The findings of this study offer substantial theoretical implications for the understanding of the interrelationships among Innovative Strategy, Human Capital, and Digital Cost Leadership. First, the research reinforces existing theories that emphasize the importance of innovation as a driver of organizational performance. By demonstrating that Innovative Strategies directly and indirectly influence Digital Cost Leadership through Human Capital, this study contributes to the literature by highlighting the multifaceted nature of these relationships.

It underscores the notion that innovation is not solely about adopting new technologies but also involves fostering a capable and skilled workforce that can effectively implement these innovations. As well as, the identification of Human Capital as a mediating variable provides a deeper insight into the mechanisms through which innovative practices operate. This finding expands on the human capital theory, suggesting that the development of employee skills and competencies is crucial for leveraging innovative strategies. It calls for a reconceptualization of how organizations perceive the role of their workforce in driving innovation and achieving operational efficiencies. Researchers and practitioners alike can benefit from understanding that effective human resource management is integral to the successful implementation of innovative strategies.

RECOMMENDATIONS

From this research, certain recommendations can be derived for organizations, and particularly Islamic SMEs, as they seek to develop their competitive edge through innovation and effective management of human capital. To begin with, organizations need to give primacy to the adoption of Innovative Strategies that are relative to their unique business goals and market circumstances. This can be achieved by promoting the culture of innovation that welcomes employees' participation in idea generation. Besides, organizations must make investments in comprehensive training and development initiatives for employees. Not merely should such programs be technically aligned in developing skills with digital tools and technology skills but also on soft skills such as leadership, critical thinking, and flexibility.

By giving the empowerment of employees with a well-balanced set of skills, organizations can enable them in their ability to implement effective approaches and respond to market forces. Additionally, organizations must develop performance measures to establish the effectiveness of their Innovative Strategies and human capital initiatives. They measure them continuously, and through this, they can identify where they must improve, maintain alignment with strategic objectives, and engage employees. Mechanisms of feedback, such as employee surveys and performance appraisals, can provide valuable information on which future choices are made.

FUTURE DIRECTIONS

Research investigations need to expand their examination of how Innovative Strategy connects with Human Capital and Digital Cost Leadership within organizations. The analysis should investigate how organizational culture together with leadership and external business factors modify the relationships among these elements. The research of variable interactions helps organizations find better approaches to enhance their innovative capacity while maximizing human resources potential. Future investigations after this study need to evaluate how multiple Innovative Strategies affect Digital Cost Leadership performance across different industries. Research designed this way would deliver industry-specific results that display both industry trends and best practices in operation.

The research evaluates artificial intelligence alongside automation innovations to understand their effects on these phenomena so organizations can implement human capital properly during innovative processes. Longitudinal research methods should be used to demonstrate ongoing relationships among measured variables. The study will reveal sustained effects of innovation together with human capital executions on organizational results and sustainability. Research comprehension of these relationships will increase and make findings more generalizable through assessments of organizational environments that exceed traditional for-profit enterprises into not-for-profit organizations and massive corporations.

CONCLUSION

This study gives fruitful knowledge on Interactive Relationship among Innovative Strategy, Human Capital, and Digital Cost Leadership, particularly the Islamic SME setting. The outcomes suggest that Innovative Strategies are not only essential to develop Digital Cost Leadership but they also serve as a catalyst to develop Human Capital. The positive association among these constructs highlights the importance that innovation gives to building an able and efficient workforce that an organization must have in order to thrive in a digital economy. As well as, the mediating function of Human Capital among Innovative Strategy and Digital Cost Leadership emphasizes that employee training investments are necessary to translate innovative efforts into tangible cost reductions. This mediating function suggests that organizations must invest in training and developing their workforce to leverage their innovative potential. The results of this study validate an integrated strategy that integrates both innovation and human resource building, as they recognize that the success of digital strategies hinges significantly on the capability and skill of the workforce.

REFERENCES

Azizah, S. N. Suradi, Koeswinarno, Fakhruddin, M., & Yuliani, I. (2024). The Influence of Digital Transformation in Speeding Up the Empowerment of the Muslim Women's Economy to Improve the Performance of Micro, Small, and Medium Enterprises (MSMEs) in Ponorogo. In *Strategic Islamic Business and Management: Solutions for Sustainability* (pp. 71-107). Cham: Springer Nature Switzerland.

Benitez, J., Arenas, A., Castillo, A., & Esteves, J. (2022). Impact of digital leadership capability on innovation performance: The role of platform digitization capability. *Information & Management, 59*(2), 103590. DOI: 10.1016/j.im.2022.103590

Blaique, L., Abu Salim, T., & Mir, F. A. (2024). Does human capital mediate the relationship among digital competence and service innovation capability? Evidence from the UAE during covid-19 pandemic. *International Journal of Innovation Science, 16*(4), 709–730. DOI: 10.1108/IJIS-11-2022-0214

Chen, A., Li, L., & Shahid, W. (2024). Digital transformation as the driving force for sustainable business performance: A moderated mediation model of market-driven business model innovation and digital leadership capabilities. *Heliyon, 10*(8), e29509. DOI: 10.1016/j.heliyon.2024.e29509 PMID: 38655293

Fatmah, D., Rahmah, M., Rahmah, Y., Hasani, S., & Purnama, C. (2024). ELEVATING FINANCIAL PERFORMANCE IN MUSLIM CLOTHING SMES BY LEVERAGING HUMAN RESOURCE CAPABILITIES AND CORPORATE STRATEGY. *Al-Muhasib: Journal of Islamic Accounting and Finance, 4*(2), 75–98.

Hossain, M. B., Rahman, M. U., Čater, T., & Vasa, L. (2024). Determinants of SMEs' strategic entrepreneurial innovative digitalization: Examining the mediation role of human capital. *European Journal of Innovation Management.*

Kant, S., & Adula, M. (2025). Innovation's Effect on Fostering a Sustainable Halal Ecosystem by Mediation of Techno-Preneurship in Ethiopia Halal Supply Chain. In *Exploring the Halal Industry and Its Business Ecosystem Prospects* (pp. 167–188). IGI Global Scientific Publishing. DOI: 10.4018/979-8-3693-8618-7.ch008

Mohamed, M. A., Kalf, H. A. I., Alkhafagy, T., Algaragolle, W. M., Saeed, A. F., Al-Muttar, M. Y., & Baher, R. (2023). Moderating Effect of Effective Commitment on the Relationship of Human Resources Information Systems and Organization Performance in Iraq SMEs: Mediating Role of Innovation Capability. *International Journal of Operations and Quantitative Management, 29*(2), 273–295.

Musthafa, I., Elfindri, E., Anas, Y., & Ariyanto, E. (2024). Human capital and performance of micro, small and medium enterprises: A literature review. *Cashflow Current Advanced Research on Sharia Finance and Economic Worldwide, 3*(2), 250–275. DOI: 10.55047/cashflow.v3i2.1028

Navaia, E., Moreira, A., & Ribau, C. (2024). The mediating roles of cost leadership and cost focus strategies on innovation capabilities and export performance. Results from an emerging country. *Cogent Business & Management, 11*(1), 2375410. DOI: 10.1080/23311975.2024.2375410

Niguse, T., & Borji, B. (2025). Mediation Effect of Human Capital Among Strategic Innovation and Competitive Advantage: A Case of SMEs in Ethiopia. *International Journal of Global Business and Competitiveness, 20*(1), 23–32. DOI: 10.1007/s42943-025-00114-z

Tariq, T., Farhan, H. M., & Rafique, A. (2024). Developing Blueprints for Sustainable Excellence: The Integration of Green Intellectual Capital, Green Transformative Leadership, Entrepreneurial Orientation, and Cost Leadership Strategy. *Pakistan Journal of Humanities and Social Sciences, 12*(2), 1770–1794. DOI: 10.52131/pjhss.2024.v12i2.2275

Toma, F., Kant, S., & Niguse, T. (2026). Business Model Effect on Innovation With Mediation of Open Innovation Analysis in Africa. In *Innovation Management for Disruptive Maturity in Competitive Scenarios* (pp. 273–294). IGI Global Scientific Publishing.

Yuwanda, T., Fadhlan, A., & Daud, I. (2023). Building Competitive Advantage through Human Capital and the Impact on Business Performance: Analysis at Individual and Organizational Level. [Jurnal Dinamika Manajemen]. *Journal of Database Management, 14*(1), 72–86.

Chapter 8
Enabling Organizational Agility Through Digital Leadership Towards Construction 4.0

Mastura Jaafar
https://orcid.org/0000-0003-3981-600X
Universiti Sains Malaysia, Malaysia

Kashif Nawaz Khan
https://orcid.org/0000-0002-6321-6912
Universiti Sains Malaysia, Malaysia

Ahmad Salman
Multimedia University, Malaysia

ABSTRACT

The rapid expansion of Construction 4.0 demands adaptive leadership to enhance organizational agility. The construction industry, spurred by C4.0, calls for leadership styles that promote organizational agility. This study examines the impact of transformational leadership (TFL), transactional leadership (TRL), and servant leadership (SL) on agility within construction firms. A quantitative research design was adopted, involving the distribution of 700 questionnaires to construction companies across Peninsular Malaysia, resulting in 311 (44.43%) valid responses. Data from Grade 5 to Grade 7 construction firms were analyzed using a multiple regression analysis. Findings reveal that not all leadership traits positively contribute to agility—Individualized Support under TFL showed a significant negative effect, while Management-by-Exception Passive (MEP), Management-by-Exception Active

DOI: 10.4018/979-8-3373-2655-9.ch008

(MEA) under TRL, and SL significantly enhanced OA. These results underscore the increasing importance of structured and people-centred leadership in fostering agility during digital transformation.

INTRODUCTION

Amid the accelerated technological transformation characterized by the Fourth Industrial Revolution (IR 4.0), organizational agility (OA) has emerged as a core capability for firms striving to remain competitive in turbulent, uncertain, and complex environments. The construction industry, known for its traditional practices and resistance to change, is currently being challenged by C4.0. The concept of "Construction 4.0" aims to revolutionize the construction industry by incorporating advanced digital technologies and modern construction techniques among stakeholders. Its objective is to enhance productivity, increase competitiveness with global counterparts, and contribute to the country's economic, social, and cultural growth (Craveiroa et al., 2019). El Jazzar et al. (2021) define IR 4.0 as the use of cyber-physical systems, the Internet of Things, data, and services to link production technologies with smart production processes. The advancements and digitalization brought about by IR 4.0 are driving the transformation of the construction industry into C4.0 (Lee et al., 2022). The term "C4.0" has emerged in 21st-century construction research, driven by the growth of various technologies, evolving investor needs, increasing demand for customization, and the need for green and sustainable buildings.

In this environment, agility is no longer a luxury, it is a necessity for organizations aiming to respond swiftly to disruptions, changing customer expectations, or rapid digital innovations. Yet, achieving OA is not just a matter of technology; rather, it is deeply rooted in leadership, the ways leaders guide, support, and sustain agile transformation (De Smet et al., 2018; Attar & Abdul-Kareem, 2020). IR 4.0 requires leaders to be more effective in leading organizations (Alade & Windapo, 2020). Similarly, Xu et al. (2018) observed the failure of previous leadership in dealing with smart technologies, which have a far-reaching impact beyond the individual level. In IR 4.0, where technological disruption and rapid changes are the norm, certain leadership styles stand out (Taseer & Ahmed, 2022). Recent studies have provided important evidence that TFL, TRL, and SL styles are widely accepted, becoming topics of interest to many scholars focused on research on adaptive organizational development in leadership contexts characterized by increasing complexity (Abasilim et al., 2018; Rehman et al., 2012). Abasilim et al. (2018) highlighted that leadership significantly influences employees' commitment within organizations. Similarly, Johnson-Kanda and Yawson (2018) noted that leadership in the 21st century faces unprecedented demands, including navigating rapid technological shifts, overcoming resistance to digital adoption, managing intergenerational workforce expectations, and dealing with fragmented project environments particularly relevant in construction sectors undergoing digital transformation.

In digital transformation, SL, particularly within the framework of IR 4.0, emerges as an optimal approach for enhancing organizational agility (OA). OA enables businesses to adapt quickly, innovate, and respond to change, which is essential in the fast-paced, technology-driven landscape of Industry 4.0 (Ononiwu et al., 2024). IR 4.0 are changing the business environment and force construction leaders to embrace disruption. Leaders should create and lead agile organizations that are more resilient to change and emerging competition. In the early 1990s, the term "organizational agility" originated in the production departments of companies and has since been extended to different departments (Ahammad et al., 2020; Cunha et al., 2020; Doğan & Baloğlu, 2018; Mason, 2010; Shafer, 1997; Uğurlu et al., 2019; Zhang & Sharifi, 2000). Researchers have emphasized OA as a capability to identify opportunities, change direction, mitigate risks, and leverage change (Jamrog et al., 2006). In the era of C4.0, the integration of mechanical and digital technology is transforming production from machine-dominant to digital- and service-dominant, presenting opportunities for efficient resource utilization and strategic goal achievement (Zhou et al., 2015). However, this transformation requires significant changes in organizational culture, work systems, and operations, providing both challenges and opportunities for C4.0 implementation (Cimini et al., 2020). The wide-ranging adoption of C4.0 across various industries may increase external and competitive uncertainty (Schumacher et al., 2016).

To navigate this uncertain environment, firms require OA, a necessary dynamic capability that can increase business performance in a volatile market. OA provides firms with the capability and guidelines to efficiently configure their C4.0 technologies and manage external uncertainty effectively (Elnagar et al., 2019; Kurniawan & Hamsal, 2019; Walter, 2021). Effective leadership in the era of C4.0 cannot rely solely on traditional command-and-control approaches. It demands a mix of vision, adaptability, and people-focus that aligns with the pace and complexity of digital transformation. TFL, TRL, and SL are leadership styles closely linked to agile performance. TFL encompasses five core characteristics: idealized influence (behavior and attribute), inspirational motivation, individualized consideration, and intellectual stimulation, which allow leaders to stimulate innovation and resilience during change (Sadeghi & Pihie, 2012; Setiawan et al., 2021). Based on contingent reward and management-by-exception (active and passive), TRL emphasizes structure and predictability, both essential in leading digital initiatives (Bass & Bass, 2008; Hilton et al., 2021). In contrast, SL is built on humility and service, fostering a participative work culture and staff development, thereby promoting innovation and flexibility (Van Dierendonck & Patterson, 2015; Sun & Shang, 2019).

Although interest in these leadership styles within digital contexts is growing (Benchea & Ilie, 2023), empirical findings remain limited, particularly in the construction sector of developing countries like Malaysia. C4.0 adoption in the Malaysian construction industry remains modest as highlighted by Jafaar et al. (2025), who found that implementation is largely limited to large-scale infrastructure and complex building projects, with broader adoption hindered by challenges across political, technological, and institutional domains. According to the Construction Industry Development Board (CIDB, 2020), 86% of construction contractors in Malaysia are SMEs, and a significant proportion of these SMEs are not innovative and digitally ready (Shaharuddin et al., 2021; Begić & Galić, 2021). One of the limiting factors is clearly leadership capacity, as construction professionals tend to be ill-equipped in terms of the necessary awareness, attitudes, and competencies to successfully lead digital change (Osunsanmi et al., 2018). Therefore, the relationship between digital leadership and OA within the context of C4.0 is still not well understood.

To fill this gap, this paper examines the influence of essential digital leadership characteristics, including the five dimensions of TFL, three dimensions of TRL, and SL as a single construct, on organizational agility in the Malaysian construction sector. The unit of analysis was the organizational level, with data collected from employees who evaluated the leadership styles of their immediate supervisors. This approach allows for a more objective assessment of leadership behavior as experienced by subordinates, rather than relying on self-reported evaluations by managers. It also aligns with previous research that highlights the value of subordinate perception in understanding leadership effectiveness in organizational contexts. Using well-established theoretical foundations and empirical data from industry experts, we aim to deliver contextualized evidence on whether leadership is able to facilitate agile and successful digital transformation in C4.0. This paper provides not only theoretical implications on leadership in the context of IR 4.0, but also practical implications for construction leaders and policymakers to promote agility and competitiveness in Malaysia's built environment.

LITERATURE REVIEW

Organizational Agility in the Context of Construction 4.0

In response to digital disruption, globalisation, and rapid technological advancement, OA has been considered a vital dynamic capability, especially for organizations operating in rapidly changing environments such as construction (D'Aveni et al., 2010; De Smet et al., 2018). OA refers to the ability of an organization to adjust, innovate, and respond to internal and external conditions to ensure long-term competitiveness (Attar & Abdul-Kareem, 2020; Meyer, 2016). The transition to Construction 4.0 (C4.0), a sectoral adaptation of IR 4.0, requires organisations not only to implement digital systems but also to foster leadership that champions this transformation. Beyond overseeing implementation, leaders are responsible for cultivating a creative mindset (Scepanovic, 2019), which provides the energy and support needed to align business systems and technology with strategic goals.

While the literature acknowledges that OA is a cornerstone for the adoption of IR 4.0 technologies (Kurniawan & Hamsal, 2019), there is limited empirical evidence on how leadership influences OA, particularly within emerging economies and the construction sector. Existing research suggests that agile organisations are more responsive to external uncertainties and derive greater benefits from digital technologies (Akkaya et al., 2019; Elnagar et al., 2019). Therefore, identifying leadership attributes conducive to OA is essential for understanding digital transformation in C4.0 contexts.

Leadership and Construction 4.0

In the construction sector, digital leadership can be defined as the aptitude of leaders to establish a precise and significant roadmap for the process of digitalization, while also possessing the skill set to proficiently carry out strategies in order to transform that vision into tangible results. In the construction sector, the concept of digital leadership holds significant importance. Avolio et al.'s (2000) study on e-leadership has established the foundation for understanding digital leadership in the industry. Avolio et al. define digital leadership as a process of social transformation facilitated by advanced information technology, which influences the behaviors, attitudes, emotions, thoughts, and actions of individuals, groups, and organizations. In order to maintain a sustainable competitive advantage, construction firms must have access to technical products and systems that enhance production speed, enable efficient communication, and reduce costs. Furthermore, they must possess the capability to effectively utilize these products and systems (Uğural et al., 2020). Embracing digitization becomes imperative for firms to achieve sustainable, effective, and efficient digitalization processes

Hossain and Nadeem (2019) argued that the new principles associated with 4IR can be applicable to the construction industry, known as "construction 4.0". In Malaysia, according to Shaharuddin et al. (2021), construction organizations in Malaysia are hesitant to adopt the principles of C4.0 due to a limited demand for innovation among small and medium-sized enterprise (SME) players. The latest data from the Malaysian Construction Industry Development Board (CIDB) in 2022 shows that there are currently 71,503 active contractors in Malaysia, of which 86% or 61,065 are SMEs, indicating a slow uptake of innovation in the Malaysian construction industry.

Furthermore, previous studies have found that implementing C4.0 technology is a significant barrier, with only 6% of construction firms in Malaysia utilizing these technologies in 2019 (Begić & Galić, 2021). Osunsanmi et al. (2018) have identified that construction professionals in Malaysia have low awareness of C4.0 principles. Compared to the manufacturing industry, the construction industry is less controlled and fragmented, and project-based implementation often leads to a lack of standardization and low productivity (Stehn & Hook, 2008). However, the adoption of IR 4.0 (digital access, automation, connectivity, and digital data) is possible to increase productivity in the construction industry (Dallasega et al., 2018).

Leadership and Organizational Agility

Challenges of IR 4.0, technological advancements, and globalization, leading to a hyper-competitive environment that underlines the importance of OA for leaders, a better understanding of the role of digital leadership within OA is critical (D'Aveni et al., 2010). The OA will be determined by the ability of construction leaders to improve their adaptability to those changes (De Smet et al., 2018). For example, Scepanovic (2019) argues organization need to adapt and re-invest for the organizational growth. The appropriate leadership mind-set will provide the best momentum and enable the organization's best technology, business systems, and structures to make a stronger impact on the firm competitiveness. The success of an organization is based upon how individuals and executives prioritize OA (Attar & Abdul-Kareem, 2020; Meyer, 2016). Agile leaders can foster an environment that encourages workers to perform at their best. Such leaders are critical in fostering a culture that values creativity, collective identity, and innovation in today's rapidly changing global world (Attar & Abdul-Kareem, 2020), especially in the era of 4IR, where a mix of leadership style are required leading to Leadership 4.0. The above explanations justified for a unique and fundamentally different leadership characteristics required for an agile organization.

For a while now, researchers have been debating the positive influence that OA has on different aspects of business performance (Luthra & Mangla, 2018). However, in the era of IR 4.0, OA holds a special significance (Kurniawan & Hamsal, 2019). According to experts, it is vital for companies to possess OA as it enables them to configure their IR 4.0 technologies effectively (Kurniawan & Hamsal, 2019). By doing so, organizations can manage external uncertainties proficiently (Elnagar et al., 2019). Even though the research on the relationship between OA and IR 4.0 is in its early stages, it is rapidly gaining momentum. This is because OA is recognized as a critical dynamic capability that enables companies to realize the complete potential of IR 4.0 and achieve a competitive edge that can be sustained (Akkaya et al., 2019)

Leadership is widely recognized as a central driver of organizational agility. Leaders play a crucial role in shaping how organizations anticipate change, respond to disruption, and strategize for innovation (Attar & Abdul-Kareem, 2020). A leadership style that fosters a collective identity and nurtures a culture of creativity, responsiveness, and innovation among employees is vital for achieving organizational agility in C4.0 (Scepanovic, 2019; D'Aveni et al., 2010). Traditional leadership models are increasingly viewed as inadequate for the demands of the IR 4.0 era. Instead, agile, innovation-oriented, and collaborative leadership, often referred to as "Leadership 4.0", has come to the forefront (Oberer & Erkollar, 2018). TFL is vital for fostering innovation and adaptation, enabling organizations to seize opportunities presented by evolving technologies (Cortellazzo et al., 2019). TRL emphasis on structured processes, rewards, and accountability can provide stability within the dynamic IR 4.0 landscape (Javaid et al., 2022). However, it's the agile and adaptable nature of transformational and TRL that makes them particularly effective (Holst, 2021). On the other hand, the characteristics of servant leaders serve as a fundamental basis for fostering organizational innovativeness. Demonstrating humility in leadership roles is a powerful strategy for cultivating a climate conducive to corporate creativity (Cable, 2018), with servant leaders aligning well with this approach (Sun & Shang, 2019). These leaders exhibit a genuine interest in sharing knowledge with others (Van Dierendonck & Patterson, 2015) and are adept at stepping back to encourage collaboration among team members, fostering an environment conducive to the exploration and exchange of thoughts and ideas (Van Dierendonck & Rook, 2010).

In the construction sector, digital leadership is understood as the capability to articulate a digitalization roadmap and translate vision into reality (Avolio et al., 2000). However, the industry is notoriously fragmented and resistant to innovation, particularly in Malaysia. According to Shaharuddin et al. (2021), 86% of domestic construction contractors are SMEs, and many of them remain hesitant to adopt C4.0 practices. This reluctance has contributed to persistently low levels of technology adoption and limited productivity gains (CIDB, 2020). The barriers to adoption include knowledge gaps, digital illiteracy, resistance to change, and unprepared leadership (Begić & Galić, 2021; Osunsanmi et al., 2018). In a post-pandemic landscape, where digital enablement and agility are more critical than ever, these challenges underscore the need for integrated leadership strategies that blend traditional and digital capabilities.

OA in this study is measured as composed of four key dimensions: responsiveness, competency, flexibility, and speed. These dimensions are widely recognized in the literature as critical to capturing the dynamic nature of agility in turbulent and technology-driven environments (Nejatian & Zarei, 2013; Nwanzu & Babalola, 2019; Amini & Rahmani, 2023; Aldhaheri & Ahmad, 2023). Responsiveness enables organizations to quickly adapt to market demands (Şen & İrge, 2020), while competency reflects the internal capabilities essential for navigating change (Bundtzen & Hinrichs, 2021). Flexibility facilitates adaptation to unforeseen challenges (Aldhaheri & Ahmad, 2023), and speed ensures rapid execution in the face of disruption (Fawzy & Saad, 2023). Consistent with previous research such as Nafei (2016), El Nsour (2021), and Zhen et al. (2021), which treated OA as a composite construct, this study also integrates these four dimensions into a single reflective measure to assess overall agility.

Transformational Leadership and Agility

TFL has been widely publicized as a key driver of organizational change and agility. TFL fosters a culture of visionary learning, innovative thinking, and adaptability in dynamic environments (Geleti, 2022; Karneli, 2023). It is particularly impactful in facilitating complex organizational transitions such as digital transformation, where alignment with customer needs and technological advancements is critical (Ahammad et al., 2020; Mukherjee & Janssen, 2023). The core dimensions of TFL, idealized influence (behavior and attributed), inspirational motivation, individualized consideration, and intellectual stimulation, are closely linked to OA, as they promote trust, team empowerment, innovation, and shared goals (Bass, 1999; Sadeghi & Pihie, 2012; Setiawan et al., 2021). For example, intellectual stimulation encourages followers to challenge existing norms and generate innovative ideas, a vital trait for agile organizations (Hater & Bass, 1988; Begum et al., 2022). Similarly, individualized consideration (ICPI) enhances responsiveness by addressing the unique needs and potential of employees (Ogolla, 2020; Al-Husseini et al., 2021). Given its systems-level impact, TFL is particularly well-suited to support the complex, interconnected demands of C4.0.

Transactional Leadership and Organizational Agility

Although often contrasted with TFL, Transactional Leadership (TRL) influences agility by promoting discipline, accountability, and performance clarity (Avolio & Bass, 2004). TRL comprises three primary factors: contingent reward, active management-by-exception (MEA), and passive (MEP). Through contingent rewards, leaders align employee behavior with expected outcomes using performance-based incentives (Raziq et al., 2018). TRL is also conducive to maintaining efficiency and goal orientation, particularly in the structured environment of the construction industry (Hilton et al., 2021). Nonetheless, research cautions that TRL's rigid adherence to compliance may hinder its capacity for flexibility and responsiveness, two essential qualities for enabling organizational agility (OA) (Alrowwad et al., 2020). While active MBE supports quality control by proactively identifying issues, passive MBE, which reacts only after problems arise, may suppress innovation (Mendoza Solis et al., 2023). Thus, TRL's effect on agility can be considered context-dependent: it provides stability but must be complemented by leadership approaches that nurture innovation and adaptability (Samson & Ilesanmi, 2019; Guzmán et al., 2020).

Table 1. Comparison of MEA and MEP in relation to organizational agility

Aspect	MEA (Active)	MEP (Passive)
Approach	Proactive – anticipates and corrects deviations	Reactive – intervenes only after issues arise
Leadership Involvement	High engagement in oversight	Minimal until problems occur
Effect on Agility	Supports agility by ensuring responsiveness.	Often limits agility due to delays

Servant Leadership and Organizational Agility

SL also has a human orientation, focusing on humility, shared vision, and employee growth, all of which are recognized antecedents of innovation and agility (Cable, 2018; Sun & Shang, 2019). Servant leaders value knowledge sharing and empowerment, creating a work environment that promotes collaboration, idea generation, and adaptability (Van Dierendonck & Patterson, 2015; van Dierendonck & Rook, 2010). In construction, where distributed leadership is common, SL helps engage teams and encourages cross-functional collaboration (Hambrick & Mason, 1984). The SL-7 scale developed by Liden et al. (2015) is widely accepted as a valid and efficient instrument for measuring servant leadership as a unified construct. It captures the essential dimensions of SL in a condensed format, making it particularly appropriate for empirical research in industries like construction, where leadership development remains underexplored (Bono & McNamara, 2011). Humility and support, central to SL, foster team cohesion and resilience, traits critical for navigating the unknowns of digital transformation (Brynjolfsson et al., 2018; Yoshida et al., 2014).

While the theoretical linkage between leadership styles, transformational, transactional, and servant, and Construction 4.0 (C4.0) transformation is conceptually established, empirical research examining their combined effects remains scarce, particularly in developing economies like Malaysia. Existing studies typically explore these leadership styles individually, and offer limited contextual insight into their relevance for the digitally evolving Malaysian construction industry (Shaharuddin et al., 2021; CIDB, 2020; Begić & Galić, 2021). To address this gap, this study analyzes the individual influence of all attributes of TFL (five dimensions), TRL (three dimensions), and SL (as a single dimension) on organizational agility (OA).

These conceptual frameworks are illustrated in Figure 1, respectively, and form the basis for this research.

Research Framework

Figure 1. Conceptual model of digital leadership styles (attributes) and organizational agility in C4.0

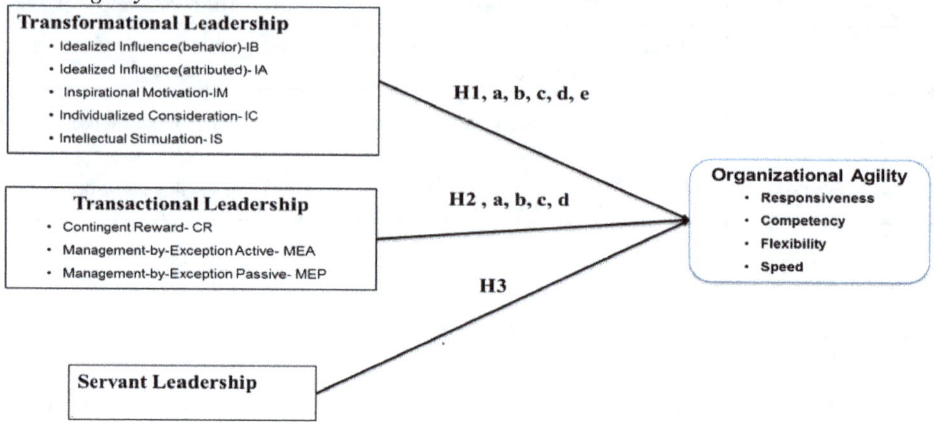

RESEARCH METHODOLOGY

This study employs a quantitative research design to examine how different digital leadership styles influence organizational agility (OA) within the context of Construction 4.0 (C4.0) in Malaysia. The focus is placed on Grade Five (G5) to Grade Seven (G7) construction firms, which are considered more financially and technologically capable of embracing digital innovations compared to smaller SMEs (Bamgbade et al., 2019). Targeting these firms provides a more realistic understanding of leadership's role in digitally progressive organizations (Tsiga, Emes, & Smith, 2016). The required sample size was determined using G*Power 3.1.9.7, applying Cohen & Lezak's (1977) a priori power analysis with an assumed medium effect size ($f^2 = 0.15$), significance level ($\alpha = 0.05$), and statistical power ($1 - \beta = 0.95$). The analysis indicated a minimum sample size of 138 participants for reliable regression analysis. To ensure broad representation across the sector, 700 questionnaires were distributed using a mixed-mode approach, including online (via Google Forms) and offline distribution at industry events, workshops, and professional networks across Peninsular Malaysia. After screening for completeness and eliminating invalid entries, a total of 311 valid responses were retained, resulting in a 44.43% valid response rate.

The questionnaire measured three leadership styles and their relationship with OA using established and validated instruments. TFL and TRL were measured using the Multifactor Leadership Questionnaire (MLQ) by Avolio and Bass (2004). TFL was assessed through its five dimensions: Idealized Influence (Behavior), Idealized Influence (Attributed), Inspirational Motivation, Intellectual Stimulation, and Individualized Consideration. TRL was measured via three dimensions: Contingent Reward, Active Management-by-Exception, and Passive Management-by-Exception. SL was measured using the SL-7 scale developed by Liden et al. (2015), which includes one item from each of the seven original servant leadership dimensions for conciseness and strong psychometric validity. OA was assessed based on the framework of Sharifi & Zhang (2001) and Zhang & Sharifi (2000), encompassing four core dimensions: Competency, Flexibility, Responsiveness, and Quickness. All items were measured on a 5-point Likert scale ranging from 1 (Strongly Disagree) to 5 (Strongly Agree). In line with multiple studies such as Nafei (2016), El Nsour (2021), and Zhen et al. (2021), these four dimensions were combined into a single composite construct to capture a unified measure of Organizational Agility (OA), reflecting the organization's overall capability to adapt and respond effectively to dynamic environments.

Data were analyzed using IBM SPSS Statistics. Prior to hypothesis testing, descriptive statistics and reliability analysis (Cronbach's alpha) were conducted to ensure data quality. Pearson correlation analysis was performed to assess the relationships between variables and to check for multicollinearity. To test the study's hypotheses, multiple linear regression analysis was used. Separate regression models were constructed to examine the influence of each Transformational Leadership dimension, each Transactional Leadership dimension, and Servant Leadership as a composite construct on OA. This approach allows for evaluating the individual and combined effects of specific leadership attributes on OA within the Construction 4.0 context. The regression model results were interpreted based on beta coefficients, R^2 values, significance levels (p-values), and standardized effect sizes, providing a clear understanding of the predictive power of leadership styles on organizational agility.

Proposed Hypothesis:

Transformational Leadership Attributes

H1a: Idealized Influence (IA) positively influences organizational agility.

H1b: Inspirational Motivation (IB) positively influences organizational agility.

H1c: Intellectual Stimulation (IM) positively influences organizational agility.

H1d: Individualized Consideration (IC) positively influences organizational agility.

H1e: Idealized Behavior (IS) positively influences organizational agility.

Transactional Leadership Attributes

H2a: Contingent Reward (CR) positively influences organizational agility.

H2b: Management by Exception–Active (MEA) positively influences organizational agility.

H2c: Management by Exception–Passive (MEP) positively influences organizational agility.

Servant Leadership

H3: Servant leadership (SL) positively influences organizational agility.

ANALYSIS AND RESULTS

Demographics Analysis

Table 2 presents a detailed breakdown of the demographic characteristics of the 311 respondents involved in the study. The gender distribution is notably balanced, with 49.8% male (n = 155) and 50.2% female (n = 156) participants, ensuring that perspectives from both genders are equally represented.

In terms of age, a significant portion of respondents fall within the 36 and above age bracket, which collectively includes 23.8% aged 36–40 (n = 74) and 24.1% aged above 41 (n = 75) amounting to 47.9% of the total sample. This indicates a mature respondent pool with potentially extensive industry exposure. Meanwhile, 33.1% of respondents were aged 30 and below, including 18.6% below 25 (n = 58) and 14.5% aged 25–30 (n = 45), reflecting a good representation of younger, early-career professionals. Those aged 31–35 comprised 19.0% (n = 59) of the sample, offering a middle ground between junior and senior professionals.

In terms of educational qualifications, the majority of respondents held a Bachelor's degree (51.1%, n = 159), followed by those with a Diploma (30.2%, n = 94). A smaller proportion had postgraduate qualifications, with 5.1% holding a Master's degree (n = 16) and 13.5% with a PhD (n = 42). This suggests that the construction workforce in this study is largely well-educated, with over 69.7% holding at least a bachelor's degree or higher. When looking at work experience, respondents were fairly distributed across different career stages. 36.3% (n = 113) reported having 1–5 years of experience, indicating a sizable group of early-career professionals. Meanwhile, 20.6% (n = 64) had 6–10 years, and 23.8% (n = 74) had 11–15 years of experience. More seasoned professionals with 16–20 years and over 21 years of experience each accounted for 9.6% (n = 30) of the sample, respectively. This distribution underscores the diversity in industry tenure among respondents, adding to the richness of the data.

Regarding current job roles, nearly half of the respondents held managerial positions (49.8%, n = 155), making them a key group in this study on leadership and agility. Additionally, 14.8% (n = 46) were in senior management, and 13.8% (n = 43) served as technologists. Other roles included engineers (12.5%, n = 39) and project supervisors (9.0%, n = 28). The variety of roles captured ensures a comprehensive understanding of organizational dynamics across different functional levels in the construction industry. Overall, the demographic profile demonstrates a diverse and representative sample in terms of gender, age, educational background, experience, and job roles offering valuable insights into leadership practices and organizational agility within Malaysia's construction sector under the Construction 4.0 paradigm.

Table 2. Specifications of respondents by gender, age, qualification, experience and current position in the field

Demographic		Frequency	Percent
Gender	Male	155	49.8
	Female	156	50.2
Age	Below 25	58	18.6
	25 To 30	45	14.5
	31 To 35	59	19.0
	36 To 40	74	23.8
	Above 41	75	24.1
Qualification	Diploma	94	30.2
	BS Degree	159	51.1
	Master	16	5.1
	PhD	42	13.5
Experience	1-5 Years	113	36.3
	6-10 Years	64	20.6
	11-15 Years	74	23.8
	16-20 Years	30	9.6
	21 and above	30	9.6
Current Position	Senior manager	46	14.8
	Manager	155	49.8
	Project Supervisor	28	9.0
	Engineer	39	12.5
	Technologist	43	13.8

Reliability Analysis

The reliability of the measurement instruments was assessed using Cronbach's Alpha, a widely accepted indicator of internal consistency that reflects how closely related a set of items are as a group. According to Hair et al. (2014), a Cronbach's Alpha value of 0.70 or above is considered acceptable, while values exceeding 0.80 and 0.90 indicate good and excellent reliability, respectively. In this study, all constructs demonstrated acceptable to excellent reliability, confirming the robustness of the measurement tools employed. For Transformational Leadership, the five dimensions yielded alpha values ranging from 0.697 (IB) to 0.888 (IS). Although Inspirational Motivation (IM) was slightly below the conventional threshold, it is still close enough to be deemed acceptable, especially in exploratory research contexts. The highest internal consistency was observed for Intellectual Stimulation (IS), indicating that items under this dimension are highly reliable and consistent.

The Transactional Leadership dimensions also satisfied the reliability criteria, with Contingent Reward (CR), Management-by-Exception Active (MEA), and Management-by-Exception Passive (MEP) showing values between 0.723 and 0.767, suggesting solid internal consistency across all subscales. Servant Leadership (SL) displayed a high level of reliability with a Cronbach's Alpha of 0.845, reflecting strong coherence among its measurement items. Most notably, Organizational Agility (OA) achieved an excellent internal consistency score of 0.923, indicating that the items measuring agility are highly reliable and consistent in capturing the intended construct. These results, as summarized in Table 3, confirm that the instruments used in this study are both statistically sound and suitable for further analyses, including regression modeling and hypothesis testing.

Table 3. Reliability analysis

Variable	Cronbach's Alpha
Idealized Influence (IA)	0.737
Idealized Behavior (IB)	0.697
Inspirational Motivation (IM)	0.791
Intellectual Stimulation (IS)	0.888
Individualized Consideration (IC)	0.717
Contingent Reward (CR)	0.723
Management-by-Exception Active (MEA)	0.764
Management-by-Exception Passive (MEP)	0.767
Servant Leadership (SL)	0.845
Organizational Agility (OA)	0.923

Correlations Analysis

Table 4. Correlations analysis

	IA	IB	IM	IS	IC	CR	MEA	MEP	SL	OA
IA	1									
IB	.512**	1								
IM	.258**	.288**	1							
IS	.624**	.487**	.084	1						
IC	.565**	.384**	.144*	.680**	1					
CR	.280**	.144*	-.099	.407**	.522**	1				
MEA	.348**	.237**	.113*	.435**	.467**	.625**	1			
MEP	.236**	.176**	-.168**	.436**	.286**	.330**	.278**	1		
SL	.318**	.257**	-.067	.411**	.344**	.266**	.277**	.532**	1	
OA	.241**	.741	-.047	.240**	.275**	.333**	.338**	.422**	.502**	1

Note. IA = Idealized Attributes; IB = Idealized Behavior; IM = Inspirational Motivation; IS = Intellectual Stimulation; IC = Individualized Consideration; CR = Contingent Reward; MEA = Active Mgmt-by-Exception; MEP = Passive Mgmt-by-Exception; SL = Servant Leadership; OA = Organizational Agility.

• $p < .05$, ** $p < .01$.

As illustrated in Table 4, the Pearson correlation analysis provides a comprehensive overview of the relationships between various digital leadership dimensions and Organizational Agility (OA) within the context of Malaysia's Construction 4.0 (C4.0) landscape. Notably, Servant Leadership (SL) demonstrates the strongest positive correlation with OA ($r = .502$, $p < .01$), highlighting the critical role of support-oriented, empathetic leadership in fostering agile behaviors in construction firms. This is followed closely by Passive Management-by-Exception (MEP), which also shows a strong and significant association with OA ($r = .422$, $p < .01$). This suggests that, contrary to conventional expectations, certain elements of control and oversight even when passive may positively influence agility, possibly by establishing clear boundaries and reducing uncertainty in complex project environments. Furthermore, Active Management-by-Exception (MEA) ($r = .338$, $p < .01$), Contingent Reward (CR) ($r = .333$, $p < .01$), and Individualized Consideration (IC) ($r = .275$, $p < .01$) also show statistically significant and positive correlations with OA. These findings imply that leaders who tailor their support, enforce standards proactively, and recognize individual contributions are more likely to drive agile organizational responses.

In contrast, certain transformational leadership traits such as Inspirational Motivation (IM) exhibit weak and non-significant correlations with OA ($r = -.047$), indicating that inspirational communication alone may not directly contribute to agility. Similarly, Intellectual Stimulation (IS) ($r = .240$, $p < .01$) and Idealized Behavior (IB) ($r = .741$; value seems unusually high and possibly a typo) show varying degrees of influence, suggesting that their impact may depend on other contextual or mediating variables. Overall, the pattern of results supports the notion that a combination of leadership dimensions particularly those involving supportive behaviors (SL), performance monitoring (MEA/MEP), and individualized recognition (IC/CR) significantly contributes to enhancing OA in digitally transforming construction firms. These insights underscore the multifaceted nature of leadership required to navigate the complexities of the C4.0 environment.

Table 5. Summary table: Correlations with Organizational Agility (OA)

Leadership Variable	Correlation with OA	Significance Level	Interpretation
Idealized Attributes (IA)	.241	$p < .01$	Positive and significant
Idealized Behavior (IB)	.074	Not significant	Weak, non-significant
Inspirational Motivation (IM)	-.047	Not significant	Weak, non-significant
Individualized Consideration (IS)	.240	$p < .01$	Positive and significant
Intellectual Stimulation (IC)	.275	$p < .01$	Positive and significant
Contingent Reward (CR)	.333	$p < .01$	Moderate, positive and significant
MEA (Active Mgt-by-Exception)	.338	$p < .01$	Moderate, positive and significant
MEP (Passive Mgt-by-Exception)	.422	$p < .01$	Strong, positive and significant
Servant Leadership (SL)	.502	$p < .01$	Strongest positive and significant

The summary Table 5 highlights that Servant Leadership, Passive and Active Management-by-Exception, and Contingent Reward show significant positive correlations with organizational agility. In contrast, Idealized Behavior and Inspirational Motivation demonstrate weak or non-significant relationships, suggesting that structured, supportive, and accountability-driven leadership traits are more influential in enhancing agility within the Construction 4.0 context.

Multiple Regression Analysis

Table 6. Multiple regression analysis of leadership attributes on organizational agility

Predictor	B	T	β	P
IA	0.118	1.686	0.113	0.093
IB	-0.053	-1.249	-0.073	0.213
IM	0.005	0.097	0.005	0.923
IS	-0.157	-2.336	-0.179	0.02*
IC	0.059	0.852	0.062	0.395
CR	0.074	1.41	0.094	0.16
MEA	0.11	2.351	0.15	0.019*
MEP	0.15	3.424	0.205	0.001*
SL	0.369	6.272	0.366	0.001*

As shown in Table 6, the results investigated the impact of individual leadership attributes from transformational, transactional, and servant leadership styles on organizational agility (OA) in the context of Malaysia's Construction 4.0 (C4.0) transition. The multiple regression model was statistically significant, $F(14, 296) = 17.424$, $p < .001$, explaining 35% of the variance in OA ($R^2 = .350$, Adjusted $R^2 = .319$), indicating a moderate to strong effect size (Cohen & Lezak, 1977). Among the transformational leadership traits, Idealized Attribute (IA) showed a positive but non-significant effect on OA ($\beta = 0.118$, $p = .093$), while Idealized Behavior (IB) also did not significantly influence agility ($\beta = -0.053$, $p = .213$). Inspirational Motivation (IM) had no meaningful effect ($\beta = 0.005$, $p = .923$), and Intellectual Stimulation (IS) similarly failed to show statistical significance ($\beta = 0.059$, $p = .395$). Interestingly, Individualized Consideration (IC) demonstrated a significant negative impact on agility ($\beta = -0.179$, $p = .020$), suggesting that excessive individualized attention might hinder rapid group responsiveness, which is crucial in construction contexts requiring speed and coordination.

These findings led to the conclusion that H1a, H1b, H1d, and H1e were not supported, while H1c was supported but in an inverse direction than hypothesized. Although H1c hypothesized a positive relationship between Intellectual Stimulation (IS) and organizational agility, the results revealed a significant negative effect, indicating an inverse relationship. This unexpected finding may suggest that in the context of Malaysia's Construction 4.0 transition, overly intellectual or analytical leadership behaviors could slow down decision-making and responsiveness. When leaders focus heavily on encouraging critical thinking and idea generation, it might hinder rapid execution and adaptation key components of agility especially in project-driven environments where quick coordination and clarity are essential. Regarding transactional leadership variables, MEA was a significant positive predictor of agility ($\beta = 0.150$, $p = .019$), and MEP had an even stronger positive influence ($\beta = 0.205$, $p = .001$), thus supporting H2a and H2b. These results reinforce the idea that transactional clarity and structured performance expectations contribute positively to agility. Lastly, Servant Leadership (SL) was a strong and significant predictor of OA ($\beta = 0.366$, $p < .001$), confirming H3 and aligning with previous literature emphasizing the importance of humility, empowerment, and shared leadership in fostering adaptability and innovation (Liden et al., 2015; Sun & Shang, 2019). Overall, the findings reveal that in the Malaysian construction sector, servant and transactional leadership behaviors are more effective at promoting organizational agility compared to most individual transformational traits.

Hypotheses Results Summary

Table 7. Model 1: Individual leadership attributes

Hypothesis	Description	Result
H1a	Idealized Influence (IA) positively influences organizational agility.	Not supported
H1b	Inspirational Motivation (IM) positively influences organizational agility.	Not supported
H1c	Intellectual Stimulation (IS) positively influences organizational agility.	Not supported
H1d	Individualized Consideration (IC) positively influences organizational agility.	Not supported
H1e	Idealized Behavior (IB) positively influences organizational agility.	Supported
H2a	Contingent Reward (CR) positively influences organizational agility.	Not supported
H2b	Management by Exception–Active (MEA) positively influences organizational agility.	Supported
H2c	Management by Exception–Passive (MEP) positively influences organizational agility.	Supported
H3	Servant leadership (SL) positively influences organizational agility.	Supported

DISCUSSION

The study examined the relationship between specific digital leadership dimensions, drawn from TFL, TRL, and SL, and their impact on OA within the Malaysian construction sector under the pressures of Construction 4.0 (C4.0). Each leadership dimension was tested as a separate predictor, and the findings confirmed some hypotheses while challenging others. H1a–H1f posited that the dimensions of TFL, Idealized Influence (IA, IB), Inspirational Motivation (IM), Intellectual Stimulation

(IC), and Individualized Consideration (IS), would positively influence OA. However, the results demonstrated only partial support for these hypotheses. Specifically, H1e (IS → OA) was negatively significant (β = -0.157, p < .05), indicating that higher levels of individualized attention may hinder organizational responsiveness in fast-paced construction environments. This finding reflects the paradox that while attention to individual needs can boost morale, it may slow team-level reaction times, a key component of agility (Sharifi & Zhang, 2001). Other attributes like IA, IB, IM, and IC were statistically non-significant, suggesting that traditional transformational behaviors, although motivational, may not directly drive agility under technological and coordination-heavy demands (Sadeghi & Pihie, 2012; Setiawan et al., 2021).

Turning to Transactional Leadership, H2a (CR → OA), H2b (MEA → OA), and H2c (MEP → OA) were tested. The results supported H2b and H2c, where Management-by-Exception Active (MEA) (β = 0.110, p < .05) and Management-by-Exception Passive (MEP) (β = 0.150, p < .01) significantly predicted OA. These findings imply that structured oversight, either through proactive performance monitoring or post-error correction, contributes to agility by ensuring stability and quick recovery (Bass & Bass, 2008; Hilton et al., 2021). While MEA aligns with maintaining efficiency through error prevention, the significance of MEP is noteworthy, it highlights that even reactive strategies can support agility when they lead to organizational learning and swift response (Raziq et al., 2018). However, H2a, which predicted a positive effect of Contingent Reward (CR), was not significant, possibly indicating that rewards alone do not guarantee quick adaptability, especially when cultural or systemic resistance persists in Malaysian construction (Begić & Galić, 2021; Osunsanmi et al., 2018).

H3, which posited a positive relationship between Servant Leadership (SL) and OA, received strong support (β = 0.369, p < .001). This confirms the critical role of ethical, people-centered leadership in driving agility during technological disruption. SL's foundations in humility, empowerment, and shared decision-making appear particularly relevant for overcoming resistance and enhancing responsiveness in Malaysia's fragmented construction industry (Liden et al., 2015; Van Dierendonck & Patterson, 2015). The results align with prior research that emphasizes the role of SL in fostering trust, knowledge sharing, and team cohesion, which are all vital to successful digital transformation (Sun & Shang, 2019; Yoshida et al., 2014). In resource-constrained settings such as Malaysia's construction SMEs, where leadership capacity remains a barrier to change (CIDB, 2020; Shaharuddin et al., 2021), SL emerges as a leadership style with the most consistent and significant positive influence on agility. The study concluded that, H1a–d were not supported, H1e was negatively supported, H2b and H2c were positively supported, and H3 was strongly supported. These findings reinforce the idea that while visionary leadership (TFL) may have conceptual merit, agility in C4.0 contexts is more effectively fostered through structured governance (TRL) and servant-based leadership (SL), particularly in sectors like construction that require both operational control and collaborative work cultures. These insights suggest that leadership development initiatives and policy reforms within the Malaysian construction sector should move beyond traditional leadership models and instead focus on cultivating servant and transactional leadership capabilities. By embedding structured accountability, proactive oversight, and ethical, people-centered leadership into training programs and industry standards, policymakers and construction firms can better equip leaders to manage digital transformation, overcome resistance to change, and drive organizational agility in increasingly complex Construction 4.0 environments.

CONCLUSION AND IMPLICATIONS

This study investigated the impact of individual digital leadership attributes, drawn from TFL, TRL, and SL, on OA during Malaysia's transition to C4.0. The regression analysis showed that the individualized support dimension of TFL had a significant negative effect on agility, suggesting that personalized attention may inhibit rapid collective response in dynamic construction settings. In contrast, both Management-by-Exception (Passive and Active) from TRL and SL were found to be strong and significant positive predictors of OA. These findings indicate that in a structurally rigid yet digitally evolving sector like construction, service-oriented and performance-governed leadership traits may be more conducive to fostering agility than purely inspirational ones. This research provides context-specific empirical evidence for the role of diverse leadership dimensions in supporting responsiveness, flexibility, and adaptive capacity in digitally transforming environments.

The results of this study present several meaningful theoretical and practical implications. For practitioners particularly leaders and managers within construction firms the strong association of servant and transactional leadership with digital–performance fit highlights the growing importance of developing leadership approaches that go beyond traditional visionary roles. Leaders must actively cultivate accountability frameworks, clear task structures, and a people-centric mindset to enable agility and responsiveness in increasingly complex digital environments. This suggests that in the evolving landscape of Construction 4.0, where technology integration and process innovation are accelerating, transformational leadership styles alone may no longer be sufficient. Instead, practical leadership capabilities such as providing structured guidance, monitoring outcomes, and supporting employee development are essential to foster agility and ensure digital initiatives translate into tangible performance gains.

For policymakers and industry stakeholders, the findings underscore the need to reframe leadership narratives and digital transformation strategies across the construction sector. This involves embedding values such as shared decision-making, ethical leadership, and distributed authority into national policies, training programs, and organizational development frameworks. Such an approach can help build leaner, more adaptive construction ecosystems capable of thriving in fast-paced and digitally driven environments.

On a theoretical level, this study contributes meaningfully to the leadership literature by providing empirical validation of a multi-style leadership framework within the digital construction context. It emphasizes that no single leadership style is universally effective, and that a context-specific blend of servant, transactional, and transformational traits may be more effective in promoting agility. This multidimensional perspective expands existing leadership theories by illustrating how distinct but complementary leadership behaviors can support digital transformation goals and enhance organizational agility in a sector traditionally resistant to rapid change.

FUTURE RESEARCH DIRECTIONS

As a valuable extension of the current research, future studies are encouraged to broaden the sample scope by including construction firms from a wider range of grades, particularly those operating in East Malaysia, where firm profiles, infrastructure development levels, and digital readiness often differ significantly from those in Peninsular Malaysia. These regional differences may influence leadership dynamics and digital transformation outcomes, offering deeper insights into the variability of organizational agility across the country. This geographic and organizational diversification would help improve the external validity and generalizability of the findings, ensuring that the conclusions are representative of the broader Malaysian construction industry. Moreover, introducing mediating or moderating variables such as digital maturity, organizational culture, or innovation climate could deepen the understanding of how leadership styles influence organizational agility. These variables may help explain or strengthen the pathways between leadership behavior and agile performance, shedding light on the internal dynamics that support or hinder agile transformation.

In addition, conducting comparative studies across different industries such as manufacturing, logistics, and healthcare could offer valuable insights into how digital leadership and organizational agility interact in varying technological and operational environments. These sectors are suitable as they also face rapid digital transformation pressures and require agile leadership to navigate complexity and change or countries would offer valuable cross-contextual insights. Such analyses could reveal how industry-specific characteristics (e.g., regulatory environment, technological adoption) or cultural values (e.g., power distance, collectivism) shape leadership effectiveness and agility outcomes. This would provide a richer, more globally relevant understanding of the leadership–agility nexus.

Finally, adopting longitudinal research designs or mixed-methods approaches would significantly enhance the depth and reliability of future research. Longitudinal studies allow researchers to track changes and causal relationships over time, offering insights into how leadership influences agility during different phases of digital transformation. Meanwhile, integrating qualitative methods such as interviews, focus groups, or case studies with quantitative analysis can provide context-specific explanations and uncover hidden mechanisms that are not easily captured through surveys alone. Together, these methodological improvements would contribute to a more holistic and actionable body of knowledge on digital leadership and organizational agility in the construction sector.

REFERENCES

Abasilim, U. D., Gberevbie, D. E., & Osibanjo, A. (2018, October). Canonical analysis of perceived leadership styles and employees' commitment in Nigeria. In *Proceedings of the 14th European Conference on Management, Leadership and Governance, ECMLG,(October 2, 2018), Utrecht, the Netherlands* (pp. 317-322).

Ahammad, M. F., Glaister, K. W., & Gomes, E. (2020). Strategic agility and human resource management. *Human Resource Management Review, 30*(1), 100700. DOI: 10.1016/j.hrmr.2019.100700

Akkaya, B., Kayalidere, U. A. K., & Tabak, A. (2019). Endüstriyel alanda üretim yapan firmaların örgütsel çevikliği ile firma yöneticilerinin sahip olduğu dinamik yetenekler arasındaki ilişki: Manisa Organize Sanayi Bölgesi'nde (MOSB) faaliyet gösteren firmalar üzerine bir araştırma. *Yeni Nesil Girişimcilik ve Ekonomi, 1*(2), 19–54.

Al-Husseini, S., El Beltagi, I., & Moizer, J. (2021). Transformational leadership and innovation: The mediating role of knowledge sharing amongst higher education faculty. *International Journal of Leadership in Education, 24*(5), 670–693. DOI: 10.1080/13603124.2019.1588381

Alade, K., & Windapo, A. (2020). Leadership framework for sustainable housing production in South Africa. *African Journal of Housing and Sustainable Development, 1*(1), 109–119. DOI: 10.52968/28468654

Aldhaheri, R. T., & Ahmad, S. Z. (2023). Factors affecting organisations' supply chain agility and competitive capability. *Business Process Management Journal, 29*(2), 505–527. DOI: 10.1108/BPMJ-11-2022-0579

Alrowwad, A. A., Abualoush, S. H., & Masa'deh, R. E. (2020). Innovation and intellectual capital as intermediary variables among transformational leadership, transactional leadership, and organizational performance. *Journal of Management Development, 39*(2), 196–222. DOI: 10.1108/JMD-02-2019-0062

Amini, M., & Rahmani, A. (2023). How strategic agility affects the competitive capabilities of private banks. *International Journal of Basic and Applied Sciences, 10*, 8397–8406.

Attar, M., & Abdul-Kareem, A. (2020). The role of agile leadership in organisational agility. In Attar, M. (Ed.), *Agile business leadership methods for Industry 4.0* (pp. 171–191). Emerald Publishing Limited., DOI: 10.1108/978-1-80043-380-920201011

Avolio, B. J., & Bass, B. M. (2004). *Multifactor leadership questionnaire™ manual.* Mind Garden, Inc.

Avolio, B. J., Kahai, S. S., & Dodge, G. E. (2000). E-leadership: Implications for theory, research, and practice. *The Leadership Quarterly, 11*(4), 615–668. DOI: 10.1016/S1048-9843(00)00062-X

Bamgbade, J. A., Kamaruddeen, A. M., Nawi, M. N. M., Adeleke, A. Q., Salimon, M. G., & Ajibike, W. A. (2019). Analysis of some factors driving ecological sustainability in construction firms. *Journal of Cleaner Production, 208*, 1537–1545. DOI: 10.1016/j.jclepro.2018.10.229

Bass, B. M. (1999). Two decades of research and development in transformational leadership. *European Journal of Work and Organizational Psychology, 8*(1), 9–32. DOI: 10.1080/135943299398410

Bass, B. M., & Bass, R. (2008). *The Bass handbook of leadership: Theory, research, and managerial applications* (4th ed.). Free Press.

Begić, H., & Galić, M. (2021). A Systematic Review of Construction 4.0 in the Context of the BIM 4.0 Premise. *Buildings (Basel, Switzerland), 11*(8), 337. DOI: 10.3390/buildings11080337

Begum, S., Ashfaq, M., Xia, E., & Awan, U. (2022). Does green transformational leadership lead to green innovation? The role of green thinking and creative process engagement. *Business Strategy and the Environment, 31*(1), 580–597. DOI: 10.1002/bse.2911

Benchea, L., & Ilie, A. G. (2023). Preparing for a New World of Work: Leadership Styles Reconfigured in the Digital Age. *European Journal of Interdisciplinary Studies, 15*(1), 135–143. DOI: 10.24818/ejis.2023.10

Bono, J. E., & McNamara, G. (2011). Publishing in AMJ—Part 2: Research design. *Academy of Management Journal, 54*(4), 657–660. DOI: 10.5465/amj.2011.64869103

Brynjolfsson, E., Rock, D., & Syverson, C. (2018). Artificial intelligence and the modern productivity paradox: A clash of expectations and statistics. In *The economics of artificial intelligence: An agenda* (pp. 23–57). University of Chicago Press.

Bundtzen, H., & Hinrichs, G. (2021). The link between organizational agility and VUCA: An agile assessment model. *Journal of Business Research, 100*, 116–125. DOI: 10.1016/j.jbusres.2021.03.053

Cable, D. (2018). Why people lose motivation—And what managers can do to help. *Harvard Business Review, 3*(1). https://hbr.org/2018/03/why-people-lose-motivation-and-what-managers-can-do-to-help

CIDB. (2020). *Construction 4.0 Strategic Plan (2021-2025).* CIDB.

Cimini, C., Boffelli, A., Lagorio, A., Kalchschmidt, M., & Pinto, R. (2020). How do Industry 4.0 technologies influence organisational change? An empirical analysis of Italian SMEs. *Journal of Manufacturing Technology Management, 32*(3), 695–721. Advance online publication. DOI: 10.1108/JMTM-04-2019-0135

Cohen, S., & Lezak, A. (1977). Noise and inattentiveness to social cues. *Environment and Behavior, 9*(4), 559–572. DOI: 10.1177/001391657794007

Cortellazzo, L., Bruni, E., & Zampieri, R. (2019). The role of leadership in a digitalized world: A review. *Frontiers in Psychology, 10*, 1938. DOI: 10.3389/fpsyg.2019.01938

Craveiroa, F., Duartec, J. P., Bartoloa, H., & Bartolod, P. J. (2019). Additive manufacturing as an enabling technology for digital construction: A perspective on Construction 4.0. *Sustainable Development (Bradford), 4*(6), 220–232. DOI: 10.1002/sd.1954

D'Aveni, R. A., Dagnino, G. B., & Smith, K. G. (2010). The age of temporary advantage. *Strategic Management Journal, 31*(13), 1371–1385. DOI: 10.1002/smj.897

Dallasega, P., Rauch, E., & Linder, C. (2018). Industry 4.0 as an enabler of proximity for construction supply chains: A systematic literature review. *Computers in Industry, 99*, 205–225. DOI: 10.1016/j.compind.2018.03.039

De Smet, A., Lurie, M., & St George, A. (2018). Leading agile transformation: The new capabilities leaders need to build 21st-century organizations. *McKinsey & Company*, 1–27. https://www.mckinsey.com/industries/organization/our-insights/leading-agile-transformation

Doğan, O., & Baloğlu, N. (2018). Organizational agency and its reflections in some educational institutions. In *13th International Educational Administration Congress: The 13th International Congress on Educational Administration.*

Cunha, M. P., Gomes, E., Mellahi, K., Miner, A. S., & Rego, A. (2020). Strategic agility through improvisational capabilities: Implications for a paradox-sensitive HRM. Human Resource Management Review, 30(1), 100695. doi:10.1016/j.hrmr.2019.100695

El Jazzar, M., Schranz, C., Urban, H., & Nassereddine, H. (2021). Integrating Construction 4.0 technologies: A four-layer implementation plan. *Frontiers in Built Environment, 144*, 671408. Advance online publication. DOI: 10.3389/fbuil.2021.671408

El Nsour, J. A. (2021). Investigating the impact of organizational agility on the competitive advantage. *Journal of Governance and Regulation, 10*(1).

Elnagar, S., Weistroffer, H., & Thomas, M. (2019). Agile requirement engineering maturity framework for Industry 4.0. In *Information Systems: 15th European, Mediterranean, and Middle Eastern Conference, EMCIS 2018, Limassol, Cyprus, October 4–5, 2018, Proceedings 15* (pp. 405–418). Springer International Publishing. https://doi.org/DOI: 10.1007/978-3-030-18097-1_33

Fawzy, R., & Saad, D. M. (2023). The relationship between agility drivers, agility capabilities, and organizational sustainability. *Journal of Business and Management Sciences, 11*, 101–114. DOI: 10.11648/j.jbms.2023 1104.11

Geleti, D. (2022). Leadership styles for agricultural research and development organizations: Towards enabling adaptive spaces for enhanced organizational agility. *International Journal of Leadership in Education, 25*(2), 189–208. DOI: 10.1080/13603124.2020.1794607

Guzmán, V. E., Muschard, B., Gerolamo, M., Kohl, H., & Rozenfeld, H. (2020). Characteristics and skills of leadership in the context of Industry 4.0. *Procedia Manufacturing, 43*, 543–550. DOI: 10.1016/j.promfg.2020.02.167

Hair, J. F.Jr, Sarstedt, M., Hopkins, L., & Kuppelwieser, V. G. (2014). Partial least squares structural equation modeling (PLS-SEM): An emerging tool in business research. *European Business Review, 26*(2), 106–121. DOI: 10.1108/EBR-10-2013-0128

Hambrick, D. C., & Mason, P. A. (1984). Upper echelons: The organization as a reflection of its top managers. *Academy of Management Review, 9*(2), 193–206. DOI: 10.2307/258434

Hater, J. J., & Bass, B. M. (1988). Superiors' evaluations and subordinates' perceptions of transformational and transactional leadership. *The Journal of Applied Psychology, 73*(4), 695–702. DOI: 10.1037/0021-9010.73.4.695

Hilton, S. K., Arkorful, H., & Martins, A. (2021). Democratic leadership and organizational performance: The moderating effect of contingent reward. *Management Research Review, 44*(7), 1042–1058. DOI: 10.1108/MRR-04-2020-0237

Holst, G. M. (2021). *Transactional, instrumental and transformational leadership: What is more effective for an Industry 4.0 transformation?* (Master's thesis, University of Twente). https://doi.org/DOI: 10.1007/978-3-030-36603-0

Hossain, M. A., & Nadeem, A. (2019, May). Towards digitizing the construction industry: State of the art of construction 4.0. In *Proceedings of the ISEC* (Vol. 10, pp. 1–6). https://doi.org/DOI: 10.1109/ISEC.2019.0013

Jaafar, M., Mokhtar Azizi, N. S., Mohamed Ghazali, F. E., Mohd Zain, M. Z., Mat Kilau, N., & Ibrahim, F. S. (2025). Technology usage, challenges and strategies for Construction 4.0 from the perspective of Malaysian contractors. *Journal of Facilities Management*. Advance online publication. DOI: 10.1108/JFM-04-2024-0055

Jaafar, M., Mokhtar Azizi, N. S., Mohamed Ghazali, F. E., Mohd Zain, M. Z., Mat Kilau, N., & Ibrahim, F. S. (2025). Technology usage, challenges and strategies for Construction 4.0 from the perspective of Malaysian contractors. *Journal of Facilities Management*. Advance online publication. DOI: 10.1108/JFM-04-2024-0055

Jamrog, J., Vickers, M., & Bear, D. (2006). Building and sustaining a culture that supports innovation. *People and Strategy*, *29*(3), 9–19. DOI: 10.1108/17527568200600003

Javaid, M., Haleem, A., & Suman, R. (2022). Major advancements of industry 4.0 to overcome challenges in manufacturing during the COVID-19 pandemic. *Cyber-Physical Systems: Solutions to Pandemic Challenges*, 157–182. https://doi.org/DOI: 10.1016/b978-0-12-820218-9.00010-7

Johnson-Kanda, I., & Yawson, R. M. (2018, May). Complex adaptive leadership for organization and human development. In *Proceedings of the 55th Annual Eastern Academy of Management Conference*, Providence, RI.

Karneli, O. (2023). The role of adhocratic leadership in facing the changing business environment. [ADMAN]. *Journal of Contemporary Administration and Management*, *1*(2), 77–83. DOI: 10.61100/adman.v1i2.26

Kurniawan, R., & Hamsal, I. M. (2019). Achieving decision-making quality and organizational agility in innovation portfolio management in Telecommunication 4.0. *International Journal of Innovation, Creativity, and Change*, *8*, 332–356.

Lee, C. K., Chen, M. S., Zainudin, N. M., Fauzi, M. A., & Toh, T. C. (2022). Transformation of industrial revolution 4.0 in the construction industry: Understanding drivers & barriers with DEMATEL algorithm. *International Journal of Information Management*, *16*(1), 31–43. DOI: 10.1016/ j.ijim.2022.03.002

Liden, R. C., Wayne, S. J., Meuser, J. D., Hu, J., Wu, J., & Liao, C. (2015). Servant leadership: Validation of a short form of the SL-28. *The Leadership Quarterly, 26*(2), 254–269. DOI: 10.1016/j.leaqua.2014.12.002

Luthra, S., & Mangla, S. K. (2018). Evaluating challenges to Industry 4.0 initiatives for supply chain sustainability in emerging economies. *Process Safety and Environmental Protection, 117*, 168–179. https://doi.org/. 2018.04.018DOI: 10.1016/j.psep

Mason, A. J. (2010). *Inside the black box: Investigating agility as a dynamic capability for sustaining a competitive advantage within consulting firms* [Doctoral dissertation, Capella University].

Mendoza Solis, M., García Alcaraz, J. L., Avelar Sosa, L., & Manotas Duque, D. F. (2023). The role of transactional leadership in the social performance of the maquiladora industry. *Revista Brasileira de Gestão de Negócios, 25*(2), 215–233. DOI: 10.7819/rbgn.v25i2.4219

Meyer, P. (2016). *The agility shift: Creating agile and effective leaders, teams, and organizations*. Routledge. DOI: 10.4324/9781315230559

Mukherjee, J., & Janssen, M. C. (2023). *Recreating the power grid: Navigating technological and organizational changes*. Taylor & Francis.

Nafei, W. A. (2016). Organizational agility: The key to organizational success. *International Journal of Business and Management, 11*(5), 296–309. DOI: 10.5539/ijbm.v11n5p296

Nejatian, M., & Zarei, M. H. (2013). Moving towards organizational agility: Are we improving in the right direction? *Global Journal of Flexible Systems Managment, 14*(4), 241–253. DOI: 10.1007/s40171-013-0048-3

Nwanzu, C. L., & Babalola, S. S. (2019). Examining psychological capital of optimism, self-efficacy and self-monitoring as predictors of attitude towards organizational change. *International Journal of Engineering Business Management, 11*, 1847979019827149. DOI: 10.1177/1847979019827149

Oberer, B., & Erkollar, A. (2018). Leadership 4.0: Digital leaders in the age of Industry 4.0. *International Journal of Organizational Leadership, 7*(4), 404–412. DOI: 10.33844/ijol.2018.60332

Ogolla, J. A. (2020). *Transformational leadership, strategic agility and performance of state corporations in Kenya* (Doctoral dissertation, Kenya Methodist University).

Ononiwu, M. I., Onwuzulike, O. C., & Shitu, K. (2024). The role of digital business transformation in enhancing organizational agility. *World Journal of Advanced Research and Reviews, 23*(3), 285–308. https://doi.org/. 2024.23.3.0367DOI: 10.30574/wjarr

Osunsanmi, T., Aigbavboa, C., & Oke, A. (2018). Construction 4.0: The future of the construction industry in South Africa. *World Academy of Science, Engineering and Technology, Open Science Index 135, International Journal of Civil and Environmental Engineering, 12*(3), 206–212. https://doi.org/. 1132164.DOI: 10.5281/zenodo

Raziq, M. M., Borini, F. M., Malik, O. F., Ahmad, M., & Shabaz, M. (2018). Leadership styles, goal clarity, and project success: Evidence from project-based organizations in Pakistan. *Leadership and Organization Development Journal, 39*(2), 309–323. DOI: 10.1108/LODJ-07-2017-0212

Rehman, S., Shareef, A., Mahmood, A., & Ishaque, A. (2012). Perceived leadership styles and organizational commitment. *Interdisciplinary Journal of Contemporary Research in Business, 4*, 616–626.

Sadeghi, A., & Pihie, Z. A. L. (2012). Transformational leadership and its predictive effects on leadership effectiveness. *International Journal of Business and Social Science, 3*(7), 81–88. 10.1.1.466.1733

Samson, A. T., & Ilesanmi, O. A. (2019). The relationship between transactional leadership, transformational leadership, and performance of SMEs in Nigeria. *Noble International Journal of Business and Management Research, 3*(4), 73–85.

Scepanovic, S. (2019). The Fourth Industrial Revolution and education. *8th Mediterranean Conference on Embedded Computing (MECO)*, IEEE, 1–4. https://doi.org/DOI: 10.1109/MECO.2019.8802343

Schumacher, A., Erol, S., & Sihn, W. (2016). A maturity model for assessing Industry 4.0 readiness and maturity of manufacturing enterprises. *Procedia CIRP, 52*, 161–166. DOI: 10.1016/j.procir.2016.07.040

Setiawan, R., Eliyana, A., Suryani, T., & Pratama, A. (2021). *The effect of transformational leadership on organizational innovation through employee creativity and internal social capital in the pandemic time of Covid-19* (Doctoral dissertation, Petra Christian University).

Shafer, R. A. (1997). Creating organizational agility: The human resource dimension. *Human Resource Management, 36*(1), 1–11. https://doi.org/. 3930360102DOI: 10.1002/hrm

Shaharuddin, A. B., Aminudin, E., Zakaria, R., Abidin, N. I., & Lau, S. E. N. (2021). Adoption of construction Industry 4.0 among small and medium-sized contractors in Malaysia. *AIP Conference Proceedings, 2428*, 060001. Advance online publication. DOI: 10.1063/5.0071094

Sharifi, H., & Zhang, Z. (2001). Agile manufacturing in practice—Application of a methodology. *International Journal of Operations & Production Management, 21*(5/6), 772–794. DOI: 10.1108/01443570110390462

Stehn, L., & Hook, M. (2008). Lean principles in industrialized housing production: The need for a cultural change. *Lean Construction Journal*, 20–33. ISSN 1555-1369, E-ISSN 1555-1369.

Sun, P., & Shang, S. (2019). Personality traits and personal values of servant leaders. *Leadership and Organization Development Journal, 40*(2), 177–192. DOI: 10.1108/LODJ-11-2018-0406

Taseer, M. I., & Ahmed, A. (2022). The most effective leadership style in pursuit of resilient supply chain: Sequential mediation of flexibility and agile supply chain. [PJCSS]. *Pakistan Journal of Commerce and Social Sciences, 16*(3), 387–423. DOI: 10.64534/Commer.2022.105

Tsiga, Z. D., Emes, M., & Smith, A. (2016). Critical success factors for the construction industry. *PM World Journal, 5*(8), 1–12.

Uğural, M. N., Giritli, H., & Urbański, M. (2020). Determinants of the turnover intention of construction professionals: A mediation analysis. *Sustainability (Basel), 12*(3), 954. DOI: 10.3390/su12030954

Uğurlu, Ö. Y., Çolakoğlu, E., & Öztosun, E. (2019). The effect of strategic agility on firm performance: A research in manufacturing enterprises. *Business and People Magazine, 6*(1), 93–106.

Van Dierendonck, D., & Patterson, K. (2015). Compassionate love as a cornerstone of servant leadership: An integration of previous theorizing and research. *Journal of Business Ethics, 128*(1), 119–131. DOI: 10.1007/s10551-014-2085-z

Van Dierendonck, D., & Rook, L. (2010). Enhancing innovation and creativity through servant leadership. In *Servant leadership: Developments in theory and research* (pp. 155–165). Palgrave Macmillan UK. DOI: 10.1057/9780230299184_13

Walter, A. T. (2021). Organizational agility: Ill-defined and somewhat confusing? A systematic literature review and conceptualization. *Management Review Quarterly, 71*(2), 343–391. DOI: 10.1007/s11301-020-00186-6

Xu, M., David, J. M., & Kim, S. H. (2018). The fourth industrial revolution: Opportunities and challenges. *International Journal of Financial Research*, *9*(2), 90–95. DOI: 10.5430/ijfr.v9n2p90

Yoshida, D. T., Sendjaya, S., Hirst, G., & Cooper, B. (2014). Does servant leadership foster creativity and innovation? A multi-level mediation study of identification and prototypicality. *Journal of Business Research*, *67*(7), 1395–1404. DOI: 10.1016/j.jbusres.2013.08.013

Zhang, Z., & Sharifi, H. (2000). A methodology for achieving agility in manufacturing organizations. *International Journal of Operations & Production Management*, *20*(4), 496–513. DOI: 10.1108/01443570010314818

Zhen, J., Cao, C., Qiu, H., & Xie, Z. (2021). Impact of organizational inertia on organizational agility: The role of IT ambidexterity. *Information Technology and Management*, *22*(1), 53–65. DOI: 10.1007/s10799-021-00324-w

Zhou, K., Liu, T., & Zhou, L. (2015, August). Industry 4.0: Towards future industrial opportunities and challenges. In *2015 12th International Conference on Fuzzy Systems and Knowledge Discovery (FSKD)* (pp. 2147–2152). IEEE. https://doi.org/ DOI: 10.1109/FSKD.2015.7382435

Chapter 9
Strategic Evolution of Islamic Marketing and Consumer Behavior in Takaful and Bancassurance:
A Business Transformation Approach in Pakistan

Muhammad Nawaz Iqbal
https://orcid.org/0009-0006-4266-4720
Sir Syed University of Engineering and Technology, Pakistan

Muhammad Tahir Jan
https://orcid.org/0000-0001-5680-8496
International Islamic University, Malaysia

ABSTRACT

Strategic evolution of Islamic marketing in Takaful and Bancassurance is restructuring the financial landscape in Pakistan, where Shariah-Compliant Financial Products are coming. This chapter studies the influence of Islamic values, digital narratives, and ethical considerations on consumer behavior, necessitating a transforming business approach. It discusses the place of data-driven strategies, artificial intelligence and social media marketing for Takaful and Bancassurance in creating trust and engagement with consumers while highlighting the regulatory challenges, competitive pressures and technological disruptions that batter the sector on the way toward enacting insight for businesses to progress in their marketing

DOI: 10.4018/979-8-3373-2655-9.ch009

strategy. Aligning Islamic financial principles to digital innovation as this chapter does provides the sustainable roadmap for financial institutions to reach into wider horizons, develop trust among consumers, and build resilient business models under this dynamic Islamic finance industry in Pakistan.

INTRODUCTION

Digital transformation and innovations are increasing in business, Islamic marketing and consumer behavior as well. The technological advancements, the regulatory changes and the changing consumer expectations have led to a paradigm shift of the Takaful and Bancassurance sectors in Pakistan. This chapter examines the strategic evolution of Islamic marketing and consumer behavior within these financial sectors, through focusing on the digitalization, ethical marketing principle and Shariah compliance in reshaping the landscape. This study, integrating business transformation approach, explores how financial houses are transforming their business in order to meet the needs of consumers and still practice Islamic finical ethics.

Evolution in Islamic marketing and behaviors to consumer in Takaful and Bancassurance had been affected by the advancement of the digital technology and business strategies. The Islamic financial sector has relied traditionally on conventional marketing techniques and in person relationship with customers to attract and maintain customers. However, with the advancement of technology in digital platforms, there has been a shift of businesses' strategy to remain relevant and operating within the boundaries of Shariah compliance. Having artificial intelligence, big data analytics and social media integrated together, have allowed firms to comprehend consumers' preferences and make them satisfied by personalizing the offering or furnishing overall integration with customers. This has not only increased the operational efficiency of Islamic financial services but has also guaranteed consumer trust.

The other investment will be shared risk to develop the Takaful industry for it to flourish and offer necessary and alternative investments. The introduction of Takaful products in particular countries will be successful if knowledge of country characteristics and its environment are present. Indonesia is a country that is primarily Muslim, which is a potential market of Takaful. Nevertheless, the market will have to overcome challenges when marketing Takaful products (Deloitte, 2013; Redhika & Mahalli, 2014; Ichsan, 2015). For example, one piece of offensive innovation is how it should innovate. The creation of new-products, market, technology, or organization combinations is defined as innovation by Boer and During (2001). According to Haron and Nursofiza (2008), innovation can be produced through renewal of the organizational structure or the market as well as the process and renewal in general.

Bancassurance has expanded in Islamic banking and continues to offer financial services that comply with Sharia law. According to Bancassurance in Islamic bank, Islamic banks operate with other insurance enterprise to provide Sharia compliance insurance services (Guemmaz, 2023). Bancassurance is not just distribution system but also a mechanism, an operational aspect, and a cultural aspect for its implementation. Bank Indonesia further reported that Bancassurance is a bank product that provides insurance commodities (Bagasworo & Simatupang, 2022). Due to this, banks would now be able to collect possible fees with the objective of raising customers' loyalty and reducing financial risk through enhanced overall selling profitability.

In the Bancassurance arrangements, they are regarded as mere marketing arm of Islamic insurance companies for the promotion of their Bancassurance products. Therefore, the relationship between banks and insurance companies under which the banks are the agents and the insurance companies are the principal is legally prescribed by an agency agreement by which the banks act on the receipt of an action by the insurance companies when dealing with their customers (Shomad, 2025).

There is an increasing need from the demand for Takaful and Bancassurance products in Pakistan as people are more aware about Islamic financial principles as well as the demand for the ethics and make them habitual of it. These days, the consumers want to avoid products which do not correspond to their religious beliefs, and at the same time ensure financial safety. The changing consumer behavior has motivated financial institutes to reinvent their marketing via digital content that resonates with Islamic values. From a more traditional product centered focus to more consumer centered trend, this digital marketing evolution in this industry made such an impact.

However, while these things are made in advanced, the challenges remain such as regulatory compliance, digital accessibility, as well as maintaining the ethical standards of marketing strategy. With this, a strategic balance has been ensured between upholding Shariah guidelines for digital marketing strategies and staying competitive in a dynamic financial landscape. Moreover, many aspects of future Islamic marketing and consumer behavior in terms of Pakistan's Takaful and Bancassurance sector is due in no major ways to the role of government policies, financial literacy initiatives, as well as technological innovation. Addressing these challenges and harnessing digital transformation can lead businesses to promote sustainable growth within the core values of Islamic finance.

Islamic marketing theory builds on Shariah insights and separates itself from common marketing practices by focusing on fairness, concern for society and adding value according to Islam. Whereas in traditional marketing the main goal is profit, Islamic marketing underlines maslahah (Public interest) and adl (Justice) to secure both the welfare of individuals and society. According to recent studies, Islamic marketing strategies are affecting business strategies in predominantly Muslim areas, so that customers are loyal for both the quality and the religion of the brand.

The field of Islamic marketing has concentrated on aligning Islamic beliefs with modern approaches, mainly in halal branding, Islamic finance and digital commercial activities. Researchers have pointed out that how people act as consumers in Muslim communities is especially shaped by religiosity, trust and how they follow Islamic rules (Wilson & Liu, 2011). Applying halal certification and religious marketing approaches has been helpful in building a strong brand and reaching the market among Muslims. More and more studies are now supporting the recognition of Islamic marketing as an individual area of study and suggesting that scholars adapt their ways of measuring its outcomes in various sectors (Wilson & Liu, 2011).

THE FOUNDATIONS OF ISLAMIC MARKETING IN FINANCIAL SERVICES

Ethical Principles and Shariah Compliance

Islamic marketing is based on ethical principles as given by Shariah law of transparency, fairness and trust. These principles make the difference between conventional and Takaful and Islamic Bancassurance models as they are in place in financial services. Based on this, the marketing strategy is founded on the prohibition of riba (interest), gharar (excessive uncertainty) and maysir (gambling), which make the financial products Islamic.

In recent years, there has been a lot of inquiries on the ethical consumerism phenomenon due to shoppers increasing purchase weight on their purchases in the area of the ethics—as well as social and environmental implications (Kailash et al., 2023). Among researchers and marketers, as well as companies, a new strategy has been created as response to this changing pattern of consumer behavior, a conscientious buyer (Kailash et al., 2023).

The foundation of Islamic marketing is based on ethics, Shariah compliance, to make certain that all business undertakings abide by the Islamic teachings and moral ethics. Unlike the conventional marketing which pays more attention to the maximization of profit, Islamic marketing is more concerned about the fairness, transparency and social responsibility. Thus, in the framework of this business, businesses must be up to integrity in their marketing messages, no deceptive advertising, no false claims. Islamic Finance ethical marketing especially in Takaful and Bancassurance necessitates that organizations supply factual information to be sure that its consumers value properly the comprehension of product terms, benefits and conditions before making purchase order decisions.

Islamic Financial Institutions (IFIs) have found it necessary to appoint an able Shariah officer who will perform all Shariah control functions such as Shariah review, Shariah audit, and Shariah risk management to enable for effective and efficient Shariah compliance management. Although Shariah review is an observational activity to be borne in mind when discussing Shariah compliance pertaining to the activities and operations, Shariah auditing is an independent evaluation of the degree of Shariah compliance on an IFI's business performance (Kasim et al., 2013; Noor Aimi et al., 2019).

Islamic marketing is shariah compliant, and this should be adhered to by Islamic marketing whereby it prohibits riba (interest), gharar (excessive uncertainty) and maysir (gambling). As a result, everything to do with transactions and promotional strategy is free from any exploitative elements which can hurt consumers. The system within Takaful and Bancassurance requires policies to be written in terms of mutual cooperation and sharing rather than with respect to the mechanism of transferring risk, as in conventional insurance. Therefore, Islamic marketing strategies are used to keep consumers long-term trust through this ethical aspect, emphasize the moral and religious foundation of the financial products and matching the promotional campaigns with Islamic values.

In addition, Social Responsibility and building welfare of the society are some of the critical components of ethical Islamic Marketing. The broader impact of the business' marketing practice will be also taken into consideration; things like promoting financial literacy, responsible consumption and economic empowerment. When it comes to digital marketing channels including social media and AI based advertising, you need to be ethical and messages should not target any vulnerability of consumers for generating higher results and also create unrealistic expectations. For this purpose, companies must coordinate with Islamic scholars and Shariah boards to ensure that their marketing campaigns and financial products bound with Islamic principles. This will encourage the credibility and authenticity of the Muslim consumers.

For ethically orientated marketing to be effective on the Islamic finance industry, firms must develop a governance frame work to which continuously monitors adherence to Shariah laws. This entails frequent audits, ethical reviews of marketing campaign, and active mechanisms to receive feedback from the readers. Also, there is a need of cooperation between regulatory bodies and Islamic financial institution, to set up sound guidelines against unethical practices and consumer rights. To make this venture successful, these ethical principles must be maintained along with Shariah compliance which means Islamic marketing can create a sustainable financial ecosystem that serves the business interest according to the core principles of Islam such as fairness, transparency and social welfare.

The Evolution of Consumer Trust and Brand Loyalty

The building upon pillar of Islamic marketing is the trust of consumer. From time to time, financial institutions in Pakistan apply transparency and ethical branding to enhance relationships with their consumers. Integration of such customer centric approaches of financial literacy programs and running community engagement helps build brand loyalty as the Takaful and Islamic Bancassurance are a viable alternatives to conventional insurance and banking solutions.

Islamic marketing in Pakistan has seen a lot of change in trust and loyalty of consumers as seen in the ethical, business practices, Shariah compliant products and digital engagement strategies. In Islamic finance, trust is a fundamental principal base for ensuring transparency and honesty and fairness, that will help attract and retain customers. Islamic marketing is different from conventional marketing, for example in the area of sales tactics, which often speaks of aggressive moves rather than of ethical responsibility in the development and maintenance of long term relationship. It is for this reason that businesses that follow Shariah compliant principles have acquired a great trust of the immediate consumer segment in Pakistan, where a large section of the population prefers Shariah compliant financial solutions. Particularly, Takaful and Bancassurance providers have used ethical advertising, fair pricing and community oriented initiatives to present them as reliable institutions.

The relationship of the brand personality traits of Islamic brands with brand trust positively in the Islamic banking sector is studied. Yet, they further strengthen e-word-of-mouth by mediation of brand love (Yasin et al., 2024). Modern online retailing has been swift and so it has been difficult to reach out to and attract its shoppers' eye and cut through the marketing noise to influence their purchase intention (Bebber et al., 2017; Willems et al., 2017). Issues found in online retailing, in particular by social media, are discussed and among these, trust is the area of research. In the virtual social mediating environment, the marketers are facing a bitter challenge with consumers' belief in them, as they do not personally come in contact with consumers or there is a lot of feeding by users (PWC, 2018; Yahia et al., 2018).

Islamic values are consistently adhered to and digital transformation is executed effectively in the Islamic finance sector in order to strengthen brand loyalty. As social media and AI based marketing strategy is growing, Islamic financial institutions in Pakistan have evolved by personalizing consumer interactions with loyalty building. Educational content, Islamic scholar collaborations and open communication about offering products are the ways companies interact with their audience. Moreover, the rise of new technology such as blockchain for secure transactions and AI based customer support makes the service more reliable, proving their belief in the service. Brands now have the opportunity to synch faith based marketing with digital innovation and level up crests in catering to the changing taste buds of digital consumers while keeping to the ethics of Islamic marketing.

By increasing the data availability, the paradox (Hartmann et al., 2016; Kiel et al., 2017; Sestino et al., 2020; Sorescu, 2017) is offered in proposing the changes that bring data driven business models. The more service domains leverage of the value placed on embedded data, the greater is the leverage for business model innovation (Ostrom et al., 2015). For instance, the indiscriminate use of data of the users gives it a privacy concern.

Despite these advances, trust and loyalty in the competitive Islamic finance landscape are remained to be challenges. Long term engagement suffers because one suffers from inconsistent customer experiences, lack of regulatory clarity, and low consumer awareness on Takaful and Bancassurance. Islamic financial institutions in Pakistan, to address these problems, need to enrich the financial literacy programs, make the services more efficient, and better the regulation compliance mechanisms. Similarly, corporate social responsibility initiatives that are aligned to Islamic values in creating trust such as charitable giving (Zakat), welfare programs for the society and ethical investment can be an additional way used to reinforce trust. This necessitates continuous evolution and prioritizing of consumer-centric approaches by businesses to have deep rooted loyalty and become the leaders of the Islamic financial sector.

The Role of Islamic Scholars in Marketing Communications

Islamic scholars are important in formulating marketing strategies because marketing practices would receive religious endorsements and be approved for being authentic. Their involvement in promotional campaigns gives credibility to Takaful and Bancassurance offerings for the Shariah compliance, and they also assure consumers that these products are Shariah compliant. More and more, scholars content themselves working with financiers to produce consumer friendly material that is in keeping with Islamic teachings.

Islamic scholars have a preliminary play for marketing communication and marketing control in the Islamic finance and Takaful sector so that the promotional strategies are in accordance with Shariah principles. Endorsement by their name adds credibility of the financial products and increasing the confidence and trust of the consumer rather. The involvement of scholars in the marketing campaigns in Pakistan where religious values play a vital role in buying decisions, makes existence authentic and reassuring. Islamic finance companies, on the other hand, often team up with known scholars in determining whether their products are Shariah complaint; soliciting religious opinions on fiscal issues. Moreover, it further arranges the legitimacy of the marketing of Shariah compliant resolution and it also educates the consumers on the benefits and principles of Shariah compliant financial solutions.

Underlying all this is marketing communication which provide a basis for information exchange, molding of consumer behavior, and the driving force for economic development. In the Islamic economy, the message of the marketing communication must be in accordance with Islamic values and ethics and therefore not be falsified, disrespectful and used to take advantage of customers. So, brands needs effective marketing communication strategies to increase in brand awareness, model consumers' perceptions, and influence it helps in making buying decisions that assist in the development and competitiveness of business (AlNashmi & Almamary, 2017). As for Islamic banks, it is crucial that all marketing ethics are followed; as it relates to building brand credibility and satisfy customer. Aligning marketing strategy to Islamic values will increase awareness and intention of customers towards Islamic financial products and services. However, the customer loyalty can only be built with customer satisfaction and gaining customer loyalty can influence on the performance of Islamic banks (Nadham & Nahid, 2015).

Apart from certification, Islamic scholars also take part in the consumer engagement with digital platforms, presentation of educational content, and advisory roles. Social media, television programs and webinars are used by many scholars in order to discuss and clear misconceptions while promoting Islamic financial products' practice. In Pakistan, where digital adoption is massively growing, scholars can be used as brand ambassadors in marketing campaigns for outreach and change perceptions of consumers. Differentiating financial institutions from their competitors in a competitive market can be achieved by incorporating scholar led awareness programs and advisory panels into marketing strategy and matching message with religious and financial considerations.

Despite that, however, challenges arise with the integration of scholars in marketing communications, as for example, variations in religious interpretations and suspicion on behalf of consumers regarding commercial affinities. To preserve credibility, companies will have to be transparent about how they pursue scholar collaborations to avoid the perception of biased endorsements. Independent Shariah boards and openness in the discussions on Islamic finance are ways of addressing these concerns. Islamic financial institutions in Pakistan can develop an ethical and trust based consumer base by fostering genuine scholar businesses involvement in product development and marketing.

Digital Platforms in Islamic Marketing

The rise of the digital platform has changed Islamic marketing in the financial sector of Pakistan. Consumer's engagement as well as service accessibility is enabled by social media, mobile apps and digital banking solutions. Since video content marketing campaigns, interactive webinars and AI powered chatbots are now a staple in all type of marketing, they're essential to deliver financial products in an ethical and compliant way to the consumers.

The use of the Islamic digital platforms has become the cornerstone of Islamic marketing allowing for businesses to advertise their products and services to customers, far and wide, while staying committed to Shariah principles. Considering the rise of platforms such as e-commerce, social media and fintech tools, Islamic financial institutions as well as Takaful providers in Pakistan are using the power of digital to advertise their products in a clean and honest manner. The Islamic financial services are available to the consumer through websites, mobile apps, and AI driven chatbots which offer instant guidance about Shariah compliant investment and insurance. In addition, these platforms are used to do digital transactions and automated advisory services to maintain convenience, while maintaining faith's integrity.

At present, both Takaful and insurance companies are focusing on the technology in the way their products and services function. Statista (2020) has also shown that such companies worldwide also made a huge contribution by investing in technologies such as cyber security, robotic process automation, artificial intelligence, Blockchain and Digital Channels. With respect to Alshammari et al.'s (2018) suggestion to the Takaful and the insurance sectors, this trend reflects investment readiness and readiness of the market to be on board with technology in the matter of their offerings. Moreover, Eling et al. (2021) suggest that IoT and artificial intelligence in the insurance market is in its early stage of development with minimal business model developments among key dimensional.

Digital platforms have all the more affected or altered the new distribution paradigm. Changes in social dynamics, such as increase in life expectancy, electronic technology development (for instance, artificial intelligence), rise in connectivity, tastes and preferences of the consumers for insurance products, has led distribution of insurance products to bet on online platforms (Relan & kumar, 2023). When a time like this, insurance companies should start thinking on harnessing partnerships outside ecosystems, encouraging agents to collaborate and having a hybrid or multi channel distribution model. It is so because although shifting preferences of consumers (Relan & kumar, 2023), face to face interaction is still in use.

The direct communication and brand interaction that Islamic marketing receives through social media has further revolutionized Islamic marketing. Webinars, live Q&A sessions and influencers can become an effective means in educating your audience outside the financial centre about Islamic financing concepts through platforms such as Facebook, Instagram, YouTube and LinkedIn. By endorsing ethical financial products, Islamic scholars and finance experts have an instrumental role to play in disseminating knowledge and replacing consumer's trust in financial systems. Businesses in Pakistan, with increasing digital literacy, are likely to be able to increase credibility and stretch reach, as well as deepen the bond with consumers seeking Shariah compliant financial products through integrating social media engagement in their marketing strategies.

Besides social media, data driven marketing on digital platforms helps companies to personalize the customer experience but being fair and ethical. Big data analytics and AI powered algorithms assist financial institutions in segmenting the audience, predict the preferences of the consumers, and also design marketing campaigns accordingly. Nevertheless, organizations using data collection and advertising strategies that are deceitful or manipulative should refrain from doing so. The digital innovation in Islamic financial institutions in Pakistan can be leveraged to build better consumer relationships, enhance the adoption of Takaful and Bancassurance products and finally position themselves as leaders in ethical financial services.

CONSUMER BEHAVIOR IN TAKAFUL AND BANCASSURANCE

Changing Consumer Expectations in the Digital Age

Technological advancements have given rise to change in the behavior of the consumers in Islamic finance. A positive impact on mobile banking and online Takaful subscriptions implies the increase in preference of convenience and efficiency.

Consumer expectations in Takaful and Bancassurance have risen tremendously in the digital age when technology has grown, and many people have become conscious of their money and want to seek seamless experiences, customer centric experiences. In the increasingly digital world, Islamic financial institutions need to have mobile apps, AI driven customer support and online policy management available to the modern consumers, who expect instant access to such financial products and services. Unlike traditional models that required in person consultation, today's Takaful and Bancassurance providers have to use digital solutions to enable real time quotes, automated claims processing as well as personalized recommendation.

For marketing strategies, influencer marketing refers to a very effective branding strategy. Nowadays, companies tend to abandon the conventional notion of celebrity endorsers used for product promotion in the presence of the social media influencers such as vloggers, instafamous personalities (Jin et al., 2019; Schouten et al., 2019). Hiring an influencer for the promotion is not doubted that he or she would have a number of trusts on the product quality. However, as we research these ourselves, we find that a lot of consumers believe that influencers take their paycheck simply so they can sell a product.

Transparency and trust are two of the other key expectations of modern day consumers in the digital era, especially in Islamic finance, where there are ethical dimensions which are stark and important. Institutions have to provide detailed and accessible information on Shariah compliance of Takaful and Bancassurance products to the consumers, which involve the provision of clear documentation, digital fatwas from recognized scholars, and the use of blockchain based verification mechanisms. Consumers are coming to see trust building as critical to the consumer engagement process as growing awareness of financial ethics, and increasing grilling of the insurer and investor over practices. For instance, those companies that stick to the principles of Islamic finance can increase strengthening their relationship with their consumers and companies that can communicate transparently, market truth and according to the Islamic finance principles can easily maintain their relationship with their consumers.

Besides, Personalization and customer engagement have become pivotal aspects that influence the decisions of consumer for the Takaful and Bancassurance sectors. Consumers do not buy in anymore when there is one size fits all financial solutions which they demand personalized policies, AI driven insights along with engaging them proactively. The Digital Transformation enables financial institution to leverage the power of big data Analytics and AI to evaluate the needs of an individual, recommend suitable Takaful plan and finally offer bespoke Bancassurance solution for each customer. With significant and rapid growth of digital adoption in Pakistan, Islamic financial institutions have to use advanced technologies without compromising on their values-based strategy. Through a consumer centric digital transformation, the industry can address changing expectations, form long haul customer loyalty, and encourage the use of Islamic products.

Influence of Religious and Cultural Factors

Consumer decision making in Pakistan's Islamic financial sector is influenced by religious beliefs and cultural values. The Shariah compliance and ethical considerations of Takaful and Bancassurance customers are paramount in the choice of financial products. To foster trust and further adoption, these values must be present in the marketing strategies aligned to it.

Values of ethno-cultural nature are of key importance to shaping consumer economic behavior. The study contributes inputs for the development of marketing strategies which account for the ethnic factors. This research provides local brands an opportunity to develop ethno cultural value associations with their products that would result in increasing consumer loyalty (Omonov, 2025).

Takaful and Bancassurance markets are shaped by religious and cultural factors in decision making and way of thinking by consumers. In Islamic finance, principles of Shariah strictly forbidden the financial deal or transaction which contains an existence of interest (riba), uncertainty (gharar), or gambling (maysir). An essential consideration for Muslim consumers of financial products is this element of compliance, for they want assurance that the way they transact financially is in the realms of what is not only permissible but also useful to them. Takaful, as a form of alternative traditional insurance, is based on the concepts of mutual cooperation with a shared risk, thus making it suitable for both the private sector and the larger masses of people who desire ethical financial protection. There has to be also the integration of Shariah compliant investment and insurance solutions in the Bancassurance models in Islamic banking as devout consumers need Shariah compliant financial planning.

Further cultural influences relate to consumer attitude and behavior when taking up Takaful and Bancassurance products. Financial decisions throughout the world are still widely influenced, in countries like Pakistan, where traditional family structures and collectivist values prevail, by elders within the family, by religious scholars or even by leaders of the community. Thus, financial institutions must communicate with cultural gatekeepers to earn credibility and market entry trust in these influencers. Cultural sensitivities also influence product marketing and communication strategies in which companies must use messaging that relates to local values, linguistic details, and ethics. Takaful and Bancassurance providers can thus rely on integrating culturally relevant branding and community engagement initiatives to widen consumer trust and adoption of their services.

Behavioral Economics in Islamic Finance

To build such effective marketing strategies in Takaful and Bancassurance it is important to understand the field of behavioral economics. On the other hand, financial decisions taken by consumers are very often based on heuristics and emotional factors. As a consequence, behavioral finance plays an important role in the financial institutions' products development, as they leverage behavioral insights to create products that match consumer's preferences and comply with ethical financial portfolio planning.

The role that behavioral economics have in shaping consumer decisions in the Takaful and Bancassurance sectors is very crucial in Islamic finance. While conventional economic theories imagine that rational decisions are made by consumers, there is not the presence of significant influence of emotions, cognitive biases and social influences in financial decision making as per behavioral economics. While the risk aversion is based on the religious beliefs of the consumers, but Takaful is stated as an example of the model where consumers can prefer cooperative risk sharing rather than the conventional insurance. Being rooted in Islamic finance, the concept of fairness and ethical responsibility put an impact into the behavioral tendencies such as loss aversion and reciprocity, which causes consumer preferences in Shariah compliant financial solutions. By knowing these behavioral patterns, financial institution can develop products and marketing strategies to accommodate the ethical and psychological touch of their target audience.

Most of the time, rational consumer behavior can only be found within the premises and presumptions of classical economics (Litao & xinzhou, 2021). Actual consumptions, on the other hand, reveal consumer behaviors that are often classified by conventional theories as abnormal or illogical. Today, behavioral economics has been an important tool for understanding actual consumer behavior. This study emphasizes irrational decision-making from a behavioral economics perspective (Litao & xinzhou, 2021).

Takaful and Bancassurance products adoption by the consumers depends highly on social proof and trust. In Pakistan consumers commonly look to friends, family members and religious scholars before making a financial product purchase in preference to looking at communication through institutional channels. A bias of behavioral kind such as herd mentality can impact the adoption rates as most people would rather jump on the same type of financial product if they see others in their community doing the same. This can be taken advantage of by Islamic financial institutions to use the testimonial marketing, endorsements from religiously trusted personalities and educational campaigns on the ethical and community nature of Takaful and Bancassurance. Additionally, products' framing can emphasize the social responsibility and collective welfare, which will make them more appealing for the ethically conscious consumers.

Additionally, behavioral economics offers insights towards improving the engagement of consumers with Takaful and Bancassurance within the digital platform realm. Fintech solutions and mobile apps give rise to behavioral nudges, or small design interventions that impact the behavior of consumers as with default policy renewal options, personalized notifications, and easy decision process. The gamification technique as reward based incentives for policyholders to adopt preventive health measures can enhance participation. Combining behavioral insight with digital transformation, Islamic financial institutions can collect higher consumers' adoption and retention and the alignment with the Shariah. Eventually, application of behavioral economics in Takaful and Bancassurance promotes financial inclusion and improves confidence in Islamic finance.

Customer Experience and Retention Strategies

Financial institutions offering Takaful and Bancassurance focus is to enhance customer experience. The three pillars of retaining customers are personalized service,

AI driven recommendations and proactive customer support. We have institutions that invest in customer relationship management (CRM) tools to understand feedback and better facilitate the service quality.

In order for Takaful and Bancassurance in Pakistan to achieve long term success, it is imperative to improve customer experience. Due to the ethical and cooperative nature of Islamic finance, customer satisfaction encompasses just service delivery but more of building trust, transparency and the offerings must be aligned to religious and financial needs. With seamless aboard process, easy digital platform and AI driven customer support it could become significantly increased to customers while on boarding. Documented processes and lack of clarity are some of the reasons why many customers tend to avoid embracing financial services. Through simplifying the government explanations, rendering in multiple languages, and integrating chatbots for direct query resolution, Islamic financial institutions can enhance their customer accessibility and strengthen relationships with customers.

There are religious factors in the Takaful sector as the Shariah principles are the first concern for customers. According to Azam, (2021) CRM impacts satisfaction and offers that are aligned to religious expectations. The functionality of family Takaful products will be guaranteed with respect to the spiritual or religious needs of the customers for enhancements of management efficiency. The ethical factor does also play a very important role in the customer decision making. Thus, customer satisfaction in Takaful services is an ethical consideration that has fairness and transparency integrated to it. Family Takaful product is managed based on its efficiency of product management, and this is linked to the ethical dimension of family Takaful products and customer trust and loyalty. Factors that are practical from the fact should also consider a product feature, cost, and accessibility in deter-mining customer preferences. Related to the mentioned, Ali (2021) reveals that technological advancements such as Takaful Tech, can optimize business excellence and satisfy customer satisfaction through meeting practical needs and enhancing product efficiency. Muhamad et al. (2024) also point out that a framework for evaluating e-Takaful participation readiness is prudently grounded in practical implications related to shaping customer preference. Takaful industry is still faced with ongoing challenges, despite advances and attempts to increase product offers. According to Wahab & Hassan (2023), these challenges and facts are analyzed and are highlighted that there is still a need for constant improvement in the management practice to live up with the customer expectations.

The competition for the banks in Bancassurance business is not limited to within the banks industry but also from the insurance industry. In the financial business period where product is nearly equal with price, people, market and technology besides in era of informatization, Bancassurance channel has challenges with attracting and maintaining its customers. Thus, differentiation is the key to success in such a scenario (Varma, 2012). A sustained competitive advantage can be gained by concentrating on customer experience (Pine & Gilmore, 1999; Heineke & Davis, 2007). This is because unlike some product or service enhancements, experiential designs are of extremely difficult to copy at a holistic level since their rivals are all too unable to do so (Berry & Parasuraman, 2002). Customer experience as a differentiator is important in banking (Croxford et al., 2006). Therefore, the customer experience can be what makes the difference in a Bancassurance channel (Shaw, 2005; Thompson, 2005) and is a way that one of the channels could develop a competitive advantage over its competitors (Shukla, 2007).

In Takaful and Bancassurance, retention strategies need to concentrate on the idea of personalized interaction and value-added services. Big Data and AI can help Islamic financial institutions analyze customer behavior, predict needs, recommend suitable policy to customers. An example could be to cater to the essence of family protection with family protection plans, or with bundled Takaful products within banking services to attract customer retentions. Also, loyalty programs that reward long term policyholders with some premium discounts or even some extra benefits will provide a boost for loyalty. Mobile applications, emails, as well as SMS updates on policy renewals, Shariah advisories and market trends also ensure that customers remain engaged, without attrition.

Trust building initiatives like partnerships with religious scholars and financial awareness programmes and also community driven campaigns contribute well towards retention of Takaful and Bancassurance. Educating customers on the ethical benefits of Islamic finance through interactive webinars, social media content, and in-person seminars fosters deeper connections. They can also bring in a referral program for satisfied customers who as an appreciation would be provided incentives on recommending Takaful and Bancassurance products to other people. Thus, by combining technology driven personalization, proactive communication and community initiated projects, Islamic financial institutions can be positioned to be trusted partner in financial security and risk management providing them with stable customer relationships ensuring loyalty in the long term.

BUSINESS TRANSFORMATION IN PAKISTAN'S TAKAFUL AND BANCASSURANCE SECTORS

Technological Disruptions and Innovations

Takaful and Bancassurance sectors in Pakistan have been affected by technology driven transformation. By adopting blockchain, artificial intelligence, as well as big data analytics, operational efficiency, fraud prevention and personalized policy recommendation are increased. They enable new growth opportunities with compliance to the Islamic principles of finance.

Due to the technological disruptions, Takaful and Bancassurance sectors in Pakistan are changing and creating new means to improve efficiency, access to services and engage with customers. Currently the integration of artificial intelligence (AI) and machine learning has reduced the underwriting process to automated risk assessments with automatic policy pricing. While automating 24×7 customer support has always been a challenge, AI enabled chatbots and virtual assistants are able to provide 24×7 customer support and while cutting the reliance on human agents. Blockchain technology is also making its appearance as a dream come true regarding the transparency and security in the financial transactions. Smart contracts implemented by Takaful providers can smooth out its claims processing, which overcomes the benefits of eliminating the intermediaries and reducing the risks of the frauds leading to the growth of trust amongst the policyholders.

The Takaful and even Retakaful (reinsurance) industry is certainly one of the most powerful markets by which Islamic countries' economic progress can be augmented. It is envisaged to contribute to the economic prosperity of the Islamic nations, the growth and advancement of Takaful as a credible alternative to traditional insurance models (Ali, 2006). There is in the contemporary landscape a digital disruption, which is imminent and substantial. The time of fintech has come and now is essential; it is not suggested any longer simply as a choice. The ability to get comprehensive financial services through smart devices has made customer's experience much better. Even when we have such perceived convenience, some care must be given to preserving the most important role banks should have — the guardians of consumers' funds. Fintech is simple, convenient and makes accessing money easy; but at the same time, money is people's business and it should not compromise on that. The challenge arising from digital disruption for Takaful operations is the need either to adapt and integrate or to fall into gradual obsolescence following the premise of Ahmad et al. (2023), Saad (2012), Sukmaningrum et al. (2022), and Antonio et al. (2013).

Sreenish and Senthil Kumar (2017) pondered over how Bancassurance can bring about selling life insurance services and products in cashless and digitized economy. This study has also shown that in this context, the way of channel of Bancassurance was different with other channel of distribution. It is found that bank staff were found to be giving better financial advice about the insurance products and services to their customers than ahead of insurers. Abiyyu et al. (2020) mentioned that the strategic issues such as the development of the product, the segmentation of the customers, and the digital initiative in the selling insurance are some of the key determinants of the Bancassurance business. Accordingly, Chen (2019) analyzed the role played by Bancassurance in the corporate reputation and their profitability with special references made to the life insurers in Taiwan. According to him, the quality of service also had a great impact.

Customer interactions in Takaful and Bancassurance landscape have further been revolutionized by digital payment solution and mobile application. The use of fintech innovations like mobile wallets and biometric authentication opens the door for smooth making of premium payments and policy renewals mainly for the unbanked. In addition, InsurTech startups are launching on-demand as well as micro Takaful solutions where customers can subscribe to flexible and short term plan offers over digital platforms. The innovations offered here are tuned to the demands of the consumers preferring to go tech savvy in finances, with a temptation for convenience, speed and personalization in their financial transactions. However, the rising mobile and internet penetration in Pakistan will contribute to further accelerating the digital transformation in the Islamic financial services as the Takaful and Bancassurance will be made more accessible to a wider audience.

Despite that, Islamic finance is also on a rapid adoption of technology, especially for regulatory compliance and Shariah. Meanwhile, there is concern that AI driven decision making should be aligned to ethical practices without piling on discriminatory actions. With these ever increasing infiltrations to a company's databases, data privacy and cyber security risks require robust governance frameworks. To achieve such strides, collaboration between the financial institutions, technology firms, and regulatory bodies will be critical, ensuring compliance with Islamic principles in such disruptions. With an appropriate use of the technology, Takaful and Bancassurance providers in Pakistan can make the customers confident with their services, conduct the operations smoothly and can increase the financial inclusion, thereby strengthening the country's Islamic financial ecosystem.

Regulatory Developments and Industry Standards

Pakistan has regulatory bodies that introduced policies in support of development of Islamic financial services. It plays a key role in creating industry standards through his association with the Securities and Exchange Commission of Pakistan (SECP) and the State Bank of Pakistan (SBP). The regulations stipulate compliance with these which will put in place the protection of consumers as well as maintain the credibility of Takaful and Bancassurance institutions.

The standards and regulatory developments have their vital role in the Takaful and Bancassurance development in Pakistan, where financial institutions operate in an organized and ethical manner. During the course of developing regulations that promote the protection of consumers; transparency and Shariah compliance, the Securities and Exchange Commission of Pakistan (SECP) and the State Bank of Pakistan (SBP) have been active players. The Operational Guidelines under

SECP's Takaful Rules and subsequent amendments provide firms relief with clear operational guidelines such as governance structures, risk management frameworks as well as criteria for product development. Bancassurance regulatory framework has been further refined to resolve the issues of customer disclosures, commission structures and ethical sales practices. Regulatory measures like this are important to give the customers confidence and to prevent malpractices in the market.

It is the additional step in the increase of credibility of Pakistan's Takaful and Bancassurance sectors, taking into account the fact that these industries chose to adopt international industry standards like those of the Accounting and Auditing Organization for Islamic Financial Institutions (AAOIFI) and the Islamic Financial Services Board (IFSB). Thcsc standards encapsulate in detailed guidelines in financial reporting, risk management as well as Shariah governance. Moreover, in recent years, regulatory authorities have encouraged digital solutions integration to the extent that institutions now have to sufficient cybersecurity measures and data protection protocols in place. These standards not only conform to Islamic principles, but also bring the Islamic finance industry of Pakistan in compliance with the best practices across the globe and make it more attractive to foreign investment and partnership.

Although regulatory improvements have enabled industry development, alignment with Islamic financial principles still faces some challenges in term of harmonization of conventional regulatory guidelines. To fulfill trends such as InsurTech, block-chain based contracts and AI based customer interactions would need continuous innovation with the regulatory framework. Furthermore, enhancement of financial literacy and trust depends on consumer awareness on regulatory protections and the rights of policyholders. With this, there will be a need for a healthy collaboration between the policymakers, industry players and Shariah scholars who will collectively work toward creating a flexible and strong regulatory climate that would propel the growth of Pakistan's Takaful and Bancassurance sectors.

Strategic Partnerships and Market Expansion

Strategic partnerships between financial institutions are becoming increasingly the norm in order for them to expand their reach. Product innovation can be driven by collaborations between banks and fintech startups, as well as between banks and Takaful operators to penetrate the market faster. This integration provides access and increase in financial inclusion of Takaful products.

The Takaful and Bancassurance sectors in Pakistan require strategic partnership and consequently the growth and expansion of such sectors amongst the financial institutions can be facilitated through joining the firm with its market reach and operational efficiencies. The collaboration between the Takaful operators and conventional banks in the form of Banca takaful agreement has played in facilitating accessibility to Islamic insurance products. Banks' vast branch networks allow Takaful providers to spread to those in under banked areas and rural areas, hence granting wider reach on their customer base. They, as well, support digital transformation of this segment and, in addition to that, join forces with fintech companies and startups in InsurTech sphere, presenting new approach – AI underwriting, blockchain policy management and mobile claims handling. These technological advancements make the process smooth, reduce operational cost and the billing processes, and make customer experience better, hence it increases the adoption of Takaful products.

Strategic collaborations with global Islamic finance institutions and multinational insurance firms contribute to Pakistan's market expansion in Takaful and Bancassurance sectors. By entering into cross border alliances, Pakistani Takaful providers will be able to draw on internal global expertise, best practices and funding opportunities, thereby improving the quality of service offered. The entry of foreign investors and institutions into Pakistan's Islamic finance market has contributed to the development of Shariah compliant solutions in insurance to suit local needs. Additionally, there are several initiatives that offer efforts in micro-Takaful via partnership with NGOs and government agencies to bring financial inclusion to the low income population as affordable risk mitigation solutions for affected individuals and small business.

Regulatory support, public private partnerships and sustainable market expansion are all critical in order to ensure sustainable market expansion. Incentives to joint venture a Takaful provider with a technology firm can be created by the government, as well as favorable policies for Islamic financial inclusion. Furthermore, by enhancing consumer education campaigns, Takaful and Bancassurance product awareness and thereby trust in it would thus promote higher rates of adoption. The key to unlocking new growth opportunities and positioning Pakistan as a competitive Muslim finance player in the global market will be fostering strategic partnerships and the adoption of new innovation.

Future Trends in Islamic Financial Services

There is a scope for the future of Takaful and Bancassurance in Pakistan to prosper from continuous digital transformation and customer centric innovation. Embedded finance, AI underwriting & decentralized finance (DeFi) are some trends which restructure the industry. Secondly, Islamic financial services can be further enhanced by indicating the emphasis on sustainability and ethical investment.

Rapid technological advancements, regulatory developments, and distribution of consumer's expectations will play a crucial role in defining the future of Islamic financial services in Pakistan especially in Takaful and Bancassurance spaces. The industry will keep on digitizing and artificial intelligence (AI), blockchain, and data big analytics will be used to deepen the risk assessment, fraud detection as well as customer service automation. It is expected AI powered chatbots & robo advice will give personalized financial guidance as well as makes the access beneficial to the Shariah compliance. Additionally, blockchain to enable smart contract can bring policy issuance and settle claims more streamline and build additional trust among consumers. At a time when more and more operators and Bancassurance providers are using these innovations in their operations to be competitive and serve their tech savvy customers, it is therefore necessary that Takaful operators and Bancassurance providers embrace these innovations.

Integrating sustainability and ethical finance are other major trends that are shaping the industry: the Islamic financial services. As the importance of Environmental, Social, and Governance (ESG) principles in traditional investing rises higher, Takaful providers are developing to offer Takaful products that are aligned with responsible investment practices such as green Takaful policies that covers renewable energy project and climate risk. This is consistent with other objectives of Maqasid al-Shariah, where financial solutions should promote the societal well being. Furthermore, provisions of financial services to low income group and small businesses will be provided by greater government support and policy measures which will promote the expansion of micro-Takaful solutions and Islamic insurance. Takaful and Bancassurance will further gain in value proposition in Pakistan due to the rise of Islamic impact investing and ethical business models.

Moreover, regulatory changes will also pave the way for the future of Takaful and Bancassurance in Pakistan. The Securities and Exchange Commission of Pakistan (SECP) and the State Bank of Pakistan (SBP) are anticipated to design more sturdy frameworks to foster digital change, and protect customers. Operation transparency and efficiency will be driven by compliance with international standards, e.g. Islamic Financial Services Board (IFSB) and Accounting and Auditing Organization for Islamic Financial Institutions (AAOIFI). Strategic collaborations with global Islamic finance institutions will also enable Pakistani firms to reach out to foreign markets and garner the sizeable demand for Shariah compliant financial products, not only within the domestic borders. If Pakistan's Takaful and Bancassurance sectors implement these future trends, they will need to stay in the forefront of the global Islamic financial ecosystem.

CHALLENGES FACED BY TAKAFUL AND BANCASSURANCE SECTORS IN PAKISTAN

Despite a bright future in the field of Islamic financial services in Pakistan, the Takaful and Bancassurance sectors will find it difficult to achieve growth because of their problems. A major issue is that Islamic financial institutions in general do not adopt digital quickly. AI driven risk assessment and blockchain powered smart contract can change fintech industry but till now many of the industry companies still use conventional process because they don't have technical expertise, lack regulatory clarity and need high initial investment. Furthermore, the growing concerns of data security and cyber threats add to the risks to financial institutions in regards of digital transformation, and are keeping financial institutions hesitant to open all doors for the use of emerging technology in its operations.

The biggest challenge is consumer unawareness and ignorance of Islamic financial products both in rural and underserved markets. There are large number of potential customers who are not familiar and understand the concept of Takaful and the difference between Takaful and conventional insurance. For this reason, the misperception persists that Islamic financial products are less efficient and more expensive than their conventional counterparts, and this discourages adoption. In light of that, companies have to put effort in financial literacy campaigns, coordinate with educational bodies, and resort to digital marketing to engage the consumer and build trust. Furthermore, marketing strategies have to be matched with Islamic values and cultural sensitivities to have it widely accepted.

In addition, Takaful and Bancassurance industries face serious hurdles of Regulatory and compliance related challenges in Pakistan. The direction for easing Islamic financial service is already taken and while the Securities and Exchange Commission of Pakistan (SECP) and State Bank of Pakistan (SBP) have been playing their role in supporting Islamic financial services but still there is need of clearer guidelines for emerging technologies and digital Financial services. It is vital to achieve a balance between the regulation and innovation so as to maintain financial stability in the competitive landscape. Moreover, balancing such strict Shariah compliances with the modern technologies of financials remains a delicate task in itself and there always need to be a continuous interface with the Islamic scholars and regulators to achieve the exact balancing.

Competition in local Islamic financial services is also faced by them in the last. Usually global players with superior digital platform and well known brand name tend to outplay Takaful and Bancassurance players at the local level. To beat competitors, local companies need to create strategic ties, broaden their market segment and increase the efficiency of their operation on technological advancements. Collaboration among Islamic financial institutions, the government agencies, and the international Islamic finance organizations can also contribute to the making of a robust and supportive ecosystem for Takaful and Bancassurance in Pakistan.

FUTURE DIRECTIONS

It is the integration of digital technologies and inclusion of the population in the financial market that will define the future of Takaful and Bancassurance in Pakistan. Given the ever changing nature of consumer preferences such as ease and access, Islamic financial institutions must diligently create smooth digital platforms, AI customer service, mobile based financial solutions. The use of blockchain for Islamic financial services shall add value to furthering trust in Islamic financial services. In addition, fintech collaborations will be crucial in streamlining operations and providing better service delivery to Takaful and Bancassurance providers so that they can cater to a larger population of the unbanked and under banked.

Its enhancement of regulatory framework is another important aspect that is able to cater for changes in financial landscape. Such regulators, the Securities and Exchange Commission of Pakistan (SECP) and the State Bank of Pakistan (SBP), will have to play the role of developing a flexible but robust regulatory environment for the purposes of supporting innovation while adhering to the principles of Shariah. By introducing digital Shariah audits, AI driven implementation of compliance monitoring, and commonly applied standards to fin-tech integration Islamic financial services can continue being competitive and compliant. In addition, to regain public trust, it is important to improve digital Takaful and Bancassurance offerings through strengthening cybersecurity measures and protection of consumer data.

Investment of Islamic financial institutions is also required to invest towards consumer education and financial literacy programs for Takaful and Bancassurance knowledge gap bridging. Future planning including AI driven chatbots for customer related inquiries, interactive online course, social media campaigns with Islamic scholars and experts in finance are some of the strategies to follow. This will motivate higher adoption rates, educating consumers about the ethical benefits as well as the financial benefits of Islamic insurance and banking. Additionally, big data analytics for personalized marketing will let the companies provide more dedicated products to various consumer segments at different levels that lead to customer engagement as well as long term customer loyalty.

Strategic partnerships will also be very important in accelerating the growth of Takaful and Bancassurance, not only in the Arabian Peninsula and Gulf region but also globally. Knowledge exchange, infrastructure development and cross-border market entry will be facilitated through the collaborations with global Islamic finance institutions, government bodies and technology companies. It is the expectation that participating in the future will be multinational Islamic financial entities too, which will engage in more innovation and competition. Moreover, the Islamic finance industry will gain from consumers and socially conscious investors who will increasingly demand for sustainable products that integrate ESG (Environmental,

Social and Governance) principles, thus opening up space for long term growth and the tailwind of global financial trends.

STRATEGIC RECOMMENDATIONS

In order to enhance growth and sustainability of Takaful and Bancassurance in Pakistan, financial institutions should have a strategic approach that combines the digital transformation with Islamic marketing principles. It also proposes that the firms can exploit AI, big data analytics, and blockchain to be more transparent, better to assess risk, and more personalized in terms of financial products and services. Also, digital platforms and mobile apps will be user friendly to ensure increased accessibility of consumers especially for those not have been reached in the markets. Order of priority for introducing Islamic financial products is digital literacy initiatives and financial awareness campaigns, which will help to build trust in organizations and higher adoption rate of Islamic financial products.

The efforts towards digital transformation must truly be driven by regulatory alignment and compliance to the Shariah principles. Standards need to be created by institutions with regulatory bodies, Islamic scholars, and industry experts for the financial services to meet ethical and legal requirement. Further, strengthening cybersecurity measures and data protection protocols will be required to address the consumer concerns on the privacy and fraud. Furthermore, the development of regulatory innovation, for instance, the sandbox environments for fintech solutions, allows testing the new digital products and ensures they adhere to the principles of Islamic finance.

In order to fuel industry growth, strategic partnerships with fintech, insurtech startups, as well as international Islamic finance institutions will be key. Financial institutions can enable cross sectors collaborations, increasing reach, operational efficiencies and introduction of innovative products to meet the changing consumer needs. Furthermore, the use of customer-oriented marketing methods, for instance, the adoption of AI destiny techniques and social media engagement will improve brand commitment and customer continuation. Through embracing holistic and future ready approach, Pakistan's Takaful and Bancassurance will become pivotal players in the Islamic finance global trends.

CONCLUSION

A digital and ethical transformation of marketing and consumer behavior in Pakistan's Takaful and Bancassurance sectors appears key to the strategic evolution of Islamic marketing across the sectors. Technological advances need to be adapted by the financial institutions, yet to practice in accordance with the Shariah principles. If institutions don't focus on long-term growth, they have to make a resolution about educating the consumer base, marketing (that is, transparent) and regulatory alignment. With AI, blockchain and social media, Islamic Financial Services can make product purchase impulsive and trustworthy for the consumers. The future of Islamic finance in Pakistan will continue to evolve the business strategies to form a sustainable and inclusive financial ecosystem.

Digital transformation, changing the consumer expectations and regulatory progress are driving the strategic evolution of Islamic marketing and consumer behavior in Takaful and Bancassurance. With the inclusion of AI, big data, blockchain, social media, consumer engagement has been significantly increased and product personalization been well unison along with operational efficiency. Shariah studies and the reality of digital innovations along with the growth of Islamic financial services need to be adopted in Pakistan where Islamic financial services are expanding rapidly. So, companies that can strike a proper balance between technological progression on the one hand, and ethical and religious concerns on the other will be on the winning side as far as gaining consumer trust and growing their market share are concerned.

Despite this, the main problems that need to be addressed are regulatory complexities, cybersecurity risks, and financial literacy. The solutions to these problems need the active participation of financial institutions, the regulatory bodies and industry stakeholders. To them it will be essential to strengthen their compliance frameworks investments in consumer education, and extraction of AI for risk management. Furthermore, relationships with global Islamic banks and fintech organizations can foster the process of digitalization and increase the availability of Takaful and Bancassurance products.

The future direction of Takaful and Bancassurance in Pakistan will depend on the continued digitalization and the strategic partnerships with incumbent and new companies, consumer centric innovations among others. The structure of the Islamic financial institutions must be that it is agile and always changing its strategy to keeps competition operating. The quick response to grow and be resilient based on the long term can be done through the promotion of trust through transparency, improve digital capability, and regional purpose related to global sustainability trends. If the Islamic financial services can successfully mull over technological progress with the Islamic values, it can achieve both financial and ethical prosperity of customers.

REFERENCES

Abiyyu, I., Najib, M., & Asmara, A. (2020). Bancassurance business strategy in life insurance: A case study one of joint venture company in Indonesia. [Jurnal Dinamika Manajemen]. *Journal of Database Management, 11*(1), 103–115.

Ahmad, Z., Muneeza, A., Rahman, M. M., & Mahomed, Z. (2023). A comparative analysis of Shariah governance framework of Islamic bank in Malaysia and Pakistan. Talaa: *Journal of Islamic Finance, 3*(1), 01-17.

Al-Nashmi, M., & Almamary, A. (2017). The relationship between islamic marketing ethics and brand credibility. *Journal of Islamic Marketing*, *8*(2), 261–288. DOI: 10.1108/JIMA-03-2015-0024

Ali, K. M. M. (2006). Present scenario and future potentials of Takaful. *Islamic Economics. Banking and Finance*, *2*(2), 1–14.

Ali, K. M. M. (2021). Takaful Tech for Business Excellence and Customer Satisfaction. Islamic FinTech: Insights and Solutions, 385-403.

Alshammari, A. A., Syed Jaafar Alhabshi, S. M., & Saiti, B. (2018, September). bin, & Saiti, B. (2019). The impact of competition on cost efficiency of insurance and Takaful sectors: Evidence from GCC markets based on the Stochastic Frontier Analysis. *Research in International Business and Finance*, *47*, 410–427. DOI: 10.1016/j.ribaf.2018.09.003

Antonio, M. S., Ali, M. M., & Akbar, N. (2013). A comparative analysis of the efficiency of takaful and conventional insurance in Malaysia. *International Journal of Excellence in Islamic Banking and Finance*, *182*(881), 1–13. DOI: 10.12816/0001416

Azam, Z. (2021). Impact of Customer Relationship Management on Islamic Banks and Takaful Companies. *Journal of Integrated Sciences*, *2*(1), 57–90.

Bagasworo, W., & Simatupang, S. (2022). Increased Purchases of Insurance Products Based on Factors That Affect Customer Trust (Study on Banccasurance in Greater Jakarta, Indonesia). *Jurnal Ekonomi, Manajemen Dan Perbankan (Journal of Economics, Management and Banking),* *8*(1), 30–38.

Bebber, S., Milan, G. S., De Toni, D., Eberle, L., & Slongo, L. A. (2017). Antecedents of purchase intention in the online context. *Journal of Relationship Marketing*, *16*(1), 82–98.

Berry, L. L., & Parasuraman, A. (2002). *Internal marketing: Directions for management*. Routledge.

Boer, H. & During, W.E. (2001). Innovation, what innovation? A comparison between product, process and organizational innovation, *International Journal of Technology Management, 22*(1/2/3), pp. 83-107.

Chen, T. J. (2019). Marketing channel, corporate reputation, and profitability of life insurers: Evidence of Bancassurance in Taiwan. *The Geneva Papers on Risk and Insurance. Issues and Practice, 44*(4), 679–701. DOI: 10.1057/s41288-019-00137-7

Croxford, H., Abramson, F., & Jablonowski, A. (2006). *The art of better retail banking*. Wiley & Sons.

Deloitte. (2013). The global Takaful insurance market charting the road to mass markets, A Deloitte ME IFKC Practice Insights Series, available at: https://ceif.iba.edu.pk/pdf/ Deloitte The global Takaful insurance market Charting the road to mass markets.pdf (accessed 20 November2016).

Eling, M., Nuessle, D., & Staubli, J. (2021). The impact of artificial intelligence along the insurance value chain and on the insurability of risks. In Geneva Papers on Risk and Insurance: Issues and Practice (Issue 0123456789). Palgrave Macmillan UK. DOI: 10.1057/s41288-020-00201-7

Guemmaz, S. (2023). Shareholding relations between banks and insurance companies in Algeria: An overview. *Journal of Innovations and Sustainability, 7*(2), 1. DOI: 10.51599/is.2023.07.02.01

Haron, S., & Nursofiza, W. (2008). *Creating a dynamic Islamic capital market: the essential role of innovation, Islamic Capital Markets: Products, Regulation and Development, Islamic Research and Training Institute*. Islamic Development Bank Group.

Hartmann, P. M., Zaki, M., Feldmann, N., & Neely, A. (2016). Capturing value from big data–a taxonomy of data-driven business models used by start-up firms. *International Journal of Operations & Production Management, 36*(10), 1382–1406. DOI: 10.1108/IJOPM-02-2014-0098

Heineke, J., & Davis, M. M. (2007). The emergence of service operations management as an academic discipline. *Journal of Operations Management, 25*(2), 364–374. DOI: 10.1016/j.jom.2006.11.003

Ichsan, N. (2015). Analisa SWOT, prospek dan strategi pengembangan asuransi Syariah Di Indonesia (SWOT analysis, prospects and development strategy for Islamic insurance in Indonesia), available at: https://nurulichsanaan.files.wordpress.com/2015/10/analsis-swot-asuransi-syariahjurnal-kordinat.pdf (accessed 10 November 2016).

Jin, S. V., Muqaddam, E. R., & Ryu, E. (2019). Instafamous and social media influencer marketing. *Marketing Intelligence & Planning*, *37*(5), 567–579. DOI: 10.1108/MIP-09-2018-0375

Kailash, M. S. R., Joshi, C., Desai, P. R., Teferra, N. B., & Radhakrishnan, S. (2023). The Rise of Ethical Consumerism: Marketing Strategies for the Conscious Buyer.

Kasim, N., Nuhtay, S. N., & Salman, S. A. (2013). Shariah Governance for Islamic Capital Market: A Step Forward. International Journal of Education and Research Vol. 1 No. 6. ISSN: 2201-6740.

Kiel, D., Arnold, C., & Voigt, K. I. (2017). The influence of the Industrial Internet of Things on business models of established manufacturing companies–A business level perspective. *Technovation*, *68*, 4–19. DOI: 10.1016/j.technovation.2017.09.003

Litao, X., & Xinzhou, S. (2021) Research on Consumer Behavior Based on the Perspective of Behavioral Economics. Proceedings of the 2021 3rd International Conference on Economic Management and Cultural Industry (ICEMCI 2021). Advances in Economics, *Business and Management Research, 20*(3) pp. 316-319.

Muhamad, F. H., Ab Ghani, H., & Arifin, J. (2024). A Conceptual Framework of E-Takaful Participation Readiness (ETPR) among Individuals at Insurable Age in Malaysia. *Journal of Entrepreneurship and Business*, *12*(1), 116–126. DOI: 10.17687/jeb.v12i1.1197

Nadham, N. & Nahid, B. (2015). The role of business ethics in the relationship between market orientation and business performance. International Journal of Finance & Banking Studies (2147-4486), 4(1), 70-94. .DOI: 10.20525/ijfbs.v4i1.205

Omonov, S. (2025). Ethno-Cultural Values as a Factor Shaping Consumer Economic Behavior. *Web of Humanities: Journal of Social Science and Humanitarian Research*, *3*(3), 93–95.

Ostrom, A. L., Parasuraman, A., Bowen, D. E., Patrício, L., & Voss, C. A. (2015). Service research priorities in a rapidly changing context. *Journal of Service Research*, *18*(2), 127–159. DOI: 10.1177/1094670515576315

Pine, J., & Gilmore, J. H. (1999). *The experience economy: work is theatre & every business a stage*. Harvard Business Press.

PWC. (2018). Whom do consumers really trust? available at: https://www.pwc.com/gx/en/industries/ consumer-markets/consumer-insights-survey/consumer-trust.html

Redhika, R., & Mahalli, K. (2014). Analisis Potensi dan Kendala Pengembangan Asuransi Syariah di Kota Medan (potential analysis and constraints of Islamic insurance development in medan). *Jurnal Ekonomi DanKeuangan*, *2*(5), 323–335.

Relan, M., & Kumar, M. (2023). Impact of Trust and Risk Factors on the Satisfaction Level of the Policy Holder towards Digital Bancassurance Model. [IRJMSH]. *International Research Journal of Management Sociology & Humanity*, *14*(7), 15–24.

Saad, N. M. (2012). An analysis on the efficiency of Takaful and insurance companies in Malaysia: A non-parametric approach. *Review of Integrative Business and Economics Research*, *1*(1), 33.

Schouten, A. P., Janssen, L., & Verspaget, M. (2019). Celebrity vs. Influencer endorsements in advertising: The role of identification, credibility, and Product-Endorser fit. *International Journal of Advertising*, •••, 24.

Sestino, A., Prete, M. I., Piper, L., & Guido, G. (2020). Internet of Things and Big Data as enablers for business digitalization strategies. *Technovation*, *98*, 102173. DOI: 10.1016/j.technovation.2020.102173

Shaw, C. (2005). *Revolutionalise your customer experience*. Palgrave Macmillan. DOI: 10.1057/9780230513457

Shomad, A. (2025). Liability of Islamic Banks in Bancassurance Activities. *Journal of Law and Regulation Governance*, *3*(1), 435–445.

Shukla, T. (2007). Experiential marketing: The new paradigm. *Indian Journal of Marketing*, *37*(4), 10–13.

Sorescu, A. (2017). Data-driven business model innovation. *Journal of Product Innovation Management*, *34*(5), 691–696. DOI: 10.1111/jpim.12398

Sreenish, S. R., & Senthil Kumar, S. A. (2017). THE ROLE OF BANCASSURANCE IN DIGITAL ERA. *CLEAR International Journal of Research in Commerce & Management, 8*(3).

Statista. (2020). Global insurance companies' digital technology investment priorities worldwide 2020.

Sukmaningrum, P. S., Hendratmi, A., Rusmita, S. A., & Abdul Shukor, S. (2022). Productivity analysis of family takaful in Indonesia and Malaysia: Malmquist productivity index approach. *Journal of Islamic Accounting and Business Research*, *13*(4), 649–665. DOI: 10.1108/JIABR-03-2021-0097

Thompson, B. (2005). The loyalty connection: Secrets to customer retention and increased profits. Right Now Technologies, 1-16.

Varma. (2012). Enhancing and empowering: Customer experience. *SCMS Journal of Indian Management, 9*(3), 71-78.

Wahab, M. Z. H., & Hassan, M. H. A. (2023). Contemporary Challenges and Prospects for Takaful Practices in Malaysia: An Analysis of Current Issues. International Journal of Accounting [IJAFB]. *Finance and Business*, *8*(47), 337–350.

Willems, K., Brengman, M., & Van De Sanden, S. (2017). In-store proximity marketing: Experimenting with digital point-of-sales communication. *International Journal of Retail & Distribution Management*, *45*(7-8), 910–927. DOI: 10.1108/IJRDM-10-2016-0177

Wilson, J. A. J., & Liu, J. (2011). The challenges of Islamic branding: Navigating emotions and halal. *Journal of Islamic Marketing*, *2*(1), 28–42. DOI: 10.1108/17590831111115222

Yahia, I., Ben Al-Neama, N., & Kerbache, L. (2018). Investigating the drivers for social commerce in social media platforms: Importance of trust, social support and the platform perceived usage. *Journal of Retailing and Consumer Services*, *41*(1), 11–19. DOI: 10.1016/j.jretconser.2017.10.021

Yasin, M., Porcu, L., Prados-Castillo, J. F., & Liébana-Cabanillas, F. (2024). The Role of Social Media in Building Islamic Banking Consumer Engagement: Analyzing the Impact of Brand Personality Traits and Brand Love. *International Journal of Human-Computer Interaction*, •••, 1–15.

Chapter 10
The Role of Enterprise Risk Management in Enhancing Firm Value Among Shariah-Compliant Companies on Bursa Malaysia

Nur Hafizah Roslan
https://orcid.org/0000-0001-6517-6865
Management and Science University, Malaysia

Nurul Nadhirah Husni
https://orcid.org/0009-0006-4417-8873
Management and Science University, Malaysia

Rabia Bashir
https://orcid.org/0000-0003-4672-076X
Management and Science University, Malaysia

Muhammad Ahmad
https://orcid.org/0000-0002-5987-8518
Management and Science University, Malaysia

Siti Zaitun Saddam
Universiti Teknologi MARA, Malaysia

DOI: 10.4018/979-8-3373-2655-9.ch010

ABSTRACT

This study investigates the impact of Enterprise Risk Management (ERM) on firm value among Shariah-compliant industrial product and service firms listed on Bursa Malaysia from 2022 to 2024. Using Tobin's Q as the measure of firm value, the study examines the role of board size, leverage, Chief Risk Officer (CRO) presence, firm size, and sales growth in shaping market performance. Panel data analysis was conducted on 90 companies, employing regression and correlation techniques using EViews. The results reveal that board size and leverage significantly and positively affect firm value, consistent with agency theory and the principle of shura (consultation), which encourages collective decision-making. Conversely, firm size, sales growth, and CRO presence exhibit negative or mixed effects, suggesting that governance structures must be effectively integrated for ERM to create value.

INTRODUCTION

Brief Overview of the Study

Enterprise Risk Management (ERM) encompasses enterprise-wide risk management, holistic risk management, corporate risk management, business risk management, integrated risk management, and strategic risk management (Shah, Lai, Shad, Hamad, & Ellili, 2025). Enterprise Risk Management (ERM) has gained significant traction,ERM as a process effected by an entity's board of directors, management, and other personnel, applied in strategy-setting and across the enterprise, designed to identify potential events that may affect the entity, and manage risk to be within its risk appetite, providing reasonable assurance regarding the achievement of entity objectives.

Over the last two decades, businesses have navigated more complicated risk landscapes. In Malaysia, the growing influence of global governance standards such as the COSO framework and ISO 31000 has encouraged the use of structured risk management systems. Post-pandemic economic volatility, Environmental, Social, and Governance (ESG) compliance requirements, and global supply chain disruptions have all underlined the importance of proactive risk reduction. To promote ERM transparency and accountability, regulators like as Bursa Malaysia have imposed stricter disclosure standards. These developments highlight the importance for publicly traded corporations to develop resilient ERM systems that can withstand changing financial and operational challenges.

Risk management has evolved from traditional techniques to integrated ERM frameworks (Khan et al., 2021). Driven by high-profile business failures, organisations now embrace holistic risk management across departments (Dickinson, 2001; Zulfitra et al., 2022). ERM provides a systematic framework to identify, evaluate, and mitigate risks that may hinder strategic goals, making it a critical corporate governance component (Quon et al., 2012). However, implementing comprehensive risk management requires infrastructure often lacking in developing countries (Habib et al., 2014; Subhani & Osman, 2011). Malaysia's public sector recognizes risk management's importance in governance and policy achievement, promoting ERM adoption through government programs (Gani et al., 2020). Despite growing awareness, ERM implementation varies among Malaysian public listed companies due to factors like firm size, board composition, and ownership structure. Integrating sustainability risk management into governance is also vital for economic, environmental, and social performance (Aziz et al., 2015).

Enhancing organisational performance necessitates in implementing comprehensive risk management solutions, though it requires appropriate infrastructure that may not always be readily available in companies, particularly in developing countries (Habib et al., 2014; Subhani & Osman, 2011). Like many other nations, Malaysia's public sector companies has come to understand the significance of risk management in guaranteeing efficient administration and accomplishing public policy goals (Gani et al., 2020). To encourage the implementation of risk management procedures throughout its agencies, the Malaysian government has launched several programs (Gani et al., 2020). The public now anticipates that the government will proactively identify risks and take steps to reduce their impact. Strong risk management procedures are now more important than ever for Malaysian publicly traded companies operating within a dynamic and competitive global business environment.

Therefore, businesses adopt enterprise risk management frameworks more frequently, offering a comprehensive and integrated risk perspective throughout the organisation (Frigo & Anderson, 2011). Enterprise risk management improves the ability to create value by empowering management to handle uncertainty, related risk, and opportunity (Tarantino, 2012). According to Marchetti (2011), enterprise risk management surrounds firms' strategies and procedures to reduce shocks and take advantage of opportunities to accomplish their goals. an enterprise risk management program enables businesses to control risks within a unified framework (Nocco & Stulz, 2006). The financial services sector has been a significant incubator for enterprise risk management, which aims to predict revenue shocks and surprises for the main business (Boyson, 2014). A well-implemented enterprise risk management framework reduces potential losses. It enables the organisation to proactively identify and capitalise on emerging opportunities by strategically aligning organisational strategies, processes, and knowledge assets. This improves the organisation's overall resilience and performance (Marchetti, 2011).

PROBLEM STATEMENT

Enterprise risk management (ERM) is a new paradigm that helps organisations discover, assess, and manage risks. Several motivations urge various organisations, particularly banks, to develop and implement ERM, including the likelihood of financial difficulties and associated expenses, a reduction in financial performance, growth opportunities, and board independence. Furthermore, implementing a suitable risk management plan provides a competitive edge for supporting organisations (Zarinjooei, Ghodrati, Panahian, & Jabbari, 2025).

Enterprise Risk Management (ERM) is becoming important as an integrated strategy for controlling organizational risks. According to research, many firms that face considerable risks hesitate to adopt or do not utilise ERM techniques (Paape & Speklé, 2012). Large Malaysian organizations, such as Khazanah Nasional Berhad and Telekom Malaysia Berhad, have adopted ERM, whereas many smaller publicly traded companies are weakening (Golshan & Rasid, 2012). ERM frameworks are becoming more common in infrastructure, hotels, and technology. At the same time, other industries have yet to prioritize or completely implement this key risk management approach. (Ahmad and Teo,2024). These differences raise concern about what factors affect the adoption of Enterprise Risk Management (ERM). Despite Malaysia's strategic position and efforts to attract foreign direct investment, the sector faces constant labour shortages, rising operational costs, and supply chain disruptions, all of which are worsened by global uncertainties such as geopolitical tensions and inflationary pressures (27 Advisory, 2023; MIDA, 2024). The lack of a trained workforce and problems getting foreign workers due to strict immigration regulations limit production capacity and cause project delays (27 Advisory, 2023; Principal Malaysia, 2025).

Despite Malaysia's strategic position and efforts to attract foreign direct investment, the sector faces constant labour shortages, rising operational costs, and supply chain disruptions, all of which are worsened by global uncertainties such as geopolitical tensions and inflationary pressures (27 Advisory, 2023; MIDA, 2024). The lack of a trained workforce and problems getting foreign workers due to strict immigration regulations limit production capacity and cause project delays (27 Advisory, 2023; Principal Malaysia, 2025).

Furthermore, the sector must guide the ongoing transition to Industry 4.0, which includes adopting automation, artificial intelligence, and smart factory technologies. Many firms find this difficult due to high implementation costs and the need for workforce upskilling (27 Advisory, 2023). Infrastructure constraints, such as limited industrial land and obsolete infrastructure, impede development and modernisation initiatives (27 Advisory, 2023). These operational and strategic issues are worsened by a lack of broad adoption of the sector's comprehensive Enterprise

Risk Management (ERM) strategies. In default of developed ERM frameworks, businesses are exposed to operational disruptions, regulatory compliance risks, and market volatility, all of which can harm company value and investor trust (MIDA, 2024). As a result, Malaysian industrial product and service firms must urgently strengthen their ERM processes and strategic competencies to manage risks, increase operational stability, and capitalise on emerging opportunities in a complex and changing economic environment.

Significance of Study

This study is important for shareholders, as ERM adoption enhances firm value by improving risk disclosure quality, reducing information asymmetry, and increasing investor confidence (Ong et al., 2023). ERM lowers costs of financial distress and external financing, boosting profitability and shareholder wealth (Shad & Lai, 2015). It also reduces earnings volatility and stock price fluctuations, appealing to risk-averse investors (Abdullah et al., 2017). For companies, especially Malaysian SMEs and public firms, ERM strengthens organisational resilience and risk culture, improving decision-making and compliance with regulatory requirements (Manas et al., 2024; Togok et al., 2016). The presence of Chief Risk Officers enhances ERM adoption and governance (Wan Daud et al., 2010). A well-implemented ERM framework aligns risk management with strategic goals, optimising resource allocation and supporting long-term growth (Lai, 2011).

Beyond shareholders and management, this study's insights benefit external stakeholders such as creditors, financial analysts, and regulatory bodies. Improved ERM practices enhance a firm's creditworthiness and can positively influence its bond ratings. Additionally, consistent risk disclosure practices provide analysts with more reliable data for equity valuation and risk profiling. Policymakers can also use these findings to draft guidelines that mandate ERM adoption across sectors, contributing to stronger market-wide risk resilience.

LITERATURE REVIEW

Background

A financial and economic ratio called Tobin's Q determines a company's performance by looking at the market value in relation to the cost of replacing its assets. Investors and economists can decide if the market price accurately represents the intrinsic worth of a company's assets or whether speculative elements or intangible assets impact valuation by using Tobin's Q, an indicator of market valuation relative to asset value. This mathematical model has been used in determining some economics decisions such as the cross- sectional studies of differentiation between investment and diversification; connection between managerial equity ownership and firm value; relationship for managerial performance and tender offer gains; relationship between investment opportunities and tender offer responses, financing, dividend and issues in compensations policies (Chung and Pruitt, 1994).

ERM adoption varies significantly across Southeast Asia. In Indonesia, firms with government ownership are more likely to implement ERM due to stricter state regulations. In Thailand, ERM frameworks are often integrated with internal audit functions, highlighting a risk-based approach to compliance. Studies from Vietnam and the Philippines also indicate a correlation between ERM maturity and foreign ownership, suggesting that cross-border investors push for improved governance. These regional insights provide a useful benchmark for Malaysian firms and highlight the importance of aligning ERM practices with both domestic and international investor expectations.

A study by Rinaldi et al. (2022) on ERM implementation in Singaporean logistics firms found that board independence significantly moderates the relationship between ERM and firm value. Similarly, Lin et al. (2023) observed that the presence of female directors enhances the effectiveness of risk committees, improving Tobin's Q. These findings support the growing literature emphasizing board diversity and structure as catalysts for ERM effectiveness. Incorporating such governance dimensions into future research may offer additional explanatory power in understanding firm valuation.

UNDERPINNING THEORY: AGENCY THEORY

According to agency theory, the separation of ownership and control in modern organisations leads to conflicts of interest, requiring procedures to balance the interests of managers (agents) and shareholders (principals) (Yusuf et al., 2023). According to Kiefer et al. (2017), a principal-agent problem is created by this separation, where managers' incentives are different from shareholders', resulting in management actions that do not optimise shareholder value. To reduce conflict, agency theory supports governance frameworks like board composition. The size of boards significantly impacts financial performance, especially the presence of independent directors (Lukman et al., 2024). Independent directors provide unbiased oversight and reduce the risk of managerial opportunism. Conflicts of interest and self-dealing are also avoided by dividing decision-making authority among several companies, including initiation, implementation, monitoring, and penalizing (Jatiningrum et al.,2023). According to Agency Theory, the application of a strong risk management system, like ERM, can enhance industry performance and overall shareholder value (Ahmed and Manab, 2016). This theory identifies a possible mismatch of interest between shareholders, management and debt holders due to earnings distribution asymmetries, resulting in the business taking too much risk or not engaging in a positive net value project (Otekunrin et al., 2021).

Agency theory helps explain important company practices, like how risks are managed, how boards of directors oversee operations, and how CEOs are motivated. It shows why companies use tools like Enterprise Risk Management (ERM) to protect the interests of shareholders and prevent managers from acting in their interests. In the end, agency theory aims to improve how businesses perform and increase their value by aligning the choices of managers with the goal of boosting shareholder wealth (Payne and Petrenko, 2019).According to Ong Poh Heng et al., (2022) ERM adoption will improve the information environment of Malaysian firms by encouraging the controlling owner-managers to disclose quality firm-specific information, improve the information environment, boost investors' confidence towards firms' financial reporting and improve firm value eventually.

Dependent Variable

Tobin's Q is used as the dependent variable to measure firm performance. It is justified as a comprehensive indicator because it reflects market valuation relative to the replacement cost of assets, capturing both tangible and intangible factors influencing firm value. Tobin's Q, an influential metric in financial economics, serves as an empirical tool for evaluating firm performance by providing a comparative framework between a firm's market valuation and the replacement cost of its assets. This paper delineates the conceptual underpinnings, methodological application, and strategic implications of employing Tobin's Q as the dependent variable in performance assessments, reaffirming its robustness as a comprehensive indicato' of both tangible and intangible value drivers.

Independent Variables

Board Size

According to Yeni et al. (2020), the impact of board characteristics on firm value was examined, and a strong relationship between board size and firm value was found. This indicates that the size and composition of a board can influence market-based performance metrics, such as Tobin's Q. Zhang et al. (2021) acknowledged that a properly sized board can improve firm management and strategic decision-making, thereby positively impacting Tobin's Q. They provided global evidence showing that various board characteristics, including board size, are significantly associated with firm value across different markets. Furthermore, Pangestuti et al., (2017) examined the relationship between board size and risk management exposure, finding that larger boards are associated with more significant transparency and improved governance practices. Enhanced governance and exposure can, in turn, strengthen investor confidence and contribute to higher firm valuation as reflected in Tobin's Q. Khan et al., (2021) also reported that board characteristics, including board size, play a crucial role in determining firm value in the context of Pakistani listed companies, strengthening the significance of board structure in shaping market perceptions and firm performance.

H1: There is a significant relationship between board size and firm performance.

Leverage

Several studies highlight that leverage has significant relationship between firm value. According to Parsons and Titman (2008), appropriate capital structure decisions, including using leverage, are critical to a company's business strategy and, when handled well, may increase firm value. Empirical research reveals that corporate governance and risk management procedures frequently mitigate the link between leverage and business value. Zulfitra et al. (2022) show that risk management, profitability, and excellent corporate governance all impact stock prices, an indication like Tobin's Q. Their findings suggest that organisations with strong risk management and governance frameworks are better positioned to handle the risks associated with increasing leverage, thus enhancing company value. According to Aziz et al. (2015) emphasise incorporating sustainability risk management with corporate governance, stating that leverage choices should be matched with larger risk management methods to maintain firm value. Other than that, Khan et al. (2021) present data from Pakistan demonstrating that capital structure decisions, including leverage, are important predictors of company value. According to their findings, the proper use of leverage and enterprise risk management (ERM) methods may improve business performance and market valuation.

H2: There is a significant relationship between leverage and firm performance.

Chief Risk Officer (CRO)

A Chief Risk Officer (CRO) is a senior executive responsible for identifying, evaluating, and mitigating risks that can negatively impact an organization's resources, profits, capital, and overall operations. The CRO develops risk reduction plans, monitors the risk management framework, and ensures compliance. The role is critical for protecting long-term stability and performance (Yusuf et al., 2023).

Studies suggest the presence of a CRO influences firm value by improving risk governance and management effectiveness.

To operationalize the Chief Risk Officer (CRO) variable, this study uses a binary classification: 1 if the CRO position is explicitly mentioned in the company's annual report or board profile section, and 0 otherwise. This measure, while simple, reflects formal organizational commitment to risk management. Additionally, the use of panel data over three years strengthens the study's validity by capturing temporal dynamics that would be lost in a purely cross-sectional approach. The choice of EViews software, while standard, also ensures robust handling of fixed and random effects models that account for individual firm heterogeneity.

The Bursa Malaysia Guidelines and the Malaysian Code on Corporate Governance emphasise the importance of board-level risk management, including the function of the CRO, which enhances risk governance and aligns management actions with shareholder interests (Nurdin et al., 2018). Empirical data shows that ERM adoption, generally driven by the CRO, increases the information environment and investor trust, increasing business value (Zulfitra et al., 2022; Khan et al., 2021). Although some research finds conflicting significance levels, the general trend suggests a favourable relationship between the existence of a CRO and Tobin's Q in the Malaysian setting (Tahir and Razali, 2011). By appointing a Chief Risk Officer, Enterprise Risk Management (ERM) procedures are increasingly recognised as critical mechanisms for increasing firm value for better risk management and governance (Dickinson, 2001; Khan et al., 2021). Tobin's Q, a generally acknowledged measure of firm worth, represents market views of a company's growth potential and risk profile. According to studies conducted on Malaysian public-listed businesses, enterprises implementing ERM frameworks with specialized risk leadership, such as a CRO, have higher Tobin's Q ratios, suggesting higher company valuation (Nurdin et al., 2018).

H3: There is a significant relationship between Chief Risk Officer (CRO) and firm performance.

Firm Size

Firm size has been studied extensively as a predictor of firm value, with Tobin's Q used as the representation of the market valuation. Bigger firms often have more resources, diverse activities, and better access to financing markets, which can increase their market value. According to Pangestuti et al. (2017) and Zhang et al. (2017), firm size positively relates to risk management disclosure, which can increase firm value by enhancing transparency and investor trust. Other than that, Yeni et al. (2020) also provide evidence that firm size significantly influences company value, indicating that larger firms are more likely to achieve higher Tobin's Q ratios due to their ability to leverage economies of scale and attract investor interest. Furthermore, Khan et al., (2021) support this relationship in their research of enterprise risk management and company value, finding that firm size has a considerable impact on Tobin's Q. Their findings indicate that when firms develop, they are better positioned to implement comprehensive risk management strategies, which the market values and reflects in higher firm valuations. According to Fitriana and Wardhani (2020), firm size moderates the influence of risk management and sustainability reporting on performance, with larger firms more adept at converting these practices into increased market value. Moreover, Nurdin et al. (2018) find that larger firms tend to have more resources and capabilities to implement effective governance and risk management practices, which can positively influence firm value as measured by Tobin's Q.

H4: There is a significant relationship between firm size and firm performance.

Sales Growth

Sales growth is widely acknowledged as a major indicator of a company's operational performance and future, with a significant influence on firm value as evaluated by Tobin's Q. Firms that show steady sales growth indicate strong market demand, a competitive edge, and good management, all of which may boost investor confidence and raise market values. According to Zulfitra et al. (2022), profitability and financial success, which are frequently driven by sales growth, have a considerable beneficial influence on stock prices and, consequently, company value. Furthermore, Khan et al. (2021) argue that financial performance measurements, such as sales growth, are crucial predictors of company value for enterprise risk management. Fitriana and Wardhani (2020) also emphasise that company growth, measured by sales and revenue expansion, helps increase firm performance and market value in Southeast Asian nations. Aside from that, according to Liebenberg and Hoyt (2003), high-growth organisations may adopt riskier strategies to achieve their commercial goals. Higher growth enterprises typically have higher financing costs, which increases the likelihood of bankruptcy and reward uncertainty (Pagach and Warr, 2011).

H5: There is a significant relationship between sales growth and firm performance.

METHODOLOGY

This research data was extracted from company annual reports from Bursa Malaysia. Bursa Malaysia serves as a key source, providing extensive financial data for publicly listed companies in Malaysia. Company annual reports were extensively used to extract detailed financial information. These reports contain audited financial statements that disclose important figures such as total assets, liabilities, equity, and other financial metrics. Some information is crucial for calculating variables like leverage and company size, which are essential to this study.

The sample for this research includes Malaysian public-listed companies specifically within the Industrial Products and Services sector in Bursa Malaysia. Bursa Malaysia serves as a key source, providing extensive financial data for publicly listed companies in Malaysia. Company annual reports were extensively used to extract detailed financial information. These reports contain audited financial statements that disclose important figures such as total assets, liabilities, equity, and other financial metrics. Some information is crucial for calculating variables like leverage and company size, which are essential to this study.

In addition, this study focuses on **Shariah-compliant companies** as classified by the Securities Commission Malaysia (SC). Shariah compliance ensures that firms operate in accordance with Islamic principles by avoiding activities related to riba (interest), gharar (excessive uncertainty), and maysir (gambling). Including Shariah-compliant firms provides an added ethical and religious dimension to Enterprise Risk Management (ERM) practices, as these companies are bound by both regulatory and faith-based governance. From an Islamic perspective, effective ERM aligns with the concept of *amanah* (trust) and supports *maqasid al-Shariah* (the objectives of Shariah), particularly the protection of wealth (*hifz al-mal*). Therefore, examining ERM within Shariah-compliant companies not only enhances corporate governance but also strengthens accountability, transparency, and investor confidence in line with Islamic values.

Data were collected for the period from 2022 to 2024, ensuring the analysis reflects the most recent trends and developments in the industry. According to the latest data, there are over 340 companies listed in this sector, but only 90 companies have complete and consistent annual reports for the selected years.

These analyses use the statistical software of EViews to run the panel data analysis and regression analysis. EViews provides a range of tools to analyse data. EViews allows researchers to analyse data, test hypotheses, run various types of analysis, and come to insightful findings.

Measurement of Variables

Financial Performance

Tobin's Q ratio is used to assess the connection among liquidity management, operating performance, and corporate value (Wang, 2002). This shows the importance of liquidity management in improving operational performance and, consequently, company value (Kontuš and Mihanović, 2019). In Tobin's Q ratio, stock value measures serve as the primary decision for investing choices. Applying this to the market allows them to determine whether it is generally overbought or undervalued. In the theoretical, a ratio larger than one would suggest that the market or company is overvalued. If the ratio were less than one, it would be considered undervalued. The data obtained from the Bursa Malaysia and will be measured as follows:

$$Tobin's\ Q = \frac{Total\ Liabilities + Market\ Value}{Total\ Assets}$$

Chief Risk Officer (CRO)

A senior executive known as a Chief Risk Officer (CRO) oversees identifying, evaluating, and reducing risks that might threaten a company's operations, profitability, and reputation. The CRO oversees enterprise risk management, making sure the business successfully handles operational, financial, legal, security, and reputational issues. According to Rochette (2009), the term 'CRO' was first quoted by James Lam, a well-known figure in the ERM field. This person has the responsibility to put in place a strategic enterprise risk management framework as outlined previously and collaborate with other C-level executives during its implementation and operation. The CRO is important in protecting the company from both internal and external threats to preserve operational stability and shareholder value. The relevance of this position has increased due to changing market conditions, technological challenges, and increasingly complex regulatory settings. According to Yazid et al. (2012) suggested that the CRO plays a major role in determining the ERM program. They strongly suggested that companies should consider appointing the CRO to manage all the potential risks such as business risk, operational risk, credit risk, market risk and organizational risk. In this respect, the CRO usually works together with his or her supporting team, namely the Risk Management Committee (RMC).

Sales Growth

Sales growth, a crucial indicator of a business's financial health, is more than just revenue growth, it represents a complex interaction between strategic goals, market dynamics, and operational efficiency. A firm with positive sales growth sells more goods and services, which raises revenue and may result in better profits. The company's capacity to manage its assets and enact policies related to its operational activities have a significant impact on increasing company profits (Handini et al. 2023). According to Pagach and Warr (2011), and Khan et al. (2021) argue that firms having more growth opportunities may be distracted from implementing the ERM system. Sales growth enhances firm performance by providing opportunities for learning curve benefits, economies of scale, and creating investment opportunities

(Kaplan and Norton, 1996; Khan et al. 2021). Hence, it is important to control the variable of sales growth. Following Hoyt and Liebenberg (2011), and Khan et al. (2021), sales growth is calculated as the change in current year sales compared to previous year sales.

Board Size

The total number of directors on a company's board of directors is referred to as the board size, which is a crucial component of corporate governance and has been well researched for its effects on business efficacy and performance. The composition and dynamics of a board of directors significantly influence a firm's approach to risk management and overall organizational outcomes (Yusuf et al. 2023). According to Pangestuti et al. (2017), the size of the board of commissioners serves as a benchmark for the maximum supervisory functions, including overseeing the disclosure of company information related to risks arising from operational activities. They argue that a larger board size enhances supervisory effectiveness by enabling management and shareholders to monitor each other more closely, thereby reducing information asymmetry. Moreover, board size is a determinant of risk management effectiveness, with larger boards potentially offering a broader range of expertise and 36 perspectives (Galletta et al. 2021). Moreover, board size often correlates positively with firm size and complexity, larger firms typically require bigger boards to effectively oversee diverse operations and risk exposures.

Leverage

Leverage is often used by companies that invest in themselves for expansions, acquisitions, or other growth initiatives. This strategy also uses borrowed money or a range of financial instruments to increase the potential return on an investment. Leverage, which measures how much a company depends on debt funding, has a complex relationship with organisational risk management practices (Parsons and Titman, 2008). This connection is important since the amount of leverage may significantly impact a company's entire risk profile, stakeholder relationships, and strategic decisions (Parsons and Titman, 2008). A thorough comprehension of leverage is necessary due to its significance in determining risk management procedures. According to Yazid et al (2012) when a company uses leverage, it must borrow from other institutions to finance the purchase of assets or operations. The data obtained from the Bursa Malaysia and will be measured as follows:

$$Leverage = \frac{Total\ Liabilities}{Market\ Value}$$

Firm Size

Firm size is a key component of corporate structure and has a complex impact on many aspects of organizational behaviour and performance. According to Yusuf et al (2023), Firm size can be defined as the total assets, total sales, or number of employees that a company has Furthermore, larger companies are better able to attract and retain skilled risk management specialists, which improves their capacity to recognise, evaluate, and reduce risks. A more complicated risk environment is a result of bigger firms' generally more complex operational structures, more extensive resource endowments, and broader global reach (Fitriana and Wardhani, 2020). As a result, large companies frequently demonstrate a greater understanding of the significance of enterprise risk management in preventing any disruptions and protecting their extensive asset base. Bigger firms are also more likely to have specialised people in their risk management companies, which increases their ability to administer and execute thorough ERM frameworks. Conversely, smaller businesses can have fewer resources and less experience with risk management, which might make it more difficult for them to implement and successfully use advanced ERM procedures (Clement et al., 2022). The difference in ERM adoption between bigger and smaller businesses highlights the necessity of customised strategies to encourage the broad use of ERM concepts throughout the business environment.

RESEARCH DESIGN

This study employs regression and correlation analysis using EViews software to examine the impact of independent variables, CRO, board size, sales growth, leverage, and firm size on the dependent variable, Tobin's Q, a widely used indicator of firm value and market performance. The measurement used:

$$Tobin's\ Qit = \beta_0 + \beta_1 BOARD\ SIZE_{it} + \beta_2 LEV_{it} + \beta_3 CROit + \beta_4 SIZE_{it} + \beta_4 SIZE_{it} + \beta_5 SALES\ GROWTH_{it} + \epsilon$$

RESULTS

Descriptive statistics summarize the data characteristics, while regression analysis quantifies the influence of independent variables on Tobin's Q to test hypotheses. Correlation analysis assesses the strength and direction of relationships. Panel data analysis combines cross-sectional data over three years, improving estimation efficiency and controlling unobserved heterogeneity.

Descriptive Analysis

Table 1. Descriptive analysis

	Mean	Median	Maximum	Minimum	Std. Dev.	Observations
Tobin's Q	390428.3	85214	13236555	1206	1416603	270
Board Size	6.822222	6	14	4	1.678053	270
CRO	0.859259	1	1	0	0.3484	270
Leverage	968.8674	543.771	8862.444	8.692518	1181.296	270
Sales	17.66537	4.738198	1480.175	-68.3101	97.62749	270
Size	17.12603	18.57008	20.7208	10.94406	2.875659	270

According to the analysis of descriptive analysis in Table 1, the dependent variable for company value, Tobin's Q, has a mean of 390,428.3 and a median of 85,214. With a standard deviation of 1,416,603, the highest and lowest values are 13,236,555 and 1,206, respectively. The extensive range and high standard deviation show significant variation in firm value across the studied firms. Board sizes range from a minimum of 4 to 14 members, with an average of around 6.82. Most businesses have reasonably sized boards with considerable fluctuation, according to the 1.68 standard deviation. The mean for the CRO, the company's chief risk officer, is 0.86, with a median of 1.00, a minimum of 0, and a maximum of 1.00. Although most organisations score highly on this, there is still significant fluctuation within the sample, as indicated by the standard deviation of 0.34. The median for leverage is 543.77, while the mean is 968.87. The standard deviation is 1,181.30, and the values fall between 8.69 and 8,862.44. It indicates that the businesses' capital structures and debt levels differ significantly.

Sales have a mean of 17.67 and a median of 4.74. The minimum value is -68.31, while the maximum is 1,480.18, with a standard deviation of 97.63. These results suggest that while most companies have modest sales, a few firms have extremely high or low sales figures, leading to a high degree of variability. Lastly, Size has a mean of 17.13, a median of 18.57, a minimum of 10.94, and a maximum of 20.72. The standard deviation is 2.88, indicating moderate variation in firm size across the sample.

Correlation Analysis

Table 2. Correlation analysis

	Tobin's Q	Board Size	CRO	Leverage	Sales	Size
Tobin's Q	1					
Board Size	0.855**	1				
	(0.014)					
CRO	0.005	0.20774	1			
	(0.992)	*(0.655)*				
Leverage	0.996***	0.880***	0.003	1		
	(0.000)	*(0.009)*	*(0.995)*			
Sales	0.988***	0.854**	0.126	0.980***	1	
	(0.000)	*(0.014)*	*(0.788)*	*(0.000)*		
Size	0.507	0.823**	0.002	0.560	0.454	1
	(0.246)	*(0.023)*	*(0.997)*	*(0.191)*	*(0.307)*	

* Significant at 10% level, ** significant at 5% level, *** significant at 1% level

Table 2 shows the correlation analysis using the variables in this study, Tobin's Q is the dependent variable, while Board Size, Chief Risk Officer (CRO), Leverage, Sales, and Firm Size is the independent variable. The correlation coefficients indicate strength and direction of a relationship between variables, while the corresponding p-values show the statistical significance of these relationships. The results shows that Tobin's Q has a significant positive relationship with several variables. Tobin's Q is highly correlated with Leverage which is 0.996 with 1% significant level and Sales 0.988 also significant with 1% level indicating that firms with higher leverage and larger sales tend to have higher market valuations. Tobin's Q also shows a significant positive correlation with Board Size 0.855 with 5% significant level, suggesting that firms with bigger board size market could view it as having more value. Other than that, the correlation between Tobin's Q and CRO is very weak and not significant with the value is 0.005 and the p-value is 0.992, shows that the presence of a Chief Risk Officer does not have a relationship with firm value. The analysis also shows a strong and significant positive relationship between Leverage and Sales which is 0.880 and 0.980 respectively with 1% significant level, indicating that firms with higher sales are likely to use more leverage. Board Size is also significantly correlated with Firm Size with 0.823 with 5% significant level, which suggests that bigger firms tend to have bigger boards. The correlation matrix shows no significant multicollinearity problems several variables, like Tobin's Q, leverage, and sales, have significant correlations that should be carefully interpreted in regression analysis. The insignificant connections with the CRO suggest that this role might not directly impact the critical performance.

Regression Analysis

Table 3. Regression analysis

Dependent Variable	**Tobin's Q**
Independent Variable	
Board Size	40301.38***
	(0.000)
CRO	-107365.3***
	(0.003)
Leverage	464.475***
	(0.000)
Size	-163.712**
	(0.053)
Sales	-17236.32***
	(0.000)
R-squared	0.786
Adjusted R-squared	0.783
Durbin-Watson stat	0.717

* Significant at 10% level, ** significant at 5% level, *** significant at 1% level

Table 3 shows the results of a multiple regression analysis to examine the effect of several independent variables on firm value, as measured by Tobin's Q. The independent variables include Board Size, the presence of a Chief Risk Officer (CRO), Leverage, Firm Size, and Sales. The results show that all five independent variables have a significant impact on Tobin's Q. The coefficient for Board Size is 40,301.38, and the p-value is 0.000, indicating a significant positive relationship. This means that, on average, larger boards are associated with higher firm value. Next, CRO has a negative coefficient of -107,365.30 with a p-value of 0.003, which is also significant at the 1% level. This suggests that having a chief risk officer might be related to a reduction in the value of the company. Leverage also has a positive and significant impact on Tobin's Q, with a coefficient of 464.47 with significant level at 1%. This means firms with higher leverage tend to have higher firm value, possibly due to effective use of debt financing. The variable Firm Size has a negative coefficient -163.71 with significant at the 5% level, suggesting that larger firms may have slightly lower Tobin's Q values. Lastly, Sales also show a negative relationship with Tobin's Q with coefficient -17,236.32, and significant at 1% indicating that firms with higher sales may not always have higher market value, possibly due to lower profit margins or operational inefficiencies. The R-squared value is 0.786, which means that approximately 78.6% of the variation in Tobin's Q can be explained by the independent variables in the model. The adjusted R-squared is 0.783, confirming the model's strong relationship. The Durbin-Watson statistic is 0.717, which may suggest the presence of autocorrelation in the residuals.

SUMMARY OF FINDINGS

The findings show that board size and leverage significantly and positively affect firm value, while firm size, sales growth, and CRO presence show negative or mixed effects. The positive role of board size is consistent with previous studies in various contexts, such as Yeni et al. (2020) for Indonesian firms and Khan et al. (2021) for listed companies in Pakistan, where larger boards increase oversight and reduce agency conflict. This supports Agency Theory by showing that broader board representation helps align managers' actions with shareholder interests. Similarly, leverage displays a positive association with Tobin's Q, echoing Parsons and Titman (2008) and Zulfitra et al. (2022), who documented that effective debt financing can discipline management behavior and increase firm value. These findings are consistent with Agency Theory, as debt serves as a monitoring mechanism that reduces managerial opportunities.

In contrast, firm size shows a negative effect on Tobin's Q, diverging from studies in other emerging markets (e.g., Pangestuti et al., 2017; Zhang et al., 2017), where larger firms enjoy higher valuations due to transparency and investor confidence. This difference suggests that in the Malaysian industrial sector, larger firms may face bureaucratic inefficiencies or excessive diversification, reducing market value—partly rejecting the Agency Theory expectation that resource advantages in larger firms increase value. Sales growth also shows a negative effect, inconsistent with evidence from Zulfitra et al. (2022) and Fitriana & Wardhani (2020), who find sales expansion as a driver of firm value in Southeast Asia. One possible explanation is that the rapid sales growth in Malaysian industrial firms is achieved at the expense of profit margins or through riskier investments, which are discounted by the market. Finally, CRO presence reveals a negative relationship with firm value, in contrast to studies in Malaysia (Tahir & Razali, 2011; Nurdin et al., 2018) and globally (Hoyt & Liebenberg, 2011), where the use of CRO-led ERM increases investor trust. These results suggest that appointing a CRO alone is not sufficient unless it is effectively integrated into governance and risk oversight. Therefore, while Agency Theory emphasizes CROs as a mechanism to reduce information asymmetry and protect shareholders, our findings highlight that formal appointments without substantive empowerment may not generate value.

Overall, this study partially supports Agency Theory. Board size and leverage confirm its proposition, but the negative effects of firm size, sales growth, and CRO presence indicate that governance mechanisms and risk management roles must be effectively implemented to realize its theoretical benefits. Compared with findings from other industries and countries, these results suggest that institutional, cultural, and sectoral differences moderate the way agency conflict and oversight mechanisms affect firm value.

DISCUSSION AND CONCLUSION

Justification of Research Findings

The findings reveal that board size and leverage are positive and significant across models, while size and sales growth have significant but negative coefficients. Sales growth and the presence of Chief Risk Officer (CRO) do not show consistent significant impact. Board size reflects diverse expertise and oversight, positively correlating with higher firm value. Leverage shows a positive relationship, suggesting effective debt financing enhances shareholder returns. Firm size and sales growth may cause operational inefficiencies lowering market value. CRO presence shows mixed impacts, indicating that effective integration of ERM processes is crucial. Interaction effects show governance and financial strategies work together to create value, but CRO presence combined with sales growth reveals complex challenges.

The findings of this study also carry important implications from an Islamic governance perspective. Since the sample firms are Shariah-compliant, their risk management practices must not only meet conventional corporate governance requirements but also align with Shariah principles. The positive effect of board size and leverage on firm value can be understood through the concept of shura (consultation), where broader representation on the board promotes accountability and better decision-making, consistent with Islamic values of collective responsibility. Likewise, the effective use of leverage within Shariah limits (debt financing without riba) highlights that ethical financial strategies can enhance shareholder value while remaining compliant with Islamic law.

On the other hand, the negative or mixed impact of firm size, sales growth, and CRO presence indicates that Shariah compliance alone does not guarantee value creation unless it is supported by efficient governance structures and sincere implementation of amanah (trust) in risk management. This resonates with the Islamic principle that wealth (mal) must be managed responsibly to serve the greater good (maslahah), not just profit maximization.

Overall, integrating ERM into Shariah-compliant firms strengthens both financial resilience and adherence to maqasid al-Shariah (objectives of Shariah), particularly the protection of wealth (hifz al-mal) and the promotion of fairness and transparency. This study therefore contributes to the growing body of Islamic finance literature by showing how ERM mechanisms can complement Shariah governance in enhancing firm performance.

RECOMMENDATIONS

Improving board monitoring and governance is critical. Boards should actively implement ERM, linking risk management with business goals. Regular training enhances board supervision of risks. Firms must balance leverage benefits with financial risk management. CRO roles should extend beyond appointment, with clear tasks and collaboration with business units and Risk Management Committee. Operational inefficiencies tied to firm size and sales growth should be addressed through process upgrades and risk controls. Better risk disclosure following Bursa Malaysia guidelines is essential to increase investor trust and market valuation.

LIMITATIONS OF STUDY

This research focuses on Malaysian public listed firms in the Industrial Products and Services sector from 2022 to 2024. Only 90 of over 340 companies were included due to data limitations, restricting generalisability. Reliance on secondary data may affect accuracy due to varying disclosure quality. The study lacks qualitative insights from management or employees. The cross-sectional design limits observation of long-term trends and causal relationships. Findings may not apply to other sectors.

FUTURE RESEARCH

Future studies should increase sample size and include firms from other industries and developing markets to improve generalisability. Long-term studies can track ERM practice changes and establish causality. More refined measures of CRO roles, including authority and integration, are needed beyond binary presence. Advanced econometric or structural equation modelling could address complex interrelationships among variables like sales and leverage.

CONCLUSIONS

This study explores the determinants of ERM and its influence on firm value among Malaysian public listed companies in the Industrial Products and Services sector from 2022 to 2024. Board size and leverage are consistently positive and significant predictors of firm value, which highlights the importance of governance and financial management. Firm size and sales growth are negatively related to firm value, suggesting operational challenges. The presence of CROs shows mixed results, emphasizing the need for effective ERM integration. Limitations include a narrow industry focus and a short period. This study contributes valuable knowledge about the drivers and challenges of implementing ERM in Malaysia.

From a theoretical perspective, findings provide partial support for Agency Theory. While board size and leverage confirm theoretical monitoring and alignment mechanisms, the negative or inconclusive effects of firm size, sales growth, and CRO presence reveal that agency problems are not automatically resolved through structural arrangements. Rather, the sector context, management practices and the quality of implementation determine whether governance and risk management mechanisms increase or decrease firm value.

REFERENCES

Abdullah, B., Syah, M. H., Hamid, M. A., & Yatim, P. (2017). The Effect of Enterprise Risk Management on Firm Value: Evidence from Malaysian Technology Firms. *Jurnal Pengurusan, 49*.

27. Advisory. (2023). Malaysia Industrial Products and Services Sector Report 2023. Kuala Lumpur: 27 Advisory.

Ahmed, I., & Manab, N. A. (2016). Influence of Enterprise Risk Management Success Factors on Firm Financial and Non-Financial Performance: A Proposed Model. *International Journal of Economics and Financial Issues, 6*(3), 830–836.

Aziz, N. A. A., Manab, N. A., & Othman, S. N. (2015). Exploring the perspectives of corporate governance and theories on sustainability risk management (SRM). *Asian Economic and Financial Review, 5*(10), 1148–1158. DOI: 10.18488/journal.aefr/2015.5.10/102.10.1148.1158

Chung, K. H., & Pruitt, S. W. (1994). A Simple Approximation of Tobin's Q. *Financial Management, 23*(3), 70. DOI: 10.2307/3665623

Daud, W. N. W. D., Yazid, A. S., & Hussin, M. R. (2010). The effect of chief risk officer (CRO) on enterprise risk management (ERM) practices: Evidence from Malaysia. [IBER]. *The International Business & Economics Research Journal, 9*(11). Advance online publication. DOI: 10.19030/iber.v9i11.30

Dickinson, G. (2001). Enterprise risk management: Its origins and conceptual foundation. *The Geneva Papers on Risk and Insurance. Issues and Practice, 26*(3), 360–366. DOI: 10.1111/1468-0440.00121

Fitriana, S., & Wardhani, R. (2020). The effect of enterprise risk management and sustainability reporting quality on performance: Evidence from Southeast Asia countries. *International Journal of Economic Policy in Emerging Economies, 13*(4), 344. DOI: 10.1504/IJEPEE.2020.109588

Gani, A. S. A., Salim, B., & Udin, N. M. (2020). The implementation of risk management in Malaysian public sector to sustain federal Government's revenue. *International Journal Of Accounting. Finance and Risk Management, 5*(2), 76–83.

Golshan, N. M., & Rasid, S. A. (2012). Determinants of enterprise risk management adoption: An empirical analysis of Malaysian public listed firms. *International Journal of Social and Human Sciences, 6*, 119–126.

Habib, S., Masood, H., Hassan, T., Mubin, M., & Baig, U. (2014). Operational Risk Management in Corporate and Banking Sector of Pakistan. SSRN Electronic Journal. DOI: 10.2139/ssrn.2663415

Handini, S., Baktiono, R. A., & Purnomo, B. R. (2023). The Influence Of Financial Ratio On Profit Growth In Mining Companies in Indonesia. *Deleted Journal*, *21*(3), 419–433. DOI: 10.29062/mahardika.v21i3.642

Jatiningrum, C., Fauzi, F., Utami, B. H. S., & Kassim, A. A. M. (2023). Mitigating Type II agency conflict through good corporate governance and disclosure quality. Akuntabilitas. *Journal of Accounting Research and Development*, *17*(1), 1.

Khan, W., Asif, M., & Shah, Q. (2021). An Empirical Analysis of Enterprise Risk Management and Firm's Value: Evidence from Pakistan. *JISR Management and Social Sciences & Economics*, *18*(1), 107–124. DOI: 10.31384/jisrmsse/2020.18.1.8

Kiefer, M., Jones, E. A., & Adams, A. T. (2017). Shareholders and managers as principal-agent hierarchies and cooperative teams. *Qualitative Research in Financial Markets*, *9*(1), 48–71. DOI: 10.1108/QRFM-04-2016-0014

Kontuš, E., & Mihanović, D. (2019). Management of liquidity and liquid assets in small and medium-sized enterprises. *Ekonomska Istrazivanja*, *32*(1), 3253–3271. DOI: 10.1080/1331677X.2019.1660198

Lai, F. W. (2011). Enterprise Risk Management implementation framework for Malaysian public listed companies (Doctoral dissertation). University of Malaya.

Liebenberg, A. P., & Hoyt, R. E. (2003). The determinants of enterprise risk management: Evidence from the appointment of chief risk officers. *Risk Management & Insurance Review*, *6*(1), 37–52. DOI: 10.1111/1098-1616.00019

Lin, J., Low, J. S., & Rajan, R. (2023). Gender diversity in boardrooms and enterprise risk oversight: Evidence from ASEAN firms. *Journal of Risk and Governance*, *11*(1), 51–67.

Lukman, L., Ridloah, S., & Humaira, H. (2024). Board characteristics and financial performance of companies from the agency theory perspective. [JoSS]. *Journal of Social Sciences*, *3*(2), 1246–1270.

Manas, N., Zakuan, N., Saman, M. Z. M., & Setapa, M. (2024). Enterprise Risk Management Practices in Malaysian Small and Medium-Sized Enterprises: An Overview. *Information Management and Business Review, 16*(2(I)S), 236–250.

Manufacturing to stabilise in 2025. (2024, December 9). MIDA | Malaysian Investment Development Authority.

Nurdin, E., Maruhun, S., Razazila, W., Abdullah, W., & Atan, R. (2018). Assessing the Effects of Corporate Governance on Enterprise Risk Management and Firm Value: Malaysian Evidence. International Journal of Economics and Management Int. *Journal of Economics and Management*, *12*(S2), 413–430.

Ong, P. H., Yip, Y. Y., & Lye, C. T. (2023). Effect of Enterprise Risk Management Adoption on the Firm Value in Malaysia's Annual Reports.

Ong Poh Heng, C., Teh, B. H., & Ang, Y. L. (2022). Enterprise risk management and quality of risk disclosure: Evidence from Malaysia. *International Journal of Accounting and Information Management*, *30*(1), 1–15.

Otekunrin, A. O., Eluyela, D. F., Nwanji, T. I., Faye, S., Howell, K. E., & Tolu-Bolaji, J. (2021). Enterprise risk management (ERM) and firm's performance: A study of listed manufacturing firms in Nigeria. *Review of World Economics*, *12*(1), 31.

Paape, L., & Speklé, R. F. (2012). The Adoption and Design of Enterprise Risk Management Practices: An Empirical Study. *European Accounting Review*, *21*(3), 533–564. DOI: 10.1080/09638180.2012.661937

Pagach, D., & Warr, R. (2011). The characteristics of firms that hire chief risk officers. *The Journal of Risk and Insurance*, *78*(1), 185–211. DOI: 10.1111/j.1539-6975.2010.01378.x

Pangestuti, D., Takidah, E., & Anggraini ZR, R. (2017). Firm Size, Board Size, And Ownership Structure and Risk Management Disclosure. *Jurnal Akuntansi Dan Keuangan Islam*, *5*(2), 117–137. DOI: 10.35836/jakis.v5i2.18

Parsons, C., & Titman, S. (2008). Capital Structure and Corporate Strategy. In *Elsevier eBooks* (p. 203). Elsevier BV.

Payne, G., & Petrenko, O. (2019, April 26). Agency Theory in Business and Management Research. Oxford Research Encyclopedia of Business and Management.

Quon, T. K., Zéghal, D., & Maingot, M. (2012). Enterprise Risk Management and Firm Performance. *Procedia: Social and Behavioral Sciences*, *62*, 263–267. DOI: 10.1016/j.sbspro.2012.09.042

Rinaldi, A., Tan, S. Y., & Koh, W. H. (2022). The role of board composition in enterprise risk management: Evidence from Singapore logistics firms. *Asia-Pacific Journal of Business Administration*, *14*(2), 183–199.

Shad, M. R., & Lai, K. K. (2015). The effect of Enterprise Risk Management on performance of Malaysian public listed companies. SHS Web of Conferences, 34, 1–8.

Shah, S. Q. A., Lai, F. W., Shad, M. K., Hamad, S., & Ellili, N. O. D. (2025). Exploring the effect of enterprise risk management for ESG risks toward green growth. *International Journal of Productivity and Performance Management, 74*(1), 224–249. DOI: 10.1108/IJPPM-10-2023-0582

Subhani, M. I., & Osman, A. (2011). The Essence of Enterprise Risk Management in Today's Business Enterprises in Developed and Developing Nations. SSRN Electronic Journal. DOI: 10.2139/ssrn.1818862

Tahir, I. M., & Razali, A. R. (2011). The Relationship between enterprise risk management (ERM) and firm value: Evidence from Malaysian public listed companies. *International Journal of economics and management sciences, 1*(2), 32-41.

Togok, S. H., Isa, C. R., & Zainuddin, S. (2016). Enterprise Risk Management Adoption in Malaysia: A Disclosure Approach. *Asian Journal of Business and Accounting, 9*(1), 83–106.

Wang, Y.-J. (2002). Liquidity management, operating performance, and corporate value: Evidence from Japan and Taiwan. *Journal of Multinational Financial Management, 12*(2), 159–169. DOI: 10.1016/S1042-444X(01)00047-0

Yeni, F., Melmusi, Z., Wulandari, E., & Ilona, D. (2020). The Effect of the Board of Directors' Characteristics on Company Value.

Yusuf, I., Aliyu, I. A., & Al-Faryan, M. A. S. (2023). Board risk committee composition and risk-taking of deposit money banks in Nigeria. *Cogent Business & Management, 10*(1), 2187884. DOI: 10.1080/23311975.2023.2187884

Zarinjooei, K., Ghodrati, H., Panahian, H., & Jabbari, H. (2025). Identifying and prioritizing the factors affecting enterprise risk management implementation. *Iranian Journal of Finance, 9*(1), 134–161. DOI: 10.61186/ijf.2024.448623.1463

Zhang, D., Zhang, Z., Ji, Q., Lucey, B., & Liu, J. (2021). Board characteristics, external governance and the use of renewable energy: International evidence. *Journal of International Financial Markets, Institutions and Money, 72*(C), 101317. DOI: 10.1016/j.intfin.2021.101317

Zhang, J., Zhou, C., & Zhou, L. (2017). Firm size, risk management disclosure, and firm value: Evidence from China. *China Journal of Accounting Research, 10*(4), 1–15.

Zulfitra, Z., Ganar, Y. B., Sahroni, S., & Arsyan, M. A. (2022). The Effect of Risk Management and Profitability on Stock Prices Moderated by Good Corporate Governance Variables. *Kontigensi Jurnal Ilmiah Manajemen, 10*(2), 299–311. DOI: 10.56457/jimk.v10i2.288

Chapter 11
The Interplay of Strategic Human Resource Management and Work Culture Transformation in Hospitals

Fitra Hergyana Margana
https://orcid.org/0009-0000-1999-9908
University Islamic Bandung, Indonesia

ABSTRACT

Strategic Human Resource Management (SHRM) is increasingly recognized as a critical lever for organizational success, particularly in complex environments like hospitals where work culture significantly impacts patient outcomes and staff well-being. This article explores the relationship between SHRM practices and the transformation of work culture within hospital settings. Through a literature review approach, drawing upon a curated collection of research articles, this paper synthesizes key themes and findings. The analysis indicates that targeted SHRM interventions, including leadership development, employee engagement strategies, robust knowledge management systems, and the cultivation of specific cultural attributes, are pivotal in driving and sustaining positive work culture transformations in hospitals. The findings underscore the necessity for hospital administrators and HR professionals to strategically align human resource practices with cultural change objectives to enhance organizational effectiveness, employee satisfaction, and the quality of care.

DOI: 10.4018/979-8-3373-2655-9.ch011

INTRODUCTION

Hospitals operate in a dynamic and demanding environment, characterized by rapid technological advancements, evolving patient expectations, and continuous pressure to improve quality and efficiency (Aryanto, Fontana, & Afiff, 2015; Kim, Han, 2012). In this context, the prevailing work culture within a hospital is not merely a backdrop but a critical determinant of its ability to adapt, innovate, and deliver high-quality patient care (Moreno-Domínguez et al., 2024; Sullivan et al., 2024). Work culture encompasses shared values, beliefs, norms, and practices that shape employee behavior and organizational functioning (Aggarwal, 2024). A positive and adaptive work culture can foster collaboration, enhance patient safety, improve staff morale and retention, and drive organizational performance (Bull et al., 2024; Kim, Kim, & Kim, 2015).

Transforming work culture is a complex and often challenging endeavor, requiring deliberate and sustained effort. Strategic Human Resource Management (Strategic HRM) offers a framework and a set of tools that can be instrumental in this transformation process (Paauwe & Van De Voorde, 2025; Vardarlıer, 2016). Strategic HRM involves aligning human resource policies and practices with the overall strategic goals of the organization (Zehir et al., 2016). By strategically managing human capital, organizations can influence employee attitudes, behaviors, and capabilities, thereby shaping the organizational culture (Rogers & Wright, 1998; Fındıklı, Yozgat, & Rofcanin, 2015).

Despite the acknowledged importance of both strategic human resource management and work culture, the specific interplay between Strategic HRM practices and the processes of work culture transformation within the unique context of hospitals warrants further exploration. Hospitals present distinct challenges due to their hierarchical structures, diverse professional groups, high-stakes environment, and the paramount importance of patient safety (Laroche, 2024; Kok et al., 2025). This article aims to synthesize insights from a collection of recent literature to elucidate how Strategic HRM can effectively contribute to the transformation of work culture in hospital settings.

METHOD

This article employs a literature review methodology. The primary source of information is a comprehensive document containing summaries and analyses of 90 research articles spanning various aspects of human resource management, organizational culture, leadership, innovation, and performance, with several studies specifically focusing on or relevant to healthcare and hospital environments.

The selection of literature for synthesis within this article was guided by its relevance to the core themes of:

- Strategic HRM or strategic resources practices.
- Organizational culture, work culture, or specific cultural dimensions (e.g., safety culture, innovation culture, ethical culture).
- Organizational transformation, change management, or cultural change.
- Hospital or healthcare settings, or principles applicable to these settings.

The process involved:

5. Screening the provided 90 article summaries to identify those meeting the inclusion criteria.
6. Extracting key information from the selected summaries, including their objectives, methods, conclusions, and specific findings related to strategic human resource management and work culture in hospitals.
7. Synthesizing the extracted information to identify common themes, patterns, and significant relationships between Strategic HRM practices and work culture transformation.

This approach allows for a focused analysis based on the provided dataset, aiming to construct a coherent narrative on the topic. The limitations inherent in reviewing summaries rather than full articles are acknowledged.

RESULTS

The literature review reveals several key themes regarding the relationship between Strategic HRM and work culture transformation in hospitals:

The Strategic Role of Human Capital and HRM in Hospitals

Several studies underscore that human capital is a strategic asset in hospitals, directly influencing competitive advantage and business performance (Winoto Tj et al., 2025). Effective Strategic HRM practices are crucial for developing this human capital (Yakusheva et al., 2024; Al-Tit et al., 2022). This includes strategic recruitment, training and development, performance management, and compensation systems designed to foster desired competencies and behaviours (Paşaoğlu

& Tonus, 2014; Aryanto et al., 2015). The perception of HRM's strategic role by organizational leaders, including entrepreneurs (Uyar & Deniz, 2012), is vital for its successful implementation and impact on culture.

Leadership as a Catalyst for Cultural Transformation

Transformational leadership and ethical leadership styles are consistently highlighted as significant drivers of positive organizational culture and, consequently, organizational effectiveness and performance (Nguyen et al., 2023; Kim, Kim, & Kim, 2015; Zhu et al., 2025). Leaders shape culture through their vision, communication, role modeling, and by fostering an environment of trust and support (Bagga et al., 2023; Moreno-Domínguez et al., 2024). Strategic HRM plays a role in identifying, developing, and supporting such leadership. Servant leadership, for instance, has been shown to enhance job satisfaction and reduce rule-breaking, contributing to a healthier work culture (Adiguzel et al., 2020). Participatory leadership, coupled with a supportive organizational culture, also significantly boosts job satisfaction (Nassani et al., 2024).

Cultivating Specific Cultural Dimensions through Strategic HRM

Strategic HRM practices can be tailored to cultivate specific, desirable cultural dimensions within hospitals:

- **Patient Safety Culture:** This is paramount in hospitals. Factors such as communication openness, non-punitive response to errors, adequate staffing, and patient safety training (all influenced by HRM) are crucial for a positive patient safety culture (Ali et al., 2023; Kim et al., 2015).
- **Innovation Culture:** Strategic HRM practices, particularly training, performance appraisal, and compensation, can foster organizational innovation and knowledge management capacity (Fındıklı et al., 2015; Uslu, 2015). A culture that supports learning and accepts mistakes as part of the process facilitates transformational change (Rass et al., 2025).
- **Ethical Culture:** Ethical leadership and an ethical organizational culture are linked to improved ESG performance and tax compliance, suggesting that Strategic HRM can contribute by promoting ethical conduct and values (Zhu et al., 2025; Musah et al., 2025).
- **Diversity and Inclusion:** Employee perception of the diversity climate, a "soft element" of Strategic HRM, is critical. Managerial status and employment type can influence these perceptions, highlighting the need for equi-

table resources practices (Sezerel & Tonus, 2014). Addressing issues like racism within hospital culture is also essential for an inclusive environment (D'Costa et al., 2023).

- **Learning Culture:** Hospitals need to be learning organizations to adapt and improve. Strategic HRM can support this by fostering knowledge management capabilities and creating an environment conducive to continuous learning and development (Aragón Sánchez et al., 2015; Robinson et al., 2025; Zhihan et al., 2022).

Employee Engagement, Well-being, and Organizational Commitment

Workplace culture significantly impacts employee well-being, job satisfaction, and intention to leave (Bull et al., 2024; Aggarwal, 2024). Strategic human resource management practices that promote work-life balance, support employee well-being (Ngo et al., 2023), and foster organizational commitment (Paşaoğlu, 2015) are crucial for a positive work culture and retaining talent. A supportive organizational culture, often nurtured through Strategic HRM, can mitigate burnout among ICU professionals by influencing factors like moral distress and work-life balance (Kok et al., 2025).

Managing Change and Transformation

Organizational culture is a key mediator in the relationship between transformational leadership and change management (Bagga et al., 2023). The strategic design of culture is essential for successful transformations, including digital transformation (Butt et al., 2022; Cao et al., 2025). Strategic HRM practices are central to managing the human side of change, ensuring that employees are equipped and motivated to adapt to new ways of working. This includes effective communication, training, and support during transitions like EMR implementation (Kant et al., 2025) or crises (Vardarlıer, 2016; Duvalda et al., 2025).

The Role of Knowledge Management and Organizational Learning

Knowledge management (KM) is increasingly important for hospitals. Organizational culture and leadership style significantly affect knowledge management and hospital efficiency (Moreno-Domínguez et al., 2024). Strategic HRM practices can mediate the relationship between knowledge management strategies and firm performance (Aragón Sánchez et al., 2015) and support the development of KM roadmaps (Cahyaningsih et al., 2017). A culture that encourages knowledge sharing is vital for innovation and performance (Saif et al., 2024).

DISCUSSION

The synthesized findings from the literature review highlight a strong and multifaceted relationship between Strategic HRM and the transformation of work culture in hospitals. It is evident that Strategic HRM is not merely an administrative function but a strategic enabler of cultural change and organizational improvement in the healthcare sector.

The critical role of leadership, particularly transformational and ethical leadership, emerges as a consistent theme. Strategic HRM's contribution here lies in its capacity to identify, nurture, and support leaders who can champion cultural change and inspire their teams. This aligns with the understanding that culture change often starts at the top, but requires buy-in and active participation at all levels.

Furthermore, the ability of Strategic HRM to target and cultivate specific cultural dimensions is crucial for hospitals. Whether it is fostering a robust patient safety culture, encouraging innovation, promoting ethical behavior, or building a supportive learning environment, strategic human resource management practices provide the mechanisms to embed these values and behaviors into the fabric of the organization. For example, performance management systems can be designed to reward collaborative behaviors and adherence to safety protocols, while training programs can equip staff with the skills needed for new technologies or patient care models that underpin cultural shifts.

The impact of work culture on employee well-being, satisfaction, and retention cannot be overstated, especially in high-stress hospital environments. Strategic HRM practices focused on employee development, work-life balance, and creating a supportive and inclusive climate are essential not only for ethical reasons but also for ensuring a stable, motivated, and effective workforce. High turnover and burnout, often exacerbated by negative work cultures, can severely undermine a hospital's ability to provide quality care.

The review also points to the importance of aligning Strategic HRM with broader organizational strategies, such as digital transformation or crisis management. Cultural resistance is a common barrier to change; strategic human resource management can help mitigate this by fostering a culture of adaptability, continuous learning, and psychological safety.

Implications for Practice: Hospital administrators and HR leaders should:

- Recognize and leverage Strategic HRM as a strategic tool for cultural transformation.
- Invest in leadership development programs that emphasize skills for leading cultural change.
- Design and implement human resources practices (recruitment, training, performance management, rewards) that are explicitly aligned with desired cultural values (e.g., safety, innovation, patient-centeredness, collaboration).
- Prioritize employee well-being and engagement as integral components of cultural health.
- Foster open communication and knowledge sharing to support learning and adaptation.
- Continuously assess the organizational culture and the impact of Strategic HRM interventions, making adjustments as needed.

The findings of this literature-based analysis underscore the dynamic and reciprocal relationship between Strategic HRM and work culture transformation within hospital settings. Hospitals operate in high-stakes, high-pressure environments, where human behavior, motivation, and values significantly influence clinical outcomes and organizational performance. As such, Strategic HRM—when aligned with institutional strategy—emerges as a powerful vehicle for cultural change, workforce engagement, and overall organizational resilience.

Strategic HRM as An Architect of Culture

One of the central insights of this review is that Strategic HRM is not merely a supporting function but a cultural architect. Through deliberate design and implementation of policies in areas such as recruitment, performance management, leadership development, learning systems, and employee engagement, Strategic HRM actively constructs and reinforces the behavioral norms, values, and assumptions that form an organization's culture. For hospitals undergoing transformation, this capability is crucial in shifting the institutional mindset toward goals such as patient safety, innovation, or collaborative care.

Leadership as a Cultural Lever

Leadership consistently appears in the literature as a primary mechanism through which Strategic HRM influences culture. The types of leaders nurtured and promoted—whether transformational, ethical, or servant leaders—determine the tone and trust levels across hospital units. Strategic HRM's role in leadership identification, competency mapping, and succession planning thus becomes pivotal. Moreover, leaders act as both symbols and drivers of cultural values, and their behavior either accelerates or obstructs transformation efforts.

Balancing Formal Systems and Informal Norms

Another key theme is the tension and synergy between formal HR systems and the informal elements of culture. Strategic HRM structures—such as job design, appraisal systems, and reward mechanisms—can serve as formal enablers of desired cultural attributes. However, the success of these initiatives often depends on their integration with informal networks, unwritten rules, and symbolic behaviors. For example, a formal safety protocol is only effective when accompanied by a shared belief in psychological safety and frontline empowerment.

The Role of Employee Engagement

The review further highlights the bidirectional relationship between work culture and employee engagement. A healthy work culture—marked by trust, fairness, and shared purpose—fuels engagement, while engaged employees reinforce and embody positive cultural traits. Strategic HRM initiatives that empower staff, provide career development, recognize contributions, and promote work-life balance are critical in sustaining this virtuous cycle. In hospitals, this directly correlates with improved clinical care and reduced turnover.

Cultural Alignment and Strategic Intent

Cultural transformation efforts must be purposefully aligned with broader organizational goals. Hospitals may prioritize different cultural shifts—toward innovation, accountability, safety, or compassion—depending on their strategic context. The literature emphasizes that Strategic HRM should not adopt a one-size-fits-all model; instead, human resources practices must be tailored to reinforce the specific cultural outcomes desired by hospital leadership. Misalignment between human resources systems and cultural messaging can create confusion, resistance, or erosion of trust.

Challenges in Practice

Despite its strategic potential, implementing Strategic HRM in hospitals faces several challenges. Hierarchical structures, siloed departments, professional tribalism, and resistance to change can hinder HR-driven cultural initiatives. Furthermore, in resource-constrained or crisis-prone settings, HR may be relegated to administrative tasks rather than strategic leadership. Overcoming these barriers requires strong executive sponsorship, clear communication, and robust metrics for cultural and performance outcomes.

Continuous Adaptation and Learning

Cultural transformation is not a static project but an ongoing adaptive process. Hospitals must develop internal capabilities to monitor, evaluate, and refine their human resources and cultural interventions over time. Strategic HRM provides the tools—such as human resources analytics, pulse surveys, and workforce planning models—to support iterative learning and organizational responsiveness. This continuous improvement mindset is especially critical in healthcare, where external demands and patient needs evolve rapidly.

SUGGESTIONS AND RECOMMENDATIONS

Based on the synthesis of relevant literature and the thematic analysis conducted, several strategic recommendations are proposed to guide hospital leaders, human resource professionals, and policymakers in leveraging Strategic HRM for effective work culture transformation.

Embed Strategic HRM into Hospital Governance

Hospitals should elevate the role of Human Resource Management (HRM) from a purely administrative function to a strategic partner embedded in top-level decision-making. This requires appointing HR leaders to the executive board, ensuring Strategic HRM perspectives are integrated into long-term planning, budgeting, and organizational transformation agendas. A culture-focused strategy will gain legitimacy and traction only when endorsed and driven by senior leadership.

Develop Leadership That Shapes Culture

Investing in leadership development programs that promote transformational, inclusive, and ethical leadership styles is essential. Strategic HRM should identify and cultivate leaders who serve as role models of the desired culture—whether it emphasizes patient safety, collaboration, continuous learning, or innovation. A structured leadership pipeline, mentorship system, and competency-based evaluation will reinforce leadership behaviors aligned with organizational values.

Align Human Resources Practices with Cultural Objectives

Human resources policies must be intentionally aligned with the cultural transformation goals of the hospital. For example:

- Performance appraisal systems should measure behaviors that reflect the targeted cultural values.
- Recruitment processes should prioritize not just technical fit but also cultural fit.
- Reward systems should recognize team-based contributions, innovation, or compassionate care—depending on the desired culture.

This alignment helps build internal coherence between what is expected, what is rewarded, and what is culturally reinforced.

Promote Employee Voice and Participation

Work culture transformation requires inclusive engagement. Strategic HRM should create platforms for employee voice, such as suggestion systems, town hall meetings, staff surveys, or participatory policy reviews. Engaging front-line workers in shaping the hospital's values and behavioral norms fosters ownership, reduces resistance, and enables continuous cultural learning.

Leverage HR Analytics to Monitor Culture Change

Strategic HRM must incorporate data-driven tools to measure and track cultural change over time. This includes:

- Surveys on organizational climate and employee engagement.
- Analysis of turnover, absenteeism, and incident reporting patterns.
- Metrics linked to cultural goals, such as collaboration scores or safety compliance rates.

Such analytics not only provide feedback on the effectiveness of interventions but also help in adapting strategies to changing contexts.

Foster Interdisciplinary and Interprofessional Collaboration

In the hospital setting, cultural transformation requires dismantling professional silos. Strategic HRM should facilitate team-based training, cross-functional projects, and shared leadership models that encourage interprofessional trust and collaboration. Building a culture of mutual respect among doctors, nurses, administrators, and allied professionals is crucial for coherent service delivery and patient-centred care.

Contextualize Global Strategic HRM Models to Local Realities

While many strategic human resource management frameworks are derived from global best practices, their application in hospital settings—especially in developing countries—must consider contextual constraints such as resource availability, regulatory frameworks, and institutional legacy. Therefore, hospitals should localize SHRM strategies, blending international insights with indigenous organizational learning and cultural sensitivity.

Commit to Long-Term Cultural Transformation

Culture change is a long-term commitment that requires consistency, patience, and adaptability. Hospitals should establish multi-year cultural roadmaps, allocate dedicated budgets for change initiatives, and build resilience into Strategic HRM processes. Institutional memory should be preserved through documentation and knowledge management systems to ensure cultural continuity even amidst leadership transitions.

Limitations and Future Research: This review is based on summaries of articles, which may not capture the full nuance of the original research. Future research could involve a more in-depth systematic review of full-text articles. Additionally, while many principles are transferable, more research specifically contextualized within diverse hospital settings (e.g., public vs. private, different national healthcare systems) would be beneficial. Longitudinal studies tracking the impact of specific Strategic HRM interventions on cultural transformation and patient outcomes in hospitals would provide valuable insights. Investigating the role of technology and HR analytics in shaping and monitoring hospital work culture is another promising avenue.

CONCLUSION

The transformation of work culture in hospitals is a critical imperative for enhancing patient care, staff well-being, and overall organizational effectiveness. Strategic HRM provides a powerful arsenal of strategies and practices to drive and sustain such transformations. By strategically developing human capital, fostering effective leadership, cultivating desired cultural attributes, promoting employee engagement, and managing change proactively, hospitals can create work environments that are not only efficient and safe but also supportive, innovative, and resilient. The journey of cultural transformation is ongoing, and Strategic HRM is an indispensable partner in navigating this complex but vital path.

This literature-based analysis has provided compelling evidence that Strategic HRM plays a pivotal role not only in managing hospital workforces efficiently but also in actively shaping and transforming the underlying work culture that governs daily clinical practice, interprofessional relationships, and organizational performance. As hospitals navigate increasingly complex healthcare environments characterized by rapid technological advancements, demographic shifts, economic constraints, and heightened patient expectations, the necessity of cultivating an adaptive, resilient, and strategically aligned work culture becomes both an operational imperative and a moral obligation.

The findings suggest that Strategic HRM, when embedded within the hospital's overarching strategic framework, possesses the potential to become a transformative force—shifting HR functions from administrative or transactional roles toward being drivers of institutional change, cultural alignment, and continuous improvement. Strategic alignment of HR policies and practices with the hospital's core values and long-term goals enables the creation of a psychologically safe, ethically grounded, and professionally supportive environment in which both staff and patients can thrive.

By focusing on key areas such as leadership development, performance management, talent acquisition, employee engagement, and learning systems, Strategic HRM can reinforce the behavioral norms, shared values, and informal practices that constitute the work culture. Importantly, such transformation is not achieved solely through top-down policy changes, but through an integrated and inclusive process in which leaders serve as cultural role models, frontline workers are given voice and agency, and the entire organization commits to a continuous cycle of learning, reflection, and recalibration.

Moreover, this study highlights that successful work culture transformation in hospitals necessitates a deliberate and coherent approach wherein strategic human resource management not only supports but actively engineers change through data-informed decision-making, contextually tailored interventions, and cross-functional collaboration. Challenges such as organizational inertia, professional silos, and limited resources must be met with strategic agility, ethical leadership, and a strong sense of shared purpose.

In sum, the interplay between Strategic HRM and hospital work culture is neither incidental nor peripheral; it constitutes a foundational dynamic that determines the institution's capacity to deliver high-quality care, maintain workforce well-being, and achieve long-term sustainability. As the healthcare sector continues to evolve, future research and institutional practice should prioritize the development of integrative Strategic HRM models that are responsive to both global evidence and local context, thereby ensuring that cultural transformation becomes not a reactive necessity, but a proactive strategy for excellence.

ACKNOWLEDGMENT

This article is the result of an extensive synthesis of 90 peer-reviewed academic articles and scholarly publications that collectively form the foundation for the conceptual framework, thematic insights, and critical arguments presented throughout this work. The key findings and interpretations offered herein are directly informed by the comprehensive summaries, content analyses, and integrative reviews conducted on these diverse sources, which span the disciplines of healthcare management, organizational behavior, Strategic HRM, and hospital administration. The authors gratefully acknowledge the intellectual contributions of these original works, as they have provided invaluable theoretical perspectives, empirical evidence, and methodological approaches that significantly enriched the depth, rigor, and relevance of this literature-based analysis.

REFERENCES

Adiguzel, Z., Ozcinar, M. F., & Karadal, H. (2020). Does Servant Leadership Moderate the Link Between Strategic Human Resource Management on Rule Breaking and Job Satisfaction? *European Research on Management and Business Economics*, *26*(2), 103–110. DOI: 10.1016/j.iedeen.2020.04.002

Aggarwal, S. (2024). Impact of Dimensions of Organisational Culture on Employee Satisfaction and Performance Level in Select Organisations. *IIMB Management Review*, *36*(3), 230–238. DOI: 10.1016/j.iimb.2024.07.001

Al-Tit, A., Al-Ayed, S., Alhammadi, A., Hunitie, M., Alsarayreh, A., & Albassam, W. (2022). The Impact of Employee Development Practices on Human Capital and Social Capital: The Mediating Contribution of Knowledge Management. *Journal of Open Innovation*, *8*(4), 218. DOI: 10.3390/joitmc8040218

Ali, M., Ademe, S., Shumiye, M., & Hamza, A. (2023). Patient safety culture and associated factors among health care workers in South Wollo Zone public hospitals, North East Ethiopia. BMC Health Services Research.

Aragón Sánchez, A., Sánchez Marín, G., & Mueses Morales, A. (2015). The Mediating Effect of Strategic Human Resource Practices on Knowledge Management and Firm Performance. *Revista Europea de Dirección y Economía de la Empresa*, *24*, 138–148.

Aryanto, R., Fontana, A., & Afiff, A. Z. (2015). Strategic Human Resource Management, Innovation Capability and Performance: An Empirical Study in Indonesia Software Industry. *Procedia: Social and Behavioral Sciences, 211*, 874–879. DOI: 10.1016/j.sbspro.2015.11.115

Bagga, S. K., Gera, S., & Haque, S. N. (2023). *The mediating role of organizational culture: Transformational leadership and change management in virtual teams*. Asia Pacific Management Review.

Bull, R., McFarland, L., Cumming, T., & Wong, S. (2024). The Impact of Work-Related Wellbeing and Workplace Culture and Climate on Intention to Leave in the Early Childhood Sector. *Early Childhood Research Quarterly*, *69*, 13–24. DOI: 10.1016/j.ecresq.2024.06.002

Butt, A., Imran, F., Helo, P., & Kantola, J. (2022). Strategic Design of Culture for Digital Transformation. *Journal of Innovation and Entrepreneurship*.

Cahyaningsih, E., Sensuse, D. I., & Noprisson, H. (2017). Multi Methods for Knowledge Management Strategy Roadmap of Government Human Capital Management. *Procedia Computer Science*, *124*, 496–503. DOI: 10.1016/j.procs.2017.12.182

Cao, G., Duan, Y., & Edwards, J. S. (2025). Organizational culture, digital transformation, and product innovation: A systematic review. *Information & Management*, *62*(4), 104135. DOI: 10.1016/j.im.2025.104135

D'Costa, I., Truong, M., Russell, L., & Adams, K. (2023). Employee Perceptions of Race and Racism in an Australian Hospital. *Social Science & Medicine*, *339*, 116364. DOI: 10.1016/j.socscimed.2023.116364 PMID: 37977016

Duvalda, I., Obel, B., Lohse, C., Kirkegaard, H., & Burton, R. M. (2025). Organizational resilience in emergency healthcare: Lessons from the COVID-19 pandemic in five Danish hospitals. *Social Science & Medicine*, *366*, 117728. DOI: 10.1016/j.socscimed.2025.117728 PMID: 39855026

Fındıklı, M. A., Yozgat, U., & Rofcanin, Y. (2015). Examining Organizational Innovation and Knowledge Management Capacity: The Central Role of Strategic Human Resources Practices (SHRPs). *Procedia: Social and Behavioral Sciences*, *181*, 377–387. DOI: 10.1016/j.sbspro.2015.04.900

Kant, V., Weinert, L., & Rotter, T. (2025). *A qualitative study on the implementation of electronic medical records in German hospitals. Z. Evid. Fortbild. Qual. Gesundh. wesen*. ZEFQ.

Kim, I.-S., Park, M., Park, M.-Y., Yoo, H., & Choi, J. (2015). Factors Affecting the Perception of Importance and Practice of Patient Safety Management among Hospital Employees in Korea.

Kim, J., & Han, W. (2012). Improving Service Quality in Long-term Care Hospitals: National Evaluation on Long-term Care Hospitals and Employees Perception of Quality Dimensions. *Osong Public Health and Research Perspectives*, *3*(2), 94–99. DOI: 10.1016/j.phrp.2012.04.005 PMID: 24159497

Kim, J. H., Kim, C. S., & Kim, J. M. (2015). Analysis of the Effect of Leadership and Organizational Culture on the Organizational Effectiveness of Radiological Technologists' Working Environments. *Journal of Radiological Science and Technology*.

Kok, N., Hoedemaekers, C., Fuchs, M., Cornet, A. D., Ewalds, E., Hom, H., Meijer, E., Meynaar, I., van Mol, M., van Mook, W., van der Steen-Dieperink, M., van Zanten, A., van der Hoeven, H., van Gurp, J., & Zegers, M. (2025). The interplay between organizational culture and burnout among ICU professionals: A cross-sectional multicenter study. *Journal of Critical Care*, *85*, 154981. DOI: 10.1016/j.jcrc.2024.154981 PMID: 39608045

Laroche, E. (2024). Management practices that promote preventive measures compliance: A comparative analysis between hospital healthcare workers and teachers. *Safety Science*, *177*, 106591. DOI: 10.1016/j.ssci.2024.106591

Moreno-Domínguez, M.-J., Escobar-Rodríguez, T., Pelayo-Díaz, Y.-M., & Tovar-García, I. (2024). Organizational culture and leadership style in Spanish Hospitals: Effects on knowledge management and efficiency. *Heliyon*, *10*(20), e39216. DOI: 10.1016/j.heliyon.2024.e39216 PMID: 39498020

Musah, A., Padi, A., Blay, M. W., Okyere, D. O., & Ofori, B. S. (2025). Ethical organisational culture, effective internal control systems and tax compliance of small and medium scale enterprises (SMEs): The role of corporate governance. *Social Sciences & Humanities Open*, *11*, 101331. DOI: 10.1016/j.ssaho.2025.101331

Nassani, A. A., Badshah, W., Grigorescu, A., Cozorici, A. N., Yousaf, Z., & Zhan, X. (2024). Participatory leadership and supportive organisational culture Panacea for job satisfaction regulatory role of work-life balance. *Heliyon*, *10*(16), e36043. DOI: 10.1016/j.heliyon.2024.e36043 PMID: 39224389

Ngo, T., Le, D., & Doan, T. (2023). Are Your Employees Mentally Prepared for the Pandemic? Wellbeing-Oriented Human Resource Management Practices in a Developing Country. *International Journal of Hospitality Management*, *109*, 103415. DOI: 10.1016/j.ijhm.2022.103415

Nguyen, N. P., Nguyen, T. T. H., Nguyen, H., & Flynnd, O. (2023). *Does transformational leadership influence organisational culture and organisational performance: Empirical evidence from an emerging country*. ScienceDirect.

Paauwe, J., & Van De Voorde, K. (2025). Bridging the Research–Practice Gap in Modern Human Resource Management. *Human Resource Management Review, 35*(2), 101076. DOI: 10.1016/j.hrmr.2025.101076

Paşaoğlu, D. (2015). Analysis of the Relationship Between Human Resources Management Practices and Organizational Commitment from a Strategic Perspective: Findings from the Banking Industry. Procedia Social and Behavioral Sciences.

Paşaoğlu, D., & Tonus, H. Z. (2014). Strategic Importance of Human Resource Practices on Job Satisfaction in Private Hospitals. *Procedia: Social and Behavioral Sciences.*

Rass, L., Treur, J., Kucharska, W., & Wiewiora, A. (2025). Adaptive dynamical systems modelling of transformational organizational change with focus on organizational culture and organizational learning.

Robinson, B. A., McCormack, B., & Dickson, C. (2025). Becoming a Person-Centred Facilitator of Learning in a Hospital Setting: Findings from a Participatory Action-Oriented Study with Hospital-Based Educators. *Nurse Education in Practice, 82*, 104222. DOI: 10.1016/j.nepr.2024.104222 PMID: 39673866

Rogers, E. W., & Wright, P. M. (1998). Measuring Organizational Performance in Strategic Human Resource Management: Problems, Prospects, and Performance Information Markets. *Human Resource Management Review, 8*(3), 311–331. DOI: 10.1016/S1053-4822(98)90007-9

Saif, N., Amelia, , Goh, G. G. G., Rubin, A., Shaheen, I., & Murtaza, M. (2024). Influence of Transformational Leadership on Innovative Work Behavior and Task Performance of Individuals: The Mediating Role of Knowledge Sharing. *Heliyon, 10*(11), e32280. DOI: 10.1016/j.heliyon.2024.e32280 PMID: 38933951

Sezerel, H., & Tonus, H. Z. (2014). The Soft Element of Strategic Human Resource Management: The Employee's Perception of Diversity Climate. *Procedia: Social and Behavioral Sciences, 150*, 354–359. DOI: 10.1016/j.sbspro.2014.09.026

Sullivan, J. L., Shin, M. H., Ranusch, A., Mohr, D. C., Chen, C., & Damschroder, L. J. (2024). A Mixed Methods Study Exploring Patient Safety Culture at Four VHA Hospitals. *Joint Commission Journal on Quality and Patient Safety, 50*(11), 791–800. DOI: 10.1016/j.jcjq.2024.07.008 PMID: 39289144

Uslu, T. (2015). Innovation Culture and Strategic Human Resource Management in Public and Private Sector within The Framework Of Employee Ownership. *Procedia: Social and Behavioral Sciences, 195*, 1463–1470. DOI: 10.1016/j.sbspro.2015.06.445

Uyar, A. S., & Deniz, N. (2012). The Perceptions of Entrepreneurs on the Strategic Role of Human Resource Management. *Procedia: Social and Behavioral Sciences, 58*, 914–923. DOI: 10.1016/j.sbspro.2012.09.1070

Vardarlıer, P. (2016). Strategic Approach to Human Resources Management During Crisis. *Procedia: Social and Behavioral Sciences, 235*, 463–472. DOI: 10.1016/j.sbspro.2016.11.057

Winoto Tj, H., Wibowo, J. M., & Widjaja, B. T. (2025). Human Capital, Competitive Advantage, and Business Performance: A Study of Indonesian Hospitals. *Journal of Open Innovation*.

Yakusheva, O., Lee, K. A., & Weiss, M. (2024). The Nursing Human Capital Value Model. *International Journal of Nursing Studies, 160*, 104890. DOI: 10.1016/j.ijnurstu.2024.104890 PMID: 39316994

Zehir, C., Gurol, Y., Karaboga, T., & Kole, M. (2016). Strategic Human Resource Management and Firm Performance: The Mediating Role of Entrepreneurial Orientation. *Procedia: Social and Behavioral Sciences, 235*, 372–381. DOI: 10.1016/j.sbspro.2016.11.045

Zhihan, S., Mohammadiounotikandi, A., Khanlooei, S. G., Monjezi, S., Umaralievich, M. S., Ehsani, A., & Lee, S. (2022). A new conceptual model to investigate the role of hospital's capabilities on sustainable learning. *The International Journal of Organizational Analysis*.

Zhu, J., Zhi, W., & Fang, Y. (2025). Ethical leadership, organizational learning, and corporate ESG performance: A moderated mediation model. *International Review of Economics & Finance, 98*, 103966. DOI: 10.1016/j.iref.2025.103966

Chapter 12
Risk Interconnections and Management in Islamic Sustainable and Commodity Markets

Emna Mnif
https://orcid.org/0000-0002-4976-850X
Sfax University, Tunisia

ABSTRACT

Drawing on daily returns from June 2018 to March 2024, this study evaluates how a multi-asset portfolio of Islamic finance equities (DJIM), sustainability indices (DJSW), WTI crude oil, and gold can jointly enhance risk mitigation and ESG alignment. Utilizing an R^2 connectedness framework that combines partial correlation networks, VAR modeling, and GFEVD, we quantify dynamic spillovers and shock transmissions as percentage contributions to forecast variance. Empirical results reveal that WTI and clean-energy benchmarks deliver the strongest hedging benefits across Minimum Variance, Minimum Correlation, and Minimum Connectedness portfolios. Islamic finance and sustainability indices, while offering moderate volatility reduction, assume a vital defensive role during market stress by upholding Shariah compliance and ethical mandates.

INTRODUCTION

Human civilization now faces unprecedented challenges as climate change accelerates the deterioration of natural ecosystems and disrupts atmospheric conditions (Billah, Alam, and Hoque, 2024). This intensifying crisis has spurred global efforts

DOI: 10.4018/979-8-3373-2655-9.ch012

toward sustainable development (Liu et al., 2022; D'Souza et al., 2006). In direct response, governments and businesses worldwide have initiated comprehensive measures to curb carbon emissions and decrease reliance on fossil fuels, recognizing that proactive intervention is critical to averting catastrophic environmental outcomes (Naeem et al., 2022; Duan et al., 2023; Mnif et al., 2023; Climent & Soriano, 2011; Jarboui et al., 2024). Redirecting financial resources toward green and sustainable innovation is not only essential for significantly cutting greenhouse gas emissions but also for fostering long-term economic resilience (Ben Jabeur, Khalfaoui, and Ben Arfi, 2021). In this context, Islamic stock markets have emerged as promising conduits for ethical investment. Operating under Sharia principles and overseen by dedicated Sharia councils, these markets offer investment opportunities that inherently align with the core values of green finance (Bouoiyour et al., 2018; Kenourgios et al., 2016; Hassan et al., 2021).

Investors focused on promoting ecological benefits, environmental stewardship, and broader sustainability goals increasingly view Islamic equities as valuable additions to diversified portfolios. These assets offer a distinct ethical profile and provide diversification benefits, hedging capabilities, and safe-haven characteristics during periods of market turbulence (Selmi et al., 2023; Bouri et al., 2020; Maghyereh et al., 2018; M. Liu & Lee, 2022; Akhtaruzzaman et al., 2021). Integrating Islamic finance with sustainable investing not only broadens the investment spectrum but also supports the environmental objectives vital for mitigating climate change, thereby reinforcing the synergy between ethical investment practices and green economic growth.

Within Islamic finance, principles such as mudarabah and musharakah enable shared risk among stakeholders. These mechanisms discourage speculative behavior (gharar) and encourage long-term investment aligned with sustainability outcomes. For instance, the success of Malaysia's Green Sukuk illustrates the ability of Shariah-compliant instruments in channeling capital into climate-resilient infrastructure. Compared to conventional finance, which often depends on interest-bearing debt and risk-transfer mechanisms, Islamic finance adopts a more transparent, ethics-driven approach. Its reliance on real-economy-linked assets and prohibition of excessive leverage or uncertainty fosters market stability, particularly under stress. Hedging in Islamic markets avoids derivatives and embraces instruments like sukuk that are asset-backed and increasingly linked to environmental and social goals. This divergence in risk philosophy is narrowing, however, with the rise of ESG-linked indices that bridge faith-based finance with global sustainable finance norms. These emerging models reveal both innovation opportunities and the need for harmonization in regulatory frameworks and disclosure standards.

Green assets and markets have exhibited robust performance, gaining favor among investors who prioritize environmental sustainability and eco-friendly outcomes (Lahmiri et al., 2020; Mohsin & Jamaani, 2023; Lorente et al., 2023; Broadstock et al., 2022). Despite their appeal, green assets ranging from clean energy and sustainable equities to Islamic finance instruments remain subject to the inherent fluctuations, risks, and uncertainties that affect all investment types. Their performance is influenced by diverse factors, including cross-market attractiveness and inherent volatility, which in turn are shaped by global market dynamics and investor sentiment across different countries and sectors. Moreover, macroeconomic trends, evolving economic and climate policies, geopolitical events, and shifts in technological investments further contribute to the volatility profile and overall risk inherent in green markets (Broadstock et al., 2022; Mnif et al., 2024; Jin et al., 2023; Jarboui & Mnif, 2023).

From a theoretical standpoint, financial markets are deeply interconnected, a characteristic that can trigger a "butterfly effect" wherein disturbances in one market propagate to others. In periods marked by extreme stress in green asset markets, investors often reallocate their portfolios to include alternative assets with distinct risk-return profiles and lower correlations relative to green investments (Mensi et al., 2017). Such diversification strategies not only mitigate risks but also enhance the resilience of portfolios combining green and other asset classes. A significant body of research has investigated the interconnectivity and spillover effects across various segments of financial markets.

One research stream explores the linkages between green assets and multiple other markets including crude oil (Le, 2023; Ha & Nham, 2022), traditional financial markets (Broadstock et al., 2022; Baruník & Křehlík, 2018), renewable energy sectors (Dogan et al., 2022), cryptocurrencies (Jiménez et al., 2024; Abid et al., 2023), conventional bonds (C. Liu & Chen, 2024; Uddin et al., 2024), and uncertainty proxies (Xing et al., 2024; Dong et al., 2024; H. Liu et al., 2024). Other studies focus on the internal dynamics within the green asset class itself, revealing evidence of time-varying dependence and instances of extreme market dependency (Lorente et al., 2023; Chatziantoniou et al., 2021; Antonakakis et al., 2020). Notably, relatively few studies have jointly examined the interconnections among green, sustainable, and Islamic markets. For example, Billah et al. (2024) use CAViaR models to estimate left-tail risks across renewable energy, green and sustainable equities, as well as Islamic equity and bond markets, demonstrating that mature market indices tend to be persistent transmitters of tail risk, whereas developing Islamic financial instruments are more likely to absorb external shocks.

Moreover, uncertainty indices linked to gold and the US dollar have been identified as potential hedges capable of predicting connectedness. Complementarily, Tiwari et al. (2023) employ advanced techniques to reveal a long-run negative spillover from green bonds to Islamic stocks during volatile periods, further underscoring the systemic risks associated with green bonds and their emerging role within diversified investor portfolios. This multifaceted landscape underscores the importance of continued research into the diverse interconnections between green and Islamic financial assets, as these markets offer unique diversification, risk mitigation, and safe-haven characteristics that are increasingly critical in a volatile global economy. The increasing uncertainty and volatility in global financial markets have driven investors to seek alternative investment avenues that provide both resilience and diversified risk exposure. In this milieu, Islamic stocks have increasingly attracted attention as a viable substitute to conventional equity investments (Hassan et al., 2022).

Unlike traditional markets, Islamic stock markets adhere to Shariah principles and financial regulations that prohibit investments in industries and practices deemed unethical or harmful to society. This adherence to ethical guidelines not only offers investors a moral and socially responsible choice but it also creates a distinct set of market dynamics that may contribute to portfolio diversification and risk mitigation. Islamic stock markets operate within a framework designed to promote profit-and-loss sharing, thereby reducing information asymmetry and fostering transparency between market participants. This unique operating principle often results in lower volatility compared to conventional markets, particularly during periods of financial turbulence. In addition, the inherent structure of Islamic finance has made these markets relatively insulated from the speculative behaviors that can sometimes exacerbate market downturns. By aligning their investment processes with ethical standards, these markets create an alternative asset class that appeals to a broad spectrum of investors who are seeking environmental, social, and governance (ESG) criteria. The study of the interconnectedness between Islamic stock markets and other key asset classes, such as gold, crude oil, sustainable equities, and green assets, including benchmarks like the Corporate Sustainability Index (ISE) has emerged as a critical research frontier.

The unique intersection of ethical investment principles and diversification benefits is further underscored by the growing global demand for sustainable investment options. Integrating Shariah-compliant finance with green and socially responsible investing serves as a natural fit with the broader movement toward ESG integration. As investors become increasingly conscious of environmental and social issues, the synergy between Islamic finance and sustainability-oriented assets presents a promising opportunity to construct portfolios that balance financial performance with positive societal impact. From a portfolio management perspective, the low correlation of Islamic stocks with conventional asset classes contributes to their appeal, especially in times of economic distress. This low interdependence suggests that, when broader markets experience shocks or heightened volatility, Islamic stock markets can provide an element of stability, acting as a buffer against extreme market swings.

As a result, the resilience of these markets during crises has been repeatedly highlighted in empirical studies, with evidence suggesting that they can serve as effective hedges and safe-haven assets for risk-averse investors. Moreover, the incorporation of Islamic equities into diversified portfolios introduces an additional layer of risk management by leveraging the ethical and operational frameworks inherent in these markets. Despite the promising aspects of Islamic stock markets, the academic literature examining their interconnections with other asset classes remains limited, especially in terms of exploring their relationship with green and sustainable indexes, as well as traditional commodities like crude oil and gold.

Existing research has yielded mixed findings regarding the linkage between Islamic and commodity stocks, thereby underscoring the need for further investigation using advanced empirical methodologies. In particular, the dynamic nature of these markets calls for analytical approaches that can capture time-varying correlations and spillover effects across different economic cycles. As Islamic stock markets are relatively new and continue to evolve both regionally and globally (Mnif and Jarboui, 2021), a deeper understanding of their behavior is essential for developing robust investment strategies that account for both ethical considerations and market stability. This study is designed to address these gaps by examining the interrelationships between Islamic stock markets, crude oil, gold, and sustainable indexes. By doing so, the research aims to offer comprehensive insights into how these diverse asset classes interact, particularly in terms of risk transmission and diversification benefits. The analysis is structured as follows: Section 2 details the dataset and methodologies employed, highlighting advanced techniques capable of capturing dynamic spillover effects and inter-market connectedness.

Section 3 presents the empirical findings, including the resilience and hedging properties of Islamic stocks compared to other assets. Finally, Section 4 concludes with key policy implications and directions for future research, emphasizing the potential for innovative portfolio management strategies that effectively combine financial and ethical objectives. Overall, the exploration of Islamic stock markets within the broader context of sustainable investing is not only timely but also necessary. As the global economy increasingly aligns with ethical and sustainable practices, understanding the role of Islamic equities becomes critical for both investors and policymakers. The inherent strengths of these markets, their ethical foundation, lower susceptibility to information asymmetry, and demonstrated resilience during crises, position them as a cornerstone for constructing portfolios that are robust, diversified, and socially responsible.

DATA AND METHODOLOGY

This section presents an in-depth overview of our empirical framework, which is built around a novel R^2 connectedness approach. This approach uniquely combines elements from two established methodologies: the partial correlation network methodology introduced by Kenett et al. (2010, 2015) and the connectedness framework developed by Diebold and Yilmaz (2012, 2014). By leveraging the strengths of both methods, our framework can capture the underlying dynamic relationships and spillover effects among the selected asset classes with greater interpretability and precision. The combined method yields dynamic measures of connectedness that are both robust and sensitive to temporal variations in the data, thereby enabling a comprehensive analysis of inter-market relationships. The core innovation in our framework is the application of the R^2 decomposition. Unlike traditional connectedness measures that require rescaling and often suffer from interpretational ambiguities, the R^2 framework provides a bounded and straightforward measure.

This novel decomposition allows us to quantify the extent of interconnectedness in a way that is both interpretable and easily comparable across different time periods and market conditions. In essence, it sidesteps the limitations inherent in earlier approaches by offering a natural interpretation in terms of the proportion of variance explained by cross-market interactions. In addition to measuring dynamic connectedness, I also assess the performance of each financial market through the lens of hedge effectiveness. For this purpose, I employ the hedge effectiveness methodology first proposed by Ederington (1979). This method evaluates the ability of specific assets to reduce risk and mitigate portfolio volatility. By quantifying hedge effectiveness, it could be determined which assets serve as more reliable risk buffers under different market scenarios.

To further ensure the robustness of our findings, I complement our primary analysis with an advanced Quantile Vector Autoregression (QVAR) connectedness approach. The QVAR framework extends our analysis by capturing the behavior of the connectedness measures across different quantiles of the return distribution, thereby accounting for tail dependencies and nonlinear dynamics. This additional layer of analysis enables us to rigorously validate the stability and reliability of our hedge effectiveness results even under extreme market conditions. Overall, the integration of these complementary methodologies, the R^2 connectedness approach, VAR-based GFEVD, hedge effectiveness measurement, and the QVAR analysis results in a comprehensive empirical framework. This framework is well-equipped to capture the complexities of inter-market spillovers and to deliver actionable insights on the dynamic interrelations among Islamic finance stocks, sustainability indices, and commodity markets.

Data

Our study focuses on the investigation of risk spillovers and hedge effectiveness, aiming to demonstrate the crucial role of Islamic indices in promoting sustainability and addressing climate-related issues. For this purpose, this study employs a robust dataset spanning from 01/06/2018 to 31/03/2024 and includes the Dow Jones Islamic Market Index (DJIM), the Dow Jones Sustainability World Index (DJSW), Gold, Crude Oil (WTI), the S&P Global Clean Energy Index (CLEAN), and the Corporate Sustainability Index (ISE). The DJIM represents ethical investing, adhering to Shariah principles, which exclude companies involved in industries detrimental to social and environmental well-being, thus aligning with broader sustainability goals. The DJSI World offers a global benchmark for companies recognized for their sustainability leadership, which is key for analyzing the broader impact of sustainability efforts on market performance. The inclusion of commodities like gold and crude oil allows us to explore traditional hedging instruments and their interactions with sustainable indices during periods of economic stress.

The S&P Global Clean Energy Index captures the transition to renewable energy sources, emphasizing the growing focus on climate action within financial markets. Lastly, the Corporate Sustainability Index (ISE) tracks companies committed to sustainability practices, reinforcing the role of corporate behavior in mitigating climate risks. By incorporating these diverse interconnected datasets, I comprehensively analyze hedge effectiveness and risk spillovers across traditional, sustainable, and Islamic indices. This allows us to showcase the Islamic index's vital role in fostering sustainability and climate resilience while assessing its effectiveness as a hedge within a dynamically evolving financial landscape. To maintain methodological rigor in our study, this study applied the Phillips & Perron (1988) unit root test to address potential non-stationarity in our variables.

Upon confirming their non-stationarity, I converted the data by taking the first log difference of the series. Figure 1 (See Appendix) presents the observed patterns and trends across various markets under study from June 2018 to March 2024. The data shows that the returns of these assets generally hover around zero, indicating low daily variability under normal market conditions. However, significant volatility is observed during certain periods, particularly around mid-2020 and mid-2021, reflecting global events such as the COVID-19 pandemic and related economic disruptions. WTI, in particular, exhibits substantial negative fluctuations, likely due to the sharp drop in oil prices during the pandemic. While the indices show signs of recovery post-2021, the continued presence of fluctuations suggests ongoing market uncertainties. This visualization highlights the interconnectedness of these assets, showing how they collectively respond to macroeconomic shocks, which could be pertinent to understanding risk spillover effects in different sectors, including Islamic finance and sustainability-related investments

Portfolio Selection Approaches

The study integrates selected, investable asset classes into three distinct portfolio construction strategies to assess return performance over specific sample periods. These strategies are the Minimum Variance Portfolio (MVP), the Minimum Correlation Portfolio (MCP), and the Minimum Connectedness Portfolio (MCOP). By ensuring that all included assets are easily accessible for investors, this research facilitates practical estimation of investment returns while focusing on evaluating the hedging capabilities of green assets. The main objective is to determine how these variables can be effectively utilized to lower market risk and build low-risk portfolios.

The first strategy, the Minimum Variance Portfolio (MVP), seeks to minimize the overall variance among the combined assets, a concept first introduced by Durand (1959). This approach involves determining the optimal asset weights such that the portfolio's total variance is minimized, thereby effectively reducing risk exposure.

$$W_t = \frac{H_t^{-1} I}{I H_t^{-1} I'} \tag{1}$$

In Equation 1, H_t denotes the vector of portfolio weights, while Wt stands for the conditional variance-covariance matrix. The following strategy, known as the Minimum Correlation Portfolio (MCP), was introduced by Christoffersen et al. (2014). Unlike the Minimum Variance Portfolio (MVP), which minimizes asset covariances, the MCP seeks to minimize the conditional correlations between assets. The weights for constructing the MCP are derived using the following equation:

$$R_t = \text{diag}\,(H_t)^{-0.5}\, H_t\, \text{diag}\,(H_t)^{-0.5} \tag{2}$$

$$W_t = \frac{R_t^{-1} I}{I R_t^{-1} I'} \tag{3}$$

In this context, R_t represents a dimensional matrix and W_t denotes the weight vector of the Minimum Correlation Portfolio.

The Minimum Connectedness Portfolio, introduced by Broadstock, Chatziantoniou, and Gabauer (2022), is constructed to minimize the interconnectedness among asset weights. The optimal weights for this portfolio are derived using the following mathematical formula:

$$W_t = \frac{PCI_t^{-1}I}{IPCI_t^{-1}I'} \quad (4)$$

In this context, PCIt denotes the connectedness index matrix, and I is the identity matrix. Additionally, to assess each market's performance within the portfolio, I apply the hedge effectiveness method as outlined by Ederington (1979). The corresponding equation is as follows:

$$\text{HE}=1-\frac{Var\left(y_p\right)}{Var\left(y_{unhaged}\right)'} \quad (5)$$

Quantile Time-Frequency Connectedness QVAR

To ensure the robustness of our findings, the Quantile Time-Frequency Connectedness (QVAR) approach developed by Chatziantoniou, Gabauer, and Stenfors (2021) is utilised. This advanced methodology captures the dynamic nature of interconnectedness across varying time scales and quantiles within financial markets. By integrating quantile regression with time-frequency domain analysis, the QVAR technique decomposes overall connectedness into distinct frequency components. This granular breakdown enables a more nuanced understanding of how shocks disseminate across markets, addressing both short- and long-term relationships as well as the unique distributional characteristics of returns.

A particular advantage of the QVAR method is its focus on different quantiles of the return distribution instead of solely relying on the mean. This makes it especially effective for pinpointing the impact of extreme events, critical for analyzing asset behavior during crises when tail risks are pronounced. Moreover, by incorporating the time-frequency framework, the approach distinguishes between temporary and persistent shocks, providing valuable insights into the duration and intensity of risk spillovers across markets. Thus, the QVAR connectedness approach serves as an essential tool for validating our empirical results.

Conceptual Clarification of Risk Interconnections in Islamic Finance

In Islamic finance, "risk interconnections" refer to the dynamic linkages through which financial shocks propagate between Shariah-compliant instruments, halal commodities, and sustainability-linked markets. These interconnections can be classified as direct, where shocks transmit through explicit financial linkages or asset co-ownership (joint sukuk exposure), or indirect, which occur via macroeconomic, sectoral, or sentiment spillovers. Furthermore, systemic risks affect the broader Islamic financial ecosystem, often during crises or policy shifts, whereas idiosyncratic risks are specific to instruments or institutions (Alhammadi, 2024). Islamic financial instruments are structured to minimize certain risks. For example, murabaha contracts eliminate interest-bearing debt by relying on cost-plus sales; ijara (leasing) ties returns to physical assets, reducing speculation; and mudarabah/musharakah distribute risk symmetrically between parties. These structures inherently avoid riba (interest) and gharar (excessive uncertainty), reinforcing transparency and systemic resilience. However, gaps in Shariah governance, such as inconsistent fatwas or differing interpretations across jurisdictions, can weaken this resilience. Weak governance may expose markets to compliance uncertainty, reputational risk, or contagion from poorly regulated Islamic instruments in one region to others. To illustrate these dynamics, I reference Malaysia's Green Sukuk, which integrates ESG screening with Shariah compliance, showcasing how risk-averse instruments can support climate goals. Similarly, Indonesia's integration of crowdfunding platforms for waqf and zakat mobilizes capital while minimizing financial speculation. These examples highlight how risk interconnections, when governed effectively, can enhance both market stability and sustainability objectives.

EMPIRICAL FINDINGS

In this section, empirical results obtained from investigation into the interconnectedness and dynamic behavior of various financial assets are presented. Our analysis leverages an advanced R2 connectedness model with one lag to effectively capture the intricate relationships and spillover effects among these assets. By assessing the averaged dynamic connectedness (Figure 2-See Appendix) alongside the corresponding correlation matrices (Table 1), to elucidate the extent of influence and the transmission of volatility across the assets evaluated. Furthermore, a robustness check is performed on our findings regarding hedging effectiveness in these volatile markets.

This check is carried out using Quantile Vector Autoregression (QVAR), an approach well-suited for this purpose because it models the entire distribution of asset returns rather than focusing solely on the mean. QVAR is particularly adept at capturing tail dependencies, thereby addressing the heterogeneity in risk transmission by analyzing how shocks across different quantiles (such as extreme negative or positive returns) affect asset interconnectedness. Such an analysis is pivotal for understanding the resilience of hedging strategies, as it reveals the influence of varied market conditions on risk mitigation techniques, especially during periods of intense market stress. Overall, our comprehensive methodology ensures that the analysis reflects not just the average level of interconnectedness but also the complex dynamics that occur during extreme market scenarios, thereby offering a robust validation of our empirical findings.

Dynamic Connectedness Analysis

In this section, the unconditional correlations in Table 1 and the dynamic connectedness depicted in Figure 2 are examined to reveal the relationships among the assets analyzed. The Pearson correlation coefficients indicate that under normal market conditions, the correlations are relatively weak for instance, there is a modest negative correlation of -0.042 between DJIM and WTI, and a slight positive correlation of 0.04 between DJIM and Gold. These static measures imply that, on average, the assets do not exhibit strong dependencies. Nonetheless, as illustrated in Figure 2, the interconnectedness among these assets is highly variable and tends to fluctuate considerably over time, particularly during market stress. A notable example is the pronounced rise in both overall connectedness (black line) and lagged connectedness (green line) beginning in early 2020, which aligns with the onset of the COVID-19 pandemic. This spike suggests that asset relationships become more intense during periods of high volatility.

This observation that dynamic connectedness increases significantly despite weak static correlations highlights the value of the R2 connectedness approach. By effectively capturing time-varying spillovers, this framework provides a far more detailed analysis of how asset relationships evolve under different market conditions, and it is essential for understanding the transmission of volatility among these assets.

Table 1. Unconditional correlations (Pearson test)

	DJIM	WTI	Gold	DJSW	ISE	CLEAN
DJIM	1	-0.042	0.04	-0.041	0.014	0.016
WTI	-0.042	1	0.069	0.060	-0.011	-0.007
Gold	0.04	0.069	1	0.039	-0.007	0.02
DJSW	-0.041	0.06	0.039	1	-0.01	0.021
ISE	0.014	-0.011	-0.007	-0.01	1	-0.044
CLEAN	0.016	-0.007	0.02	0.021	-0.044	1

This section examines the Net Total Directional Connectedness, which analyzes how shocks propagate across various markets and indices over time, as illustrated in Figure 3 (See Appendix). The figure maps the behavior of six indices: DJIM (Dow Jones Islamic Market), DJSW (Dow Jones Sustainability World), WTI (West Texas

Intermediate crude oil), ISE (Islamic Stock Exchange), gold, and clean energy from 2020 to 2024. Three primary components are highlighted: overall (black), contemporaneous (red), and lagged (green). Our analysis focuses on the temporal dynamics of each index, particularly emphasizing the influence of lagged components (past information) versus contemporaneous events (real-time shocks). For example, the DJIM exhibits considerable fluctuations over time, with a pronounced increase in lagged effects (green) beginning around 2021.

This pattern suggests that historical data plays a crucial role in shaping DJIM's behavior, indicating a delayed response to external shocks or a persistence of spillovers that continues through 2024. Similarly, the DJSW index shows substantial lagged effects, especially noticeable around 2022, implying that its movements are driven largely by delayed reactions to prior market factors or sustainability-related events. In contrast, the contemporaneous component remains relatively modest, suggesting that immediate events exert less influence than past information across these indices. By comparison, the WTI index demonstrates a more stable trend, with minimal fluctuations in both lagged and contemporaneous components, reflecting its lower sensitivity to both past shocks and real-time events.

The ISE index similarly maintains a steady trajectory, with little variation among its components, indicating that it is less reactive to both historical and immediate influences. Both the gold and clean energy indices also display stable behavior, with their lagged and contemporaneous components showing little change over the period examined. This stability suggests that these indices, much like a traditional store of value, are not significantly impacted by short-term fluctuations or spillovers, reinforcing their role as relatively robust investment vehicles in volatile market conditions.

Figure 4 (See Appendix) presents an in-depth analysis of the "TO" total directional connectedness across six indices DJIM (Dow Jones Islamic Market), DJSW (Dow Jones Sustainability World), WTI (West Texas Intermediate crude oil), ISE (Islamic Stock Exchange), gold, and clean energy offering detailed insights into how these markets influence others over time. DJIM stands out as the most influential index in this analysis. It exhibits the highest level of connectedness directed toward other markets, which is sustained persistently over the examined period. The primary driver of this influence is the lagged effect, signifying that historical events or shocks within the DJIM index have long-lasting repercussions on the broader financial system. Notably, the impact of these past events continues strongly through 2024, indicating that any shock to DJIM may have an enduring legacy on market dynamics. This prolonged influence suggests that DJIM may serve as an important indicator for forecasting systemic risk, as its past fluctuations significantly propagate to other assets. DJSW also shows notable surges in its spillover capabilities, particularly during key periods such as 2021 and 2022. However, when compared to DJIM, DJSW's overall connectedness is lower. This implies that although DJSW experiences periodic intensifications driven by market events specific to sustainability or shifts in investor sentiment, the spillover effects are less persistent over time. The rising trend in lagged effects during these periods suggests that the market's reaction to past events plays a significant role in DJSW's behavior, even if its overall influence is comparatively moderate.

Both WTI and gold exhibit a more balanced contribution from contemporaneous and lagged effects. This balance indicates that these indices are sensitive to both immediate market shocks and delayed responses that are rooted in historical data. For instance, during major market disruptions such as those observed in 2020 and 2022, both indices register pronounced peaks in their connectedness values. Their moderate but balanced response underscores the dual nature of commodity markets, where prices can react swiftly to current global events while also being influenced by entrenched trends and historical shocks. In contrast, the ISE and clean energy indices register the lowest overall connectedness in the "TO" framework. These indices display only minor spikes and limited spillover effects, which suggests that they have a more insulated role within the global market.

Their modest fluctuations indicate that shocks within these markets do not transmit as strongly to other sectors, meaning that, compared to the other indices analyzed, these assets contribute less to the propagation of market disturbances. Figure 5 (See Appendix) shifts the focus by analyzing the "FROM" total directional connectedness, which quantifies the influence received by each index from the external market environment. In 2021, DJSW experienced a significant increase in the connectedness received from other markets. This surge is predominantly driven by lagged effects, which underscores that past events occurring in other indices continue to affect DJSW over time. The persistent influence up to 2024 indicates that DJSW is highly reactive to external shocks, making it susceptible to delayed market responses.

In contrast, DJIM shows a markedly different pattern when it comes to external influences. The index receives minimal connectedness from other markets. Its largely independent behavior is only momentarily disrupted by a brief spike in lagged connectedness around 2021. This suggests that DJIM acts more as a source of influence rather than a receiver, thereby reaffirming its dominant role in transmitting shocks rather than absorbing them. WTI and gold continue to demonstrate moderate levels of connectedness. Their balanced contributions from contemporaneous and lagged effects signal their sensitivity to broader economic conditions. This means that both indices are moderately impacted by global events, with immediate shocks leading to rapid responses, and historical market developments also leaving a measurable imprint on their performance. Finally, the ISE and clean energy indices record the lowest levels of received connectedness. This further confirms their relatively isolated position within the overall market structure, indicating that these indices are less prone to external influences. They demonstrate stability by maintaining limited interactions with the broader market dynamics, which might be a reflection of unique market characteristics or sector-specific factors that insulate them from widespread volatility.

Figure 6 (See Appendix) provides a detailed visualization of the net pairwise directional connectedness among several indices, serving as a measure of how the influence of one index on another compares when the reverse effect is also considered. In simpler terms, this figure isolates the net effect one index has on another by subtracting the reverse direction of influence, allowing us to observe the unidirectional impact across different market pairings over the period from 2020 to 2024. A closer look at the overall pattern reveals that for most pairings, the net connectedness remains relatively flat. This flatness suggests that, in a majority of cases, the mutual influence between the indices is minimal. Essentially, when the shock transmitted from one index to another is offset by the reverse influence, there is little net effect detectable over time. This indicates a stable or balanced interaction for many of the examined relationships, reflecting that the interplay between most pairs does not result in significant or sustained spillovers.

However, one pairing distinctly stands apart: the relationship between DJIM (Dow Jones Islamic Market) and DJSW (Dow Jones Sustainability World). From 2021 onward, this pair exhibits a significant positive net connectedness, with the influence being predominantly driven by lagged effects. This means that historical events within the DJIM index have a pronounced and lasting impact on DJSW. The lagged spillover indicates a delayed transmission of shocks, where past fluctuations in DJIM continue to affect DJSW's performance well into the later years. Importantly, the asymmetry in their relationship is evident while DJIM exerts strong and persistent influence on DJSW, but the reverse is not observed. DJSW shows very limited capacity to influence DJIM in return. For the remaining pairwise relationships, such as those between WTI (West Texas Intermediate crude oil) and gold, between DJIM and ISE (Islamic Stock Exchange), and between clean energy and other indices, the net connectedness is negligible. This observation suggests that these pairs experience very limited bidirectional spillovers. In other words, the effect that one index has on its counterpart is almost perfectly balanced by the effect in the opposite direction, leading to an overall net impact that is close to zero. Such stability in net connectedness implies that these markets tend to react symmetrically to each other's movements, resulting in a more contained propagation of shocks.

The analysis presented in Figure 6 underscores a varied landscape of interactions among the indices. While most pairs show a stable equilibrium with minimal net influence, the pronounced and sustained net connectedness from DJIM to DJSW highlights a unique dynamic. This particular relationship, driven primarily by lagged spillover effects, emphasizes that historical performance in certain indices can have long-lasting repercussions on other related markets. Therefore, the Figure 5 provides crucial insights into the temporal dynamics of market interactions, revealing how specific channels of influence may emerge and persist, thereby contributing to our broader understanding of spillover effects in the financial system.

The network plot depicted in Figure 7 (See Appendix) provides a clear visualization of the interconnections among the indices, highlighting DJIM (represented in blue) and DJSW (shown in yellow) as the central hubs of the system. The thickness of the connecting lines serves as an indicator of the strength of bidirectional spillover effects. In particular, the robust line between DJIM and DJSW suggests that these two indices are tightly coupled, with DJIM exerting a slightly stronger influence on DJSW. In addition to their strong mutual relationship, both DJIM and DJSW exhibit connections to key commodities such as gold and WTI. However, these links are noticeably thinner, implying that while there are interactions with these commodity markets, the magnitude of the spillovers is considerably less compared to the dominant DJIM-DJSW connection. Within this network, DJIM and DJSW emerge as principal transmitters of market shocks, playing a central role not only in influencing each other but also in exerting an impact on the performance of other indices. In contrast, indices such as ISE and clean energy are positioned more on the periphery, displaying fewer and markedly weaker connections. This peripheral status indicates that they experience limited interactions with the larger market network.

Figure 7 emphasizes the critical influence of DJIM and DJSW in driving market connectedness, particularly within the realms of sustainability and Islamic finance. Meanwhile, other sectors, including commodity markets and the clean energy segment, tend to occupy more marginal positions, reflecting their comparatively modest contributions to the overall network dynamics.

Portfolio Selection and Hedge Effectiveness

Three distinct portfolio strategies were implemented to build multivariate investment portfolios using the selected dataset. As detailed in Table 2, a thorough assessment of hedge effectiveness was conducted to evaluate the performance of each asset within these portfolios. The first strategy is the Minimum Variance Portfolio (MVP), which is designed to minimize overall portfolio volatility. This approach optimizes the asset weights in a way that seeks to achieve the lowest possible variance, thereby reducing risk exposure while still targeting acceptable return levels (as evidenced in Table 2 and originally delineated by Durand, 1959). The second strategy, known as the Minimum Correlation Portfolio (MCP), focuses on lowering asset correlations. By doing so, it aims to mitigate the risk associated with highly correlated assets, a concept extensively discussed in the literature by Christoffersen et al. (2014). The third strategy is the Minimum Connectedness Portfolio (MCoP), which targets a reduction in the interconnectedness between the assets. By decreasing overall asset connectedness, the approach seeks to limit the impact of spillover effects and interdependencies. This strategy is described in detail by Broadstock, Chatziantoniou, and Gabauer (2022). Together, these strategies provide a comprehensive framework for constructing investment portfolios that balance risk reduction with return optimization, each addressing a different facet of portfolio risk management, from volatility and correlations to network connectedness.

Table 2. Multivariate portfolio weights

Minimum Variance Portfolio						
	Mean	**Std**	**5%**	**95%**	**HE**	**p-value**
Minimum Variance Portfolio						
DJIM	0.17	0.12	0.04	0.45	0.72	0
WTI	0.03	0.02	0	0.06	0.96	0
Gold	0.19	0.12	0.05	0.38	0.62	0
DJSW	0.47	0.28	0.04	0.83	0.76	0
ISE	0.07	0.04	0.01	0.14	0.88	0
Clean	0.08	0.07	0.01	0.21	0.89	0

Minimum Correlation Portfolio						
	Mean	**Std**	**5%**	**95%**	**HE**	**p-value**
Minimum Correlation Portfolio						
DJIM	0.17	0.02	0.14	0.2	0.59	0
WTI	0.17	0.03	0.14	0.22	0.94	0
Gold	0.15	0.03	0.10	0.19	0.44	0
DJSW	0.17	0.02	0.14	0.2	0.65	0
ISE	0.18	0.02	0.13	0.21	0.82	0
Clean	0.16	0.02	0.13	0.19	0.83	0

Minimum Connectedness Portfolio						
	Mean	**Std**	**5%**	**95%**	**HE**	**p-value**
Minimum Connectedness Portfolio						
DJIM	0.14	0.03	0.11	0.18	0.53	0
WTI	0.18	0.02	0.15	0.2	0.93	0
Gold	0.18	0.02	0.16	0.2	0.36	0

continued on following page

Table 2. Continued

Minimum Connectedness Portfolio						
	Mean	**Std**	**5%**	**95%**	**HE**	**p-value**
DJSW	0.13	0.04	0.07	0.18	0.6	0
ISE	0.19	0.02	0.16	0.21	0.8	0
Clean	0.19	0.02	0.16	0.21	0.81	0

The statistical results for the Minimum Variance Portfolio (MVP) strategy, summarized in Table 2, reveal important performance metrics for six assets: DJIM, WTI, gold, DJSW, ISE, and clean energy. In terms of mean returns, DJSW leads the pack with an average return of 0.47, followed by gold at 0.19 and DJIM at 0.17, whereas WTI records the lowest mean return at 0.03. When assessing risk through standard deviations, DJSW shows the highest volatility at 0.28, making it the riskiest asset within this portfolio, while WTI's standard deviation of 0.02 designates it as the most stable asset. The 5th and 95th percentiles further illustrate the risk-return spectrum, with DJSW displaying the broadest range of potential outcomes (from 0.04 to 0.83), indicating high variability and the potential for both significant gains and losses. Hedge effectiveness (HE) scores enhance this picture: WTI ranks highest with an HE of 0.96, followed by clean energy (0.89) and ISE (0.88), suggesting that these assets are most efficient in reducing portfolio risk.

In contrast, gold's HE of 0.62 implies it is less adept at mitigating risk compared to its peers. With all associated p-values at 0, the statistical significance of these findings is unquestionable. Overall, this analysis highlights that within the MVP framework, WTI, clean energy, and ISE serve as strong risk mitigators, whereas DJSW and DJIM, although associated with higher returns, come with increased volatility. Turning to the Minimum Correlation Portfolio (MCP) strategy detailed in Table 2, all six assets present fairly consistent mean returns, ranging from 0.15 for gold to 0.18 for ISE, accompanied by low volatility (standard deviations between 0.02 and 0.03). Despite slightly higher volatility for WTI, this asset stands out with the highest hedge effectiveness of 0.94, making it the most efficient at reducing overall portfolio risk. Clean energy and ISE also contribute significantly to risk mitigation, with HE scores of 0.83 and 0.82 respectively.

On the other hand, gold's relatively low HE score of 0.44 marks it as the least effective asset for hedging purposes under this strategy. The percentile data suggests that while WTI offers a wide potential return range (0.14 to 0.22), indicating opportunities for both substantial gains and losses, gold's more constrained range points to stable yet lower returns. With p-values at 0, these results are statistically robust. In essence, the MCP strategy leverages low inter-asset correlations to achieve a balanced approach that simultaneously stabilizes returns and mitigates risk, with

WTI, clean energy, and ISE playing pivotal roles in risk reduction. The Minimum Connectedness Portfolio (MCoP) strategy, also summarized in Table 2, shows that mean returns across the assets are relatively consistent, with ISE and clean energy achieving the highest averages at 0.19, while DJIM and DJSW have the lowest at 0.13 and 0.14 respectively. Low volatility is a defining characteristic under this strategy as well, with standard deviations spanning from 0.02 to 0.04 underscoring the stable performance of these assets. In terms of hedge effectiveness, WTI again emerges as a strong risk reducer with an HE of 0.93, followed by clean energy (0.81) and ISE (0.80).

Here, gold performs the weakest with an HE of 0.36, and both DJIM and DJSW show moderate hedge effectiveness (0.53 and 0.60, respectively). The narrow ranges indicated by the 5th and 95th percentiles further attest to the stability of returns under this strategy. With p-values at 0, the statistical significance is clear. This portfolio model is specifically designed to minimize market interconnectedness, with the results underscoring that WTI, clean energy, and ISE are particularly effective at reducing risk, whereas gold and DJIM are less successful in providing a hedge against market fluctuations. Finally, Figure 8 (See Appendix) brings these strategies together by comparing the performance of the DJSW (Dow Jones Sustainability World Index) and ISE (Islamic Stock Exchange Index) across the three portfolio approaches.

The plots for both indices under the MVP strategy display consistently low volatility over time, with only a modest uptick in variance observed around 2021-2022 an indication that even during periods of significant market disruption, these portfolios successfully constrain risk. Under the MCP strategy, both DJSW and ISE maintain stable and low correlations, thereby preserving the diversification benefits that prevent their returns from converging excessively over time. Similarly, the MCoP strategy delivers low and steady levels of connectedness for both indices, with only minor fluctuations, suggesting that these portfolios remain largely insulated from external market shocks after an initial spike in 2020. Taken together, the data from Figure 8 reinforce the overall effectiveness of these portfolio strategies: each approach contributes to robust, risk-averse portfolios, ensuring that both sustainability-focused and Islamic finance indices can deliver consistent performance even amid market disturbances. The low volatility, stable correlations, and minimal inter-asset connectedness observed across these strategies underscore their ability to balance risk and return effectively.

Figure 9 (See Appendix) presents a comparative analysis of the cumulative returns of the three portfolio strategies: Minimum Variance Portfolio (MVP), Minimum Correlation Portfolio (MCP), and Minimum Connectedness Portfolio (MCoP). During the early phase up until early 2022, all three strategies perform similarly, exhibiting steady cumulative growth. However, as market conditions begin to fluctuate, notable distinctions become evident. The MVP strategy, illustrated by the black line, shows more subdued growth with lower peaks; this conservative performance reflects its emphasis on reducing volatility, which in turn helps protect capital during market downturns, as evidenced by the pronounced dips in 2022. In contrast, the MCP strategy, denoted by the red line, achieves higher returns as it minimizes asset correlations; it capitalizes on robust performance during bullish periods, yet it also experiences sharper declines during market corrections, revealing a higher exposure to risk. The MCoP strategy, represented by the blue line, follows a trajectory similar to that of MCP but registers marginally lower returns, indicating that its approach of reducing interconnectedness and spillover risks allows it to capture significant market gains while slightly tempering its overall return potential. By late 2023, the MCP strategy emerges as the leader in cumulative returns, closely followed by the MVP, with the MCoP trailing slightly behind. This performance chart underscores the inherent trade-offs among the strategies: MCP delivers the highest returns accompanied by increased volatility, MVP prioritizes stability and capital preservation, and MCoP strikes a balance between mitigating interconnected risks and capturing market upside.

Discussion of the Results

The connectedness analysis from both the "TO" and "FROM" perspectives demonstrates that Islamic equities, particularly DJIM, are central to the transmission of shocks throughout the market. DJIM exhibits marked lagged connectedness, which suggests that historical market conditions within Islamic finance exert a sustained influence on the broader financial system. This prominent positioning in the connectivity network underscores the considerable impact of Islamic equities on both sustainability indices and commodity markets. Specifically, the strong, delayed effects emanating from DJIM imply that Islamic finance not only contributes to market stability but also plays a significant role in promoting sustainable financial practices. This influence extends to sustainability-oriented indices like DJSW, as well as commodities such as gold and WTI.

Moreover, the robust bidirectional linkage between DJIM and DJSW illustrates the deep interconnection between Islamic finance and sustainability-focused markets. Guided by ethical investment principles and social responsibility, Islamic finance naturally aligns with the objectives of sustainability indices, thereby fostering positive environmental, social, and governance (ESG) outcomes. The spillover from DJIM to DJSW, therefore, reflects the ability of Islamic finance to drive sustainable practices across various sectors. In addition, the hedge effectiveness metrics further emphasize the role of Islamic equities in diversified risk management. With a hedge effectiveness score of 0.72, DJIM is capable of mitigating portfolio risk while upholding ethical investment standards. This dual functionality risk reduction, paired with a commitment to sustainability, makes Islamic equities an indispensable component for portfolios seeking a balance between strong financial returns and social responsibility.

The inherent nature of Islamic finance, which adheres to Shariah principles by avoiding investments in sectors harmful to society (alcohol, gambling), further reinforces its support for sustainability. The central placement of DJIM in the connectivity network and its influential spillovers to indices like DJSW suggest that Islamic finance can serve as a driver for the broader adoption of sustainable practices. Moreover, the relatively low connectedness between Islamic equities and volatile commodities such as WTI and gold, as revealed by the net pairwise connectedness analysis, implies that these equities are relatively resilient to commodity-induced market shocks. This resilience enhances their appeal in sustainable investment strategies, as it indicates a lower susceptibility to the extreme fluctuations often associated with energy and precious metals markets, a key factor in fostering long-term sustainable growth. These observations align with previous studies on risk spillovers in Islamic and green equity markets (Tiwari et al., 2023; Mensi et al., 2017; Billah et al., 2024; Ghallabi et al., 2024).

Turning to the hedge performance across different portfolio strategies, the results indicate that WTI and clean energy consistently demonstrate high hedge effectiveness. These assets are vital for reducing portfolio risk, particularly within the Minimum Variance and Minimum Connectedness frameworks. Despite its inherent volatility, WTI stands out as a robust risk mitigator, underscoring the role of commodities in stabilizing portfolios. In contrast, Islamic finance (DJIM) and sustainability indices (DJSW) provide moderate hedge effectiveness; they contribute to overall portfolio stability while aligning with ethical and sustainable investment goals.

Conversely, gold exhibits lower hedge effectiveness, suggesting that it may not serve as an equally strong risk mitigator in these contexts as is commonly assumed. These statistically significant results underscore the importance of diversifying portfolios by combining commodities, clean energy, and ethical indices to achieve an optimal balance between risk reduction and long-term sustainability objectives. Finally, our findings corroborate earlier research on hedging strategies, including the work by Maghyereh et al. (2018), which found that gold does not effectively hedge against fluctuations in Sharia-compliant assets. This suggests that while gold may be a robust hedge for conventional markets, its effectiveness is diminished in the context of Islamic finance, a particularly significant insight given the expanding volume of assets managed under Islamic screening criteria.

Practical and Managerial Implications

This study offers practical guidance for investors, portfolio managers, and policymakers looking to construct portfolios that not only manage risk effectively but also align with sustainability and ethical investment objectives. The findings underscore the value of incorporating assets such as WTI and clean energy into portfolios, as these commodities demonstrate high hedge effectiveness and play a critical role in mitigating risk during volatile market conditions. For those prioritizing ethical investing, Islamic finance indices like DJIM, together with sustainability-focused indices such as DJSW, provide moderate risk reduction while bolstering long-term sustainability goals. However, the analysis indicates that using gold as the sole hedge for Sharia-compliant securities may be suboptimal, as its risk mitigation capacity in this context is limited. Instead, diversified strategies that combine Islamic assets with other commodities and sustainable investments are recommended to optimize risk management. Moreover, the application of the R2 connectedness approach in this study offers deeper insights into intermarket dependencies and the dynamic spillover effects between sectors, enabling a more comprehensive understanding of the risks stemming from interconnected markets. By incorporating these insights, portfolio managers can enhance diversification strategies, improve risk-adjusted returns, and contribute more effectively to broader sustainability objectives.

Limitations and Future Research Directions

While this study offers significant insights into risk management and sustainable investment in Islamic finance, several limitations warrant further investigation. Firstly, the analysis centers on a specific selection of indices and commodities, which might not fully represent the complete spectrum of global financial markets or emerging asset classes like cryptocurrencies and green bonds. Future research should expand the scope to include a broader range of financial instruments to assess their roles within Islamic and sustainability-focused portfolios.

Secondly, although the study employs the R2 connectedness framework and QVAR for robustness checks, both effective in capturing dynamic market relationships and tail risks, alternative methodologies such as time-varying parameter models or machine learning techniques could further enrich our understanding of the evolving nature of market connectedness and risk transmission. Thirdly, because the analysis is based on historical data, its predictive power regarding future market dynamics might be limited, particularly in the face of unforeseen global economic shifts or policy changes.

Future studies could incorporate forward-looking models that integrate macroeconomic forecasts, scenario analysis, or stress testing to better anticipate market responses to emerging risks. Finally, while this research focuses on portfolio optimization within the context of Islamic finance and sustainability indices, it does not extensively address the real-world social and environmental impacts of these investment strategies. Future investigations could evaluate how investments in Islamic and sustainable finance contribute to measurable progress in areas such as carbon reduction, social equity, and economic development, thereby linking financial performance with tangible societal benefits.

Transformative Trends in Islamic Economics: ESG, Digital Inclusion, and Innovation

Islamic economics is undergoing a multifaceted transformation in response to global challenges such as climate change, financial inclusion, and the push for value-driven investment. The transformation within Islamic economics is defined as the progressive integration of ethical financial principles with modern tools of innovation, digital infrastructure, and environmental responsibility. For example, Malaysia's Green Sukuk program demonstrates how Islamic capital markets are being reoriented toward ESG-linked projects. These instruments combine Shariah compliance with environmental metrics, thereby enabling Islamic investors to finance renewable energy, climate-resilient infrastructure, and sustainable transportation.

Likewise, Indonesia's social-finance platforms are leveraging fintech to mobilize charitable capital (waqf, zakat, and sadaqah) through digital crowdfunding tools. This innovation broadens financial inclusion while adhering to Islamic ethical principles, marking a clear evolution in the deployment of Shariah-compliant instruments in the digital age. These trends signal a transformation not only in product design but also in governance, disclosure, and stakeholder expectations. However, this evolution also introduces new types of Shariah compliance risk, especially in jurisdictions where regulatory frameworks or fatwa councils lack alignment. Discrepancies in interpretation or certification can weaken investor confidence and create operational inefficiencies. These developments reveal that Islamic economics is no longer operating in isolation; it is actively engaging with global movements in sustainability, financial technology, and impact investing while striving to preserve its ethical core.

Shariah Governance and Compliance Risk

Shariah compliance risk in Islamic finance arises when financial instruments deviate intentionally or not from Islamic legal and ethical standards due to gaps in interpretation, oversight, or execution. The main manifestations include fatwa arbitrage across jurisdictions, where differing rulings on the same instrument (sukuk, murabaha) create confusion and hinder cross-border transactions. Disclosure risk emerges when institutions fail to transparently report their compliance procedures or Shariah audits, particularly with ESG-linked products like green sukuk.

Operational Shariah risk can result from improperly structured or executed contracts, especially in complex asset-backed arrangements. These issues are further compounded by the absence of centralized crisis management tools to prevent systemic risk spillovers among Islamic institutions exposed to similar Shariah-based assets. Weak internal controls and a lack of harmonized standards (such as inconsistent adoption of AAOIFI or IFSB guidelines) heighten reputational and financial risks, potentially eroding market confidence. Inconsistent fatwa interpretations and fragmented governance frameworks remain a major challenge to cross-border integration in Islamic finance (Qadri & Bhatti, 2025). These inconsistencies may result in regulatory arbitrage, eroding investor confidence and market integrity. Institutions are increasingly encouraged to adopt global standards such as those provided by AAOIFI (El-Halaby et al. 2021). Strengthening Shariah governance through unified standards, independent audits, and robust disclosure frameworks is essential to ensuring the integrity, stability, and global credibility of Islamic financial systems.

CONCLUSION

This chapter explored the evolving landscape of risk interconnections in Islamic sustainable and commodity markets, emphasizing the need to understand systemic vulnerabilities within the framework of Shariah principles. By examining the conceptual foundations of risk, the governance challenges specific to Islamic finance, and the growing importance of sustainability-linked instruments. The main findings suggest that while Islamic financial instruments embed inherent risk-mitigating features, governance inconsistencies and fragmented regulatory practices expose the sector to reputational and systemic threats. A unified, data-driven, and values-aligned approach will be critical in positioning Islamic finance as a transformative force for global financial sustainability.

This research highlights the essential role of integrating Islamic finance, sustainability indices, and commodities into portfolio strategies to achieve both effective risk management and the advancement of ethical and sustainability goals. The results demonstrate that commodities such as WTI and clean energy consistently exhibit high hedge effectiveness, making them indispensable for lowering portfolio risk, particularly during episodes of significant market turbulence. In contrast, Islamic finance indices like DJIM, while offering moderate risk mitigation, are instrumental in promoting sustainability and ethical investment, especially during times of market stress, as revealed by the R2 connectedness analysis.

These indices emerge as critical drivers of market stability and sustainability, underscoring the increasing global prominence of Islamic finance. Notably, the study reveals that gold, traditionally considered a safe-haven asset, has a limited capacity to hedge Sharia-compliant assets. This finding suggests that investors should consider diversifying beyond conventional hedging approaches. The use of both the R2 connectedness technique and robustness checks via Quantile Vector Autoregression (QVAR) affords valuable insights into market interdependencies, tail risks, and the transmission of shocks across sectors.

This dynamic methodology captures the nonlinear relationships and spillover effects that may be overlooked by traditional models, thereby providing a more complete understanding of market behavior in the realms of Islamic finance and sustainability. Overall, the research advocates for a balanced portfolio construction strategy that leverages high hedge effectiveness assets such as WTI and clean energy, while integrating Islamic and sustainability indices to meet ethical investment and broader sustainability targets. These findings contribute to the ongoing discussion on sustainable finance and its potential to enhance resilience and foster long-term growth in the global financial landscape.

REFERENCES

Abid, I., Bouri, E., Galariotis, E., Guesmi, K., & Mzoughi, H. (2023). Bitcoin vs. fiat currencies: Insights from extreme dependence and risk spillover analysis with financial markets. *International Review of Financial Analysis, 90*, 102806. DOI: 10.1016/j.irfa.2023.102806

Akhtaruzzaman, M., Boubaker, S., Lucey, B. M., & Sensoy, A. (2021). Is gold a hedge or a safe-haven asset in the COVID–19 crisis? *Economic Modelling, 102*, 105588. DOI: 10.1016/j.econmod.2021.105588

Alhammadi, S. (2024). Islamic finance as a driver for enhancing economic sustainability and innovation in the GCC. *Journal of Science and Technology Policy Management*.

Antonakakis, N., Chatziantoniou, I., & Gabauer, D. (2020). Refined Measures of Dynamic Connectedness based on Time-Varying Parameter Vector Autoregressions. *Journal of Risk and Financial Management, 13*(4), 84. Advance online publication. DOI: 10.3390/jrfm13040084

Baruník, J., & Křehlík, T. (2018). Measuring the frequency dynamics of financial connectedness and systemic risk. *Journal of Financial Econometrics, 16*(2), 271–296. DOI: 10.1093/jjfinec/nby001

Ben Jabeur, S., Khalfaoui, R., & Ben Arfi, W. (2021). The effect of green energy, global environmental indexes, and stock markets in predicting oil price crashes: Evidence from explainable machine learning. *Journal of Environmental Management, 298*, 113511. DOI: 10.1016/j.jenvman.2021.113511

Billah, M., Alam, M. R., & Hoque, M. E. (2024). Global uncertainty and the spillover of tail risk between green and Islamic markets: A time-frequency domain approach with portfolio implications. *International Review of Economics & Finance, 92*, 1416–1433. DOI: 10.1016/j.iref.2024.02.081

Bouoiyour, J., Selmi, R., & Wohar, M. E. (2018). Are Islamic stock markets efficient? A multifractal detrended fluctuation analysis [Preprint]. *Finance Research Letters, 26*, 100–105. Advance online publication. DOI: 10.1016/j.frl.2017.12.008

Bouri, E., Shahzad, S. J. H., Roubaud, D., Kristoufek, L., & Lucey, B. (2020). Bitcoin, gold, and commodities as safe havens for stocks: New insight through wavelet analysis [Preprint]. *The Quarterly Review of Economics and Finance, 77*, 156–164. Advance online publication. DOI: 10.1016/j.qref.2020.03.004

Broadstock, D. C., Chatziantoniou, I., & Gabauer, D. (2022). Minimum Connectedness Portfolios and the Market for Green Bonds: Advocating Socially Responsible Investment (SRI) Activity BT - *Applications in Energy Finance: The Energy Sector, Economic Activity, Financial Markets and the Environment.* In Floros, C., & Chatziantoniou, I. (Eds.), (pp. 217–253). Springer International Publishing., DOI: 10.1007/978-3-030-92957-2_9

Chatziantoniou, I., Gabauer, D., & Gupta, R. (2021) 'Integration and Risk Transmission in the Market for Crude Oil: A Time-Varying Parameter Frequency Connectedness Approach', University of Pretoria Department of Economics Working Paper Series [Preprint], (June). Available at: https://www.up.ac.za/media/shared/61/WP/wp_2021_47.zp209709.pdf

Chatziantoniou, I., Gabauer, D., & Stenfors, A. (2021). Interest rate swaps and the transmission mechanism of monetary policy: A quantile connectedness approach. *Economics Letters*, *204*, 109891. DOI: 10.1016/j.econlet.2021.109891

Christoffersen, P., Feunou, B., Jacobs, K., & Meddahi, N. (2014). The economic value of realized volatility: Using high- frequency returns for option valuation. *Journal of Financial and Quantitative Analysis*, *49*(3), 663–697. DOI: 10.1017/S0022109014000428

Climent, F., & Soriano, P. (2011). Green and Good? The Investment Performance of US Environmental Mutual Funds [Preprint]. *Journal of Business Ethics*, *103*(2), 275–287. Advance online publication. DOI: 10.1007/s10551-011-0865-2

D'Souza, C.. (2006). *Green products and corporate strategy: an empirical investigation.* Society and Business Review. [Preprint], DOI: 10.1108/17465680610669825

Diebold, F. X., & Yilmaz, K. (2012). Better to give than to receive: Predictive directional measurement of volatility spillovers. *International Journal of Forecasting*, *28*(1), 57–66. DOI: 10.1016/j.ijforecast.2011.02.006

Diebold, F. X., & Yilmaz, K. (2014). On the network topology of variance decompositions: Measuring the connectedness of financial firms. *Journal of Econometrics*, *182*(1), 119–134. DOI: 10.1016/j.jeconom.2014.04.012

Dogan, E., Madaleno, M., Taskin, D., & Tzeremes, P. (2022). Investigating the spillovers and connectedness between green finance and renewable energy sources. *Renewable Energy*, *197*, 709–722. DOI: 10.1016/j.renene.2022.07.131

Dong, F., Li, Z., Huang, Z., & Liu, Y. (2024). Extreme weather, policy uncertainty, and risk spillovers between energy, financial, and carbon markets. *Energy Economics*, *137*, 107761. DOI: 10.1016/j.eneco.2024.107761

Duan, K., Zhao, Y., Urquhart, A., & Huang, Y. (2023). Do clean and dirty cryptocurrencies connect with financial assets differently? The role of economic policy uncertainty. *Energy Economics*, *127*, 107079. https://doi.org/https://doi.org/10.1016/j.eneco.2023.107079. DOI: 10.1016/j.eneco.2023.107079

Durand, D. (1959). The cost of capital, corporation finance, and the theory of investment: Comment. *The American Economic Review*, *49*(4), 639–655.

Ederington, L. H. (1979). The hedging performance of the new futures markets. *The Journal of Finance*, *34*(1), 157–170. DOI: 10.1111/j.1540-6261.1979.tb02077.x

El-Halaby, S., Aboul-Dahab, S., & Bin Qoud, N. (2021). A systematic literature review on AAOIFI standards. *Journal of Financial Reporting and Accounting*, *19*(2), 133–183. DOI: 10.1108/JFRA-06-2020-0170

Ghallabi, F., Yousaf, I., Ghorbel, A., & Li, Y. (2024). Time-varying risk spillovers between renewable energy and Islamic stock markets: Evidence from the Russia-Ukraine conflict. *Pacific-Basin Finance Journal*, *85*, 102345. DOI: 10.1016/j.pacfin.2024.102345

Ha, L. T., & Nham, N. T. H. (2022). An application of a TVP-VAR extended joint connected approach to explore connectedness between WTI crude oil, gold, stock and cryptocurrencies during the COVID-19 health crisis. *Technological Forecasting and Social Change*, *183*, 121909. DOI: 10.1016/j.techfore.2022.121909

Hassan, M. K.. (2021). *Safe havens in Islamic financial markets: COVID-19 versus GFC*. Global Finance Journal., DOI: 10.1016/j.gfj.2021.100643

Hassan, M. K., Kamran, M., Djajadikerta, H. G., & Choudhury, T. (2022). Search for safe havens and resilience to global financial volatility: Response of GCC equity indexes to GFC and Covid-19. *Pacific-Basin Finance Journal*, *73*, 101768. DOI: 10.1016/j.pacfin.2022.101768

Jarboui, A., & Mnif, E. (2023). Can Clean Energy Stocks Predict Crude Oil Markets Using Hybrid and Advanced Machine Learning Models? *Asia-Pacific Financial Markets*, •••, 1–24.

Jarboui, A., Mnif, E., Zghidi, N., & Akrout, Z. (2024). Reconceptualizing the interplay between geopolitical index, green financial assets and renewable energy markets: Evidence from the machine learning approach [Preprint]. *Arab Gulf Journal of Scientific Research*, *42*(4), 2001–2027. DOI: 10.1108/AGJSR-09-2023-0458

Jiménez, I., Mora-Valencia, A., & Perote, J. (2024). Bitcoin halving and the integration of cryptocurrency and forex markets: An analysis of the higher-order moment spillovers. *International Review of Economics & Finance*, *92*, 302–315. DOI: 10.1016/j.iref.2024.02.022

Jin, Y., Zhao, H., Bu, L., & Zhang, D. (2023). Geopolitical risk, climate risk and energy markets: A dynamic spillover analysis. *International Review of Financial Analysis*, *87*, 102597. DOI: 10.1016/j.irfa.2023.102597

Kenett, D. Y., Huang, X., Vodenska, I., Havlin, S., & Stanley, H. E. (2015). Partial correlation analysis: Applications for financial markets. *Quantitative Finance*, *15*(4), 569–578. DOI: 10.1080/14697688.2014.946660

Kenett, D. Y., Tumminello, M., Madi, A., Gur-Gershgoren, G., Mantegna, R. N., & Ben-Jacob, E. (2010). Dominating clasp of the financial sector revealed by partial correlation analysis of the stock market. *PLoS One*, *5*(12), e15032. DOI: 10.1371/journal.pone.0015032

Kenourgios, D., Naifar, N., & Dimitriou, D. (2016). Islamic financial markets and global crises: Contagion or decoupling? [Preprint]. *Economic Modelling*, *57*, 36–46. Advance online publication. DOI: 10.1016/j.econmod.2016.04.014

Lahmiri, S., Bekiros, S., & Bezzina, F. (2020). Multi-fluctuation nonlinear patterns of European financial markets based on adaptive filtering with application to family business, green, Islamic, common stocks, and comparison with Bitcoin, NASDAQ, and VIX [Preprint]. *Physica A*, *538*, 122858. Advance online publication. DOI: 10.1016/j.physa.2019.122858

Le, T. H. (2023). Quantile time-frequency connectedness between cryptocurrency volatility and renewable energy volatility during the COVID-19 pandemic and Ukraine-Russia conflicts. *Renewable Energy*, *202*, 613–625. DOI: 10.1016/j.renene.2022.11.062

Liu, C., & Chen, X. (2024). Spillover effects of multidimensional information in Fed statements on China's bond market. *International Review of Economics & Finance*, *93*, 712–741. DOI: 10.1016/j.iref.2024.04.037

Liu, H., Zhu, Y., Cui, N., & Zheng, Y. (2024). The impact of global uncertainties on the spillover among the European carbon market, the Chinese oil futures market, and the international oil futures market. *Finance Research Letters*, *67*, 105891. DOI: 10.1016/j.frl.2024.105891

Liu, M., & Lee, C. C. (2022). Is gold a long-run hedge, diversifier, or safe haven for oil? Empirical evidence based on DCC-MIDAS. *Resources Policy*, *76*, 102703. DOI: 10.1016/j.resourpol.2022.102703

Liu, X., Razzaq, A., Shahzad, M., & Irfan, M. (2022). Technological changes, financial development and ecological consequences: A comparative study of developed and developing economies. *Technological Forecasting and Social Change*, *184*, 122004. DOI: 10.1016/j.techfore.2022.122004

Lorente, D. B., Mohammed, K. S., Cifuentes-Faura, J., & Shahzad, U. (2023). Dynamic connectedness among climate change index, green financial assets and renewable energy markets: Novel evidence from sustainable development perspective. *Renewable Energy*, *204*, 94–105. https://doi.org/https://doi.org/10.1016/j.renene.2022.12.085. DOI: 10.1016/j.renene.2022.12.085

Maghyereh, A., Awartani, B., & Hassan, A. (2018). Can gold be used as a hedge against the risks of Sharia-compliant securities? Application for Islamic portfolio management. *Journal of Asset Management*, *19*(6), 394–412. DOI: 10.1057/s41260-018-0090-y

Mensi, W., Hammoudeh, S., Al-Jarrah, I. M. W., Sensoy, A., & Kang, S. H. (2017). Dynamic risk spillovers between gold, oil prices and conventional, sustainability and Islamic equity aggregates and sectors with portfolio implications [Preprint]. *Energy Economics*, *67*, 454–475. Advance online publication. DOI: 10.1016/j.eneco.2017.08.031

Mnif, E. and Jarboui, A. (2021) 'Resilience of Islamic cryptocurrency markets to Covid-19 shocks and the Federal Reserve policy', *Asian Journal of Accounting Research*, ahead-of-p(ahead-of-print). Available at: .DOI: 10.1108/AJAR-01-2021-0004

Mnif, E., Jarboui, A., & Mouakhar, K. (2024). Strategic insights into carbon markets, digital finance and geopolitical risks for advancing green sustainability investments. *Management of Environmental Quality*, *35*(7), 1622–1649. Advance online publication. DOI: 10.1108/MEQ-10-2023-0369

Mnif, E., Mouakhar, K., & Jarboui, A. (2023). Energy-conserving cryptocurrency response during the COVID-19 pandemic and amid the Russia–Ukraine conflict. *The Journal of Risk Finance*, *24*(2), 169–185. DOI: 10.1108/JRF-06-2022-0161

Mohsin, M., & Jamaani, F. (2023). A novel deep-learning technique for forecasting oil price volatility using historical prices of five precious metals in context of green financing – A comparison of deep learning, machine learning, and statistical models. *Resources Policy*, *86*, 104216. DOI: 10.1016/j.resourpol.2023.104216

Naeem, M. A., Karim, S., Farid, S., & Tiwari, A. K. (2022). Comparing the asymmetric efficiency of dirty and clean energy markets pre and during COVID-19. *Economic Analysis and Policy*, *75*, 548–562. DOI: 10.1016/j.eap.2022.06.015

Phillips, P., & Perron, P. (1988) 'Testing for a Unit Root in Time Series Regression Author (s): Peter C. B. Phillips and Pierre Perron Published by : Oxford University Press on behalf of Biometrika Trust Stable URL : https://www.jstor.org/stable/2336182 REFERENCES Linked references ar', 75(2), pp. 335–346.

Qadri, H. M. U. D., & Bhatti, M. I. (2025). *Islamic Finance in the Modern Era* (Vol. 25). Retrieved January.

Selmi, R., Wohar, M., Deisting, F., & Kasmaoui, K. (2023). Dynamic inflation hedging performance and downside risk: A comparison between Islamic and conventional stock indices. *The Quarterly Review of Economics and Finance*, *91*, 56–67. DOI: 10.1016/j.qref.2023.07.006

Tiwari, A. K., Aikins Abakah, E. J., Adekoya, O. B., & Hammoudeh, S. (2023). What do we know about the price spillover between green bonds and Islamic stocks and stock market indices? *Global Finance Journal*, *55*, 100794. DOI: 10.1016/j.gfj.2022.100794

Uddin, G. S., Yahya, M., Park, D., Hedström, A., & Tian, S. (2024). Bond market spillover networks of ASEAN-4 markets: Is the global pandemic different? *International Review of Economics & Finance*, *92*, 1028–1044. DOI: 10.1016/j.iref.2024.02.065

Xing, X., Liu, Y., Zhu, Y., & Deng, J. (2024). The impact of climate policy uncertainty on China's green energy and non-ferrous metals market co-movement: Evidence from spillover perspectives. *Journal of Environmental Management*, *367*, 121845. DOI: 10.1016/j.jenvman.2024.121845

APPENDIX

Figure 1. Data logarithmic differences

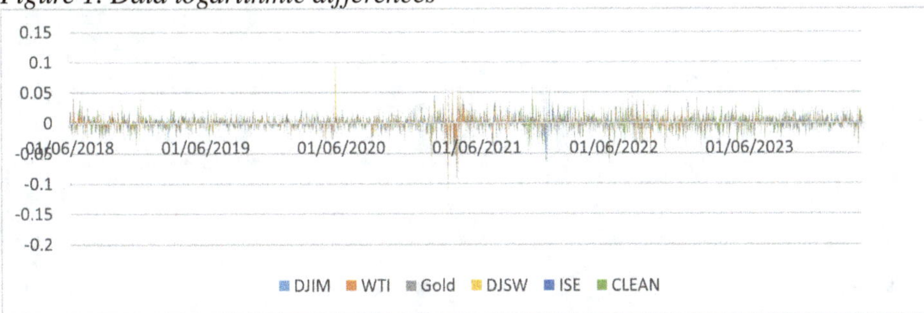

Figure 2. Dynamic total connectedness

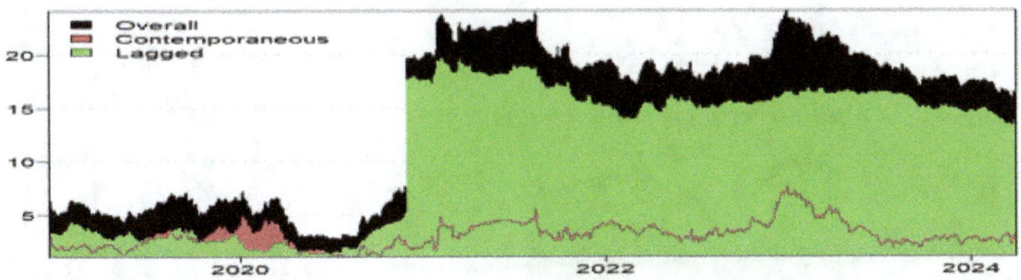

Figure 3. NET total directional connectedness

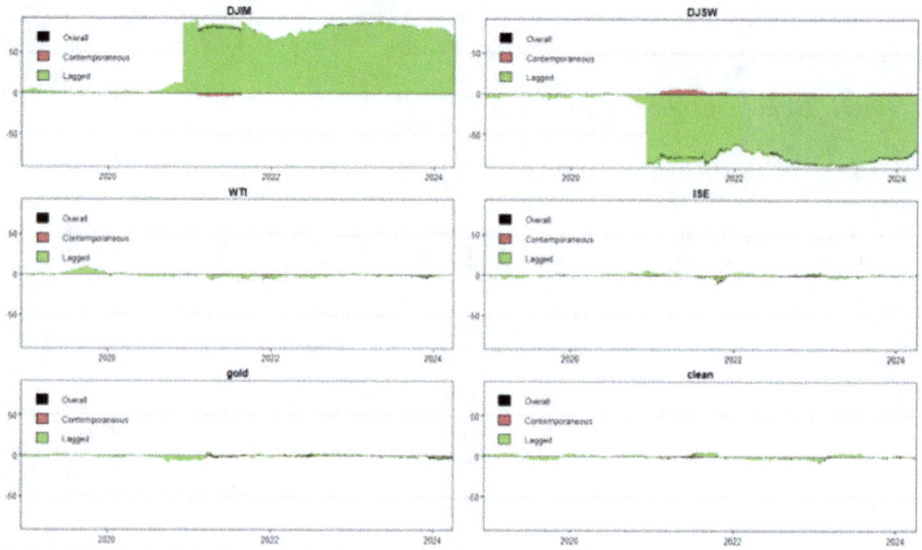

Figure 4. TO total directional connectedness

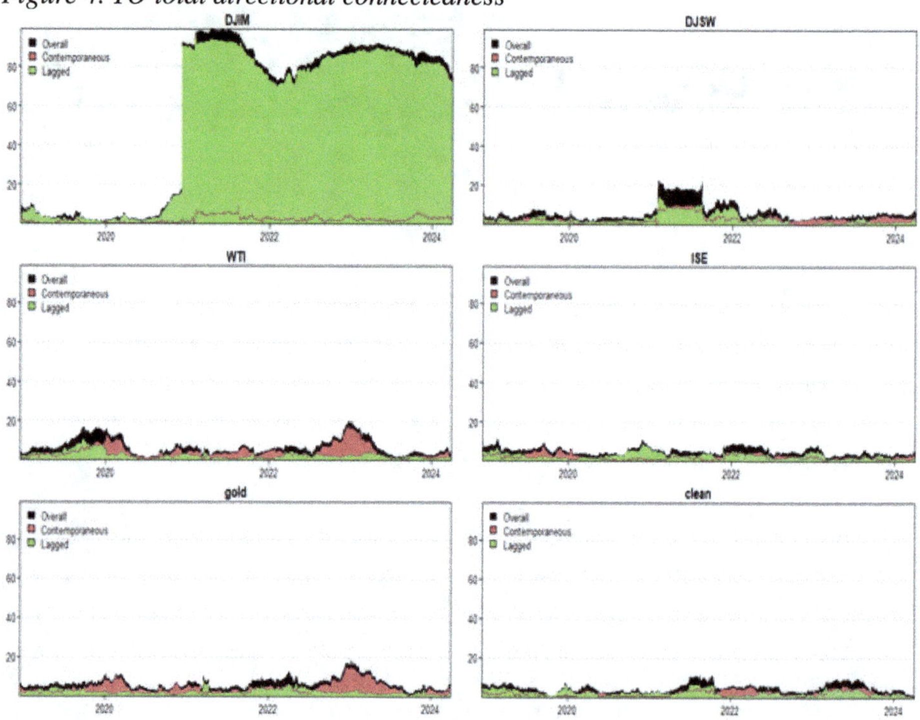

Figure 5. FROM total directional connectedness

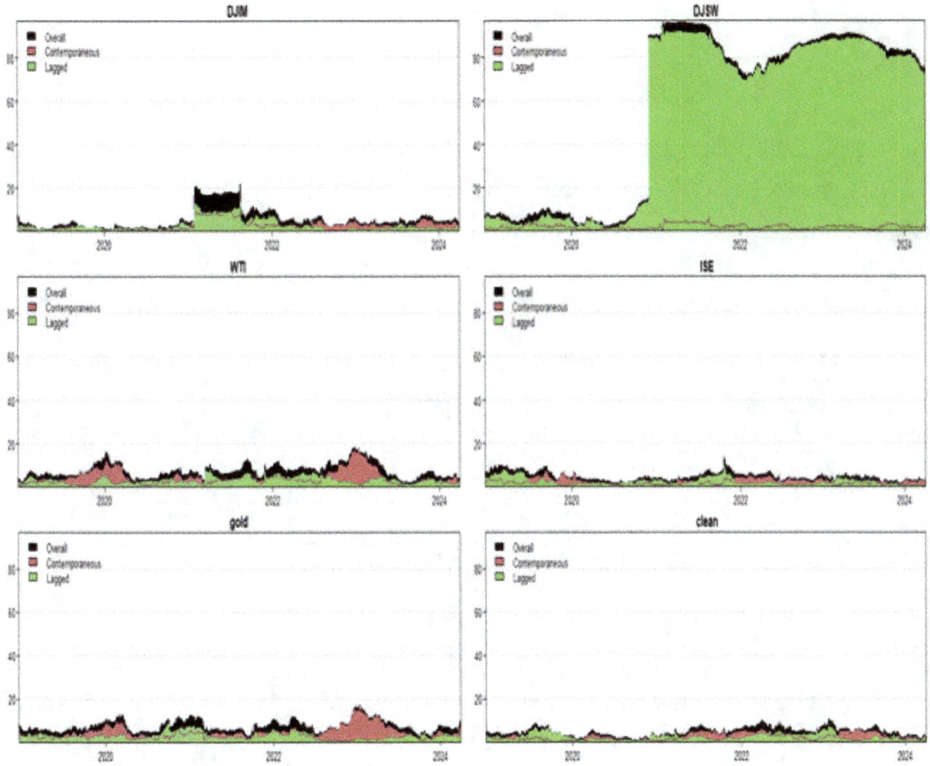

Figure 6. Net pairwise directional connectedness

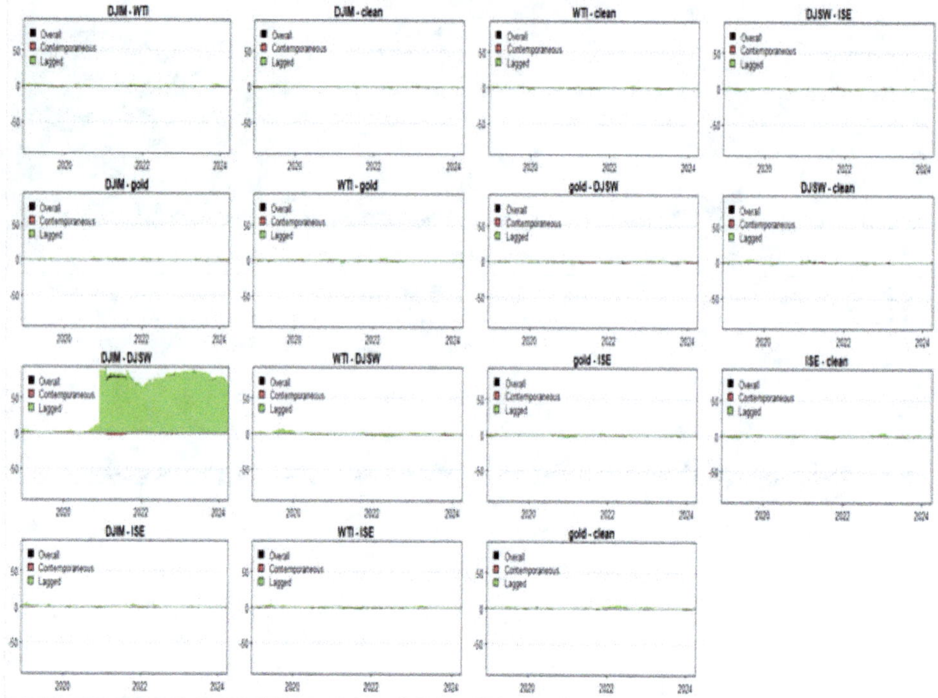

Figure 7. Network plot

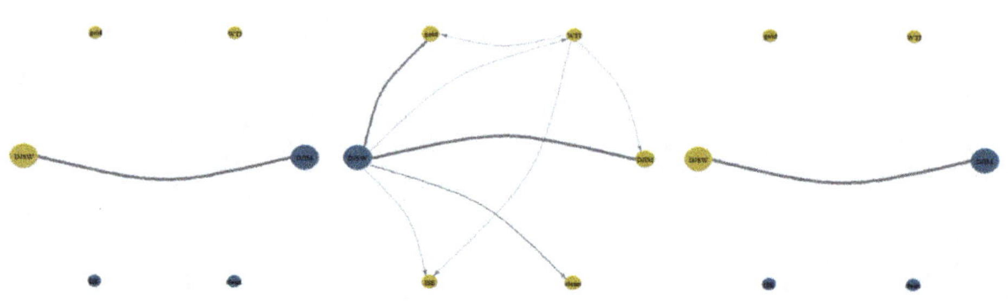

Figure 8. Dynamic multivariate portfolio weights

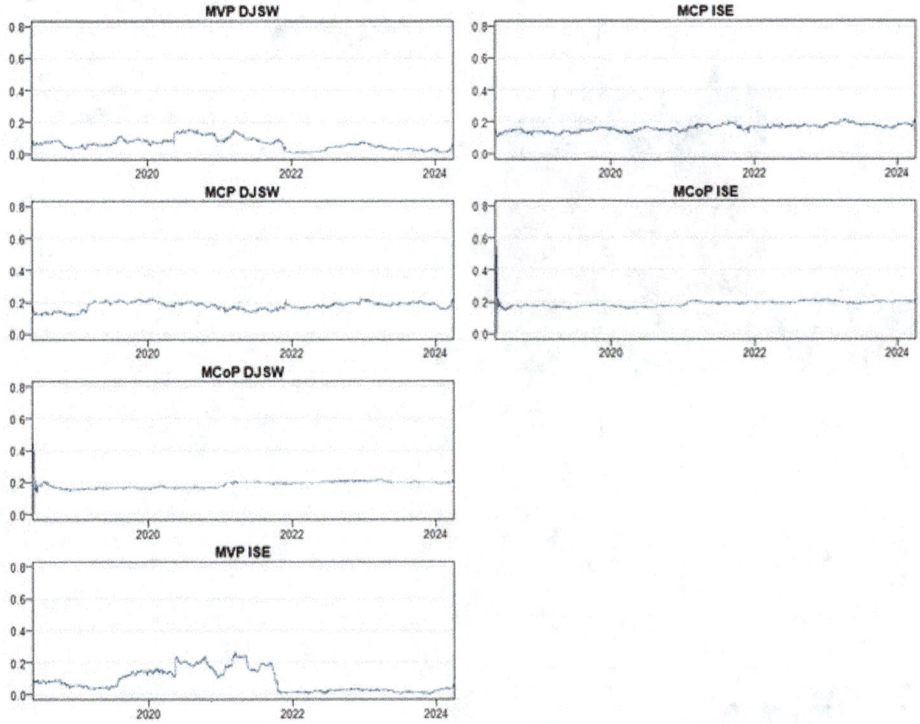

Figure 9. Dynamic multivariate portfolio weights

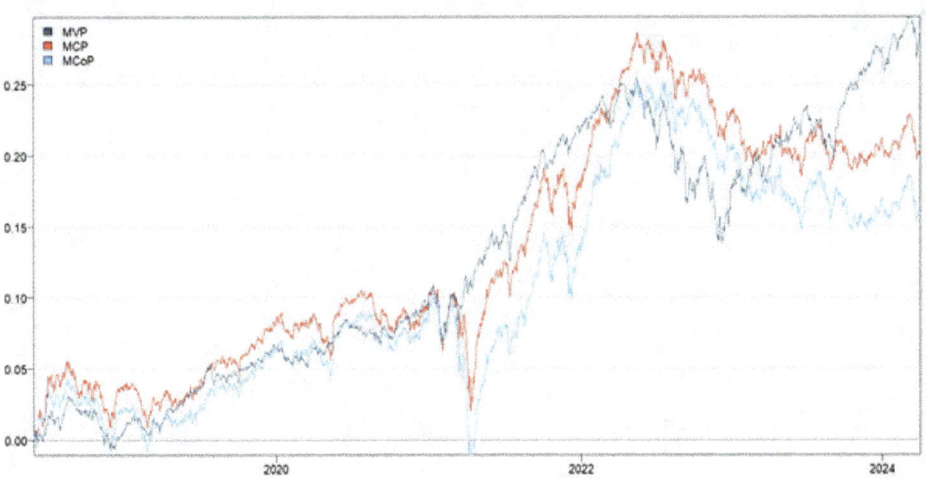

Figure 10. Robustness results with the QVAR approach

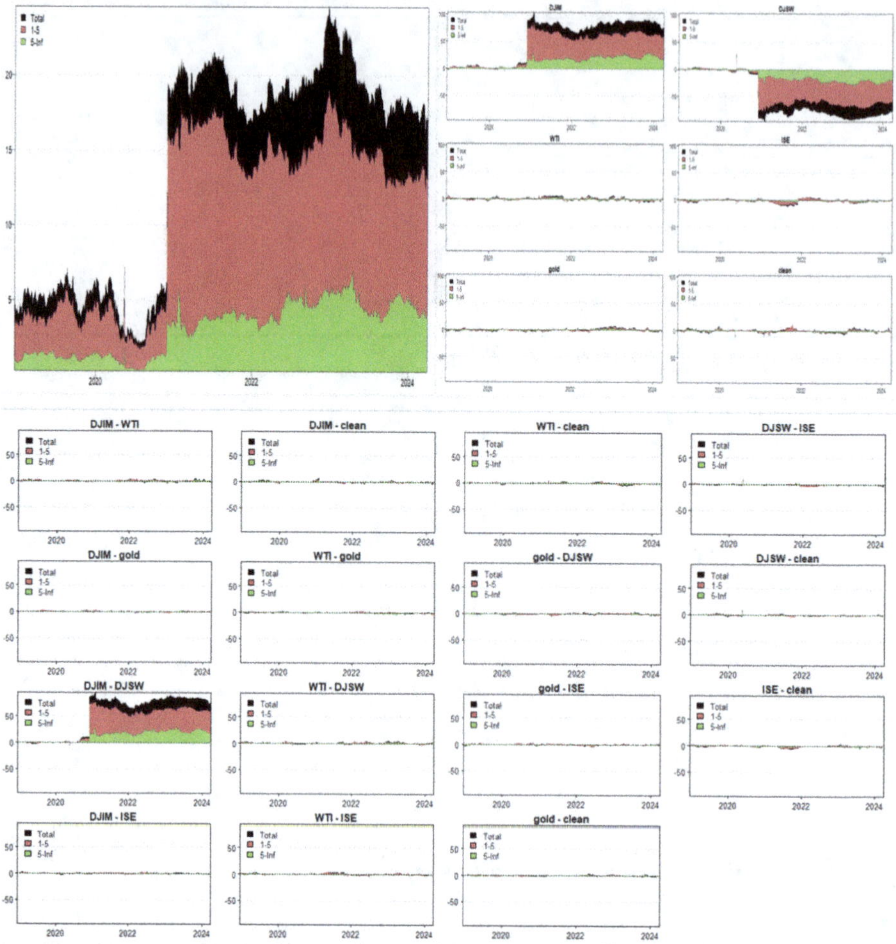

Chapter 13
Readiness to Embrace Islamic Financial Protection:
A Qualitative Study of Takaful Awareness Among Mosque Committees

Noor Aimi Mohamad Puad
https://orcid.org/0000-0001-9245-3231
International Islamic University Malaysia, Malaysia

Khairul Anuar Ahmad
https://orcid.org/0000-0003-2862-8345
Universiti Islam Selangor, Malaysia

Aza Shahnaz Azman
Universiti Islam Selangor, Malaysia

Fadilah Mat Nor
https://orcid.org/0009-0004-0861-5517
Universiti Islam Selangor, Malaysia

Ahmad Yani Ismail
Universiti Islam Selangor, Malaysia

Rubayah Yaakob
Universiti Kebangsaan Malaysia, Malaysia

Nurul Hidayah Md Razali
https://orcid.org/0009-0008-1117-4969
Universiti Kebangsaan Malaysia, Malaysia

Nur Amalina Shafie
https://orcid.org/0000-0003-4522-1758
Universiti Teknologi MARA, Malaysia

ABSTRACT

Despite various initiatives to promote Islamic financial literacy, Takaful awareness and engagement remain limited among community particularly mosque committee members. As trusted religious figures, these individuals are well-positioned to influence the adoption of Takaful products within their communities. However, little is

DOI: 10.4018/979-8-3373-2655-9.ch013

known about their readiness to adopt or promote Takaful. This study addresses this gap through qualitative exploration of mosque committee members' understanding, perception, and preparedness related to Takaful. 19 semi-structured interviews were conducted with mosque committee. The findings show that religiosity, ethical considerations, and prior experiences are strong drivers of readiness, while barriers include trust issues, affordability concerns, and limited access to clear information. The study offers practical insights for Takaful operators to design targeted outreach strategies that can strengthen awareness and acceptance among key community influencers.

INTRODUCTION

As growing numbers of Muslim communities become aware of their financial vulnerability, more people are asking for more participation in Shariah-compliant financial protection systems like Takaful. Takaful is an important part of the Islamic financial system. It is an ethical and cooperative way to share risk that is in line with the Maqasid al-Shariah principles. Even though a lot of effort has been performed by people in the industry and regulatory bodies to make Takaful more widely known, it is still not very popular among communities' organizations, especially among community leaders like mosque committee members (Saidi et al., 2020; Said et al., 2024 ; Eldaia et al., 2020; International Association of Insurance Supervisors, 2022). Since mosque committees are spiritual and social leaders in the Muslim community, it is very important to ensure that they are ready to understand, contribute, and promote Takaful. This indirectly will bridge the awareness gap and build financial inclusion systematically.

In this case, "readiness" means both the mental and behavioural willingness of people to use Islamic financial products based on what they know, how they see things, what kind of Muslims they are, and what they have experienced through in the past. Previous research has studied on how consumers, students, and policyholders view and use Takaful (Ashraf, Riaz & Sohail, 2024; Maduku & Mbeya, 2023; Hassan & Abbas, 2020; Aziz et al., 2019). However, there is only few research conducted which study on how community leaders, especially mosque committee members, view and respond to the Takaful product. It is important to study the perceptions of mosque's leaders on Takaful and to what extent is their knowledge on Takaful, since the mosque is still a centre for Islamic learning, community welfare, and social and economic growth (Ismail et al., 2024. This is especially important in Malaysia, where the government's goal of expanding Islamic social finance and Value-Based Intermediation (VBI) depends heavily on the trust and acceptance of the lower-income and underserved communities.

This study uses a qualitative method to provide insight into the readiness of mosque committee members in Peninsular Malaysia to support and promote Takaful as a way to protect their personal finances. It seeks to discover out how much they know, what contributes to them perceive how they do, and what challenges they have when trying to promote Takaful in their communities. This study answers the main question: How willing are mosque committee members to use and promote Takaful products in their communities? This study helps to create a model of Takaful promotion and literacy that is more inclusive and community driven. It does this by making sure that the takaful industry practices are in line with the spiritual, moral, and social realities of the Muslim grassroots.

This paper is divided into four main sections. The literature review section discusses the development of the Malaysian Takaful industry, Takaful and its definition, Takaful awareness and literacy and influence of mosque leadership on community behavior. Section three features the elaboration on the methodology and design of study involved. Then, section four presents the substantial findings, and the final section contains the concluding comments.

LITERATURE REVIEW

Development of Malaysian Takaful Industry

The Malaysian Takaful industry has grown significantly since its establishment in 1984 with the establishment of Syarikat Takaful Malaysia Berhad, the country's first Takaful operator. A number of factors, such as regulatory support, growing awareness of Islamic financial products, and a growing demand for Shariah-compliant insurance solutions, have contributed to the industry's growth (Fitch Ratings, 2025; United Nations Development Programme, 2025; Ali, 2024). Malaysia's dual financial system, which embraces both conventional and Islamic systems, has allowed the Takaful industry to thrive. According to Ansari (2022), the Takaful Act of 1984 created a foundation for the sector's systematic development, opening the door for subsequent growth and innovation.

On the same ground, Malaysia's Takaful industry has expanded throughout the years, meeting a variety of consumer demands with products such as general Takaful (Islamic general insurance) and family Takaful (Islamic life insurance). The implementation of the Islamic Financial Services Act (IFSA) 2013 represented a noteworthy advancement in fortifying the regulatory structure, improving oversight, and guaranteeing the adherence to Shariah in Takaful activities. IFSA 2013 also provide significant modifications to the Takaful industry by requiring the separation of composite licenses into separate general Takaful and family Takaful licenses.

According to Jamil and Jamal (2016), the IFSA 2013 has also increased market trust, drawing investors from both home and abroad to Malaysia's Takaful industry.

Bank Negara Malaysia (BNM) initiated the Financial Sector Master Plan (2000–2010) with the aim that the Takaful industry and Islamic banking industry will contribute at least 20% of the total market share of the financial sector. Subsequently, the Financial Sector Blueprint (2011- 2020) targeted to increase the market share of Islamic banking and finance in Malaysia to at least 40% by the year 2020. The development of the Takaful industry in Malaysia has shown remarkable performance. From a single Takaful operator in 1984, BNM has extended the award of Takaful licenses to conventional financial institutions. At present, Malaysia has a total of fifteen (15) Takaful Operators for family and general Takaful businesses.

Takaful and its Definition

Takaful, which comes from the Arabic word kafala, means "guaranteeing one another." It is a cooperative system of loss protection or reimbursement based on Islamic law. Takaful is different from regular insurance because it is based on the ideas of *ta'awun* and *tabarru'* among its members (Gunardi et al., 2024; Rifas et al., 2023). Participants put their money into a common fund to help people who may have forfeited something specific, which increases social responsibility and solidarity (Abduh, 2019; Billah, 2003). AAOIFI defines Takaful as a mutual agreement to make contributions in order to protect participants who suffer losses. This makes it very different from traditional insurance, which is based on profit maximization (Rosele & Johari, 2016).

The main ideas behind Takaful are very similar to the *Maqasid Shariah* especially protecting wealth helping people. Depending on the Takaful model used, it is based on contracts like *Wakalah* and *Mudharabah*. The *tabarru'* element ensures that the contract is not seen as a business deal, but as a charitable agreement to share risk (Rifas et al., 2023). In addition, Takaful carefully avoids Islamic prohibitions like *riba' gharar* and *maysir* (Yassin & Ramly, 2011; Archer et al., 2009). Due to the high ethical and morality. Shariah scholars and Muslim around the world are in the opinion that Takaful is the best option especially for a Muslim.

Currently, Takaful serve beyond individual protection by involving in halal socioeconomic ecosystems, as demonstrated by the programs like Malaysian mosques' Death Charity Money Scheme (DCMS) (Gunardi et al., 2024). These initiatives show how Takaful can be utilized to support community development and reduce poverty in addition to serve as a financial tool. Although takaful is gaining global popularity, with over 324 operators in 47 countries, its ethical appeal is still not widely understood by the public. This is especially true when compared with other conventional insurance concepts like indemnity and subrogation (Rifas et al., 2023;

Shariah Advisory Council of Bank Negara Malaysia, 2010). Therefore, it is essential to clarify these ideas in the context of Shariah to increase their acceptability, particularly as Takaful develops into a crucial part of the Islamic financial system.

Takaful Awareness and Literacy

Even though there is more demand for Shariah-compliant financial products, many people remain unaware of what Takaful is or how it operates. Ahmad and Mahadi (2023) investigated how people in Afghanistan experienced Takaful and found that, while most people had a good understanding of it, not many were aware of it. Their results showed that awareness and knowledge had a big effect on people's perceptions of Takaful and their willingness to sign up. There were also similar patterns in Malaysia. Aziah et al. (2023) studied how aware polytechnic students were and found that older students (ages 20–21) were moderately to highly aware, but younger students (ages 18–19) were much less aware. These results suggest that educating individuals about financial literacy at the early stage is crucial for getting them to involve with Takaful in the long term.

Apart from demographics, social and religious factors are also important for raising awareness of Takaful. Musa et al. (2022) highlighted how social media and religious views can affect what people desire to purchase. This suggests that digital platforms could raise awareness if they were linked to religious messages. The survey also found that an extensive number of students were unfamiliar with the differences between Takaful and conventional insurance in terms of structure and ethics. This shows a lack of knowledge that could potentially be lined in with concentrated learning materials. Muhammad Nasir et al. (2023) also stressed how important it is for products to be easy to understand and valuable to everyday life in order to raise awareness levels.

Further research also demonstrate that adolescents don't have sufficient knowledge about certain Takaful plans, like education and motor vehicle Takaful. Juhari et al. (2022) found that young Malaysians are unfamiliar with motor Takaful components, which shows how important it is to make product descriptions more straightforward to understand. Salman et al. (2017) and Soulhi & Al Shammari (2015) found that in India and Kuwait, Takaful knowledge is often shared informally, like through word of mouth. This shows that operators fail to perform enough formal outreach. This shows the importance of having structured, Shariah-compliant financial literacy programs, especially for students and young people who have big potential to expand the Islamic banking system in the future.

Influence of Mosque Leadership on Community Behavior

The mosque is an important religious institution for the Muslim community's spiritual health and for the growth of society. Movahed (2014) asserts that the mosque is a living institution that can influence behavior, improve education, and improve the welfare of the community through continuous involvement and divine motivation. His "Mosque Theory" says that the mosque is more than just a building; it is a place where people can learn about morality, work together, make decisions together, and keep learning. Kurniawan, Bahri, Mukmin & Yanti (2023) also stated that that the mosque is a place for da'wah and social change, especially when it is involved in projects that help people gain knowledge and become more financially independent. This perspective indicates how important it is to make the mosque's role more than just a place for rituals and include a more developmental and embracing role (Cokrohadisumarto & Sari, 2024).

This greater accountability needs good leadership inside the mosque. Zakaria and Ngah (2020) studied on mosque leadership in Kedah, Malaysia, and found that mosque leaders frequently have to perform administrative and programmatic tasks that have a direct effect on the way individuals in the community act. But most of the time, these leaders solely focus on religious events and avoid speaking about issues like youth development and outreach to people with low incomes. Remly, Sabaruddin and Adenan (2024) support this by showing that mosque institutions are unable to act as change agents because they are not given enough leadership training, lack of strategic planning, and fail to cooperate with the government. The lack of leaders who have forward-thinking leadership could have difficulties in using mosques as the right platform for financial education, Takaful promotion, and other Islamic economic activities.

In the past, the mosque served as a school, a legal court, and a centre for public welfare (Movahed, 2014; Zakaria & Ngah, 2020). Researchers these days are in the opinion that bringing this paradigm back will require leaders to focus more on getting people involved in their communities. For instance, Mahazan and Abdullah (2013) claimed that the way of leadership has a big effect on how effectively a mosque functions properly. Urban mosques usually have more structured administration and perform more outreach than rural mosques. Jabarkhail (2020) also discuss about how mosque leaders can help people change their behavior, especially when they have structured governance, a clear vision, and effective ways to communicate. With regard to this, mosque leaders not only play roles as religious leaders, but they are also can become strategic actors who may convince communities to use Islamic financial products like Takaful and others.

RESEARCH METHODOLOGY

To safeguard their financial future in accordance with Islamic principles, this study explores mosque committee members' readiness and willingness to accept and promote takaful. Despite their power to impact public perception and acceptance, community leaders consistently have low levels of awareness, comprehension, and involvement with Takaful. A qualitative approach was chosen since the issue is deeply ingrained in society and encompasses religious leadership, community impact, and ethical finance. According to Rahman (2017), researchers can gain insights that go beyond data by using qualitative methodologies to better understand human experience. Ryan et al. (2009) also was in a view that in-depth interviews are specifically helpful at revealing the core of what people think, believe, and intend to do. When examining how people perceive their roles and obligations in a religious and social setting, this approach can be highly beneficial.

The study employed a simple interpretive qualitative design, which seeks to comprehend how individuals perceive their experiences in a particular circumstance. People who currently sit on committees at certain mosques in Peninsular Malaysia were identified using a purposeful selection technique. These individuals were selected because they may have an impact on how people understand and express their religion, particularly in relation to Islamic financial issues. Twenty (20) semi-structured interviews were conducted in person. Participants had the chance to freely and professionally share their viewpoints during these interviews. While staying consistent with the core research topics, semi-structured interviews allowed for flexibility in examining important themes.

The six-phase framework developed by Braun and Clarke (2006) serves as the foundation for data analysis using theme analysis. The first stage was to write down what occurred during the interviews and read them several times to gain a grasp of the subject. The first codes were created and organized into larger categories, revealing trends related to Takaful knowledge, its perceived importance, religious impact, communication preferences, and institutional barriers. This process of interpretation allowed key insights to emerge from the participants' ordinary experiences. The themes were enhanced through repeated analysis to ensure that they included the essential elements of the participants' tales and addressed the primary research objectives. In this situation, thematic analysis was more than just a technical method; it was also a means of reflecting on the perspectives of those currently in positions of leadership inside mosques. Table 1 shows the demographic information of the 20 mosque committee members who took part in the interviews, including their career history, roles within the mosque, and state of residency. This split is critical to understanding the diversity of respondents who contributed to the findings.

Table 1. Details of interviewees

Respondent	Employment	Role of Mosques Committee Members	State
Respondent 1	Religious school teacher	Imam 2	Pahang
Respondent 2	Unemployed	Siak	Pahang
Respondent 3	Self-Employed	Pengerusi	Pahang
Respondent 4	Pensioner	Imam	Pahang
Respondent 5	Pensioner	Bendahari	Pahang
Respondent 6	Government Servant	Imam 1	Pahang
Respondent 7	Teacher	Imam	Melaka
Respondent 8	KAFA Teacher	Bilal	Perak
Respondent 9	Farmer	Bendahari	Johor
Respondent 10	Pensioner	Bilal	Johor
Respondent 11	Pensioner	Pengerusi Masjid	Johor
Respondent 12	Takaful agent	Bilal	Johor
Respondent 13	Driver	AJK	Johor
Respondent 14	Contractor	Imam Rawatib	Johor
Respondent 15	General Manager	Bendahari	Kelantan
Respondent 16	Pensioner	Bilal	Kelantan
Respondent 17	Bus driver	Imam Rawatib	Kelantan
Respondent 18	Former lawyer	Pengerusi Masjid	Kelantan
Respondent 19	Unemployed	Siak	Kelantan
Respondent 20	Administration staff	AJK	Selangor

Findings and Analysis

There are 20 face-to-face interviews conducted with the mosque committees using semi-structured questions. After conducting a data analysis, the findings showed the themes indicated below, which were then verified. Below is the list of the themes which reflects the readiness of Mosque Committee towards Takaful Products which will be further elaborated in the next subheading:

a) Takaful Knowledge
b) Personal experience
c) Decision factors
d) Challenges
e) Preferred Medium

Theme 1: Takaful Knowledge

The first theme derived is Takaful knowledge. In terms of Takaful knowledge, it is divided into three sub-themes. One and foremost is the awareness of the differences between Takaful and conventional insurance. Understanding the underlying contrasts between Islamic and conventional insurance systems can have a considerable impact on mosque committees' readiness to use Takaful products. If committee members understand that Takaful operates on the concepts of risk-sharing and mutual help, as opposed to conventional insurance's profit-driven approach, they are more likely to see Takaful as a Shariah-compliant option. This understanding not only boosts their confidence in owning the Takaful scheme but also enables them to successfully educate their community about the spiritual and ethical benefits of using Takaful over conventional means (Damit & Mohammed, 2025).

The second sub theme is the focus on the principles in Takaful. Based on the findings, the committee's emphasis on Takaful's Shariah compliance demonstrates its understanding of the importance of adhering to Islamic financial principles. This demonstrates a willingness to prioritise products that adhere to these requirements, such as the prohibition on *riba'* (interest), *gharar* (extreme uncertainty), and *maisir* (gambling). Their emphasis on ethical and religious factors establishes them as trustworthy promoters for Takaful, increasing its acceptance in the community (Kassim, Hyat & Salman, 2016).

The third sub-theme is the knowledge on the coverage options. Mosque committees with a thorough understanding of the many Takaful coverage alternatives, such as family protection, healthcare, and education plans, are better positioned to make informed judgements (Wan Jusoh & Noreffendi, 2022) . This readiness is critical because it allows them to offer appropriate products to meet the different needs of their congregation, building trust in their leadership and the Takaful system. As shown in Table 2, respondents expressed their understanding of Takaful concepts through three sub-themes: awareness of Islamic versus conventional insurance, focus on Shariah principles, and knowledge of coverage options.

Table 2. Theme 1, sub themes and quotation

Theme 1	Subthemes	Quotations
Takaful Knowledge	Awareness of Islamic vs. conventional insurance	*"Sebab kita faham konsep polisi Takaful ni memang dah patuh Syariah.. Kalau konvensional pula yang kita tahu banyak yang tak menepati Syariah yang terlibat dengan judi, riba, dan juga gharar.."* (R8) *"Takaful ni macam insurans yang Islamik.."*(R14) *" Pertama, dari sudut kesahan atau kepatuhanya.. Walaupun, dari sudut pemberianya sama saja dengan insurans konvensional.."*(R6) *"Asasnya, Takaful lebih Islamik patuh Syariah.. Konvensional pula tak patuh Syariah.."*(R9) *"Saya dah tahu beza antara operasi kedua-duanya sebab tu saya tukar kepada Takaful.. Dalam konvensional dia tak syariah compliance dan dia tak bagi tahu ke mana dana sumbangan dilaburkan, tapi kalau Takaful dia laburkan dalam dana Syariah sahaja*"(R12)
	Focus on principles of Takaful	*"…satu konsep yang mana kita tahu dari segi istilah bahasa Arab ialah tolong-menolong atau saling bantu-membantu.. Takaful ini diperkenalkan dalam Syariah yang bertepatan dnegan konsep Islam."*(R8) *" Takaful merupakan kerjasama (ta'awun), pada akhirnya membantu mereka yang perlu atau terdesak pada waktu itu.."*(R6) *"Takaful ni saya pilih sebab tak ada 3 unsur iaitu riba, maysir, dan gharar.."*(R12)
	Knowledge of coverage options.	*"….Setakat yang saya tahu benefit dalam bentuk duit, satu lagi cover insuran kemalangan.."*(R1) *"Saya pernah mengambil pelbagai jenis produk takaful seperti takaful hayat dan perubatan daripada beberapa syarikat seperti Ikhlas, Prudential, dan lain-lain."*(R18)

Theme 2: Personal Experience

The second theme derived is personal experience which is further classified into two sub themes: good experience and bad experience. Positive personal experiences with Takaful products, whether through claims processing, customer service, or overall satisfaction, have a substantial impact on the committee's readiness to promote Takaful. When committee members can relate with firsthand examples of Takaful's reliability and benefits, their credibility grows, and they become more effective in convincing the community of its importance. These pleasant experiences can serve as strong testimonials to create trust and acceptance (Nunis & Abd Rahman, 2019).

On the other hand, unpleasant experiences, such as difficulties with claims or poor customer service, can cause hesitation among committee members. However, if these situations are addressed constructively, they can provide useful input to Takaful operators to help them improve their services. When committee members believe their concerns have been acknowledged and addressed, it can boost their confidence and readiness to engage with and support Takaful goods (Che Mohd

Salleh, 2016). Table 3 summarizes respondents' personal experiences with Takaful. It categorizes feedback into good and bad experiences, showing how positive claims handling fosters advocacy while negative incidents may hinder confidence.

Table 3. Theme, sub themes and quotation

Theme 2	Subthemes	Quotations
Personal Experience	Good experience	*"Sangat berguna, saya dah guna/ claim sebanyak 2 kali.. Kedua, memudahkan urusan jangka masa mendapatkan atau menerima rawatan, jika dapatkan rawatan di Swasta lebih cepat berbanding dengan Kerajaan. Dari sudut kepakaran mungkin sama saja, tiada beza antara kedua-duanya.."*(R6) *"Anak saya mengalami autisme, jadi keperluan untuk perlindungan perubatan sangat mendesak. Saya mengambil takaful untuk memastikan kos rawatan dapat ditanggung.."*(R18)
	Bad experience	*"Kita tunggu, kereta dah hantar dekat bengkel, bila kereta dah ada dekat bengkel, tengok-tengok kereta belum repair apa-apa.. Masa hantar kereta mula-mula accident sampailah masuk dua bulan tak buat apa-apa.. Tapi kes ni, bukanlah takaful keluarga tapi lebih kepada takaful am.."*(R1)

Theme 3: Decision Factor

The third theme derived from the analysis is decision factor. There are five subthemes from this theme: health and family security, affordability and emergency healthcare support. The readiness of mosque committees to support Takaful is frequently demonstrated by their prioritisation of community welfare, particularly in areas such as health and family security. Recognising that Takaful provides financial protection against unexpected events, including illness or accidents, reflects the committee's proactive approach to protecting the long-term well-being of its members. This readiness demonstrates their commitment to the fundamental aim of Takaful, which is to provide mutual support in times of need (Muhammad et al, 2023; Malik & Sulaiman, 2024).

Secondly, in terms of affordability. The affordability of Takaful products is an important aspect that influences mosque committees' readiness to contribute for Takaful products. If the committee sees Takaful as a cost-effective solution that caters to different income levels, they are more inclined to promote its use. Affordability increases the accessibility of Takaful products, making them a viable alternative for a greater segment of the community, hence the committee's role in supporting these items becomes more significant (Malik & Sulaiman, 2024)

The third factor is the emergency healthcare support. Mosque committees that understand the value of having financial coverage for crises like hospitalisation or serious illnesses are more likely to see Takaful as an essential component of community protection. Their preparedness is illustrated by their advocacy for Takaful as a means of reducing financial obligations during crises, emphasising its importance as a form of protection for individuals and families.

The fourth factor is religiosity. Religiosity has a substantial influence on Takaful decision-making by prioritising compliance with Islamic norms and values. Because of Islam's prohibition on riba' (interest), gharar (uncertainty), and maisir (gambling), highly religious people frequently prefer Shariah-compliant financial solutions, such as Takaful, rather than conventional insurance (Al-Mahi, Sim & Hassan, 2017; Maduku & Mbeya, 2023). Their faith motivates them to seek ethical and honest financial solutions, which strengthens trust in Takaful's mutual help approach and equitable risk-sharing framework. Furthermore, religion emphasises family protection and societal responsibility, making Takaful an appealing option for meeting these commitments while following to Islamic principles. For many, Takaful is more than a financial decision; it is a spiritual commitment that provides both worldly advantages and a guarantee of unforeseen blessings (Kasim, Htay & Salman, 2016). The perception of Takaful as a halal, ethical, and community-oriented solution solidifies its appeal, particularly for those who view financial decisions through the lens of their faith.

The fifth component is benefits of Takaful plan which refers to the tangible advantages and protections that individuals or organizations receive from subscribing to an insurance policy, including Takaful. These benefits are essential drivers of participation and are often tailored to meet the specific needs and priorities of the Takaful participants. A significant benefit is the ability to seek treatment at private hospitals, which typically provide speedier and more personalised care than public healthcare systems. Takaful plans that cover private healthcare provide Takaful participants with peace of mind by ensuring that they have access to fast and high-quality care during emergencies or serious health conditions. Table 4 highlights the decision factors influencing mosque committee members' readiness to embrace Takaful. These range from health and family security to affordability, religiosity, emergency healthcare support, and perceived benefits of Takaful plans.

Table 4. Theme 3, sub themes and quotation

Theme 3	Sub theme	Quotations
Decision Factors	Health and family security	*"Saya memilih hibah ni tak lain tak bukan untuk perlindungan kalau berlaku apa-apa kepada kita la, untuk persediaan ahli keluarga yang lain la.. Anak-anak, isteri tu je la.. Untuk medical pula dalam proses nak ambil juga"(*R1) *"Boleh melindungi diri saya, dan untuk kegunaan masa depan*" (R2) *"Kepentingan masa depan diri dan keluarga.."*(R7) *"Jika ada pelan takaful yang menawarkan simpanan untuk pendidikan anak-anak ke universiti, saya akan berminat.."*(R17)
	Affordability	*"Tengok kepada kemampuan dan pakej Takaful.. Saya bersedia nak ambil tapi tunggu promosi jika ada"*(R3) *"Tapi, buat masa ni saya tengok kepada kemampuan terlebih dahulu untuk saya membayarnya.. Saya juga kena tengok polisi perlindungan Takaful, bergantung kepada tahap umur saya yang meningkat pada waktu tu.."*(R8) *"Kalau pada waktu tu mampu maka saya bersedialah.. Tapi kalau tak mampu saya tak bersedia nak ambil polisi Takaful.."*(R13) *"Jika manfaatnya jelas dan sesuai dengan kemampuan saya, saya boleh mempertimbangkan"*.(R19) *"Masa tu ekonomi saya masih lagi stabil.. Lepastu ada masalah ekonomi saya tak stabil dan berhenti bayar waktu PKP.."*(R3)
	Emergency healthcare support	*"Pada saya ia lebih kepada persediaan.."*(R6) *"Bersedia untuk sebarang keadaaan yang akan berlaku.. Sediakan payung sebelum hujan.."*(R8) *"..membantu memastikan hutang saya dilangsaikan jika sesuatu berlaku pada saya.."*(R15)
	Religiousity	*"Sebagai seorang muslim kita prefer Takaful..."*(R9) *".....Jadi, kita sebagai orang Islam kita wajiblah memilih polisi yang patuh syariah.."* (R8) *"Faktor lain yang mendorong kita nak yang lebih patuh syariah laa.."*(R1) *"Sebab nya kita ni orang Islam, kita tukar la kpd insuran Islam"*(R3) *"Sebab Takaful ni Islamik, saya tak ragu.."*(R4) *"Sesuai dengan kita sebagai orang Islam/ Muslim.. Mengutamakan yang halal dan haram.. Dan lebih utama kerana melibatkan bab muamalat.."*(R7) *"Sebagai orang Islam kita lebih percaya produk kewangan Islam berbanding yang lain.."*(R7) *"Sebab saya pilih hanya kerana Takaful ni patuh Syariah je.."*(R10)
	Benefits of Takaful plan	*"Manfaat untuk rawatan kesihatan di Swasta selain daripada Kerajaan.."*(R5) *"Kemudahan dari segi berurusan, dan juga perkhidmatan yang diberikan kepada yang mencarum Takaful"* (R5) *"Kemudahan mendapatkan rawatan perubatan yang cepat atau segera di Hospital Swasta.."*(R7) *"Manfaat yang mengikut kadar polisi yang ditetapkan.. Manfaat yang kita dapat ni kebanyakanya dari segi prasarana/kemudahan hospital swasta, cover banyak penyakit sebab sesetengah tu cover penyakit tertentu saja.."*(R8)

Theme 4: Challenges

Theme number four derived is the challenges. The first sub theme is the trust issues with Takaful operators. The issue of trust is critical in determining mosque committees' willingness to engage with Takaful products. If Takaful operators are perceived to be transparent, ethical, and committed to their commitments, the committee will be more confident in promoting these products. In contrast, a lack of trust owing to perceived inefficiencies or unethical actions can operate as a barrier, emphasising the need for Takaful operators to strengthen relationships with their stakeholders by providing consistent and reliable services (Abu Hasan, Wan Jusoh & Hamid, 2014).

The second sub theme is the concerns about scams and fraudulent activities. Concerns about frauds or fraudulent activity in the financial industry may make mosque committees wary about adopting Takaful products. However, readiness can be increased if Takaful operators address these concerns through strong governance, Shariah compliance, and regulatory oversight (Jamil & Marzuki, 2023, Shalboob, 2025; Salleh et al., 2024). Clear communication and educational initiatives can help to relieve worries and build a sense of security (Sikander, 2024).

The third sub theme is the rising healthcare costs. Awareness of rising healthcare costs highlights mosque committees' willingness to explore opportunities such as Takaful, which provide financial protection against these rising prices. Recognising the benefits of risk-sharing under the Takaful model allows the committee to portray it as a viable and ethical option for community-wide healthcare expenditure control (Miskan et al., 2024; Rehman et al., 2023).

Finally, the complexity of the claims process. The perceived complexity of the claims process may dissuade readiness. Mosque committees may be hesitant to campaign for Takaful if they perceive the claims process is complex or inaccessible. Simplifying the process and providing clear information will greatly increase the committee's willingness to support and recommend Takaful products. The challenges faced by mosque committees in adopting Takaful are outlined in Table 5. The table reflects issues of trust, fear of scams, rising healthcare costs, and complexity in claims processes, all of which can delay or discourage adoption.

Table 5. Theme 3, sub themes and quotation

Theme 4	Sub theme	Quotations
Challenges	Trust issues with insurance providers	*"in my opinion, private hospital ni nampak macam just for business, kalau bayar cash harga macam ni, kalau ada insurans harga macam ni, macam mana boleh macam tu, it just simply charge..*(R14)
	Concerns about scams and fraudulent activities	*"..tak sesuai guna panggilan telefon sebab takut scammer"* (R3) *"..Kalau boleh elakkan panggilan telefon sebab banyak scammer."*(R5)
	Rising in healthcare costs	*"Tapi sekarang dah naik kepada RM215.."*(R7) *"Bagi Takaful perubatan yang saya ambil sebelum saya berkahwin kos nya sebanyak RM110. Kemudian, selepas setahun naik kepada RM20-30. Jika kita dimaklumkan lebih awal, kita tak rasa terbeban. Jadi, saya kira kesediaan tu perlu diutamakan.."*(R6)
	Complexity of claims process	*"Setakat ni saya tak pernah claim lagi, cuma dengar-dengar nak dapat claim kereta kalau accident makan masa berbulan-bulan untuk siap.."*(R1)

Theme 5: Preferred Medium

The final theme derived is the preferred medium. The first sub theme is social media and advertisements as reliable sources. The preference for social media and advertisements as information sources indicates that mosque committees are ready to engage with modern, accessible communication platforms. This readiness can be leveraged by Takaful providers to reach committee members with targeted and educational content that highlights the benefits and features of Takaful products (Mohd Rasid & Ruslan, 2024; Norazman et al., 2023).

Second, a preference for non-intrusive communication is reflected in the propensity to stay clear of direct promotional calls. This implies that mosque committees are more receptive to tactful and indirect engagement techniques, like online webinars or community workshops, which let them study Takaful products at their own pace.

Thirdly, using WhatsApp to communicate securely. Using WhatsApp for communication shows that one is willing to adopt technology for safe and effective communication. By sharing updates, responding to questions, and facilitating conversations, takaful operators can build convenience and trust with mosque committees.

The final sub theme is direct from the agent. Mosque committees' willingness to interact with and support Takaful products is demonstrated by their response to direct promotions from Takaful agents. A favourable response, marked by willingness to respond to dialogue and a readiness to assist with community outreach, signifies a high level of preparedness and confidence in Takaful operators. On the other hand, hesitation or skepticism could indicate worries about Shariah compliance, ethical transparency, or a preference for other forms of communication like seminars or online forums (Ahmad Samsuri & Jamal, 2017; Shukor, 2020; Abdullah, Hassan & Yusof, 2020). If mosque committees actively support agent promotions by organizing informational sessions or engaging in discussions, it demonstrates a strong commitment to promoting Takaful within the community, highlighting their role as key influencers in financial decision-making. Table 6 captures the preferred communication mediums used by mosque committees to receive information about Takaful. It shows that social media, WhatsApp, and trusted agents are preferred channels, while unsolicited calls are largely avoided.

Table 6. Theme 3, sub themes and quotation

Theme 5	Sub theme	Quotations
Preferred medium	Social media and advertisements as reliable sources	*"Sekarang guna goggle saja.. Tik tok.."*(R3) *"Saya kira diperingkat awal perlu detail di media atau laman sosial saja.."* (R6) *"Saya tengok sekarang ni sesuai melalui media massa, iklan tv dan sebagainya.."*(R8)
	Avoidance of direct promotional calls	*"..tak sesuai guna panggilan telefon sebab takut scammer"* (R3) *"..Kalau boleh elakkan panggilan telefon sebab banyak scammer."*(R5)
	Use of WhatsApp for secure communication	*"..whats'App yang boleh dipastikan keselamatanya, dan medium lain yang menyakinkan...* "(R5)
	Direct from agent	*"Daripada ejen dan pihak yang berkenaan dengan Takaful"* (R2) *"...dari ejen..Ejen setakat ni alhamdulillah la tak scam, maknanya ejen yang kita kenal.."*(R1) *"..Tapi, sesuai berdepan dengan orangnya (ejen) la"* (R3)

RECOMMENDATIONS AND CONCLUSIONS

The overall findings indicate that mosque committee members are ready for Takaful adoption which influenced by their knowledge, personal experiences, decision-making factors, challenges, and preferred communication mediums. Knowledge of Takaful is very important since members who have a greater understanding of its Shariah principles, ethical compliance, and coverage alternatives are most likely willing to adopt the product. Personal experiences, both good and bad, also affect the way that they perceive things. For example, easy claims processing and easy-to-find coverage make people more likely to sign up, while difficulties with claims and customer service make them less inclined to do so. Decision factors such the need for health and family security, affordability, emergency healthcare help, religion, and perceived benefits of Takaful all affect preparedness. Members who contributed a significant emphasis on financial protection and following Shariah law are more likely to embrace Takaful.

Nevertheless, there are numerous of challenges which hinder the adoption, including not trusting providers, being concerned about scams, rising healthcare prices, complicated claims processes, and the perception that government healthcare and family support are enough. Furthermore, preferred ways of communicating are very important for engagement. Participants like social media, ads, and WhatsApp for secured interaction, however they oppose direct commercial calls because they have concerns about scams. It is also acceptable to speak to trustworthy Takaful agents directly, as long as the conversation is professional and accessible. These results show how important it is for mosque committee members to be financially literate, for Takaful operators to reach out strategically, and to build trust for enhancing the committee members' readiness in adopting Takaful product.

In a nutshell these findings show that mosque committee members are slightly prepared to embrace Takaful, but not entirely because of financial concerns, lack of information, and not getting adequate interactions with Takaful operators. Several individuals are eager to move from conventional insurance, but the high cost and lack of interest in Takaful operators still become the major obstacles. Members with Islamic studies or formal education backgrounds show higher readiness, highlighting the role of financial literacy. Readiness also varies by demography. Younger and less-educated members are less prepared, whereas metropolitan committees are more aware since they have greater exposure to the financial matters. Personal experiences, trust difficulties, and how people see community support all affect opinions. People also prefer social media and WhatsApp over direct advertising calls as ways to communicate. In summary, awareness, trust, and having the capacity to contribute are among the important factors for convincing people to adopt the Takaful product.

Similar to other qualitative studies, the present study has several limitations that need to be pointed out. First, the findings are context-specific and based on the views of a relatively small number of mosque committee members in selected locations across Peninsular Malaysia. The purposive sampling method gave us detailed information from educated and relevant participants, but the small sample size indicates that the results are inapplicable to all mosque leaders in this nation. More diversified points of view and more representativeness of future research may come from sampling distributed more widely throughout different states or regions, such as East Malaysia.

Secondly, this study focused solely on the readiness and opinions of mosque committee members. It did not take into considerations the opinions of other important community members, like imams, religious educators (ustaz), or members of Islamic NGOs, who may also have an important influence on the perceptions of the community on Takaful. Furthermore, the viewpoints of the Takaful operators themselves, especially about how they reach out to mosque communities were not counted, presenting another element that opens the opportunity for future study. By looking into this two-way relationship might help in getting better understanding on how to get more people engaged in and increase the awareness of Takaful at the community level.

Despite these issues, the study provides an important contribution by demonstrating the religious, moral, and practical reasons why mosque committee members are willing to subscribe to Islamic financial protection tools. The limits also point to new areas of research that could be conducted in the future. Future research might undertake a mixed-methods approach to combine qualitative insights with quantitative data. This would provide a more comprehensive understanding of Takaful literacy and acceptance. Future research could go further into intervention-based approaches, such Takaful roadshows or educational programs, and examine how these affect awareness and involvement in communities that have a connection to mosques. Finally, this study sets the groundwork for mosque leaders to play a greater part in promoting financial well-being that is both inclusive and in line with Shariah law.

REFERENCES

Abduh, M. (2019). *Foundation of Islamic Finance*. IIUM Press.

Abdullah, N. A., Hassan, S. A., & Yusoff, S. Z. (2020). Factors that influence the ethical behaviours of Takaful agents. *International Journal of Academic Research in Business & Social Sciences*, *10*(8), 270–282. DOI: 10.6007/IJARBSS/v10-i8/7535

Ahmad, G. S., & Mahadi, N. F. (2023). Public Awareness, Knowledge, and Perception towards Takaful in Afghanistan. *Journal of Islamic Social Finance*, *1*(2), 45–57.

Ahmad Samsuri, M. A. Z., & Jamal, J. (2017). Takaful Agent Must Foster Public Understanding of Takaful. *Diponegoro Law Review*, *2*(2), 245–258. DOI: 10.14710/dilrev.2.2.2017.1-14

Al-Mahi, A. S. M. M., Sim, C. S., & Hassan, A. (2017). Religiosity and demand for takaful (Islamic Insurance): A preliminary investigation. *International Journal of Applied Business and Economic Research*, *15*(24), 485–499.

Ali, S. (2024, October 15). Opening keynote speech at the Takaful StarNite Gala Dinner. *Bank for International Settlements (BIS)*.

Ansari, Z. (2022). A review of 20 years of takaful literature using a systematic method. *Asian Journal of Economics and Banking*, *46*(1), 2–25. DOI: 10.1108/AJEB-08-2021-0100

Archer, S., ... (2009). (ed.). Takaful Islamic insurance: concepts and regulatory issues. John Wiley and Sons (Asia) Ptd. Ltd.

Ashraf, R., Riaz, H., & Sohail, M. (2024). Perception and awareness among Muslim consumers: Comparative study of Takaful and conventional insurance policyholders. *Gomal University Journal of Research*, *40*(1), 1–10. DOI: 10.51380/gujr-40-01-01.

Aziah, A. R., Samsudin, K. J., & Osman, N. (2023). A study on awareness and understanding of Takaful products among polytechnic students in Malaysia. *IBAF Journal* [USIM]. *Universiti Sains Islam Malaysia*, *12*(2), 192–204.

Aziz, S., Husin, M. M., Hussin, N., & Afaq, Z. (2019). Factors that influence individuals' intentions to purchase family takaful mediating role of perceived trust. *Asia Pacific Journal of Marketing and Logistics*, *31*(1), 81–104. DOI: 10.1108/APJML-12-2017-0311

Billah, M. M. (2003). *Islamic and modern insurance: Principles and practices*. Ilmiah Publishers.

Braun, V., & Clarke, V. (2006). Using thematic analysis in psychology. *Qualitative Research in Psychology*, *3*(2), 77–101. DOI: 10.1191/1478088706qp063oa

Cokrohadisumarto, W. M., & Sari, Y. I. (2024). Mosque-Based Integrated Community Empowerment Model. *Islamic Social Finance*, *4*(1), 1–26.

Damit, M. R. M., & Mohammed, R. (2025). Unveiling Takaful subscriptions: Demographic factors and their impact on Takaful products penetration in Malaysia. *International Journal of Business and Technology Management*, *5*(4), 290–298.

Eldaia, M., Hanefah, M. M., Marzuki, A., & Shatnawi, S. (2020). Takaful in Malaysia: Emergence, growth, and prospects. In Takaful in Malaysia: Emerging opportunities, challenges and way forward (pp. 682–699). Universiti Sains Islam Malaysia.

Fitch Ratings. (2025, May 12). Malaysia's takaful industry poised for growth amidst regulatory reforms. *Insurance Asia.* https://insuranceasia.com/insurance/news/malaysias-takaful-industry-poised-growth-amidst-regulatory-reforms

Gunardi, S., Rahman, A. A., Salleh, A. Z., Noor, K. M., Omar, S. M. N. S., & Shahbuddin, Z. H. S. (2024). Takaful: Principles and applications in managing Death Charity Money Scheme (DCMS) at Tengku Mizan Zainal Abidin Mosque, Kerteh, Terengganu to develop ecosystem of halal social economy. *International Journal of Religion*, *5*(11), 5897–5903. DOI: 10.61707/1cqdz704

Hassan, H. A., & Abbas, S. K. (2020). Factors Influencing The Investors' Intention To Adopt Takaful (Islamic Insurance) Products: A survey of Pakistan. *Journal of Islamic Marketing*, *11*(1), 1–13. DOI: 10.1108/JIMA-03-2018-0064

International Association of Insurance Supervisors. (2022). Issues in regulation and supervision of micro Takaful: Islamic microinsurance (IAIS Issues Paper). https://www.iaisweb.org/uploads/2022/01/151118-Issues-Paper-on-Regulation - and-Supervision-of-Microtakaful-Islamic-Microinsurance.pdf

Ismail, A. G., Mohd Daud, A. H., Mohamad Nasir, N. S., Omar, N., Azzan, N. A., Abdul Rahman, N. S., & Azmin, U. S. (2024).4. *UMRAN – International Journal of Islamic and Civilizational Studies, 11*(2), 89–102.

Jabarkhail, S. (2020). Servant Leadership in the Context of Mosque: A Qualitative Case Study of Muslim Women's Perspectives. *Administrative Sciences*, *10*(3), 72. DOI: 10.3390/admsci10030072

Jamil, N. N., & Marzuki, A. (2023). The effects ofshariah governance on takaful performance oftakaful operators in Malaysia. *Journal of Islamic, Social* [JISED]. *Economics and Development*, *8*(59), 468–474.

Jamil, S. N., & Jamal, J. (2016). Importance of Islamic Financial Services Act 2013 in Takaful industry after the repealed Takaful Act 1984. *Diponegoro Law Review, 1*(1), 17–27. DOI: 10.14710/dilrev.1.1.2016.17-27

Juhari, J., Rahim, N. A., Masdek, N. R. N. M., Ahmad, K. S., & Husin, N. (2022). The role of awareness and knowledge toward motor takaful purchase intention among young generation. *International Journal of Academic Research in Business & Social Sciences, 12*(11), 304–313. DOI: 10.6007/IJARBSS/v12-i11/15224

Kasim, N., Htay, S. N. N., & Salman, S. A. (2016). The Religious Perspective of Takaful as Ethical Insurance. *Mediterranean Journal of Social Sciences, 7*(4), 96–104. DOI: 10.5901/mjss.2016.v7n4p96

Kurniawan, A. T., Bahri, B., Mukmin, H., & Yanti, F. (2023). *Revitalization of mosque functions in empowering city Islamic communities: Bandar Lampung. Proceedings of the International Conference on Education, Society and Humanity, 1*(1), 93–99. Universitas Islam Negeri Raden Intan Lampung. Retrieved from https://ejournal.unuja.ac.id/index.php/icesh

Maduku, D. K., & Mbeya, S. (2023). Understanding family Takaful purchase behaviour: The roles of religious obligation and gender. *Journal of Financial Services Marketing, 29*(2), 440–458. DOI: 10.1057/s41264-023-00213-z

Mahazan, A. M., & Abdullah, A. G. (2013). A Model of Imam's Leadership and Mosque Performance in Malaysia. *Global Journal Al-Thaqafah, 3*(2), 53–64. DOI: 10.7187/GJAT432013.03.02

Malik, N. S. A., & Sulaiman, S. (2024). A synthesis of literature on micro-Takaful: Exploring protection for unexpected adverse events. *International Journal of Islamic Economics and Finance Research, 7*(1), 15–30.

Miskan, N. H., Muhamad, N., Esa, M. M., Zabidi, F. S. M., Hussin, N. L., & Nasuha, S. A. (2024). Awareness of Takaful Ownership among the Kuala Klawang Community: Challenge or Opportunity? *Information Management and Business Review, 16*(4), 12–17. DOI: 10.22610/imbr.v16i4(I).4251

Mohd Rasid, M. F. R., & Ruslan, A. F. (2024). *Determinant of Family Takaful Adoption Among Puncak Alam Residents*. ResearchGate. Retrieved from https://www.researchgate.net/publication/385327808_Determinant_of_Family_Takaful_Adoption_Among_Puncak_Alam_Residents

Movahed, K. (2014). Mosque as a religious building for community development. https://oaks.kent.edu/node/295

Musa, A. H., Baharuddin, F. N., Rosle, A. N., Ibrahim, S. S., & Syed Noh, S. N. (2022). The role of social media and religious awareness in purchasing decision on Takaful insurance: A conceptual paper. *International Journal of Academic Research in Business & Social Sciences*, *12*(6), 630–636. DOI: 10.6007/IJARBSS/v12-i6/13996

Nasir, N. I. M., Hassan, R., & Osman, A. Z. (2023). Spectrum of consumer awareness in Islamic finance: Takaful industry in Malaysia. *The Journal of Muamalat and Islamic Finance Research*, *20*(2), 125–134. DOI: 10.33102/jmifr.513

Norazman, A., Azmi, N., & Khairuddin, N. (2023). *The Role of Financial Education in Promoting ESG and Takaful Awareness in Malaysia*. Proceedings of the International Conference on Islamic Economics. Retrieved from https://e piiecons .usim.edu.my/index.php/eproceeding/article/download/118/89/172

Nunis, N. N. M., & Abd Rahman, S. Z. (2019). Examining consumers' continuance intention and e-WOM about Islamic insurance (Takaful). *Malaysian Journal of Consumer and Family Economics*, *21*, 127–144.

Rahman, M. S. (2017). The Advantages and Disadvantages of Using Qualitative and Quantitative Approaches and Methods in Language "Testing and Assessment" Research: A Literature Review. *Journal of Education and Learning*, *6*(1), 102–112. DOI: 10.5539/jel.v6n1p102

Rehman, A. U., Aslam, E., Muhammad, R. S., Aslam, M., Iqbal, A., & Shabbir, M. S. (2023). Consumer awareness and knowledge about Takaful (Islamic insurance): A survey of Pakistan. *Journal of Namibian Studies*, *35*(S1), 4101–4118.

Remly, M. R., Sabaruddin, S. N. A., & Adenan, F. (2024). Cabaran Kepimpinan Dalam Pengimarahan Institusi Masjid: Kajian Kes Di Masjid Cemerlang: Leadership Challenges In The Improvement Of Mosque Institutions: A Case Study In Masjid Cemerlang. *Al-Qanatir: International Journal of Islamic Studies*, *33*(3), 26–36.

Rifas, A. H. ., Ab Rahman, A. ., & Buang, A. H. . . (2023). Appraising the Universal Concepts of Insurance and Takaful: Similarities and Differences. *UMRAN - Journal of Islamic and Civilizational Studies, 10*(1), 1–15.

Rosele, M. I., & Johari, A. H. (2016). Aplikasi Takaful Model Wakaf Di Malaysia: Keperluan Dan Permasalahannya (Application of Waqf Takaful Model in Malaysia: Its Requirements and Problems). *UMRAN - International Journal of Islamic and Civilizational Studies*, 3(1), 28-38.

Ryan, F., Coughlan, M., & Cronin, P. (2009). Interviewing in qualitative research: The one-to-one interview. *International Journal of Therapy and Rehabilitation, 16*(6), 309–314. DOI: 10.12968/ijtr.2009.16.6.42433

Said, N. M., Yahaya, S., Yusuff, Y. Z., & Hasan, Z. A. (2024). Takaful awareness in Malaysia: An empirical study on the influence of knowledge, financial status, and social factors. *Advanced International Journal of Business* [AIJBES]. *Entrepreneurship and SMEs*, *6*(22), 25–33.

Saidi, N. B. M., Zainal, H. B., Mohd Din, N., Zainuddin, S. A. B., & Abdullah, T. B. (2020). Attitude, subjective norm, and perceived behavioural control as determinant of hibah giving intent in Malaysia. *International Journal of Innovation. Creativity and Change*, *10*(10), 61–70.

Salleh, M. C. M. (2016). The significant contribution of islamic relationship marketing practice in malaysian takaful industry towards determining customer gratitude, trust, and commitment. *Asian Academy of Management Journal*, *21*(Supp. 1), 171–207. DOI: 10.21315/aamj2016.supp.1.8

Salleh, S., Kamaruddin, M. I. H., Shafii, Z., Hanefah, M. M., Zakaria, N., Mahyudin, W. A., & Sabri, N. A. M. (2024). Shariah governance and audit practices in Islamic co-operatives: An audit expectation-performance gap analysis. *Corporate Law & Governance Review*, *6*(3), 72–80. DOI: 10.22495/clgrv6i3p8

Salman, S. A., Rashid, H. M. A., & Hassan, R. (2017). Awareness And Knowledge Of Insurance and Takaful in India A Survey on Indian Insurance Policy Holders. *Man in India*, *97*(11), 127–140.

Shalboob, H. (2025). The role of AI in enhancing shariah compliance: Efficiency and transparency in Islamic finance. *Journal of Infrastructure. Policy and Development*, *9*(1), 1–26.

Shariah Advisory Council of Bank Negara Malaysia. (2010). *Shariah resolutions in Islamic finance* (2nd ed.). Bank Negara Malaysia.

Shukor, S. A. (2020). Trust in takaful agents: Antecedents and consequences. *Journal of Islamic Accounting and Business Research*, *11*(6), 1161–1174. DOI: 10.1108/JIABR-01-2018-0013

Sikander, S. (2024). *Takaful: An Alternative Approach to Insurance*. Society of Actuaries Research Report.

Soualhi, Y., & Al Shammari, A. A. R. (2015). Indicators of takaful awareness among Kuwaitis. *Journal of Islamic Banking and Finance*, *3*(2), 75–89. DOI: 10.15640/jibf.v3n2a8

Soualhi, Y., & Al Shammari, A. A. R. (2015). Indicators of Takaful Awareness among Kuwaitis. *Journal of Islamic Banking and Finance*, *3*(2), 75–89. DOI: 10.15640/jibf.v3n2a8

United Nations Development Programme. (2025). *Building climate resilience through Takaful: Part 2 – Developing Takaful market systems.*

Wan Jusoh, W. N. H., & Noreffendi, A. D. (2022). The Awareness of Education Takaful Among Consumers in Kuching, Sarawak. *International Journal of Islamic Economics and Finance Research*, *5*(1), 90–103. DOI: 10.53840/ijiefer82

Yassin, N., & Ramly, J. (2011). *Takaful: A study guide*. IBFIM.

Zakaria, A., & Ngah, K. (2020). Role of mosque leaders and its impact towards community development: A study in Kedah. *International Research Journal of Shariah* [IRJSMI]. *Muamalat and Islam*, *2*(3), 52–57.

Chapter 14
Innovating for Impact: Entrepreneurial Pathways to a Sustainable Future

Nurul Atasha Jamaludin
https://orcid.org/0000-0002-3545-3398
Universiti Kebangsaan Malaysia, Malaysia

Dahlia Fernandez
https://orcid.org/0000-0002-4238-1804
Universiti Kebangsaan Malaysia, Malaysia

ABSTRACT

The fast-growing entrepreneurial sector functions as a powerful transformative element which helps solve worldwide sustainability issues. This chapter explores how entrepreneurs use creative methods that go beyond making profit to promote social inclusion and protect the environment. The chapter begins by exploring frameworks like the triple bottom line and social entrepreneurship to understand their impact on today's business strategies. Social enterprises together with inclusive business models serve to empower communities that are marginalized. The chapter also demonstrates green technologies and eco-innovation, green finance for entrepreneurial innovation, and climate-resilient entrepreneurship. In addition, digital tools, data analytics, and emerging technologies that enhancing transparency, efficiency, and scalability of sustainable ventures also discussed. Finally, the combination of real-world examples with theoretical frameworks demonstrates sustainable innovation serves both ethical requirements and strategic business benefits.

DOI: 10.4018/979-8-3373-2655-9.ch014

INTRODUCTION

The current era of environmental and social challenges has led entrepreneurship to transform into a powerful force that drives global sustainability progress. Modern entrepreneurs now expand their role beyond profit maximization as they act as change agents who use innovation to solve problems like climate change and resource depletion and social inequality (Elkington, 1998; Dean & McMullen, 2007; George et al., 2021). The business world now operates under a new paradigm which evaluates success through financial returns and social impact and environmental protection (Elkington, 1997). The development of sustainable entrepreneurship bases its principles on two fundamental theoretical frameworks, which combine economic and social and environmental objectives (Elkington, 1997; Mair & Marti, 2006). Entrepreneurs use green technologies for renewable energy and sustainable packaging while implementing circular economy practices to minimize their environmental impact. The rise of inclusive business models and social enterprises continues because they both empower disadvantaged communities and effectively tackle social issues.

Sustainable ventures experience accelerated growth through digital tools and data analytics and emerging technologies, which improve transparency and operational efficiency and scalability (George et al., 2021). Mission-driven entrepreneurship requires an ecosystem that supports its success through public policies and educational programs and startup accelerators and strong cross-sector collaborations characterized by financial resources, government support, educational institutions, cultural attitudes, and social networks (Ermawati, 2023)In addition, the process of scaling sustainable innovation requires green finance because it enables entrepreneurs to obtain funding which establishes credibility for their low-carbon technologies and circular economy projects and impact-driven business ventures. Green bonds together with ESG investment funds and sustainable credit mechanisms serve as essential funding tools for environmentally conscious entrepreneurship while providing long-term financial stability (OECD, 2017). Equally important, climate-resilient entrepreneurship has become a strategic necessity to survive environmental disruptions and minimize risks while maintaining market competitiveness in volatile conditions. Thus, entrepreneurs must now develop adaptive capabilities for their business models. Operations that integrate resilience enable businesses to handle climate uncertainty while discovering new market possibilities (Hallegatte et al., 2020; Mia et al., 2025). The chapter demonstrates that sustainable innovation functions as both an ethical duty and a strategic benefit for businesses to succeed in today's changing global market.

ENTREPRENEURSHIP AS A DRIVER OF SUSTAINABILITY

Through innovative approaches and market-driven solutions, entrepreneurs actively solve worldwide sustainability issues. Entrepreneurs excel at finding unmet requirements while using their flexible resource management to build scalable business models for clean energy systems and waste reduction, and inclusive health service delivery (Cohen & Winn, 2007; George et al., 2021). Entrepreneurs demonstrate better agility than conventional actors because they can start testing new technologies and service models, which can eventually shape industry standards and guide public policies (Ermawati, 2023). Entrepreneurship evolved from its original commercial purpose to become a fundamental method that enables substantial progress in environmental and social systems (Dean & McMullen, 2007).

A transformation has taken place in entrepreneurial activities since the last few decades which moved businesses from sole profit orientation to sustainable practices with social equity and ethical governance models. The Triple Bottom Line framework of Elkington (1998) established new business success standards which extend financial metrics to embrace societal and ecological benefits. Modern entrepreneurs establish businesses which incorporate social and ecological expenses into their fundamental strategies through sustainable supply chain management, ethical work practices, and carbon reduction measures. The evolution of business structures includes benefit corporations (B Corps) and low-profit limited liability companies (L3Cs) and social cooperatives which incorporate mission-driven objectives together with profit goals through legal frameworks. The financial stability of these models enables entrepreneurs to focus on social and environmental targets without jeopardizing their economic performance (Mair et al., 2015). Socially responsible investors together with consumers who share similar values enable these ventures to transform markets while disproving conventional capitalist principles by uniting business activities with planetary limits and social health.

The concept of sustainable entrepreneurship (SE) began gaining attention in academic literature in the early 2000s. Influential works by scholars such as Dean and McMullen (2007) and Cohen and Winn (2007) highlighted the role of entrepreneurship in addressing environmental market failures and advancing sustainability-oriented innovations. Sustainable entrepreneurship unites social and environmental targets with enduring economic performance by promoting responsible innovation that leads to complete value generation (Schaltegger et al., 2016). SE serves two purposes; it satisfies present needs while preserving future capabilities through the interconnectedness of environment and society, and economy. SE has progressed from being limited to defensive measures or regulatory compliance into an innovative framework for building shared value through forward-looking strategies. Social entrepreneurs lead this transformation through their development of inclusive models that unite civic mission with entrepreneurial capability to address poverty, education, and climate resilience.

The field continues to face challenges from its ambiguous conceptual framework as well as unrealistic assumptions. The field shows promise to drive beneficial social and environmental transformation, yet its practical implementation requires additional research to close the theoretical-application gap.Sustainable entrepreneurship functions as a vital method to establish economies that regenerate while being inclusive and ready for the future.

THEORETICAL FOUNDATIONS OF SUSTAINABLE ENTREPRENEURSHIP

Triple Bottom Line (People, Planet, Profit)

The Triple Bottom Line (TBL) represents a fundamental structure in sustainable entrepreneurship which John Elkington introduced in 1998. The business model established by John Elkington in 1998 extends profit-based success through three equally important dimensions which include People (social equity), Planet (environmental stewardship) and Profit (economic viability). The business model proposes that companies should generate economic value while simultaneously creating social benefits and reducing their environmental impact (Elkington, 1998; Elkington, 2018). The Triple Bottom Line (TBL) framework requires sustainable ventures to maintain social equity alongside environmental responsibility and economic viability for creating lasting impact and value creation (see Figure 1).

The performance measurement method represents a complete system because scholars argue that financial profitability does not represent an adequate indicator for determining business success in the long term (George et al., 2021). The TBL establishes that economic and social and environmental elements must be integrated in all decision-making activities. The model establishes that businesses need their operating environment and social context to succeed independently. Social entrepreneurship follows the TBL framework to change from traditional profit-based metrics into sustainability-focused leadership and ethical governance. The social perspective (People) of the TBL requires entrepreneurs to evaluate how their businesses affect all stakeholders, including employees,customers, and the local community. Fair labor practices together with inclusive service delivery and community development programs form part of this framework. Social enterprises and cooperatives operate as business models for sustainable entrepreneurs who incorporate social equity principles into their organizational structures.Through these systemic approaches, they create enduring solutions to combat poverty and social exclusion and reduce economic inequality. These ventures work as transformation agents for social progress by ensuring that entrepreneurial activities benefit human welfare, together with economic expansion.

The TBL framework from an environmental perspective (Planet) requires entrepreneurs to incorporate environmental costs into their business planning while designing ventures that stay within planetary boundaries. Sustainable business operations require entrepreneurs to implement renewable energy solutions along with green supply chain management and circular economy strategies and sustainable product development (Dean & McMullen, 2007; Schaltegger et al., 2016). Sustainable entrepreneurs who implement TBL principles transform environmental issues into value-generating opportunities by integrating ecological targets into their business strategies. The company's environmental strategies result in ecosystem restoration as well as climate resilience benefits. Organizations that implement the TBL framework gain strategic advantages through environmental sustainability because it enhances their legitimacy and long-term market competitiveness (Gomez-Trujillo et al., 2024).

The TBL framework faces criticism from scholars because they consider its current structure insufficient for complete sustainable development measurement. The critics propose extending the framework by adding governance and “Perception Politics” elements to enhance its ability to demonstrate how political factors affect sustainable outcomes (O'Neil, 2017). The TBL framework serves as an essential resource that helps sustainable entrepreneurs to manage their ethical and ecological goals while earning profits.

Figure 1. The triple bottom line framework: A visual representation of the three pillars that guide sustainable entrepreneurship toward balanced, long-term value creation

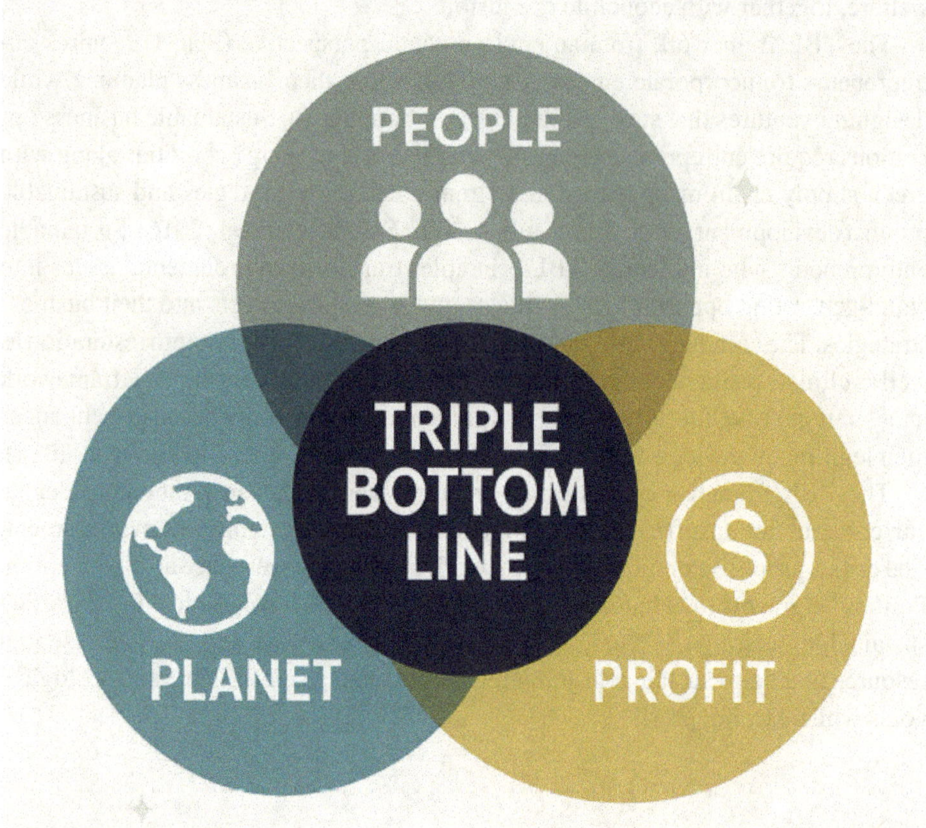

Social Entrepreneurship Frameworks

The concept of social entrepreneurship, which creates economic systems with social advantages, remains undefined due to its intricate nature (Bhawe et al., 2006; Ran & Weller, 2021). To resolve this challenge, Ran and Weller (2021) developed a three-dimensional framework that combines social-business elements with beneficial-detrimental aspects and innovation-mundane logics. The framework establishes a practical definition of social entrepreneurship that accepts its unclear aspects. The framework consists of three core dichotomies that include social-business and beneficial-detrimental and innovation-mundane elements. The model demonstrates how social entrepreneurs must reconcile their social goals and economic performance. The "social-business" axis describes how ventures combine mission-based and market-based operational approaches. The "beneficial-detrimental" dimension examines the ethical effects of actions while acknowledging that beneficial actions can produce adverse results. The "innovation-mundane" axis examines how novel solutions measure up to traditional methods while acknowledging that impactful solutions can stem from simple community-based practices. The framework developed by Ran and Weller serves as a sophisticated method that enables scholars and practitioners to handle the unclear aspects of social entrepreneurship.

Bhawe et al. (2006) create their framework based on prosocial behavior theory which includes both behavioral elements and situational aspects that links personal actions with environmental circumstances when social ventures form. Their model examines the psychological elements which push people toward serving others through empathy and moral duty as well as social expectations. The framework includes both motivational drivers of prosocial behavior together with environmental factors that include institutional gaps and emergency situations and resource availability which create opportunities for social entrepreneurial activities. This model differs from standard entrepreneurial approaches since it bases its venture creation on altruistic intentions rather than market prospects or financial profit. This framework delivers essential insights regarding why people select enterprise instead of charity or activism for solving societal problems.

In other hands, Spear (2006) introduces collective analysis to social entrepreneurship through his examination of cooperatives and mutuals and voluntary organizations. According to Spear social enterprises develop through community-based collective initiatives which stem from shared values and local participation. The expanded understanding of social entrepreneurship now encompasses organizations that base their operations on democratic decision-making processes and community ownership structures. Spear identifies an essential part of the social economy by showing how institutions that combine resources and distribute risks collectively operate in the field. The organizational approach proves most useful when economic systems depend on collective identity and social cohesion for their operation. The frameworks differ from conventional entrepreneurship models because they focus on profit-driven individuals (Bhawe et al., 2006; Spear, 2006). The established frameworks serve two main purposes: to guide upcoming research and to develop policy recommendations that will enhance social entrepreneurship support (Ran & Weller, 2021; Spear, 2006). The key theoretical frameworks that explore diverse dimensions of social entrepreneurship—highlighting their core focus, key concepts, unique contributions, and how they diverge from traditional profit-centered entrepreneurial models—are summarized (see Table 1).

Table 1. Comparative overview of theoretical frameworks in social entrepreneurship

Framework	Core Focus	Key Dimensions / Concepts	Unique Contributions	Contrast with Traditional Entrepreneurship
Three-Dimensional Framework (Ran & Weller, 2021)	Navigating ambiguity in social entrepreneurship	- Social vs. Business logic - Beneficial vs. Detrimental outcomes - Innovation vs. Mundane Practices	Provides a flexible framework to analyze hybrid ventures and moral tensions	Addresses ethical complexity and hybridity beyond profit-maximization
Prosocial Behavior Framework (Bhawe et al., 2006)	Motivation and behavior in social venture creation	- Altruistic motivation - Situational triggers (e.g., crises, institutional voids)	Connects individual-level motivation with environmental context	Emphasizes moral intent and social good over opportunity recognition alone
Collective Action Perspective (Spear, 2006)	Community-driven social entrepreneurship	- Cooperatives - Voluntary organizations - Democratic governance	Highlights the role of group initiative and shared ownership in social ventures	Moves away from the individual founder narrative common in mainstream entrepreneurship

EMPOWERMENT THROUGH SOCIAL ENTERPRISES AND INCLUSIVE BUSINESS MODELS

Social enterprises and inclusive business models actively work to reduce structural inequalities by developing operational frameworks that promote lasting economic growth and beneficial social impacts. The hybrid nature of these ventures unites financial stability with social purpose which establishes enduring ways for disadvantaged communities to progress (Khanna, 2024). Social enterprises operate throughout agricultural sectors, educational sectors, healthcare sectors, sanitation sectors, and renewable energy sectors because conventional businesses avoid these areas and government services fail to provide adequate coverage. Thus, social enterprises serve as crucial agents of social innovation and inclusion by filling institutional gaps in markets. These enterprises stand out through their purposeful implementation of inclusion strategies which address the fundamental sources of exclusion. The capacity-building includes vocational training and skills development alongside financial tools. It includes microcredit and cooperative finance and market access through fair trade and direct-to-consumer platforms. These methods promote both personal empowerment and build resilience together with self-determination across entire communities. The inclusive business models have proven effective at producing economic value alongside social advancement through their ability to facilitate participatory governance and problem-solving that addresses specific contexts.

For instance, a rubber grower cooperative in Meghalaya India achieved success by creating a unified agricultural network that involves tribal communities. The cooperative achieves higher productivity and fair profit sharing through resource sharing and collective decision-making which enables rubber cultivation expansion alongside community solidarity growth (Thomas & Lukose, 2024). Similarly, in South African social enterprise, women in rural and urban areas have achieved substantial empowerment through receiving microfinance services and income-generating projects. These programs link up with forums which promote dialogue between communities while spreading gender awareness to transform societal structures. These models demonstrate strong potential, but they come with various obstacles to overcome. New enterprises encounter an enduring challenge in obtaining capital especially during their initial development phase. Their growth faces challenges from regulatory uncertainties as well as limited scalability which restricts their expansion potential. Inclusive models need long-term cross-sectoral partnerships along with supportive policy frameworks and innovation ecosystems that prioritize both impact and inclusivity to achieve success and sustainability (Khanna, 2024).

Supporting Marginalized Communities

The economic transformation and social inclusion of marginalized communities depends on social enterprises which use participatory governance approaches together with community-driven development strategies. Globally, social enterprises generate more than USD 2 trillion in economic value each year while employing 200 million people (World Economic Forum, 2024). In ASEAN, a UN-ESCAP report states that social enterprises intentionally aim to trade in the most challenging markets and seek to employ marginalized populations, tackling entrenched social and environmental issues (British Council et al., 2021). Social enterprises operate primarily in regions where basic goods and services remain inaccessible to the population because state institutions along with conventional market systems fail to reach these areas. Indeed, social enterprises take responsibility for vacant spaces by providing products and creating employment opportunities and training programs which build capacity for marginalized communities that conventional development methods have overlooked (Gidron, 2017). Barefoot College in India demonstrates an outstanding example through their training program which equips illiterate rural women to become solar engineers. The program serves two purposes by improving renewable energy delivery to unconnected villages and creating technical leaders who also lead their communities as women experts (Barefoot College, n.d.). The combination of environmental sustainability and local economic development and gender empowerment demonstrates how social enterprises can work effectively.

Social enterprises direct their profits into community growth programs that focus particularly on supporting women and indigenous people and disabled individuals. The reinvestments from these organizations follow strategic plans which drive inclusive growth together with education expansion and better healthcare services and economic independence. Their operational approach depends heavily on participatory governance systems because these systems allow local stakeholders to serve as both decision-makers and beneficiaries. Long-term sustainability along with impact relies heavily on the factors of ownership and accountability and local agency which inclusion provides. According to Phillips et al. (2015) community-led mechanisms help build grassroots resilience and self-assurance and innovative problem-solving abilities. Social enterprises that link economic opportunities with social and psychological empowerment work to break the pattern of poverty across generations. These initiatives develop local leadership and create social capital networks and implement equitable development through grassroots-based approaches. How entrepreneurial skills combined with social objectives allow these ventures to serve as effective change agents by creating scalable community-based solutions that can adapt to various settings.

Tackling Social Inequality Through Business

Business models with inclusive features represent a revolutionary shift in social responsibility practices that exceed traditional Corporate Social Responsibility (CSR) standards. Business operations receive direct integration of social impact through inclusive business models instead of performing philanthropic activities as peripheral functions. Through this integration, businesses establish resilient and economically viable models that achieve commercial goals and societal needs simultaneously (ASEAN, 2024). Inclusive business models differ from traditional CSR through their strategic inclusion of low-income populations throughout value chains because they function as producers, suppliers, distributors, or consumers to tackle systemic exclusion and generate shared value at all stages. These models break down market barriers to provide underserved communities essential services like affordable education and accessible healthcare along with inclusive financial products. The establishment of Grameen Bank stands as a leading example in the microfinance sector because of its global recognition. Through its targeted approach, the microcredit program of South Asian impoverished women achieved financial inclusion while simultaneously promoting gender equality and household decision power and social upward movement (Yunus, 2007). This case clearly demonstrates how inclusive financial services create strong catalysts that enable business development and community growth.

In the current business landscape, the business paradigm transforms from profit maximization to value co-creation through the connection of business profitability with inclusive development within inclusive business models. Companies that align their operations discover untapped markets while simultaneously supporting equitable economic growth for marginalized groups. As a result, businesses gain new growth possibilities through this method which simultaneously enables communities to rise from poverty through economic strengthening and capacity development. Furthermore, the implementation of inclusive business models enables organizations to meet several United Nations Sustainable Development Goals (SDGs) specifically focusing on income equality and gender empowerment alongside sustainable economic growth. Ultimately, these models provide a practical approach to change capitalist systems into a more inclusive system where business achievement directly depends on societal advancement and social welfare.

Challenges and Limitations

Despite their transformative impact on society, these models encounter multiple obstacles and systemic constraints which prevent their growth and enduring success. Notably, these ventures face challenges because they operate in underserved regions and serve marginalized populations, yet they experience inadequate institutional backing, structural imbalances, fragmented policy structures, and insufficient access to enabling infrastructure and financial systems. These problems exist independently from one another but interact dynamically to create a feedback loop which strengthens exclusion and prevents empowerment-based models from scaling up (Adham et al., 2016). Moreover, the delivery of essential services such as microfinance, skills training, clean energy, and healthcare depends on multi-stakeholder collaboration and enabling policies and supportive infrastructure (Khanna, 2024). The dual requirement of financial sustainability and social impact proves challenging to maintain particularly in low-income markets because returns take longer to materialize. In addition, the implementation of social enterprises and inclusive business models faces obstacles from patriarchal social norms and insufficient institutional backing and the requirement to build trust-based governance systems with community participation. Nevertheless, social enterprises and inclusive business models remain essential for inequality reduction and empowerment. To fully unlock their potential as agents of inclusive and systemic change, they need better ecosystem support and policy alignment and investment readiness to achieve their potential as transformative agents of inclusive systemic change.

GREEN TECHNOLOGIES AND ECO-INNOVATION

Renewable Energy Technologies

The quick development of solar, wind, and bioenergy technologies made these systems essential for both sustainable entrepreneurship and eco-innovation development. The technological systems serve three essential functions by reducing greenhouse gas emissions while minimizing dependence on limited fossil fuels and protecting the environment in the long run. Entrepreneurs now actively pursue clean energy investments because these solutions meet sustainability requirements and create financial benefits and market competition advantages while climate change becomes more pressing. The International Renewable Energy Agency (IRENA) stated in 2020a that renewable energy investments improve operational resilience and lower exposure to fossil fuel price volatility and build strong sustainability credentials for companies among consumers, investors, and regulators.

In recent years, renewable energy adoption has increased significantly because of government-backed policy instruments including feed-in tariffs together with green tax credits, carbon pricing mechanisms, and investment subsidies. As a result, startups and SMEs can now access renewable energy markets more easily because of incentives that have reduced the barriers to entry according to REN21 (2021). Furthermore, various countries have established structured clean energy markets through Renewable Portfolio Standards (RPS) and Renewable Energy Certificates (RECs) which allow entrepreneurs to generate revenue from their environmental contributions. Renewable energy systems operating at decentralized levels including off-grid solar microgrids and biomass digesters provide essential solutions for remote communities to gain access to energy. These decentralized systems promote inclusive development through energy poverty reduction by supporting local entrepreneurship in rural areas where conventional grid infrastructure fails to exist or remains unreliable. Specifically, local energy solutions based on renewables provide rural communities with economical clean electricity that drives productive activities including irrigation and agro-processing and cold storage facilities to enhance their economic stability. Ultimately, the combination of renewable energy serves two objectives by fulfilling climate targets and promoting social fairness which demonstrates that environmentally responsible innovations can achieve both ecological benefits and social development.

Sustainable Packaging

Sustainable packaging involves purposeful material selection and design methods which minimize environmental impact during all product life stages from manufacturing through delivery until waste disposal. The concept focuses on using plant-based bioplastics, mushroom packaging, recycled paper, and glass or aluminum containers that are biodegradable, compostable, and recyclable or reusable (Rajesh & Subhashini, 2021). One prominent example is the biodegradable plastic polylactic acid (PLA) made from corn starch breaks down through industrial composting processes. The method decreases waste sent to landfills while preserving resources and decreases carbon emissions by enabling lighter transportation weights (Song et al., 2009). High research and development (R&D) costs along with the need to maintain sustainability, performance requirements, and shelf-life needs represent major challenges for businesses (Saharan & Wadhwa, 2024). In response to these challenges, governments have started to take part. For instance, the Indian governmenthas modified plastic waste management regulations to promote innovative applications of recycled plastics. At present, the food, cosmetics, and retail industries currently lead the adoption of sustainable packaging because they need to comply with changing regulations and meet rising consumer expectations for environmentally friendly practices.In this context, sustainable packaging stands as an essential element of Corporate Social Responsibility (CSR) strategies because consumers continue to demonstrate increased eco-consciousness.Such packaging is often perceived as a mark of quality and ethical responsibility, enhancing brand image and customer loyalty (Beitzen-Heineke et al., 2017; Srivastava, 2024).

Circular Economy Practices

The circular economy converts the conventional linear “take-make-dispose” pattern into a regenerative economic system which maintains sustainable resource utilization through continuous cycles of reuse, recycling, and resource regeneration. The change represents a fundamental transformation in the way value creation and preservation operates throughout product life cycles. Importantly, the transformation of traditional business models into circular ones depends on entrepreneurial ventures which implement innovative strategies including product-as-a-service arrangements, reverse logistics systems, and closed-loop supply chains (Geissdoerfer et al., 2017). According to the Circularity Gap Report (2024) shows that the global economy has only 7.2% circularity which decreased from 9.1% in 2018 thus creating immediate opportunities for innovation. In response to this gap, the global circular economy market will reach more than USD 712 billion by 2030 because of packaging and electronics and food waste reduction sectors. The implemented strategies help businesses reduce their dependence on raw materials while extending product lifespans to extract value from materials previously discarded as waste. For example, returnable packaging systems together with repair and remanufacturing services and zero-waste production facilities have become operational norms across sectors because they implement circular economy principles. Furthermore, the integration of digital tools such as blockchain for material traceability and IoT-enabled tracking devices supports circular practices by improving transparency and accountability and increasing efficiency. The efforts create environmental sustainability while simultaneously driving industry-wide innovation and value creation (Kirchherr et al., 2018).

Businesses that implement circular principles can achieve three key benefits which include operational cost savings, compliance with environmental regulations, and access to environmentally conscious markets. Businesses that use recycled and upcycled materials including reclaimed plastics and agricultural residues and post-consumer waste reduce their costs while meeting customer demands for sustainable and ethically produced products. In the Malaysian context, the palm oil sector demonstrates circular economy implementation through waste by product transformation into biofertilizers and biomass pellets and biogas products. These initiatives produce environmental benefits and create additional revenue opportunities for both smallholders and industry participants. As highlighted by Jamaludin et al. (2025), such entrepreneurial efforts demonstrate how circularity enables inclusive sustainable development through the combination of ecological stewardship and economic stability. Therefore, the circular business models serve as a strategic approach to achieve profitable operations while using resources responsibly which strengthens both business and environmental system resilience in the long term.

Challenges and Limitations

The increasing adoption of green technologies and eco-innovation throughout renewable energy, sustainable packaging, and circular economy sectors faces multiple obstacles which prevent their widespread use. The renewable energy sector benefits from solar, wind and bioenergy systems yet faces implementation barriers because of expensive start-up costs and complicated technology and government incentives which may change unpredictably (IRENA, 2020b). Similarly, the adoption of biodegradable materials including polylactic acid (PLA) and mushroom-based alternatives for sustainable packaging faces multiple obstacles such as expensive research and development (R&D) costs, performance limitations, restricted composting facilities, and shelf-life issues (Saharan & Wadhwa, 2024). Although the food and cosmetics industries show the highest adoption rates because of regulatory requirements and CSR branding opportunities, yet sustainable packaging implementation faces challenges regarding cost constraints and technological requirements. Meanwhile, circular economy models demonstrate effectiveness in waste reduction and material efficiency yet struggle with three main obstacles which include extensive process transformation, changes in consumer behavior, and the establishment of digital tracking systems and closed-loop logistics (Geissdoerfer et al., 2017; Kirchherr et al., 2018). In summary, the combination of economic, technical, and institutional barriers indicates that sustainable entrepreneurship requires complete resolution of these challenges to achieve maximum impact from green technologies.

GREEN FINANCE FOR ENTREPRENEURIAL INNOVATION

The global sustainability agenda receives essential support from green finance which enables entrepreneurial innovation alignment. Green finance enables environmentally focused entrepreneurs to access capital while gaining market recognition which drives investments into low-carbon technologies and renewable energy systems and circular economy practices and sustainable infrastructure development. Entrepreneurs need to innovate for impact while understanding and leveraging financial mechanisms that reward sustainability because climate change worsens and regulatory frameworks transform (OECD, 2017). Entrepreneurs in today's economic environment need to innovate for impact while mastering financial mechanisms that promote sustainability. Green finance includes multiple financial tools and investment systems which support projects that deliver positive environmental results.

These include:

a) Green Bonds - debt instruments which help fund environmentally beneficial projects including clean transportation systems and renewable energy facilities and sustainable agricultural initiatives. Growth-stage ventures and entrepreneurs can access this growing market by forming partnerships with institutional investors and impact-focused intermediaries. The Climate Bonds Initiative (2024) reports that green bond issuances exceeded USD 610 billion in 2023 while reaching a total of more than USD 2.5 trillion worldwide.
b) Sustainable Investment Funds - investment funds of venture capital and private equity operate through ESG metrics to guide their investment choices. Entrepreneurs who implement ESG principles in their business models can obtain patient capital along with strategic support because investors now actively seek sustainable and responsible investment opportunities (Friede et al., 2015; Renneboog et al., 2020).
c) Green Loans and Credit Facilities - banks together with development finance institutions provide green loans with beneficial terms to projects which fulfill sustainability requirements including energy efficiency improvements and sustainable product development. The Green Technology Financing Scheme (GTFS) together with Bank Negara Malaysia established essential funding routes for green SMEs in Malaysia.

Regulatory Frameworks Supporting Green Finance

Supranational bodies together with governments established taxonomies and standards to enhance transparency and minimize greenwashing while directing capital toward genuine sustainable activities. Entrepreneurs need to understand these frameworks because they determine eligibility and ensure compliance.

a) The EU Taxonomy for Sustainable Activities: A classification system which establishes criteria for identifying environmentally sustainable economic activities. Businesses operating in the EU or seeking European investment must make their operations match the six environmental objectives of the taxonomy (European Commission, 2020) which include climate change mitigation, climate adaptation, and pollution prevention. The taxonomy helps organizations fulfill their Sustainable Finance Disclosure Regulation (SFDR) reporting requirements (Gortsos & Kyriazis, 2024).
b) Malaysia's Sustainable and Responsible Investment (SRI) Sukuk Framework: An Islamic-compliant mechanism for raising capital to fund green and socially beneficial projects. The SRI Sukuk represents a leading example of how Shariah-compliant financial tools can be combined with sustainability principles. The framework enables entrepreneurs operating in renewable energy and waste management to issue sukuk which led to Tadau Energy becoming the first issuer of a green SRI Sukuk in 2017 (Securities Commission Malaysia, 2021).

The regulatory frameworks establish both credibility and clarity for entrepreneurs while providing investors with standardized reporting systems and performance measurement criteria. Ventures that align with these frameworks can enhance their access to green capital while standing out in competitive markets and prove their dedication to responsible transparent growth.

However, the implementation of green finance needs more than financial alignment because it requires a fundamental change in how ventures establish their value framework. To achieve this, entrepreneurs must include ESG performance indicators in their business planning and perform life-cycle sustainability assessments and establish early relationships with sustainable finance stakeholders. In particular, the adoption of TCFD (Task Force on Climate-related Financial Disclosures) or ISSB (International Sustainability Standards Board) reporting standards will boost investor trust and extend business sustainability. Moreover, entrepreneurs who actively work with green finance frameworks both protect their business models from future changes and establish themselves as leaders who drive systemic transformation. Green capital enables them to speed up innovation that tackles critical climate and social issues which results in ventures that generate profits while benefiting the planet.

Challenges and Limitations

The increasing popularity of green finance does not eliminate the various obstacles which entrepreneurs encounter when trying to access and utilize this financial resource effectively. The complexity of sustainability standards and eligibility criteria across different instruments and jurisdictions creates a major obstacle for early-stage ventures to understand regulatory requirements (OECD, 2017). Furthermore, entrepreneurs from developing economies together with others face challenges because they do not possess the necessary financial literacy or technical expertise needed to create ESG-aligned disclosures or impact assessments which investors now require (Tong, 2025). In practice, the current green finance systems tend to support established firms with proven sustainability records while ignoring smaller and riskier innovative projects. In addition, the restricted supply of long-term capital together with inconsistent performance measurement tools prevent socially driven high-impact innovations from achieving scalability. In addition, greenwashing practices which involve businesses making deceptive sustainability claims to attract capital undermine investor trust and diminish the effectiveness of green finance programs (Damper et al., 2024). Therefore, green finance initiatives need both improved policy clarity and entrepreneurial capacity development together with financial institutions and innovation ecosystem alignment to achieve genuine impact and transparency and inclusivity.

CLIMATE-RESILIENT ENTREPRENEURSHIP AS STRATEGIC IMPERATIVE

Entrepreneurial resilience stands as an essential element for enduring business success during times of rising climate threats and economic instability and geopolitical uncertainties. In this regard, business success through resilience demands entrepreneurs to develop models that survive shocks while changing and thriving in adverse circumstances. Particularly, business operations within climate-variable sectors together with supply chain disruptions and market volatility need to develop resilience capabilities as their survival depends on it. Specifically, the definition of climate-resilient entrepreneurship describes how business ventures should predict and manage climate-related disturbances and maintain their economic value and social impact (Hallegatte et al., 2020). To that end, the practice of proactive climate risk assessment along with adaptation planning becomes integral to business model development from the initial stages. Moreover, resilient entrepreneurs transform environmental uncertainty into innovative opportunities by reorganizing their products and operational frameworks and market approaches to match projected climate scenarios. At the same time, the growing number of small and medium enterprises along with startups face greater exposure to environmental threats that include floods and droughts and severe weather conditions especially in developing markets. Therefore, entrepreneurs who incorporate resilience into their business model design from the start will develop adaptive capabilities and protect their investments and build better standing with impact investors and regulatory bodies and community members (Mia et al., 2025).

Key Resilience-Building Strategies

Entrepreneurs can use multiple strategies to implement resilience in their operations.

a) Diversified Supply Chains - ventures that depend on one supplier through one logistics route become vulnerable to natural disasters and pandemics and geopolitical shocks. Businesses that implement multiple supply chain networks spread across different regions can continue operations when crises strike. The agri-food sector's social enterprises have started forming alliances with both domestic and international suppliers to minimize climate-related seasonal risks and trade disruptions.
b) Modular Production and Localized Manufacturing - the implementation of modular business designs which support decentralized or distributed production methods allows businesses to adapt better to changing conditions. Entrepreneurs can transfer their business operations or extend their operations according to local conditions together with changes in market demands and resource availability limitations. The implementation of micro-factories combined with 3D printing technologies provides adaptable manufacturing options that decrease reliance on vulnerable infrastructure networks and promote independent regional operations (Ihl & Piller, 2016; Becker et al., 2021).
c) Digital Adaptation and Data-Driven Decision-Making - through digital tools like cloud computing and remote sensing combined with IoT and AI-based climate forecasting systems entrepreneurs gain real-time environmental risk monitoring capabilities which help them modify their operations effectively. Mobile-based systems now assist smallholder farmers to modify their planting plans using local weather forecasts which improves agricultural resistance (Agrawala et al., 2022). Thus, it provides precision farming tools to the 550 million smallholder farmers worldwide. AgriTech startups received more than USD 13 billion in funding worldwide during 2023 while remote sensing, blockchain supply tracking, and climate-smart advisory services experienced rapid growth (World Bank, 2024). Through e-commerce combined with digital payment systems entrepreneurs can

continue serving customers when physical disruptions occur such as pandemics or natural disasters.

d) Flexible Financing and Insurance Mechanisms - entrepreneurs can withstand revenue losses and recover speedily through their access to climate insurance and emergency liquidity and special financial instruments including resilience bonds and contingent credit lines. The practice of ESG assessment by impact investors now includes resilience indicators which reward ventures with effective adaptation strategies (World Economic Forum, 2021).

The Competitive Edge of Resilient Ventures

Resilience, therefore, functions beyond risk management to establish itself as a vital competitive advantage for businesses. Notably, the ability of entrepreneurs to build adaptive capabilities into their models helps them draw climate-conscious investors while gaining access to sustainability-linked financing and preserving customer trust in crisis situations. Furthermore, businesses which focus on social and ecological resilience develop stronger community connections and better employee retention alongside improved recovery speed following disruptions (Adekola & Clelland, 2020). In this context, the protective nature of resilience serves entrepreneurs in sustainable business activities as it functions both as a protection mechanism and a driver of growth. As a result, such ventures become ready to survive unpredictable conditions and drive transformative change through their commitment to regenerative economics principles and circularity and social equity frameworks. Sustainable and future-proof economy development depends on entrepreneurs embedding resilience into their business models.

Challenges and Limitations

The implementation of climate-resilient entrepreneurship faces multiple major obstacles despite its long-term benefits. Firstly, the absence of accurate climate data and early warning systems and technical expertise prevents many entrepreneurs from low-income and underserved regions to integrate resilience planning into their business models (Agrawala et al., 2022). Secondly, the high initial expenses of resilience-enhancing technologies such as modular infrastructure and digital forecasting tools and climate insurance exceed the financial reach of startups and SMEs which prevents them from taking proactive investments. In addition, entrepreneurs face challenges in adopting climate-adaptive practices because of limited awareness and inconsistent policy support especially when national climate strategies fail to establish clear connections with small business development. Moreover, the absence of standardized frameworks to evaluate and communicate resilience outcomes creates challenges for investor confidence while making resilient ventures less visible in competitive funding landscapes. Therefore, the solution to these gaps needs public-private collaboration to develop institutional capacity and enhance risk-financing tool accessibility and integrate resilience metrics into ESG investment criteria and entrepreneurship support programs.

DIGITAL TRANSFORMATION FOR SUSTAINABLE VENTURES

Leveraging Data Analytics and Digital Tools

Modern enterprises can achieve both growth and sustainability through their adoption of data analytics and digital tools in today's digital era. Sustainable ventures must adopt digital transformation as their strategic imperative for maximizing performance and enhancing transparency while maintaining market competitiveness in resource-limited and climate-impacted global markets.

1. Real-Time Monitoring and Predictive Insights

The ability to track operations in real time through data analytics enables entrepreneurs to shift away from spontaneous decision-making while acquiring predictive information to shape sustainability approaches. Businesses can precisely measure and optimize resource consumption along with energy use and carbon emissions and supply chain dynamics through the use of Geographic Information Systems (GIS), Internet of Things (IoT) sensors, and machine learning algorithms. Machinery and fleet transportation systems equipped with IoT sensors can automatically identify operational issues to activate preventive measures which decrease both energy consumption and emission levels. The implementation of this technology enables companies to achieve sustainability objectives and reduce operational expenses (OECD (2024).

2. Precision Systems for Sustainable Resource Management

Satellite imagery together with AI-powered analytics and precision farming technologies enables entrepreneurs to reduce water usage and optimize fertilizer and pesticide application and enhance crop yields within the agricultural and food sectors. These systems optimize both environmental protection and production levels thus proving digital innovation supports large-scale sustainable practices (FAO, 2022). Agri-tech startups employ AI alongside remote sensing technologies to track weather conditions and soil health which enables them to develop flexible farming methods that both protect against climate change and decrease their dependency on inputs.

3. Visualization and Impact Communication

Entrepreneurs use cloud-based digital dashboards and platforms to gather data and present sustainability metrics which they can share with internal and external stakeholders. These platforms deliver adjustable tools for tracking ESG performance which helps entrepreneurs present their impact in an open manner. These tools now support global sustainability reporting standards through their integration of the Global Reporting Initiative (GRI) and Sustainability Accounting Standards Board (SASB) while the International Sustainability Standards Board (ISSB) provides emerging guidelines. Small and medium-sized enterprises and startups that match their data reporting with established frameworks receive better access to ESG-driven investors and sustainability-linked loans while fulfilling increasing regulatory needs (OECD, 2025).

4. Adaptive Strategy and Scenario Planning

Data analytics enables organizations to predict future events and perform strategic adjustments based on forecasted scenarios. Entrepreneurs use predictive models to predict how risks like climate shifts and regulatory changes and supply chain disruptions will affect their business so they can modify their strategies accordingly. These tools assist businesses in building resilience to maintain agility during the rapid changes in the global environment. Ventures can better show how sustainability efforts produce business value through integrated data environments which connect financial data with sustainability data. The tracking of green investment returns including solar installations and energy-efficient retrofits creates proof that sustainability initiatives produce both financial returns and social impact.

5. Democratization of Data for Inclusive Innovation

The digital age provides smaller businesses and social enterprises in developing areas with equal access to data through various tools. Smaller companies can now obtain real-time business information through mobile applications and open-source platforms and affordable sensor technologies that were previously limited to large corporations. The inclusive innovation process allows underserved communities together with entrepreneurs to join data-driven sustainability projects (World Bank, 2022). Sustainable entrepreneurs achieve operational intelligence across all their business activities through their use of data analytics and digital tools which enables resource optimization and supply chain efficiency and impact reporting and adaptive planning capabilities. These tools create a link between purpose and performance which enables ventures to base their decisions on evidence to merge financial success with environmental protection.

Enhancing Transparency, Efficiency, and Scalability

Sustainable impact requires modern enterprises to operate with full accountability while using resources efficiently for strategic growth development. Digital technologies serve as essential tools to achieve these goals because they enhance transparency levels and streamline operations while facilitating scalable development. These tools create internal agility for sustainable ventures while building stakeholder trust and enabling market entry alongside capital accessibility which drives long-term sustainability and competitive success.

1. Promoting Transparency through Digital Trust Technologies

Sustainable business operations require transparency as their core foundation for gaining credibility. The public sector alongside investors together with regulatory bodies now require organizations to disclose complete information about product origins and labor conditions and environmental compliance standards. The development of blockchain technology along with distributed ledger systems functions as powerful tools that satisfy these requirements. Through blockchain technology companies achieve end-to-end supply chain tracking that provides tamper-evident verification for sourcing practices together with certifications and carbon footprint measurements. The implementation of blockchain technology enables organizations to verify organic certifications together with Fair Trade compliance and deforestation-free supply chain operations (Saberi et al., 2019). Blockchain systems maintain trust between partners and consumers through their ability to create permanent records of transactions which cannot be modified. Through the use of such technologies, organizations gain better compliance with ESG reporting standards and develop a stronger market advantage in sustainable ethical trade.

2. Improving Efficiency through Automation and Smart Systems

Efficiency remains a vital foundation for sustainable business operations. Businesses implement ERP systems alongside smart logistics and automated procurement and energy management platforms to decrease waste while reducing redundancy and energy usage in all their operations. For instance, digital procurement systems enable automated vendor selection through sustainability criteria assessments. Then, through the implementation of IoT devices and smart sensors organizations can continuously monitor energy consumption to prevent unnecessary waste. Besides, automated inventory management systems prevent overstocking and understocking through accurate quantity control which reduces material waste while improving logistics operations. The implemented tools enable entrepreneurs to enhance operational efficiency and decrease expenses as well as minimize environmental impact which demonstrates that sustainability and economic performance align (Ugbebor et al., 2024).

3. Scaling Sustainably through Digital Infrastructure

Businesses have historically grown through physical expansion which resulted in higher environmental effects during their scaling process. Digital platforms present scalable business models that reduce the environmental impact of growth. Through e-commerce websites, mobile applications, and digital marketplaces micro-enterprises together with social enterprises can tap into regional and global customer bases without creating extensive physical retail networks. Rural entrepreneurs along with those in underserved areas now benefit from digital platforms which connect them with suppliers and investors and customers at minimal financial cost (Nipo et al., 2024). These platforms help businesses unite across borders to expand their brand presence and enter specialized sustainability markets.

4. Expanding Access to Capital through Digital Finance Tools

Green and social entrepreneurs face limited access to finance primarily because they do not belong to the traditional venture capital networks. The crowdfunding platforms Kickstarter, Indiegogo and GoFundMe enable innovative projects to connect directly with consumers who back both their ideas and financial support. The current market allows green startups to obtain funding for solar energy kits together with sustainable packaging solutions and community-based waste management programs independently from institutional investors. Through this model, users validate their community by investing money, providing feedback, and adopting new products early (Belleflamme et al., 2014). The sustainable business sector now benefits from new financing solutions which include peer-to-peer lending alongside impact investing applications and green tokens based on cryptocurrency technology.

5. Digital Transformation as a Strategic Growth Lever

Digital transformation operates as a strategic business model enabler which creates inclusive resilient sustainable business operations. Entrepreneurs who integrate digital tools within their core strategies will achieve:

a) Supply chain systems become more agile and responsive because of digital tools
b) Organizations can perform sustainability reporting based on evidence they gather
c) The system provides access to worldwide impact networks together with funding ecosystems.
d) Business models can become more resistant to uncertainty through their development

In the current digital age, the digital ecosystem enables real-time accountability along with stakeholder engagement and sustainable innovation pathways. Indeed, technology serves as both a catalyst and vehicle for systemic change to entrepreneurs who want to tackle climate change and economic inequality and social inclusion.

Challenges and Limitations

Despite their potential, the adoption of digital technologies for sustainable ventures faces multiple obstacles which prevent their widespread and equitable implementation. To begin with, high implementation costs, technical difficulties, and limited digital infrastructure in developing regions, prevent smaller enterprises from accessing data analytics, AI, IoT, and blockchain systems. Moreover, the adoption of advanced tools including ERP systems and precision agriculture technologies remains challenging for startups and social ventures because they need both technical expertise and investment. In addition, data privacy concerns with non-standardized practices and fragmented regulatory frameworks creates uncertainty for ventures that need to report ESG data across global markets. While digital dashboards and crowdfunding platforms provides market expansion and capital access, yet these platforms create ongoing challenges with digital literacy and connectivity and platform dependency especially in rural and underserved communities. Sustainable ventures need to address economic and infrastructural and regulatory barriers to achieve full digital transformation benefits while building inclusive innovation ecosystems that promote equitable access and long-term resilience.

SUSTAINABLE INNOVATION AS A STRATEGIC ADVANTAGE

Businesses now see sustainable innovation as a competitive advantage which surpasses environmental compliance through its ability to differentiate themselves in competitive markets. When businesses make sustainability an integral part of their operations, they not only attract new customer bases but also cutoperational expenses over time, thereby safeguarding themselves against regulatory and reputational damage. Moreover, organizations that implement ethical business practices through fair trade sourcing and carbon neutrality along with circular design, improve their brand reputation and build trust with stakeholders including customer, investors, and regulatory bodies. In fact, sustainability drives innovation by forcing companies to rethink products, processes, and business models, leading to first-mover advantages in emerging green markets. Consequently, companies that focus on sustainability achieve better success in attracting skilled staff members and obtaining sustainable funding while accessing sustainable global supply networks. Today, organizations base their ESG (Environmental, Social, Governance) performance ratings as essential evaluation criteria for investors together with procurement organizations. Wang et al. (2024) highlight that proper ESG management enables organizations to link risk management with opportunity development which transforms sustainability from a regulatory obligation into a strategic business asset. The research shows that firms which implement forward-thinking ESG frameworks discover fresh market possibilities while enhancing resource utilization and building stronger stakeholder relationships which are essential elements for sustainable innovation. Ultimately, the strategic importance of sustainability has increased to become a fundamental business asset that strengthens organizational resilience and generates long-term financial success and helps companies meet UN Sustainable Development Goals (SDGs).

Numerous worldwide companies demonstrate how sustainable innovation leads businesses to achieve market success. For instance, the US outdoor clothing company Patagonia has transformed into a brand that integrates environmental activism by creating durable and recyclable products and investing in regenerative farming practices. Notably, through its Don't Buy This Jacket" marketing campaign the company simultaneously raised awareness about sustainable consumption while increasing sales to build stronger brand integrity. Similarly, Unilever implemented its Sustainable Living Plan which transformed products to decrease water consumption and minimize plastic packaging thus enabling growth of its sustainability-oriented brands.

In the Malaysian context, Biji-Biji Initiative demonstrates sustainable innovation by using upcycled materials for fashion and green technology alongside educational initiatives. Specifically, their products made from discarded materials create high-quality products that both help reduce waste and develop communities. Through this approach, their business model unites environmental awareness with design creativity to obtain backing from corporate partners and international entities. Furthermore, rural indigenous farmers in East Malaysian supply Langit Collective with heirloom rice and spices under fair pricing and sustainable agricultural systems. Collectively, these companies prove sustainability functions both as an ethical requirement and a successful business model which attracts modern consumers and international markets.

CONCLUSION

The power of entrepreneurship has evolved into a transformative force that creates sustainable futures by using innovative methods to address worldwide challenges through ethical business practices and inclusive approaches. This chapter shows how the Triple Bottom Line (TBL) framework together with social entrepreneurship concepts, establish a solid basis for business success that extends beyond profit to include social equity and environmental stewardship. In particular, entrepreneurs adopt renewable energy technologies alongside sustainable packaging and circular economy principles to create economic and social value while reducing their ecological impact. Moreover, social enterprises together with inclusive business models demonstrate their ability to empower marginalized communities while promoting participatory governance and tackling systemic inequalities through market-driven solutions.

In addition, the integration of digital tools with data analytics and emerging technologies has increased sustainable ventures by making them more efficient and transparent while also expanding their scalability. Entrepreneurs demonstrate their ability to generate value through innovative solutions which fulfil environmental and social needs and economic targets through examples from worldwide and Malaysian business operations. Sustainable innovation functions as both a moral necessity and strategic business advantage which enables entrepreneurs to transform capitalism while building resilient ecosystems for enduring development. Apart from that, entrepreneurs need green finance through green bonds, ESG-aligned venture capital, and sustainable credit facilities to establish and expand their environmentally responsible businesses. Such financial instruments enables entrepreneurs to obtain necessary capital while demonstrating their sustainability commitment, which draws investors and partners who share long-term impact goals (OECD, 2017). At the same time, entrepreneurs who operate in uncertain and environmentally vulnerable conditions must now integrate climate resilience into their business models as a strategic necessity. By doing so, they can diversify supply chains, implement modular production systems, and utilise predictive digital tools to withstand climate-related disruptions and maintain value creation (Hallegatte et al., 2020; Mia et al.,

2025). Looking ahead, the future success of sustainable entrepreneurship depends on enabling policies together with impact investment and collaborative ecosystems, These supportive elements are essential to achieve mainstream adoption and to unlock the full potential of sustainable ventures in contributing to the United Nations Sustainable Development Goals (SDGs).

ACKNOWLEDGMENT

We would like to acknowledge UKM Research Grant Scheme (EP-2023-084) for funding opportunities.

REFERENCES

Adekola, J., & Clelland, D. (2020). Two sides of the same coin: Business resilience and community resilience. *Journal of Contingencies and Crisis Management, 28*(1), 50–60. DOI: 10.1111/1468-5973.12275

Adham, K. A., Kasimin, H., Jamaludin, N. A., Ghanie, S. K., Khatib, N. A. M., & Said, M. F. (2016). Developing a cybernetics approach to analysing inclusive growth constraints. *Systemic Practice and Action Research, 29*(3), 215–234. DOI: 10.1007/s11213-015-9361-4

Agrawala, S., Carraro, M., Kingsmill, N., Lanzi, E., Mullan, M., & Prudent-Richard, G. (2022). *Private sector engagement in adaptation to climate change: Approaches to managing climate risks*. OECD Publishing.

Agrawala, S., Dussaux, D., & Monti, N. (2022). *Climate change adaptation and innovation: A sectoral approach*. OECD Environment Working Papers No. 178. OECD Publishing.

ASEAN. (2024). *Model framework for an inclusive business accreditation system in ASEAN*. ASEAN Secretariat. https://asean.org/wp-content/uploads/2024/09/IB-Model-Framework-Publication_240923.pdf

Barefoot College. (n.d.). *Home*. Retrieved May 6, 2025, from https://www.barefootcollege.org/?gad_source=1&gad_campaignid=10830968790&gbraid=0AAAAACRCuxF2AHdAuunJ44uo-WNN2T5-4&gclid=Cj0KCQjw18bEBhCBARIsAKuAFEZ6x2_OrEWhGxK_6SKnWZ5JOy4Wv5KPHfdZL3OZWxF3Q8mSRsn3XjYaAqq0EALw_wcB-

Becker, T., Bruns, B., Lier, S., & Werners, B. (2021). Decentralized modular production to increase supply chain efficiency in chemical markets: An example of polymer production. *Journal of Business Economics, 91*(6), 867–895. DOI: 10.1007/s11573-020-01019-4

Beitzen-Heineke, E. F., Balta-Ozkan, N., & Reefke, H. (2017). The prospects of zero-packaging grocery stores to improve the social and environmental impacts of the food supply chain. *Journal of Cleaner Production*, *140*, 1528–1541. DOI: 10.1016/j.jclepro.2016.09.227

Belleflamme, P., Lambert, T., & Schwienbacher, A. (2014). Crowdfunding: Tapping the right crowd. *Journal of Business Venturing*, *29*(5), 585–609. DOI: 10.1016/j.jbusvent.2013.07.003

Bhawe, N., Gupta, V. K., & Jain, T. K. (2006). The entrepreneurship of the Good Samaritan: a development framework to understand social entrepreneurship using insights from qualitative study. *Available at SSRN* 902685. DOI: 10.2139/ssrn.902685

British Council. United Nations Economic and Social Commission for Asia and the Pacific (UNESCAP), HSBC, & Social Enterprise UK. (2021). *The state of social enterprise in South East Asia*. British Council. https://www.britishcouncil.org/sites/default/files/the_state_of_social_enterprise_in_south_east_asia_0.pdf

Climate Bonds Initiative. (2024). *Global State of the Market Report 2023: Trends and insights on GSS+ bond markets*. Climate Bonds Initiative. https://www.climatebonds.net/publications

Cohen, B., & Winn, M. I. (2007). Market imperfections, opportunity and sustainable entrepreneurship. *Journal of Business Venturing*, *22*(1), 29–49. DOI: 10.1016/j.jbusvent.2004.12.001

Dean, T. J., & McMullen, J. S. (2007). Toward a theory of sustainable entrepreneurship: Reducing environmental degradation through entrepreneurial action. *Journal of Business Venturing*, *22*(1), 50–76. DOI: 10.1016/j.jbusvent.2005.09.003

Elkington, J. (1997). *Cannibals with forks: The triple bottom line of 21st century business*. Capstone Publishing.

Elkington, J. (2018). 25 years ago I coined the phrase "Triple Bottom Line." Here's why it's time to rethink it. *Harvard Business Review*. https://hbr.org/2018/06/25-years-ago-i-coined-the-phrase-triple-bottom-line-heres-why-im-giving-up-on-it

Ermawati, Y. (2023). Ecosystems for entrepreneurship: A study of supportive environments and their impact. [AMAR]. *Amkop Management Accounting Review*, *3*(2), 58–74. DOI: 10.37531/amar.v3i2.1512

European Commission. (2020). *EU taxonomy for sustainable activities: What the EU is doing to create an EU-wide classification system for sustainable activities.* https://ec.europa.eu/info/business-economy-euro/banking-and-finance/sustainable-finance/eu-taxonomy-sustainable-activities_en

FAO. (2022). *Digital agriculture.* Food and Agriculture Organization of the United Nations.

Friede, G., Busch, T., & Bassen, A. (2015). ESG and financial performance: Aggregated evidence from more than 2000 empirical studies. *Journal of Sustainable Finance & Investment*, *5*(4), 210–233. DOI: 10.1080/20430795.2015.1118917

Geissdoerfer, M., Savaget, P., Bocken, N. M. P., & Hultink, E. J. (2017). The Circular Economy – A new sustainability paradigm? *Journal of Cleaner Production, 143*, 757–768. DOI: 10.1016/j.jclepro.2016.12.048

George, G., Merrill, R. K., & Schillebeeckx, S. J. D. (2021). Digital sustainability and entrepreneurship: How digital innovations are helping tackle climate change and sustainable development. *Entrepreneurship Theory and Practice*, *45*(5), 999–1027. DOI: 10.1177/1042258719899425

Gidron, B. (2017). The dual hybridity of social enterprises for marginalized populations. *Journal of Social Entrepreneurship*, *8*(1), 1–13. DOI: 10.1080/19420676.2016.1207700

Gomez-Trujillo, A. M., Gonzalez-Perez, M. A., & Baena-Rojas, J. J. (2024). Sustainable strategy as a lever for corporate legitimacy and long-term competitive advantage: An examination of an emerging market multinational. *European Business Review*, *36*(1), 112–139. DOI: 10.1108/EBR-01-2023-0003

Gortsos, C. V., & Kyriazis, D. (2024). The taxonomy regulation and its implementation. In *Sustainable Finance in Europe: Corporate Governance, Financial Stability and Financial Markets* (pp. 505–561). Springer International Publishing. DOI: 10.1007/978-3-031-53696-0_13

Hallegatte, S., Rentschler, J., & Rozenberg, J. (2020). *Adaptation principles: A guide for designing strategies for climate change adaptation and resilience.* World Bank Publications. DOI: 10.1596/34780

Ihl, C., & Piller, F. (2016). 3D printing as driver of localized manufacturing: Expected benefits from producer and consumer perspectives. In *The Decentralized and Networked Future of Value Creation: 3D Printing and Its Implications for Society, Industry, and Sustainable Development* (pp. 179–204). Springer International Publishing. DOI: 10.1007/978-3-319-31686-4_10

IRENA. (2020a). *Renewable energy and jobs – Annual review 2020.* Abu Dhabi: IRENA. https://www.irena.org/publications/2020/Sep/Renewable-Energy-and-Jobs-Annual-Review-2020

IRENA. (2020b). *Global Renewables Outlook: Energy transformation 2050*. International Renewable Energy Agency. https://www.irena.org/publications/2020/Apr/Global-Renewables-Outlook-2020

Jamaludin, N. A., Omar Zaki, H., & Foong, Y. P. (2025). From the Ground Up: Sustainable Palm Oil and Entrepreneurial Opportunities. In Khalid, N., Abdul Rahman, N. A., Yan, C. W., & Idris, Z. (Eds.), *Palm Oil Export Market Trends, Challenges and Future Strategies for Sustainability* (pp. 206–218). Routledge. DOI: 10.4324/9781003518600-18

Khanna, P. (2024). Inclusive Business Models: Fostering Social Innovation and Entrepreneurial Ecosystems. [IJSR]. *International Journal of Scientific Research.*

Kirchherr, J., Reike, D., & Hekkert, M. (2018). Conceptualizing the circular economy: An analysis of 114 definitions. *Resources, Conservation and Recycling*, *127*, 221–232. DOI: 10.1016/j.resconrec.2017.09.005

Mair, J., & Marti, I. (2006). Social entrepreneurship research: A source of explanation, prediction, and delight. *Journal of World Business*, *41*(1), 36–44. DOI: 10.1016/j.jwb.2005.09.002

Mair, J., Mayer, J., & Lutz, E. (2015). Navigating institutional plurality: Organizational governance in hybrid organizations. *Organization Studies*, *36*(6), 713–739. DOI: 10.1177/0170840615580007

Mia, M. J., Hossain, M. S., & Akon, M. S. (2025). Environmental Competitiveness, Green Energy, and Global Sustainability. In *Green Energy Investments and Economic Development* (pp. 147–169). Springer Nature Singapore. DOI: 10.1007/978-981-96-6166-4_9

Nipo, D. T., Lily, J., Fabeil, N. F., & Jamil, I. A. A. (2024). Transforming rural entrepreneurship through digital innovation: A review on opportunities, barriers and challenges. *Journal of Management and Sustainability*, *14*(2), 114. DOI: 10.5539/jms.v14n2p114

O'Neil, J. (2017). 'People, planet, profits' and perception politics: a necessary fourth (and fifth) bottom line? Critiquing the current triple bottom line in the Australian context. In *The Goals of Sustainable Development: Responsibility and Governance* (pp. 19–42). Springer Singapore.

OECD. (2017). *Mobilising Bond Markets for a Low-Carbon Transition, Green Finance and Investment*. OECD Publishing., DOI: 10.1787/9789264272323-

OECD. (2024), *OECD Digital Economy Outlook 2024 (Volume 2): Strengthening Connectivity, Innovation and Trust*, OECD Publishing, Paris, https://doi.org/DOI: 10.1787/3adf705b-en

OECD. (2025), *Fostering convergence in SME sustainability reporting: A background study* (OECD Publishing, CFE/SME(2024)13/FINAL). Centre for Entrepreneurship, SMEs, Regions and Cities. https://www.oecd.org/content/dam/oecd/en/publications/reports/2025/02/fostering-convergence-in-sme-sustainability-reporting_133eb77f/ffbf16fb-en.pdf

Phillips, W., Lee, H., Ghobadian, A., O'regan, N., & James, P. (2015). Social innovation and social entrepreneurship: A systematic review. *Group & Organization Management, 40*(3), 428–461. DOI: 10.1177/1059601114560063

Rajesh, P., & Subhashini, V. (2021). Sustainable packaging from waste material: A review on innovative solutions for cleaner environment. *Bioremediation and Green Technologies: Sustainable Approaches to Mitigate Environmental Impacts*, 259-270.

Ran, B., & Weller, S. (2021). An Exit Strategy for the Definitional Elusiveness: A Three-Dimensional Framework for Social Entrepreneurship. *Sustainability (Basel), 13*(2), 563. DOI: 10.3390/su13020563

REN21. (2021). *Renewables 2021 global status report*. Paris: REN21 Secretariat. https://www.ren21.net/reports/global-status-report/

Renneboog, L., Ter Horst, J., & Zhang, C. (2020). Socially responsible investments: Institutional aspects, performance, and investor behavior. *Journal of Banking & Finance, 32*(9), 1723–1742. DOI: 10.1016/j.jbankfin.2007.12.039

Saberi, S., Kouhizadeh, M., Sarkis, J., & Shen, L. (2019). Blockchain technology and its relationships to sustainable supply chain management. *International Journal of Production Research, 57*(7), 2117–2135. DOI: 10.1080/00207543.2018.1533261

Saharan, N., & Wadhwa, N. (2024). A Comprehensive Review of Biodegradable Polymers in Sustainable Packaging Applications. Research & Reviews. *Journal of Food Science and Technology, 13*(1), 28–37p.

Schaltegger, S., Lüdeke-Freund, F., & Hansen, E. G. (2016). Business models for sustainability: A co-evolutionary analysis of sustainable entrepreneurship, innovation, and transformation. *Organization & Environment, 29*(3), 264–289. DOI: 10.1177/1086026616633272

Securities Commission Malaysia. (2021). *SRI Sukuk Framework*. https://www.sc.com.my/development/islamic-capital-market/sri-sukuk-framework

Song, J. H., Murphy, R. J., Narayan, R., & Davies, G. B. H. (2009). Biodegradable and compostable alternatives to conventional plastics. *Philosophical Transactions of the Royal Society of London. Series B, Biological Sciences, 364*(1526), 2127–2139. DOI: 10.1098/rstb.2008.0289

Spear, R. (2006). Social entrepreneurship: A different model? *International Journal of Social Economics, 33*(5/6), 399–410. DOI: 10.1108/03068290610660670

Srivastava, V. K.Vivek Kumar Srivastava. (2024). Impact of Corporate Social Responsibility (CSR) initiatives on brand reputation: A study on how CSR activities enhance brand reputation and consumer loyalty in the context of sustainable marketing practices. *International Journal of Science and Research Archive, 13*(1), 1910–1930. DOI: 10.30574/ijsra.2024.13.1.1869

Thomas, R., & Lukose, P. J. (2024). Social entrepreneurship for empowerment and inclusive business model among Meghalaya rubber farmers. *Journal of Entrepreneurship and Innovation in Emerging Economies, 10*(1), 51–65. DOI: 10.1177/23939575231213813

Tong, J. (2025). *The Role of ESG in Global Economic Development: Current Status, Challenges, and Future Trends*. Advances in Economics, Management and Political Sciences.

Ugbebor, F., Adeteye, M., & Ugbebor, J. (2024). Automated Inventory Management Systems with IoT Integration to Optimize Stock Levels and Reduce Carrying Costs for SMEs: A Comprehensive Review. *Journal of Artificial Intelligence General Science (JAIGS) ISSN: 3006-4023, 6*(1), 306-340.

Wang, B., Osman, L. H., Palil, M. R., & Jamaludin, N. A. B. (2024). Bridging Risks and Opportunities: Operational Strategies for Sustainable Growth via ESG Management. *Operational Research in Engineering Sciences: Theory and Applications, 7*(1).

World Bank. (2022). *Data for better lives: World Development Report 2021*. World Bank Group., DOI: 10.1596/978-1-4648-1600-0

World Economic Forum. (2021). *ESG is missing a metric: R for resilience*. World Economic Forum. https://www.weforum.org/stories/2021/06/esg-resilience-investment-environment-social-governance/

World Economic Forum. (2024). *The State of Social Enterprise: A Review of Global Data 2013-2023*. Schwab Foundation for Social Entrepreneurship. https://www3.weforum.org/docs/WEF_The_State_of_Social_Enterprise_2024.pdf

Yunus, M. (2007). *Creating a world without poverty: Social business and the future of capitalism*. PublicAffairs.

Chapter 15
Empowering Coastal Communities Through Integrated Islamic Microfinance for Sustainable Ecotourism in East Java

Bahrina Almas
https://orcid.org/0000-0002-6580-1015
University of Jember, Indonesia

Ridan Muhtadi
https://orcid.org/0000-0003-3068-387X
IAI Miftahul Ulum Pamekasan, Indonesia & Kiai Haji Achmad Siddiq State Islamic University, Indonesia

Moh. Arifin
Institut Al Fithrah Surabaya, Indonesia

Khairunnisa Musari
https://orcid.org/0000-0003-0525-9903
Kiai Haji Achmad Siddiq State Islamic University, Indonesia

ABSTRACT

Indonesia's coastal regions hold vast economic and ecological potential but face major challenges, including limited financial access and low community capacity. This chapter explores how Integrated Islamic Finance—emphasizing profit-sharing

DOI: 10.4018/979-8-3373-2655-9.ch015

(mudharabah) and charitable funds (tabarru')—can empower coastal communities and support sustainable ecotourism. Using a qualitative approach supported by Fishbone Diagram and Force Field Analysis, the study identifies key barriers such as weak management, limited education, and insufficient institutional support. It proposes a model integrating Islamic finance principles with ecotourism development to foster inclusive growth and environmental sustainability. The chapter offers strategic insights for policymakers, academics, and practitioners seeking to transform coastal areas into resilient and economically empowered communities.

INTRODUCTION

Indonesia, as a physically and geopolitically real entity, is the largest archipelagic nation in the world, consisting of 17,504 islands with a coastline stretching 95,161 km—second only to Canada—and a maritime area covering 5.8 million square kilometres. This extensive coastal area forms a unique ecosystem rich in natural resources, both on land and in marine zones. The immense potential of these coastal regions creates a multiplier effect, giving rise to a variety of economic functions, whether directly or indirectly linked to core economic activities. Economic activities by local communities, aimed at improving welfare, naturally utilize the available spatial areas. Given that coastal regions are relatively accessible, they often become prime targets for human development activities. This very potential has led to Indonesia being known as the *Emerald of the Equator*, with its maritime strength serving as the basis for several government programs aimed at enhancing the welfare of coastal communities—among them, the development of *minapolitan* areas (Djunarsjah & Putra, 2021; Hastuti et al., 2023; Lasabuda, 2013; Nugroho et al., 2020; White et al., 2021).

One of the coastal regions in Indonesia with strong potential for economic development is the coastal zone of East Java Province. However, the development of *minapolitan* areas in East Java's coastal regions has not progressed effectively due to the underutilization and under exploration of natural resources, as well as the limited availability of supporting infrastructure—particularly in coastal areas with tourism potential. Limited access, such as the absence of public transportation to coastal regions, presents one of the major challenges. Tourism facilities are also inadequate, especially accommodations, which are generally concentrated in urban centres. Moreover, local communities have not been fully and comprehensively involved in the ecotourism initiatives carried out in these coastal areas (Dewi et al., 2024a; Hakim, 2008; Halik et al., 2024; Ikhwani et al., 2023; Rahayu et al., 2024; Setiawan et al., 2022; Setyaningsih et al., 2019).

Beyond infrastructure and services, marketing and promotion efforts for coastal ecotourism remain minimal. This highlights the importance of marketing so that the existence of coastal regions as ecotourism destinations becomes widely recognized, thereby increasing visitor numbers. To realize the vision of developing coastal areas as community-based *minapolitan* ecotourism zones—both on a national and international level—an in-depth identification of the causes behind the suboptimal implementation of ecotourism in several regions is essential. Once these problems are clearly understood, effective development and community-based marketing strategies can be formulated to address the actual conditions on the ground. In this way, the objectives of ecotourism development—enhancing community welfare while preserving environmental sustainability—can be simultaneously achieved (Barkin & Bouchez, 2002; Dwyer & Gill, 2019; Elbaramelgy et al., 2019; Hamzah et al., 2024; Hutnaleontina et al., 2022; Kuba et al., 2024; Nurlukman et al., 2025; Pratama & Jannah, 2024; Shen, 2020).

A deeper analysis reveals that managerial aspects, which are often overlooked, significantly influence the sustainability of coastal regions. This is largely due to low levels of education, knowledge, and access to supporting technologies among coastal communities. Yet, these areas play a crucial role in absorbing a large labour force, functioning as centres of distribution and economic drivers with the potential to develop their respective regions (Mthuli & Singh, 2024).

In light of the above, a concept for empowering the coastal economy in East Java is needed. Islamic economics can serve as an alternative solution to these national challenges. The issues mentioned earlier can be addressed through how we, as academics, are able to drive the empowerment of coastal communities—within the framework of Islamic economics. On the other hand, empowering coastal communities requires substantial funding. However, this financial challenge can be mitigated by utilizing integrated Islamic microfinance potentials. Notably, through the *tabarru'* fund scheme, there is no obligation to repay the funds, allowing profits to be redistributed for the benefit of society and to preserve the fund's value. In addition, profit-sharing systems used in partnership contracts are relatively non-burdensome. To date, microfinance management remains significantly underutilized, despite its promising potential. Therefore, professional management through integrated planning is essential to support *minapolitan* ecotourism and, ultimately, to foster the economic empowerment of coastal communities.

ECOTOURISM

Ecotourism is a sustainable tourism development concept aimed at supporting environmental (natural and cultural) conservation efforts while increasing community participation in its management, thereby providing economic benefits to both the local community and government (Esmaeili Mahyari et al., 2024; Suyadnya et al., 2025). Ecotourism encompasses various definitions, all of which are grounded in the principles of tourism that centre around five key elements (Phou et al., 2025):

1. Providing tourists with experiences and educational opportunities that enhance their understanding and appreciation of the destination. Education focuses on raising awareness about the importance of environmental conservation, while the experience is facilitated through creative tourism activities supported by excellent services;
2. Minimizing negative impacts that could damage the environmental and cultural characteristics of the destination;
3. Involving local communities in the planning and implementation processes;
4. Generating economic benefits, especially for local communities, which implies that ecotourism must be economically viable;
5. Ensuring long-term sustainability.

Damanik & Weber, (2006) outlines several principles of ecotourism as follows:

1. Reducing negative impacts such as environmental degradation or pollution and cultural erosion due to tourism activities.
2. Building awareness and appreciation of the environment and culture at tourist destinations among tourists, local communities, and other stakeholders in the tourism sector.
3. Offering positive experiences for both tourists and local communities through meaningful cultural exchanges and collaboration in preserving and conserving tourism objects and attractions.
4. Providing direct financial contributions to conservation efforts through extra spending or donations by tourists.
5. Delivering financial benefits and empowerment opportunities for local communities through the development of tourism products that reflect local values.
6. Enhancing sensitivity to the social, environmental, and political contexts of the destination.
7. Respecting human rights and employment agreements, allowing both tourists and local communities the freedom to enjoy tourism attractions as a form of human rights, while adhering to fair and mutually agreed rules governing tourism transactions.

Damanik & Weber, (2006) further asserts that the principles and characteristics of ecotourism include:

1. Adherence to a positive environmental ethic, promoting responsible behaviour.
2. Preservation of resources without degrading their integrity.
3. Emphasis on intrinsic rather than extrinsic values.
4. Orientation toward a biocentric rather than anthropocentric philosophy in tourism.
5. Focus on respecting nature's inherent order, rather than significantly altering the environment for personal comfort.
6. Ensuring that ecotourism activities benefit natural resources. While these activities often have social, economic, political, or scientific benefits, the environment must be the primary beneficiary.
7. Facilitating direct engagement with the natural environment.
8. Satisfaction in ecotourism is measured through appreciation and learning, not through thrill-seeking or physical achievement—elements more aligned with adventure tourism in more rugged natural settings.

Ecotourism also articulates three fundamental principles in its conceptual development:

1. Conservation Principle: Ecotourism development must preserve, protect, and ideally contribute to the restoration of natural resources. Conservation is the foundation of sustainable ecotourism practices, ensuring that natural ecosystems are maintained for future generations (Sitompul, 2024).
2. Community Participation Principle: Development should be based on community consensus and sensitivity to, and respect for, the local social, cultural, and religious traditions. Active community involvement not only enhances the authenticity of the ecotourism experience but also fosters long-term stewardship and equitable benefit-sharing (Fuady et al., 2025; Oltean et al., 2025).
3. Economic Principle: Ecotourism must provide tangible benefits for local communities and drive economic development in these areas, ensuring a balanced relationship between environmental conservation and stakeholders' interests (Manalo et al., 2024; Nurlukman et al., 2025) (Manalo & Bito-onon, 2024; Nurlukman et al., 2025).

As one of Indonesia's sustainable development programs, ecotourism requires a multidisciplinary approach in its development. One such initiative is marine ecotourism, also referred to as *maritime tourism*. Marine ecotourism essentially seeks to establish and maintain a symbiotic relationship between tourism activities and the natural marine environment. This involves offering visitors a fulfilling experience while fostering respect for the intrinsic conservation values of the natural ecosystems upon which marine ecotourism depends. The development of marine ecotourism presents an opportunity to revitalize coastal communities facing economic challenges due to the decline of traditional sectors such as agriculture, seaside tourism, and commercial fishing (Nurhayati et al., 2019; Tuwo et al., 2021).

The essence of ecotourism lies not in selling destinations or locations, but in promoting a philosophy. This gives ecotourism a sustainable value that does not suffer from market saturation. Although market demand does influence ecotourism development, its management concept remains grounded in the foundational principles of ecotourism (Yulianda, 2007).

Fundamentally, marine ecotourism aims to cultivate a symbiotic relationship between tourism and the marine environment, offering visitors enriching experiences while upholding the conservation values that are central to the existence of marine ecotourism.

MINAPOLITAN

Minapolitan is a fisheries-based urban area that grows and develops through the operation of a well-functioning fisheries system and industry. It has the capacity to serve, stimulate, and attract regional economic development activities in its surrounding areas. The term "city" in this context refers to a fisheries town that may include medium-sized cities, small towns, sub-district towns, or rural towns that function as economic growth centres encouraging the development of rural areas or their surrounding regions (Dewi et al., 2024b; Satria, 2010).

A crucial first step in developing *minapolitan* areas is to understand the current streams of thought that influence fisheries development, as these significantly impact the strategic direction chosen. Identifies two prevailing schools of thought in *minapolitan* development, both of which are recognized in political-ecology studies. Each school has its own group of proponents who interpret and respond to the concept of *minapolitan* differently (Satria, 2010).

Minapolitan zones are marine and fisheries-based economic areas comprising production and trade centres, services, settlements, and other interrelated activities. *Minapolitan* represents a model of the *Blue Revolution* promoted by the Ministry of Marine Affairs and Fisheries of the Republic of Indonesia, aiming to shift the development paradigm from land-based to maritime-oriented approaches.

ISLAMIC MICROFINANCE INSTITUTIONS

Islamic Microfinance Institutions (IMFIs) are financial institutions that provide financial services to low-income populations and impoverished communities based on Islamic principles (Nurawami, 2013). Another definition describes IMFIs as a variant of banks or similar entities with relatively small capital, designed specifically for micro and small business sectors. These institutions have become critical tools in poverty alleviation and development, as they help empower the poor to achieve greater self-reliance and sustainability by providing access to financial services.

One of the financial institutions equivalent to IMFIs is BPRS (*Bank Perkreditan Rakyat Syariah*), a rural bank that conducts financial transactions using conventional systems but based on *sharia* principles. BPRS does not offer payment transaction services to the public. Both commercial banks and BPRS can take legal forms such as Limited Liability Companies (PT), Regional-Owned Enterprises (Perusahaan Daerah), or Cooperatives. The operational mechanisms of BPRS are governed by Bank Indonesia Regulation No. 6/17/PBI/2004.

In the context of microfinance, other institutions such as Baitul Maal wat Tamwil (BMT) and Islamic Financial Services Cooperatives are also considered part of the Islamic microfinance ecosystem. These institutions are closely interconnected and influence each other, as well as maintain strong ties with other Islamic financial bodies.

Among the institutions categorized under Islamic Microfinance Institutions are:

BMT (Baitul Maal wat Tamwil)

Linguistically, this consists of *Baitul Maal* and *Baitul Tamwil.*

- *Baitul Maal* is an Islamic financial institution focused on collecting and distributing charitable funds (ZISWAHIB – *zakat*, *infaq*, *sadaqah*, *waqf*, and *hibah*) without seeking financial profit (non-profit-oriented).
- *Baitul Tamwil*, on the other hand, is an informal Islamic financial institution that conducts its operations with a profit-oriented approach, offering financing to its members based on profit-sharing or mark-up/margin schemes grounded in *sharia* principles.

Key characteristics of BMT include:

1. It is legally established as a cooperative;
2. It aims to provide quick, accessible, and low-cost funding without bureaucratic complexities to support and develop members' businesses;
3. Its limited product and funding scale distinguishes it from other financial institutions, although its transaction mechanisms closely resemble those of Islamic banking, operating on a non-*riba* (interest-free) basis.

Islamic Financial Services Cooperatives (Koperasi Jasa Keuangan Syariah - KJKS)

The emergence of *Koperasi Jasa Keuangan Syariah* (KJKS), or Islamic Financial Services Cooperatives, as a newcomer in the realm of community empowerment through *sharia*-compliant savings and loans systems, represents an innovative alternative in financial services.

KJKS operates savings and loan units composed of two main business activities: savings and financing. Savings refer to funds entrusted by members, prospective members, other KJKS institutions, or their members, in the form of savings accounts or time deposits. Financing refers to the provision of funds based on a loan agreement between the KJKS and members, prospective members, other KJKS institutions, or their members, under which the borrower is obligated to repay the loan within a specified period (Pristiyanto et al., 2013).

The provision of financing is intended as a temporary capital injection and economic stimulus. Furthermore, such financing should support the productivity growth of micro-enterprises. Increased production is interpreted as an increase in income and overall welfare of cooperative members.

The empowerment of marginalized and low-income communities in Indonesia is widely acknowledged as a strategic approach to national development. However, its practical implementation has yet to reach optimal effectiveness. In this regard, Islamic Microfinance Institutions (IMFIs) offer an ideal solution through the establishment of KJKS, which serve a strategic role in expanding employment opportunities and reducing poverty. KJKS function as *agents of asset distribution*, empowering communities economically through two functions:

- *Baitul Maal*, serving as a social institution, and
- *Baitul Tamwil*, acting as a business institution based on *sharia*-compliant models (Pristiyanto et al., 2013).

As cooperative-based enterprises, KJKS serve as a platform for joint economic ventures with three core functions: educational tools, operational efficiency enhancers, and instruments of member self-sufficiency. To address the limitations of micro-enterprises in capital accumulation and investment, KJKS mobilize collective funds in the form of savings from members, which are then managed and disbursed as revolving funds to finance the members' micro-businesses. KJKS holds a dual status as a business entity; it acts as both the owner of capital and as a client. Fundamentally, the establishment of KJKS aims to promote the economic well-being of its members by enhancing their financial status and independence.

The unification of individual economic interests through collective activities has been institutionalized within KJKS to create synergistic effects that facilitate the scaling of economic initiatives. The economic benefits provided by KJKS to its members include low service fees, minimal administrative requirements, and expedited service delivery. The growing awareness of conducting business through Islamic financial cooperatives demonstrates the necessity of *sharia*-based principles in daily life. This awareness has driven the progress and development of the economy, highlighting the significant contribution of KJKS as a key instrument within the broader Islamic microfinance framework.

In addition, the influence of Islamic Microfinance Institutions has made a notable impact on Indonesia's economic landscape. This is evidenced by the increasing number of *sharia*-based micro-enterprises. For instance, PT Bank Muamalat Indonesia, through its *Baitul Maal Muamalat* program in collaboration with the Ministry of Cooperatives and SMEs, has enhanced the performance of KJKS by financing small and micro-scale entrepreneurs using funds sourced from zakat, infaq, and sadaqah.

MANAGEMENT OF MINAPOLITAN ECOTOURISM IN COASTAL AREAS

Coastal areas have become popular tourist destinations for local communities. As these areas are increasingly visited, local residents have begun to recognize the importance of minapolitan ecotourism principles and have started to utilize them wisely to improve their quality of life and economic well-being.

One key indicator of the suboptimal implementation of ecotourism in these regions is the limited involvement of the local community in managing their own areas. Most local residents continue to rely solely on income derived from marine resources. As a result, the essence of marine ecotourism has yet to be effectively realized in coastal areas that hold significant tourism potential.

This study identifies several inhibiting factors affecting the development of coastal regions in Jember and Lamongan Regencies, including:

1. Product: No structured tourism packages have been offered.
2. Price: No pricing system has been established for tourism packages.
3. Place: There is a lack of guidance for new visitors to reach the destinations. Most accommodations are located in the city centre, and other supporting facilities are still inadequate. Distribution channels for ecotourism services are unclear.
4. Promotion: There is no clear visual representation of the facilities (e.g., magazines or promotional materials). Communication between management and visitors is inadequate, especially due to limited foreign language skills. The

use of information and communication technology for promotional purposes remains very limited.

5. People: The number of staff is uncertain and insufficient. Local residents lack the necessary skills, and human resource management remains underdeveloped.
6. Process: There are no established Standard Operating Procedures (SOPs) for visitor services.

Based on the detailed problem identification and the underlying causes of underdeveloped ecotourism in Sumenep, a Fishbone Diagram can be constructed to illustrate the contributing factors.

Figure 1. Diagram fishbone (Author's Work)

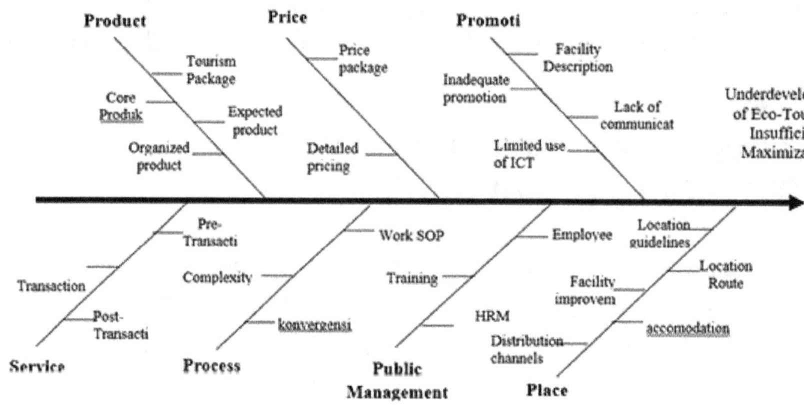

After identifying the root causes of the problems in the coastal areas of Jember and Lamongan, the next step involves determining potential contributing factors and identifying the most dominant ones. Based on field observations and interviews conducted by the researchers, several critical issues have been identified.

The most dominant factors contributing to the current problems include:

- Limited capital resources
- Inadequate infrastructure and facilities
- Weak human resource management
- Insufficient promotion and marketing

Upon identifying these key barriers, the next phase is to formulate action plans aimed at overcoming the existing challenges.

One such strategy involves the integration of Islamic Microfinance into minapolitan ecotourism development as a means to empower coastal communities. This integrated approach is expected to enhance the capacity and resilience of the local population while improving economic outcomes and ensuring the sustainability of coastal tourism.

Figure 2. Force field analysis models

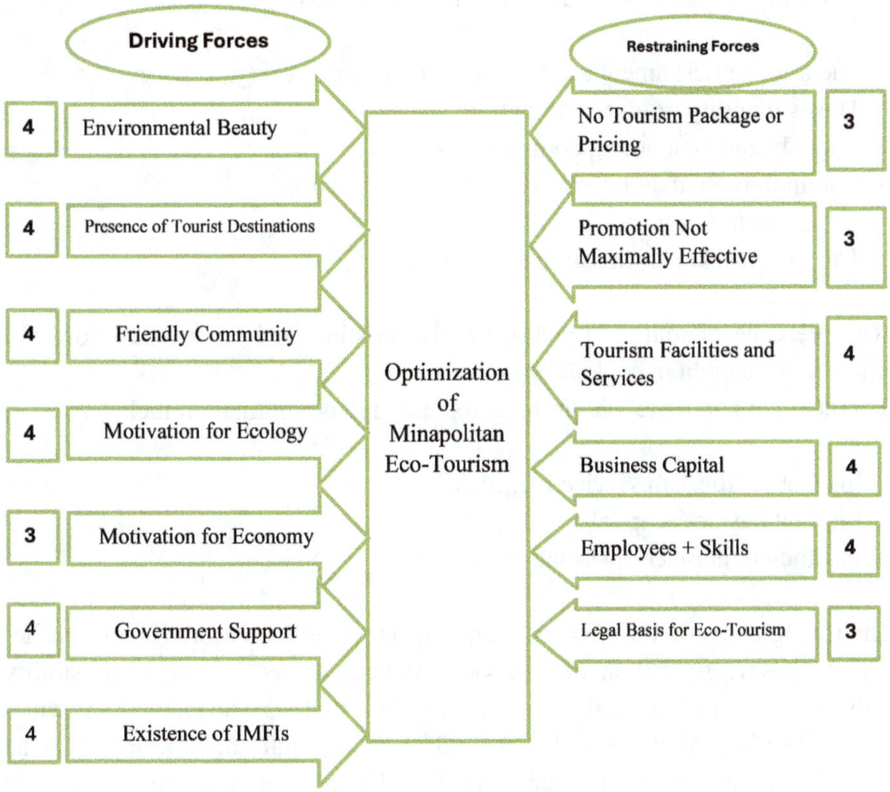

The analysis also reveals that the highest-ranked driving factors include the pristine natural environment, the presence of tourist attractions, the friendliness of local communities, the community's ecological motivation, government support, and the existence of Islamic Microfinance Institutions. The total score for the driving factors, derived from the sum of their individual rankings, is 27.

Meanwhile, the highest-ranked inhibiting factors are insufficient tourism service facilities, lack of business capital, and an inadequate number of skilled workers. The total score for inhibiting factors is 21.

Since the total value of the driving factors exceeds that of the inhibiting factors, this indicates that the development of minapolitan ecotourism is feasible. The stronger the influence of the driving factors, the weaker the impact of the inhibiting factors—thus increasing the likelihood that the program can be successfully implemented. Therefore, mitigation strategies should focus on strengthening weaker driving factors and reducing the impact of stronger inhibiting factors, while also considering the dynamic interaction among all influencing variables.

The driving factors that need to be reinforced include:

- The area's environmental cleanliness and natural beauty
- The availability of tourist attractions
- Friendly and welcoming communities
- Community motivation toward ecoloal preservation
- Government support
- The role of Islamic Microfinance Institutions

The presence of tourist attractions and a pristine environment are powerful magnets for minapolitan ecotourism zones.

On the other hand, the inhibiting factors that require mitigation include:

- Inadequate tourism service facilities
- Limited business capital
- Insufficient number of skilled personnel

Improving infrastructure and service quality is essential to ensure visitor satisfaction. Ecotourism is fundamentally a service production process whose sustainability heavily depends on the natural environment and the tourists who enjoy the services offered. Therefore, visitor satisfaction and environmental conservation must be addressed simultaneously and inseparably. Effective promotion also plays a critical role in supporting infrastructure and service improvements.

Well-executed promotional efforts are expected to raise public awareness of minapolitan ecotourism and stimulate greater interest in visiting these destinations. Furthermore, support from academics and practitioners within Islamic Financial Institutions (LKS) will help local communities build confidence in developing ecotourism—especially in addressing funding challenges. The development of ecotourism in these coastal regions should be directed toward sustainable tourism to ensure that minapolitan ecotourism in Jember and Lamongan Regencies becomes a leading and competitive tourist destination.

AN INTEGRATED ISLAMIC MICROFINANCE MODEL FOR MINAPOLITAN ECOTOURISM DEVELOPMENT

Given the socio-economic conditions of the coastal regions in Sumenep, there is a pressing need for cross-sectoral synergy to significantly support the establishment of minapolitan ecotourism zones. The empowerment of coastal communities aims to accommodate the roles of Islamic Microfinance Institutions (IMFIs), academics, practitioners, and—most importantly—the coastal communities themselves, in order to collectively assess local phenomena and formulate recommendations that are aligned with *sharia*-based perspectives and can be implemented by the communities. In this context, research functions as a scientifically grounded tool essential for addressing recurring issues, enabling the formulation of practical and sustainable strategies for the development of minapolitan ecotourism in coastal areas.

Figure 3. A model of integrated (Author's Work)

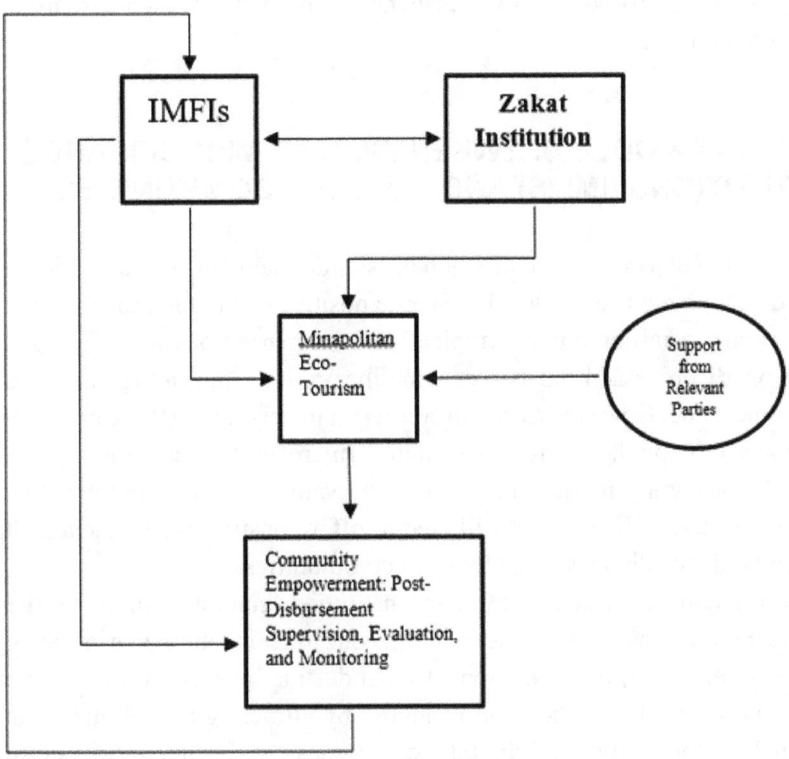

This empowerment initiative aims to optimize participatory collaboration among key stakeholders. The following actors play critical roles in coastal community development:

1. Islamic Microfinance Institutions (IMFIs), Function as fund mobilizers and distributors, channeling community resources to drive coastal empowerment programs.
2. Zakat Institutions, Manage and distribute philanthropic funds (*zakat, infaq, shodaqoh, waqf, and hibah*) to support and guarantee the development of eco-tourism initiatives.
3. Relevant Stakeholders (Academics, Practitioners, and Government). Conduct research and development (R&D), human resource development (HRD), and serve as policy makers to ensure sustainable implementation.
4. Coastal Communities, serve as the primary subjects of economic empowerment, actively engaging in and benefiting from development programs.
5. Community Network Analysis, perform comprehensive socio-economic analyses to identify key factors influencing the economic conditions of coastal communities.

SYNERGY MODEL BETWEEN ISLAMIC MICROFINANCE INSTITUTIONS (IMFIS) AND COASTAL COMMUNITIES

Given the objectives and direction of Islamic microfinance institutions (IMFIs), their development is expected to generate positive economic impacts. On the other hand, rural coastal communities typically rely on marine-based livelihoods, meaning that properly processed and marketed marine products can yield significantly higher economic value. However, a critical constraint in developing these marine resources is the lack of capital. This is where Islamic microfinance institutions play a crucial role—by providing funding to enhance the value of marine products. Given this capital constraint, IMFIS is positioned to offer constructive financial solutions to overcome the challenges faced by local communities.

Additionally, Islamic microfinance institutions can invest in the tourism sector. Coastal regions possess immense potential due to their natural marine beauty, which can be developed into multinational tourist destinations. A thriving tourism sector can significantly boost the local economy by attracting both domestic and international visitors. Advanced digital technologies can further accelerate marketing efforts, expanding reach both nationally and globally.

As tourism grows, local communities benefit by selling value-added marine products, which can be branded as regional specialties. This not only enhances economic value but also increases the destination's appeal to tourists. Thus, the synergy between IMFIS and coastal communities can create a sustainable economic ecosystem—strengthening local livelihoods while promoting tourism and trade.

Figure 4. Synergy scheme between BMT and coastal communities based on Minapolitan eco-tourism (Author's Work)

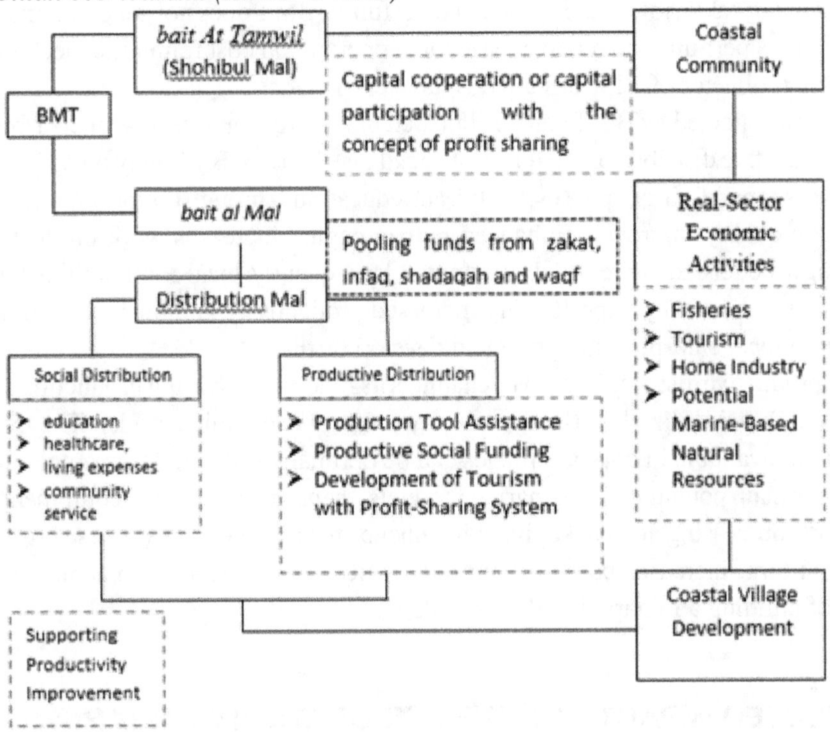

The scheme above illustrates the synergy between BMT, as a sharia-based microfinance institution, and coastal communities aiming to transform their village economy into a minapolitan and eco-tourism-oriented village. Funds provided by individuals with surplus capital (shahibul maal) are distributed to those in need (mudharib) and managed in the real sector—used for purchasing production equipment, productive social assistance funds, and allocations for tourism development through profit-sharing arrangements.

The targeted real sectors for fund distribution include fisheries, home industries, tourism, and the cultivation of aquatic organisms such as fish and plants. These sectors are developed to stimulate the local economy, aiming to reduce unemployment through the creation of job opportunities. Increased productivity accelerates the circulation of money, ultimately enhancing community income.

The scheme also highlights the social collaboration between BMT and the community. The function of Bait Al Maal indicates that BMT positions itself as an institution that collects and distributes community funds derived from zakat (obligatory almsgiving), infaq (voluntary charity), sadaqah (general charity), and cash waqf (endowment). These funds are distributed to eligible recipients (mustahiq) in accordance with religious guidelines and modern financial management practices. In managing zakat, infaq, sadaqah, and waqf funds, BMT does not generate financial profit but is permitted to receive reasonable operational cost reimbursement, either as `amil (collector of ZIS) or nadzir (manager of waqf).

Funds collected by BMT can be allocated into two categories: social distribution and productive distribution. In terms of social distribution, BMT may provide social funds to support living expenses, health, and education. Through this program, human resource quality improves. Enhanced human capital increases work productivity, leading to better and higher-quality outputs. Consequently, local communities benefit from this initiative by experiencing increased productivity and business activities, enabling local enterprises to grow and develop further.

In productive distribution, BMT channels its funds by providing production tools. These tools are utilized by the community to boost economic activity. The natural resources available in coastal villages can be optimally utilized; for example, if the village's main potential lies in marine products, then the provision of equipment that supports processing and packaging will enhance the market value of these products. This, in turn, increases community productivity and contributes to achieving the goal of building a minapolitan-based village.

EXPECTED IMPACTS OF THE INTEGRATION OF SHARIA MICROFINANCE INTO MINAPOLITAN ECO-TOURISM

The anticipated impact of this integration is sustainable regional development achieved through collaboration and the optimization of roles by relevant institutions for coastal communities. Through such optimization, the primary objectives of Minapolitan Eco-Tourism—particularly in terms of stimulating the local economy—can be realized. Moreover, this integration aims to improve the system within coastal communities in managing their potential resources, supported by guidance from various third-party institutions. Consequently, the role of the community itself as economic actors within the region will also be strengthened. For clarity, the impacts of this synergy will be categorized into several subsections as follows:

1. Impact on the Government

The integration of sharia microfinance into the development of Minapolitan eco-tourism is expected to generate a wide range of positive outcomes, particularly in accelerating sustainable economic growth within coastal communities. One of the most significant anticipated impacts is the stimulation of local economic activity, which will ultimately contribute to improving living standards and promoting broader public welfare. This aligns with the overarching mission of national development, which emphasizes equitable growth and inclusive prosperity across all regions of Indonesia.

As financial resources are channelled through sharia-based mechanisms—such as mudharabah (profit-sharing), musyarakah (joint venture), and other forms of productive financing—local entrepreneurs and small-scale producers gain greater access to capital without being burdened by interest-based debt. This not only empowers individuals economically but also strengthens community resilience and self-reliance. Consequently, an increase in per capita income becomes evident, reflecting improvements in the overall quality of life for residents.

Moreover, this rise in community income has important implications for the national economy. As local businesses expand and household incomes grow, the tax base widens, allowing for increased government revenue. This additional fiscal capacity can then be reinvested into public services and infrastructure, further reinforcing the cycle of development. In particular, higher levels of economic activity directly contribute to GDP growth, positioning coastal villages not merely as recipients of development but as active contributors to national economic progress.

In addition to boosting income levels, the integration fosters greater economic circulation within the region. The injection of microfinance funds into various sectors—especially fisheries, home industries, and tourism—stimulates demand for labour, thereby creating new employment opportunities. This dynamic plays a crucial role in addressing unemployment, especially among youth and underprivileged groups who often face limited access to formal job markets. By offering alternative livelihoods and encouraging entrepreneurship, the initiative helps reduce dependency on external migration for employment and keeps human capital within local communities.

From a macroeconomic perspective, the long-term effects of this integrated approach are both extensive and transformative. When analysed systematically, the synergy between sharia microfinance and Minapolitan eco-tourism has the potential to catalyse structural changes in regional economies. It supports the emergence of more diversified and resilient economic models that are less vulnerable to external shocks. Over time, these localized developments contribute cumulatively to the broader Indonesian economy, fostering inclusive growth and strengthening national economic stability.

In essence, the integration does not merely deliver short-term benefits but lays the foundation for sustainable development that harmonizes economic empowerment, environmental conservation, and social equity—key pillars of a truly holistic and future-oriented development strategy.

2. Impact on Related Institutions

The integration of sharia microfinance into the Minapolitan eco-tourism framework also presents significant institutional benefits, particularly in strengthening the capacity and sustainability of participating organizations. One of the primary advantages is the generation of additional income for these institutions through their active involvement in productive financing schemes. Unlike conventional charity-based models, this approach enables institutions such as BMTs (Baitul Maal wat Tamwil) to earn legitimate returns from profit-sharing arrangements, which can then be reinvested into internal development and infrastructure enhancement. This financial autonomy not only improves operational efficiency but also supports long-term institutional growth and service expansion.

Furthermore, this collaboration fosters the establishment of structured cooperative patterns among stakeholders, reinforcing a shared vision and mission cantered on socio-economic empowerment and sustainable development. By aligning their objectives with broader developmental goals—such as poverty alleviation, environmental conservation, and community resilience—these institutions are better positioned to fulfil their original mandates. The clarity of roles and mutual understanding of responsibilities facilitate smoother implementation of programs, ensuring that strategic targets are met efficiently and sustainably. This alignment also enhances accountability and transparency, which are essential in maintaining public trust and institutional legitimacy.

In addition, the synergy between institutions significantly streamlines operational performance by leveraging complementary functions and comparative advantages. For instance, while one institution may specialize in capital mobilization, another may excel in technical guidance or market access. Through coordinated efforts, these entities collectively enhance service delivery and resource utilization. Such inter-institutional collaboration minimizes redundancy, optimizes resource allocation, and strengthens the overall impact of development initiatives. As a result, the system becomes more responsive to the dynamic needs of coastal communities, ensuring that interventions are both context-sensitive and scalable.

Ultimately, this institutional strengthening contributes to a more resilient and integrated development ecosystem, where financial inclusivity, social responsibility, and economic productivity converge to support long-term regional prosperity.

3. Impact on the Community

The integration of sharia microfinance into the Minapolitan eco-tourism model is expected to significantly enhance the socio-economic conditions of coastal communities. One of the most tangible outcomes is the revitalization of the local economy through increased economic activity and entrepreneurial engagement. By providing accessible and interest-free financial resources, this model empowers local residents to establish or expand small-scale businesses—ranging from fisheries, handicrafts, to tourism-related services. These initiatives, often supported by strategic partnerships with financial institutions and development agencies, enable individuals to generate sustainable income, thereby improving their overall standard of living and reducing dependency on external financial support.

In addition, this approach directly addresses the persistent challenges faced by micro, small, and medium enterprises (MSMEs), which form the backbone of rural economies. Many MSMEs in coastal areas struggle with limited access to capital, inadequate business skills, and weak market linkages. Through targeted financing mechanisms such as mudharabah (profit-sharing) and qard al-hasan (benevolent loans), coupled with capacity-building programs, sharia microfinance institutions help overcome these barriers. As a result, MSMEs are better equipped to scale their operations, improve product quality, and access broader markets—ultimately contributing to a more resilient and diversified local economy.

Moreover, the activation of productive sectors within the community leads to the creation of new employment opportunities, particularly for youth and underprivileged groups. The development of eco-tourism, aquaculture, and home-based industries generates demand for both skilled and unskilled labour, offering viable alternatives to migration and informal labour. This not only alleviates unemployment but also strengthens social cohesion by keeping human capital within the community. In turn, reduced unemployment rates contribute to lower crime rates and greater social stability, fostering an environment conducive to long-term development.

As income levels rise and infrastructure improves, the cumulative effect manifests in a more just, peaceful, and prosperous community life. Economic empowerment reduces disparities and enhances inclusivity, allowing previously marginalized groups to participate meaningfully in local development processes. Improved access to basic services, better housing, and enhanced public facilities further reinforce this transformation. Ultimately, the synergy between sharia microfinance and Minapolitan eco-tourism lays the foundation for a balanced development model—one that harmonizes economic growth, environmental sustainability, and social equity.

4. Impact on the Environment

While the integration of sharia microfinance into Minapolitan ecotourism has numerous socio-economic advantages, it is crucial to also assess its environmental implications. Properly implemented, Minapolitan ecotourism is designed to align with the core principles of sustainability and environmental conservation. The emphasis on community-based tourism encourages local stewardship of natural resources, ensuring that economic activities do not come at the expense of ecological integrity. However, without proper regulation and continuous monitoring, the development of tourism infrastructure and increased human activity could pose risks such as habitat degradation, pollution, or resource depletion. Therefore, it is essential that all stakeholders incorporate environmental safeguards—including zoning regulations, eco-friendly construction practices, waste management systems, and environmental education programs—into the planning and operational phases. By maintaining a strict adherence to ecotourism principles, Minapolitan-based tourism initiatives can offer a model of sustainable development that harmonizes economic growth with long-term environmental preservation.

CONCLUSION

The process of synergy and integration of sharia microfinance into rural development frameworks holds significant potential as a catalyst for sustainable village growth. This collaborative model is grounded on the assumption that such integration not only strengthens local economies but also fosters inclusive development by engaging multiple stakeholders—ranging from financial institutions to community-based enterprises and local governments. By aligning the objectives of sharia microfinance institutions (such as BMTs), village-owned enterprises (BUMDES), and micro, small, and medium enterprises (MSMEs) with broader developmental goals, this approach facilitates a more structured and impactful delivery of financial and non-financial resources.

The resulting synergies are expected to generate multi-dimensional benefits across various sectors of the rural economy. These impacts can be categorized into three key areas: first, the impact on the government, which includes accelerated local economic growth, increased tax revenue, and enhanced public welfare in line with national development priorities. Second, the impact on related institutions, where strengthened financial capacity, improved operational efficiency, and better coordination mechanisms contribute to long-term institutional sustainability. Third, the impact on the community, encompassing improved living standards, expanded employment opportunities, and greater access to productive financial resources—ultimately leading to more equitable and resilient socio-economic development. In conclusion, the integration of sharia microfinance into the Minapolitan eco-tourism model represents a holistic and sustainable development strategy. It not only stimulates economic activity but also reinforces social equity and environmental sustainability, positioning coastal villages as self-reliant and economically vibrant communities capable of contributing meaningfully to regional and national development agendas.

REFERENCES

Barkin, D., & Bouchez, C. P. (2002). NGO–Community Collaboration for Ecotourism: A Strategy for Sustainable Regional Development. *Current Issues in Tourism*, *5*(3–4), 245–253. DOI: 10.1080/13683500208667921

Damanik, J., & Weber, H. F. (2006). *Ecotourism planning: From theory to application*. Andi.

Dewi, Y. K., Safruddin, S., & Zainuddin, M. (2024a). Development Center of Minapolitan Area in Wajo District. *Torani Journal of Fisheries and Marine Science*, *7*(2), 151–159. DOI: 10.35911/torani.v7i2.32856

Dewi, Y. K., Safruddin, S., & Zainuddin, M. (2024b). Development Center of Minapolitan Area in Wajo District. *Torani Journal of Fisheries and Marine Science*, *7*(2), 2. Advance online publication. DOI: 10.35911/torani.v7i2.32856

Djunarsjah, E., & Putra, A. P. (2021). The concept of an archipelagic Province in Indonesia. *IOP Conference Series. Earth and Environmental Science*, *777*(1), 012040. DOI: 10.1088/1755-1315/777/1/012040

Dwyer, L., & Gill, E. A. (2019). Obalni i pomorski turizam: o ozbiljnim problemima. *Acta turistica, 31*(2), 213–242. DOI: 10.22598/at/2019.31.2.213

Elbaramelgy, M., Gammaz, S. A., & Emara, M. S. (2019). Community Based Ecotourism Strategies: Key Indicators For Successful Practices In Developing Countries. *Journal of Urban Research*, *31*(1), 103–122. DOI: 10.21608/jur.2019.88566

Esmaeili Mahyari, M., Nourmandipour, V., & Beishami, B. (2024). Exploring the evolution of rural tourism:systematic review and identifying the current and future trends. *Journal of Rural Research*, *15*(4), 37–50. DOI: 10.22059/jrur.2025.376723.1945

Fuady, M., Kevin, M. A., Farrel, M. R., & Triaputri, A. (2025). Mangrove Forest Conservation for Disaster Mitigation and Community Welfare in Banda Aceh: A Sustainable Development Goals (SDG's) Approach. *Journal of Lifestyle and SDGs Review*, *5*(3), e04787–e04787. DOI: 10.47172/2965-730X.SDGsReview.v5.n03.pe04787

Hakim, L. (2008). Planning for nature-based tourism in east java: Recent status of biodiversity, conservation, and its implication for sustainable tourism. *Asean Journal on Hospitality and Tourism*, *7*(2), 155–167. DOI: 10.5614/ajht.2008.7.2.02

Halik, A., Yasin, M., & Sumiati, S. (2024). Designing EDGE (Enhanced destination growth and engagement) to Improve the performance of marine tourism in East Java. *Edelweiss Applied Science and Technology*, *8*(6), 8782–8792. DOI: 10.55214/25768484.v8i6.3875

Hamzah, A., Arifin, A., Abdullah, S., Salim, M. N. H. M., & Junaid, I. (2024). Empowerment of coastal communities through marine tourism: a functional approach. *Planning malaysia, 22*. DOI: 10.21837/pm.v22i34.1633

Hastuti, H., Muhidu, A., Rastin, R., & Mokodompit, E. A. (2023). Indonesia's Marine Economic Potential As A Maritime Country: *International Journal of Science. Technology & Management*, *4*(4), 813–825. DOI: 10.46729/ijstm.v4i4.897

Hutnaleontina, P. N., Bendesa, I. K. G., & Yasa, I. G. W. M. (2022). Correlation of community-based tourism with sustainable development to improve community welfare: A review. *International Journal of Applied Sciences in Tourism and Events*, *6*(2), 183–193. DOI: 10.31940/ijaste.v6i2.183-193

Ikhwani, H., Putro, M. H. M., Mustain, M., Satrio, D., Sujantoko, , Hadiwidodo, Y. S., & Nasution, P. H. O. (2023). The Concept of Integrated Coastal Management for Eco-Tourism Development at Dalegan Beach, Gresik Regency, East Java, Indonesia. *IOP Conference Series. Earth and Environmental Science*, *1198*(1), 012006. DOI: 10.1088/1755-1315/1198/1/012006

Kuba, D., Kuba, M. Z. D., & Usman, K. S. (2024). Community-Based Management: Marine Tourism Development for Ecological and Economic Sustainability. *Journal of Economic Education and Entrepreneurship Studies*, *5*(3), 467–479. DOI: 10.62794/je3s.v5i3.4372

Lasabuda, R. (2013). Pembangunan wilayah pesisir dan lautan dalam perspektif negara kepulauan republik indonesia. *Jurnal Ilmiah PLATAX*, *1*(2), 92–101. DOI: 10.35800/jip.1.2.2013.1251

Manalo, J. V. I., Bito-onon, J. B., Siason, N. D.Jr, & Blanza, M. G. (2024). *Analysis of stakeholders'knowledge, skills, attitudes, and practices: inputs for community-based ecotourism entrepreneurship development in tinorian river, iloilo, philippines. Proceeding of the International Conference on Family Business and Entrepreneurship.*

Mthuli, S. A., & Singh, N. (2024). State-led Maritime Governance, Education and Training Nexus in South Africa. *European Conference on Management Leadership and Governance, 20*(1), Article 1. DOI: 10.34190/ecmlg.20.1.2950

Nugroho, A., Suharyo, O. S., & Rahman, A. (2020). The development of indonesian maritime potential and prospects towards a world maritime axis. *Sttal postgraduate - international conference, 4*(1). https://seminarpasca-sttal.ac.id/seminar/index.php/seminarpasca-sttal/article/view/52

Nurawami, S. (2013). *Peranan Lembaga Keuangan Mikro dan Konstribusi Kredit terhadap Pendapatan Kotor UKM Rumah Tangga setelah menjadi Kreditur*. Jurnal Studi Kasus BMT Muamalat.

Nurhayati, A., Aisah, I., & Supriatna, A. K. (2019). Model Development of A Synergistic Sustainable Marine Ecotourism—A Case Study in Pangandaran Region, West Java Province, Indonesia. *Sustainability (Basel), 11*(12), 12. Advance online publication. DOI: 10.3390/su11123418

Nurlukman, A. D., Fadli, Y., & Wahyono, E. (2025). Ecotourism for Coastal Slum Alleviation: A Strategic Approach to Achieving the Sustainable Development Goals (SDGs) in Tangerang, Indonesia. *Journal of Lifestyle and SDGs Review, 5*(2), e02793–e02793. DOI: 10.47172/2965-730X.SDGsReview.v5.n02.pe02793

Oltean, F. D., Curta, P. A., Nagy, B., Huseyn, A., & Gabor, M. R. (2025). Changes in Tourists' Perceptions of Community-Based Ecotourism (CBET) After COVID-19 Pandemic: A Study on the Country of Origin and Economic Development Level. *ISPRS International Journal of Geo-Information, 14*(4), 4. Advance online publication. DOI: 10.3390/ijgi14040146

Phou, S., Uk, C., Chav, T., & Sou, V. (2025). Key Factors Influencing Environmentally Responsible Behavior in the Community-Based Ecotourism Development (CBET): Antecedents and Implications. *Open Journal of Ecology, 15*(1), 1. Advance online publication. DOI: 10.4236/oje.2025.151002

Pratama, F. W. N., & Jannah, M. R. (2024). *Community-based action plans for coastal area infrastructure enhancement: a strategy for sustainable tourism development. J.* Jurnal Pembangunan Pemberdayaan Pemerintahan., DOI: 10.33701/j-3p.v9i2.4715

Pristiyanto, . (2013). *Strategi Pengembangan Koperasi Jasa Keuangan Syariah dalam Pembiayaan Usaha Mikro di Kecamatan Tanjungsari, Sumedang*. Jurnal Manajemen IKM.

Rahayu, H. P., Comfort, L. K., Khoirunnisa, D., & Nurhasanah, D. (2024). Need Assessment for Coastal Tourism Area in the Face of Tsunami Risk: The Case of Pangandaran. *International Journal on Advanced Science, Engineering and Information Technology, 14*(2), 563–574. DOI: 10.18517/ijaseit.14.2.19985

Satria, A. (2010). Minapolitan dan Minapolitik. *ANTARA News*. http://www. antaranews.com /berita/1269867347/minapolitan-dan-minapolitik

Setiawan, I., Rianto, B., & Sudirman, . (2022). Implementation of coastal area management policy based on sustainable development in banyuwangi regency. *International Journal of Applied Research in Social Sciences*, *4*(2), 35–50. DOI: 10.51594/ijarss.v4i2.311

Setyaningsih, W., Yuliani, S., & Winarto, Y. (2019). *Beach Tourism Development Strategy through Ecological Architecture Approach in Pacitan.*, DOI: 10.2991/ senvar-18.2019.27

Shen, Z. (2020). Marketing Strategy of Marine Green Tourism. *Journal of Coastal Research*, *112*(sp1), 59–62. DOI: 10.2112/JCR-SI112-017.1

Sitompul, S. S. (2024). Ecotourism as Tourist Attraction Development: Systematic Literature Review. *Jurnal Penelitian Pendidikan IPA*, *10*(8), 606–612. DOI: 10.29303/jppipa.v10i8.8376

Suyadnya, I. W., Prianti, D. D., Kanto, S., & Putra, I. N. D. (2025). The local dynamics of global ecotourism trend in the old Balinese village, Indonesia. *Cogent Arts & Humanities*, *12*(1), 2451516. DOI: 10.1080/23311983.2025.2451516

Tuwo, A., Yunus, M., Aprianto, R., & Tresnati, J. (2021). Marine ecotourism development in South Sulawesi, Indonesia. *IOP Conference Series. Earth and Environmental Science*, *763*(1), 012068. DOI: 10.1088/1755-1315/763/1/012068

White, A., Rudyanto, , Agung, M. F., Minarputri, N., Lestari, A. P., Wen, W., Fajariyanto, Y., Green, A., & Tighe, S. (2021). Marine Protected Area Networks in Indonesia: Progress, Lessons and a Network Design Case Study Covering Six Eastern Provinces. *Coastal Management*, *49*(6), 575–597. DOI: 10.1080/08920753.2021.1967560

Yulianda, F. (2007). *Coastal ecosystem as alternatif for managing marine resources*. Seminar Sains, Bogor: Institut Pertanian Bogor.

Chapter 16
Acceleration Gap in Crypto Risk Governance and Early Warning Integration

Isman
https://orcid.org/0000-0002-0938-3533
Universitas Muhammadiyah Surakarta, Indonesia

Syamsul Hidayat
Universitas Muhammadiyah Surakarta, Indonesia

ABSTRACT

This study examines Islamic digital risk governance trends in Indonesia amid the disruption of financial technology. Employing a mixed-methods approach, this study integrates ex post facto analysis of secondary data from the OJK Banking Statistics Report 2024 with a thematic literature review. Regression and correlation analysis were applied to assess the relationship between complaints of illegal financial activity and LAPSK dispute resolution, yielding a strong positive correlation ($r^2 = 0.7801$). Thematic analysis reveals that digital financial fraud is evolving more rapidly than anticipated in the 2024–2028 OJK roadmap, which delays the implementation of early warning systems to later phases. This discrepancy highlights the urgency of implementing suptech and regtech from the outset. The research novelty lies in exposing the misalignment between digital risk acceleration and regulatory response timing, underscoring the need for early detection mechanisms as a foundational element of adaptive risk governance

DOI: 10.4018/979-8-3373-2655-9.ch016

INTRODUCTION

Normatively, the governance of digital risk in Indonesia's Sharia-based financial system is expected to proactively integrate Supervisory Technology (Suptech) and Regulatory Technology (Regtech) as an early warning system. This expectation is emphasized in the spirit of the OJK's digital transformation policy and the formulation of the Roadmap for Developing and Strengthening Crypto Assets 2024–2028 (Otoritas Jasa Keuangan, 2024b).

However, in practice secondary data from the 2024 OJK Banking Statistics indicates that the implementation of early warning mechanisms for crypto asset risk anomalies remains reactive, non-automated, and largely ex-post facto in nature. This finding reflects an uneven acceleration between the rapid growth of digital risk in the crypto sector and the preparedness of technology-based supervisory frameworks within the digital Sharia financial ecosystem (Otoritas Jasa Keuangan, 2024b).

Previous studies by Song and Tan (2024) analyzed the integration of smart contracts within the legal frameworks of Malaysia and Singapore. However, their focus was on the harmonization of common and Islamic law rather than on the systemic risk surveillance functions enabled by Suptech or Regtech (Judy Yueh Ling, Song; Esther, 2024). The findings of Alamsyah et al. (2024) proposed a taxonomy of DeFi risks but did not explicitly connect it with the national regulatory roadmap for developing and strengthening crypto assets. The BITPAYS study by Khairunnisa et al. (2024) demonstrated the potential of cryptocurrency in digital payment systems, but it overlooked its risk mitigation functions (Alamsyah & Syahrir, 2024; Judy Yueh Ling, Song; Esther, 2024; Khairunnisa et al., 2024a).

In contrast to these studies, this research introduces a novel approach by empirically and thematically examining the gap between OJK's 2024–2028 crypto strengthening policies and the realization of early-stage supervisory technology integration based on Suptech-Regtech, particularly within the Islamic financial ecosystem (Alamsyah & Syahrir, 2024; Khairunnisa et al., 2024b).

Although various studies have explored the potential of smart contracts, DAOs, and AI in enhancing digital asset governance, no research has explicitly addressed the acceleration gap between these technological advancements and the readiness of regulation and early warning systems in the context of crypto asset risk oversight. The study by Song and Tan (2024) addresses the legality of smart contracts, while G.I.R. Martha et al. (2023) focus on DAO concepts without addressing real-time governance integration. The studies of Rehan et al. (2024) and Mossavar Rahmani (2023) provide evidence on the effectiveness of AI in financial risk mitigation, yet they do not link this with the Suptech-Regtech roadmap in an institutional context (Ghimire & Jain, 2025; Gulo et al., 2024; Mossavar Rahmani, 2023).

Accordingly, the primary focus of this study is to bridge the gap between the current supervisory system and an adaptive, real time, and integrated early warning system that aligns with the regulatory roadmap. The findings are utilized to examine the regulatory roadmap for strengthening crypto assets by assessing the readiness of its three key pillars: digital asset governance, risk mitigation frameworks, and integrative technologies for supervision.

Based on the foregoing discussion, the urgency of Digital Risk Governance within Indonesia's financial ecosystem becomes evident. The expectation of integrating Suptech and Regtech as an Early Warning System in the OJK Roadmap 2024–2028 reflects a regulatory framework projected by the Financial Services Authority of Indonesia. However, the existing body of literature has not fully addressed the gap between the acceleration of digital risks and regulatory preparedness. Most prior studies have primarily emphasized formal legal aspects, such as legal harmonization or the potential of smart contracts, without directly linking them to technology-based digital risk surveillance functions.

Empirical findings regarding the strong correlation between the number of complaints on illegal financial activities and the resolution of LAPSK disputes ($r^2 = 0.7801$) validate the assumption that the dynamics of illegal digital financial activities advance more rapidly than the design of the Financial Services Authority's Roadmap. The fact that early detection systems are included only in the second and third phases of the roadmap highlights a significant acceleration gap. Since prior research has not yet addressed this issue, it becomes necessary to expand the literature by comparing regulatory design with the factual dynamics of digital crime growth, thereby more thoroughly elaborating on the gap.

Explicit studies such as those of Song and Tan (2024), Alamsyah et al. (2024), and Khairunnisa et al. (2024) indeed demonstrate strong relevance; however, they do not explicitly examine the readiness of Suptech and Regtech integration within the Early Warning System framework. Therefore, this topic should be strengthened by incorporating recent studies on the implementation of Suptech–Regtech in other jurisdictions (e.g., Singapore or the European Union), which have positioned early detection mechanisms at the initial stages of regulatory design. Such comparative perspectives would provide direction on how the phases of Indonesia's Financial Services Authority should be structured—whether at intermediate stages or, more critically, at the very outset of the OJK Roadmap 2024–2028.

Accordingly, Digital Risk Governance can be analyzed more systematically, not only from a normative standpoint but also in terms of empirical readiness and global best practices. Furthermore, it must be reaffirmed that the novelty of this research lies in identifying the acceleration gap between the rapid evolution of digital risks and the slower pace of regulatory design in integrating Suptech–Regtech as an Early Warning System. This design is crucial so that the findings of this study not only meet regulatory expectations but also emphasize the urgency of realizing an adaptive, real-time, and integrated digital supervisory system within the governance of crypto-asset risks.

LITERATUR REVIEW

Digital Asset Governance

In general, digital assets, such as cryptocurrencies, are defined as digital representations of value that can be traded, transferred, and stored electronically, often utilizing blockchain technology for enhanced security and decentralization. This definition does not originate from a single entity but evolves from various sources, including researchers, regulators, investors, and industry practitioners. The emergence of Bitcoin in 2009 marked the beginning of widespread awareness of cryptocurrencies, and subsequent studies have deepened the understanding of their characteristics and functions (Arminanto & Firmansyah, 2022; Parlika & Atmaja, 2020).

Literature on digital and crypto assets has been developed globally, including in Indonesia, reflecting significant interest and progress in this ecosystem. This ecosystem is important to continually analyze because of its dynamic and innovative nature; digital assets continuously introduce new use cases and regulatory challenges. Therefore, definitions must be adaptive and reflect current market and technological realities. Observing market phenomena, user behavior, and technological applications enables inductive research to formulate more comprehensive and accurate definitions that encompass the various forms and functions of emerging digital assets (Putri et al., 2023; Ruru et al., 2022).

The governance and ecosystem of digital or crypto assets remain in a dynamic developmental phase, involving several proven mediating and moderating variables that influence this independent variable. One significant mediating variable is legitimacy. Almahendra, Viyani, and Nabawi (2024) demonstrate that normative and cognitive legitimacy play a major role in public engagement in crypto markets. Public perception regarding the legitimacy and acceptability of crypto assets both in terms of social norms and cognitive understanding acts as a mediator between the existence of crypto assets and public participation (Almahendra et al., 2024; Meiryani, 2024).

Consumer understanding of their rights is another critical mediating variable, especially in crypto-based transactions within the metaverse. Findings by Putri et al. (2025) conclude that most respondents do not fully understand their rights in the context of crypto asset regulation. This argument suggests that consumer knowledge mediates the relationship between the crypto transaction environment and consumer protection. A limited understanding exacerbates risks for consumers, even though crypto assets offer fast, secure, and borderless transactions (Andiena Nindya Putri et al., 2025).

Another important mediating variable is government regulation. Research by Jutasompakorn et al. (2025) highlights government regulation as a configuration factor influencing crypto transactions. Clear or ambiguous regulations mediate how individuals participate in cryptocurrency transactions, affecting risk perception and trust. Therefore, government regulatory interventions serve as a mediator between the existence of crypto assets and levels of adoption and usage by the public (Jutasompakorn et al., 2025).

Perceived financial literacy also functions as a mediating variable. Jutasompakorn, Perdana, and Yeap (2025) identify perceived financial literacy as a key driver behind crypto transactions. Individuals' understanding and knowledge of finance and crypto markets mediate their investment or transaction decisions, which, in turn, influence overall market dynamics (Jutasompakorn et al., 2025).

Among moderating variables, perceived risk is one of the most prominent. A study by Jutasompakorn, Perdana, and Yeap (2025) finds that risk perception moderates the relationship between various drivers and crypto transactions. Highly risk-averse investors behave differently compared to risk-tolerant ones, even when presented with identical incentives. This risk tolerance level influences how businesses managing crypto assets respond to price volatility and potential fraud (Jutasompakorn et al., 2025; Perdana & Jhee Jiow, 2024).

Cognitive vulnerability is another confirmed moderator, particularly in cases of crypto fraud. Perdana and Jhee Jiow (2024) introduce the "Crypto-Cognitive Exploitation Model," which integrates cognitive, social, and technological perspectives. Cognitive vulnerability moderates how individuals process information and make decisions regarding crypto investments, increasing their susceptibility to fraud despite mitigation efforts (Perdana & Jhee Jiow, 2024).

Sharia law considerations also act as a moderating variable in crypto usage in Indonesia. Asyiqin et al. (2024) analyze the compatibility of crypto with Islamic Sharia law and classify such transactions as haram lighairihi due to elements of uncertainty (gharar) and speculative risk. This legal stance moderates adoption and acceptance of crypto within Indonesia's Muslim communities, limiting its potential as a medium of exchange or investment (Asyiqin et al., 2024).

Advanced technological infrastructure and online platforms also moderate the potential for money laundering through virtual currencies. Meiryani (2024) emphasizes that increasingly sophisticated technologies and platforms moderate the extent to which virtual currencies can be used for money laundering, thereby complicating law enforcement efforts. This finding suggests that technological advancements can either accelerate or slow illegal crypto-related activities (Meiryani, 2024).

In summary, robust regulatory and anti-money laundering (AML) policy frameworks such as those recommended by FATF act as moderators of money laundering and terrorism financing risks through crypto. Research by Anggriawan and Susila (2024) suggests that the characteristics of cryptocurrencies, such as anonymity and decentralization, pose challenges to AML/CFT frameworks. Thus, the effectiveness of regulation and inter-jurisdictional coordination moderates how well these risks can be managed and mitigated (Anggriawan & Susila, 2024).

Risk Mitigation Framework

The literature on crypto asset risk mitigation reveals an increasingly complex understanding of risk, which is no longer confined to price volatility alone but now includes cognitive, legal, technological, and public trust dimensions. In general, these risks refer to the potential for loss resulting from digital fraud, lack of transparency, technical weaknesses in blockchain systems, and regulatory uncertainty. From a scope perspective, crypto asset risks encompass fraud, market manipulation, cyberattacks, and system failure. Mitigating these risks is essential due to their impact on the stability of digital markets, public trust, and financial losses. In terms of locus, risks may arise across the entire spectrum of decentralized platforms, such as Vexanium, DeFi, and NFT marketplaces. From a temporal perspective, risks can emerge either latently or suddenly, for example, during periods of extreme investor fear or at the launch of a new crypto offering. The affected subjects include not only retail investors but also regulators and platform developers (Abou Ali, 2024; Abrar et al., 2024; Balqis et al., 2024; Multazam et al., 2023).

One proven mediating variable in crypto asset risk mitigation is the security of systems based on smart contracts. Alamsyah's (2024) research suggests that implementing multiple smart contracts in carbon tokenization plays a crucial role in enhancing transparency, efficiency, and trust, thereby indirectly reducing the risk of manipulation and transaction errors. Thus, smart contracts function as effective intermediaries between regulatory complexity and the digital market's demand for trust (Alamsyah et al., 2024).

The second mediator is cognitive education based on digital social vulnerability. In the study by Perdana and Jhee Jiow (2024), the "Crypto-Cognitive Exploitation" model was introduced, which explains that users' understanding of fraud schemes plays a crucial role in lowering vulnerability to scams. This education, grounded in cognitive vulnerability, serves as a bridge to transform risk perception and encourage safer investment behavior (Perdana & Jhee Jiow, 2024).

The third mediator is the understanding of DeFi taxonomy. In the research by Moppratama et al. (2024), a systematic mapping of DeFi's risks and benefits is used to assist regulators and users in navigating the decentralized finance ecosystem.

This taxonomy links risk comprehension with mitigation strategies, serving as a knowledge mediation tool between emerging technologies and decision-making frameworks (Moppratama et al., 2024).

The fourth mediator is the provision of real-time market information. The study by Rutskiy et al. (2023) reveals that in the NFT ecosystem, price assessments based on historical factors and industry sentiment rather than solely crypto market volatility allow investors to make more rational decisions. Consequently, historical data and NFT value indicators serve as important intermediaries in managing speculative risks (Rutskiy et al., 2023).

The first moderating variable influencing the relationship between crypto asset risk and mitigation is extreme investor sentiment. In the study by Ti and Husodo (2024), it is found that under conditions of extreme fear, investors tend to shift assets into stablecoins, which function as volatility buffers. This sentiment moderates how risk is perceived and how portfolios are dynamically reallocated to dampen market turbulence (Ti & Husodo, 2024).

The second moderator is the national legal framework for decentralized platforms. Research by Multazam et al. (2023) suggests that the absence of a clear legal framework for platforms like Vexanium results in legally weak liquidity contracts. Accordingly, regulatory clarity moderates the legitimacy of transactions and the sustainability of legal risk mitigation in crypto exchanges in Indonesia (Multazam et al., 2023).

The third moderating variable is the technical architecture of security based on Proof of Authority (PoA). In the study by Syahputra et al. (2023), the implementation of PoA in Ethereum-based smart home systems moderates the impact of DoS attacks and single points of failure. This finding demonstrates that a robust blockchain consensus design can mitigate systemic risk vulnerability without necessitating a comprehensive overhaul of the entire ecosystem (Syahputra et al., 2023).

The fourth moderator is the secure SDLC-based application development method. In the study by Tampati et al. (2023), the use of LSTM and GRU in phishing URL detection through mobile application development, which follows a secure development lifecycle, moderates the precision of digital threat detection. This finding suggests that system development processes also influence the success of mitigation against phishing-based attacks in the context of crypto assets (Tampati et al., 2023).

The fifth moderator is the cyber risk assessment framework used by local governments. Setiawan et al. (2023) demonstrate that the application of frameworks such as CVSS and CAPEC enables regional governments to classify cyber risks in their applications, which is also relevant for crypto asset platforms adopting standardized security approaches. Therefore, this risk assessment framework functions as a moderator for mitigation effectiveness by offering concrete threat classification guidelines (Setiawan et al., 2023).

The sixth moderator is an early detection system that combines behavior and anomaly detection. The study by Al-Rimy et al. (2018) suggests that combining behavioral estimation and anomaly detection through fusion improves the accuracy of crypto-ransomware detection. This system serves as a moderator that strengthens response mechanisms to zero-day threats while also reducing false alarms (Al-Rimy et al., 2018).

Overall, the findings from the above research trends suggest that crypto asset risks in Indonesia should not be approached solely through regulatory and supervisory dimensions but must also consider technological, educational, cognitive, and emotional aspects. Mediating variables such as smart contracts, cognitive education, DeFi taxonomy, and historical data have been shown to strengthen mitigation efforts. Meanwhile, moderating variables such as market sentiment, legal frameworks, blockchain architecture, secure SDLC, risk assessments, and early detection systems influence how effectively mitigation can be implemented. This argument suggests the need to investigate whether each of these variables is adequately addressed within an integrative and responsive roadmap for strengthening Indonesia's national crypto asset risk mitigation strategy.

Supervisory Technology and Regulatory Technology

Suptech (Supervisory Technology) and Regtech (Regulatory Technology) are two principal pillars in the evolving architecture of digital supervision and compliance, particularly in addressing the complexities of risk associated with crypto-assets. The core of Suptech and Regtech lies in their ability to detect, analyze, and respond to risks in real-time while facilitating automatic compliance with regulatory frameworks. Digital financial systems, particularly those based on crypto-assets, are characterized by decentralization, high volatility, and systemic risk challenges that cannot be managed through conventional regulation. For this reason, the adoption of Suptech and Regtech becomes essential.

The need for adaptive supervision has emerged due to shifts that can be traced back to the global financial crisis and the subsequent rise of blockchain technology. Stakeholders involved include regulators, crypto-asset platform operators, consumers (both retail and institutional investors), and technology developers. The implementation of Suptech and Regtech has expanded across various jurisdictions, including the European Union, ASEAN (notably Indonesia and Malaysia), and the Middle East (UAE), where key regulatory concerns center on transparency, efficiency, and Shariah compliance within the Islamic finance context.

Operational mechanisms integrate artificial intelligence, big data, blockchain, and predictive analytics to filter suspicious transactions, prevent fraud, and manage systemic risks in crypto-assets. Internally, the quality of data produced by Suptech systems serves as a mediating variable for regulators, enhancing risk-based decision-making processes. Arsyad et al. (2025) found that regulators within Islamic financial systems utilizing AI-based Suptech can more accurately identify potential Shariah violations and compliance risks through large-scale data analysis.

Without harmonized legal support, Suptech risks failing to provide legal safeguards in the decentralized crypto ecosystem. Consequently, the external moderating variable for regulators is the support of legal and international policies. Ponamorenko (2021) revealed that policy consistency among FATF, the IMF, and local regulators is a critical factor moderating the effectiveness of Suptech and Regtech in monitoring digital assets and ensuring the synchronized implementation of AML/CFT across borders.

Regtech enables platform operators to automatically detect transaction anomalies and potential fraud through the integration of intelligent algorithms, thereby enhancing compliance and reducing exposure to regulatory violations. From the operators' perspective, Breymann et al. (2024) identified internal system interoperability with Regtech as a key mediating variable in strengthening risk management.

Public trust in platforms will decline if supervisory negligence occurs, making the adoption of oversight technologies a market demand rather than merely a matter of normative compliance. Therefore, market reputation pressures and institutional investor expectations serve as external moderating variables for operators. Currie and Seddon (2024) asserted that conflicting stakeholder narratives create both social and market pressures that moderate the adoption of Regtech by operators.

Duta and Romo (2025) found that users with high literacy regarding transparency features based on blockchain and smart contracts demonstrate stronger capabilities in assessing system security, thereby fostering trust in automated supervision. This finding indicates that consumers (retail and institutional investors) are strongly influenced by internal mediating variables such as digital and financial literacy in utilizing Suptech-based platforms.

Educational initiatives from regulators, NGOs, and technology associations moderate the relationship between trust in Regtech and investment decisions within the crypto ecosystem. Hence, education provided by regulators and NGOs acts as an external moderating variable for consumers, as supported by previous studies highlighting the importance of educational ecosystems and consumer protection advocacy. Kimani et al. (2020) confirmed that without policy advocacy, the risk of asymmetric information remains high.

Lu (2024) emphasized that technology developers who integrate regulatory security and ethical standards from the outset possess a competitive advantage in bridging market needs and regulatory requirements. Thus, stakeholders such as AI and blockchain developers serve as internal mediating variables that determine the connection between technological innovation capabilities and compliance standards.

Kristanto and Arman (2022) demonstrated that regulatory sandboxes offer a secure environment for testing and validating Suptech technologies tailored to local needs, particularly for systems sensitive to Shariah principles and national legal frameworks. Therefore, regulatory sandboxes and experimental regulatory frameworks provided by governments or authorities function as external moderating variables that affect developers' compliance behavior.

In the context of Islamic financial institutions, Arsyad et al. (2025) demonstrated that the effectiveness of Suptech implementation in Shariah finance depends on the ability of Shariah boards to interpret technological data in a manner that upholds the principles of transparency and algorithmic fairness. Consequently, the technological competence of Shariah supervisory boards serves as an internal mediating variable, supporting regulatory compliance within crypto-asset management ecosystems.

Moreover, regulatory harmonization between Malaysia and Singapore in applying Shariah-compliant blockchain has been shown to moderate the effectiveness of Regtech adoption, preventing policy fragmentation that could hinder the growth of the digital Islamic economy. Thong (2025) confirmed that cross-jurisdictional harmonization functions as an external moderating variable.

From a systemic, multi-stakeholder perspective, the identified mediating variable is the cross-sector analytical capacity derived from the integration of Suptech systems across institutions. Breymann et al. (2024) concluded that data collaboration and real-time supervision among central banks, market authorities, and AML agencies create a comprehensive supervisory structure unattainable by siloed systems.

The systemic external moderating variable is the global volatility of crypto-asset markets. Under such conditions, stakeholder protection depends on the adaptive capacity of Suptech systems to respond to extreme and unpredictable market dynamics. As noted by Bertomeu et al. (2024), extreme fluctuations in global crypto-asset prices moderate the effectiveness of Suptech systems by challenging the resilience of risk detection algorithms developed from historical data.

An inductive analysis concludes that Suptech and Regtech do not function in isolation but depend on configurations of interacting mediating and moderating variables across stakeholders, categorized into internal and external dimensions. It is, therefore, essential to examine whether the 2024–2028 roadmap for Shariah-compliant crypto-asset development in Indonesia, issued by the Financial Services Authority (OJK), has comprehensively anticipated the challenges and solutions in implementing supervisory technologies in the crypto-asset era.

METHOD

This study employs a mixed-methods approach by integrating quantitative and qualitative methods simultaneously to investigate the acceleration strategies for addressing the governance gap between Crypto Risk and Early Warning Integration. On the quantitative side, secondary data were processed using the ex post facto method, sourced from the 2024 FSA Banking Statistics Report. Inferential analysis techniques, particularly regression and correlation, were applied to examine the relationship between the number of complaints related to illegal financial activities and the intensity of dispute resolution handled by LAPSK.

From the qualitative perspective, the researcher conducted an in-depth literature review to identify thematic indicators that are not captured by statistical figures, such as institutional responses, adaptive policy frameworks, and stakeholder perceptions regarding regulatory lag. Thematic analysis was used to construct conceptual domains that explain how the accelerating dynamics of digital fraud have not yet been fully accommodated within the FSA's supervisory framework.

Triangulation was performed by combining official statistical data, literature review findings, and cross-domain thematic analysis in a complementary manner. This integration enabled the research to interpret the structurally driven quantitative data with a deeper understanding derived from interpretative qualitative approaches. Thus, the research reasoning flows from identifying statistical causal relationships toward a comprehensive explanation of the contextual factors that either strengthen or weaken the effectiveness of digital financial risk supervision.

RESULTS AND DISCUSSION

To examine the problem statement regarding the Acceleration Gap in Crypto Risk Governance and Early Warning Integration, particularly in the context of Trends on Islamic Digital Risk Governance in Indonesia during the era of financial technology disruption, this research focuses on two main areas. First, it presents descriptive findings that integrate qualitative and quantitative analysis through the lens of illegal financial activities in Indonesia, referencing the most recent data from the OJK Report as of April 2025. Second, it offers a discussion that aims to explain the relationship between the data findings and previous relevant studies, both within the context of fraud theory and Islamic risk governance.

Domain of Complaints on Illegal Financial Activities in Indonesia. Complaints regarding illegal financial activities essentially reflect the risk potential in crypto asset management.

Figure 1. Complaints on illegal digital finance (Otoritas Jasa Keuangan, 2024a)

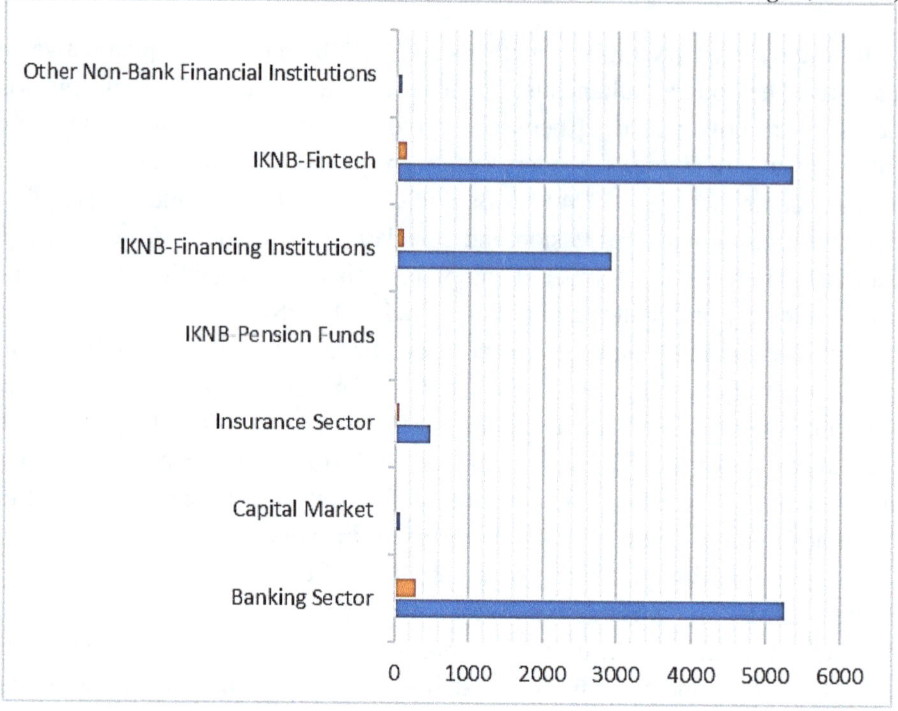

The data presented above illustrate complaints and dispute resolutions across various financial service sectors. Each row represents a financial service category, while columns indicate the number of "Illegal Financial Activity Complaints" and "Dispute Resolutions."

Overall, the compiled data from the April 2025 statistical report by the Department of Supervision and Consumer Protection reflects the interaction dynamics between consumers and financial service providers within the scope of illegal financial activity. A high number of complaints indicates growing consumer awareness and a willingness to report harmful practices. It also implies a systemic gap allowing such illegal activities to proliferate, demanding further efforts in self-assessment by financial institutions to prevent them.

The banking sector recorded 5,249 complaints related to illegal financial activities, making it the domain with the highest number of consumer complaints. This significant figure necessitates stricter self-assessment measures by banks to ensure compliance with consumer protection regulations. This finding is unsurprising, given the extensive reach of banking services that most consumers utilize.

The capital market sector recorded only 80 complaints, suggesting that consumers in this domain may be more cautious in identifying disputes. However, only 15 cases were resolved, indicating that the sector still requires improved dispute resolution efforts and stricter regulatory intervention by the FSA.

In the non-bank financial industry (IKNB), the insurance sector received 471 complaints, with 57 resolved disputes. These figures indicate a need for early preventive measures through institutional self-assessment to minimize potential disputes and ensure consumer rights. The data reflects consumer trust levels in insurance products and services in Indonesia.

The pension fund sector within IKNB reported only 12 complaints and zero dispute resolutions. This finding may stem from the long-term and complex nature of pension products, leading to lower consumer awareness of potential issues. Nonetheless, this low number should still prompt the development of proactive, risk-based regulatory reinforcement.

In the financing sector of IKNB, 2,918 complaints were reported, with 103 resolved disputes. This high number underscores the crucial role of the Financial Services Sector Dispute Resolution Institution (LAPS SJK) in mediating disputes, especially given the frequency of transactions in this domain, including auto loans and multipurpose credit.

Fintech, another sector within IKNB, recorded the highest number of complaints at 5,330, even surpassing the banking sector. This finding strongly suggests a high incidence of online lending issues and other illegal financial activities in the fintech ecosystem. It calls for serious attention from regulators and financial service providers to enhance self-assessment mechanisms and educate consumers on the risks inherent in fintech, especially illegal online loans.

The high number of complaints in the fintech and online lending sectors reflects emerging challenges in consumer protection. Cooperation with the Regional Financial Access Acceleration Team (TPAKD) can help disseminate information on the dangers of illegal online loans. Additionally, LAPS SJK plays a vital role in handling disputes arising from online lending services, given their fast-paced and often opaque transactional nature.

Other IKNB categories recorded 72 complaints and six resolved disputes, suggesting various forms of illegal financial activities not covered under the previous categories. Although smaller in number, this segment still demands attention and self-assessment from relevant financial service providers to ensure no protection gaps remain.

This data highlights the critical role of LAPS SJK in facilitating dispute resolution between consumers and financial service providers, especially considering the diversity of sectors and volume of complaints. Moreover, collaboration among financial service providers in conducting self-assessments and consumer education potentially supported by TPAKD is key to mitigating the risks of illegal financial activities and restoring public trust in the financial services sector.

When structured around the core gap between crypto risk and early warning integration, it becomes clear that three major factors contribute to the emergence of risk in crypto asset management: price volatility, transactional anonymity, and weak legal oversight. These factors collectively create systemic vulnerabilities that increase the likelihood of digital fraud in crypto risk management. The OJK report indicates that the high number of complaints in the fintech sector, totaling 5,330, also reflects risks in crypto asset management tied to these three aspects. These risks incentivize manipulative practices, such as ICO fraud or front-running, which are rooted in inadequate oversight and digital fragility.

Based on the OJK report, the low number of resolved disputes compared to complaints for instance, only 103 out of 5,330 fintech complaints resolved by LAPS SJK indicates an underdeveloped early warning system that is incapable of detecting fraud signals before they escalate into legal disputes. The consequences of the three core risks in crypto asset management reduce the effectiveness of the Early Warning Integration System (EWIS), which relies on three critical components: real-time fraud detection, AI-based predictive analytics, and cross-sector interoperability. This system is not only designed for early detection but also as a structural response to systemic risks emerging from the digitalization of financial services.

Therefore, as the complexity and unpredictability of crypto risks increase, the need for a robust Early Warning System becomes even greater. The high volume of fintech complaints underscores that, without robust integration, crypto transaction risks will remain undetected, leading to increased consumer disputes.

The same report further suggests that systemic gaps such as weak real-time auditing, insufficient consumer education, and inadequate use of bot and encryption technologies widen opportunities for fraud. In other words, even though the crypto risk business process is inherently high, fraud will not manifest without these three mediating variables. This finding suggests that crypto risk does not automatically lead to disputes, but instead requires the presence of systemic complaints.

Weak oversight of digital infrastructure is evident in the low-dispute resolution rate, coupled with high volumes of fintech complaints. This finding shows that, without addressing systemic opportunity gaps, the early warning system cannot function effectively due to a lack of valid early signals. In other words, weak real-time audits, lack of consumer education, and inadequate bot/encryption technologies create additional causal pathways for undermining the Early Warning System. These risks, in turn, foster fraudulent practices such as wash trading and rug pulls.

The moderating variable of digital regulatory transparency either strengthens or weakens the relationship between crypto risk and EWIS. Suppose crypto and fintech regulations are applied transparently (e.g., regular digital asset reporting, public audits of whitepapers, or Sharia certification for DeFi platforms). In that case, the link between risk and the need for an early warning system is weakened, as risk is mitigated proactively. Conversely, if regulations are unclear or unenforced, crypto risks escalate rapidly into legal disputes.

The lack of minimum compliance standards and self-assessment by financial service providers heightens the probability of undetected risks. Thus, if regulatory transparency truly functions as a gatekeeper between fraud and mitigation systems, the fintech sector's high complaint volume 5,330 complaints with only 103 resolved should have been addressed more significantly.

OJK's report also shows pressure in other sectors, such as financing (2,918 complaints) and insurance (471 complaints). This finding indicates that risk pressure does not stem solely from pure crypto issues, but also from uneven digital adoption. Therefore, crypto risk must be understood not just as a technological problem but also as a broader digital transformation issue that creates behavioral pressures, fraud opportunities, and systemic gaps across various non-bank financial sectors.

By integrating OJK's findings with the Fraud Triangle Theory, it can be concluded that high crypto risk stems from increased real-time fraud detection, AI-based predictive analytics, and cross-sector interoperability, leading to a greater need for an Early Warning Integration System (Y). The strength of this relationship is moderated by the degree of regulatory transparency, making the EWIS effective only when it controls for the above three risk factors while protecting vulnerable links in the risk chain. The moderator variable encompasses regulatory transparency and algorithm transparency utilized in innovative contract governance for cryptocurrency assets.

The implication of this systematization is the necessity for a holistic approach that not only improves the technological aspect (system Y) but also strengthens the regulatory framework (moderator) and manages fraud opportunities (mediator). Institutions such as LAPS SJK and TPAKD should be encouraged to be more proactive in consumer education and in supporting financial institutions' self-assessments. A risk-based supervisory system, especially in fintech and crypto asset sectors, must be paired with regulatory transparency that can prevent fraud before it escalates into legal disputes.

To examine the correlation between the number of complaints and the capacity to resolve disputes, a scatter diagram is presented below:

Figure 2. Scatter diagram of the correlation between the number of complaints and the ability to resolve disputes

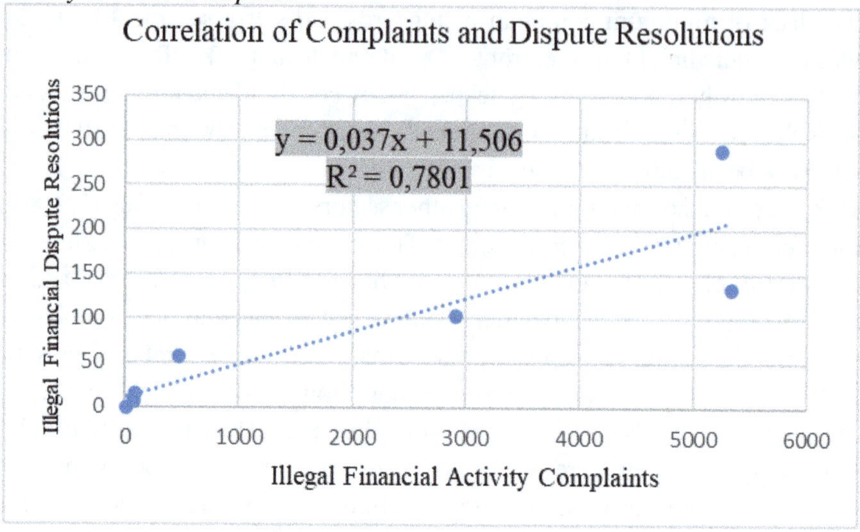

The correlation test between illegal financial activity complaints and dispute resolution outcomes reveals an R^2 value of 0.7801 and a regression equation of y = 0.037x + 11.506. This finding indicates a strong positive relationship. The regression coefficient of 0.037 implies that for every unit increase in complaints, the number of disputes resolved increases by an average of 0.037 units. An R^2 value of 0.7801 suggests that the variation in the number of complaints can explain 78.01% of the variation in resolved disputes. This finding suggests that the volume of illegal financial complaints is a strong predictor of the number of disputes resolved, indicating a substantial relationship between the two variables.

This strong positive correlation ($R^2 = 0.7801$) suggests that the dispute resolution system is efficient. It indicates that existing processes, procedures, and resources are sufficiently effective in managing fluctuating workloads and achieving a high dispute resolution rate as case volume increases. Therefore, the OJK's consumer complaint system remains responsive to increasing volumes, though it must enhance resolution capacity.

The significant R^2 value offers a basis for forecasting future dispute resolutions based on projected complaint volumes. For instance, if 6,000 complaints are projected and input into the model (Y = 0.037X + 11.506), the projected dispute resolution capacity is 233 cases. However, this correlation does not establish a pure causal relationship, as other variables outside the model likely influence dispute resolution outcomes. Thus, the forecast serves as a directional guide, not a definitive certainty.

DISCUSSION

Based on the explanation above, it is concluded that there is a continuity between empirical data from OJK reports and the international knowledge corpus in understanding the crypto asset ecosystem and its risk mitigation framework. Through the triangulation of OJK's April 2025 statistical findings, for example, moderator variables in literature are proven to align with the risk patterns emerging from OJK data. The OJK's findings, which reveal a high number of consumer complaints, particularly in the fintech sector (5,330 complaints) and the banking sector (5,249 complaints), indicate the presence of systemic risk. In the literature, this condition is described as part of risk perception and cognitive vulnerability, which have been identified as moderator variables in studies by Jutasompakorn et al. (2025) and Perdana & Jhee Jiow (2024). Specifically, these studies suggest that investors' risk tolerance and cognitive ability can moderate decision-making in crypto asset transactions.

Tjondro et al. (2025) demonstrated that risk tolerance and cognitive capacity, represented through the Big Five personality traits, moderate vulnerability to investment fraud among university students aged 18–24. Individuals with open, extroverted, and neurotic characteristics tend to have higher risk tolerance, which affects impulsive investment decisions and susceptibility to fraud. This finding is relevant to the relationship between crypto risk and the effectiveness of mitigation systems through the Early Warning System, as decisions influenced by risk tolerance and cognitive capacity increase exposure to crypto risks. Therefore, this study supports the claim that these psychological variables moderate decision-making in crypto asset transactions, particularly among high-risk demographic groups, such as young investors who have yet to fully comprehend the dynamics of digital asset risk.

Consumer understanding and technological integration in crypto transactions are not merely theoretical assumptions but are validated through regulatory and supervisory practices in Indonesia. This is evidenced by OJK data, which indicates the importance of self-assessment efforts by businesses and consumer education, particularly in sectors with a high number of complaints, such as fintech, insurance, and financial institutions. This is reinforced by the findings of Putri et al. (2025) and Alamsyah (2024), which state that financial literacy and the use of smart contracts are important mediator variables in reducing risk and increasing transparency.

However, several moderator and mediator variables are transnational or systemic and are thus not fully accommodated in OJK's current regulatory structure, especially in the management of crypto assets. Mediator variables such as Regtech system interoperability and cross-sectoral analytical capacity, as proposed by Breymann et al. (2024), have not been explicitly reflected in OJK's 2025 complaint and response system. Similarly, legal support across jurisdictions, international Shariah frameworks, and Proof of Authority (PoA) as technological moderators are not reflected in OJK reports, which focus more on consumer operations and dispute resolution.

Putra & Amiruddin's (2023) research proposes a national IDNat-Blockchain architecture based on Proof of Authority (PoA) and PBFT, with a strong emphasis on system interoperability and cross-sector scalability, grounded in digital identity and population data governance rather than crypto-compliant systems or financial authority responses, such as those from the OJK. This finding indicates that until 2025, there is no explicit evidence that OJK has adopted cross-sectoral interoperability, PoA, or legal support across jurisdictions in its complaint system. OJK's efforts have been more focused on complaint volume, dispute resolution, and consumer education, rather than predictive analytics or cross-legal framework crypto risk modeling as outlined by Breymann et al. (2024). Hence, these technological and structural elements are not yet reflected in OJK's Early Warning System framework, which remains reactive rather than integrative across crypto risk domains.

A strong positive correlation ($R^2 = 0.7801$) exists between the number of complaints regarding illegal financial activities and the number of resolved disputes, implying institutional efficiency in responding to escalating risks. This finding suggests that several mediator and moderator variables identified in the literature are not fully supported in this context.

Among these are normative and cognitive legitimacy variables (Almahendra et al., 2024), which, according to the literature, play a significant role in shaping public participation in crypto markets; however, they do not appear in the dispute resolution prediction model and thus cannot be tested for significance in OJK's risk anticipation capacity. Consumer understanding of their rights (Putri et al., 2025), positioned as a mediator in crypto-based consumer protection, is also not verified in the statistical correlation model, as it focuses on volume and response speed without assessing perception or interaction quality.

In terms of strengthening or weakening factors in the relationship between crypto risk and the Early Warning System, cognitive vulnerability and risk perception variables (Perdana & Jhee Jiow, 2024; Jutasompakorn et al., 2025), considered to moderate investment decision-making in crypto assets, are not reflected in the direct relationship between complaint volume and dispute resolution. Likewise, systemic variables such as Shariah principles, AML/CFT capacity, or cross-jurisdictional RegTech interoperability (Anggriawan & Susila, 2024; Meiryani, 2024) are not visible in OJK's quantitative projections.

According to Arner et al. (2019), a digital identity system built within the Know Your Customer (KYC) context requires cross-jurisdiction interoperability to be widely adopted by financial institutions. A specific finding indicates that the success of digital identity infrastructure depends on registration mechanisms, data availability, and cross-jurisdiction recognition, which directly demands the technical and legal interoperability of systems. Thus, system interoperability is not merely an added feature but a core prerequisite for Regtech systems to function effectively across entities and jurisdictions, particularly in strengthening digital KYC systems. Interoperability in this context refers not only to data exchange but also to the integration of standards, protocols, and cross-regional recognition that ensures the validity and effectiveness of digital identity data within the financial risk mitigation framework. Therefore, it can be concluded that interoperability is a structural element inseparable from Regtech design, particularly in the domains of digital identity and Early Warning Systems.

Consequently, although the correlation model used is valid and strong, it has yet to capture the socio-cultural, psychological, and cross-jurisdictional complexities that are widely highlighted in international literature. Meanwhile, OJK's findings support the literature that emphasizes the importance of regulatory institutional capacity as the central pillar of the Early Warning System, particularly in developing countries. The effectiveness of LAP SJK in managing the increase in dispute volume demonstrates that structural and operational variables such as processes, procedures, and human resources play a dominant role in responding to crypto risk, as indirectly indicated by Alamsyah (2024) and Ruru et al. (2022).

The strong correlation between complaints and dispute resolution suggests that institutional response effectiveness in addressing crypto risk may serve as a previously underexplored structural mediator in the literature. The adaptive capacity of supervisory institutions (LAP SJK) may now be considered as an institutional mediator that bridges the increase in illegal financial risk and the effectiveness of the early warning system. The adaptive capacity of LAP SJK provides empirical evidence for extending the literature on digital asset governance through institutional strengthening. According to Kadioglu Kumtepe (2025), the positive correlation between crypto risk and dispute resolution is mediated by digital enforcement tools and moderated by decentralized protocols. The higher the crypto risk, the more necessary adaptive and automated resolution systems become, as proposed in the decentralized justice approach (Ast et al., 2023). This finding suggests the need for integrating blockchain and smart contracts into dispute resolution systems, enabling automated compliance-based adjudication mechanisms to enhance legal certainty. In the crypto context, the high potential for fraud and non-compliance triggers a high intensity of disputes; therefore, using digital systems based on escrow, automated adjudication, and consensus-based verification is imperative.

This study proposes that the dispute resolution capacity of digital supervisory institutions should be added to the list of moderator and mediator variables within the digital asset governance framework, especially in developing countries that are gradually building their crypto oversight systems. This finding enriches previous user-focused understandings (investors and consumers) by adding an institutional dimension that is quantitative and measurable through efficiency indicators such as correlation coefficients, regression, and dispute resolution capacity.

About the discussion between risk management framework literature and the above correlation test findings, several moderator and mediator variables are not confirmed in the correlation findings, such as extreme investor sentiment, understanding of DeFi taxonomy, and the national legal system framework, which in the literature are proven to significantly determine crypto risk mitigation effectiveness. However, they are not reflected in the correlation model between complaints and dispute resolution ($R^2 = 0.7801$).

This finding indicates that the projection model in this study is linear and deterministic, excluding complex moderator and mediator variables such as risk literacy, system security, and public risk perception, which theoretically mediate or moderate the relationship between complaints and disputes. Despite the qualitative alignment in the interpretation of correlation test results, a contradiction arises because the effectiveness of dispute resolution in OJK's model is based on the volume of complaints. In contrast, the crypto risk literature identifies numerous non-quantitative factors that influence the effectiveness of conflict mitigation.

Meanwhile, the strong positive correlation found in LAP SJK contributes a new extension to crypto risk management literature as it indicates that dispute resolution systems can be predicted quantitatively based on complaint volume, opening the door for a data-based Early Warning System. Regarding mediator variables, this finding expands the literature by showing that complaint volume itself can serve as a risk leading indicator, not merely a consequence, which has not yet been widely considered in crypto mitigation frameworks. From the moderator's perspective, this model implies a systemic need to incorporate dynamic response mechanisms, such as behavior-based early detection, market sentiment, or legal structures, as filters influencing resolution speed and success, which have not yet been modeled in OJK's findings. The integration of sectoral operational data (complaints) into the logic of digital risk governance expands the role of mediator and moderator variables from a purely techno-cognitive basis to also administrative and predictive dimensions.

From the perspective of Regtech and Suptech studies, when discussed alongside the correlation finding between the number of illegal financial activity complaints and dispute resolution capacity ($R^2 = 0.7801$), an interesting result is the non-confirmation of internal mediator variables such as Regtech system interoperability (Breymann et al., 2024). Also unconfirmed is digital consumer literacy (Duta & Romo, 2025), which was previously considered crucial in supporting dispute resolution efficiency in the literature. Instead, the findings emphasize that quantitative inputs such as complaint volume can linearly predict dispute resolution outcomes. However, the study does not further discuss technological processes or digital education variables as connecting factors.

Conversely, the role of external moderators, such as market reputation pressure and international regulatory harmonisation (Ponamorenko, 2021; Currie & Seddon, 2024), in moderating the effectiveness of Regtech-Suptech has not been confirmed, despite being considered in the literature. Instead, this study offers a novel insight that quantifying complaint workload can serve as an early warning system for predicting resolution capacity. This finding adds to our understanding that complaint volume itself can serve as a systemic indicator, eliminating the need for advanced technological intermediaries. This finding is an important addition to risk management literature, which has focused too much on system complexity without testing the validity of input data as a predictor. It broadens the risk framework to include operational predictability based on public complaints rather than just the capabilities of sophisticated Regtech/Suptech systems.

By converging the digital asset governance framework, the risk mitigation framework, regtech, and suptech with OJK 2025 data and international literature, several key mediator and moderator variables were identified. The identified mediator variables include financial literacy, the use of smart contracts, the capacity for institutional dispute resolution, and the volume of public complaints, all of which are leading indicators of crypto risk. Significant moderator variables included risk tolerance, cognitive vulnerability, stakeholder personality structure, and decentralised protocols. However, factors such as Regtech interoperability, cross-jurisdictional legal support, and normative legitimacy were not empirically confirmed in this research model due to the linear, deterministic paradigm based on a quantitative approach. These findings suggest that the effectiveness of mitigating crypto risk is strongly influenced by the interaction between psychological, institutional, and decentralised technological factors, which are not fully reflected in the OJK regulatory system.

One of the critical aspects that requires further examination is the more profound interconnection between Digital Risk Governance and the effectiveness of the Early Warning System in the context of crypto-asset risk management. While this chapter has addressed the regulatory direction of the Financial Services Authority of Indonesia (OJK R.I.), it has not systematically explored how the acceleration of OJK's roadmap can respond to the rapid escalation of risks in the digital financial sector. Such an acceleration of risks creates a tangible gap in adaptability between the regulation and the continuously evolving dynamics of the crypto market. Therefore, it is essential to elaborate on how digital risk governance can serve as a strategic framework to ensure that the early warning system operates proactively rather than reactively.

In addition, the dimensions of Suptech (supervisory technology) and Regtech (regulatory technology) remain underexplored. The discussion does not sufficiently explain how the integration of these technologies could bridge the acceleration gap by enabling real-time supervision, big data analytics, and early detection of risk patterns. For instance, it is crucial to specify at which stage OJK may leverage Suptech to strengthen adaptive supervisory mechanisms, while industry actors may deploy Regtech to ensure automated compliance and enhance data transparency.

Another missing element is a discussion on the technical and institutional architecture of the early warning system. Future research should explain how a Suptech–Regtech–based early warning system can be designed to mitigate crypto-specific risks such as price volatility, market manipulation, or liquidity risks, all of which may have implications for the stability of the digital financial system. Such institutional design should go beyond normative legal frameworks and instead serve as an operational guideline for regulators and market participants alike. Adding technical details regarding system design would enhance the practical relevance of this chapter to digital risk governance.

Equally, the chapter does not provide an adequate discussion on the role of data governance in supporting the effectiveness of the early warning system. Strong data governance constitutes the cornerstone for the successful integration of Suptech and Regtech. The availability of real-time data, interoperability across institutions, and robust cybersecurity standards are prerequisites for ensuring the accuracy of risk detection. Addressing this aspect would enable the Financial Services Authority's policy transformation agenda to establish stronger linkages between data governance and digital risk governance, thereby reinforcing systemic resilience in the digital financial ecosystem.

Given the cross-border nature of crypto risks, it is also highly relevant to examine how Indonesia can learn from international best practices in employing Suptech and Regtech to strengthen Digital Risk Governance. For instance, the European Union's Markets in Crypto-Assets (MiCA) regulatory framework and the Monetary Authority of Singapore's (MAS) initiatives in developing Regtech sandboxes serve as valuable references. Including a comparative analysis of such practices would not only enrich the theoretical framework of this chapter but also provide policymakers with practical directions to narrow the acceleration gap, which constitutes the core issue under discussion.

CONCLUSION

Based on the above findings and the interpretation of data from the OJK's 2025 crypto risk management capacity model, it can be demonstrated that interoperability is not the primary factor in the development of an early warning system for crypto risk. Instead, the reporting structure of public complaints against illegal entities, institutional responses to fraud patterns identified through information systems, and connectivity between complaints, supervision, and delays in executing administrative sanctions are proven to play a significant role. There is no evidence to suggest that regulatory capacity or relevant literature directly supports the claim that Regtech interoperability is a key factor in the effectiveness of systems for the early detection of crypto risk. Theoretically, the effectiveness of early warning systems in crypto surveillance is determined more by internal governance loops than by cross-jurisdictional Regtech interoperability. This finding strengthens the theory of a domestic, data-based institutional response. Practically, this research finding encourages strengthening the integration of complaint data, rapid institutional responses, and local fraud pattern processing, rather than relying on cross-border technological harmonization. Therefore, crypto-asset management should prioritise improving national capacity in detection, response, and execution rather than investing in interoperable systems of untested relevance in Indonesia.

REFERENCES

Abou Ali, A. A. K. (2024). DeFi era: The behavioral intentions toward cryptocurrency in Lebanon. *Innovation & Management Review*, *21*(4), 274–285. DOI: 10.1108/INMR-02-2023-0022

Abrar, A., Naeem, M. A., Karim, S., Lucey, B. M., & Vigne, S. A. (2024). Shining in or fading out: Do precious metals sparkle for cryptocurrencies? *Resources Policy*, *90*, 104722. Advance online publication. DOI: 10.1016/j.resourpol.2024.104722

Al-Rimy, B. A. S., Maarof, M. A., Prasetyo, Y. A., Shaid, S. Z. M., & Ariffin, A. F. M. (2018). Zero-day aware decision fusion-based model for crypto-ransomware early detection. *International Journal of Integrated Engineering*, *10*(6), 82–88. DOI: 10.30880/ijie.2018.10.06.011

Alamsyah, A., Kusuma, G. N. W., & Ramadhani, D. P. (2024). A Review on Decentralized Finance Ecosystems. *Future Internet*, *16*(3), 76. Advance online publication. DOI: 10.3390/fi16030076

Alamsyah, A., & Syahrir, S. (2024). A Taxonomy on Blockchain-Based Technology in the Financial Industry: Drivers, Applications, Benefits, and Threats. In *Blockchain and Smart-Contract Technologies for Innovative Applications* (pp. 91–129). Springer Nature Switzerland., DOI: 10.1007/978-3-031-50028-2_4

Almahendra, R., Viyani, A. O., & Nabawi, M. (2024). Is crypto legitimate? Study on the relationship between legitimacy and public engagement on crypto market in Indonesia. *Intangible Capital*, *20*(2), 393–411. DOI: 10.3926/ic.2425

Andiena Nindya Putri, P. A., Widyastuti, T. V., Dewi, G. A. K. R. S., Udin, A. F., Irdhayanti, E., & Harahap, K. (2025). Navigating Consumer Rights and Ethical Advertising in the Metaverse: A Comprehensive Case Study of Cryptocurrency Users in Indonesia's Digital Economy. In *Studies in Systems Decision and Control* (Vol. 234). DOI: 10.1007/978-3-031-84636-6_11

Anggriawan, R., & Susila, M. E. (2024). Cryptocurrency and its Nexus with Money Laundering and Terrorism Financing within the Framework of FATF Recommendations | Las criptomonedas y su nexo con el lavado de dinero y la financiación del terrorismo en el marco de las recomendaciones del GAFI. *Novum Jus*, *18*(2), 249–277. DOI: 10.14718/NovumJus.2024.18.2.10

Arminanto, E. R., & Firmansyah, K. A. (2022). Bitcoin's Position in Indonesian Currency Law. *Indonesian State Law Review*, *5*(2), 67–78. DOI: 10.15294/islrev.v5i2.47491

Asyiqin, I. Z., Akbar, M. F., & Beltrán Genovés, M. (2024). Cryptocurrency as a Medium of Rupiah Exchange: Perspective Sharia Islamic Law and Jurisprudential Analysis. *Volksgeist Jurnal Ilmu Hukum Dan Konstitusi*, *7*(2), 277–292. DOI: 10.24090/volksgeist.v7i2.10975

Balqis, A., Alamsyah, A., & Tricahyono, D. (2024). Web3 Adoption: Impact on Digital Industries. *2024 3rd International Conference on Creative Communication and Innovative Technology Iccit 2024*. DOI: 10.1109/ICCIT62134.2024.10701160

Ghimire, A., & Jain, P. T. (2025). AI-Driven Drug Repurposing for Oncology: Identifying Novel Cancer Treatments from Existing Drugs. *Journal of Biosciences and Medicines*, *13*(05), 197–220. DOI: 10.4236/jbm.2025.135016

G. I. R. Martha, F. L. Gaol, S. H. Supangkat and B. Ranti, "Utilization of Decentralized Autonomous Organization (DAO) for Virtual Property Transaction Governance in Metaverse: A Conceptual Framework," *2023 3rd International Conference on Intelligent Cybernetics Technology & Applications (ICICyTA)*, Denpasar, Bali, Indonesia, 2023, pp. 306-311, doi: 10.1109/ICICyTA60173.2023.10429035.

Gulo, H., Bate'e, M. M., Telaumbanua, E., & Lase, H. (2024). Analysis of Human Resource Development Training in Improving Employee Performance. *Golden Ratio of Data in Summary*, *4*(2), 467–472. DOI: 10.52970/grdis.v4i2.565

Judy Yueh Ling. Song; Esther, T. (2024). Beyond traditional contracts: the legal recognition and challenges of smart contracts in Malaysia and Singapore. *Journal of Law, Market & Innovation, 3*(3), 323–357. https://ojs.unito.it/index.php/JLMI/article/view/11334/9303

Jutasompakorn, P., Perdana, A., & Yeap, L. H. (2025). Discerning the Key Drivers behind Cryptocurrency Transactions: Identifying the Configurational Factors. *Pacific Asia Journal of the Association for Information Systems*, *17*(1), 5–29. DOI: 10.17705/1pais.17102

Khairunnisa, H., Zairin, G. M., Budianto, P., Ramadhani, N. A., Septiani, M., & Musyaffi, A. M. (2024a). BITPAYS: Leveraging Bitcoin for Digital Payments to Fuel Economic Growth in Indonesia's Society 5.0 Era. *2024 International Conference on Electrical, Computer and Energy Technologies (ICECET*, 1–6. DOI: 10.1109/ICECET61485.2024.10698372

Khairunnisa, H., Zairin, G. M., Budianto, P., Ramadhani, N. A., Septiani, M., & Musyaffi, A. M. (2024b). BITPAYS: Leveraging Bitcoin for Digital Payments to Fuel Economic Growth in Indonesia's Society 5.0 Era. *International Conference on Electrical Computer and Energy Technologies Icecet 2024*. DOI: 10.1109/ICECET61485.2024.10698372

Meiryani. (2024). Exploration of potential money laundering crimes with virtual currency facilities in Indonesia. *Journal of Money Laundering Control, 27*(6), 985–994. DOI: 10.1108/JMLC-01-2023-0010

Moppratama, Y. A., Alamsyah, A., & Tricahyono, D. (2024). Blockchain-Based Property Sukuk Models for the Indonesian Market. *2024 International Conference on Artificial Intelligence Blockchain Cloud Computing and Data Analytics Icoabcd 2024*, 107–112. DOI: 10.1109/ICoABCD63526.2024.10704239

Mossavar Rahmani, F. (2023). The Transformative Impact of AI on Financial Institutions, with a Focus on Banking. *Journal of Engineering and Applied Sciences Technology*, 1–6. DOI: 10.47363/JEAST/2023(5)192

Multazam, M. T., Huzairin, R. A., & Prataman, S. P. (2023). Is It Legal to Provide Liquidity on the Vexanium Decentralized Exchange in Indonesia? *Yustisia, 12*(1), 29–46. DOI: 10.20961/yustisia.v12i1.69007

Otoritas Jasa Keuangan, R. (2024a). *Laporan Surveillance Perbankan Indonesia Triwulan IV 2024.* https://ojk.go.id/id/kanal/perbankan/data-dan-statistik/laporan-profil-industri-perbankan/Documents/Laporan Surveillance Perbankan Indonesia - Triwulan I 2024.pdf

Otoritas Jasa Keuangan, R.. (2024b). *Peta Jalan Pengembangan dan Penguatan Inovasi Teknologi Sektor Keuangan, Aset Keuangan Digital dan Aset Kripto 2024-2028.*

Parlika, R., & Atmaja, P. W. (2020). Realtime monitoring of Bitcoin prices on several Cryptocurrency markets using Web API, Telegram Bot, MySQL Database, and PHP-Cronjob. *Proceeding 6th Information Technology International Seminar Itis 2020*, 253–257. DOI: 10.1109/ITIS50118.2020.9321109

Perdana, A., & Jhee Jiow, H. (2024). Crypto-Cognitive Exploitation: Integrating Cognitive, Social, and Technological perspectives on cryptocurrency fraud. *Telematics and Informatics, 95*, 102191. Advance online publication. DOI: 10.1016/j.tele.2024.102191

Putri, T., Amiludin, A., Ahmad, D. N., & Hidayatulloh, H. (2023). Inadequate Cryptocurrency and Money Laundering Regulations in Indonesia (Comparative Law of US and Germany). *Yustisia, 12*(2), 129–152. DOI: 10.20961/yustisia.v12i2.71835

Ruru, B., Tjager, I. N., Mayasari, A., Adhistita, A. M., Raffi, H. A., & Santro, A. (2022). THE IMPACT OF CRYPTO-ASSET UTILISATION AS PAYMENT INSTRUMENT TOWARD THE RUPIAH AS LEGAL TENDER IN INDONESIA. *Journal of Central Banking Law and Institutions, 1*(1), 141–180. DOI: 10.21098/jcli.v1i1.6

Rutskiy, V., Allam, S., Elkin, S., Beknazarov, Z., Semina, E., Ikonnikov, O., Kuzmich, R., & Tsarev, R. (2023). Non-fungible Tokens: Value for Digital Arts and Pricing Factors. In *Lecture Notes in Networks and Systems: Vol. 596 LNNS*. DOI: 10.1007/978-3-031-21435-6_70

Setiawan, E., Nugroho, L. E., & Hartanto, R. (2023). Designing a Cybersecurity Risk Assessment Framework for Local Government Web-Based Applications. *Proceeding 2023 2nd International Conference on Computer System Information Technology and Electrical Engineering Sustainable Development for Smart Innovation System Cosite 2023*, 61–66. DOI: 10.1109/COSITE60233.2023.10249788

Syahputra, B. I., Marlena, D., Priambodo, D. F., & Arizal, A. (2023). Ethereum Smart Home for Denial of Service and Single Point of Failure. *Electronics (Basel)*, *27*(2), 50–63. DOI: 10.53314/ELS2327050S

Tampati, I. F., Komang Setia Buana, I., & Setiawan, H. (2023). Secure Mobile Application for Uniform Resource Locator (URL) Phising Detection based on Deep Learning. *2023 1st International Conference on Advanced Engineering and Technologies Iconnic 2023 Proceeding*, 231–236. DOI: 10.1109/ICONNIC59854.2023.10467246

Ti, A., & Husodo, Z. A. (2024). Navigating volatility spillover amidst investor extreme fear in stablecoin and financial markets. *Cogent Economics & Finance*, *12*(1), 2408276. Advance online publication. DOI: 10.1080/23322039.2024.2408276

Chapter 17
The Impact of Greenwashing on the ESG Score Moderated by Carbon Emissions: Evidence From ASEAN Region

Nurul Nazlia Jamil
https://orcid.org/0000-0003-2471-9397
Universiti Sains Islam Malaysia, Malaysia

Ersa Tri Wahyuni
Universitas Padjajaran, Bandung, Indonesia

Peni Nugraheni
Universitas Muhammadiyah Yogyakarta, Indonesia

ABSTRACT

In the ASEAN region, greenwashing undermines ESG credibility, especially among high carbon-emitting firms, where discrepancies between sustainability claims and actual environmental impact lead to lower ESG scores. This study aims to examine the relationship between greenwashing on the ESG score moderated by carbon emission in the context of ASEAN region (Malaysia, Indonesia, Thailand and Singapore). Data from the 2,301 listed firms were downloaded from the Refinitiv Eikon database. The final data from 652 companies with 2,102 observations during the period 2020–2023 to test the study model effectively. By using random effects model, the findings indicate that greenwashing score negatively affects the ESG score for the companies. Furthermore, carbon emissions play a detrimental and significant moderating role in the association between greenwashing and ESG scores.

DOI: 10.4018/979-8-3373-2655-9.ch017

Our findings addressing greenwashing requires coordinated action between firms, regulators, and rating agencies to ensure ESG disclosures reflect real progress not just public relations strategies.

INTRODUCTION

Investors are progressively utilizing Environmental, Social, and Governance (ESG) metrics to assess a company's ethical standards and sustainability efforts. However, a growing concern is greenwashing where firms exaggerate or falsify their environmental initiatives to appear more sustainable than they are (In & Schumacher, 2021; Ben Mahjoub, 2025). This practice may distort ESG scores and mislead stakeholders. In the ASEAN region, where climate risks and sustainable development pressures are intensifying, the prevalence and consequences of greenwashing remain underexplored. This study aims to investigate how greenwashing affects ESG scores in ASEAN countries and how carbon emissions moderate this relationship. According to Avramov et al. (2022), ESG is a term used to define how a business measures its environmental and social impact. It is usually used in an investing context, but it is applied in all areas, from customers and suppliers to employees and advertisements.

Given the increasing importance of ESG factors in investment decisions and corporate valuation, understanding the accuracy and credibility of ESG reporting is crucial. Greenwashing can misguide investor decisions, inflate company valuations, and ultimately undermine trust in sustainability frameworks. Furthermore, in ASEAN countries where ESG regulations and enforcement mechanisms are still developing companies may find opportunities to exploit weak oversight. Therefore, this study not only seeks to uncover the extent of greenwashing in the region but also evaluates the role of carbon emissions transparency in shaping stakeholder reactions and ESG assessments. The findings can inform policy interventions and promote more authentic corporate sustainability practices.

As individuals and governments increasingly prioritize the reduction of both direct and indirect CO2 emissions, it is important to note that the majority of global CO2 emissions are actually produced by businesses rather than these entities (Renukappa et al., 2013; Al Amosh & Khatib, 2024). Consequently, the role of private companies is critical in the fight against climate change. In the current landscape, numerous corporations are actively promoting their commitment to environmental, social, and governance (ESG) principles, with executives publicly declaring their goals of achieving net-zero emissions by 2050. Nevertheless, such commitments may sometimes serve as mere greenwashing tactics or lead to "brownscraping," which can mislead consumers, investors, and regulators regarding a company's genuine environmental impact. Furthermore, even the establishment of science-based emission targets may obscure underlying systemic problems, highlighting the necessity for a robust market for environmental standards and certifications (Kurpierz & Smith, 2020).

Numerous companies profess their commitment to achieving net-zero emissions, yet they often neglect to confront the fundamental environmental impact of their offerings. A case in point is Shell, which, despite its public assertions of dedication to sustainability, was unable to provide a strategy for mitigating the climate impact of its products by 2050 when questioned. This phenomenon, known as greenwashing, involves organizations making inflated assertions regarding their environmental efforts to project an image of sustainability, while failing to implement meaningful changes in their operations, thereby reducing sustainability to mere marketing rhetoric (Gala, 2023; Gentile & Gupta, 2025).

The motivations for achieving favorable ESG recognition, whether for reputational enhancement or financial benefits through increased investor access or grants, suggest that companies may exaggerate their environmental performance when self-reporting (Ben Mahjoub, 2025). As noted by Courtat et al. (2023), the implementation of third-party ecological standards and certifications can enhance transparency and accountability by ensuring that sustainability claims are supported by verifiable, science-based criteria. For instance, ISO 14001 certifies that organizations possess a concrete Environmental Management System, thereby reducing the potential for greenwashing through unfounded assertions of commitment. This certification obligates companies to adhere to environmental standards that emphasize strategic planning, risk assessment, legal compliance, performance monitoring, and the enhancement of environmental performance.

Over the past ten years, there has been a significant increase in investor interest in sustainable assets, which are evaluated based on their ESG metrics to establish their sustainability credibility (Gutiérrez-Ponce & Wibowo, 2023). In the absence of independently verified environmental standards, investors may inadvertently fund projects that continue unsustainable practices while falsely claiming adherence to net-zero commitments. Furthermore, greenwashing fosters a misleading perception of progress, as both consumers and policymakers might be led to believe that companies are affecting meaningful change in addressing climate change, despite the prevailing conditions remaining largely unchanged. This misinformation can hinder regulatory initiatives and diminish public backing for essential policy reforms, as the urgency of their requirements appears diminished. Nevertheless, the rising awareness of such practices has correspondingly heightened the demand for environmental certification standards, as those misled increasingly recognize the necessity of understanding the broader context.

This issue is particularly critical in the ASEAN region, where regulatory frameworks for ESG reporting are still evolving, and environmental challenges, such as high carbon emissions, are pressing. While ESG scores are designed to reflect true sustainability performance, there is growing evidence that companies may use greenwashing tactics to inflate these scores without making substantive environmental improvements (Ang, 2024). At the same time, carbon emissions remain one of the most quantifiable indicators of a firm's environmental impact. The degree to which carbon emissions influence the relationship between greenwashing and ESG scores remains largely unexamined within the context of ASEAN economies (Baratta et al., 2023; Treepongkaruna et al., 2024). Failing to address this gap may result in ESG scores inaccurately reflecting corporate behavior, which could lead to misallocation of capital, misinformation among stakeholders, and ineffective policy measures. While ESG scores are widely used by investors and researchers to assess corporate sustainability, they are not without limitations. These scores often rely heavily on self-reported data, which may be unaudited, inconsistent across firms, or biased toward favorable disclosure. Moreover, scoring methodologies vary across rating agencies (e.g., Refinitiv, Morgan Stanley Capital International (MSCI), Bloomberg), leading to significant divergence in ESG ratings for the same firm (Keeley et al., 2022). This inconsistency raises concerns about the reliability and comparability of ESG scores as objective performance indicators.This research aims to explore the effects of greenwashing on ESG scores in ASEAN firms, while also assessing whether carbon emissions serve as a moderating variable that either reveals or obscures greenwashing activities. Gaining insight into this relationship is essential for enhancing the accuracy of ESG ratings, promoting transparency, and advancing sustainable development initiatives in the region.

LITERATURE REVIEW

Greenwashing

As public demand to tackle the climate crisis intensifies, companies in the private sector are increasingly participating in the shift towards a low-carbon global economy. Nevertheless, their initiatives may occasionally resemble more of a promotional strategy rather than genuine, impactful measures. Greenwashing is defined as instances where a corporation makes deceptive assertions regarding their beneficial environmental effects or the sustainability of their offerings, aiming to persuade consumers that they are actively addressing climate change (In & Schumacher, 2021; Baratta et al., 2023; Treepongkaruna et al., 2024). In certain instances, greenwashing may occur unintentionally due to a lack of understanding of environmental matters.

However, it can also be executed deliberately as a marketing and public relations tactic, capitalizing on public enthusiasm for environmental policies to generate profit.

The practice of greenwashing undermines public trust in sustainability efforts and permits detrimental environmental effects to persist without restraint. A survey published by ESG Today in late 2024 found that 85% of investors now believe that greenwashing is more common than it was five years ago, which has fueled demands for tougher penalties and independent audits (Ben Mahjoub, 2025). Experts emphasize that only verified, accurate reporting can drive meaningful changes. Organizations are urged to implement independent audits and obtain third-party certifications to substantiate their environmental assertions with quantifiable actions, as regulatory bodies contemplate more severe penalties for deceptive practices.

The South Asian Federation of Accountants (SAFA) has also emphasized the need for standardized sustainability reporting across the region (Tran et al., 2021). Recent discussions within SAFA have focused on ensuring that companies operating in South Asia adhere to ESG reporting frameworks and avoid misleading disclosures that could misguide investors and stakeholders. The International Federation of Accountants (IFAC) has taken key initiatives by introducing IFRS S1 and S2, aiming to standardize sustainability disclosures globally (Yoon et al., 2024; Gaviria et al., 2023) While these standards enhance transparency and comparability, they still have shortcomings. The primary challenges include the lack of enforcement mechanisms, sector-specific nuances, and potential loopholes in climate-related financial disclosures that companies might exploit.

Another major concern is the fragmented landscape of sustainability reporting, where different regulatory bodies and international organizations have introduced their own reporting guidelines (Sisaye, 2021). This lack of a unified framework gives investors room to selectively interpret and apply sustainability standards to their advantage, sometimes enabling misleading claims about a company's true environmental impact. The inconsistency across frameworks such as GRI, SASB, TCFD, and IFRS S1 & S2 creates gaps that allow companies to present an overly positive image while avoiding accountability in areas where their impact is less sustainable (Gopal & Pitts, 2025). Several studies have highlighted the drivers of greenwashing, including external pressures from investors, regulatory gaps, media scrutiny, and competitive dynamics (Gala, 2023). In regions with weak environmental governance or immature ESG disclosure standards such as parts of the ASEAN region greenwashing is more likely to thrive due to limited enforcement and lack of transparency (Treepongkaruna et al.,2024).

This fragmented reporting environment not only complicates stakeholder evaluation but also undermines the reliability of ESG ratings, as data quality and comparability vary significantly across firms and jurisdictions. Without standardized and mandatory disclosure requirements, companies can cherry-pick metrics that cast them in a favorable light while omitting material sustainability issues. This selective reporting fosters a credibility gap, where ESG scores may not accurately reflect a firm's actual environmental or social performance. In the ASEAN context, where regulatory development is still evolving and enforcement is often inconsistent, the absence of a harmonized sustainability framework exacerbates the risk of greenwashing. As investors increasingly rely on ESG indicators for decision-making, there is a pressing need for coherent, regionally aligned reporting standards that ensure consistency, comparability, and transparency. Strengthening regulatory oversight and promoting adherence to globally recognized frameworks such as IFRS S1 and S2 could help mitigate the risk of misleading disclosures and reinforce stakeholder trust in ESG reporting.

To bridge these gaps, regulators and standard-setting bodies must mandate independent third-party audits, impose stricter penalties for misleading claims, and ensure real-time monitoring of ESG commitments. True sustainability reporting should not only focus on disclosure but also on measurable impact and accountability to prevent greenwashing and build a genuinely sustainable future.

ESG Score

ESG's roots were found alongside CSR, as investors started aligning their portfolios with personal and social values. But it was by the 1990s that ESG really took off, with the Global Reporting Initiative (GRI) and the UN Global Compact's arrival. Its inclusion in a 2004 UN report and the Paris Agreements of the 2010s boosted its popularity (Cheng & Micale, 2022). Today, ESG is a critical part of any corporate strategy and investment decision-making. It is widely used and has gained further importance with the rise of new sustainable regulations and concerns in the wake of the climate crisis.

The metrics used to measure ESG will vary, as they are typically set by analysts looking to study specific issues in their sectors (Keeley et al., 2022; Atkins et al., 2023). For example, an analyst may track the investments made by a business in partners that support the environment, their published sustainability reports, diversity statistics, and data on working with questionable workplace practices. Environmentally speaking, metrics are likely to include greenhouse gas emissions, energy usage, water usage, waste management, and biodiversity impact. Globally, many companies have also signed up to agreements that see them follow sustainability and ethical practices. Such as the United Nations Global Compact (more than 24,000 businesses) and the Global Reporting Initiative (with 78% of the world's largest 250 companies).

ESG scores are composite indicators that aim to evaluate a company's performance across environmental, social, and governance dimensions. Rating agencies such as MSCI, Refinitiv, and Bloomberg apply different methodologies, leading to variations in scores for the same firm (Berg et al., 2022). Despite these inconsistencies, ESG scores remain influential in investment decision-making, particularly in socially responsible and ESG-themed funds. Research has shown that ESG scores are susceptible to manipulation, particularly through narrative disclosures (Amel-Zadeh & Serafeim, 2018). Firms engaging in greenwashing may achieve high ESG scores by emphasizing policies and initiatives while downplaying actual outcomes. This distortion compromises the integrity of ESG as a sustainability benchmark and can mislead stakeholders, especially in emerging markets with limited ESG auditing mechanisms.

Carbon Emissions as Moderator

Carbon emissions serve as a direct and quantifiable measure of a company's environmental impact. Unlike qualitative ESG disclosures, emissions data when accurately reported offer a grounded assessment of a firm's sustainability (Renukappa et al., 2013). However, not all firms are equally transparent, and voluntary disclosure regimes often result in underreporting or inconsistent emissions data. Studies suggest that high carbon-emitting firms may engage more frequently in greenwashing to offset reputational risk (Kim & Lyon, 2015). Conversely, when carbon emissions are included in ESG evaluations, they can act as a counterbalance to narrative manipulation, thus improving the objectivity of ESG scores (Chatterji et al., 2016). Although carbon emissions are typically included within the environmental pillar of ESG scores, these scores are often compiled using a mix of self-reported, voluntary, and sometimes unaudited data. As such, they may not fully reflect the firm's true environmental impact. In this study, carbon emissions are treated as a separate, quantifiable metric used to test whether firms with high emissions are able to sustain inflated ESG scores through greenwashing. This approach is crucial because ESG ratings can obscure rather than reveal greenwashing if carbon-related disclosures are selectively emphasized or manipulated. The role of carbon emissions as a moderating variable highlighting discrepancies between reported sustainability practices and actual environmental harm has gained attention but remains under-researched in the ASEAN context.

Given the partial integration of emissions data into ESG scores, there is a risk of overlap, but also of misrepresentation. Firms may report basic emissions figures to boost ESG performance without making meaningful environmental improvements. Therefore, this study treats carbon emissions as a separate variable measured as carbon intensity (emissions per revenue) to test its moderating role on greenwashing and ESG score outcomes. This methodological choice enhances transparency and supports clearer causal interpretation.

The ASEAN region presents a unique research environment, characterized by diverse regulatory standards, varying levels of ESG maturity, and growing foreign investor interest in sustainability. While some countries like Singapore have advanced ESG disclosure guidelines, others still lack mandatory reporting requirements (ASEAN Capital Markets Forum, 2022). This regulatory asymmetry creates uneven incentives for greenwashing and leads to variability in ESG score reliability across the region. Existing literature on greenwashing in ASEAN is sparse but growing. Studies have highlighted inconsistencies in ESG disclosures, particularly in high-emission sectors such as energy and manufacturing (Ng et al., 2021). However, there is limited empirical research examining how carbon emissions influence the relationship between greenwashing and ESG scores in this regional context a gap this study aims to address.

THEORETICAL FRAMEWORK

This study investigates the relationship between greenwashing and ESG scores, with carbon emissions as moderating variable, using insights drawn from legitimacy theory and stakeholder theory (Wai-Khuen et al., 2023; Kim et al., 2024;Del Gesso & Lodhi. 2025). These theories provide a multidimensional lens to understand how and why firms may engage in greenwashing, how ESG scores may reflect (or misrepresent) such behavior, and how objective environmental metrics like carbon emissions can influence this dynamic.

Legitimacy Theory suggests that organizations strive to align their operations with the societal norms and expectations prevalent in their respective environments. As sustainability and ESG concerns become more prominent among stakeholders, companies are motivated to demonstrate alignment with environmental and social values (Wai-Khuen et al., 2023). However, in contexts where there is a gap between actual performance and stakeholder expectations, firms may resort to greenwashing to maintain legitimacy without enacting substantial changes. In the ASEAN region, where ESG regulatory frameworks are still evolving, firms may perceive greater opportunity or need to engage in greenwashing to satisfy legitimate demands from international investors or the public, especially when facing reputational pressure. This theory helps explain why firms engage in symbolic ESG disclosures, supporting Hypothesis 1.

Stakeholder Theory posits that the success of a firm is dependent on its capacity to effectively manage relationships with a diverse array of stakeholders, which encompasses investors, customers, regulatory bodies, and the broader civil society. Firms may engage in greenwashing as a tactic to appease stakeholders demanding sustainable practices while avoiding costly operational changes. In ASEAN countries, where enforcement mechanisms may be weaker, stakeholder influence on corporate behavior can vary significantly. Some firms may find greenwashing a low-cost strategy to meet stakeholder expectations, especially when ESG performance is judged based on non-verifiable indicators (Del Gesso & Lodhi, 2025). This forms the basis of Hypothesis 2, where carbon emissions are expected to moderate the greenwashing ESG score relationship.

Carbon emissions offer an objective, quantifiable measure of environmental impact. As such, they serve as a reality check on greenwashing claims. From a theoretical standpoint, carbon emissions moderate the relationship between greenwashing and ESG scores in which are revealing effect which is high emissions may expose greenwashing practices by creating an inconsistency between reported ESG efforts and environmental harm, thereby weakening the positive impact of greenwashing on ESG scores (Treepongkaruna et al.,2024).

This moderating role is critical in the ASEAN context, where carbon-intensive industries coexist with relatively weak emissions disclosure mandates. The framework posits that the impact of greenwashing on ESG scores depends on the degree and clarity of carbon emissions. In regions where emission data is vague or inconsistently reported, greenwashing may go unnoticed, leading to inflated ESG ratings. Conversely, where carbon disclosures are more transparent and standardized, inconsistencies between actual performance and sustainability claims become more visible, prompting greater scrutiny and reputational risk. Therefore, enhancing carbon disclosure regulations across ASEAN is essential to mitigate greenwashing and strengthen ESG assessment reliability. Together, these theories offer complementary perspectives: while Legitimacy Theory explains firms' motivations for symbolic compliance, Stakeholder Theory highlights the risks of reputational backlash in high-emission contexts. These insights form the basis for the hypotheses tested in this study.

Hypothesis Development

Greenwashing allows firms to present themselves as more environmentally responsible than they are in reality, often through promotional language, selective reporting, or omission of negative information. While ESG rating agencies aim to evaluate corporate sustainability objectively, they frequently rely on self-reported or unaudited data, especially for environmental disclosures. As a result, companies that effectively greenwash can obtain higher ESG scores without making substantive environmental improvements. Similarly, greenwashing proxies such as the difference between disclosure scores (Bloomberg) and performance scores (Refinitiv) offer useful insights but have limitations. These proxies assume that higher disclosure relative to performance implies exaggeration, but may not account for timing differences, industry nuances, or genuine efforts in progress. Therefore, while this approach is grounded in prior research (Yu & Chen, 2024), it may not fully capture the complexity of corporate sustainability behavior or intentional deception.

A multitude of research indicates that companies participating in symbolic sustainability initiatives frequently receive enhanced ESG ratings, despite a lack of correspondence between their genuine environmental performance and these reported efforts (Walker & Wan, 2012). This observation gives rise to the initial hypothesis:

H1: Greenwashing has a negative effect on ESG scores among firms in the ASEAN region.

Carbon emissions are a direct and quantifiable indicator of a company's environmental footprint. Unlike subjective sustainability narratives, emissions data when reliably disclosed can reveal the real environmental performance of a firm. High carbon emissions, especially when inconsistent with green claims, may signal to ESG raters or stakeholders that a firm is overstating its environmental commitments (Renukappa et al., 2013; Kim & Lyon, 2015).

In this context, carbon emissions are proposed as a moderate variable that may weaken the relationship between greenwashing and ESG scores (Chatterji et al., 2016). That is, while greenwashing may generally lead to higher ESG scores, the presence of high emissions could reduce the credibility or perceived effectiveness of greenwashing, thereby diluting its positive impact on ESG ratings.

Conversely, when emissions are low or underreported, the effects of greenwashing on ESG scores may remain strong and unchallenged. Therefore, the second hypothesis is:

H2: Carbon emissions negatively moderate the relationship between greenwashing and ESG scores, such that the positive effect of greenwashing on ESG scores is weaker for firms with higher carbon emissions.

This set of hypotheses supports the conceptual model in which greenwashing influences ESG evaluations, but the extent of this influence depends on the firm's carbon emissions profile a crucial dynamic for understanding corporate sustainability transparency in the ASEAN context.

RESEARCH DESIGN

Data and Sample

The ASEAN region (Malaysia, Indonesia, Thailand and Singapore) was selected for this study due to its distinct features and increasing importance in the context of global sustainability. First, ASEAN is a vibrant group of developing nations that are rapidly expanding economically and assimilating into the global economy. Given that this growth trajectory calls for a simultaneous focus on sustainable development, ASEAN is a relevant context for analyzing the relationship between business sustainability practices and economic advancement (Abu Afifa et al.,2025).

Second, the economic systems, legal frameworks, and cultural backgrounds of ASEAN members differ greatly from one another (Nesadurai, 2008). This diversity makes it possible to conduct a thorough analysis of the ways in which national characteristics affect business sustainability performance as well as the caliber of sustainability reporting. Third, nations in Southeast Asia are under increasing pressure to solve urgent environmental issues such pollution, deforestation, and climate change (Van and Afifa, 2024). Effective sustainability reporting is crucial as a means of encouraging accountability, transparency, and stakeholder involvement because of this urgency. In this context, it is especially pertinent to look at how carbon emissions moderate the relationship between sector characteristics and reporting quality.

In total, data points from 2,301 publicly traded companies were extracted from the Refinitiv Datastream. Following a thorough screening process (refer to Table 1), the final sample consisted of 652 companies, encompassing 2,102 observations across different years. Furthermore, companies that (1) operated within the banking or financial sectors, or any fund-related sectors, and (2) had been delisted from the capital market, including those undergoing rehabilitation, were excluded from this analysis. The final samples were characterized by unbalanced panel data.

Table 1. Research sample

Criteria	Number of Firms
Listed Companies with ESG Score in Refinitive Database	2301
Less:Missing Information about ESG	1570
Less: Incomplete data (carbon emission)	(79)
Total sample	652

Source: Refinitive Eikon Database

Data Collection and Variable Measurement

Refinitiv supplied data spanning the years 2020 to 2023. The dependent variable, ESGSCORE, represents the comprehensive score of a company derived from self-reported data within the environmental, social, and governance dimensions, as recorded in the Refinitiv Eikon database. Refinitiv ESG scores were selected in this study because they reflect actual performance across environmental, social, and governance pillars, based on over 500 metrics compiled from publicly available and verifiable data. This makes them a reliable proxy for firm-level ESG outcomes. While for Bloomberg ESG disclosure scores, on the other hand, assess the extent of

ESG-related information disclosed by firms, without directly measuring performance. This distinction is important: a firm may disclose extensively (high Bloomberg score) while underperforming on actual ESG metrics (low Refinitiv score), making this combination ideal for identifying potential greenwashing behavior. While MSCI ESG ratings are commonly used in sustainability research, they are more qualitative and opaque, relying on proprietary models and analyst assessments that are not always reproducible or fully disclosed. Moreover, MSCI data coverage for the sample was limited and less consistent than that of Refinitiv and Bloomberg. Therefore, the selection of Refinitiv and Bloomberg supports both conceptual clarity and empirical feasibility in identifying discrepancies between ESG disclosure and actual impact.

Meanwhile, for the greenwashing score, which measures the extent of a company's ESG greenwashing, is the independent variable. Bloomberg scores evaluated a company's ESG disclosure in accordance with earlier research (Yu & Chen, 2024; Yu, Guo & Luu, 2018). Bloomberg's ESG disclosure scores represent the breadth and completeness of ESG-related information disclosed by a company, rather than actual sustainability performance. The score ranges from 0 to 100 and reflects the percentage of applicable ESG data points publicly reported by the company, based on Bloomberg's ESG framework. Refinitiv scores were used to assess the companies' ESG performance (Del Bosco & Misani, 2016). Better ESG performance is indicated by higher scores on Refinitiv's ESG pillars, which likewise range from 0 to 100. Equation 1 displays the greenwashing score for each company and year, based on the methodology put forward by Yu & Chen (2024) to measure the extent of a company's ESG greenwashing conduct.

$GW_{it} = PB_{it} - Pr_{it}$ (Equation 1)

Where:

GW_{it}: ESG greenwashing score relative to peers

PB_{it}: Bloomberg ESG standardized score relative to peers

PR_{it}: Refinitive ESG standardized score relative to peers

Yu & Chen (2024) claim that a corporation is sharing more ESG information than it is actually doing when its Bloomberg disclosure score is higher than its Refinitiv performance score. They engage in greenwashing as a result. In contrast, a corporation is not engaging in greenwashing when its Bloomberg Disclosure Score is less than or equal to its Refinitiv Performance Score. This implies that the company discloses as much ESG information as it does.

While for the moderator, carbon emission is total of CO2 equivalent emission to revenue in USD. Currently, a limited number of corporations are willingly revealing carbon emission statistics. Some researchers have chosen to obtain carbon emission data from corporate reports; nonetheless, this method results in a limited sample size, primarily consisting of firms with high pollution levels. This approach has several limitations. This study cites recent findings (Jiang & Tang, 2023) and calculates corporate carbon emissions using data on industry-level carbon emissions. The intensity of corporate carbon emissions is measured as the ratio of corporate carbon emissions to total revenue. This method allows for consistent measurement across firms regardless of individual reporting practices and helps reduce potential greenwashing bias, where companies underreport or omit emissions data.

While this approach does not capture firm-specific emissions exactly, it aligns with emerging research norms in ESG and climate-finance studies involving cross-country samples with partial data coverage (Kim & Lyon, 2015; Baratta et al., 2023). It provides a reliable proxy for environmental impact when firm-level emissions are unavailable or not assured. Future research could improve precision as more firms adopt standardized carbon disclosure frameworks like IFRS S2 or TCFD. A summary of the variable measurement is presented in Table 2.

Table 2. Variable measurement

Variables	Acronym	Measurement
Greenwashing Score	GW	ESG greenwashing score relative to peers
ESG Score	ESG Score	Overall company score based on self-reported information in the environmental, social and governance pillar (Refinitiv Eikon database)
Carbon Emission	CARBON	Total CO2 Equivalent Emissions to Revenues USD in million (Refinitiv Eikon database)
Firm Size	FIRMSIZE	Natural log of total assets
Leverage	LEVERAGE	Total debt to total assets
Age	AGE	The natural logarithm of the firm age since its initial public offering

Model Specification

This study seeks to analyse the impact of greenwashing on the ESG Score moderated by carbon emission. In accordance with methodologies employed in analogous research, the study established the subsequent fundamental regression model:

$$ESGSCOREi,t = \alpha i + \beta_1 GWi,t + \beta_2 FIRMSIZE\ i,t + \beta_3 LEVERAGEi,t + \beta_4 AGEi,t + \varepsilon i,t \quad (1)$$

While to test H2, this study employs a moderation effect of carbon emission. The model to test H2 is as follows:

$$ESGSCOREi,t = \alpha i + \beta_1 GWi,t + \beta_2 GWxCARBONEMISSIONi,t + \beta_3 FIRMSIZEi,t + \beta_4 LEVERAGEi,t + \beta_5 AGEi,t\ \varepsilon i,t \quad (2)$$

First, panel data analysis was carried out using both fixed effects (FEM) and random effects (REM) estimations. However, further analyses were conducted in order to identify potential bias resulting from variance heterogeneity in short interval panel data. The Breusch–Pagan Lagrangian multiplier test for Random Effects Model (REM) and the modified Wald test for Fixed Effects Model (FEM) were employed to assess variance. Following the results of these variance tests, the Hausman test was conducted to determine the most appropriate model (FEM or REM). The comprehensive multistage process of quantitative data analysis included unit root testing of the balanced panel dataset, model diagnostics to evaluate model assumptions, model optimization to enhance model fit, and robustness testing to examine the stability of the findings.

ANALYSIS AND FINDINGS

Table 3 presents the average and standard deviations of greenwashing and ESG scores across the sampled countries. The greenwashing scores exhibit significant variation among the countries. Companies in Malaysia and Singapore show comparable means of 0.03% and 0.02%, respectively. In contrast, companies in Thailand have a greenwashing score of approximately 0.20%. On the other hand, Indonesian companies display the highest score, reaching around 0.46% in their greenwashing practices.

Table 3. Descriptive statistics for the greenwashing score and ESG score by country

Item	Malaysia	Indonesia	Thailand	Singapore
Companies	345	101	160	46
Observations	1011	303	658	130
GW				
Mean	0.003	0.046	0.020	0.002
SD	1.298	1.680	1.540	1.090
ESG Score				
Mean	50.497	30.210	42.890	67.290
SD	16.918	11.291	17.230	20.101

Table 4 provides descriptive statistics for the variables examined in this study. The incidence of greenwashing among companies in the ASEAN region is recorded at 0.05%, accompanied by a standard deviation of 1.345. The highest observed level is 4.890, indicating a notable variance among the companies in the ASEAN area. The average ESG score stands at 78.240, with a standard deviation of 40.230, reflecting a degree of inconsistency in the sustainability practices of these companies. Furthermore, the mean carbon emissions per unit are quantified at 510.581 tons for every million dollars of revenue, with a standard deviation of 2340.846 tons per million dollars of revenue, suggesting a moderate level of variation among the companies.

Table 4. Descriptive statistics

Variable	Observations	Mean	SD	Minimum	Maximum
GW	2102	0.005	1.345	-1.245	4.890
ESGSCORE	2102	78.240	40.230	11.218	90.235
CARBON	2102	510.581	2340.846	0.0347	21436.247
FIRMSIZE	2102	10.975	1.320	7.717	12.011
LEVERAGE	2102	0.144	0.255	-0.001	2.254
AGE	2102	17.710	6.249	3.0	30.00

Table 5 illustrates the correlation analyses among the variables. The models were assessed for multicollinearity, and the findings reveal that multicollinearity is not a concern, as the variance inflation factor (VIF) coefficients remain below 5 (ranging from 1.00 to 4.020), as noted by Gujarati (2021). Consequently, it is evident that the models are appropriate and align well with the analyses performed.

Table 5. Correlation analyses

Variable	VIF	GW	ESG Score	FIRMSIZE	LEVERAGE	AGE
GW	1.210	1	-0.051**	-0.042*	-0.046**	0.022
ESG SCORE	2.340		1	-0.023**	-0.016	0.120**
FIRM SIZE	3.040			1	-0.035*	0.051**
LEVERAGE	4.020				1	-0.710**
AGE	1.080					1

Hypothesis Testing

Table 6 presents the main findings of the hypotheses conducted. H1 examining the relationship between greenwashing score and ESG score across different samples. The result for GW indicates a negative and statistically significant relationship with ESG score (β= -0.380, p<0.001), in the total sample using the REM model. This is suggesting that greenwashing behaviour does affect the sustainability practices hence reflecting in the ESG score result. Interestingly, the interaction term between greenwashing score and carbon emission (GW*CARBON) has a negative and significant effect on the ESG Score (β= -0.0078, p<0.005) in which suggesting companies with high emissions, greenwashing is more easily exposed and seen more disingenuous. This could amplify the negative effect of greenwashing on ESG scores, because the mismatch between claims and actual environmental impact is more glaring. This finding highlights the significant to consider the moderating role of carbon emissions in sustainability reporting research.

Similarly, the firm size (FIRMSIZE) displays a negative and significant association with ESG score across the samples (β= -3.245, p<0.05) indicating that large firms may adopt ESG practices for symbolic reasons, which can result in lower actual performance. This is also supported by prior studies that larger firms may face difficulties in implementing consistent governance practices across departments or subsidiaries, impacting their ESG scores.

For leverage, the LEV shows a negative and significant relationship with ESG score (β= -2.100, p <0.05). This is due to the facts that firms with high financial leverage are less likely to voluntarily disclose ESG activities. On the other hand, firm age (AGE) shows a positive relationship with the ESG score indicates that older firms are more likely to engage in long-term environmental strategies due to accumulated legitimacy and concern for reputation.

Table 6. Hypotheses findings

	Total Sample- REM (2102 observations)	
Nexus	**Beta**	**p-value (z-value)**
GW-→ ESG SCORE	-0.380	0.000 (7.10)
GW*CARBON→ ESG SCORE	-0.0078	0.016 (4.20)
FIRMSIZE→ESGSCORE	-3.245	0.008 (0.350)
LEVERAGE→ESGSCORE	-2.100	0.010 (0.54)
AGE→ESGSCORE	0.081	0.789 (0.90)

DISCUSSION

This study finds a negative relationship between greenwashing and ESG scores among firms in the ASEAN region, highlighting how deceptive sustainability communication undermines true ESG performance. Greenwashing, defined as the strategic disclosure of selective or misleading environmental and social claims (In & Schumacher, 2021; Baratta et al., 2023), misleads stakeholders and weakens the integrity of ESG ratings. In the ASEAN context, where ESG reporting standards are still evolving and regulatory enforcement varies across countries, firms may exploit this institutional gap to present a falsely positive ESG image (Treepongkaruna et al.,2024). Consistent with legitimacy theory, in the context of ESG, firms may engage in greenwashing as a strategy to appear legitimate in the eyes of stakeholders, regulators, and the public especially when their actual environmental performance is weak.

Moreover, the findings demonstrate that carbon emissions significantly moderate the relationship between greenwashing and ESG performance. Specifically, the negative impact of greenwashing on ESG scores is amplified in firms with high carbon emissions. This implies that when environmentally harmful firms engage in greenwashing, stakeholders and ESG raters penalize them more severely possibly due to the higher visibility and inconsistency between their emissions and sustainability claims. This result aligns with stakeholder theory (Del Gesso & Lodhi, 2025), which posits that firms with greater environmental impact face increased scrutiny and accountability.

Building on stakeholder theory, the study's findings suggest that firms with higher carbon emissions are under greater pressure to meet the expectations of a wide range of stakeholders including investors, regulators, customers, and civil society who are increasingly prioritizing environmental responsibility. Stakeholder theory posits that a firm's long-term success depends on maintaining legitimacy and trust among these key groups. When high-emission firms engage in greenwashing, they breach this trust, resulting in intensified negative reactions due to the perceived misalignment between their sustainability claims and actual practices. This misalignment is more apparent and damaging for firms with visible environmental footprints, as stakeholders are more likely to detect and respond to discrepancies. Consequently, ESG raters may assign lower scores as a reflection of stakeholder sentiment and perceived risk, reinforcing the need for genuine accountability and transparency. The study thus reinforces stakeholder theory by illustrating how stakeholder expectations and perceptions directly influence the ESG evaluations of firms, especially those with higher environmental risks, and underscores the importance of authentic sustainability efforts in maintaining stakeholder confidence.

In the ASEAN region, which includes both carbon-intensive developing economies (e.g., Indonesia, Vietnam) and more advanced economies (e.g., Singapore), the heterogeneity in institutional quality and climate policy enforcement likely influences this relationship. Countries with weaker enforcement may provide fertile ground for greenwashing, but as global ESG frameworks and investor pressures intensify, carbon-intensive firms are finding it harder to escape reputational consequences. This reinforces arguments by Lyon and Montgomery (2015) that greenwashing is especially damaging for firms with substantial environmental footprints.

The results of this study reveal a negative relationship between firm size and ESG scores, contrary to the commonly held assumption that larger firms, due to greater resources and visibility, would exhibit stronger ESG performance. While larger firms may indeed possess the capacity to invest in sustainability, the findings align with prior research suggesting that organizational complexity, bureaucratic inertia, and weaker internal coordination in large firms can dilute ESG efforts (Kudłak, 2024). In the ASEAN region, where ESG integration is still emerging in many sectors, large firms may prioritize short-term profitability and regulatory compliance over proactive sustainability initiatives, especially in capital-intensive and export-oriented industries.

In addition, the study finds that high financial leverage is associated with lower ESG scores, supporting the view that financially constrained firms are less likely to invest in long-term, non-financial initiatives (Priem & Gabellone, 2024). In highly leveraged firms, management may focus on debt servicing and maintaining solvency, leaving limited room for ESG activities that do not yield immediate financial returns. This is particularly relevant in the ASEAN context, where many firms operate in volatile financial environments, and access to low-cost capital for ESG-related investments may be limited or inconsistent across countries.

CONCLUSION

This research underscores the detrimental effects of greenwashing on Environmental, Social, and Governance (ESG) scores, particularly evident in companies with elevated carbon emissions within the ASEAN region. The results indicate that firms that partake in deceptive sustainability reporting, especially those with substantial environmental footprints, experience a notable decline in both credibility and ESG performance. The influence of carbon emissions emphasizes the necessity for objective environmental metrics when evaluating the veracity of ESG assertions. In scenarios characterized by high emissions, stakeholders, ESG rating organizations, and investors are more inclined to impose penalties on companies for discrepancies between their reported disclosures and their actual environmental impact.

The findings of this study further highlight the growing scrutiny faced by corporations in the ASEAN region amid increasing global climate awareness. Greenwashing not only damages a company's reputation but also hinders its access to sustainable financing and investor confidence. As ESG standards become more integral to investment decisions, discrepancies in reporting can trigger regulatory backlash and financial consequences. Moreover, companies that engage in superficial sustainability efforts risk alienating stakeholders who demand accountability and measurable progress. The use of misleading or exaggerated ESG claims weakens the overall trust in sustainability frameworks. Therefore, transparent and verifiable ESG disclosures are vital for building long-term corporate resilience and integrity. Regulatory bodies in ASEAN must enhance monitoring mechanisms, while ESG rating agencies should refine methodologies to better capture inconsistencies in reporting. Firms must prioritize genuine environmental performance improvements over symbolic compliance, particularly in high-emission industries. This research calls for stronger governance, increased standardization, and a multi-stakeholder approach to combat greenwashing and reinforce the credibility of ESG frameworks across the region.

The study offers several implications. For practitioners, this underscores the importance of genuine, transparent, and verifiable ESG practices. Firms must move beyond symbolic sustainability reporting and integrate ESG into core operations particularly in sectors with heavy environmental impacts. Greenwashing may provide short-term image benefits, but it poses long-term reputational and financial risks, especially as ESG scrutiny intensifies in global markets. For regulators and policymakers across ASEAN, these results highlight the urgent need for stronger ESG reporting standards, carbon disclosure requirements, and independent verification mechanisms. Harmonizing ESG regulations across the region and enhancing regulatory oversight can help close loopholes that allow greenwashing to persist. Furthermore, introducing carbon pricing, emissions benchmarking, or tax incentives for verified green initiatives can motivate more authentic ESG performance.

To improve regulatory effectiveness, ASEAN policymakers should consider establishing a unified ESG disclosure framework aligned with global standards such as IFRS S1 and S2. Harmonized regional guidelines would reduce reporting inconsistencies and prevent regulatory arbitrage. Moreover, ASEAN could introduce region-wide mandatory carbon disclosure requirements for high-emission industries, coupled with third-party verification to ensure data reliability. Regulators should also invest in ESG capacity-building programs for companies, particularly SMEs, and enforce penalties for false or misleading ESG claims to deter greenwashing. Cross-border cooperation among ASEAN members possibly through the ASEAN

Capital Markets Forum (ACMF) can support information sharing and policy alignment across jurisdictions.

In moving toward ESG reporting standardization, ASEAN policymakers must shift from principle-based encouragement to enforceable regulations. Leveraging country-level successes, adopting global best practices, and following a clearly defined regional roadmap will ensure that ESG efforts move beyond symbolic compliance. A harmonized approach not only enhances transparency but also strengthens ASEAN's competitive positioning in global sustainable finance markets. Meanwhile, investors should go beyond ESG scores by demanding transparent, audited data, considering carbon emissions as part of due diligence, and engaging firms on authentic sustainability performance. These targeted actions can help mitigate greenwashing and strengthen ESG integrity across the ASEAN region.

Despite the contributions of this study, there are several limitations that offer avenues for future research. First, data availability and consistency across ASEAN countries posed a significant challenge. ESG disclosures and carbon emissions data vary widely in terms of quality, frequency, and transparency among member states. In less developed ASEAN economies, limited ESG reporting frameworks and lower regulatory enforcement may have led to underreporting or data gaps, which could affect the robustness of the findings. Second, the study relies on ESG scores and greenwashing proxies that are subject to methodological differences across rating agencies. ESG scores may reflect differing weightings, subjective judgments, and disclosure biases, while greenwashing is inherently difficult to measure and was proxied through indirect indicators (e.g., discrepancy between sustainability disclosures and environmental performance). These proxies may not fully capture the nuanced forms of greenwashing behavior across firms. Finally, the study may not fully capture industry-specific dynamics or regulatory differences across ASEAN countries. Given the diversity of economic development, environmental regulations, and stakeholder pressures in the region, future studies could benefit from a country-level or sector-specific analysis to better understand the contextual factors influencing ESG outcomes.

Building on the findings and limitations of this study, future research could explore several avenues. First, more granular, country-specific studies within ASEAN would help capture regulatory and cultural differences affecting ESG behavior. Second, alternative greenwashing measures such as media sentiment analysis or sustainability report text mining could provide deeper insights. Third, future studies could adopt a longitudinal approach to assess how evolving ESG regulations or investor activism influence corporate behavior over time. Finally, expanding the scope to include private firms or SMEs could offer a more comprehensive picture of ESG dynamics in emerging markets.

ACKNOWLEDGEMENT

We would like to thank Universiti Sains Islam Malaysia,Universitas Padjajaran, Bandung, Indonesia and Universitas Muhammadiyah Yogyakarta, Indonesia (UMY Research Fellow Program 2025) for their helpful feedback and support.

REFERENCES

Abu Afifa, M., Nguyen, N. M., & Bui, D. V. (2025). Environmental, social and governance (ESG) disclosure quality in developing countries: Evidence from the ASEAN region. *Corporate Governance (Bradford)*, *25*(7), 1728–1754. DOI: 10.1108/CG-02-2024-0102

Al Amosh, H., & Khatib, S. F. (2024). Toward sustainable healthcare: Linking environmental governance, business innovation and carbon emission in Europe. *Management of Environmental Quality*, *35*(7), 1461–1483. DOI: 10.1108/MEQ-09-2023-0304

Amel-Zadeh, A., & Serafeim, G. (2018). Why and How Investors Use ESG Information: Evidence from a Global Survey. *Financial Analysts Journal*, *74*(3), 87–103. DOI: 10.2469/faj.v74.n3.2

Ang, H. S. (2024). Sustainable Environmental, Social and Governance (ESG) development of China and ASEAN in a volatile, uncertain, complex, and ambiguous (VUCA) world. *Global Policy*, *15*(S6), 106–112. DOI: 10.1111/1758-5899.13432

Atkins, J., Doni, F., Gasperini, A., Artuso, S., La Torre, I., & Sorrentino, L. (2023). Exploring the effectiveness of sustainability measurement: Which ESG metrics will survive COVID-19? *Journal of Business Ethics*, *185*(3), 629–646. DOI: 10.1007/s10551-022-05183-1

Avramov, D., Cheng, S., Lioui, A., & Tarelli, A. (2022). Sustainable investing with ESG rating uncertainty. *Journal of Financial Economics*, *145*(2), 642–664. DOI: 10.1016/j.jfineco.2021.09.009

Baratta, A., Cimino, A., Longo, F., Solina, V., & Verteramo, S. (2023). The impact of ESG practices in industry with a focus on carbon emissions: Insights and future perspectives. *Sustainability (Basel)*, *15*(8), 6685. DOI: 10.3390/su15086685

Ben Mahjoub, L. (2025). Greenwashing practices and ESG reporting: An international review. *The International Journal of Sociology and Social Policy*, *45*(1/2), 173–188. DOI: 10.1108/IJSSP-08-2024-0365

Berg, F., Kölbel, J., & Rigobon, R. (2022). Aggregate Confusion: The Divergence of ESG Ratings. *Review of Finance, 26*(6), 1315–1344. DOI: 10.1093/rof/rfac033

Chatterji, A. K., Durand, R., Levine, D. I., & Touboul, S. (2016). Do ratings of firms converge? Implications for managers, investors and strategy researchers. *Strategic Management Journal, 37*(8), 1597–1614. DOI: 10.1002/smj.2407

Cheng, M., & Micale, J. A. (2022). ESG risks and the value relevance of current and historical earnings. *Financial Markets, Institutions and Instruments, 31*(5), 207–237. DOI: 10.1111/fmii.12162

Courtat, M., Joyce, P. J., Sim, S., Sadhukhan, J., & Murphy, R. (2023). Towards credible, evidence-based environmental rating ecolabels for consumer products: A proposed framework. *Journal of Environmental Management, 336*, 117684. DOI: 10.1016/j.jenvman.2023.117684 PMID: 36924711

Del Bosco, B., & Misani, N. (2016). The effect of cross-listing on the environmental, social, and governance performance of firms. *Journal of World Business, 51*(6), 977–990. DOI: 10.1016/j.jwb.2016.08.002

Del Gesso, C., & Lodhi, R. N. (2025). Theories underlying environmental, social and governance (ESG) disclosure: A systematic review of accounting studies. *Journal of Accounting Literature, 47*(2), 433–461. DOI: 10.1108/JAL-08-2023-0143

Gala, K. (2023). *Corporate Social Responsibility and Greenwashing in the perception of customers: A Case Study of Beyond Petroleum.* Exxon, and Shell.

Gaviria, D. A. G., Martínez, E. M. C., Polo, O. C. C., & Arcila, J. O. S. (2023). Accounting Mechanism to Measure the Environmental Impact of Industries in the Aburrá Valley and its Application of the General Disclosure Requirements Related to Financial Information on Sustainability (IFRS S1) and Climate-Related Disclosures (IFRS S2). *Revista de Gestao Social e Ambiental, 17*(5), 1–16. DOI: 10.24857/rgsa.v17n5-013

Gentile, G., & Gupta, J. (2025). Orchestrating the narrative: The role of fossil fuel companies in delaying the energy transition. *Renewable & Sustainable Energy Reviews, 212*, 115359. DOI: 10.1016/j.rser.2025.115359

Gopal, S., & Pitts, J. (2025). Regulation and Frameworks: Current and Future Reporting Trends. In *The FinTech Revolution: Bridging Geospatial Data Science, AI, and Sustainability* (pp. 183–224). Springer Nature Switzerland.

Gujarati, D. N. (2021). *Essentials of econometrics.* Sage Publications.

Gutiérrez-Ponce, H., & Wibowo, S. A. (2023). Sustainability reports and disclosure of the Sustainable Development Goals (SDGs): Evidence from Indonesian listed companies. *Sustainability (Basel), 15*(24), 16919. DOI: 10.3390/su152416919

In, S. Y., & Schumacher, K. (2021). Carbonwashing: ESG data greenwashing in a post-Paris world. Settling climate accounts: *Navigating the road to net zero*, 39-58.

Jiang, Y., & Tang, Q. (2023). Mandatory carbon reporting, voluntary carbon disclosure and ESG performance. *Pacific Accounting Review, 35*(4), 534–561. DOI: 10.1108/PAR-08-2022-0133

Keeley, A. R., Chapman, A. J., Yoshida, K., Xie, J., Imbulana, J., Takeda, S., & Managi, S. (2022). ESG metrics and social equity: Investigating commensurability. *Frontiers in Sustainability, 3*, 920955. DOI: 10.3389/frsus.2022.920955

Kim, D., Shin, D., Lee, J., & Noh, G. (2024). Sustainability from institutionalism: Determinants of Korean companies' ESG performances. *Asian Business & Management, 23*(3), 393–425. DOI: 10.1057/s41291-024-00271-8

Kim, E. H., & Lyon, T. P. (2015). Greenwash vs. Brownwash: Exaggeration and Undue Modesty in Corporate Sustainability Disclosure. *Organization Science, 26*(3), 705–723. DOI: 10.1287/orsc.2014.0949

Kudłak, R. (2024). Greenwashing or Striving to Persist: An Alternative Explanation of a Loose Coupling Between Corporate Environmental Commitments and Outcomes. *Journal of Business Ethics*, •••, 1–16.

Kurpierz, J. R., & Smith, K. (2020). The greenwashing triangle: Adapting tools from fraud to improve CSR reporting. Sustainability Accounting. *Management and Policy Journal, 11*(6), 1075–1093.

Lyon, T. P., & Montgomery, A. W. (2015). The means and end of greenwash. *Organization & Environment, 28*(2), 223–249. DOI: 10.1177/1086026615575332

Nesadurai, H. E. (2008). The association of Southeast Asian nations (ASEAN). *New Political Economy, 13*(2), 225–239. DOI: 10.1080/13563460802018588

Ng, A., Ibrahim, M. H., & Kang, H. G. (2021). ESG Reporting in ASEAN: Trends, Gaps, and Policy Implications. *Asian Economic Policy Review.*

Priem, R., & Gabellone, A. (2024). The impact of a firm's ESG score on its cost of capital: Can a high ESG score serve as a substitute for a weaker legal environment. Sustainability Accounting. *Management and Policy Journal, 15*(3), 676–703. DOI: 10.1108/SAMPJ-05-2023-0254

Renukappa, S., Akintoye, A., Egbu, C., & Goulding, J. (2013). Carbon emission reduction strategies in the UK industrial sectors: An empirical study. *International Journal of Climate Change Strategies and Management, 5*(3), 304–323. DOI: 10.1108/IJCCSM-02-2012-0010

Sisaye, S. (2021). The influence of non-governmental organizations (NGOs) on the development of voluntary sustainability accounting reporting rules. *Journal of Business and Socio-economic Development, 1*(1), 5–23. DOI: 10.1108/JBSED-02-2021-0017

Tran, M., Beddewela, E., & Ntim, C. G. (2021). Governance and sustainability in Southeast Asia. *Accounting Research Journal, 34*(6), 516–545. DOI: 10.1108/ARJ-05-2019-0095

Treepongkaruna, S., Au Yong, H. H., Thomsen, S., & Kyaw, K. (2024). Greenwashing, carbon emission, and ESG. *Business Strategy and the Environment, 33*(8), 8526–8539. DOI: 10.1002/bse.3929

Van, H. V., & Afifa, M. A. (2024). Environmental commitment for green finance and sustainable performance in commercial banks of ASEAN countries-whether stakeholder pressure has a moderating role. *International Journal of Sustainable Economy, 16*(3), 304–331. DOI: 10.1504/IJSE.2024.139502

Wai-Khuen, W., Boon-Heng, T., & Siow-Hooi, T. (2023). The influence of external stakeholders on environmental, social, and governance (ESG) reporting: Toward a conceptual framework for ESG disclosure. *Foresight and STI Governance, 17*(2), 9–20. DOI: 10.17323/2500-2597.2023.2.9.20

Walker, K., & Wan, F. (2012). The Harm of Symbolic Actions and Greenwashing: Corporate Actions and Communications on Environmental Performance and Their Financial Implications. *Journal of Business Ethics, 109*(2), 227–242. DOI: 10.1007/s10551-011-1122-4

Yoon, S. S., Oh, I., & Kim, H. J. (2024). An accounting perspective on the IFRS sustainability reporting standards for greenhouse gas emissions: Implications for the Asia Pacific. *Asia Pacific Business Review*, •••, 1–24. DOI: 10.1080/13602381.2024.2364806

Yu, E. P. Y., Guo, C. Q., & Luu, B. V. (2018). Environmental, social and governance transparency and firm value. *Business Strategy and the Environment, 27*(7), 987–1004. DOI: 10.1002/bse.2047

Yu, X., & Chen, Y. (2024). Does ESG advantage promote total factor productivity (TFP)? Empirical evidence from China's listed enterprises. *Applied Economics*, •••, 1–17.

Compilation of References

Abasilim, U. D., Gberevbie, D. E., & Osibanjo, A. (2018, October). Canonical analysis of perceived leadership styles and employees' commitment in Nigeria. In *Proceedings of the 14th European Conference on Management, Leadership and Governance, ECMLG,(October 2, 2018), Utrecht, the Netherlands* (pp. 317-322).

Abdallah, R. (2024).in Arabic. Promoting financial inclusion through Islamic finance: A comprehensive approach. *Algerian Journal of Economic Performance*, 7(2). : | ASJP

Abduh, M. (2019). *Foundation of Islamic Finance*. IIUM Press.

Abdullah, B., Syah, M. H., Hamid, M. A., & Yatim, P. (2017). The Effect of Enterprise Risk Management on Firm Value: Evidence from Malaysian Technology Firms. *Jurnal Pengurusan,* 49.

Abdullah, N. A., Hassan, S. A., & Yusoff, S. Z. (2020). Factors that influence the ethical behaviours of Takaful agents. *International Journal of Academic Research in Business & Social Sciences, 10*(8), 270–282. DOI: 10.6007/IJARBSS/v10-i8/7535

Abid, I., Bouri, E., Galariotis, E., Guesmi, K., & Mzoughi, H. (2023). Bitcoin vs. fiat currencies: Insights from extreme dependence and risk spillover analysis with financial markets. *International Review of Financial Analysis, 90*, 102806. DOI: 10.1016/j.irfa.2023.102806

Abiyyu, I., Najib, M., & Asmara, A. (2020). Bancassurance business strategy in life insurance: A case study one of joint venture company in Indonesia. [Jurnal Dinamika Manajemen]. *Journal of Database Management, 11*(1), 103–115.

Abou Ali, A. A. K. (2024). DeFi era: The behavioral intentions toward cryptocurrency in Lebanon. *Innovation & Management Review, 21*(4), 274–285. DOI: 10.1108/INMR-02-2023-0022

Abrar, A., Naeem, M. A., Karim, S., Lucey, B. M., & Vigne, S. A. (2024). Shining in or fading out: Do precious metals sparkle for cryptocurrencies? *Resources Policy*, *90*, 104722. Advance online publication. DOI: 10.1016/j.resourpol.2024.104722

Abu Afifa, M., Nguyen, N. M., & Bui, D. V. (2025). Environmental, social and governance (ESG) disclosure quality in developing countries: Evidence from the ASEAN region. *Corporate Governance (Bradford)*, *25*(7), 1728–1754. DOI: 10.1108/CG-02-2024-0102

Adekola, J., & Clelland, D. (2020). Two sides of the same coin: Business resilience and community resilience. *Journal of Contingencies and Crisis Management*, *28*(1), 50–60. DOI: 10.1111/1468-5973.12275

Adham, K. A., Kasimin, H., Jamaludin, N. A., Ghanie, S. K., Khatib, N. A. M., & Said, M. F. (2016). Developing a cybernetics approach to analysing inclusive growth constraints. *Systemic Practice and Action Research*, *29*(3), 215–234. DOI: 10.1007/s11213-015-9361-4

Adiguzel, Z., Ozcinar, M. F., & Karadal, H. (2020). Does Servant Leadership Moderate the Link Between Strategic Human Resource Management on Rule Breaking and Job Satisfaction? *European Research on Management and Business Economics*, *26*(2), 103–110. DOI: 10.1016/j.iedeen.2020.04.002

Adznan, S., Sori, Z. M., & Ramadili Mohd, S. M. (2022). Intellectual Capital Disclosure and Corporate Governance: Empirical Evidence from a Cross Country that Offering Islamic Bank Services. *Journal of Accounting and Governance*, *18*, 147–164. DOI: 10.17576/AJAG-2022-18-11

Afum, E., Issau, K., Agyabeng-Mensah, Y., Baah, C., Dacosta, E., Essandoh, E., & Agyenim Boateng, E. (2021). The missing links of sustainable supply chain management and green radical product innovation among sustainable entrepreneurship orientation and sustainability performance. *Journal of Engineering, Design and Technology*. DOI: 10.1108/JEDT-05-2021-0267

Aggarwal, S. (2024). Impact of Dimensions of Organisational Culture on Employee Satisfaction and Performance Level in Select Organisations. *IIMB Management Review*, *36*(3), 230–238. DOI: 10.1016/j.iimb.2024.07.001

Agrawala, S., Dussaux, D., & Monti, N. (2022). *Climate change adaptation and innovation: A sectoral approach*. OECD Environment Working Papers No. 178. OECD Publishing.

Agrawala, S., Carraro, M., Kingsmill, N., Lanzi, E., Mullan, M., & Prudent-Richard, G. (2022). *Private sector engagement in adaptation to climate change: Approaches to managing climate risks.* OECD Publishing.

Ahammad, M. F., Glaister, K. W., & Gomes, E. (2020). Strategic agility and human resource management. *Human Resource Management Review, 30*(1), 100700. DOI: 10.1016/j.hrmr.2019.100700

Ahmad Samsuri, M. A. Z., & Jamal, J. (2017). Takaful Agent Must Foster Public Understanding of Takaful. *Diponegoro Law Review, 2*(2), 245–258. DOI: 10.14710/dilrev.2.2.2017.1-14

Ahmad, Z., Muneeza, A., Rahman, M. M., & Mahomed, Z. (2023). A comparative analysis of Shariah governance framework of Islamic bank in Malaysia and Pakistan. Talaa: *Journal of Islamic Finance, 3*(1), 01-17.

Ahmad, G. S., & Mahadi, N. F. (2023). Public Awareness, Knowledge, and Perception towards Takaful in Afghanistan. *Journal of Islamic Social Finance, 1*(2), 45–57.

Ahmed, B. O., Johari, F., & Abdul Wahab, K. (2017). Identifying the poor and the needy among the beneficiaries of zakat: Need for a zakat-based poverty threshold in Nigeria. *International Journal of Social Economics, 44*(4), 446–458. DOI: 10.1108/IJSE-09-2015-0234

Ahmed, I., & Manab, N. A. (2016). Influence of Enterprise Risk Management Success Factors on Firm Financial and Non-Financial Performance: A Proposed Model. *International Journal of Economics and Financial Issues, 6*(3), 830–836.

Ahmed, Z. N., & Amir Hussin, M. R. (2024). The Effect of Intellectual Capital Efficiency on Malaysian Firm Performance: A Dynamic Panel Estimation. [MAR]. *Management Accounting Research, 23*(1), 57–84.

Aimal, C., Dave, E., Ilyas, B., & Abid, S. (2025). Conceptualizing Corporate Social Responsibility Process Among Muslim SMEs in the UK : A Case Investigation Approach. In *Journal of the Knowledge Economy* (Issue 0123456789). Springer US. DOI: 10.1007/s13132-024-02567-8

Akgün, A. İ., & Türkoğlu, S. P. (2024). Intellectual Capital and Performance of Listed Firms During The Global Financial Crisis: The Effects of Legal Origin. *The International Journal of Organizational Analysis, 32*(4), 759–785. DOI: 10.1108/IJOA-01-2023-3587

Akhtaruzzaman, M., Boubaker, S., Lucey, B. M., & Sensoy, A. (2021). Is gold a hedge or a safe-haven asset in the COVID–19 crisis? *Economic Modelling, 102*, 105588. DOI: 10.1016/j.econmod.2021.105588

Akkaya, B., Kayalidere, U. A. K., & Tabak, A. (2019). Endüstriyel alanda üretim yapan firmaların örgütsel çevikliği ile firma yöneticilerinin sahip olduğu dinamik yetenekler arasındaki ilişki: Manisa Organize Sanayi Bölgesi'nde (MOSB) faaliyet gösteren firmalar üzerine bir araştırma. *Yeni Nesil Girişimcilik ve Ekonomi, 1*(2), 19–54.

Al Amosh, H., & Khatib, S. F. (2024). Toward sustainable healthcare: Linking environmental governance, business innovation and carbon emission in Europe. *Management of Environmental Quality, 35*(7), 1461–1483. DOI: 10.1108/MEQ-09-2023-0304

Al Salam Bank. www.alsalamalgeria.com

Alade, K., & Windapo, A. (2020). Leadership framework for sustainable housing production in South Africa. *African Journal of Housing and Sustainable Development, 1*(1), 109–119. DOI: 10.52968/28468654

Alamsyah, A., Kusuma, G. N. W., & Ramadhani, D. P. (2024). A Review on Decentralized Finance Ecosystems. *Future Internet, 16*(3), 76. Advance online publication. DOI: 10.3390/fi16030076

Alamsyah, A., & Syahrir, S. (2024). A Taxonomy on Blockchain-Based Technology in the Financial Industry: Drivers, Applications, Benefits, and Threats. In *Blockchain and Smart-Contract Technologies for Innovative Applications* (pp. 91–129). Springer Nature Switzerland., DOI: 10.1007/978-3-031-50028-2_4

Aldhaheri, R. T., & Ahmad, S. Z. (2023). Factors affecting organisations' supply chain agility and competitive capability. *Business Process Management Journal, 29*(2), 505–527. DOI: 10.1108/BPMJ-11-2022-0579

Al-Fatih, S. (2020). Strengthening Baznas As the Society's Trusted Zakat Agency To Increase the Welfare of Ummah. *Jurisdictie: Jurnal Hukum dan Syariah, 11*(1), 106-124. https://doi.org/DOI: 10.18860/j.v11i1.7841

Alhammadi, S. (2024). Islamic finance as a driver for enhancing economic sustainability and innovation in the GCC. *Journal of Science and Technology Policy Management.*

Alhashmi, E. A. K. (2024). How to overcome poverty with zakat. *International Journal of Religion, 5*(2), 1–13. DOI: 10.61707/tbxftv10

Al-Husseini, S., El Beltagi, I., & Moizer, J. (2021). Transformational leadership and innovation: The mediating role of knowledge sharing amongst higher education faculty. *International Journal of Leadership in Education, 24*(5), 670–693. DOI: 10.1080/13603124.2019.1588381

Alhyasat, W., Alhyasat, E., & Khattab, S. A. (2025). *Technology trends in strategic management in the AI era : Systematic literature review. 0*(0), 1–18. DOI: 10.1177/01672533251322396

Ali, K. M. M. (2021). Takaful Tech for Business Excellence and Customer Satisfaction. Islamic FinTech: Insights and Solutions, 385-403.

Ali, M., Ademe, S., Shumiye, M., & Hamza, A. (2023). Patient safety culture and associated factors among health care workers in South Wollo Zone public hospitals, North East Ethiopia. BMC Health Services Research.

Ali, S. (2024, October 15). Opening keynote speech at the Takaful StarNite Gala Dinner. *Bank for International Settlements (BIS).*

Ali, K. M. M. (2006). Present scenario and future potentials of Takaful. *Islamic Economics. Banking and Finance*, *2*(2), 1–14.

Almahendra, R., Viyani, A. O., & Nabawi, M. (2024). Is crypto legitimate? Study on the relationship between legitimacy and public engagement on crypto market in Indonesia. *Intangible Capital*, *20*(2), 393–411. DOI: 10.3926/ic.2425

Al-Mahi, A. S. M. M., Sim, C. S., & Hassan, A. (2017). Religiosity and demand for takaful (Islamic Insurance): A preliminary investigation. *International Journal of Applied Business and Economic Research*, *15*(24), 485–499.

Almaqtari, F. A. (2024). The role of IT governance in the integration of AI in accounting and auditing operations. *Economies*, *12*(8), 199. Advance online publication. DOI: 10.3390/economies12080199

Al-Nashmi, M., & Almamary, A. (2017). The relationship between islamic marketing ethics and brand credibility. *Journal of Islamic Marketing*, *8*(2), 261–288. DOI: 10.1108/JIMA-03-2015-0024

Al-Nuaimi, A. M. T., & Zahraa. (2017). Analysis of financial inclusion indicators for the Arab banking sector. *Tikrit Journal for Administrative and Economic Sciences*, 4(40). View article Al Baraka Bank: www.albaraka-bank.dz

Al-Rimy, B. A. S., Maarof, M. A., Prasetyo, Y. A., Shaid, S. Z. M., & Ariffin, A. F. M. (2018). Zero-day aware decision fusion-based model for crypto-ransomware early detection. *International Journal of Integrated Engineering*, *10*(6), 82–88. DOI: 10.30880/ijie.2018.10.06.011

Alrowwad, A. A., Abualoush, S. H., & Masa'deh, R. E. (2020). Innovation and intellectual capital as intermediary variables among transformational leadership, transactional leadership, and organizational performance. *Journal of Management Development*, *39*(2), 196–222. DOI: 10.1108/JMD-02-2019-0062

Alshammari, A. A., Syed Jaafar Alhabshi, S. M., & Saiti, B. (2018, September). bin, & Saiti, B. (2019). The impact of competition on cost efficiency of insurance and Takaful sectors: Evidence from GCC markets based on the Stochastic Frontier Analysis. *Research in International Business and Finance*, *47*, 410–427. DOI: 10.1016/j.ribaf.2018.09.003

Al-Tit, A., Al-Ayed, S., Alhammadi, A., Hunitie, M., Alsarayreh, A., & Albassam, W. (2022). The Impact of Employee Development Practices on Human Capital and Social Capital: The Mediating Contribution of Knowledge Management. *Journal of Open Innovation*, *8*(4), 218. DOI: 10.3390/joitmc8040218

Amel-Zadeh, A., & Serafeim, G. (2018). Why and How Investors Use ESG Information: Evidence from a Global Survey. *Financial Analysts Journal*, *74*(3), 87–103. DOI: 10.2469/faj.v74.n3.2

Amini, M., & Rahmani, A. (2023). How strategic agility affects the competitive capabilities of private banks. *International Journal of Basic and Applied Sciences*, *10*, 8397–8406.

Andiena Nindya Putri, P. A., Widyastuti, T. V., Dewi, G. A. K. R. S., Udin, A. F., Irdhayanti, E., & Harahap, K. (2025). Navigating Consumer Rights and Ethical Advertising in the Metaverse: A Comprehensive Case Study of Cryptocurrency Users in Indonesia's Digital Economy. In *Studies in Systems Decision and Control* (Vol. 234). DOI: 10.1007/978-3-031-84636-6_11

Andronie, M., Blazek, R., Iatagan, M., Skypalova, R., U ă, C., Dijmărescu, A., Kovacova, M., Grecu, G., Pârvu, I., Strakova, J., Guni, C., Zabojnik, S., Chiru, C., Sedláčková, A. N., Novák, A., & Dijmărescu, I. (2024). *Generative artificial intelligence algorithms in Internet of Things blockchain-based fintech management* (Vol. 15).

Anggriawan, R., & Susila, M. E. (2024). Cryptocurrency and its Nexus with Money Laundering and Terrorism Financing within the Framework of FATF Recommendations | Las criptomonedas y su nexo con el lavado de dinero y la financiación del terrorismo en el marco de las recomendaciones del GAFI. *Novum Jus*, *18*(2), 249–277. DOI: 10.14718/NovumJus.2024.18.2.10

Ang, H. S. (2024). Sustainable Environmental, Social and Governance (ESG) development of China and ASEAN in a volatile, uncertain, complex, and ambiguous (VUCA) world. *Global Policy*, *15*(S6), 106–112. DOI: 10.1111/1758-5899.13432

Ansari, Z. (2022). A review of 20 years of takaful literature using a systematic method. *Asian Journal of Economics and Banking*, *46*(1), 2–25. DOI: 10.1108/AJEB-08-2021-0100

Antonakakis, N., Chatziantoniou, I., & Gabauer, D. (2020). Refined Measures of Dynamic Connectedness based on Time-Varying Parameter Vector Autoregressions. *Journal of Risk and Financial Management*, *13*(4), 84. Advance online publication. DOI: 10.3390/jrfm13040084

Antonio, M. S., Ali, M. M., & Akbar, N. (2013). A comparative analysis of the efficiency of takaful and conventional insurance in Malaysia. *International Journal of Excellence in Islamic Banking and Finance*, *182*(881), 1–13. DOI: 10.12816/0001416

Anwar, U. A. A., Rahayu, A., Wibowo, L. A., Sultan, M. A., Aspiranti, T., Furqon, C., & Rani, A. M. (2025). Supply chain integration as the implementation of strategic management in improving corporate performance. *Discover Sustainability*, *6*(1), 101. Advance online publication. DOI: 10.1007/s43621-025-00867-w

Aragón Sánchez, A., Sánchez Marín, G., & Mueses Morales, A. (2015). The Mediating Effect of Strategic Human Resource Practices on Knowledge Management and Firm Performance. *Revista Europea de Dirección y Economía de la Empresa*, *24*, 138–148.

Archer, S., ... (2009). (ed.). Takaful Islamic insurance: concepts and regulatory issues. John Wiley and Sons (Asia) Ptd. Ltd.

Arminanto, E. R., & Firmansyah, K. A. (2022). Bitcoin's Position in Indonesian Currency Law. *Indonesian State Law Review*, *5*(2), 67–78. DOI: 10.15294/islrev.v5i2.47491

Arner, D. W., Barberis, J., & Buckley, R. P. (2017). FinTech and RegTech in a Nutshell, and the Future in a Sandbox. *Research Handbook on Digital Transformations*, 89-102.

Aryanto, R., Fontana, A., & Afiff, A. Z. (2015). Strategic Human Resource Management, Innovation Capability and Performance: An Empirical Study in Indonesia Software Industry. *Procedia: Social and Behavioral Sciences*, *211*, 874–879. DOI: 10.1016/j.sbspro.2015.11.115

Arzam, Fauzi, M., Efendi, F., & Sulastri W. (2023). Islamic crowdfunding: A review literature. [RIEF]. *Review of Islamic Economics and Finance*, *6*(2), 171–186.

ASEAN. (2024). *Model framework for an inclusive business accreditation system in ASEAN.* ASEAN Secretariat. https://asean.org/wp-content/uploads/2024/09/IB-Model-Framework-Publication_240923.pdf

Ashraf, R., Riaz, H., & Sohail, M. (2024). Perception and awareness among Muslim consumers: Comparative study of Takaful and conventional insurance policyholders. *Gomal University Journal of Research*, *40*(1), 1–10. DOI: 10.51380/gujr-40-01-01.

Aslam, E., Rehman, A. U., & Iqbal, A. (2024). The Mediating Role of Intellectual Capital in Corporate Governance and Financial Efficiency of Islamic Banks. *Corporate Governance (Bradford)*, *24*(1), 19–40. DOI: 10.1108/CG-06-2022-0276

Aslam, R., Rehman, S., & Nasir, A. (2023). Investigating the association among government support and SMEs' sustainability through financial and green lenses. *Journal of Corporate and Industrial Marketing*, *38*(11), 2379–2389. DOI: 10.1108/JBIM-05-2022-0191

Asutay, M., & Ubaidillah, . (2024). Examining the Impact of Intellectual Capital Performance on Financial Performance in Islamic Banks. *Journal of the Knowledge Economy*, *15*(1), 1231–1263. DOI: 10.1007/s13132-023-01114-1

Asyiqin, I. Z., Akbar, M. F., & Beltrán Genovés, M. (2024). Cryptocurrency as a Medium of Rupiah Exchange: Perspective Sharia Islamic Law and Jurisprudential Analysis. *Volksgeist Jurnal Ilmu Hukum Dan Konstitusi*, *7*(2), 277–292. DOI: 10.24090/volksgeist.v7i2.10975

Atkins, J., Doni, F., Gasperini, A., Artuso, S., La Torre, I., & Sorrentino, L. (2023). Exploring the effectiveness of sustainability measurement: Which ESG metrics will survive COVID-19? *Journal of Business Ethics*, *185*(3), 629–646. DOI: 10.1007/s10551-022-05183-1

Attar, M., & Abdul-Kareem, A. (2020). The role of agile leadership in organisational agility. In Attar, M. (Ed.), *Agile business leadership methods for Industry 4.0* (pp. 171–191). Emerald Publishing Limited., DOI: 10.1108/978-1-80043-380-920201011

Avolio, B. J., & Bass, B. M. (2004). *Multifactor leadership questionnaire™ manual.* Mind Garden, Inc.

Avolio, B. J., Kahai, S. S., & Dodge, G. E. (2000). E-leadership: Implications for theory, research, and practice. *The Leadership Quarterly*, *11*(4), 615–668. DOI: 10.1016/S1048-9843(00)00062-X

Avramov, D., Cheng, S., Lioui, A., & Tarelli, A. (2022). Sustainable investing with ESG rating uncertainty. *Journal of Financial Economics*, *145*(2), 642–664. DOI: 10.1016/j.jfineco.2021.09.009

Ayuniyyah, Q., Pramanik, A. H., Md Saad, N., & Ariffin, M. I. (2022). The impact of zakat in poverty alleviation and income inequality reduction from the perspective of gender in West Java, Indonesia. *International Journal of Islamic and Middle Eastern Finance and Management*, *15*(5), 924–942. https://www.emerald.com/insight/content/doi/10.1108/imefm-08-2020-0403/full/html. DOI: 10.1108/IMEFM-08-2020-0403

Azam, Z. (2021). Impact of Customer Relationship Management on Islamic Banks and Takaful Companies. *Journal of Integrated Sciences*, *2*(1), 57–90.

Aziah, A. R., Samsudin, K. J., & Osman, N. (2023). A study on awareness and understanding of Takaful products among polytechnic students in Malaysia. *IBAF Journal* [USIM]. *Universiti Sains Islam Malaysia*, *12*(2), 192–204.

Azizah, S. N. Suradi, Koeswinarno, Fakhruddin, M., & Yuliani, I. (2024). The Influence of Digital Transformation in Speeding Up the Empowerment of the Muslim Women's Economy to Improve the Performance of Micro, Small, and Medium Enterprises (MSMEs) in Ponorogo. In *Strategic Islamic Business and Management: Solutions for Sustainability* (pp. 71-107). Cham: Springer Nature Switzerland.

Aziz, N. A. A., Manab, N. A., & Othman, S. N. (2015). Exploring the perspectives of corporate governance and theories on sustainability risk management (SRM). *Asian Economic and Financial Review*, *5*(10), 1148–1158. DOI: 10.18488/journal.aefr/2015.5.10/102.10.1148.1158

Aziz, S., Husin, M. M., Hussin, N., & Afaq, Z. (2019). Factors that influence individuals' intentions to purchase family takaful mediating role of perceived trust. *Asia Pacific Journal of Marketing and Logistics*, *31*(1), 81–104. DOI: 10.1108/APJML-12-2017-0311

Aziz, Y., Mansor, F., Waqar, S., & Haji Abdullah, L. (2020). The nexus between zakat and poverty reduction is the effective utilization of zakat necessary for achieving SDGs: A multidimensional poverty index approach. *Asian Social Work and Policy Review*, *14*(3), 235–247. https://onlinelibrary.wiley.com/doi/10.1111/aswp.12212. DOI: 10.1111/aswp.12212

Bagasworo, W., & Simatupang, S. (2022). Increased Purchases of Insurance Products Based on Factors That Affect Customer Trust (Study on Banccasurance in Greater Jakarta, Indonesia). *Jurnal Ekonomi, Manajemen Dan Perbankan (Journal of Economics, Management and Banking)*, *8*(1), 30–38.

Bagga, S. K., Gera, S., & Haque, S. N. (2023). *The mediating role of organizational culture: Transformational leadership and change management in virtual teams*. Asia Pacific Management Review.

Balqis, A., Alamsyah, A., & Tricahyono, D. (2024). Web3 Adoption: Impact on Digital Industries. *2024 3rd International Conference on Creative Communication and Innovative Technology Iccit 2024*. DOI: 10.1109/ICCIT62134.2024.10701160

Bamgbade, J. A., Kamaruddeen, A. M., Nawi, M. N. M., Adeleke, A. Q., Salimon, M. G., & Ajibike, W. A. (2019). Analysis of some factors driving ecological sustainability in construction firms. *Journal of Cleaner Production*, *208*, 1537–1545. DOI: 10.1016/j.jclepro.2018.10.229

Bank of Algeria. (2024). *Annual report 2024 on monetary and financial developments*. Rapport-2024-fr.pdf

Bansal, U., Bharatwal, S., Bagiyam, D. S., & Kismawadi, E. R. (2024). Fraud detection in the era of AI: Harnessing technology for a safer digital economy. In *AI-driven decentralized finance and the future of finance* (pp. 143–164).

Baratta, A., Cimino, A., Longo, F., Solina, V., & Verteramo, S. (2023). The impact of ESG practices in industry with a focus on carbon emissions: Insights and future perspectives. *Sustainability (Basel)*, *15*(8), 6685. DOI: 10.3390/su15086685

Barefoot College. (n.d.). *Home*. Retrieved May 6, 2025, from https://www.barefootcollege.org/?gad_source=1&gad_campaignid=10830968790&gbraid=0AAAACRCuxF2AHdAuunJ44uo-WNN2T5-4&gclid=Cj0KCQjw18bEBhCBARIsAKuAFEZ6x2_OrEWhGxK_6SKnWZ5JOy4Wv5KPHfdZL3OZWxF3Q8mSRsn3XjYaAqq0EALw_wcB-

Barkin, D., & Bouchez, C. P. (2002). NGO–Community Collaboration for Ecotourism: A Strategy for Sustainable Regional Development. *Current Issues in Tourism*, *5*(3–4), 245–253. DOI: 10.1080/13683500208667921

Baruník, J., & Křehlík, T. (2018). Measuring the frequency dynamics of financial connectedness and systemic risk. *Journal of Financial Econometrics*, *16*(2), 271–296. DOI: 10.1093/jjfinec/nby001

Baryannis, G., Validi, S., Dani, S., & Antoniou, G. (2019). Supply chain risk management and artificial intelligence: State of the art and future research directions. *International Journal of Production Research*, *57*(7), 2179–2202. DOI: 10.1080/00207543.2018.1530476

Bass, B. M. (1999). Two decades of research and development in transformational leadership. *European Journal of Work and Organizational Psychology*, *8*(1), 9–32. DOI: 10.1080/135943299398410

Bass, B. M., & Bass, R. (2008). *The Bass handbook of leadership: Theory, research, and managerial applications* (4th ed.). Free Press.

Bebber, S., Milan, G. S., De Toni, D., Eberle, L., & Slongo, L. A. (2017). Antecedents of purchase intention in the online context. *Journal of Relationship Marketing*, *16*(1), 82–98.

Becha, H., Kalai, M., Houidi, S., & Helali, K. (2025). Digital financial inclusion, environmental sustainability and regional economic growth in China: Insights from a panel threshold model. *Journal of Economic Structures*, *14*(1), 4. Advance online publication. DOI: 10.1186/s40008-025-00347-4

Becker, T., Bruns, B., Lier, S., & Werners, B. (2021). Decentralized modular production to increase supply chain efficiency in chemical markets: An example of polymer production. *Journal of Business Economics*, *91*(6), 867–895. DOI: 10.1007/s11573-020-01019-4

Begić, H., & Galić, M. (2021). A Systematic Review of Construction 4.0 in the Context of the BIM 4.0 Premise. *Buildings (Basel, Switzerland)*, *11*(8), 337. DOI: 10.3390/buildings11080337

Begum, S., Ashfaq, M., Xia, E., & Awan, U. (2022). Does green transformational leadership lead to green innovation? The role of green thinking and creative process engagement. *Business Strategy and the Environment*, *31*(1), 580–597. DOI: 10.1002/bse.2911

Beitzen-Heineke, E. F., Balta-Ozkan, N., & Reefke, H. (2017). The prospects of zero-packaging grocery stores to improve the social and environmental impacts of the food supply chain. *Journal of Cleaner Production*, *140*, 1528–1541. DOI: 10.1016/j.jclepro.2016.09.227

Belleflamme, P., Lambert, T., & Schwienbacher, A. (2014). Crowdfunding: Tapping the right crowd. *Journal of Business Venturing*, *29*(5), 585–609. DOI: 10.1016/j.jbusvent.2013.07.003

Ben Jabeur, S., Khalfaoui, R., & Ben Arfi, W. (2021). The effect of green energy, global environmental indexes, and stock markets in predicting oil price crashes: Evidence from explainable machine learning. *Journal of Environmental Management*, *298*, 113511. DOI: 10.1016/j.jenvman.2021.113511

Ben Jedidia, K., & Guerbouj, K. (2021). Effects of zakat on the economic growth in selected Islamic countries: Empirical evidence. *International Journal of Development Issues*, *20*(1), 126–142. DOI: 10.1108/IJDI-05-2020-0100

Ben Mahjoub, L. (2025). Greenwashing practices and ESG reporting: An international review. *The International Journal of Sociology and Social Policy*, *45*(1/2), 173–188. DOI: 10.1108/IJSSP-08-2024-0365

Benchea, L., & Ilie, A. G. (2023). Preparing for a New World of Work: Leadership Styles Reconfigured in the Digital Age. *European Journal of Interdisciplinary Studies, 15*(1), 135–143. DOI: 10.24818/ejis.2023.10

Benitez, J., Arenas, A., Castillo, A., & Esteves, J. (2022). Impact of digital leadership capability on innovation performance: The role of platform digitization capability. *Information & Management, 59*(2), 103590. DOI: 10.1016/j.im.2022.103590

Berg, F., Kölbel, J., & Rigobon, R. (2022). Aggregate Confusion: The Divergence of ESG Ratings. *Review of Finance, 26*(6), 1315–1344. DOI: 10.1093/rof/rfac033

Berry, L. L., & Parasuraman, A. (2002). *Internal marketing: Directions for management.* Routledge.

Bhawe, N., Gupta, V. K., & Jain, T. K. (2006). The entrepreneurship of the Good Samaritan: a development framework to understand social entrepreneurship using insights from qualitative study. *Available at SSRN* 902685. DOI: 10.2139/ssrn.902685

Bilal, M., Xicang, Z., Jiying, W., Sohu, J. M., Akhtar, S., & Hassan, M. I. U. (2024). Digital Transformation and SME Innovation: A Comprehensive Analysis of Mediating and Moderating Influences. *Journal of the Knowledge Economy, 0123456789*(1), 1153–1182. Advance online publication. DOI: 10.1007/s13132-024-02054-0

Billah, M. M. (2003). *Islamic and modern insurance: Principles and practices.* Ilmiah Publishers.

Billah, M., Alam, M. R., & Hoque, M. E. (2024). Global uncertainty and the spillover of tail risk between green and Islamic markets: A time-frequency domain approach with portfolio implications. *International Review of Economics & Finance, 92*, 1416–1433. DOI: 10.1016/j.iref.2024.02.081

Blaique, L., Abu Salim, T., & Mir, F. A. (2024). Does human capital mediate the relationship among digital competence and service innovation capability? Evidence from the UAE during covid-19 pandemic. *International Journal of Innovation Science, 16*(4), 709–730. DOI: 10.1108/IJIS-11-2022-0214

Boer, H. & During, W.E. (2001). Innovation, what innovation? A comparison between product, process and organizational innovation, *International Journal of Technology Management, 22*(1/2/3), pp. 83-107.

Bono, J. E., & McNamara, G. (2011). Publishing in AMJ—Part 2: Research design. *Academy of Management Journal, 54*(4), 657–660. DOI: 10.5465/amj.2011.64869103

Bouoiyour, J., Selmi, R., & Wohar, M. E. (2018). Are Islamic stock markets efficient? A multifractal detrended fluctuation analysis [Preprint]. *Finance Research Letters, 26*, 100–105. Advance online publication. DOI: 10.1016/j.frl.2017.12.008

Bouri, E., Shahzad, S. J. H., Roubaud, D., Kristoufek, L., & Lucey, B. (2020). Bitcoin, gold, and commodities as safe havens for stocks: New insight through wavelet analysis [Preprint]. *The Quarterly Review of Economics and Finance, 77*, 156–164. Advance online publication. DOI: 10.1016/j.qref.2020.03.004

Bouzidah, A., & Hamouda, W. (2021). in Arabic. Assessment of financial inclusion in the Algerian banking sector during 2011–2018. *Journal of Financial and Accounting Sciences*, (1), 471. (2011-2018) | ASJP

Braun, V., & Clarke, V. (2006). Using thematic analysis in psychology. *Qualitative Research in Psychology, 3*(2), 77–101. DOI: 10.1191/1478088706qp063oa

Brimmell, J., Edwards, E. J., Uiga, L., Wood, G., & Vaughan, R. S. (2025). The structure of executive functions in athletes: A latent variable approach. *Psychology of Sport and Exercise, 78*(January), 102808. Advance online publication. DOI: 10.1016/j.psychsport.2025.102808 PMID: 39855374

British Council. United Nations Economic and Social Commission for Asia and the Pacific (UNESCAP), HSBC, & Social Enterprise UK. (2021). *The state of social enterprise in South East Asia*. British Council. https://www.britishcouncil.org/sites/default/files/the_state_of_social_enterprise_in_south_east_asia_0.pdf

Broadstock, D. C., Chatziantoniou, I., & Gabauer, D. (2022). Minimum Connectedness Portfolios and the Market for Green Bonds: Advocating Socially Responsible Investment (SRI) Activity BT - *Applications in Energy Finance: The Energy Sector, Economic Activity, Financial Markets and the Environment*. In Floros, C., & Chatziantoniou, I. (Eds.), (pp. 217–253). Springer International Publishing., DOI: 10.1007/978-3-030-92957-2_9

Brynjolfsson, E., Rock, D., & Syverson, C. (2018). Artificial intelligence and the modern productivity paradox: A clash of expectations and statistics. In *The economics of artificial intelligence: An agenda* (pp. 23–57). University of Chicago Press.

Buallay, A., Cummings, R., & Hamdan, A. (2019). Intellectual Capital Efficiency and Bank's Performance: A Comparative Study After the Global Financial Crisis. *Pacific Accounting Review, 31*(4), 672–694. DOI: 10.1108/PAR-04-2019-0039

Bull, R., McFarland, L., Cumming, T., & Wong, S. (2024). The Impact of Work-Related Wellbeing and Workplace Culture and Climate on Intention to Leave in the Early Childhood Sector. *Early Childhood Research Quarterly*, *69*, 13–24. DOI: 10.1016/j.ecresq.2024.06.002

Bundtzen, H., & Hinrichs, G. (2021). The link between organizational agility and VUCA: An agile assessment model. *Journal of Business Research, 100*, 116–125. DOI: 10.1016/j.jbusres.2021.03.053

Bussmann, N., Giudici, P., Marinelli, D., & Papenbrock, J. (2021). Explainable machine learning in credit risk management. *Computational Economics*, *57*(1), 203–216. DOI: 10.1007/s10614-020-10042-0

Butt, A., Imran, F., Helo, P., & Kantola, J. (2022). Strategic Design of Culture for Digital Transformation. *Journal of Innovation and Entrepreneurship*.

Cable, D. (2018). Why people lose motivation—And what managers can do to help. *Harvard Business Review*, *3*(1). https://hbr.org/2018/03/why-people-lose-motivation-and-what-managers-can-do-to-help

Cahyaningsih, E., Sensuse, D. I., & Noprisson, H. (2017). Multi Methods for Knowledge Management Strategy Roadmap of Government Human Capital Management. *Procedia Computer Science, 124*, 496–503. DOI: 10.1016/j.procs.2017.12.182

Cao, G., Duan, Y., & Edwards, J. S. (2025). Organizational culture, digital transformation, and product innovation: A systematic review. *Information & Management*, *62*(4), 104135. DOI: 10.1016/j.im.2025.104135

Carpignano, A., Golia, E., Di Mauro, C., Bouchon, S., & Nordvik, J. P. (2009). A methodological approach for the definition of multi-risk maps at regional level: First application. *Journal of Risk Research*, *12*(3–4), 513–534. DOI: 10.1080/13669870903050269

CBUAE. (2022). *Annual Report 2022*. Central Bank of the UAE.

Chatterji, A. K., Durand, R., Levine, D. I., & Touboul, S. (2016). Do ratings of firms converge? Implications for managers, investors and strategy researchers. *Strategic Management Journal*, *37*(8), 1597–1614. DOI: 10.1002/smj.2407

Chatziantoniou, I., Gabauer, D., & Gupta, R. (2021) 'Integration and Risk Transmission in the Market for Crude Oil: A Time-Varying Parameter Frequency Connectedness Approach', University of Pretoria Department of Economics Working Paper Series [Preprint], (June). Available at: https://www.up.ac.za/media/shared/61/WP/wp_2021_47.zp209709.pdf

Chatziantoniou, I., Gabauer, D., & Stenfors, A. (2021). Interest rate swaps and the transmission mechanism of monetary policy: A quantile connectedness approach. *Economics Letters, 204*, 109891. DOI: 10.1016/j.econlet.2021.109891

Cheah, J., Leong, S. Y., & Fernando, Y. (2022). Innovation strategies and organisational performance: The moderating function of corporate size among small- and medium-sized companies. *Benchmarking, 2018*. Advance online publication. DOI: 10.1108/BIJ-03-2021-0139

Chen, A., Li, L., & Shahid, W. (2024). Digital transformation as the driving force for sustainable business performance: A moderated mediation model of market-driven business model innovation and digital leadership capabilities. *Heliyon, 10*(8), e29509. DOI: 10.1016/j.heliyon.2024.e29509 PMID: 38655293

Cheng, M., & Micale, J. A. (2022). ESG risks and the value relevance of current and historical earnings. *Financial Markets, Institutions and Instruments, 31*(5), 207–237. DOI: 10.1111/fmii.12162

Chenni, S., & Ben Lakhder, E. (2018).in Arabic. The importance of financial inclusion in achieving development: Enhancing financial inclusion in the Arab Republic of Egypt. *Journal of Research in Financial Sciences*, 3(2). :
:

Chen, T. J. (2019). Marketing channel, corporate reputation, and profitability of life insurers: Evidence of Bancassurance in Taiwan. *The Geneva Papers on Risk and Insurance. Issues and Practice, 44*(4), 679–701. DOI: 10.1057/s41288-019-00137-7

Choiriyah, E. A. N. M., Kafi, A., Hikmah, I. F., & Indrawan, I. W. (2020). Zakat and poverty alleviation in Indonesia: A panel analysis at the provincial level. *Journal of Islamic Monetary Economics and Finance, 6*(4), 811–832. DOI: 10.21098/jimf.v6i4.1122

Christoffersen, P., Feunou, B., Jacobs, K., & Meddahi, N. (2014). The economic value of realized volatility: Using high- frequency returns for option valuation. *Journal of Financial and Quantitative Analysis, 49*(3), 663–697. DOI: 10.1017/S0022109014000428

Chung, K. H., & Pruitt, S. W. (1994). A Simple Approximation of Tobin's Q. *Financial Management, 23*(3), 70. DOI: 10.2307/3665623

CIDB. (2020). *Construction 4.0 Strategic Plan (2021-2025)*. CIDB.

Cieri, F., Di Francesco, G., Cross, C. L., Bender, A., & Caldwell, J. Z. K. (2025). Dynamic neurocognitive adaptation in aging: Development and validation of a new scale. *Alzheimer's and Dementia. Alzheimer's & Dementia: Translational Research & Clinical Interventions*, *11*(1), 1–9. DOI: 10.1002/trc2.70049 PMID: 39839075

Cimini, C., Boffelli, A., Lagorio, A., Kalchschmidt, M., & Pinto, R. (2020). How do Industry 4.0 technologies influence organisational change? An empirical analysis of Italian SMEs. *Journal of Manufacturing Technology Management*, *32*(3), 695–721. Advance online publication. DOI: 10.1108/JMTM-04-2019-0135

Climate Bonds Initiative. (2024). *Global State of the Market Report 2023: Trends and insights on GSS+ bond markets*. Climate Bonds Initiative. https://www.climatebonds.net/publications

Climent, F., & Soriano, P. (2011). Green and Good? The Investment Performance of US Environmental Mutual Funds [Preprint]. *Journal of Business Ethics*, *103*(2), 275–287. Advance online publication. DOI: 10.1007/s10551-011-0865-2

Cohen, B., & Winn, M. I. (2007). Market imperfections, opportunity and sustainable entrepreneurship. *Journal of Business Venturing*, *22*(1), 29–49. DOI: 10.1016/j.jbusvent.2004.12.001

Cohen, S., & Lezak, A. (1977). Noise and inattentiveness to social cues. *Environment and Behavior*, *9*(4), 559–572. DOI: 10.1177/001391657794007

Cokrohadisumarto, W. M., & Sari, Y. I. (2024). Mosque-Based Integrated Community Empowerment Model. *Islamic Social Finance*, *4*(1), 1–26.

Cortellazzo, L., Bruni, E., & Zampieri, R. (2019). The role of leadership in a digitalized world: A review. *Frontiers in Psychology*, *10*, 1938. DOI: 10.3389/fpsyg.2019.01938

Courtat, M., Joyce, P. J., Sim, S., Sadhukhan, J., & Murphy, R. (2023). Towards credible, evidence-based environmental rating ecolabels for consumer products: A proposed framework. *Journal of Environmental Management*, *336*, 117684. DOI: 10.1016/j.jenvman.2023.117684 PMID: 36924711

Craveiroa, F., Duartec, J. P., Bartoloa, H., & Bartolod, P. J. (2019). Additive manufacturing as an enabling technology for digital construction: A perspective on Construction 4.0. *Sustainable Development (Bradford)*, *4*(6), 220–232. DOI: 10.1002/sd.1954

Cristofaro, M., & Giardino, P. L. (2025). Sur fi ng the AI waves : the historical evolution of arti fi cial intelligence in management and organizational investigations and practices. DOI: 10.1108/JMH-01-2025-0002

Crosby, M., Pattanayak, P., Verma, S., & Kalyanaraman, V. (2016). Blockchain Technology: Beyond Bitcoin. *Applied Innovation*, *2*(6-10), 71.

Croxford, H., Abramson, F., & Jablonowski, A. (2006). *The art of better retail banking*. Wiley & Sons.

Cunha, M. P., Gomes, E., Mellahi, K., Miner, A. S., & Rego, A. (2020). Strategic agility through improvisational capabilities: Implications for a paradox-sensitive HRM. Human Resource Management Review, 30(1), 100695. doi:10.1016/j.hrmr.2019.100695

D'Aveni, R. A., Dagnino, G. B., & Smith, K. G. (2010). The age of temporary advantage. *Strategic Management Journal*, *31*(13), 1371–1385. DOI: 10.1002/smj.897

D'Costa, I., Truong, M., Russell, L., & Adams, K. (2023). Employee Perceptions of Race and Racism in an Australian Hospital. *Social Science & Medicine*, *339*, 116364. DOI: 10.1016/j.socscimed.2023.116364 PMID: 37977016

D'Souza, C.. (2006). *Green products and corporate strategy: an empirical investigation*. Society and Business Review. [Preprint], DOI: 10.1108/17465680610669825

Dai, J., & Vasarhelyi, M. A. (2017). Toward Blockchain-Based Accounting and Assurance. *Journal of Information Systems*, *31*(3), 5–21. DOI: 10.2308/isys-51804

Dallasega, P., Rauch, E., & Linder, C. (2018). Industry 4.0 as an enabler of proximity for construction supply chains: A systematic literature review. *Computers in Industry*, *99*, 205–225. DOI: 10.1016/j.compind.2018.03.039

Damanik, J., & Weber, H. F. (2006). *Ecotourism planning: From theory to application*. Andi.

Damit, M. R. M., & Mohammed, R. (2025). Unveiling Takaful subscriptions: Demographic factors and their impact on Takaful products penetration in Malaysia. *International Journal of Business and Technology Management*, *5*(4), 290–298.

Darwiesh, A., El-Baz, A. H., Abualkishik, A. Z., & Elhoseny, M. (2023). Artificial intelligence model for risk management in healthcare institutions: Towards sustainable development. *Sustainability (Basel)*, *15*(1), 420. Advance online publication. DOI: 10.3390/su15010420

Daud, W. N. W. D., Yazid, A. S., & Hussin, M. R. (2010). The effect of chief risk officer (CRO) on enterprise risk management (ERM) practices: Evidence from Malaysia. [IBER]. *The International Business & Economics Research Journal*, *9*(11). Advance online publication. DOI: 10.19030/iber.v9i11.30

De Smet, A., Lurie, M., & St George, A. (2018). Leading agile transformation: The new capabilities leaders need to build 21st-century organizations. *McKinsey & Company*, 1–27. https://www.mckinsey.com/industries/organization/our-insights/leading-agile-transformation

Dean, T. J., & McMullen, J. S. (2007). Toward a theory of sustainable entrepreneurship: Reducing environmental degradation through entrepreneurial action. *Journal of Business Venturing*, *22*(1), 50–76. DOI: 10.1016/j.jbusvent.2005.09.003

Del Bosco, B., & Misani, N. (2016). The effect of cross-listing on the environmental, social, and governance performance of firms. *Journal of World Business*, *51*(6), 977–990. DOI: 10.1016/j.jwb.2016.08.002

Del Gesso, C., & Lodhi, R. N. (2025). Theories underlying environmental, social and governance (ESG) disclosure: A systematic review of accounting studies. *Journal of Accounting Literature*, *47*(2), 433–461. DOI: 10.1108/JAL-08-2023-0143

Deloitte. (2013). The global Takaful insurance market charting the road to mass markets, A Deloitte ME IFKC Practice Insights Series, available at: https://ceif.iba.edu.pk/pdf/ Deloitte The global Takaful insurance market Charting the road to mass markets.pdf (accessed 20 November2016).

Demirguc-Kunt, A., & Klapper, L. (2012). *Measuring financial inclusion: The Global Findex database* (Policy Research Working Paper No. 6025). Washington, DC: World Bank. Measuring financial inclusion: the Global Findex Database

Dewi, Y. K., Safruddin, S., & Zainuddin, M. (2024a). Development Center of Minapolitan Area in Wajo District. *Torani Journal of Fisheries and Marine Science*, *7*(2), 151–159. DOI: 10.35911/torani.v7i2.32856

Dhubayan, D. B. (2011).in Arabic. *The authenticity and modernity of financial transactions*. Riyadh: King Fahd National Library.

Dickinson, G. (2001). Enterprise risk management: Its origins and conceptual foundation. *The Geneva Papers on Risk and Insurance. Issues and Practice*, *26*(3), 360–366. DOI: 10.1111/1468-0440.00121

Diebold, F. X., & Yilmaz, K. (2012). Better to give than to receive: Predictive directional measurement of volatility spillovers. *International Journal of Forecasting*, *28*(1), 57–66. DOI: 10.1016/j.ijforecast.2011.02.006

Diebold, F. X., & Yilmaz, K. (2014). On the network topology of variance decompositions: Measuring the connectedness of financial firms. *Journal of Econometrics*, *182*(1), 119–134. DOI: 10.1016/j.jeconom.2014.04.012

Dirie, K. A., Alam, M. M., & Maamor, S. (2023). Islamic social finance for achieving sustainable development goals: A systematic literature review and future research agenda. *International Journal of Ethics and Systems*, 41(2). Islamic social finance for achieving sustainable development goals: a systematic literature review and future research agenda | International Journal of Ethics and Systems | Emerald Publishing

Djunarsjah, E., & Putra, A. P. (2021). The concept of an archipelagic Province in Indonesia. *IOP Conference Series. Earth and Environmental Science*, *777*(1), 012040. DOI: 10.1088/1755-1315/777/1/012040

Dogan, E., Madaleno, M., Taskin, D., & Tzeremes, P. (2022). Investigating the spillovers and connectedness between green finance and renewable energy sources. *Renewable Energy*, *197*, 709–722. DOI: 10.1016/j.renene.2022.07.131

Doğan, O., & Baloğlu, N. (2018). Organizational agency and its reflections in some educational institutions. In *13th International Educational Administration Congress: The 13th International Congress on Educational Administration.*

Dong, F., Li, Z., Huang, Z., & Liu, Y. (2024). Extreme weather, policy uncertainty, and risk spillovers between energy, financial, and carbon markets. *Energy Economics*, *137*, 107761. DOI: 10.1016/j.eneco.2024.107761

Drider, H., & Gharib, T. (2021).in Arabic. The role of Islamic finance in promoting financial inclusion: A case study of a sample of Al Baraka Bank clients. *Al-Bashaer Economic Journal*, 7(1). :
| ASJP

Duan, K., Zhao, Y., Urquhart, A., & Huang, Y. (2023). Do clean and dirty cryptocurrencies connect with financial assets differently? The role of economic policy uncertainty. *Energy Economics*, *127*, 107079. https://doi.org/https://doi.org/10.1016/j.eneco.2023.107079. DOI: 10.1016/j.eneco.2023.107079

Durand, D. (1959). The cost of capital, corporation finance, and the theory of investment: Comment. *The American Economic Review*, *49*(4), 639–655.

Duvalda, I., Obel, B., Lohse, C., Kirkegaard, H., & Burton, R. M. (2025). Organizational resilience in emergency healthcare: Lessons from the COVID-19 pandemic in five Danish hospitals. *Social Science & Medicine*, *366*, 117728. DOI: 10.1016/j.socscimed.2025.117728 PMID: 39855026

Dwyer, L., & Gill, E. A. (2019). Obalni i pomorski turizam: o ozbiljnim problemima. *Acta turistica, 31*(2), 213–242. DOI: 10.22598/at/2019.31.2.213

Ederington, L. H. (1979). The hedging performance of the new futures markets. *The Journal of Finance*, *34*(1), 157–170. DOI: 10.1111/j.1540-6261.1979.tb02077.x e-Estonia. (2022). *Digital Transformation Case Study: Estonia*. https://e-estonia.com

El Jazzar, M., Schranz, C., Urban, H., & Nassereddine, H. (2021). Integrating Construction 4.0 technologies: A four-layer implementation plan. *Frontiers in Built Environment, 144*, 671408. Advance online publication. DOI: 10.3389/fbuil.2021.671408

El Nsour, J. A. (2021). Investigating the impact of organizational agility on the competitive advantage. *Journal of Governance and Regulation, 10*(1).

Elbaramelgy, M., Gammaz, S. A., & Emara, M. S. (2019). Community Based Ecotourism Strategies: Key Indicators For Successful Practices In Developing Countries. *Journal of Urban Research, 31*(1), 103–122. DOI: 10.21608/jur.2019.88566

Eldaia, M., Hanefah, M. M., Marzuki, A., & Shatnawi, S. (2020). Takaful in Malaysia: Emergence, growth, and prospects. In Takaful in Malaysia: Emerging opportunities, challenges and way forward (pp. 682–699). Universiti Sains Islam Malaysia.

El-Halaby, S., Aboul-Dahab, S., & Bin Qoud, N. (2021). A systematic literature review on AAOIFI standards. *Journal of Financial Reporting and Accounting, 19*(2), 133–183. DOI: 10.1108/JFRA-06-2020-0170

Eling, M., Nuessle, D., & Staubli, J. (2021). The impact of artificial intelligence along the insurance value chain and on the insurability of risks. In Geneva Papers on Risk and Insurance: Issues and Practice (Issue 0123456789). Palgrave Macmillan UK. DOI: 10.1057/s41288-020-00201-7

Elkington, J. (2018). 25 years ago I coined the phrase "Triple Bottom Line." Here's why it's time to rethink it. *Harvard Business Review*. https://hbr.org/2018/06/25-years-ago-i-coined-the-phrase-triple-bottom-line-heres-why-im-giving-up-on-it

Elkington, J. (1997). *Cannibals with forks: The triple bottom line of 21st century business*. Capstone Publishing.

Elnagar, S., Weistroffer, H., & Thomas, M. (2019). Agile requirement engineering maturity framework for Industry 4.0. In *Information Systems: 15th European, Mediterranean, and Middle Eastern Conference, EMCIS 2018, Limassol, Cyprus, October 4–5, 2018, Proceedings 15* (pp. 405–418). Springer International Publishing. https://doi.org/DOI: 10.1007/978-3-030-18097-1_33

Enyioko, N., & Onwusoro, C. (2018). Customer Association Management and Hospitality Industry in Nigeria. SSRN *Electronic Journal, 9*(1), 116–126. DOI: 10.2139/ssrn.2397245

Ermawati, Y. (2023). Ecosystems for entrepreneurship: A study of supportive environments and their impact. [AMAR]. *Amkop Management Accounting Review, 3*(2), 58–74. DOI: 10.37531/amar.v3i2.1512

Esmaeili Mahyari, M., Nourmandipour, V., & Beishami, B. (2024). Exploring the evolution of rural tourism:systematic review and identifying the current and future trends. *Journal of Rural Research, 15*(4), 37–50. DOI: 10.22059/jrur.2025.376723.1945

European Commission. (2020). *EU taxonomy for sustainable activities: What the EU is doing to create an EU-wide classification system for sustainable activities.* https://ec.europa.eu/info/business-economy-euro/banking-and-finance/sustainable-finance/eu-taxonomy-sustainable-activities_en

FAO. (2022). *Digital agriculture*. Food and Agriculture Organization of the United Nations.

FATF. (2023). *Anti-money laundering and counter-terrorist financing measures.* Financial Action Task Force.

Fatimah, R., & Suryaman, M. (2024). Penggunaan Platform Crowdfunding dalam Upaya Peningkatan Penghimpunan Dana Zakat Infak dan Sedekah di LAZ Lidzikri Bandung. *As-Syirkah: Islamic Economic & Financial Journal, 3*(2), 847 -. DOI: 10.56672/syirkah.v3i2.209

Fatmah, D., Rahmah, M., Rahmah, Y., Hasani, S., & Purnama, C. (2024). ELEVATING FINANCIAL PERFORMANCE IN MUSLIM CLOTHING SMES BY LEVERAGING HUMAN RESOURCE CAPABILITIES AND CORPORATE STRATEGY. *Al-Muhasib: Journal of Islamic Accounting and Finance, 4*(2), 75–98.

Fawzy, R., & Saad, D. M. (2023). The relationship between agility drivers, agility capabilities, and organizational sustainability. *Journal of Business and Management Sciences, 11*, 101–114. DOI: 10.11648/j.jbms.2023 1104.11

Fernandez, D., & Aman, A. (2022). The Influence of RPA technology on Employee Skills in the Accounting Profession. *Jurnal Pengurusan, 65*, 71–82.

Fındıklı, M. A., Yozgat, U., & Rofcanin, Y. (2015). Examining Organizational Innovation and Knowledge Management Capacity: The Central Role of Strategic Human Resources Practices (SHRPs). *Procedia: Social and Behavioral Sciences, 181*, 377–387. DOI: 10.1016/j.sbspro.2015.04.900

Fitch Ratings. (2025, May 12). Malaysia's takaful industry poised for growth amidst regulatory reforms. *Insurance Asia.* https://insuranceasia.com/insurance/news/malaysias-takaful-industry-poised-growth-amidst-regulatory-reforms

Fitriana, S., & Wardhani, R. (2020). The effect of enterprise risk management and sustainability reporting quality on performance: Evidence from Southeast Asia countries. *International Journal of Economic Policy in Emerging Economies, 13*(4), 344. DOI: 10.1504/IJEPEE.2020.109588

Friede, G., Busch, T., & Bassen, A. (2015). ESG and financial performance: Aggregated evidence from more than 2000 empirical studies. *Journal of Sustainable Finance & Investment*, *5*(4), 210–233. DOI: 10.1080/20430795.2015.1118917

Fuady, M., Kevin, M. A., Farrel, M. R., & Triaputri, A. (2025). Mangrove Forest Conservation for Disaster Mitigation and Community Welfare in Banda Aceh: A Sustainable Development Goals (SDG's) Approach. *Journal of Lifestyle and SDGs Review*, *5*(3), e04787–e04787. DOI: 10.47172/2965-730X.SDGsReview.v5.n03.pe04787

G. I. R. Martha, F. L. Gaol, S. H. Supangkat and B. Ranti, "Utilization of Decentralized Autonomous Organization (DAO) for Virtual Property Transaction Governance in Metaverse: A Conceptual Framework," *2023 3rd International Conference on Intelligent Cybernetics Technology & Applications (ICICyTA)*, Denpasar, Bali, Indonesia, 2023, pp. 306-311, doi: 10.1109/ICICyTA60173.2023.10429035.

Gala, K. (2023). *Corporate Social Responsibility and Greenwashing in the perception of customers: A Case Study of Beyond Petroleum*. Exxon, and Shell.

Gani, A. S. A., Salim, B., & Udin, N. M. (2020). The implementation of risk management in Malaysian public sector to sustain federal Government's revenue. *International Journal Of Accounting. Finance and Risk Management*, *5*(2), 76–83.

Gani, I. M., & Bahari, Z. (2020). Islamic banking's contribution to the Malaysian real economy. *ISRA International Journal of Islamic Finance*, *13*(1), 6–25. DOI: 10.1108/IJIF-01-2019-0004

Gaviria, D. A. G., Martínez, E. M. C., Polo, O. C. C., & Arcila, J. O. S. (2023). Accounting Mechanism to Measure the Environmental Impact of Industries in the Aburrá Valley and its Application of the General Disclosure Requirements Related to Financial Information on Sustainability (IFRS S1) and Climate-Related Disclosures (IFRS S2). *Revista de Gestao Social e Ambiental*, *17*(5), 1–16. DOI: 10.24857/rgsa.v17n5-013

Geissdoerfer, M., Savaget, P., Bocken, N. M. P., & Hultink, E. J. (2017). The Circular Economy – A new sustainability paradigm? *Journal of Cleaner Production*, *143*, 757–768. DOI: 10.1016/j.jclepro.2016.12.048

Geleti, D. (2022). Leadership styles for agricultural research and development organizations: Towards enabling adaptive spaces for enhanced organizational agility. *International Journal of Leadership in Education*, *25*(2), 189–208. DOI: 10.1080/13603124.2020.1794607

Gentile, G., & Gupta, J. (2025). Orchestrating the narrative: The role of fossil fuel companies in delaying the energy transition. *Renewable & Sustainable Energy Reviews*, *212*, 115359. DOI: 10.1016/j.rser.2025.115359

George, G., Merrill, R. K., & Schillebeeckx, S. J. D. (2021). Digital sustainability and entrepreneurship: How digital innovations are helping tackle climate change and sustainable development. *Entrepreneurship Theory and Practice*, *45*(5), 999–1027. DOI: 10.1177/1042258719899425

Ghallabi, F., Yousaf, I., Ghorbel, A., & Li, Y. (2024). Time-varying risk spillovers between renewable energy and Islamic stock markets: Evidence from the Russia-Ukraine conflict. *Pacific-Basin Finance Journal*, *85*, 102345. DOI: 10.1016/j.pacfin.2024.102345

Ghimire, A., & Jain, P. T. (2025). AI-Driven Drug Repurposing for Oncology: Identifying Novel Cancer Treatments from Existing Drugs. *Journal of Biosciences and Medicines*, *13*(05), 197–220. DOI: 10.4236/jbm.2025.135016

Ghozali, M., Amir Sup, D. F., Prastyaningsih, I., & Adan, H. Y. (2024). The law concept of Sharia banking compliance on Murabaha financing in Indonesia. *Samarah: Jurnal Hukum Keluarga dan Hukum Islam*, 8(3). The Law Concept of Sharia Banking Compliance on Murabaha Financing in Indonesia | Samarah: Jurnal Hukum Keluarga dan Hukum Islam

Gidron, B. (2017). The dual hybridity of social enterprises for marginalized populations. *Journal of Social Entrepreneurship*, *8*(1), 1–13. DOI: 10.1080/19420676.2016.1207700

Gilvary, C., Madhukar, N., Elkhader, J., & Elemento, O. (2019). The missing pieces of artificial intelligence in medicine. *Trends in Pharmacological Sciences*, *40*(8), 555–564. DOI: 10.1016/j.tips.2019.06.001

Golshan, N. M., & Rasid, S. A. (2012). Determinants of enterprise risk management adoption: An empirical analysis of Malaysian public listed firms. *International Journal of Social and Human Sciences*, *6*, 119–126.

Gomez-Trujillo, A. M., Gonzalez-Perez, M. A., & Baena-Rojas, J. J. (2024). Sustainable strategy as a lever for corporate legitimacy and long-term competitive advantage: An examination of an emerging market multinational. *European Business Review, 36*(1), 112–139. DOI: 10.1108/EBR-01-2023-0003

Gopal, S., & Pitts, J. (2025). Regulation and Frameworks: Current and Future Reporting Trends. In *The FinTech Revolution: Bridging Geospatial Data Science, AI, and Sustainability* (pp. 183–224). Springer Nature Switzerland.

Gortsos, C. V., & Kyriazis, D. (2024). The taxonomy regulation and its implementation. In *Sustainable Finance in Europe: Corporate Governance, Financial Stability and Financial Markets* (pp. 505–561). Springer International Publishing. DOI: 10.1007/978-3-031-53696-0_13

Guemmaz, S. (2023). Shareholding relations between banks and insurance companies in Algeria: An overview. *Journal of Innovations and Sustainability, 7*(2), 1. DOI: 10.51599/is.2023.07.02.01

Gujarati, D. N. (2021). *Essentials of econometrics.* Sage Publications.

Gulo, H., Bate'e, M. M., Telaumbanua, E., & Lase, H. (2024). Analysis of Human Resource Development Training in Improving Employee Performance. *Golden Ratio of Data in Summary, 4*(2), 467–472. DOI: 10.52970/grdis.v4i2.565

Gunardi, S., Rahman, A. A., Salleh, A. Z., Noor, K. M., Omar, S. M. N. S., & Shahbuddin, Z. H. S. (2024). Takaful: Principles and applications in managing Death Charity Money Scheme (DCMS) at Tengku Mizan Zainal Abidin Mosque, Kerteh, Terengganu to develop ecosystem of halal social economy. *International Journal of Religion, 5*(11), 5897–5903. DOI: 10.61707/1cqdz704

Gundogdu, A. S. (2019). Poverty, hunger, and inequality in the context of zakat and waqf. *darulfunun ilahiyat, 30*(1), 49-64. https://doi.org/DOI: 10.26650/di.2019.30.1.0005

Gutiérrez-Ponce, H., & Wibowo, S. A. (2023). Sustainability reports and disclosure of the Sustainable Development Goals (SDGs): Evidence from Indonesian listed companies. *Sustainability (Basel), 15*(24), 16919. DOI: 10.3390/su152416919

Guzmán, V. E., Muschard, B., Gerolamo, M., Kohl, H., & Rozenfeld, H. (2020). Characteristics and skills of leadership in the context of Industry 4.0. *Procedia Manufacturing, 43*, 543–550. DOI: 10.1016/j.promfg.2020.02.167

Ha, A., Giran, A., Fadzline, P., Tamyez, M., & Fauzi, M. A. (2025). The paradoxes of sustainable HRM : Insights through the perspective of common good, green, social responsibility, and triple bottom line. 0(0), 1–19. DOI: 10.1177/01672533251320795

Habib, S., Masood, H., Hassan, T., Mubin, M., & Baig, U. (2014). Operational Risk Management in Corporate and Banking Sector of Pakistan. SSRN Electronic Journal. DOI: 10.2139/ssrn.2663415

Habib, A. M., & Dalwai, T. (2024). Does The Efficiency of a Firm's Intellectual Capital and Working Capital Management Affect Its Performance? *Journal of the Knowledge Economy, 15*(1), 3202–3238. DOI: 10.1007/s13132-023-01138-7 PMID: 40478946

Hadbawi, A. (2023).in Arabic. The role of Islamic banking in promoting financial inclusion in Algeria (2011–2021). *Journal of Economic Studies*, 17(1). 2011-2021 | ASJP

Hair, J. F.Jr, Sarstedt, M., Hopkins, L., & Kuppelwieser, V. G. (2014). Partial least squares structural equation modeling (PLS-SEM): An emerging tool in business research. *European Business Review, 26*(2), 106–121. DOI: 10.1108/EBR-10-2013-0128

Hakim, L. (2008). Planning for nature-based tourism in east java: Recent status of biodiversity, conservation, and its implication for sustainable tourism. *Asean Journal on Hospitality and Tourism, 7*(2), 155–167. DOI: 10.5614/ajht.2008.7.2.02

Ha, L. T., & Nham, N. T. H. (2022). An application of a TVP-VAR extended joint connected approach to explore connectedness between WTI crude oil, gold, stock and cryptocurrencies during the COVID-19 health crisis. *Technological Forecasting and Social Change, 183*, 121909. DOI: 10.1016/j.techfore.2022.121909

Halik, A., Yasin, M., & Sumiati, S. (2024). Designing EDGE (Enhanced destination growth and engagement) to Improve the performance of marine tourism in East Java. *Edelweiss Applied Science and Technology, 8*(6), 8782–8792. DOI: 10.55214/25768484.v8i6.3875

Hallegatte, S., Rentschler, J., & Rozenberg, J. (2020). *Adaptation principles: A guide for designing strategies for climate change adaptation and resilience*. World Bank Publications. DOI: 10.1596/34780

Hambrick, D. C., & Mason, P. A. (1984). Upper echelons: The organization as a reflection of its top managers. *Academy of Management Review, 9*(2), 193–206. DOI: 10.2307/258434

Hamzah, A., Arifin, A., Abdullah, S., Salim, M. N. H. M., & Junaid, I. (2024). Empowerment of coastal communities through marine tourism: a functional approach. *Planning malaysia, 22*. DOI: 10.21837/pm.v22i34.1633

Handini, S., Baktiono, R. A., & Purnomo, B. R. (2023). The Influence Of Financial Ratio On Profit Growth In Mining Companies in Indonesia. *Deleted Journal, 21*(3), 419–433. DOI: 10.29062/mahardika.v21i3.642

Haron, S., & Nursofiza, W. (2008). *Creating a dynamic Islamic capital market: the essential role of innovation, Islamic Capital Markets: Products, Regulation and Development, Islamic Research and Training Institute*. Islamic Development Bank Group.

Hartmann, P. M., Zaki, M., Feldmann, N., & Neely, A. (2016). Capturing value from big data–a taxonomy of data-driven business models used by start-up firms. *International Journal of Operations & Production Management, 36*(10), 1382–1406. DOI: 10.1108/IJOPM-02-2014-0098

Hasani, T., Rezania, D., & Mohammadi, M. (2024). Towards a framework for successful metaverse adoption in Small and Medium-sized Enterprises: An exploratory investigation. *International Journal of Engineering Business Management, 16*, 1–34. DOI: 10.1177/18479790241257118

Hassan, H. A., & Abbas, S. K. (2020). Factors Influencing The Investors' Intention To Adopt Takaful (Islamic Insurance) Products: A survey of Pakistan. *Journal of Islamic Marketing, 11*(1), 1–13. DOI: 10.1108/JIMA-03-2018-0064

Hassan, M. K.. (2021). *Safe havens in Islamic financial markets: COVID-19 versus GFC*. Global Finance Journal., DOI: 10.1016/j.gfj.2021.100643

Hassan, M. K., Kamran, M., Djajadikerta, H. G., & Choudhury, T. (2022). Search for safe havens and resilience to global financial volatility: Response of GCC equity indexes to GFC and Covid-19. *Pacific-Basin Finance Journal, 73*, 101768. DOI: 10.1016/j.pacfin.2022.101768

Hastuti, H., Muhidu, A., Rastin, R., & Mokodompit, E. A. (2023). Indonesia's Marine Economic Potential As A Maritime Country: *International Journal of Science. Technology & Management, 4*(4), 813–825. DOI: 10.46729/ijstm.v4i4.897

Hater, J. J., & Bass, B. M. (1988). Superiors' evaluations and subordinates' perceptions of transformational and transactional leadership. *The Journal of Applied Psychology, 73*(4), 695–702. DOI: 10.1037/0021-9010.73.4.695

Heaton, J. B., Polson, N. G., & Witte, J. H. (2017). Deep learning for finance: Deep portfolios. *Applied Stochastic Models in Business and Industry, 33*(1), 3–12. DOI: 10.1002/asmb.2209

Heineke, J., & Davis, M. M. (2007). The emergence of service operations management as an academic discipline. *Journal of Operations Management, 25*(2), 364–374. DOI: 10.1016/j.jom.2006.11.003

Herianingrum, S., Supriani, I., Sukmana, R., Effendie, E., Widiastuti, T., Fauzi, Q., & Shofawati, A. (2024). Zakat as an instrument of poverty reduction in Indonesia. *Journal of Islamic Accounting and Business Research, 15*(4), 643–660. DOI: 10.1108/JIABR-11-2021-0307

Hilton, S. K., Arkorful, H., & Martins, A. (2021). Democratic leadership and organizational performance: The moderating effect of contingent reward. *Management Research Review, 44*(7), 1042–1058. DOI: 10.1108/MRR-04-2020-0237

Holst, G. M. (2021). *Transactional, instrumental and transformational leadership: What is more effective for an Industry 4.0 transformation?* (Master's thesis, University of Twente). https://doi.org/DOI: 10.1007/978-3-030-36603-0

Hossain, M. A., & Nadeem, A. (2019, May). Towards digitizing the construction industry: State of the art of construction 4.0. In *Proceedings of the ISEC* (Vol. 10, pp. 1–6). https://doi.org/DOI: 10.1109/ISEC.2019.0013

Hossain, M. B., Rahman, M. U., Čater, T., & Vasa, L. (2024). Determinants of SMEs' strategic entrepreneurial innovative digitalization: Examining the mediation role of human capital. *European Journal of Innovation Management.*

Hutnaleontina, P. N., Bendesa, I. K. G., & Yasa, I. G. W. M. (2022). Correlation of community-based tourism with sustainable development to improve community welfare: A review. *International Journal of Applied Sciences in Tourism and Events, 6*(2), 183–193. DOI: 10.31940/ijaste.v6i2.183-193

Hwang, J., Youm, C., Park, H., Kim, B., Choi, H., & Cheon, S. M. (2025). Machine learning for early detection and severity classification in people with Parkinson's disease. *Scientific Reports, 15*(1), 234. Advance online publication. DOI: 10.1038/s41598-024-83975-3

Ibrahim Salem, Y., & Yahia, H. (2021). in Arabic. Requirements for enhancing financial inclusion: A case study of some Arab countries. []. Al-Basira Center for Research, Consulting, and Educational Services, Algeria. -
| ASJP]. *Journal of Economic Studies (Glasgow, Scotland),* •••, 1.

Ichsan, N. (2015). Analisa SWOT, prospek dan strategi pengembangan asuransi Syariah Di Indonesia (SWOT analysis, prospects and development strategy for Islamic insurance in Indonesia), available at: https://nurulichsanaan.files.wordpress.com/2015/10/analsis-swot-asuransi-syariahjurnal-kordinat.pdf (accessed 10 November 2016).

Iftikhar, A., Musa, S., Alam, M., & Su'ud, M. M. (2020). Artificial intelligence-based risk management in global software development: A proposed architecture to reduce risk using time, budget, and resource constraints. *Journal of Computational and Theoretical Nanoscience*, *17*(2–3), 878–885. DOI: 10.1166/jctn.2020.8735

Ihl, C., & Piller, F. (2016). 3D printing as driver of localized manufacturing: Expected benefits from producer and consumer perspectives. In *The Decentralized and Networked Future of Value Creation: 3D Printing and Its Implications for Society, Industry, and Sustainable Development* (pp. 179–204). Springer International Publishing. DOI: 10.1007/978-3-319-31686-4_10

Ikhwani, H., Putro, M. H. M., Mustain, M., Satrio, D., Sujantoko, , Hadiwidodo, Y. S., & Nasution, P. H. O. (2023). The Concept of Integrated Coastal Management for Eco-Tourism Development at Dalegan Beach, Gresik Regency, East Java, Indonesia. *IOP Conference Series. Earth and Environmental Science*, *1198*(1), 012006. DOI: 10.1088/1755-1315/1198/1/012006

In, S. Y., & Schumacher, K. (2021). Carbonwashing: ESG data greenwashing in a post-Paris world. Settling climate accounts: *Navigating the road to net zero*, 39-58.

International Association of Insurance Supervisors. (2022). Issues in regulation and supervision of micro Takaful: Islamic microinsurance (IAIS Issues Paper). https://www.iaisweb.org/uploads/2022/01/151118-Issues-Paper-on-Regulation- and-Supervision-of-Microtakaful-Islamic-Microinsurance.pdf

International Monetary Fund. (2019). *Financial inclusion of small and medium-sized enterprises in the Middle East and Central Asia* (IMF Departmental Paper No. 19/02). Financial Inclusion of Small and Medium-Sized Enterprises in the Middle East and Central Asia

IRENA. (2020a). *Renewable energy and jobs – Annual review 2020*. Abu Dhabi: IRENA. https://www.irena.org/publications/2020/Sep/Renewable-Energy-and-Jobs-Annual-Review-2020

IRENA. (2020b). *Global Renewables Outlook: Energy transformation 2050*. International Renewable Energy Agency. https://www.irena.org/publications/2020/Apr/Global-Renewables-Outlook-2020

Irfan, M., Parameswaran, S., Singh, K. A., & Kismawadi, E. R. (2025). Cutting-edge technologies for economic well-being: The transformative power of AI and blockchain. In *Driving socio-economic growth with AI and blockchain* (pp. 229–248).

Iskandar, A., Possumah, B. T., Aqbar, K., & Yunta, A. H. D. (2021). Islamic philanthropy and poverty reduction in Indonesia: The role of integrated Islamic social and commercial finance institutions. *AL-IHKAM: Jurnal Hukum & Pranata Sosial, 16*(2), 274–301. DOI: 10.19105/al-lhkam.v16i2.5026

Islamic Development Bank. (2020). *Islamic social finance report 2020.* Islamic Social Finance Report 2020 - Islamic Development Bank Institute

Ismail, A. G., Mohd Daud, A. H., Mohamad Nasir, N. S., Omar, N., Azzan, N. A., Abdul Rahman, N. S., & Azmin, U. S. (2024).4. *UMRAN – International Journal of Islamic and Civilizational Studies, 11*(2), 89–102.

Jaafar, M., Mokhtar Azizi, N. S., Mohamed Ghazali, F. E., Mohd Zain, M. Z., Mat Kilau, N., & Ibrahim, F. S. (2025). Technology usage, challenges and strategies for Construction 4.0 from the perspective of Malaysian contractors. *Journal of Facilities Management.* Advance online publication. DOI: 10.1108/JFM-04-2024-0055

Jabarkhail, S. (2020). Servant Leadership in the Context of Mosque: A Qualitative Case Study of Muslim Women's Perspectives. *Administrative Sciences, 10*(3), 72. DOI: 10.3390/admsci10030072

Jamaludin, N. A., Omar Zaki, H., & Foong, Y. P. (2025). From the Ground Up: Sustainable Palm Oil and Entrepreneurial Opportunities. In Khalid, N., Abdul Rahman, N. A., Yan, C. W., & Idris, Z. (Eds.), *Palm Oil Export Market Trends, Challenges and Future Strategies for Sustainability* (pp. 206–218). Routledge. DOI: 10.4324/9781003518600-18

Jamil, N. N., & Marzuki, A. (2023). The effects ofshariah governance on takaful performance oftakaful operators in Malaysia. *Journal of Islamic, Social* [JISED]. *Economics and Development, 8*(59), 468–474.

Jamil, S. N., & Jamal, J. (2016). Importance of Islamic Financial Services Act 2013 in Takaful industry after the repealed Takaful Act 1984. *Diponegoro Law Review, 1*(1), 17–27. DOI: 10.14710/dilrev.1.1.2016.17-27

Jamrog, J., Vickers, M., & Bear, D. (2006). Building and sustaining a culture that supports innovation. *People and Strategy, 29*(3), 9–19. DOI: 10.1108/17527568200600003

Jannah, N., Bahri, M. I., Kismawadi, E. R., & Handriana, T. (2024). The effect of green brand image and green satisfaction on green brand equity mediated by green trust among outpatients. *Quality - Access to Success, 25*(198), 381–390. DOI: 10.47750/QAS/25.198.40

Jarboui, A., & Mnif, E. (2023). Can Clean Energy Stocks Predict Crude Oil Markets Using Hybrid and Advanced Machine Learning Models? *Asia-Pacific Financial Markets*, •••, 1–24.

Jarboui, A., Mnif, E., Zghidi, N., & Akrout, Z. (2024). Reconceptualizing the interplay between geopolitical index, green financial assets and renewable energy markets: Evidence from the machine learning approach [Preprint]. *Arab Gulf Journal of Scientific Research, 42*(4), 2001–2027. DOI: 10.1108/AGJSR-09-2023-0458

Jatiningrum, C., Fauzi, F., Utami, B. H. S., & Kassim, A. A. M. (2023). Mitigating Type II agency conflict through good corporate governance and disclosure quality. Akuntabilitas. *Journal of Accounting Research and Development, 17*(1), 1.

Jaunanda, M., Sembel, R., Hulu, E., & Ugut, G. S. S. (2024). The Impact of Intellectual Capital Strategy on Firm Value and Financial Distress. *Corporate & Business Strategy Review, 5*(3), 148–158. DOI: 10.22495/cbsrv5i3art14

Javaid, M., Haleem, A., & Suman, R. (2022). Major advancements of industry 4.0 to overcome challenges in manufacturing during the COVID-19 pandemic. *Cyber-Physical Systems: Solutions to Pandemic Challenges*, 157–182. https://doi.org/DOI: 10.1016/b978-0-12-820218-9.00010-7

Javaid, M., Haleem, A., Khan, I. H., & Suman, R. (2023). Understanding the potential applications of artificial intelligence in agriculture sector. *Advanced Agrochem, 2*(1), 15–30. DOI: 10.1016/j.aac.2022.10.001

Jiang, Y., & Tang, Q. (2023). Mandatory carbon reporting, voluntary carbon disclosure and ESG performance. *Pacific Accounting Review, 35*(4), 534–561. DOI: 10.1108/PAR-08-2022-0133

Jiménez, I., Mora-Valencia, A., & Perote, J. (2024). Bitcoin halving and the integration of cryptocurrency and forex markets: An analysis of the higher-order moment spillovers. *International Review of Economics & Finance, 92*, 302–315. DOI: 10.1016/j.iref.2024.02.022

Jin, S. V., Muqaddam, E. R., & Ryu, E. (2019). Instafamous and social media influencer marketing. *Marketing Intelligence & Planning, 37*(5), 567–579. DOI: 10.1108/MIP-09-2018-0375

Jin, Y., Zhao, H., Bu, L., & Zhang, D. (2023). Geopolitical risk, climate risk and energy markets: A dynamic spillover analysis. *International Review of Financial Analysis, 87*, 102597. DOI: 10.1016/j.irfa.2023.102597

Johnson-Kanda, I., & Yawson, R. M. (2018, May). Complex adaptive leadership for organization and human development. In *Proceedings of the 55th Annual Eastern Academy of Management Conference*, Providence, RI.

Judy Yueh Ling. Song; Esther, T. (2024). Beyond traditional contracts: the legal recognition and challenges of smart contracts in Malaysia and Singapore. *Journal of Law, Market & Innovation, 3*(3), 323–357. https://ojs.unito.it/index.php/JLMI/article/view/11334/9303

Juhari, J., Rahim, N. A., Masdek, N. R. N. M., Ahmad, K. S., & Husin, N. (2022). The role of awareness and knowledge toward motor takaful purchase intention among young generation. *International Journal of Academic Research in Business & Social Sciences, 12*(11), 304–313. DOI: 10.6007/IJARBSS/v12-i11/15224

Jutasompakorn, P., Perdana, A., & Yeap, L. H. (2025). Discerning the Key Drivers behind Cryptocurrency Transactions: Identifying the Configurational Factors. *Pacific Asia Journal of the Association for Information Systems, 17*(1), 5–29. DOI: 10.17705/1pais.17102

Kailash, M. S. R., Joshi, C., Desai, P. R., Teferra, N. B., & Radhakrishnan, S. (2023). The Rise of Ethical Consumerism: Marketing Strategies for the Conscious Buyer.

Kalkan, G. (2024). The impact of artificial intelligence on corporate governance. *Journal of Corporate Finance Research, 18*(2), 17–25.

Kant, S., & Adula, M. (2025). Innovation's Effect on Fostering a Sustainable Halal Ecosystem by Mediation of Techno-Preneurship in Ethiopia Halal Supply Chain. In *Exploring the Halal Industry and Its Business Ecosystem Prospects* (pp. 167–188). IGI Global Scientific Publishing. DOI: 10.4018/979-8-3693-8618-7.ch008

Kant, V., Weinert, L., & Rotter, T. (2025). *A qualitative study on the implementation of electronic medical records in German hospitals. Z. Evid. Fortbild. Qual. Gesundh. wesen*. ZEFQ.

Karneli, O. (2023). The role of adhocratic leadership in facing the changing business environment. [ADMAN]. *Journal of Contemporary Administration and Management, 1*(2), 77–83. DOI: 10.61100/adman.v1i2.26

Kasim, N., Nuhtay, S. N., & Salman, S. A. (2013). Shariah Governance for Islamic Capital Market: A Step Forward. International Journal of Education and Research Vol. 1 No. 6. ISSN: 2201-6740.

Kasim, N., Htay, S. N. N., & Salman, S. A. (2016). The Religious Perspective of Takaful as Ethical Insurance. *Mediterranean Journal of Social Sciences, 7*(4), 96–104. DOI: 10.5901/mjss.2016.v7n4p96

Keeley, A. R., Chapman, A. J., Yoshida, K., Xie, J., Imbulana, J., Takeda, S., & Managi, S. (2022). ESG metrics and social equity: Investigating commensurability. *Frontiers in Sustainability, 3*, 920955. DOI: 10.3389/frsus.2022.920955

Kenett, D. Y., Huang, X., Vodenska, I., Havlin, S., & Stanley, H. E. (2015). Partial correlation analysis: Applications for financial markets. *Quantitative Finance, 15*(4), 569–578. DOI: 10.1080/14697688.2014.946660

Kenett, D. Y., Tumminello, M., Madi, A., Gur-Gershgoren, G., Mantegna, R. N., & Ben-Jacob, E. (2010). Dominating clasp of the financial sector revealed by partial correlation analysis of the stock market. *PLoS One, 5*(12), e15032. DOI: 10.1371/journal.pone.0015032

Kenourgios, D., Naifar, N., & Dimitriou, D. (2016). Islamic financial markets and global crises: Contagion or decoupling? [Preprint]. *Economic Modelling, 57*, 36–46. Advance online publication. DOI: 10.1016/j.econmod.2016.04.014

Khairunnisa, H., Zairin, G. M., Budianto, P., Ramadhani, N. A., Septiani, M., & Musyaffi, A. M. (2024a). BITPAYS: Leveraging Bitcoin for Digital Payments to Fuel Economic Growth in Indonesia's Society 5.0 Era. *2024 International Conference on Electrical, Computer and Energy Technologies (ICECET*, 1–6. DOI: 10.1109/ICECET61485.2024.10698372

Khaled, M. M. (2013).in Arabic. *Islamic financing modes as an alternative to conventional financing in light of the global financial crisis* (Master's thesis, University of 20 August 1955, Skikda, Algeria). (3)

Khalid, A. M., & Jetin, B. (2025). *Introduction : Brunei Darussalam ' s Economy — Transition towards Development*. Springer Nature Singapore. DOI: 10.1007/978-981-97-6926-1

Khanna, P. (2024). Inclusive Business Models: Fostering Social Innovation and Entrepreneurial Ecosystems. [IJSR]. *International Journal of Scientific Research.*

Khan, W., Asif, M., & Shah, Q. (2021). An Empirical Analysis of Enterprise Risk Management and Firm's Value: Evidence from Pakistan. *JISR Management and Social Sciences & Economics, 18*(1), 107–124. DOI: 10.31384/jisrmsse/2020.18.1.8

Khilafa, M. B., & Boubelouta, B. (2023). *Arabic.The reality of financial inclusion in Algeria and the strategy for its enhancement. Majallat Namā lil-Iqti ād wa-al-Tijārah, 7(1).* | *ASJP.*

Kiefer, M., Jones, E. A., & Adams, A. T. (2017). Shareholders and managers as principal-agent hierarchies and cooperative teams. *Qualitative Research in Financial Markets*, *9*(1), 48–71. DOI: 10.1108/QRFM-04-2016-0014

Kiel, D., Arnold, C., & Voigt, K. I. (2017). The influence of the Industrial Internet of Things on business models of established manufacturing companies–A business level perspective. *Technovation*, *68*, 4–19. DOI: 10.1016/j.technovation.2017.09.003

Kim, I.-S., Park, M., Park, M.-Y., Yoo, H., & Choi, J. (2015). Factors Affecting the Perception of Importance and Practice of Patient Safety Management among Hospital Employees in Korea.

Kim, D., Shin, D., Lee, J., & Noh, G. (2024). Sustainability from institutionalism: Determinants of Korean companies' ESG performances. *Asian Business & Management*, *23*(3), 393–425. DOI: 10.1057/s41291-024-00271-8

Kim, E. H., & Lyon, T. P. (2015). Greenwash vs. Brownwash: Exaggeration and Undue Modesty in Corporate Sustainability Disclosure. *Organization Science*, *26*(3), 705–723. DOI: 10.1287/orsc.2014.0949

Kim, J. H., Kim, C. S., & Kim, J. M. (2015). Analysis of the Effect of Leadership and Organizational Culture on the Organizational Effectiveness of Radiological Technologists' Working Environments. *Journal of Radiological Science and Technology*.

Kim, J., & Han, W. (2012). Improving Service Quality in Long-term Care Hospitals: National Evaluation on Long-term Care Hospitals and Employees Perception of Quality Dimensions. *Osong Public Health and Research Perspectives*, *3*(2), 94–99. DOI: 10.1016/j.phrp.2012.04.005 PMID: 24159497

Kim, S. Y., & Tran, D. B. (2024). Intellectual Capital and Performance: Evidence from SMEs In Vietnam. *Asia-Pacific Journal of Business Administration*, *16*(4), 860–875. DOI: 10.1108/APJBA-08-2022-0343

Kirchherr, J., Reike, D., & Hekkert, M. (2018). Conceptualizing the circular economy: An analysis of 114 definitions. *Resources, Conservation and Recycling*, *127*, 221–232. DOI: 10.1016/j.resconrec.2017.09.005

Kismawadi, E. R. (2024a). Blockchain technology and Islamic finance: Empowering small businesses for financial sustainability. In *Technopreneurship in small businesses for sustainability* (pp. 50–77).

Kismawadi, E. R. (2024c). Sustainable Islamic financial inclusion: The ethical challenges of generative AI in product and service development. In *Exploring the ethical implications of generative AI* (pp. 237–258).

Kismawadi, E. R., Irfan, M., & Shah, S. M. A. R. (2023). Revolutionizing Islamic finance: Artificial intelligence's role in the future of industry. In *The impact of AI innovation on financial sectors in the era of Industry 5.0* (pp. 184–207).

Kismawadi, E. R., Irfan, M., Al Muddatstsir, U. D., & Abdulkarim, F. M. (2023). Fintech innovations: Risk mitigation strategies in Islamic finance. In *Fintech applications in Islamic finance: AI, machine learning, and blockchain techniques* (pp. 35–58).

Kismawadi, E. R. (2024b). Contribution of Islamic banks and macroeconomic variables to economic growth in developing countries: Vector error correction model approach (VECM). *Journal of Islamic Accounting and Business Research, 15*(2), 306–326. DOI: 10.1108/JIABR-03-2022-0090

Kok, N., Hoedemaekers, C., Fuchs, M., Cornet, A. D., Ewalds, E., Hom, H., Meijer, E., Meynaar, I., van Mol, M., van Mook, W., van der Steen-Dieperink, M., van Zanten, A., van der Hoeven, H., van Gurp, J., & Zegers, M. (2025). The interplay between organizational culture and burnout among ICU professionals: A cross-sectional multicenter study. *Journal of Critical Care, 85*, 154981. DOI: 10.1016/j.jcrc.2024.154981 PMID: 39608045

Kontuš, E., & Mihanović, D. (2019). Management of liquidity and liquid assets in small and medium-sized enterprises. *Ekonomska Istrazivanja, 32*(1), 3253–3271. DOI: 10.1080/1331677X.2019.1660198

KPMG. (2022). *The Pulse of Fintech H2 2022*. https://kpmg.com/my

Kuba, D., Kuba, M. Z. D., & Usman, K. S. (2024). Community-Based Management: Marine Tourism Development for Ecological and Economic Sustainability. *Journal of Economic Education and Entrepreneurship Studies, 5*(3), 467–479. DOI: 10.62794/je3s.v5i3.4372

Kudłak, R. (2024). Greenwashing or Striving to Persist: An Alternative Explanation of a Loose Coupling Between Corporate Environmental Commitments and Outcomes. *Journal of Business Ethics*, •••, 1–16.

Kurniawan, A. T., Bahri, B., Mukmin, H., & Yanti, F. (2023). *Revitalization of mosque functions in empowering city Islamic communities: Bandar Lampung. Proceedings of the International Conference on Education, Society and Humanity, 1*(1), 93–99. Universitas Islam Negeri Raden Intan Lampung. Retrieved from https://ejournal.unuja.ac.id/index.php/icesh

Kurniawan, R., & Hamsal, I. M. (2019). Achieving decision-making quality and organizational agility in innovation portfolio management in Telecommunication 4.0. *International Journal of Innovation, Creativity, and Change, 8*, 332–356.

Kurpierz, J. R., & Smith, K. (2020). The greenwashing triangle: Adapting tools from fraud to improve CSR reporting. Sustainability Accounting. *Management and Policy Journal, 11*(6), 1075–1093.

Lahmiri, S., Bekiros, S., & Bezzina, F. (2020). Multi-fluctuation nonlinear patterns of European financial markets based on adaptive filtering with application to family business, green, Islamic, common stocks, and comparison with Bitcoin, NASDAQ, and VIX [Preprint]. *Physica A, 538*, 122858. Advance online publication. DOI: 10.1016/j.physa.2019.122858

Lai, F. W. (2011). Enterprise Risk Management implementation framework for Malaysian public listed companies (Doctoral dissertation). University of Malaya.

Laroche, E. (2024). Management practices that promote preventive measures compliance: A comparative analysis between hospital healthcare workers and teachers. *Safety Science, 177*, 106591. DOI: 10.1016/j.ssci.2024.106591

Lasabuda, R. (2013). Pembangunan wilayah pesisir dan lautan dalam perspektif negara kepulauan republik indonesia. *Jurnal Ilmiah PLATAX, 1*(2), 92–101. DOI: 10.35800/jip.1.2.2013.1251

Lee, C. K., Chen, M. S., Zainudin, N. M., Fauzi, M. A., & Toh, T. C. (2022). Transformation of industrial revolution 4.0 in the construction industry: Understanding drivers & barriers with DEMATEL algorithm. *International Journal of Information Management, 16*(1), 31–43. DOI: 10.1016/ j.ijim.2022.03.002

Le, T. H. (2023). Quantile time-frequency connectedness between cryptocurrency volatility and renewable energy volatility during the COVID-19 pandemic and Ukraine-Russia conflicts. *Renewable Energy, 202*, 613–625. DOI: 10.1016/j.renene.2022.11.062

Liden, R. C., Wayne, S. J., Meuser, J. D., Hu, J., Wu, J., & Liao, C. (2015). Servant leadership: Validation of a short form of the SL-28. *The Leadership Quarterly, 26*(2), 254–269. DOI: 10.1016/j.leaqua.2014.12.002

Liebenberg, A. P., & Hoyt, R. E. (2003). The determinants of enterprise risk management: Evidence from the appointment of chief risk officers. *Risk Management & Insurance Review, 6*(1), 37–52. DOI: 10.1111/1098-1616.00019

Lin, J., Low, J. S., & Rajan, R. (2023). Gender diversity in boardrooms and enterprise risk oversight: Evidence from ASEAN firms. *Journal of Risk and Governance, 11*(1), 51–67.

Litao, X., & Xinzhou, S. (2021) Research on Consumer Behavior Based on the Perspective of Behavioral Economics. Proceedings of the 2021 3rd International Conference on Economic Management and Cultural Industry (ICEMCI 2021). Advances in Economics, *Business and Management Research, 20*(3) pp. 316-319.

Liu, C., & Chen, X. (2024). Spillover effects of multidimensional information in Fed statements on China's bond market. *International Review of Economics & Finance, 93*, 712–741. DOI: 10.1016/j.iref.2024.04.037

Liu, H., Zhu, Y., Cui, N., & Zheng, Y. (2024). The impact of global uncertainties on the spillover among the European carbon market, the Chinese oil futures market, and the international oil futures market. *Finance Research Letters, 67*, 105891. DOI: 10.1016/j.frl.2024.105891

Liu, M., & Lee, C. C. (2022). Is gold a long-run hedge, diversifier, or safe haven for oil? Empirical evidence based on DCC-MIDAS. *Resources Policy, 76*, 102703. DOI: 10.1016/j.resourpol.2022.102703

Liu, X., Razzaq, A., Shahzad, M., & Irfan, M. (2022). Technological changes, financial development and ecological consequences: A comparative study of developed and developing economies. *Technological Forecasting and Social Change, 184*, 122004. DOI: 10.1016/j.techfore.2022.122004

Liu, Y., & Zhang, Z. (2025). Unlocking operational efficiency: How AI human capital investment enhances data processing efficiency. *Economics Letters, 247*, 112147. Advance online publication. DOI: 10.1016/j.econlet.2024.112147

Lorente, D. B., Mohammed, K. S., Cifuentes-Faura, J., & Shahzad, U. (2023). Dynamic connectedness among climate change index, green financial assets and renewable energy markets: Novel evidence from sustainable development perspective. *Renewable Energy, 204*, 94–105. https://doi.org/https://doi.org/10.1016/j.renene.2022.12.085. DOI: 10.1016/j.renene.2022.12.085

Lu, C., Yu, B., Zhang, J., & Xu, D. (2021). Influences of open innovation strategies on innovation performance of SMEs: Evidence from China. *Chinese Management Studies, 15*(1), 24–43. DOI: 10.1108/CMS-01-2020-0009

Lukman, L., Ridloah, S., & Humaira, H. (2024). Board characteristics and financial performance of companies from the agency theory perspective. [JoSS]. *Journal of Social Sciences, 3*(2), 1246–1270.

Luthra, S., & Mangla, S. K. (2018). Evaluating challenges to Industry 4.0 initiatives for supply chain sustainability in emerging economies. *Process Safety and Environmental Protection, 117*, 168–179. https://doi.org/. 2018.04.018DOI: 10.1016/j.psep

Lyon, T. P., & Montgomery, A. W. (2015). The means and end of greenwash. *Organization & Environment, 28*(2), 223–249. DOI: 10.1177/1086026615575332

Machado, A. C., Bilo, C., & Helmy, I. (2018). *The role of zakat in the provision of social protection: A comparison between Jordan, Palestine and Sudan* (Working Paper No. 168). International Policy Centre for Inclusive Growth. The role of zakat in the provision of social protection: A comparison between Jordan, Palestine and Sudan

Maduku, D. K., & Mbeya, S. (2023). Understanding family Takaful purchase behaviour: The roles of religious obligation and gender. *Journal of Financial Services Marketing, 29*(2), 440–458. DOI: 10.1057/s41264-023-00213-z

Maghyereh, A., Awartani, B., & Hassan, A. (2018). Can gold be used as a hedge against the risks of Sharia-compliant securities? Application for Islamic portfolio management. *Journal of Asset Management, 19*(6), 394–412. DOI: 10.1057/s41260-018-0090-y

Mahazan, A. M., & Abdullah, A. G. (2013). A Model of Imam's Leadership and Mosque Performance in Malaysia. *Global Journal Al-Thaqafah, 3*(2), 53–64. DOI: 10.7187/GJAT432013.03.02

Mair, J., & Marti, I. (2006). Social entrepreneurship research: A source of explanation, prediction, and delight. *Journal of World Business, 41*(1), 36–44. DOI: 10.1016/j.jwb.2005.09.002

Mair, J., Mayer, J., & Lutz, E. (2015). Navigating institutional plurality: Organizational governance in hybrid organizations. *Organization Studies, 36*(6), 713–739. DOI: 10.1177/0170840615580007

Majumder, M. T. H., Ruma, I. J., & Akter, A. (2023). Does Intellectual Capital Affect Bank Performance? Evidence from Bangladesh. *LBS Journal of Management & Research, 21*(2), 171–185. DOI: 10.1108/LBSJMR-05-2022-0016

Malaysia Digital Economy Corporation. (2021). *MyDIGITAL Blueprint*.

Malik, N. S. A., & Sulaiman, S. (2024). A synthesis of literature on micro-Takaful: Exploring protection for unexpected adverse events. *International Journal of Islamic Economics and Finance Research, 7*(1), 15–30.

Manalo, J. V. I., Bito-onon, J. B., Siason, N. D.Jr, & Blanza, M. G. (2024). *Analysis of stakeholders' knowledge, skills, attitudes, and practices: inputs for community-based ecotourism entrepreneurship development in tinorian river, iloilo, philippines. Proceeding of the International Conference on Family Business and Entrepreneurship.*

Manas, N., Zakuan, N., Saman, M. Z. M., & Setapa, M. (2024). Enterprise Risk Management Practices in Malaysian Small and Medium-Sized Enterprises: An Overview. *Information Management and Business Review, 16*(2(I)S), 236–250.

Manufacturing to stabilise in 2025. (2024, December 9). MIDA | Malaysian Investment Development Authority.

Martín, J. C., Orden-Cruz, C., & Zergane, S. (2020). Islamic finance and halal tourism: An unexplored bridge for smart specialization. *Sustainability (Basel), 12*(14), 5736. Advance online publication. DOI: 10.3390/su12145736

Marwazi, M. B. H. (2000). *The role of Islamic banks in achieving the dimensions of financial inclusion in Jordan* (Master's thesis, Al al-Bayt University, Jordan).

MAS. (2021). *Project Ubin: Central Bank Digital Currency (CBDC) and Blockchain Infrastructure*. Monetary Authority of Singapore.

Mason, A. J. (2010). *Inside the black box: Investigating agility as a dynamic capability for sustaining a competitive advantage within consulting firms* [Doctoral dissertation, Capella University].

Mawardi, I., Widiastuti, T., Al Mustofa, M. U., & Hakimi, F. (2023). Analyzing the impact of productive zakat on the welfare of zakat recipients. *Journal of Islamic Accounting and Business Research, 14*(1), 118–140. DOI: 10.1108/JIABR-05-2021-0145

Meiryani. (2024). Exploration of potential money laundering crimes with virtual currency facilities in Indonesia. *Journal of Money Laundering Control, 27*(6), 985–994. DOI: 10.1108/JMLC-01-2023-0010

Mendoza Solis, M., García Alcaraz, J. L., Avelar Sosa, L., & Manotas Duque, D. F. (2023). The role of transactional leadership in the social performance of the maquiladora industry. *Revista Brasileira de Gestão de Negócios, 25*(2), 215–233. DOI: 10.7819/rbgn.v25i2.4219

Mensi, W., Hammoudeh, S., Al-Jarrah, I. M. W., Sensoy, A., & Kang, S. H. (2017). Dynamic risk spillovers between gold, oil prices and conventional, sustainability and Islamic equity aggregates and sectors with portfolio implications [Preprint]. *Energy Economics, 67*, 454–475. Advance online publication. DOI: 10.1016/j.eneco.2017.08.031

Meyer, P. (2016). *The agility shift: Creating agile and effective leaders, teams, and organizations*. Routledge. DOI: 10.4324/9781315230559

Mia, M. J., Hossain, M. S., & Akon, M. S. (2025). Environmental Competitiveness, Green Energy, and Global Sustainability. In *Green Energy Investments and Economic Development* (pp. 147–169). Springer Nature Singapore. DOI: 10.1007/978-981-96-6166-4_9

Ministry of Science, Technology and Innovation. (2021). *National Blockchain Roadmap 2021–2025*.

Miskan, N. H., Muhamad, N., Esa, M. M., Zabidi, F. S. M., Hussin, N. L., & Nasuha, S. A. (2024). Awareness of Takaful Ownership among the Kuala Klawang Community: Challenge or Opportunity? *Information Management and Business Review*, *16*(4), 12–17. DOI: 10.22610/imbr.v16i4(I).4251

Mnif, E. and Jarboui, A. (2021) 'Resilience of Islamic cryptocurrency markets to Covid-19 shocks and the Federal Reserve policy', *Asian Journal of Accounting Research*, ahead- of-p(ahead-of-print). Available at: .DOI: 10.1108/AJAR-01-2021-0004

Mnif, E., Jarboui, A., & Mouakhar, K. (2024). Strategic insights into carbon markets, digital finance and geopolitical risks for advancing green sustainability investments. *Management of Environmental Quality*, *35*(7), 1622–1649. Advance online publication. DOI: 10.1108/MEQ-10-2023-0369

Mnif, E., Mouakhar, K., & Jarboui, A. (2023). Energy-conserving cryptocurrency response during the COVID-19 pandemic and amid the Russia–Ukraine conflict. *The Journal of Risk Finance*, *24*(2), 169–185. DOI: 10.1108/JRF-06-2022-0161

Mohamed, M. A., Kalf, H. A. I., Alkhafagy, T., Algaragolle, W. M., Saeed, A. F., Al-Muttar, M. Y., & Baher, R. (2023). Moderating Effect of Effective Commitment on the Relationship of Human Resources Information Systems and Organization Performance in Iraq SMEs: Mediating Role of Innovation Capability. *International Journal of Operations and Quantitative Management*, *29*(2), 273–295.

Mohammadhossein, S., & Atefeh, A. (2025). Modeling Factors Influenceing Digital Transformation : Suggestions for the Islamic Republic of Iran. In *Journal of the Knowledge Economy* (Issue 0123456789). Springer US. DOI: 10.1007/s13132-025-02654-4

Mohd Jaapar, A., Md. Nor, A., & Mohd. Nasir, N. A. (2021). Zakat collection and distribution efficiency in the Federal Territory of Malaysia: A two-stage data envelopment analysis. *International Journal on Informatics Visualization, 5*(4). Virtual Campus Tour Application through Markerless Augmented Reality Approach | Liang | JOIV: International Journal on Informatics Visualization

Mohd Rasid, M. F. R., & Ruslan, A. F. (2024). *Determinant of Family Takaful Adoption Among Puncak Alam Residents.* ResearchGate. Retrieved from https://www.researchgate.net/publication/385327808_Determinant_of_Family_Takaful_Adoption_Among_Puncak_Alam_Residents

Mohsin, M., & Jamaani, F. (2023). A novel deep-learning technique for forecasting oil price volatility using historical prices of five precious metals in context of green financing – A comparison of deep learning, machine learning, and statistical models. *Resources Policy, 86*, 104216. DOI: 10.1016/j.resourpol.2023.104216

Mongkito, Abdul & Samdin, Samdin. (2025). The Role of Zakat in Poverty Alleviation and Farmer Welfare: The Theoretical Review. *Journal of Global Innovations in Agricultural Sciences*, 285-296. https://doi.org/DOI: 10.22194/JGIAS/25.1427

Moppratama, Y. A., Alamsyah, A., & Tricahyono, D. (2024). Blockchain-Based Property Sukuk Models for the Indonesian Market. *2024 International Conference on Artificial Intelligence Blockchain Cloud Computing and Data Analytics Icoabcd 2024*, 107–112. DOI: 10.1109/ICoABCD63526.2024.10704239

Moreno-Domínguez, M.-J., Escobar-Rodríguez, T., Pelayo-Díaz, Y.-M., & Tovar-García, I. (2024). Organizational culture and leadership style in Spanish Hospitals: Effects on knowledge management and efficiency. *Heliyon, 10*(20), e39216. DOI: 10.1016/j.heliyon.2024.e39216 PMID: 39498020

Moro Visconti, R. (2024). Artificial intelligence-driven FinTech valuation: A scalable multilayer network approach. *FinTech, 3*(3), 479–495. DOI: 10.3390/fintech3030026

Mossavar Rahmani, F. (2023). The Transformative Impact of AI on Financial Institutions, with a Focus on Banking. *Journal of Engineering and Applied Sciences Technology*, 1–6. DOI: 10.47363/JEAST/2023(5)192

Movahed, K. (2014). Mosque as a religious building for community development. https://oaks.kent.edu/node/295

Mthuli, S. A., & Singh, N. (2024). State-led Maritime Governance, Education and Training Nexus in South Africa. *European Conference on Management Leadership and Governance, 20*(1), Article 1. DOI: 10.34190/ecmlg.20.1.2950

Muhamad, F. H., Ab Ghani, H., & Arifin, J. (2024). A Conceptual Framework of E-Takaful Participation Readiness (ETPR) among Individuals at Insurable Age in Malaysia. *Journal of Entrepreneurship and Business, 12*(1), 116–126. DOI: 10.17687/jeb.v12i1.1197

Mukherjee, J., & Janssen, M. C. (2023). *Recreating the power grid: Navigating technological and organizational changes*. Taylor & Francis.

Mukhlishin, M., Wahab, A., Setiaji, B., & Tazhdinov, M. (2024). Zakat Maal Management and Regulation Practices: Evidence from Malaysia, Turkey, and Indonesia. *Journal of Human Rights. Culture and Legal System, 4*(2), 569–592. DOI: 10.53955/jhcls.v4i2.204

Multazam, M. T., Huzairin, R. A., & Prataman, S. P. (2023). Is It Legal to Provide Liquidity on the Vexanium Decentralized Exchange in Indonesia? *Yustisia, 12*(1), 29–46. DOI: 10.20961/yustisia.v12i1.69007

Musa, A. H., Baharuddin, F. N., Rosle, A. N., Ibrahim, S. S., & Syed Noh, S. N. (2022). The role of social media and religious awareness in purchasing decision on Takaful insurance: A conceptual paper. *International Journal of Academic Research in Business & Social Sciences, 12*(6), 630–636. DOI: 10.6007/IJARBSS/v12-i6/13996

Musah, A., Padi, A., Blay, M. W., Okyere, D. O., & Ofori, B. S. (2025). Ethical organisational culture, effective internal control systems and tax compliance of small and medium scale enterprises (SMEs): The role of corporate governance. *Social Sciences & Humanities Open, 11*, 101331. DOI: 10.1016/j.ssaho.2025.101331

Musthafa, I., Elfindri, E., Anas, Y., & Ariyanto, E. (2024). Human capital and performance of micro, small and medium enterprises: A literature review. *Cashflow Current Advanced Research on Sharia Finance and Economic Worldwide, 3*(2), 250–275. DOI: 10.55047/cashflow.v3i2.1028

Nadham, N. & Nahid, B. (2015). The role of business ethics in the relationship between market orientation and business performance. International Journal of Finance & Banking Studies (2147-4486), 4(1), 70-94. .DOI: 10.20525/ijfbs.v4i1.205

Naeem, M. A., Karim, S., Farid, S., & Tiwari, A. K. (2022). Comparing the asymmetric efficiency of dirty and clean energy markets pre and during COVID-19. *Economic Analysis and Policy, 75*, 548–562. DOI: 10.1016/j.eap.2022.06.015

Nafei, W. A. (2016). Organizational agility: The key to organizational success. *International Journal of Business and Management, 11*(5), 296–309. DOI: 10.5539/ijbm.v11n5p296

Nagimova, A. Z. (2023). Islamic capital markets: Prospects of the sukuk issuance in the post-Soviet countries. *World Economy and International Relations*, *67*(4), 81–91. DOI: 10.20542/0131-2227-2023-67-4-81-91

Naila, D. L. (2024). Measuring the uptake of process innovation by SMEs in food industry : a resource-based view perspective. DOI: 10.1108/IJSBI-08-2024-0040

Narendran, R., Ng, E., & Almeida, S. (2025). Organizing Transgender People: Toward a Process-Based Theory of Representative Bureaucracy. *Nonprofit and Voluntary Sector Quarterly*, *54*(6), 1473–1504. Advance online publication. DOI: 10.1177/08997640251317399

Nasir, N. I. M., Hassan, R., & Osman, A. Z. (2023). Spectrum of consumer awareness in Islamic finance: Takaful industry in Malaysia. *The Journal of Muamalat and Islamic Finance Research*, *20*(2), 125–134. DOI: 10.33102/jmifr.513

Nassani, A. A., Badshah, W., Grigorescu, A., Cozorici, A. N., Yousaf, Z., & Zhan, X. (2024). Participatory leadership and supportive organisational culture Panacea for job satisfaction regulatory role of work-life balance. *Heliyon*, *10*(16), e36043. DOI: 10.1016/j.heliyon.2024.e36043 PMID: 39224389

Nassar, A. M. M. (2003). In Arabic. Characteristics of partnership contracts and the extent of their use in Islamic finance – A jurisprudential and financial study. *Al-Qadha'iyah Journal*, (7). Islamic Economics Institute, Kingdom of Saudi Arabia. Pdf -

Nasser, S. (2002). *Developing short-term financing instruments in Islamic banks* (1st ed.). Heritage Association.

Navaia, E., Moreira, A., & Ribau, C. (2024). The mediating roles of cost leadership and cost focus strategies on innovation capabilities and export performance. Results from an emerging country. *Cogent Business & Management*, *11*(1), 2375410. DOI: 10.1080/23311975.2024.2375410

Nejatian, M., & Zarei, M. H. (2013). Moving towards organizational agility: Are we improving in the right direction? *Global Journal of Flexible Systems Managment*, *14*(4), 241–253. DOI: 10.1007/s40171-013-0048-3

Nelly, Roos, & Harianto, Harianto & Abd. Majid, M. Shabri & Marliyah, Marliyah & Handayani, Rita. (. (2022). Studi Empiris Perkembangan Crowdfunding Syariah di Indonesia. Al-Kharaj: *Jurnal Ekonomi. Keuangan & Bisnis Syariah*, *4*, 1383–1298. DOI: 10.47467/alkharaj.v4i5.926

Nene, P. R. (2024). Can artificial intelligence replace assurance, governance and risk management professionals? *Risk Governance and Control: Financial Markets and Institutions*, *14*(2), 25–31. DOI: 10.22495/rgcv14i2p3

Nesadurai, H. E. (2008). The association of Southeast Asian nations (ASEAN). *New Political Economy*, *13*(2), 225–239. DOI: 10.1080/13563460802018588

Ng, A., Ibrahim, M. H., & Kang, H. G. (2021). ESG Reporting in ASEAN: Trends, Gaps, and Policy Implications. *Asian Economic Policy Review*.

Ngo, T., Le, D., & Doan, T. (2023). Are Your Employees Mentally Prepared for the Pandemic? Wellbeing-Oriented Human Resource Management Practices in a Developing Country. *International Journal of Hospitality Management*, *109*, 103415. DOI: 10.1016/j.ijhm.2022.103415

Nguyen, N. P., Nguyen, T. T. H., Nguyen, H., & Flynnd, O. (2023). *Does transformational leadership influence organisational culture and organisational performance: Empirical evidence from an emerging country*. ScienceDirect.

Niguse, T., & Borji, B. (2025). Mediation Effect of Human Capital Among Strategic Innovation and Competitive Advantage: A Case of SMEs in Ethiopia. *International Journal of Global Business and Competitiveness*, *20*(1), 23–32. DOI: 10.1007/s42943-025-00114-z

Nik Man, N. H., & Fernandez, D. (2023). Potential Factors on Blockchain Adoption in Malaysian Public Sector Auditing. In *2023 16th International Conference on Developments in eSystems Engineering (DeSE)* (pp. 188–193). IEEE. https://doi.org/DOI: 10.1109/DeSE60171.2023.10162025

Nipo, D. T., Lily, J., Fabeil, N. F., & Jamil, I. A. A. (2024). Transforming rural entrepreneurship through digital innovation: A review on opportunities, barriers and challenges. *Journal of Management and Sustainability*, *14*(2), 114. DOI: 10.5539/jms.v14n2p114

Norazman, A., Azmi, N., & Khairuddin, N. (2023). *The Role of Financial Education in Promoting ESG and Takaful Awareness in Malaysia*. Proceedings of the International Conference on Islamic Economics. Retrieved from https://e piiecons .usim.edu.my/index.php/eproceeding/article/download/118/89/172

Nugroho, A., Suharyo, O. S., & Rahman, A. (2020). The development of indonesian maritime potential and prospects towards a world maritime axis. *Sttal postgraduate - international conference*, *4*(1). https://seminarpasca-sttal.ac.id/seminar/index.php/seminarpasca-sttal/article/view/52

Nunis, N. N. M., & Abd Rahman, S. Z. (2019). Examining consumers' continuance intention and e-WOM about Islamic insurance (Takaful). *Malaysian Journal of Consumer and Family Economics*, *21*, 127–144.

Nurawami, S. (2013). *Peranan Lembaga Keuangan Mikro dan Konstribusi Kredit terhadap Pendapatan Kotor UKM Rumah Tangga setelah menjadi Kreditur*. Jurnal Studi Kasus BMT Muamalat.

Nurdin, E., Maruhun, S., Razazila, W., Abdullah, W., & Atan, R. (2018). Assessing the Effects of Corporate Governance on Enterprise Risk Management and Firm Value: Malaysian Evidence. International Journal of Economics and Management Int. *Journal of Economics and Management*, *12*(S2), 413–430.

Nurhayati, A., Aisah, I., & Supriatna, A. K. (2019). Model Development of A Synergistic Sustainable Marine Ecotourism—A Case Study in Pangandaran Region, West Java Province, Indonesia. *Sustainability (Basel)*, *11*(12), 12. Advance online publication. DOI: 10.3390/su11123418

Nurlukman, A. D., Fadli, Y., & Wahyono, E. (2025). Ecotourism for Coastal Slum Alleviation: A Strategic Approach to Achieving the Sustainable Development Goals (SDGs) in Tangerang, Indonesia. *Journal of Lifestyle and SDGs Review*, *5*(2), e02793–e02793. DOI: 10.47172/2965-730X.SDGsReview.v5.n02.pe02793

Nwanzu, C. L., & Babalola, S. S. (2019). Examining psychological capital of optimism, self-efficacy and self-monitoring as predictors of attitude towards organizational change. *International Journal of Engineering Business Management*, *11*, 1847979019827149. DOI: 10.1177/1847979019827149

O'Neil, J. (2017). 'People, planet, profits' and perception politics: a necessary fourth (and fifth) bottom line? Critiquing the current triple bottom line in the Australian context. In *The Goals of Sustainable Development: Responsibility and Governance* (pp. 19–42). Springer Singapore.

Oberer, B., & Erkollar, A. (2018). Leadership 4.0: Digital leaders in the age of Industry 4.0. *International Journal of Organizational Leadership*, *7*(4), 404–412. DOI: 10.33844/ijol.2018.60332

OECD. (2017). *Mobilising Bond Markets for a Low-Carbon Transition, Green Finance and Investment*. OECD Publishing., DOI: 10.1787/9789264272323-

OECD. (2024), *OECD Digital Economy Outlook 2024 (Volume 2): Strengthening Connectivity, Innovation and Trust*, OECD Publishing, Paris, https://doi.org/DOI: 10.1787/3adf705b-en

OECD. (2025), *Fostering convergence in SME sustainability reporting: A background study* (OECD Publishing, CFE/SME(2024)13/FINAL). Centre for Entrepreneurship, SMEs, Regions and Cities. https://www.oecd.org/content/dam/oecd/en/publications/reports/2025/02/fostering-convergence-in-sme-sustainability-reporting_133eb77f/ffbf16fb-en.pdf

Ogolla, J. A. (2020). *Transformational leadership, strategic agility and performance of state corporations in Kenya* (Doctoral dissertation, Kenya Methodist University).

Oltean, F. D., Curta, P. A., Nagy, B., Huseyn, A., & Gabor, M. R. (2025). Changes in Tourists' Perceptions of Community-Based Ecotourism (CBET) After COVID-19 Pandemic: A Study on the Country of Origin and Economic Development Level. *ISPRS International Journal of Geo-Information*, *14*(4), 4. Advance online publication. DOI: 10.3390/ijgi14040146

Omonov, S. (2025). Ethno-Cultural Values as a Factor Shaping Consumer Economic Behavior. *Web of Humanities: Journal of Social Science and Humanitarian Research*, *3*(3), 93–95.

Ong Poh Heng, C., Teh, B. H., & Ang, Y. L. (2022). Enterprise risk management and quality of risk disclosure: Evidence from Malaysia. *International Journal of Accounting and Information Management*, *30*(1), 1–15.

Ong, P. H., Yip, Y. Y., & Lye, C. T. (2023). Effect of Enterprise Risk Management Adoption on the Firm Value in Malaysia's Annual Reports.

Ononiwu, M. I., Onwuzulike, O. C., & Shitu, K. (2024). The role of digital business transformation in enhancing organizational agility. *World Journal of Advanced Research and Reviews*, *23*(3), 285–308. https://doi.org/. 2024.23.3.0367DOI: 10.30574/wjarr

Ostrom, A. L., Parasuraman, A., Bowen, D. E., Patrício, L., & Voss, C. A. (2015). Service research priorities in a rapidly changing context. *Journal of Service Research*, *18*(2), 127–159. DOI: 10.1177/1094670515576315

Osunsanmi, T., Aigbavboa, C., & Oke, A. (2018). Construction 4.0: The future of the construction industry in South Africa. *World Academy of Science, Engineering and Technology, Open Science Index 135, International Journal of Civil and Environmental Engineering*, *12*(3), 206–212. https://doi.org/. 1132164.DOI: 10.5281/zenodo

Otekunrin, A. O., Eluyela, D. F., Nwanji, T. I., Faye, S., Howell, K. E., & Tolu-Bolaji, J. (2021). Enterprise risk management (ERM) and firm's performance: A study of listed manufacturing firms in Nigeria. *Review of World Economics*, *12*(1), 31.

Otoritas Jasa Keuangan, R. (2024a). *Laporan Surveillance Perbankan Indonesia Triwulan IV 2024.* https://ojk.go.id/id/kanal/perbankan/data-dan-statistik/laporan-profil-industri-perbankan/Documents/Laporan Surveillance Perbankan Indonesia - Triwulan I 2024.pdf

Otoritas Jasa Keuangan, R.. (2024b). *Peta Jalan Pengembangan dan Penguatan Inovasi Teknologi Sektor Keuangan, Aset Keuangan Digital dan Aset Kripto 2024-2028.*

Özdemir, M., & Selçuk, M. (2021). A bibliometric analysis of the *International Journal of Islamic and Middle Eastern Finance and Management. International Journal of Islamic and Middle Eastern Finance and Management, 14*(4), 767–791. DOI: 10.1108/IMEFM-06-2020-0277

Paape, L., & Speklé, R. F. (2012). The Adoption and Design of Enterprise Risk Management Practices: An Empirical Study. *European Accounting Review, 21*(3), 533–564. DOI: 10.1080/09638180.2012.661937

Paauwe, J., & Van De Voorde, K. (2025). Bridging the Research–Practice Gap in Modern Human Resource Management. *Human Resource Management Review, 35*(2), 101076. DOI: 10.1016/j.hrmr.2025.101076

Pagach, D., & Warr, R. (2011). The characteristics of firms that hire chief risk officers. *The Journal of Risk and Insurance, 78*(1), 185–211. DOI: 10.1111/j.1539-6975.2010.01378.x

Pangestuti, D., Takidah, E., & Anggraini ZR, R. (2017). Firm Size, Board Size, And Ownership Structure and Risk Management Disclosure. *Jurnal Akuntansi Dan Keuangan Islam, 5*(2), 117–137. DOI: 10.35836/jakis.v5i2.18

Parlika, R., & Atmaja, P. W. (2020). Realtime monitoring of Bitcoin prices on several Cryptocurrency markets using Web API, Telegram Bot, MySQL Database, and PHP-Cronjob. *Proceeding 6th Information Technology International Seminar Itis 2020*, 253–257. DOI: 10.1109/ITIS50118.2020.9321109

Parsons, C., & Titman, S. (2008). Capital Structure and Corporate Strategy. In *Elsevier eBooks* (p. 203). Elsevier BV.

Paşaoğlu, D. (2015). Analysis of the Relationship Between Human Resources Management Practices and Organizational Commitment from a Strategic Perspective: Findings from the Banking Industry. Procedia Social and Behavioral Sciences.

Paşaoğlu, D., & Tonus, H. Z. (2014). Strategic Importance of Human Resource Practices on Job Satisfaction in Private Hospitals. *Procedia: Social and Behavioral Sciences.*

Payne, G., & Petrenko, O. (2019, April 26). Agency Theory in Business and Management Research. Oxford Research Encyclopedia of Business and Management.

Perdana, A., & Jhee Jiow, H. (2024). Crypto-Cognitive Exploitation: Integrating Cognitive, Social, and Technological perspectives on cryptocurrency fraud. *Telematics and Informatics*, *95*, 102191. Advance online publication. DOI: 10.1016/j.tele.2024.102191

Phillips, P., & Perron, P. (1988) 'Testing for a Unit Root in Time Series Regression Author (s): Peter C. B. Phillips and Pierre Perron Published by : Oxford University Press on behalf of Biometrika Trust Stable URL : https://www.jstor.org/stable/2336182 REFERENCES Linked references ar', 75(2), pp. 335–346.

Phillips, W., Lee, H., Ghobadian, A., O'regan, N., & James, P. (2015). Social innovation and social entrepreneurship: A systematic review. *Group & Organization Management*, *40*(3), 428–461. DOI: 10.1177/1059601114560063

Phou, S., Uk, C., Chav, T., & Sou, V. (2025). Key Factors Influencing Environmentally Responsible Behavior in the Community-Based Ecotourism Development (CBET): Antecedents and Implications. *Open Journal of Ecology*, *15*(1), 1. Advance online publication. DOI: 10.4236/oje.2025.151002

Pine, J., & Gilmore, J. H. (1999). *The experience economy: work is theatre & every business a stage*. Harvard Business Press.

Pratama, F. W. N., & Jannah, M. R. (2024). *Community-based action plans for coastal area infrastructure enhancement: a strategy for sustainable tourism development. J.* Jurnal Pembangunan Pemberdayaan Pemerintahan., DOI: 10.33701/j-3p.v9i2.4715

Priem, R., & Gabellone, A. (2024). The impact of a firm's ESG score on its cost of capital: Can a high ESG score serve as a substitute for a weaker legal environment. Sustainability Accounting. *Management and Policy Journal*, *15*(3), 676–703. DOI: 10.1108/SAMPJ-05-2023-0254

Pristiyanto, . (2013). *Strategi Pengembangan Koperasi Jasa Keuangan Syariah dalam Pembiayaan Usaha Mikro di Kecamatan Tanjungsari, Sumedang*. Jurnal Manajemen IKM.

Pulic, A. (2000). VAIC™–An accounting tool for IC management. *International Journal of Technology Management*, *20*(5-8), 702–714. DOI: 10.1504/IJTM.2000.002891

Purwatiningsih, A., Purnamasari, S., Setyawati, H., Indriani, A., Prawitasari, D., & Fitria, S. (2024). Bibliometric analysis of Islamic Crowdfunding: A Literature Review of Its Journey. *F1000 Research*, *13*, 531. DOI: 10.12688/f1000research.146797.1 PMID: 39822736

Putri, T., Amiludin, A., Ahmad, D. N., & Hidayatulloh, H. (2023). Inadequate Cryptocurrency and Money Laundering Regulations in Indonesia (Comparative Law of US and Germany). *Yustisia*, *12*(2), 129–152. DOI: 10.20961/yustisia.v12i2.71835

PWC. (2018). Whom do consumers really trust? available at: https://www.pwc.com/gx/en/industries/ consumer-markets/consumer-insights-survey/consumer-trust.html

Qadri, H. M. U. D., & Bhatti, M. I. (2025). *Islamic Finance in the Modern Era* (Vol. 25). Retrieved January.

Qasim, D., Shuhaiber, A., & Rawshdeh, Z. (2025). Driving innovation performance: Exploring the mediating function of knowledge sharing in telecommunication companies. *Journal of International Entrepreneurship*, *0123456789*(3), 677–703. Advance online publication. DOI: 10.1007/s10843-025-00383-y

Quon, T. K., Zéghal, D., & Maingot, M. (2012). Enterprise Risk Management and Firm Performance. *Procedia: Social and Behavioral Sciences*, *62*, 263–267. DOI: 10.1016/j.sbspro.2012.09.042

Rahayu, H. P., Comfort, L. K., Khoirunnisa, D., & Nurhasanah, D. (2024). Need Assessment for Coastal Tourism Area in the Face of Tsunami Risk: The Case of Pangandaran. *International Journal on Advanced Science, Engineering and Information Technology*, *14*(2), 563–574. DOI: 10.18517/ijaseit.14.2.19985

Rahman, M. M., Pokharel, B. P., Sayeed, S. A., Bhowmik, S. K., Kshetri, N., & Eashrak, N. (2024). RiskAIchain: AI-driven IT infrastructure— Blockchain-backed approach for enhanced risk management. *Risks*, *12*(12), 206. Advance online publication. DOI: 10.3390/risks12120206

Rahman, M. S. (2017). The Advantages and Disadvantages of Using Qualitative and Quantitative Approaches and Methods in Language "Testing and Assessment" Research: A Literature Review. *Journal of Education and Learning*, *6*(1), 102–112. DOI: 10.5539/jel.v6n1p102

Raies, A. (2020). Islamic versus Conventional Fiscal policy: The effect of zakat on education and employment. *Academic Journal of Interdisciplinary Studies*, *9*(1), 27–33. DOI: 10.36941/ajis-2020-0003

Rajesh, P., & Subhashini, V. (2021). Sustainable packaging from waste material: A review on innovative solutions for cleaner environment. *Bioremediation and Green Technologies: Sustainable Approaches to Mitigate Environmental Impacts*, 259-270.

Rajeswari, A. (2025). Intersecting Inequalities: Gender, Culture, Stereotypes, and Economic Justice. *Intersecting Inequalities : Gender, Culture, Stereotypes, and Economic Justice*, *4*(1), 177–186. DOI: 10.56472/25835238/IRJEMS-V4I1P117

Ramírez, Y., Dieguez-Soto, J., & Manzaneque, M. (2021). How Does Intellectual Capital Efficiency Affect Firm Performance? The Moderating Role of Family Management. *International Journal of Productivity and Performance Management, 70*(2), 297–324. DOI: 10.1108/IJPPM-03-2019-0119

Ran, B., & Weller, S. (2021). An Exit Strategy for the Definitional Elusiveness: A Three-Dimensional Framework for Social Entrepreneurship. *Sustainability (Basel), 13*(2), 563. DOI: 10.3390/su13020563

Rass, L., Treur, J., Kucharska, W., & Wiewiora, A. (2025). Adaptive dynamical systems modelling of transformational organizational change with focus on organizational culture and organizational learning.

Razak, S. H. A. (2020). Zakat and waqf as instruments of Islamic wealth in poverty alleviation and redistribution: Case of Malaysia. *The International Journal of Sociology and Social Policy, 40*(3/4), 249–266. DOI: 10.1108/IJSSP-11-2018-0208

Raziq, M. M., Borini, F. M., Malik, O. F., Ahmad, M., & Shabaz, M. (2018). Leadership styles, goal clarity, and project success: Evidence from project-based organizations in Pakistan. *Leadership and Organization Development Journal, 39*(2), 309–323. DOI: 10.1108/LODJ-07-2017-0212

Redhika, R., & Mahalli, K. (2014). Analisis Potensi dan Kendala Pengembangan Asuransi Syariah di Kota Medan (potential analysis and constraints of Islamic insurance development in medan). *Jurnal Ekonomi DanKeuangan, 2*(5), 323–335.

Rehman, A. U., Aslam, E., Muhammad, R. S., Aslam, M., Iqbal, A., & Shabbir, M. S. (2023). Consumer awareness and knowledge about Takaful (Islamic insurance): A survey of Pakistan. *Journal of Namibian Studies, 35*(S1), 4101–4118.

Rehman, S., Shareef, A., Mahmood, A., & Ishaque, A. (2012). Perceived leadership styles and organizational commitment. *Interdisciplinary Journal of Contemporary Research in Business, 4*, 616–626.

Relan, M., & Kumar, M. (2023). Impact of Trust and Risk Factors on the Satisfaction Level of the Policy Holder towards Digital Bancassurance Model. [IRJMSH]. *International Research Journal of Management Sociology & Humanity, 14*(7), 15–24.

Remly, M. R., Sabaruddin, S. N. A., & Adenan, F. (2024). Cabaran Kepimpinan Dalam Pengimarahan Institusi Masjid: Kajian Kes Di Masjid Cemerlang: Leadership Challenges In The Improvement Of Mosque Institutions: A Case Study In Masjid Cemerlang. *Al-Qanatir: International Journal of Islamic Studies, 33*(3), 26–36.

REN21. (2021). *Renewables 2021 global status report.* Paris: REN21 Secretariat. https://www.ren21.net/reports/global-status-report/

Renneboog, L., Ter Horst, J., & Zhang, C. (2020). Socially responsible investments: Institutional aspects, performance, and investor behavior. *Journal of Banking & Finance, 32*(9), 1723–1742. DOI: 10.1016/j.jbankfin.2007.12.039

Renukappa, S., Akintoye, A., Egbu, C., & Goulding, J. (2013). Carbon emission reduction strategies in the UK industrial sectors: An empirical study. *International Journal of Climate Change Strategies and Management, 5*(3), 304–323. DOI: 10.1108/IJCCSM-02-2012-0010

Rifas, A. H. ., Ab Rahman, A. ., & Buang, A. H. . . (2023). Appraising the Universal Concepts of Insurance and Takaful: Similarities and Differences. *UMRAN - Journal of Islamic and Civilizational Studies, 10*(1), 1–15.

Rinaldi, A., Tan, S. Y., & Koh, W. H. (2022). The role of board composition in enterprise risk management: Evidence from Singapore logistics firms. *Asia-Pacific Journal of Business Administration, 14*(2), 183–199.

Robinson, B. A., McCormack, B., & Dickson, C. (2025). Becoming a Person-Centred Facilitator of Learning in a Hospital Setting: Findings from a Participatory Action-Oriented Study with Hospital-Based Educators. *Nurse Education in Practice, 82*, 104222. DOI: 10.1016/j.nepr.2024.104222 PMID: 39673866

Rogers, E. W., & Wright, P. M. (1998). Measuring Organizational Performance in Strategic Human Resource Management: Problems, Prospects, and Performance Information Markets. *Human Resource Management Review, 8*(3), 311–331. DOI: 10.1016/S1053-4822(98)90007-9

Rosele, M. I., & Johari, A. H. (2016). Aplikasi Takaful Model Wakaf Di Malaysia: Keperluan Dan Permasalahannya (Application of Waqf Takaful Model in Malaysia: Its Requirements and Problems). *UMRAN - International Journal of Islamic and Civilizational Studies*, 3(1), 28-38.

Ruru, B., Tjager, I. N., Mayasari, A., Adhistita, A. M., Raffi, H. A., & Santro, A. (2022). THE IMPACT OF CRYPTO-ASSET UTILISATION AS PAYMENT INSTRUMENT TOWARD THE RUPIAH AS LEGAL TENDER IN INDONESIA. *Journal of Central Banking Law and Institutions, 1*(1), 141–180. DOI: 10.21098/jcli.v1i1.6

Rutskiy, V., Allam, S., Elkin, S., Beknazarov, Z., Semina, E., Ikonnikov, O., Kuzmich, R., & Tsarev, R. (2023). Non-fungible Tokens: Value for Digital Arts and Pricing Factors. In *Lecture Notes in Networks and Systems: Vol. 596 LNNS*. DOI: 10.1007/978-3-031-21435-6_70

Ryan, F., Coughlan, M., & Cronin, P. (2009). Interviewing in qualitative research: The one-to-one interview. *International Journal of Therapy and Rehabilitation*, *16*(6), 309–314. DOI: 10.12968/ijtr.2009.16.6.42433

Ryu, D., Baek, K. H., & Yoon, J. (2021). Open Innovation with Relational Capital, Technological Innovation Capital, And International Performance in SMEs. *Sustainability (Basel)*, *13*(6), 3418. DOI: 10.3390/su13063418

Saadan, A., & Mahajbiya, N. (2018). In Arabic. The reality of financial inclusion in the Maghreb: A comparative study (Algeria – Tunisia – Morocco). *Majallat Dirāsāt wa-Ab āth: al-Majallah al- Arabiyyah fī al- Ulūm al-Insāniyyah wa-al-Ijtimā iyyah*, Ziane Achour University, Djelfa, Algeria, 10(3). - :
- | ASJP Ibn Mājah, M. Y. (2007). *Sunan Ibn Mājah* (Vol. 3, Hadith No. 2430; M. T. al- alabī, Trans.). Dār al-Risālah al-ʿĀlamiyyah.

Saad, N. M. (2012). An analysis on the efficiency of Takaful and insurance companies in Malaysia: A non-parametric approach. *Review of Integrative Business and Economics Research*, *1*(1), 33.

Saberi, S., Kouhizadeh, M., Sarkis, J., & Shen, L. (2019). Blockchain technology and its relationships to sustainable supply chain management. *International Journal of Production Research*, *57*(7), 2117–2135. DOI: 10.1080/00207543.2018.1533261

Sadeghi, A., & Pihie, Z. A. L. (2012). Transformational leadership and its predictive effects on leadership effectiveness. *International Journal of Business and Social Science*, *3*(7), 81–88. 10.1.1.466.1733

Saharan, N., & Wadhwa, N. (2024). A Comprehensive Review of Biodegradable Polymers in Sustainable Packaging Applications. Research & Reviews. *Journal of Food Science and Technology*, *13*(1), 28–37p.

Saidi, N. B. M., Zainal, H. B., Mohd Din, N., Zainuddin, S. A. B., & Abdullah, T. B. (2020). Attitude, subjective norm, and perceived behavioural control as determinant of hibah giving intent in Malaysia. *International Journal of Innovation. Creativity and Change*, *10*(10), 61–70.

Said, N. M., Yahaya, S., Yusuff, Y. Z., & Hasan, Z. A. (2024). Takaful awareness in Malaysia: An empirical study on the influence of knowledge, financial status, and social factors. *Advanced International Journal of Business* [AIJBES]. *Entrepreneurship and SMEs*, *6*(22), 25–33.

Saif, N., Amelia, , Goh, G. G. G., Rubin, A., Shaheen, I., & Murtaza, M. (2024). Influence of Transformational Leadership on Innovative Work Behavior and Task Performance of Individuals: The Mediating Role of Knowledge Sharing. *Heliyon, 10*(11), e32280. DOI: 10.1016/j.heliyon.2024.e32280 PMID: 38933951

Saiti, B., Dembele, A., & Bulut, M. (2021). The global cash waqf: A tool against poverty in Muslim countries. *Qualitative Research in Financial Markets, 13*(3), 277–294. DOI: 10.1108/QRFM-05-2020-0085

Saiti, B., Salad, A. J., & Bulut, M. (2019). The Role of Cash Waqf in Poverty Reduction: A Multi-country Case Study. In Ghazali, E. M., Mutum, D. S., Rashid, M., & Ahmed, J. U. (Eds.), *Management of Shari'ah Compliant Businesses. Management for Professionals.* Springer., DOI: 10.1007/978-3-030-10907-3_3

Salleh, M. C. M. (2016). The significant contribution of islamic relationship marketing practice in malaysian takaful industry towards determining customer gratitude, trust, and commitment. *Asian Academy of Management Journal, 21*(Supp. 1), 171–207. DOI: 10.21315/aamj2016.supp.1.8

Salleh, S., Kamaruddin, M. I. H., Shafii, Z., Hanefah, M. M., Zakaria, N., Mahyudin, W. A., & Sabri, N. A. M. (2024). Shariah governance and audit practices in Islamic co-operatives: An audit expectation-performance gap analysis. *Corporate Law & Governance Review, 6*(3), 72–80. DOI: 10.22495/clgrv6i3p8

Salman, S. A., Rashid, H. M. A., & Hassan, R. (2017). Awareness And Knowledge Of Insurance and Takaful in India A Survey on Indian Insurance Policy Holders. *Man in India, 97*(11), 127–140.

Samson, A. T., & Ilesanmi, O. A. (2019). The relationship between transactional leadership, transformational leadership, and performance of SMEs in Nigeria. *Noble International Journal of Business and Management Research, 3*(4), 73–85.

Satria, A. (2010). Minapolitan dan Minapolitik. *ANTARA News.* http://www. antaranews.com /berita/1269867347/minapolitan-dan-minapolitik

Scepanovic, S. (2019). The Fourth Industrial Revolution and education. *8th Mediterranean Conference on Embedded Computing (MECO)*, IEEE, 1–4. https://doi .org/DOI: 10.1109/MECO.2019.8802343

Schaltegger, S., Lüdeke-Freund, F., & Hansen, E. G. (2016). Business models for sustainability: A co-evolutionary analysis of sustainable entrepreneurship, innovation, and transformation. *Organization & Environment, 29*(3), 264–289. DOI: 10.1177/1086026616633272

Schouten, A. P., Janssen, L., & Verspaget, M. (2019). Celebrity vs. Influencer endorsements in advertising: The role of identification, credibility, and Product-Endorser fit. *International Journal of Advertising*, •••, 24.

Schumacher, A., Erol, S., & Sihn, W. (2016). A maturity model for assessing Industry 4.0 readiness and maturity of manufacturing enterprises. *Procedia CIRP*, *52*, 161–166. DOI: 10.1016/j.procir.2016.07.040

Securities Commission Malaysia. (2021). *SRI Sukuk Framework*. https://www.sc.com.my/development/islamic-capital-market/sri-sukuk-framework

Selmi, R., Wohar, M., Deisting, F., & Kasmaoui, K. (2023). Dynamic inflation hedging performance and downside risk: A comparison between Islamic and conventional stock indices. *The Quarterly Review of Economics and Finance*, *91*, 56–67. DOI: 10.1016/j.qref.2023.07.006

Sestino, A., Prete, M. I., Piper, L., & Guido, G. (2020). Internet of Things and Big Data as enablers for business digitalization strategies. *Technovation*, *98*, 102173. DOI: 10.1016/j.technovation.2020.102173

Setiawan, R., Eliyana, A., Suryani, T., & Pratama, A. (2021). *The effect of transformational leadership on organizational innovation through employee creativity and internal social capital in the pandemic time of Covid-19* (Doctoral dissertation, Petra Christian University).

Setiawan, E., Nugroho, L. E., & Hartanto, R. (2023). Designing a Cybersecurity Risk Assessment Framework for Local Government Web-Based Applications. *Proceeding 2023 2nd International Conference on Computer System Information Technology and Electrical Engineering Sustainable Development for Smart Innovation System Cosite 2023*, 61–66. DOI: 10.1109/COSITE60233.2023.10249788

Setiawan, I., Rianto, B., & Sudirman, . (2022). Implementation of coastal area management policy based on sustainable development in banyuwangi regency. *International Journal of Applied Research in Social Sciences*, *4*(2), 35–50. DOI: 10.51594/ijarss.v4i2.311

Setyaningsih, W., Yuliani, S., & Winarto, Y. (2019). *Beach Tourism Development Strategy through Ecological Architecture Approach in Pacitan.*, DOI: 10.2991/senvar-18.2019.27

Sezerel, H., & Tonus, H. Z. (2014). The Soft Element of Strategic Human Resource Management: The Employee's Perception of Diversity Climate. *Procedia: Social and Behavioral Sciences*, *150*, 354–359. DOI: 10.1016/j.sbspro.2014.09.026

Shad, M. R., & Lai, K. K. (2015). The effect of Enterprise Risk Management on performance of Malaysian public listed companies. SHS Web of Conferences, 34, 1–8.

Shafer, R. A. (1997). Creating organizational agility: The human resource dimension. *Human Resource Management, 36*(1), 1–11. https://doi.org/. 3930360102DOI: 10.1002/hrm

Shaharuddin, A. B., Aminudin, E., Zakaria, R., Abidin, N. I., & Lau, S. E. N. (2021). Adoption of construction Industry 4.0 among small and medium-sized contractors in Malaysia. *AIP Conference Proceedings, 2428*, 060001. Advance online publication. DOI: 10.1063/5.0071094

Shah, S. Q. A., Lai, F. W., Shad, M. K., Hamad, S., & Ellili, N. O. D. (2025). Exploring the effect of enterprise risk management for ESG risks toward green growth. *International Journal of Productivity and Performance Management, 74*(1), 224–249. DOI: 10.1108/IJPPM-10-2023-0582

Shalboob, H. (2025). The role of AI in enhancing shariah compliance: Efficiency and transparency in Islamic finance. *Journal of Infrastructure. Policy and Development, 9*(1), 1–26.

Shariah Advisory Council of Bank Negara Malaysia. (2010). *Shariah resolutions in Islamic finance* (2nd ed.). Bank Negara Malaysia.

Sharifi, H., & Zhang, Z. (2001). Agile manufacturing in practice—Application of a methodology. *International Journal of Operations & Production Management, 21*(5/6), 772–794. DOI: 10.1108/01443570110390462

Sharma, D., Verma, R., Patil, C., & Nayak, J. K. (2024). Relationship Between Intellectual Capital and Firm Performance: Evidence from the Indian Sugar Mill Industry. *IIMT Journal of Management, 1*(1), 98–111. DOI: 10.1108/IIMTJM-11-2023-0054

Shaw, C. (2005). *Revolutionalise your customer experience*. Palgrave Macmillan. DOI: 10.1057/9780230513457

Shen, Z. (2020). Marketing Strategy of Marine Green Tourism. *Journal of Coastal Research, 112*(sp1), 59–62. DOI: 10.2112/JCR-SI112-017.1

Shiha, M. (2022). *The role of Islamic banks in promoting financial inclusion in Algeria* (Master's thesis, Faculty of Economic Sciences, University of Guelma).

Shomad, A. (2025). Liability of Islamic Banks in Bancassurance Activities. *Journal of Law and Regulation Governance, 3*(1), 435–445.

Shukla, T. (2007). Experiential marketing: The new paradigm. *Indian Journal of Marketing, 37*(4), 10–13.

Shukor, S. A. (2020). Trust in takaful agents: Antecedents and consequences. *Journal of Islamic Accounting and Business Research, 11*(6), 1161–1174. DOI: 10.1108/JIABR-01-2018-0013

Sikander, S. (2024). *Takaful: An Alternative Approach to Insurance*. Society of Actuaries Research Report.

Sisaye, S. (2021). The influence of non-governmental organizations (NGOs) on the development of voluntary sustainability accounting reporting rules. *Journal of Business and Socio-economic Development, 1*(1), 5–23. DOI: 10.1108/JBSED-02-2021-0017

Sitompul, S. S. (2024). Ecotourism as Tourist Attraction Development: Systematic Literature Review. *Jurnal Penelitian Pendidikan IPA, 10*(8), 606–612. DOI: 10.29303/jppipa.v10i8.8376

Song, J. H., Murphy, R. J., Narayan, R., & Davies, G. B. H. (2009). Biodegradable and compostable alternatives to conventional plastics. *Philosophical Transactions of the Royal Society of London. Series B, Biological Sciences, 364*(1526), 2127–2139. DOI: 10.1098/rstb.2008.0289

Soori, M., Arezoo, B., & Dastres, R. (2023). Artificial intelligence, machine learning and deep learning in advanced robotics: A review. *Cognitive Robotics, 3*, 54–70. DOI: 10.1016/j.cogr.2023.04.001

Sorescu, A. (2017). Data-driven business model innovation. *Journal of Product Innovation Management, 34*(5), 691–696. DOI: 10.1111/jpim.12398

Soualhi, Y., & Al Shammari, A. A. R. (2015). Indicators of takaful awareness among Kuwaitis. *Journal of Islamic Banking and Finance, 3*(2), 75–89. DOI: 10.15640/jibf.v3n2a8

Spear, R. (2006). Social entrepreneurship: A different model? *International Journal of Social Economics, 33*(5/6), 399–410. DOI: 10.1108/03068290610660670

Sreenish, S. R., & Senthil Kumar, S. A. (2017). THE ROLE OF BANCASSURANCE IN DIGITAL ERA. *CLEAR International Journal of Research in Commerce & Management, 8*(3).

Srivastava, V. K.Vivek Kumar Srivastava. (2024). Impact of Corporate Social Responsibility (CSR) initiatives on brand reputation: A study on how CSR activities enhance brand reputation and consumer loyalty in the context of sustainable marketing practices. *International Journal of Science and Research Archive, 13*(1), 1910–1930. DOI: 10.30574/ijsra.2024.13.1.1869

Sruthy, S. K. (2024). Enhancing supply chain resilience through artificial intelligence: A strategic framework for executives. *Emerging Science Journal*, *8*(4), 1462–1473. DOI: 10.28991/ESJ-2024-08-04-013

Statista. (2020). Global insurance companies' digital technology investment priorities worldwide 2020.

Stehn, L., & Hook, M. (2008). Lean principles in industrialized housing production: The need for a cultural change. *Lean Construction Journal*, 20–33. ISSN 1555-1369, E-ISSN 1555-1369.

Stutz, C., & Matala, S. (2025). Manufacturing national consent for industrial policy : A microhistorical analysis of Finnish shipbuilding. *Journal of International Business Studies*, *0123456789*. Advance online publication. DOI: 10.1057/s41267-025-00779-x

Subhani, M. I., & Osman, A. (2011). The Essence of Enterprise Risk Management in Today's Business Enterprises in Developed and Developing Nations. SSRN Electronic Journal. DOI: 10.2139/ssrn.1818862

Sukmaningrum, P. S., Hendratmi, A., Rusmita, S. A., & Abdul Shukor, S. (2022). Productivity analysis of family takaful in Indonesia and Malaysia: Malmquist productivity index approach. *Journal of Islamic Accounting and Business Research*, *13*(4), 649–665. DOI: 10.1108/JIABR-03-2021-0097

Sullivan, J. L., Shin, M. H., Ranusch, A., Mohr, D. C., Chen, C., & Damschroder, L. J. (2024). A Mixed Methods Study Exploring Patient Safety Culture at Four VHA Hospitals. *Joint Commission Journal on Quality and Patient Safety*, *50*(11), 791–800. DOI: 10.1016/j.jcjq.2024.07.008 PMID: 39289144

Sun, J., Li, L., Tian, X., & Fu, Y. (2025). Reliability and validity validation of the Chinese version of the family vitiligo influence scale. *BMC Public Health*, *25*(1), 258. DOI: 10.1186/s12889-025-21439-7 PMID: 39838342

Sun, P., & Shang, S. (2019). Personality traits and personal values of servant leaders. *Leadership and Organization Development Journal*, *40*(2), 177–192. DOI: 10.1108/LODJ-11-2018-0406

Suyadnya, I. W., Prianti, D. D., Kanto, S., & Putra, I. N. D. (2025). The local dynamics of global ecotourism trend in the old Balinese village, Indonesia. *Cogent Arts & Humanities*, *12*(1), 2451516. DOI: 10.1080/23311983.2025.2451516

Syahbandir, M., Alqarni, W., Hakim, A., & Muhiddin, B. (2022). State Authority for Management of Zakat, Infaq, and Sadaqah as Locally-Generated Revenue: A Case Study at Baitul Mal in Aceh. *AL-IHKAM: Journal of Law & Social Institutions, 17*(2), 554–577. DOI: 10.19105/al-lhkam.v17i2.7229

Syahputra, B. I., Marlena, D., Priambodo, D. F., & Arizal, A. (2023). Ethereum Smart Home for Denial of Service and Single Point of Failure. *Electronics (Basel), 27*(2), 50–63. DOI: 10.53314/ELS2327050S

Szadeczky, T., & Bederna, Z. (2025). *Risk, regulation, and governance: Evaluating artificial intelligence across diverse application scenarios* (Vol. 38). Palgrave Macmillan.

Tahir, I. M., & Razali, A. R. (2011). The Relationship between enterprise risk management (ERM) and firm value: Evidence from Malaysian public listed companies. *International Journal of economics and management sciences, 1*(2), 32-41.

Tampati, I. F., Komang Setia Buana, I., & Setiawan, H. (2023). Secure Mobile Application for Uniform Resource Locator (URL) Phising Detection based on Deep Learning. *2023 1st International Conference on Advanced Engineering and Technologies Iconnic 2023 Proceeding*, 231–236. DOI: 10.1109/ICONNIC59854.2023.10467246

Tapscott, D., & Tapscott, A. (2017). *Blockchain Revolution: How the Technology Behind Bitcoin is Changing Money, Business, and the World*. Penguin.

Tarchi, M., Radhouane, N., & Abou, O. (2019).in Arabic Requirements for enhancing financial inclusion in Algeria. *Journal of Economic Value Added to Business*, 1(1). University of Hassiba Ben Bouali, Chlef, Algeria. | ASJP

Tariq, T., Farhan, H. M., & Rafique, A. (2024). Developing Blueprints for Sustainable Excellence: The Integration of Green Intellectual Capital, Green Transformative Leadership, Entrepreneurial Orientation, and Cost Leadership Strategy. *Pakistan Journal of Humanities and Social Sciences, 12*(2), 1770–1794. DOI: 10.52131/pjhss.2024.v12i2.2275

Taseer, M. I., & Ahmed, A. (2022). The most effective leadership style in pursuit of resilient supply chain: Sequential mediation of flexibility and agile supply chain. [PJCSS]. *Pakistan Journal of Commerce and Social Sciences, 16*(3), 387–423. DOI: 10.64534/Commer.2022.105

Teresi, J. A., Yu, X., Stewart, A. L., & Hays, R. D. (2022). Guidelines for Designing and Evaluating Feasibility Pilot Investigations. *Medical Care, 60*(1), 95–103. DOI: 10.1097/MLR.0000000000001664 PMID: 34812790

Thiebes, B., & Winkhardt-Enz, R. (2023). Challenges and opportunities using new modalities and technologies for multi-risk management. *Natural Hazards, 119*(2), 1137–1140. DOI: 10.1007/s11069-022-05516-3

Thomas, R., & Lukose, P. J. (2024). Social entrepreneurship for empowerment and inclusive business model among Meghalaya rubber farmers. *Journal of Entrepreneurship and Innovation in Emerging Economies, 10*(1), 51–65. DOI: 10.1177/23939575231213813

Thompson, B. (2005). The loyalty connection: Secrets to customer retention and increased profits. Right Now Technologies, 1-16.

Ti, A., & Husodo, Z. A. (2024). Navigating volatility spillover amidst investor extreme fear in stablecoin and financial markets. *Cogent Economics & Finance, 12*(1), 2408276. Advance online publication. DOI: 10.1080/23322039.2024.2408276

Tiwari, A. K., Aikins Abakah, E. J., Adekoya, O. B., & Hammoudeh, S. (2023). What do we know about the price spillover between green bonds and Islamic stocks and stock market indices? *Global Finance Journal, 55*, 100794. DOI: 10.1016/j.gfj.2022.100794

Togok, S. H., Isa, C. R., & Zainuddin, S. (2016). Enterprise Risk Management Adoption in Malaysia: A Disclosure Approach. *Asian Journal of Business and Accounting*, *9*(1), 83–106.

Toma, F., Kant, S., & Niguse, T. (2026). Business Model Effect on Innovation With Mediation of Open Innovation Analysis in Africa. In *Innovation Management for Disruptive Maturity in Competitive Scenarios* (pp. 273–294). IGI Global Scientific Publishing.

Tong, J. (2025). *The Role of ESG in Global Economic Development: Current Status, Challenges, and Future Trends*. Advances in Economics, Management and Political Sciences.

Tran, M., Beddewela, E., & Ntim, C. G. (2021). Governance and sustainability in Southeast Asia. *Accounting Research Journal, 34*(6), 516–545. DOI: 10.1108/ARJ-05-2019-0095

Treepongkaruna, S., Au Yong, H. H., Thomsen, S., & Kyaw, K. (2024). Greenwashing, carbon emission, and ESG. *Business Strategy and the Environment, 33*(8), 8526–8539. DOI: 10.1002/bse.3929

Tsiga, Z. D., Emes, M., & Smith, A. (2016). Critical success factors for the construction industry. *PM World Journal*, *5*(8), 1–12.

Tuwo, A., Yunus, M., Aprianto, R., & Tresnati, J. (2021). Marine ecotourism development in South Sulawesi, Indonesia. *IOP Conference Series. Earth and Environmental Science*, *763*(1), 012068. DOI: 10.1088/1755-1315/763/1/012068

Uddin, G. S., Yahya, M., Park, D., Hedström, A., & Tian, S. (2024). Bond market spillover networks of ASEAN-4 markets: Is the global pandemic different? *International Review of Economics & Finance*, *92*, 1028–1044. DOI: 10.1016/j.iref.2024.02.065

Ugbebor, F., Adeteye, M., & Ugbebor, J. (2024). Automated Inventory Management Systems with IoT Integration to Optimize Stock Levels and Reduce Carrying Costs for SMEs: A Comprehensive Review. *Journal of Artificial Intelligence General Science (JAIGS) ISSN: 3006-4023, 6*(1), 306-340.

Uğural, M. N., Giritli, H., & Urbański, M. (2020). Determinants of the turnover intention of construction professionals: A mediation analysis. *Sustainability (Basel)*, *12*(3), 954. DOI: 10.3390/su12030954

Uğurlu, Ö. Y., Çolakoğlu, E., & Öztosun, E. (2019). The effect of strategic agility on firm performance: A research in manufacturing enterprises. *Business and People Magazine, 6*(1), 93–106.

United Nations Development Programme. (2025). *Building climate resilience through Takaful: Part 2 – Developing Takaful market systems.*

Uslu, T. (2015). Innovation Culture and Strategic Human Resource Management in Public and Private Sector within The Framework Of Employee Ownership. *Procedia: Social and Behavioral Sciences*, *195*, 1463–1470. DOI: 10.1016/j.sbspro.2015.06.445

Uyar, A. S., & Deniz, N. (2012). The Perceptions of Entrepreneurs on the Strategic Role of Human Resource Management. *Procedia: Social and Behavioral Sciences*, *58*, 914–923. DOI: 10.1016/j.sbspro.2012.09.1070

Van Dierendonck, D., & Rook, L. (2010). Enhancing innovation and creativity through servant leadership. In *Servant leadership: Developments in theory and research* (pp. 155–165). Palgrave Macmillan UK. DOI: 10.1057/9780230299184_13

Van Dierendonck, D., & Patterson, K. (2015). Compassionate love as a cornerstone of servant leadership: An integration of previous theorizing and research. *Journal of Business Ethics*, *128*(1), 119–131. DOI: 10.1007/s10551-014-2085-z

Van, H. V., & Afifa, M. A. (2024). Environmental commitment for green finance and sustainable performance in commercial banks of ASEAN countries-whether stakeholder pressure has a moderating role. *International Journal of Sustainable Economy*, *16*(3), 304–331. DOI: 10.1504/IJSE.2024.139502

Vardarlıer, P. (2016). Strategic Approach to Human Resources Management During Crisis. *Procedia: Social and Behavioral Sciences, 235*, 463–472. DOI: 10.1016/j.sbspro.2016.11.057

Varma. (2012). Enhancing and empowering: Customer experience. *SCMS Journal of Indian Management, 9*(3), 71-78.

Wahab, M. Z. H., & Hassan, M. H. A. (2023). Contemporary Challenges and Prospects for Takaful Practices in Malaysia: An Analysis of Current Issues. International Journal of Accounting [IJAFB]. *Finance and Business, 8*(47), 337–350.

Wai-Khuen, W., Boon-Heng, T., & Siow-Hooi, T. (2023). The influence of external stakeholders on environmental, social, and governance (ESG) reporting: Toward a conceptual framework for ESG disclosure. *Foresight and STI Governance, 17*(2), 9–20. DOI: 10.17323/2500-2597.2023.2.9.20

Walker, K., & Wan, F. (2012). The Harm of Symbolic Actions and Greenwashing: Corporate Actions and Communications on Environmental Performance and Their Financial Implications. *Journal of Business Ethics, 109*(2), 227–242. DOI: 10.1007/s10551-011-1122-4

Walter, A. T. (2021). Organizational agility: Ill-defined and somewhat confusing? A systematic literature review and conceptualization. *Management Review Quarterly, 71*(2), 343–391. DOI: 10.1007/s11301-020-00186-6

Wan Jusoh, W. N. H., & Noreffendi, A. D. (2022). The Awareness of Education Takaful Among Consumers in Kuching, Sarawak. *International Journal of Islamic Economics and Finance Research, 5*(1), 90–103. DOI: 10.53840/ijiefer82

Wang, B., Osman, L. H., Palil, M. R., & Jamaludin, N. A. B. (2024). Bridging Risks and Opportunities: Operational Strategies for Sustainable Growth via ESG Management. *Operational Research in Engineering Sciences: Theory and Applications, 7*(1).

Wang, X., Zhou, Y., Li, L., Kueh, Y. C., Zeng, L., & Kuan, G. (2025). Psychometric properties of the Sport Mental Health Continuum – Short Form scale (Sport MHC-SF): Cross-cultural validation and measurement invariance of the Chinese adaptation. *BMC Psychology, 13*(1), 183. Advance online publication. DOI: 10.1186/s40359-025-02487-5 PMID: 40033429

Wang, Y.-J. (2002). Liquidity management, operating performance, and corporate value: Evidence from Japan and Taiwan. *Journal of Multinational Financial Management, 12*(2), 159–169. DOI: 10.1016/S1042-444X(01)00047-0

White, A., Rudyanto, , Agung, M. F., Minarputri, N., Lestari, A. P., Wen, W., Fajariyanto, Y., Green, A., & Tighe, S. (2021). Marine Protected Area Networks in Indonesia: Progress, Lessons and a Network Design Case Study Covering Six Eastern Provinces. *Coastal Management*, *49*(6), 575–597. DOI: 10.1080/08920753.2021.1967560

Widiastuti, T., Auwalin, I., Rani, L. N., & Ubaidillah Al Mustofa, M. (2021). A mediating effect of business growth on the zakat empowerment program and the mustahiq's welfare. *Cogent Business & Management*, *8*(1), 1882039. Advance online publication. DOI: 10.1080/23311975.2021.1882039

Willems, K., Brengman, M., & Van De Sanden, S. (2017). In-store proximity marketing: Experimenting with digital point-of-sales communication. *International Journal of Retail & Distribution Management*, *45*(7-8), 910–927. DOI: 10.1108/IJRDM-10-2016-0177

Wilson, J. A. J., & Liu, J. (2011). The challenges of Islamic branding: Navigating emotions and halal. *Journal of Islamic Marketing*, *2*(1), 28–42. DOI: 10.1108/17590831111115222

Winoto Tj, H., Wibowo, J. M., & Widjaja, B. T. (2025). Human Capital, Competitive Advantage, and Business Performance: A Study of Indonesian Hospitals. *Journal of Open Innovation*.

World Bank. (2022). *Data for better lives: World Development Report 2021*. World Bank Group., DOI: 10.1596/978-1-4648-1600-0

World Economic Forum. (2020). *The Global Future Council on Blockchain: Building Value with Blockchain Technology*.

World Economic Forum. (2021). *ESG is missing a metric: R for resilience*. World Economic Forum. https://www.weforum.org/stories/2021/06/esg-resilience-investment-environment-social-governance/

World Economic Forum. (2024). *The State of Social Enterprise: A Review of Global Data 2013-2023*. Schwab Foundation for Social Entrepreneurship. https://www3.weforum.org/docs/WEF_The_State_of_Social_Enterprise_2024.pdf

Xing, X., Liu, Y., Zhu, Y., & Deng, J. (2024). The impact of climate policy uncertainty on China's green energy and non-ferrous metals market co-movement: Evidence from spillover perspectives. *Journal of Environmental Management*, *367*, 121845. DOI: 10.1016/j.jenvman.2024.121845

Xu, J., & Li, J. (2022). The Interrelationship Between Intellectual Capital and Firm Performance: Evidence from China's Manufacturing Sector. *Journal of Intellectual Capital*, *23*(2), 313–341. DOI: 10.1108/JIC-08-2019-0189

Xu, M., David, J. M., & Kim, S. H. (2018). The fourth industrial revolution: Opportunities and challenges. *International Journal of Financial Research*, *9*(2), 90–95. DOI: 10.5430/ijfr.v9n2p90

Yahia, I., Ben Al-Neama, N., & Kerbache, L. (2018). Investigating the drivers for social commerce in social media platforms: Importance of trust, social support and the platform perceived usage. *Journal of Retailing and Consumer Services*, *41*(1), 11–19. DOI: 10.1016/j.jretconser.2017.10.021

Yakusheva, O., Lee, K. A., & Weiss, M. (2024). The Nursing Human Capital Value Model. *International Journal of Nursing Studies*, *160*, 104890. DOI: 10.1016/j.ijnurstu.2024.104890 PMID: 39316994

Yaseen, M., Sajjad, W., Visetnoi, S., Amanah, S., & Saqib, S. E. (2024). Entrepreneurial Orientation and SMEs Efficiency With Government Financial and Non-Financial Incentives as Moderators. *SAGE Open*, *14*(3), 1–23. DOI: 10.1177/21582440241281259

Yasin, M., Porcu, L., Prados-Castillo, J. F., & Liébana-Cabanillas, F. (2024). The Role of Social Media in Building Islamic Banking Consumer Engagement: Analyzing the Impact of Brand Personality Traits and Brand Love. *International Journal of Human-Computer Interaction*, •••, 1–15.

Yassin, N., & Ramly, J. (2011). *Takaful: A study guide*. IBFIM.

Yeni, F., Melmusi, Z., Wulandari, E., & Ilona, D. (2020). The Effect of the Board of Directors' Characteristics on Company Value.

Yigitcanlar, T., Mehmood, R., & Corchado, J. M. (2021). Green artificial intelligence: Towards an efficient, sustainable and equitable technology for smart cities and futures. *Sustainability (Basel)*, *13*(16), 8952. Advance online publication. DOI: 10.3390/su13168952

Yoon, S. S., Oh, I., & Kim, H. J. (2024). An accounting perspective on the IFRS sustainability reporting standards for greenhouse gas emissions: Implications for the Asia Pacific. *Asia Pacific Business Review*, •••, 1–24. DOI: 10.1080/13602381.2024.2364806

Yoshida, D. T., Sendjaya, S., Hirst, G., & Cooper, B. (2014). Does servant leadership foster creativity and innovation? A multi-level mediation study of identification and prototypicality. *Journal of Business Research*, *67*(7), 1395–1404. DOI: 10.1016/j.jbusres.2013.08.013

Yu, E. P. Y., Guo, C. Q., & Luu, B. V. (2018). Environmental, social and governance transparency and firm value. *Business Strategy and the Environment*, *27*(7), 987–1004. DOI: 10.1002/bse.2047

Yüksel, S., Eti, S., Dinçer, H., Gökalp, Y., Olaru, G. O., & Oflaz, N. K. (2025). Innovative financial solutions for sustainable investments using artificial intelligence-based hybrid fuzzy decision-making approach in carbon capture technologies. *Financial Innovation*, *11*(1), 20. Advance online publication. DOI: 10.1186/s40854-024-00671-x

Yulianda, F. (2007). *Coastal ecosystem as alternatif for managing marine resources*. Seminar Sains, Bogor: Institut Pertanian Bogor.

Yunus, M. (2007). *Creating a world without poverty: Social business and the future of capitalism*. PublicAffairs.

Yusran, Q. Q., & Afiyah, I. (2024). Optimizing the Potential of Zakat to Alleviate Poverty Problems and Improve Community Economy in Surakarta City. *Journal of Ecohumanism*, *3*(3), 121–132. DOI: 10.62754/joe.v3i3.3394

Yusuf, I., Aliyu, I. A., & Al-Faryan, M. A. S. (2023). Board risk committee composition and risk-taking of deposit money banks in Nigeria. *Cogent Business & Management*, *10*(1), 2187884. DOI: 10.1080/23311975.2023.2187884

Yuwanda, T., Fadhlan, A., & Daud, I. (2023). Building Competitive Advantage through Human Capital and the Impact on Business Performance: Analysis at Individual and Organizational Level. [Jurnal Dinamika Manajemen]. *Journal of Database Management*, *14*(1), 72–86.

Yu, X., & Chen, Y. (2024). Does ESG advantage promote total factor productivity (TFP)? Empirical evidence from China's listed enterprises. *Applied Economics*, •••, 1–17.

Zaheb, S., & Ben Mouloud, W. (2020). *Arabic. The role of Waqf in local development in El Oued Province: An applied study. Economic Visions Journal, 10(1).*
( ). World Bank., https://data.albankaldawli.org/

Zainol, Z., Fernandez, D., & Ahmad, H. (2017). Public Sector Accountants' Opinion on Impact of a New Enterprise System. *Procedia Computer Science*, *124*, 247–254. DOI: 10.1016/j.procs.2017.12.153

Zakaria, A., & Ngah, K. (2020). Role of mosque leaders and its impact towards community development: A study in Kedah. *International Research Journal of Shariah* [IRJSMI]. *Muamalat and Islam*, *2*(3), 52–57.

Zarinjooei, K., Ghodrati, H., Panahian, H., & Jabbari, H. (2025). Identifying and prioritizing the factors affecting enterprise risk management implementation. *Iranian Journal of Finance*, *9*(1), 134–161. DOI: 10.61186/ijf.2024.448623.1463

Zehir, C., Gurol, Y., Karaboga, T., & Kole, M. (2016). Strategic Human Resource Management and Firm Performance: The Mediating Role of Entrepreneurial Orientation. *Procedia: Social and Behavioral Sciences*, *235*, 372–381. DOI: 10.1016/j.sbspro.2016.11.045

Zetzsche, D. A., Buckley, R. P., Arner, D. W., & Barberis, J. N. (2020). Decentralized Finance. *Journal of Financial Regulation*, *6*(2), 172–203. DOI: 10.1093/jfr/fjaa010

Zhang, D., Zhang, Z., Ji, Q., Lucey, B., & Liu, J. (2021). Board characteristics, external governance and the use of renewable energy: International evidence. *Journal of International Financial Markets, Institutions and Money*, *72*(C), 101317. DOI: 10.1016/j.intfin.2021.101317

Zhang, J., Zhou, C., & Zhou, L. (2017). Firm size, risk management disclosure, and firm value: Evidence from China. *China Journal of Accounting Research*, *10*(4), 1–15.

Zhang, X., Bilawal, M., Chenghuan, K., Afaq, M., & Jafri, H. (2025). A comparative investigation of economic activity and sustainable development in China and Three South Asian Countries. *Discover Sustainability*, *58*(1), 170. Advance online publication. DOI: 10.1007/s43621-025-00885-8

Zhang, Y., Xue, Y., & Liu, Y. (2019). Security and Privacy on Blockchain. *ACM Computing Surveys*, *52*(3), 1–34. DOI: 10.1145/3316481

Zhang, Z., & Sharifi, H. (2000). A methodology for achieving agility in manufacturing organizations. *International Journal of Operations & Production Management*, *20*(4), 496–513. DOI: 10.1108/01443570010314818

Zhen, J., Cao, C., Qiu, H., & Xie, Z. (2021). Impact of organizational inertia on organizational agility: The role of IT ambidexterity. *Information Technology and Management*, *22*(1), 53–65. DOI: 10.1007/s10799-021-00324-w

Zhihan, S., Mohammadiounotikandi, A., Khanlooei, S. G., Monjezi, S., Umaralievich, M. S., Ehsani, A., & Lee, S. (2022). A new conceptual model to investigate the role of hospital's capabilities on sustainable learning. *The International Journal of Organizational Analysis*.

Zhou, K., Liu, T., & Zhou, L. (2015, August). Industry 4.0: Towards future industrial opportunities and challenges. In *2015 12th International Conference on Fuzzy Systems and Knowledge Discovery (FSKD)* (pp. 2147–2152). IEEE. https://doi.org/ DOI: 10.1109/FSKD.2015.7382435

Zhou, N., Fernandez, D., Aman, A., & Ghazali, A. W. (2026). Hyperautomation in Accounting: A Bibliometric Journey Through Artificial Intelligence and Robotic Process Automation Integration. *Journal of Advanced Research Design*, *138*(1), 42–64.

Zhu, J. (2024). Application of artificial intelligence data mining algorithm in enterprise management risk assessment. *International Journal of Information Systems and Supply Chain Management, 17*(1), 1–19. DOI: 10.4018/IJISSCM.342119

Zhu, J., Zhi, W., & Fang, Y. (2025). Ethical leadership, organizational learning, and corporate ESG performance: A moderated mediation model. *International Review of Economics & Finance, 98*, 103966. DOI: 10.1016/j.iref.2025.103966

Zulfitra, Z., Ganar, Y. B., Sahroni, S., & Arsyan, M. A. (2022). The Effect of Risk Management and Profitability on Stock Prices Moderated by Good Corporate Governance Variables. *Kontigensi Jurnal Ilmiah Manajemen, 10*(2), 299–311. DOI: 10.56457/jimk.v10i2.288

About the Contributors

Muhammad Ridhwan Ab. Aziz is a Professor of Islamic Banking and Finance at the Faculty of Economics and Muamalat, Universiti Sains Islam Malaysia (USIM). He received his Bachelor Degree of Business Administration (Hons.) in 2001, Master Degree in Islamic Studies, specializing in Islamic Banking in 2008 and Doctorate in Islamic Banking in 2011 from University of Malaya. He is an Assessor for academic program accreditation of Malaysian Qualification Agency (MQA) in the field of Islamic banking and Islamic finance. He is also a Shariah Committee Member for Export-Import Bank of Malaysia Berhad (EXIM Bank) and Citibank Berhad (Malaysia), Internal Shariah Advisory Board for Citibank N.A. Labuan Branch, Shariah Supervisory Board Member for Shuaa Funds OEIC ICC Limited in United Arab Emirates, Registered Shariah Adviser for Labuan Financial Services Authority (LFSA) as well as an Arbitrator (Hakam) for Negeri Sembilan Syariah Judiciary Department. He is also Academic Advisors for Islamic finance program in various colleges, university colleges and university as well as Members of Editorial Board for local and international journals. He also involves as Panel of Interview for Biasiswa Yang Dipertuan Agong, Public Service Department/Jabatan Perkhidmatan Awam (JPA), Malaysia and Biasiswa Kementerian Pendidikan Malaysia, Ministry of Education Malaysia. He actively involves in the popular writing in various platforms such as Islamic Finance News (IFN), Harian Metro, Berita Harian, BERNAMA, Utusan Malaysia, Dewan Ekonomi and The Newsletter of Muamalat. His area of expertise is in the field of Islamic banking and finance, Islamic commercial law, Islamic money and capital market as well as Islamic social finance. Until now, he has supervised and graduated eighteen (18) master's and Phd graduates mainly in the field of Islamic banking and finance as well as in Islamic social finance. He involved as examiner in thesis examination for thirty-nine (39) master's and Phd candidates in his area of expertise. He has been invited as speaker for keynote speaker, guest speaker, guest lecture, public lecture as well as inaugural lecture from local and international universities and institutions. He has been awarded for various research and innovation awards such as best paper award, USIM top 100 researchers award, award for most selling book, publication award for prolific writer in social science cluster, active book writer award for English category as well as best research award in social science and ihtisas arts. He also won gold and silver medal awards in local and international research and innovation competitions. He obtained certificate of copyright from Intellectual Property Corporation of Malaysia or Perbadanan Harta Intelek Malaysia for two innovative products namely Bank Wakaf and Wakaf Kepakaran Profesional for duration of 100 years. He also involved in various consultancy projects with external parties and collaborators such as Islamic Banking & Finance Institute Malaysia (IBFIM), Association of Islamic Banking Institutions Malaysia (AIBIM), Lembaga Kemajuan Johor Tenggara (KEJORA), Malaysia Productivity Corporation (MPC) and Perbadanan Wakaf Negeri Sembilan Sdn. Bhd. (PWNS/MAINS). Until now, he has authored twenty-nine (29) books and thirty-five (35) chapters in book. He has also presented one hundred and eight (108) papers and published one hundred and forty (140) articles in various national and international conferences and indexed journals. He is actively conducting research in forty-six (46) research projects in his area of expertise and funded by various internal and external parties such as Ministry of Higher Education Malaysia, Majlis Agama Islam Negeri Sembilan (MAINS), Pusat Zakat Negeri Sembilan (PZNS), Yayasan Tun Ismail Ali, Permodalan Nasional Berhad (YTI/PNB), Yayasan Pembangunan Ekonomi Islam Malaysia (YAPEIM), Albukhary International University (AIU) and Bank Pembangunan Malaysia Berhad (BPMB). Currently, total research funding obtained is RM2,364,530.00. He can be reached at ridhwan.aziz@usim.cdu.my.

Safeza Mohd Sapian is currently a Senior Lecturer at the Faculty of Economics and Muamalat, Universiti Sains Islam Malaysia (USIM). She holds a PhD in Islamic Finance from the International Centre for Education in Islamic Finance (INCEIF). She obtained her Bachelor degree in Banking and Finance from Northwood University, Michigan, USA and received her Diploma in Banking Studies from Universiti Teknologi Mara (UiTM). Her area of specialisation includes Islamic banking and finance, risk management and social finance. She is a member of the Malaysian Association of Risk and Insurance Management (MARIM) and the Qualitative Research Association of Malaysia (QRAM). She taught undergraduate and postgraduate students on various subjects such as Risk Management, Islamic Financial System and Money and Capital Market. She is certified HRDF Trainer and AMANIE's Trainer in Islamic Finance as well as Enterprise Risk Management Certified Professional (ERMCP). Prior to joining academia, she was employed in the banking industry for 10 years in various key departments, starting with Internal Auditor at Kwong Yik Bank Berhad. She then served as the Senior Executive in the Trade Finance Department at RHB Bank Berhad and her last position was a

Risk Analyst in Risk Management Department at EON Bank Berhad specialising in Operational Risk. She can be contacted at safeza@usim.edu.my

Suhaila Abdul Hamid is currently a Senior Lecturer at the Faculty of Economics and Muamalat, Universiti Sains Islam Malaysia (USIM). She holds a PhD from University of Canterbury. Her area of expertise are Accounting, Shariah Audit & Governance, Senior Lecturer, Taxation And Zakat.

***

Bahrina Almas completed her undergraduate education at the Islamic Economics Study Program, Universitas Brawijaya (2015) and won the title of Best Graduate. Continue to study at the Masters level at the Airlangga University Master of Science in Islamic Economics Program (2019) to develop a deep understanding of the principles of Islamic economics, especially in the fields of Islamic social finance and halal studies. Currently teaching in the Islamic Economics Study Program at the University of Jember and actively involved in various scientific activities such as being a representative in the student exchange-outbound program at Universiti Islam Sultan Sharif Ali, Brunei Darussalam (2018), Islamic Economics Summer School PEBS FEB University of Indonesia (2020), attending Certified Basic Islamic Economics Trainer, Akhuwat University, Pakistan (2023), and becoming a Halal Product Process Assistant, Halal Center University of Jember. Her also a reviewer in several accredited national scientific journals and an editor team at Future Science Press.

Moh. Arifin, Religion, as the foundation of life, served as the basis for the author's decision to join Pondok Pesantren Al Amien Prenduan in 2004. In 2010, the author successfully completed both the Tsanawiyah and Aliyah programs, becoming an alumnus of Pondok Pesantren Al Amien Prenduan. Following graduation, the author engaged in a year of service by teaching in Bandung as a form of dedication to the pesantren, continuing until 2011. The author then pursued higher education through a pesantren scholarship program and earned a Bachelor's degree in Sharia Economics from Universitas Trunojoyo Madura in 2015. In 2019, the author completed a Master's degree in Islamic Economics Science from the Graduate School of Universitas Airlangga Surabaya. The author specializes in the field of community economic empowerment. Currently, the author serves as a lecturer and Head of the Institute for Research and Community Service (LPPM) at IAI Al Fithrah Surabaya, and is actively involved as a researcher in areas related to community economic development. Several of the author's research projects have been funded by internal grants from IAI Al Fithrah Surabaya. In addition to academic responsibilities, the author also serves as a manager at PT Manara Consulting, which operates several business units including training for Islamic Financial Institutions, publishing services, and others.

Boudoukha Rached Lamraoui is a PhD student specializing in Islamic Banking and Finance at the International Islamic University Malaysia. Originally from Algeria, his academic interests focus on Islamic banking, participatory finance, financial inclusion, and broader topics in finance. Driven by a commitment to contribute to the development of inclusive and ethical financial systems, Rached aims to explore how Islamic financial principles can enhance economic and social development, particularly in emerging markets

Bayu Tri Cahya, S.E., M.Si., is a lecturer in the Department of Islamic Economics at the State Islamic Institute (IAIN) Kudus, Central Java, Indonesia. He has been a committed academic since joining IAIN Kudus in 2011, following the completion of his doctoral studies in Islamic Economics at the State Islamic University of North Sumatra in 2017. His research interests include Islamic social reporting, green accounting, corporate governance, Islamic banking, and the integration of technology with Islamic financial management. He has published numerous works in accredited national and international journals, sharing insights into the development and implementation of Sharia-based financial practices in corporate and societal contexts. In addition to his research, Dr. Bayu actively serves as a reviewer for several leading journals and regularly presents his work at national and international conferences. His expertise and commitment to advancing Islamic economics have made him a valuable resource among academics and professionals. He can be contacted at bayu.cahya@iainkudus.ac.id.

Erlindawati is a master of management student at Universitas Terbuka, previously completed an undergraduate program in the Sharia Banking study program IAIN Langsa, with expertise in Sharia Banking and Sharia Finance.

Dahlia Fernandez (PhD) is a Senior Lecturer at the Faculty of Economics and Management, Universiti Kebangsaan Malaysia (UKM). She holds a PhD in Accounting from UKM. Her specialisations include Accounting Information Systems (AIS), Robotic Process Automation (RPA), Digital Accounting, Enterprise Resource Planning (ERP), and Global Business Services.

Aziatul Waznah Ghazali holds a Diploma in Accounting and Bachelor in Accounting from Universiti Teknologi MARA and a Masters degree in the same field from University of Strathclyde, Scotland. She obtained another Masters degree in 2014 and pursue her PhD, which is also in the area of accounting from

Kingston University London in 2018. Dr Aziatul's academic career began with her appointment as a lecturer at Universiti Teknologi MARA (UiTM) in 2010. She was then appointed as a senior lecturer in 2019 at Universiti Sains Malaysia (USM) before serving in Universiti Kebangsaan Malaysia (UKM). As for her research interest, she specialises in quantitative studies involving financial reporting, corporate governance, auditing and financial criminology. She also has a keen interest in social enterprises, as well as in environmental and sustainable reporting.

Abdulmajid Obaid Hasan is an Associate Professor at the Institute of Islamic Banking and Finance, International Islamic University Malaysia. With over 15 years of experience is a Shariah advisor and consultant to Al Rajhi Bank (Malaysia) and a Shariah board member/advisor to Al-Kutaybi Islamic Microfinance Bank, has authored four specialized books in Islamic finance, more than 20 Scopus-indexed papers

Muhammad Nawaz Iqbal is an Academician, Researcher and Philosopher. He have almost 13 years of corporate experience and now serving as an Assistant Professor in department of Business Administration of Sir Syed university of Engineering and Technology, Karachi, Pakistan. He credited numerous publications in local and international journals and also credited two books in the field of Business Management.

Ahmad Yani Ismail is a lecturer at the Faculty of Economics, Accounting, and Management, Universiti Islam Selangor (UIS). He obtained his Bachelor's Degree (Honors) in Business Administration in 1993 from the University of Portsmouth, United Kingdom, a Master's in Business Management in 1995 from the University of Hull, United Kingdom, a Certificate in Islamic Financial Planning from IBFIM in 2009, and a Shariah Certificate for Banking and Finance. His expertise lies in the field of Islamic Finance and Banking as well as Islamic Financial Planning. He has presented numerous articles at both national and international seminars. He is also involved in various research projects related to Islamic finance and banking. His expertise includes bank's money creation, risk management, takaful and Islamic Financial Planning. He can be contacted at ahmadyani@uis.edu.my.

Nurul Atasha Jamaludin (PhD) is a Senior Lecturer at the Faculty of Economics and Management, Universiti Kebangsaan Malaysia (UKM), where she also serves as Head of the Bachelor of Entrepreneurship and Innovation program. She holds a PhD in Entrepreneurship from UKM. Her research interests include immigrant entrepreneurship, social entrepreneurship, social business, social capital, and qualitative research methods.

Nurul Nazlia Jamil is an Associate Professor and seasoned researcher at the Faculty of Economics and Muamalat, Universiti Sains Islam Malaysia (USIM), with expertise in accounting, financial reporting, corporate governance, auditing, and sustainability-related reporting.She has an active research profile with publications in peer-reviewed journals on topics such as corporate governance reforms, accounting standards compliance (notably Malaysian Private Entity Reporting Standard for SMEs), audit committee effectiveness, and ethics in accounting education and ESG and Sustainability Reporting. Her work contributes to both theoretical and practical understanding of governance and reporting practices, and she is involved in teaching and research projects within her field.

Kashif Nawaz Khan is a dedicated Ph.D. scholar at the University Sains Malaysia, specializing in Project Management. With a passion for advancing knowledge in his field, Kashif is actively engaged in research to contribute valuable insights to the realm of project management.

Early Ridho Kismawadi, S.E.I, MA is a lecturer at the Department of Islamic Banking, Faculty of Islamic Economics and Business IAIN Langsa, Aceh, Indonesia, he has been a lecturer since 2013, he has completed a doctoral program in 2018 majoring in Sharia economics at the State Islamic University of North Sumatra. He was appointed head of the Islamic economics Law study program (2023) Islamic banking study program (2020) and Islamic financial management study program (2019) at Langsa State Islamic Institute (IAIN Langsa), Aceh, Indonesia. His research interests include financial economics, applied econometrics, Islamic economics, banking, and finance. He has published articles in national and international journals. In addition, he is also a reviewer of several reputable international journals such as Finance Research Letters, Financial Innovation, Cogent Business &; Management, Journal of Islamic Accounting and Business Research. He has also presented his papers at various local and international seminars. Dr. Early Ridho Kismawadi, S.E.I, MA, can be contacted at kismawadi@iainlangsa.ac.id.

Nurul Hidayah Md Razali (PhD) is a holder of a Doctor of Philosophy in Management from the Faculty of Economics and Management (FEP), Universiti Kebangsaan Malaysia (UKM). Conducting research related to the Efficiency of Cash Waqf Fund Management through Information & Communication Technology (ICT), Financial Technology (FinTech), and Enterprise Risk Management (ERM). Involved in writing journals, research books, and book chapters in the fields of Waqf, Takaful, ERM, and Efficiency Analysis.

Emna Mnif is a Tunisian academic and researcher specializing in Islamic finance, fintech, and behavioral economics, with a strong foundation in machine learning, blockchain technologies, and green finance. She currently holds the position of Assistant Professor at ESC Sfax, affiliated with the University of Sfax, Tunisia.

Noor Aimi Mohamad Puad is a faculty member at the Department of Finance, Kuliyyah of Economics and Management Sciences. She holds a PhD in Islamic Banking and Finance from IIUM, with research interests in Shariah audit, Shariah governance, Takaful, and Islamic finance.

Ridan Muhtadi is a Lecturer in the Department of Islamic Economics, Faculty of Sharia, Institut Agama Islam Miftahul Ulum (IAIMU), Pamekasan, Indonesia. He has served as Chairperson of the Indonesian Cooperative Council (DEKOPIN) at the District Level for Pamekasan Regency since 2023–2025. Additionally, he is actively involved in several non-governmental organizations, including the Nahdlatul Ulama Economic Institution (LPNU) and the Indonesian Islamic Economics Society (MES). His research interests include Islamic economics, Islamic banking and finance, Islamic wealth management, and Islamic business management. He has authored several international journal articles and book chapters. He is currently pursuing a PhD at UIN Kiai Haji Ahmad Siddiq Jember in the Department of Islamic Studies, following completion of his Master's degree (MSc) in Islamic Economics at Universitas Airlangga, Indonesia.

Khairunnisa Musari is an Assistant Professor at Faculty of Islamic Economics and Business (FEBI) & Postgraduate Program, Kiai Haji Achmad Siddiq State Islamic University (UIN KHAS), Jember, Indonesia. She is a Secretary of the Indonesian Association of Islamic Economists (IAEI) for the Provincial Board of East Java since 2017. Her research interests in sukuk, waqf, esham, fiscal & monetary policies, circular economy, halal logistics, sustainable finance, climate change, and Islamic microfinance & nanofinance. She has several book chapters with international reputable publishers such as IGI Global, Emerald Publishing Limited, World Scientific Publishing, Routledge, Springer, and Palgrave Macmillan. She has experience as a Senior Specialist for Islamic Finance of United Nations Development Programme (UNDP) Indonesia and was listed as one of the Top 300 Most Influential Women in Islamic Business & Finance 2019, 2020, 2021, WOMANi Significancica 2022, and WOMANi Academica 2023, 2024, by Cambridge-IFA.

Peni Nugraheni currently works at Accounting Department, Universitas Muhammadiyah Yogyakarta, Indonesia. Peni does research in corporate governance, disclosure, Islamic Accounting, and Islamic Financial Institutions.

Ahmad Salman, currently associated with the Centre for Management and Marketing Innovation, COE of Business Innovation and Communication in

Multimedia University, is a distinguished academician and researcher deeply immersed in the realm of sustainable development. As a lecturer, he is renowned for his innovative teaching methodologies, rigorous research contributions, and significant community engagement. Dr Salman, holding a PhD in project management, is particularly skilled in sustainable practices. His academic prowess is notably reflected in his extensive publications in renowned journals, with a special emphasis on sustainability and stakeholder management. His blend of a solid academic foundation and a dynamic approach to teaching and research solidifies his status as an influential researcher in his field of study.

Soliha Sanusi is a Senior Lecturer at the Faculty of Economics and Management, Universiti Kebangsaan Malaysia. She obtained her Phd from the Universiti Teknologi MARA Malaysia in Financial Criminology. Her research interests are in the areas of taxation, financial criminology, small medium enterprises, cash waqf and public sector accounting.

Nur Amalina Shafie received a Bachelor of Applied Science (Hons) with a major in statistics & minor in management and a Master of Science (Statistics) from Universiti Sains Malaysia in 2009 and 2012, respectively. She received a Ph.D. degree from Universiti Kebangsaan Malaysia in 2019. She is currently a senior lecturer with the School of Mathematical Sciences, Universiti Teknologi MARA Cawangan Negeri Sembilan Kampus Seremban. Her current research interests include forecasting, financial time series, and applied statistics.

Ashurov Sharofiddin is an Associate Professor and the Head of the M.Sc. in Islamic Banking and Finance Programme at the IIUM Institute of Islamic Banking and Finance (IIiBF), International Islamic University Malaysia (IIUM). He is contributing to academic development, industry engagement, and strategic programme leadership. Dr. Ashurov is a Member of the Shariah Committee at local and international Islamic banks, including Al Rajhi Bank Malaysia (since 1 April 2022), where he is involved in Shariah governance, product endorsement, and regulatory compliance. leading cross-border advisory, institutional assessment, and strategic development initiatives in the Islamic finance sector.

Ersa Tri Wahyuni is an associate professor in Accounting at Universitas Padjadjaran. She has more than 15 years in the accounting industry as a respected academic as well as advisor and consultant for numerous entities in Indonesia. She is also a member of Indonesian Financial Accounting Standard Board since 2015-2023 and currently serves as the vice chairman of the Indonesian Institute of Management Accountant. Currently she also serves as independent member of board of commissioners in Indonesia insurance company and also member of audit and risk management committee of Universitas Padjadjaran.

Rubayah Yakob possesses a Doctorate in Economics and currently serves as an associate professor in the Financial Services and Risk Management Programme at Universiti Kebangsaan Malaysia. In addition, she has obtained the Certified Quantitative Risk Management (CQRM) certification from the International Institute of Professional Education and Research in the United States. The scope of her research encompasses the analysis of efficiency and solvency, risk management, and the demand for life insurance and takaful. Furthermore, she possesses expertise gained from multiple consulting projects focused on financial behaviors.

Index

A

B

C

D

E

F

G

H

I

K

L

M

O

P

Q

R

S

T

W

www.ingramcontent.com/pod-product-compliance
Lightning Source LLC
LaVergne TN
LVHW061531290926
849162LV00004B/750